Batsford Chess Library

Maud Jones.
Christmas '95

BATSFORD CHESS ENDINGS

JON SPEELMAN
JON TISDALL · BOB WADE

An Owl Book
Henry Holt and Company
New York

Henry Holt and Company, Inc.
Publishers since 1866
115 West 18th Street
New York, New York 10011

Henry Holt® is a registered trademark
of Henry Holt and Company, Inc.

First published in the United States in 1993 by
Henry Holt and Company, Inc.
Originally published in Great Britain in 1993 by
B. T. Batsford Ltd.

Library of Congress Catalog Card Number: 93–77839

ISBN 0-8050-2947-8 (An Owl Book: pbk.)

First American Edition—1993

Printed in the United Kingdom
All first editions are printed on acid-free paper. ∞

10 9 8 7 6 5 4 3 2 1

Adviser: R. D. Keene, GM, OBE
Technical Editor: Andrew Kinsman

Contents

Introduction

Batsford Chess Endings has been a monumental project taking nearly a decade from conception to birth. Luckily, with the signal exception of database positions, endgame theory is fairly constant. And so the early sections I wrote on pawn endings and rook endings have needed little correction except in the very simplified "Siliconisable" examples. I have, however, added a few examples recently to bring them up to date.

Collating an encyclopaedia is a notoriously difficult process. And the team of midwives has only gelled finally in the last couple of years. As I stated above, I was personally responsible for the sections on rooks and pawns. I am delighted to have had the assistance of Bob Wade who did most of the queen endings; and Jonathan Tisdall who undertook the myriad other sections - about 40% of the book in total. We have indicated in the contents list who wrote each section. But naturally as chief editor I take ultimate responsibility for all the contents.

Since the first endgame databases in the late seventies, a considerable number of different endings have undergone the fascinating but also frequently baffling process of being subjected to total analysis. The list of databases is growing daily. And we have endeavoured, whenever possible, to check any examples which fall into these categories.

In order to consult an oracle you have to have access to it. My friend and colleague Dr John Nunn was indefatigable in his haruspications on our behalf; and displayed superhuman patience at my many requests. One should also mention Lars Rasmussen, who supplied the interface program which makes communication with the oracle itself immeasurably simpler than it would otherwise be.

There is a list of the known results for different endings following this introduction. As you will see, many types of endgame can take more than 50 moves to win. I have taken the opportunity at several places in the text to inveigh against FIDE's attempts to reconcile tournament play with this new information by extending the 50 move rule. And I am delighted that they have decided now to make everything 50 moves.

The death knell of the more complex arrangement was sounded by the startling discovery that rook and bishop v two knights can take 224 moves to win! I should add, however, that I have no objection whatsoever to study composers having their own arrangements for the sake of art. My constituency is actual players; and we certainly need protection from the wilder lunacies of Silicon-certainty.

The organization of the material should be easy to follow, as it is a very natural one. Having dealt with the basic mates, we first consider Pawn Endings, then Minor Piece Endings, before moving on to endgames with major pieces. Inside each section there is a similar progression of material, starting with no pawns (where this is non-trivial) before considering cases with one or more pawns on the board. In many types of ending there are more meaningful ways to subdivide the material than the precise number of pawns; thus subheadings such as "Pawns all on the same side" or "Outside Passed Pawns" will be found throughout the book.

The main aim of the book is to increase the reader's understanding of the practical aspects of playing endgames. Therefore top priority when allocating space has been given to the types of ending that occur most frequently in tournament play, while incorporating in the text explanations of the aims of both sides in these endings. However the reader will find plenty of articles examples, for successful endgame play by its very nature tends to possess artistic elements.

It is worth clarifying at the outset precisely what we mean by reciprocal (or mutual) zugzwang, especially since computer analysis has shown that this phenomenon crops up in many endings far more often that human intuition would suggest. Reciprocal zugzwang is a situation in which the stronger side cannot force a win if he is to move, while the weaker side loses if he must move. Note that we do not insist that the side to move must lose (as do some writers).

In such a large work there are bound to be mistakes. I hope that readers will forgive us for our Carbon-based frailty. And we would be delighted to receive correspondence about improving BCE (c/o Batsford) for inclusion in the second edition.

Finally, there are many people whom I (JS) should like to thank. My original material was hand-written and I must express my admiration for Sarah Christopher's detective work in translating a preliminary typescript into a viable version. Byron Jacobs has received a tidal wave of material from us for typesetting; I am very grateful to him for so cheerfully transforming water into print.

Throughout the gestation period, Peter Kemmis Betty has had an unreasonable but ultimately justified belief that this project could ever come to fruition. While Peter has been at the helm throughout, BCE has gone through several technical editors. I should like especially to single out Andrew Kinsman whose Caesarian enthusiasm prised the material from the various recalcitrant authors to expedite BCE's big day; and the present incumbent Graham Burgess who was there to wield the forceps.

Jonathan Speelman,
September 1993

Table of Computer Database Results

Material	Longest Win	Target Position	Percentage Winning	Starting Position	Analyst	Year
QvK	10	M	100	Ka1,Qb1 v Ke6	S	1970
RvK	16	M	100	Ka1,Rb2 v Kc3	S	1970
				Ka1,Rh8 v Kd5		
PvK	19	P	76.5	Kh3/h2/g2,Pb2 v Kg5	C	1977
QvQ	10	MW		Kb1,Qa1 v Ke1,Qg1	SZ	1979
QvR	31	MW		Kc8,Qd8 v Ke3,Rc4	S	1970
				Ka2,Qa3 v Ke4,Rh2		
RvB	18	MW		Ka4,Rc3 v Ka7,Ba6	S	1970
				Ka4,Ra3 v Ka8,Ba6		
RvN	27	MW		Kd1,Rh1 v Kb1,Ng4	S	1970
BBvK	19	M	99.97	Kh8,Bd2,Bd7 v Kd3	BVH	1984
				Ka1,Bh4,Bd1vKd2		
BNvK	33	M	99.5	Ka8,Be8,Nh2 v Kc8	DAV	1981
				Ka1,Bc1,Nb1vKc2		
QQvQ	30	M	94	Kc8,Qg2,Qh1 v Kb6,Qf5	T	1986
QRvQ	67	M	92.1	Ka8,Qh8,Rb8 v Kg6,Qa4	T	1986
QBvQ	33	M	53.4		T	1986
QNvQ	41	M	48.4		T	1986
QPvQ	59	MPW		Kd6,Qa6,Pg7 v Kc2,Qb1	KF	1973
				Kh4,Qa6,Pg7vKc2,Qb8		
QvRP	29	MT		Kh8,Qa4 v Kf8,Rf7,Pd2	SZ	1979
QvBB	71	MW	92.1	Ka8,Qa1 v Kd7,Bc5,Bd5	T	1986
QvBN	42	MW	93.1	Ka8,Qb6 v Kd7,Bd5,Ne7	T	1986
QvNN	63	MW	89.7	Kd8,Qh1 v Kd6,Ne5,Nh8	T	1986
RBvR	59	MW	40.1	Kd6,Re2,Bc8 v Ka8,Rh7	T	1985
RNvR	33	MW	35.9	Kd5,Ra6,Na5 v Kc8,Re8	T	1985
RPvR	60	MPW		Kc3,Rc4,Pb2 v Ke4/f4,Rd1	LRGKF	1976
				Kd1,Rd6,Pb2vKh6,Ra8		
				Kd1,Rd6,Pb2vKg7,Ra3		
BBvN	66	MW	91.8	Ka8,Bh1,Bh6 v Kf3,Ng2	T	1983
				Kd8,Ba1,Bb7 v Kb6,Nc6		

The table on the previous page summarises the results of computer database analysis of various endings. It was compiled by Christian Posthoff, Rainer Staudte and Michael Schlosser.

Analyst Key: Ampt (A), Bakker (B), Clarke (C), Futer (F), Golfand (G), Herschberg (H), Komisarchik (K), Aleksandrov (L), Barayev (R), Strohlein (S), Thompson (T), van der Herik (V) and Zagler (Z).

Target Position Key: Mate (M), Promotion (P), Win of a piece (W) or Transposition to a simpler, won ending (T).

White to play in all cases except QPvQ, QvRP and RPvP.
Note that the result for QPvQ is only for the case of a knight's pawn on the seventh rank, while that for QvRP is only for a centre pawn on the seventh rank.

The percentages of won positions may be misleading at first sight. These are based on random legal placings of the pieces, so White to play may, for example, simply be able to capture the black queen immediately.

Symbols

+	Check
±/∓	Better chances
+-/-+	Winning advantage
=	Equal position/Drawn
!!	Excellent move
!	Good move
!?	Interesting move
?!	Dubious move
?	Bad move
??	Blunder
+	(by diagram) White wins
-	(by diagram) Black wins

By each diagram are symbols indicating which player is to move, together with the result with correct play from White's viewpoint. When the position is less clear-cut, an assessment, again from White's viewpoint, will be given.
After many diagrams there follows analysis both with White to move and with Black to move. Then the result (or assessment) with correct play in each case appears above the appropriate letter.

Basic Mates

In this section we look at the basic checkmating techniques against a lone king. These are essential weapons in the arsenal of every player and need to be mastered.

King and Queen v King

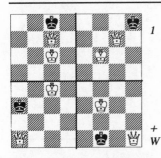

Checkmating Positions

King and queen against lone king is usually the beginner's first experience of endgames.

The lone king needs to be driven to the rim of the board to be checkmated. Sample mates appear in the quarter diagrams of diag 1.

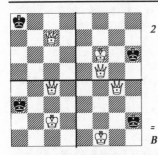

Stalemate

En route the player trying to win must guard against allow ing stalemate. For samples of stalemate see the quarter diagrams in diag 2.

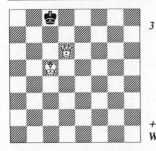

Do not be too enthusiastic to limit the black king as White in diag 3. Notice that

   1   ♞b6 is stalemate!
   1   ♞c6 is stalemate!

Play 1 ♕e7 and then next move bring the white king to c6 or b6 and give checkmate on the following move.

The Standard Technique

Proceeding from diag 4 White should make one queen move to limit the black king to one sector of the board.

   1   ♕e4

Not a check! After:

   1   ...   ♚d7

White should start to bring the slow mover, the king, near the opposing king.

2	♔b4	♚d6
3	♔b5	♚d7
4	♔c5	♚c7

Only now is a check to drive the king on to the edge appropriate.

5	♕e7+	♚c8
6	♔c6	♚b8
7	♕b7 mate	

Basic Mates

Again:

1	♕e4	♚c5
2	♔b3	♚d6
3	♔c4	♚d7
4	♔c5	♚c7
5	♕e7+	♚c8
6	♔c6	♚b8
7	♕b7 mate	

Once more:

1	♕e4	♚c5

2	♔b3	♚b5

When White could check at d5 or play:

3	♕e6	♚c5
4	♔c3	♚b5
5	♕d6	♚a5
6	♔c4	♚a4
7	♕b4 mate	

King and Rook v King

This is also always a win. The same basic technique is used as in king and queen against king: the enemy king must first be driven to the edge of the board before a mating net can be constructed. Whereas a queen can drive the king towards the edge without the help of the king, here the king must be used in conjunction with the rook to achieve this.

In diag 5 the win is quite straightforward. Both 1 ♖a4 and 1 ♖e1 would immediately restrict the black king but it is probably most logical to activate the king first:

1	♔b7	♚e4
2	♔c6	♚d4

3	♖e1	

This forces the enemy king towards the a-file.

3	...	♚c4
4	♖e4+	♚d3
5	♔d5	

Black is now boxed in to the area a1-a3-d3-d1 and White can gradually tie the noose.

5	...	♚c3
6	♖d4	

Further reducing the box.

6	...	♚c2
7	♔c4	♚b2
8	♖d2+	♚c1

The king is already forced to the edge.

9	♔c3	♚b1
10	♔b3	♚c1
11	♖d3	♚b1
12	♖d1 mate	

King and Two Bishops v King

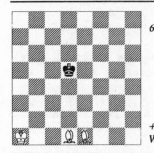

Although one bishop cannot mate a lone king, two bishops can force a win very easily.

In diag 6 the winning procedure is similar to that which we encountered in the queen and rook positions. White can gradually drive back the black king by co-ordinating the bishops to control the king's escape squares:

1	♔b2	♚e4
2	♔c3	♚d5
3	♗f3+	♚e5
4	♗g3+	♚e6
5	♔d4	

Having cut off the black

Basic Mates

king the white pieces can easily drive it into a corner.

5	...	♔f5
6	♔d5	♔f6
7	♗g4	♔g5
8	♘d7	♔f6
9	♗h4+	♔g6

Having prepared the way White is now able to push back the king into the h8-corner.

10	♔e5	♔f7
11	♔f5	♔g7
12	♗e8	♔f8
13	♗g6	♔g7
14	♗e7	♔g8
15	♔f6	♔h8
16	♗f5	♔g8
17	♔g6	♔h8
18	♘d6	♔g8
19	♗e6+	♔h8
20	♗e5 mate	

Although this may not be the quickest mate the basic technique is the same.

King and Two Knights v King

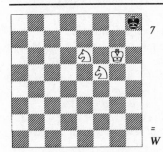

7

= W

It should be obvious that there is no way that a single knight can checkmate a lone king, but perhaps it is not so apparent that even two knights cannot force mate. Whilst there are mating positions there is no way that these can be constructed without a strong degree of cooperation by the defending side - the defender's sole task is to avoid one-move mates.

In diag 7 White has driven the black king into the corner but he cannot make further progress:

1 ♘f8

Of course 1 ♘e7 and 1 ♘h6 are stalemate.

1	...	♔g8
2	♘d7	♔h8
3	♘d6	♔g8
4	♘f6+	♔f8

Of course not 1 ... ♔h8?? 2 ♘f7 mate, but after 4 ... ♔f8 White has no way of forcing checkmate.

King, Bishop and Knight v King

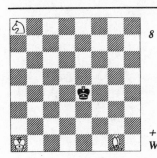

8

+ W

With bishop and knight mate can be forced, and this ending is worth careful study to develop the necessary technique since checkmate usually takes many moves and inaccurate play may result in a draw under the fifty-move rule. Checkmate can only be forced in the corners of the same colour as the bishop; in the other two corners mate is possible, as is the case with two knights, but only if the defender makes a mistake.

The winning procedure is quite involved. The first stage is to drive the enemy king to the edge of the board. Then the king must be driven into a corner and finally, assuming that it is in the "wrong" corner, the king must be pushed over to the corner of the same colour as the bishop. The technique is much more difficult than, for example, the two bishops ending, as

11

Basic Mates

here it is far from easy to cut off and drive back the defending king. The bishop and knight do not act particularly effectively as a team, and they always need the support of the king. The theme is to use the knight and king to control squares which the bishop cannot control.

1	♔b2	♚d3
2	♘c7	♚c4

Black holds back his opponent's king.

3	♘e6	♚d5
4	♘d4	♚c4
5	♔c2	♚b4

5 ... ♚d5 would be met by 6 ♔d3.

6	♔d3	♚c5
7	♗h2	

Having coordinated his forces it is clear that White has taken many squares away from the black king.

7	...	♚d5
8	♘b3	♚c6

The king must retreat, so it heads for a8. Less accurate is 8 ... ♚e6 when 9 ♔e4 would drive the black king towards the "correct" corner - h8.

9	♔c4	♚b6

9 ... ♚d7 is well met by 10 ♔d5.

10	♘c5	♚c6
11	♘a4	

We have now reached a typical situation which is similar to that after White's eighth move except White has grouped his forces better.

11	...	♚b7
12	♔b5	♚c8
13	♔c6	♚d8
14	♔d6	♚c8

Black could try to escape with 14 ... ♚e8 but after 15 ♔e6 ♚f8 16 ♗e5 or here 15 ... ♚d8 16 ♘b6 he would be driven towards h8.

15	♘b6+	♚b7
16	♔c5	♚a6
17	♔c6	♚a5
18	♗d6	♚a6
19	♗b8	

Having barred the route back to a8 White begins to drive the black king towards a1.

19	...	♚a5
20	♘d5!	♚a4

White would win more simply after 20 ... ♚a6 21 ♘b4+ ♚a5 22 ♔c5 ♚a4 23 ♔c4 ♚a5 24 ♗c7+ etc.

21	♔c5	♚b3
22	♘b4!	

A key knight move - this is a typical way of driving the king from one corner to another.

22	...	♚c3
23	♗f4	

The excellent position of the knight stops the black king escaping.

23	...	♚b3
24	♗e5	♚a4
25	♔c4	♚a5
26	♗c7+	♚a4
27	♘d3	♚a3
28	♗b6	

A fine waiting move.

28	...	♚a4
29	♘b2+	♚a3
30	♔c3	♚a2
31	♔c2	♚a3
32	♗c5+	♚a2
33	♘d3	♚a1

White has finally cornered the black king in the "correct" corner.

34	♗b4	♚a2
35	♘c1+	♚a1
36	♗c3 mate	

The reader is recommended to practise this ending in order to become fully conversant with the winning technique.

Pawn(s) v Pawn(s)

King and Pawn v King

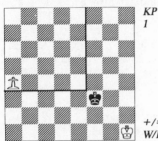

KP 1

+/= W/B

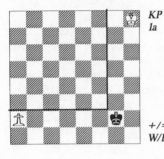

KP 1a

+/= W/B

If the attacking king is so badly placed that it takes no part at all, then this ending becomes a straight race between the defending king and the pawn.

There are two possible ways to calculate the outcome of this race:

A. The Rule of the Square

Imagine a square on the chessboard with the pawn at one of the corners and the side equal to the pawn's journey home. In diag 1, we have drawn such a square.

The defender will draw, if on his move he can get his king into the square, otherwise he will lose.

Thus in diag 1 Black to move plays:

  1   ...   ♚e4!

The king has entered the square so it is a draw.

  2   a5   ♚d5
  3   a6   ♚c6
  4   a7   ♚b7 etc

But White to move wins with:

  1   a5   ♚e4
  2   a6   ♚d5
  3   a7   ♚c6
  4   a8♕+ and wins

B. Counting

An alternative method, equally good, is to count the number of moves which the pawn and king require to reach the queening square.

Then White to move will win if his pawn requires *fewer* than the enemy king; otherwise it will be drawn.

Thus in diag 1 we count:

The pawn requires four moves to reach a8.

The king requires five moves to reach a8.

Therefore White to move wins - as we have already seen this is indeed true.

But after Black's 1 ... ♚e4! the counts are equal so it is a draw.

Counting is a very important tool in the ending. Personally I (JS) find A is an easier method; but B is also perfectly okay. However:

C. "Analysis"

"I go there, he goes there, now I go there, where is he now? ..." This is a method much beloved of beginners but we *do not* recommend it.

Diag 1a: A Slight Modification
When the pawn is on the second rank, then in view of its ability to make a jump, you must imagine that the pawn is already on the third rank.

Thus in diag 1a we draw a square as though the pawn were on a3:

White to move wins with 1 a4!.

Black to move draws with 1 ... ♚f3!.

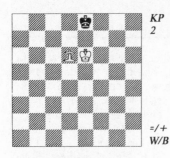

KP 2

=/+
W/B

KP 2a

=
B

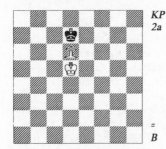

KP 3

+/+
W/B

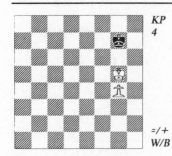

KP 4

=/+
W/B

Diag 2 is the fundamental position of king and pawn vs king and, it could well be argued, the fundamental position of endgame theory as a whole.

It is "zugzwang".

White to move can only draw.

But Black to move loses.

White to move:

| 1 | d7+ | ♚d8 |
| 2 | ♚d6 | |

This is the only move to protect the pawn but now it is stalemate.

Instead of 1 d7+ White might try to mess around a bit; but as long as Black al-

ways retreats his king *in front of the pawn* then no harm can befall him, e.g.

| 1 | ♚d5 | ♚d7 |
| 2 | ♚e5 | ♚d8! |

But not 2 ... ♚e8?? (or 1 ... ♚c8??) 3 ♚e6 ♚d8 4 d7 and wins.

| 3 | ♚e6 | ♚e8 etc. |

Black to move:

1	...	♚d8
2	d7	♚c7
3	♚e7 and 4 d8♛	

Diagram 2a:
Here Black to move must choose the right square for his king. As we have already seen, correct is 1 ... ♚d8!.

This position is always won whoever is to move.

White to move:

Although Black has the "opposition" (cf diag 4), with the white king already on the sixth rank this does not matter:

| 1 | ♚h6! |

But not 1 ♚f6? ♚h7 2 g6+?? (2 ♚f7! ♚h8 3 ♚g6! ♚g8 4 ♚h6! still wins) 2 ... ♚h8 3 ♚f7 or 3 g7+ ♚g8 4 ♚g6 and in each case it is

stalemate.

| 1 | ... | ♚h8 |

If 1 ... ♚f7 or 1 ... ♚f8 then 2 ♚h7 and White's next three moves are g6, g7, g8♛.

| 2 | g6 | ♚g8 |
| 3 | g7 and wins | |

Black to move:

| 1 | ... | ♚h8 |

1 ... ♚f8 2 ♚h7 is very similar.

| 2 | ♚f7! | ♚h7 |
| 3 | g6+ and the pawn | |

is escorted home.

When the kings face each other one square apart then the player who is *not to move* is said to have the "opposition".

It is usually an advantage to have the opposition (though not always - see also diag 20). The reason is that the player to move will have to *give way*

with his king which will allow his opponent to improve his own king position.

In diagram 4 White to move only draws since Black has the opposition. But Black to move loses.

White to move:

| 1 | ♚h5 | ♚h7! |

Or 1 ♔f5 ♚f7! (Black must not allow the enemy king to get past). Since his king's path is blocked, White has to advance his pawn prematurely.

2 g5　♚g7
3 g6　♚g8!

But not 3 ... ♚h8?? or 3 ... ♚f8?? (see diag 2).

4 ♔h6　♚h8
5 g7+　♚g8
6 ♔g6　stalemate

Black to move:

Since White has the opposition the black king must give way.

1 ...　♚h7

Or 1 ... ♚f7 2 ♔h6.

2 ♔f6!　♚g8
3 ♔g6

3 g5 ♚h7 4 ♔f7! also wins (see diag 3).

3 ...　♚h8
4 g5　♚g8
5 ♔h6!

Winning again as in diag 3.

KP 5

+/=
W/B

The white pawn will queen only if it is escorted through by the king. But in order to escort it, the white king must get in front of the pawn and seize the opposition; otherwise we will get a position like diag 2a where Black draws by choosing the right square for his king.

White to move:

1 ♔f2

Or 1 ♔d2, but he must on no account advance the pawn. White now just has time to get his king in front of the pawn and is therefore able to win.

1 ...　♚f8

Black takes the so-called "distant opposition" - the kings face each other *an odd number of squares apart* and the opponent is to move. But here that does not help him since by advancing his king, White gets a "reserve tempo" with his pawn.

2 ♔f3　♚f7
3 ♔e4　♚e6

Black has the opposition, but White has the reserve tempo move.

4 e3!　♚d6

Or 4 ... ♚f6 5 ♔d5 etc.

5 ♔f5　♚e7
6 ♔e5!

But not 6 e4? ♚f7 and Black takes the opposition and draws.

6 ...　♚d7
7 ♔f6　♚e8
8 e4　♚f8
9 e5　♚e8
10 ♔e6! and wins as in diag 3.

But not 10 e6?? ♚f8 11 e7+ ♚e8 12 ♔e6 stalemate.

Black to move:

1 ...　♚e7
2 ♔f2　♚f6

Or 2 ... ♚e6 (which also draws since the white king cannot go to e2). But not 2 ... ♚d6?? 3 ♔f3! ♚e5 4 ♔e3 when White gains the opposition and wins.

3 ♔f3　♚f5
4 ♔e3　♚e5
5 ♔d3　♚d5
6 e3

Or 6 e4+. The white king cannot make any headway so it is a draw.

6 ...　♚e5
7 e4

White can never do any better than diag 2a and so it is

Pawn(s) v Pawn(s)   ♙(♙) v ♟(♟)

a draw, e.g. 7 ... ♔e6 8 ♔d4 ♔d6 9 e5+ ♔e6 10 ♔e4 ♔e7 11 ♔d5 ♔d7 12 e6+ ♔e7 13 ♔e5 ♔e8! 14 ♔d6 ♔d8 15 e7+ ♔e8 16 ♔e6 stalemate.

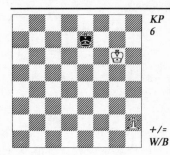

KP 6

+/= W/B

When the attacker has a rook's pawn then his winning chances are drastically reduced. This is because the defender will always draw if he can get his king in front of the pawn - h7 will always lead to stalemate whether the black king is on g8 or h8.

White can win only if:

a) The pawn queens immediately - the black king is outside the square; or

b) He can "shoulder" the enemy king away from the queening square with his own king.

White to move:

1   ♔g7!

The only move shouldering the enemy king off.

1   ...   ♔e6

2	h4	♔f5
3	h5	♔g5
4	h6 and wins	

Black to move:

1   ...   ♔f8!

Now White's only real choice is between giving stalemate and being stalemated himself!

2   ♔h7

Or 2 h4 ♔g8 3 h5 ♔h8 4 h6 ♔g8 5 h7+ ♔h8 6 ♔h6 stalemate.

2	...	♔f7
3	h4	♔f8
4	h5	♔f7
5	h6	♔f8
6	♔h8	

Or 6 ♔g6 ♔g8 etc.

6	...	♔f7
7	h7	♔f8
	stalemate	

King and Two Pawns v King

KP 7a

+ B

KP 7b

+ B

The ending of king and two v king is usually a very simple win. Even in the absence of their own king, two pawns can often defend each other. In these two half diagrams we can see the most common instances of this.

Diagram 7a

Black cannot take the b-pawn since the a-pawn would queen immediately. Therefore he must mark time with 1 ... ♔a6 when White can bring up his own king, winning easily.

Diagram 7b

1   ...   ♔h5

Or 1 ... ♔f5 2 h5!.

2   f5!

The pawns defend each other. Black's position is hopeless since if he ever tries ... ♔g7 then White can answer h5! If we assume that the white king is on a1:

2	...	♔h6
3	♔b2	♔g7
4	h5!	♔h6
5	f6! etc.	

Pawn(s) v Pawn(s)

KP
8a

=/+
W/B

In these examples White has problems because of the doubled pawns.

Diagram 8a

White to move loses a pawn at once.

1 &c3 &xb5
2 &b3

And since the white king is behind the pawn, it is a draw.

KP
8b

+/=
W/B

But Black to move loses:

1 ... &b7
2 &c5 &c7
3 b6+ &b7
4 &b5 &b8
5 &a6 &a8
6 b7+ &b8
7 b5 &c7

8 &a7 and wins

If White had played 5 &c6 then the black king would now be on a7 and 8 &c7?? would lead to stalemate. Instead 8 b8&+! &xb8 9 &b6 would win.

Diagram 8b

A rank further up, the position is drawn even with Black to move. White has not got "room" for a successful pawn sacrifice.

1 ... &g8!
2 &f6 &f8
3 g7+ &g8
4 &g6 or 4 g6 stalemate

King and Pawn v King and Pawn

KP
9

=/+
W/B

This position is decisive zugzwang. As we already know, whoever is *not to move* has the "opposition" and this decides the game.

White to move can make no progress, e.g.

1 &g5 &g7
2 &f5 &f7 etc.

But Black to move loses:

1 ... &e7

2 &g6 &e8
3 &f6 &d7
4 &f7 &d8
5 &e6 &c7
6 &e7 &c8
7 &xd6 &d8

Black has the opposition but, as we know from diag 3, with the white pawn already on the fifth rank this does not help him. White wins, e.g. 8 &e6 &e8 9 d6 &d8 10 d7 &c7 11 &e7 etc.

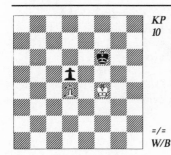

KP
10

=/=
W/B

White to move can still get nowhere. Black to move will lose his pawn exactly as in diag 9. But here, with the white pawn only on the fourth rank, that does not really matter.

1 ... &e6
2 &g5 &e7
3 &f5 &d6
4 &f6 &d7
5 &e5 &c6
6 &e6 &c7

7 &xd5

White obviously cannot gain anything by delaying the capture of this pawn.

7 ... &d7!

Black has the opposition. Here that is sufficient to draw cf diag 4, e.g. 8 &e5 &e7 9 d5 &d7 10 d6 &d8! 11 &e6 &e8 12 d7+ &d8 13 &d6 stalemate.

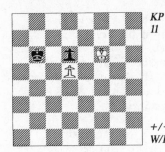

KP 11

+/+
W/B

White's king has broken through and he will always win, with, or without the move. But he must be very careful about tempi.

White to move:

1   ♔e7!
But not 1 ♔e6?? ♚c5 and Black wins!

1   ...   ♚c5
Or 1 ... ♚c7 2 ♔e6 etc.

2   ♔e6
This position is decisive zugzwang - whoever moves loses. White has carefully arranged that this should be Black.

2   ...   ♚ moves
3   ♔xd6 and wins

Black to move:

1   ...   ♚b5
Unfortunately he cannot play 1 ... ♚c4. If 1 ... ♚c5 2 ♔e6 etc or 1 ... ♚c7 2 ♔e6.

2   ♔e7!   ♚c5
3   ♔e6 and wins

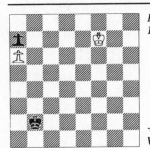

KP 12

+
W

Schlage - Ahues
Berlin 1921

It is very important to remember that a king can sometimes aim for a point via *several different shortest routes*. This is not nearly as confusing as it sounds.

In diag 12 the white king must obviously aim to take the black pawn. In order to do this he will travel via b7. But there are many different ways to get to b7.

There is the "direct route" ♔f7-e7-d7-c7-b7xa7.

Or the route which the king took in the actual game: 1 ♔e6 ♚c3 2 ♔d6? ♚d4 3 ♔c6 ♚e5 4 ♔b7 ♚d6 5 ♔xa7 ♚c7=

But White can win by using his king in two ways at once. The king can both approach the a-pawn and shoulder off his opponent.

1   ♔e6   ♚c3
2   ♔d5!
With this move he keeps the enemy king away from the vital c7-square.

2   ...   ♚d3
2 ... ♚b4 3 ♔c6 ♚a5 4 ♔b7 ♚b5 5 ♔xa7 ♚c6 6 ♔b8! etc.

3   ♔c6   ♚e4
In the game (see above) Black was able to play 3 ... ♚e5.

4   ♔b7   ♚d5
5   ♔xa7   ♚c6
6   ♔b8 and wins

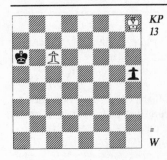

KP 13

=
W

Réti 1921

This very famous study is another example of a multi-purpose king. At first sight, it seems quite incredible that White should be able to draw. But he does so by following a "king-path", whereby he approaches both the enemy h-pawn and his own, seemingly quite useless, passed pawn.

1   ♔g7!   h4
If 1 ... ♚b6 2 ♔f6! h4 3 ♔e5 h3 4 ♔d6 h2 5 c7 and draws.

2   ♔f6!   h3
Or 2 ... ♚b6 3 ♔e5 as in the previous note.

3   ♔e6
Or 3 ♔e7.

3   ...   h2
4   c7 and draws

Pawn(s) v Pawn(s)   ♙(♙) v ♟(♟)

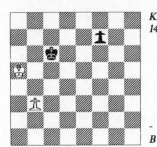

KP 14

B

Ljubojevic - Browne
Amsterdam 1972
This position could well have been a study! In time trouble Black played:

| 1 | ... | f5? |
| 2 | ♔b4 | |

And a draw was agreed. After 2 ... f4 3 ♔c3 both pawns will disappear, and if 2 ... ♔d5 3 ♔c3 ♔e4 4 ♔d2 Black also gets nowhere.

But Black could have won with the study-like, multi-purpose king move:

| 1 | ... | ♔d5!! |
| 2 | ♔b4 | |

2 b4 f5 3 b5 f4 4 b6 ♔c6! transposes into the main line.

| 2 | ... | ♔d4! |
| 3 | ♔a5 | |

Or 3 ♔a3 f5 4 ♔b2 f4 5

♔c2 ♔e3! 6 ♔d1 (if 6 b4 f3 Black is too quick) 6 ... ♔f2 7 b4 f3 8 b5 ♔g2 9 b6 f2 10 b7 f1♕+ (CHECK) and wins.

3	...	f5
4	b4	f4
5	b5	♔c5!
6	b6	♔c6
7	♔a6	

Now White will even queen first. But the white king has been forced onto a square where Black will queen *with check* and this decides the issue.

7	...	f3
8	b7	f2
9	b8♕	f1♕+
10	♔a5	

Or 10 ♔a7 ♕a1 mate.

| 10 | ... | ♕a1+ |
| 11 | ♔b4 | ♕b1+ etc. |

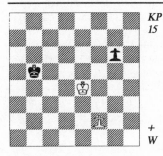

KP 15

+ W

Dobias 1926
White's task is to prevent the enemy king from attacking his pawn from the rear. This he does by the now familiar tactic of shouldering the enemy off.

| 1 | ♔d4!! | |

If 1 f4? ♔c4 2 ♔e5 ♔d3 3 ♔f6 ♔e4=. 1 ♔e5 is similar: 1 ... ♔c4 2 ♔f6 ♔d4 3 ♔xg6 ♔e4 and the pawn perishes.

Finally, if 1 ♔d5 ♔b4! White is outflanked again.

| 1 | ... | ♔c6 |

If 1 ... ♔b4 2 f4 and White has time to win the g-pawn, or 1 ... g5 2 ♔e5 ♔c5 3 ♔f5 ♔d5 4 ♔xg5 ♔e4 and, having taken the pawn on g5, White can easily support his f-pawn with 5 f4 (or 5 ♔g4).

| 2 | ♔e5 | ♔c5 |
| 3 | f4! and wins | |

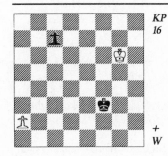

KP 16

+ W

Grigoriev 1932
Pawn endings can often transpose into queen endings or perhaps queen vs pawn. Elsewhere we shall examine the theory of queen vs pawn, but here is a foretaste, an exceptional position discovered by the great composer Grigoriev.

| 1 | ♔f5 | ♔e3 |
| 2 | ♔e5 | c6! |

2 ... ♔d3 loses simply to 3

♔d5 ♔c3 4 ♔c5 and 5 a4 etc.

3	a4	♔d3
4	a5	c5
5	a6	c4
6	a7	c3
7	a8♕	c2 (16a)

As we shall see later, the white king is outside the normal winning zone. But the black king is also misplaced and this allows White to win.

First we shall examine "normal play": if 8 ♕a3+ ♔d2

19

KP 16a

and:

a) 9 ♕b2 ♔d1 10 ♔d4 c1♕ and White cannot play 11 ♔d3;

b) 9 ♕a2 ♔c3! (but not 9 ... ♔d1? 10 ♔e4 c1♕ 11 ♔d3 and wins) 10 ♕a3+ ♔d2 etc.

Instead White plays:

8   ♕d5+!!   ♔e3

If 8 ... ♔c3 9 ♕d4+ ♔b3 10 ♕a1 etc, or 8 ... ♔e2 9 ♕a2! and now the king cannot go to c3 so 9 ... ♔d1 10 ♔e4 c1♕ 11 ♔d3 and wins.

9   ♕g2! and wins

9 ♕g2 was the only winning move. If 9 ♕d4+ ♔e2 10 ♕b2 ♔d1 etc, or 9 ♕h1 ♔d2.

+ W

King and Two Pawns v King and Pawn

KP 17

The white pawns protect each other (cf diag 7). White to move wins by first mopping up the black pawn and then queening his own. But, of course, the white king is outside the square of the pawn, (cf diag 1) so Black to move would win.

Black to move:
1 ... d3; 2 ... d2 and 3 ... d1♕.

+/– W/B

White to move

1   ♔g4   d3
2   ♔f3   d2
3   ♔e2   ♔a8
4   ♔xd2

Now in order to win, White must sacrifice the a-pawn with a8♕+ following this up with ♔a6 or ♔c6, e.g. 4 ... ♔b7 5 ♔d3 ♔a8 6 ♔c4 ♔b7 7 ♔c5 ♔a8 8 ♔b5 ♔b7 9 a8♕+ ♔xa8 10 ♔c6 (Or 10 ♔a6) 10 ... ♔b8 11 b7 ♔a7 12 ♔c7 etc.

KP 18

The white king cannot possibly stop the enemy e-pawn. But his own pawns are far advanced and, even with Black to move, he can force a win.

1   ...   e2
2   h7+   ♔h8

+ B

3   ♔f7

3 g7+ ♔xh7 4 ♔f7 would amount to the same thing.

3   ...   e1♕
4   g7+   ♔xh7
5   g8♕+   ♔h6
6   ♕g6 mate

KP 19

Protected Passed Pawns

An extra protected passed pawn will usually ensure the win. But there may be problems if the pawn is advanced either too far or too little.

Diagram 19

White can do no better than

= B

give stalemate, e.g.

1   ...   ♔b8

Or 1 ... ♔c8 2 ♔c6 ♔b8 3 b7 ♔a7 4 ♔c7 stalemate.

2   ♔c6

Since he has a rook's pawn, 2 b7 would be pointless.

2   ...   ♔c8
3   b7+   ♔b8

Pawn(s) v Pawn(s) ♟(♟) v ♟(♟)

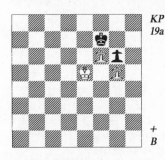

KP 19a

+ B

4 &b6 stalemate

Diagram 19a
White wins easily by sacrificing the f-pawn.

1 ... &f8
2 f7!

If 2 &e6 &e8 3 f7+ &f8 then White can still win with anything except 4 &f6??.

2 ... &xf7
2 ... &e7 3 f8♕+.

3 &d6

And White wins easily as in diag 9, viz. 3 ... &f8 4 &e6 &g7 5 &e7 &g8 6 &f6 &h7 7 &f7 &h8 8 &xg6 &g8 9 &h6! &h8 10 g6 &g8 11 g7 etc.

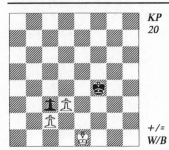

KP 20

+/= W/B

Grigoriev 1921
In contrast to diag 19, here the white pawns are not advanced far enough. There is no danger of stalemate, but White cannot get his king active for fear of ... &xc2. White to move would win easily with 1 &e2 or 1 &f2 but with Black to move it is more interesting.

1 ... &f3!

Here it would be wrong to "take the opposition". If 1 ... &e3? 2 &d1 and Black must choose between 2 ... &d4 3 &e2 and 2 ... &f3 3 &c1 &e3 4 &b1 &d4 5 &a2 and the king gets out on the queenside.

2 &d1

If 2 &f1 &e3 3 &g2 &d2! and draws.

2 ... &e3

3 &c1 &d4
4 &b1 &c5
5 &a2 &b4
6 &b1 &c5
7 &a1

Trying to confuse Black. If now 7 ... &b4? 8 &a2 &a4 9 &b1 &b4 10 &c1 &c5 11 &d1 &d4 12 &e2 and wins easily, but Black draws with:

7 ... &b5!

And now if 8 &a2 &b4! or 8 &b1 &c5! in each case drawing.

In fact this position is a rather simple example of corresponding squares - a1 corresponds to b5 - see diag 23 for some more detail on this important topic and see also diag 49.

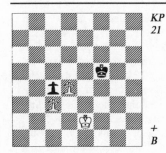

KP 21

+ B

Here White has more room. Although Black can try to defend as in diag 20, White easily breaks the coordination and wins.

1 ... &f4
2 &d2 &e4
3 &c2 &d5
4 &c1!

Black has no square for his king and the white king will soon emerge via either e3 or a3.

4 ... &e4
4 ... &c6 5 &d2 etc.

5 &b2 &d5
6 &a3 &c6
7 &b4 etc.

Pawn(s) v Pawn(s)   ♙(♙) v ♟(♟)

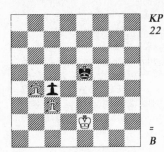

KP 22

= B

In this position, in contrast to diag 21, White does not control e5. This gives the black king more freedom of movement. And by a surprising counter-attack against the white c-pawn he is able to force a draw.

1	...	♚f4

1 ... ♚e4 is also okay.

2	♚d2	♚e4
3	♚c2	♚d5
4	♚c1	♚d6
5	♚d2	♚e6

5 ... ♚d5 is also playable. In this position Black's main aim is to *take the opposition as soon as the white king moves to the third rank*. As long as he does this (and does not allow ♚a4) then he will be okay.

6	♚e2	♚f6
7	♚f2	♚e6
8	♚g3	

If 8 ♚f3 ♚f5 or 9 ♚e3 ♚e5 and as long as the black king stays in the pawn's square, b5 will never help.

8	...	♚e5!

The only move.

9	♚g4	♚e4
10	♚g3	♚e5!

But not 10 ... ♚d3? 11 b5 ♚xc3 12 b6 ♚d2 13 b7 c3 14 b8♕ c2 15 ♕b2 ♚d1 16 ♚f2 c1♕ 17 ♕e2 mate. The white king was too near.

11	♚g4	♚e4
12	♚g5	♚d3

12 ... ♚e5 was also okay. Black can never be forced to counterattack; but why not?

13	b5	♚xc3
14	b6	♚d2
15	b7	c3
16	b8♕	c2

The position is drawn cf diag 16a, e.g.

17	♕b2	♚d1
18	♕d4+	♚c1
19	♚f4	♚b1
20	♕b4+	♚a2
21	♕c3	♚b1
22	♕b3+	♚a1! etc.

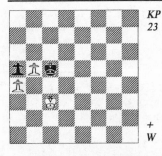

KP 23

+ W

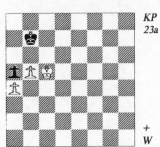

KP 23a

+ W

Protected Passed Pawn and Triangulation or Co-ordinate Squares

If the protected passed pawn is on the fifth rank then the stronger side *always* wins. In diag 23, White starts by forcing his king to the fourth rank.

1	♚d3	♚d5
2	♚e3	♚e5
3	♚f3	♚d5

Black cannot play 3 ... ♚f5 since the king would leave the square of the b-pawn: 4 b6 and wins.

4	♚f4	♚d6
5	♚e4	♚e6
6	♚d4	♚d6
7	♚c4	

Since the pawn controls c6 the king forces its way still further into the enemy camp.

7	...	♚c7
8	♚c5	

8 ♚d5 is quicker but this is more instructive.

8	...	♚b7 (23a)

Now 9 b6?? would be a terrible mistake since after 9 ... ♚a6 10 ♚c6 is stalemate. But if it were *Black to move* in diag 23a then he would clearly lose immediately, i.e. if "1" ... ♚a7 2 ♚c6 or 1 ... ♚c7 2 b6+ ♚b7 3 ♚b5. We can state this more concisely:

Diagram 23a is a position of zugzwang.

White to move wins in diagram 23a by manoeuvering to lose a move: this he does by

---

22

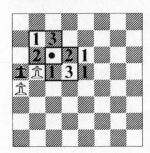

using a very important technique: triangulation.

Coordinate Squares

In diagram 23b we have marked some numbers. At first these may seem rather baffling, but in fact the idea is really quite simple.

We already know that diag 23a is a position of zugzwang:

White to move: 1 b6?? ♔a6=.

Black to move: 1 ... ♔a7 2 ♔c6 or 1 ... ♔c7 2 b6+ wins.

Working from this we can see that the positions ♔d6 vs ♔b6 and ♔d5 v ♔c7 are also zugzwang.

♔d6 v ♔b6: 1 ... ♔b7 2 ♔c5!.

But White to move cannot immediately make progress.

♔d5 v ♔c7: 1 ... ♔b6 2 ♔d6 or 1 ... ♔b7 2 ♔c5.

Again White to move cannot immediately make progress.

What about if the white king is on e5 or e6? Then in each case it can go immediately to either d5 or d6 and so the black king really wants to be on b7 in each case. Therefore both e5 and e6 correspond to b7 and we have marked them both "1".

(In fact we could also have chosen "4" for these squares since in a sense Black has no square corresponding to either of them - there is nothing magical about these numbers - they are merely an aid).

The fact that both e5 and e6 correspond to b7 suggests an idea. White marches his king to one of these squares and then marks time. Black must move his king off b7 and thus loses the co-ordination. Unfortunately c6 is not available for his king and he is therefore lost.

One further point before the solution of diag 23a. The borders around the white and black zones are merely conventional aids to identify the main area of combat - they are nothing more than that.

The solution:

1	♔d5	♔c7
2	♔e6	♔b7
3	♔e5!	

Black is now in zugzwang and must lose the co-ordination, e.g.

3	...	♔c7
4	♔d5	♔b6
5	♔d6	♔b7
6	♔c5 and wins	

Triangulation

If you do not like the idea of coordinate squares then there is a simpler way to look at this sequence.

In his 2nd-4th moves, the white king went along a triangle, thus losing a move. The black king was unable to emulate this, since c6 was unavailable to him. By losing a move, White transferred the move to Black and thus forced the win.

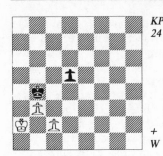

KP
24

Grigoriev 1933

White will win in this very interesting position if he can only activate his king. But he must be extremely careful about doing so.

If 1 ♔b1 ♔c3 2 ♔c1 d4 and White is in zugzwang - whichever way his king goes the black king will follow, i.e. if 3 ♔b1 d3 4 cxd3 ♔xb3! or 3 ♔d1 d3 4 cxd3 ♔xd3!.

This zugzwang position is the key to the ending. As we have seen, White to play may only draw but it is not hard to see that Black to play would lose.

What about 1 ♔b2? Black

plays 1 ... d4 2 ♔b1 (2 ♔c1 ♔c3 etc. as above) 2 ... d3! 3 c4 ♔xb3 and if 4 c5? d2 and Black wins, so White must be content with a draw.

That leaves:

    1 ♔a1!! ♔c3
1 ... d4 2 ♔b2 and wins.
    2 ♔b1 ♔b4
Or 2 ... d4 3 ♔c1 and it is Black who is in zugzwang, viz. 3 ... d3 4 cxd3 and if 4 ... ♔xb3 5 ♔d2 or 4 ... ♔xd3 5 ♔b2.
    3 ♔c1 ♔c3
    4 ♔d1 d4
Now there is obviously nothing better.
    5 ♔c1 and wins

KP
25

+
W

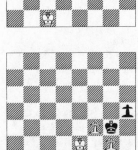

KP
25a

=/+
W/B

Grigoriev 1936

This position may look like an easy win, but White has technical problems because Black can sometimes get counterplay by taking the g-pawn and then rushing his own h-pawn home. The key to this ending is the zugzwang position of diag 25a.

    1 ♔d2
Not 1 g4? h5!.
    1 ... ♔f5
    2 ♔e3
If 2 ♔e2? ♔e4 followed by ... h5 - h4. Or 2 ♔d3? h5 3 ♔e3 ♔g4 and White is in zugzwang (see diag 25a).
    2 ... h6
2 ... h5? 3 ♔f3 or 2 ... ♔g4 3 ♔e4 etc.
    3 ♔f2!
3 ♔f3? h5 4 ♔e3 (else Black will play 4 ... h4) 4 ... ♔g4 etc. (see diag 25a).
    3 ... ♔g4
Or 3 ... ♔e4 4 ♔g2 h5 5 ♔h3 ♔f5 6 ♔h4 ♔g6 7 f5+ ♔xf5 8 ♔xh5 and wins.
    4 ♔e2!!

Not 4 ♔e3? h5; nor 4 ♔g2 h5 and 5 ... h4.
    4 ... h5
Or 4 ... ♔f5 5 ♔e3 ♔g4 6 ♔e4 etc.
    5 ♔e3 (25a)

This is a position of mutual zugzwang. White to move could only draw for if 6 ♔e4 ♔xg3 and Black queens *with check* or 6 ♔f2/e2 h4!. But, as we shall see, Black to move loses.
    5 ... ♔xg3
    6 f5

Now Black does not get his check when he queens and White is able to win (cf diags xxx).

    6 ... h4
    7 f6 h3
    8 f7 h2
    9 f8♕ h1♕
    10 ♕g7+ ♔h3
If 10 ... ♔h2 11 ♕f2!.
    11 ♕h6+ ♔g2
    12 ♕g5+ ♔h3
12 ... ♔h2 13 ♔f2; or 12 ... ♔f1 13 ♕f4+ ♔g2 14 ♕g4+ transposes.

13	♕h5+	♚g2		15	♕e2+	♚g1
14	♕g4+	♚f1		16	♕f2	mate

14 ... ♚h2 15 ♚f2.

KP 26

=/=
W/B

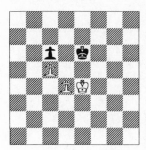

KP 26a

=/+
W/B

Blockaded Passed Pawns and the Opposition - Critical Squares

If White is to move, then Black has the opposition and draws easily. With Black to move, conversely it is White who has the opposition. But here *that does not matter* since White cannot penetrate on the queenside - he has not got enough room over there (for the explanation of the Xs on the diagram see after 3 ... ♚f7!).

White to move:

	1	♚f3	♚f7
	2	♚g3	♚e6

But not 2 ... ♚g7?? 3 d5! and wins.

	3	♚f3	♚f7!

3 ... ♚e7 would also draw (see diag 26 with Black to move). But 3 ... ♚f5 would lose! After 4 ♚e3 the black king cannot go to e5 and White manages to gain the opposition *with his king on the fourth rank.*

Why should it matter whether the white king is on the third or fourth rank when he gains the opposition? The point is that by gaining the opposition, a player forces the opposing king *to give way.* That is all very well, but it will only be important if he has to surrender an important square (or important squares).

In diag 26 we have put X's on a number of squares. These are the so-called "critical squares", which the white

king must reach in order to force the win. By inspecting the diagram you can see that White will win if he reaches any of the squares marked X (always assuming that the black king is not on the rampage at that stage).

	4	♚e3	♚e7
	5	♚e4	♚e6
	6	♚d3	♚d7

Not 6 ... ♚d5? 7 ♚e3 ♚e6 (7 ... ♚c4 8 ♚e4 is also hopeless) 8 ♚e4 and wins.

	7	♚c4	♚c7
	8	♚b4	♚b7
	9	♚a5	♚a7 etc.

Black to move

	1	...	♚f7
	2	♚d3	

If 2 ♚f3 ♚e7, or 2 ♚e4 ♚e6 or 2 ♚f4 ♚f6.

	2	...	♚e7!
	3	♚c3	♚d7
	4	♚b4	♚c7
	5	♚a5	♚b7

Black has defended the queenside - just in time - and so he draws.

Diagram 26a

Here zugzwang is decisive. White to play still cannot do anything but Black to play loses.

White to play:

	1	♚f4	♚f6
	2	♚g4	♚e6!=

But not 2 ... ♚g6?? 3 d5.

Black to play:

	1	...	♚d7

If 1 ... ♚f6 2 d5! ♚e7 3 d6+!

and wins. Or 1 ... ♚e7 2 ♚e5.

2 ♚f5!   ♚e7
3 ♚e5

White takes the opposition again and forces his king for-

ward further.

3 ...   ♚d7
4 ♚f6 and the c-pawn soon falls.

KP 27

+ B

Here there is more space on the queenside and so even the distant opposition is decisive.

1 ...   ♚g7
2 ♚e3   ♚f7
3 ♚d3

3 ♚d4 ♚f6 4 ♚d3 would also win.

3 ...   ♚f6

4 ♚d4   ♚e7
5 ♚c4   ♚d7
6 ♚b5   ♚c7
7 ♚a6! and wins

In diagram 26 the analogous square was off the board; which accounts for the different results in these two positions.

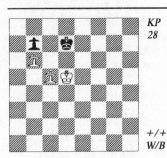

KP 28

+/+ W/B

With the white pawns so far advanced this is an easy win, even if he has to move.

1 ♚e5

But not 1 c6+? when 1 ... bxc6+ 2 ♚c5 ♚d8 3 ♚d6! would win for White. But Black would play instead 1 ... ♚c8! 2 ♚d6 ♚b8 3 ♚d7 bxc6! and draws.

1 ...   ♚c8

If 1 ... ♚e7 2 c6 ♚d8 3 cxb7! or 1 ... ♚c6 2 ♚d4 ♚d7 3 ♚d5 etc.

2 ♚e6   ♚d8
3 ♚d6   ♚c8
4 ♚e7   ♚b8
5 ♚d7   ♚a8
6 c6   bxc6
7 ♚c7 and wins

As indeed would 7 ♚xc6 or 7 ♚c8.

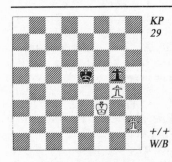

KP 29

+/+ W/B

White wins by combining two threats.

a) To get his king to e4 after which ... ♚e6 will be answered with h3! gaining the opposition.

b) To play h4 when Black cannot take it.

At the moment Black is defending against both of these threats. But in order to do this he is forced to play very exactly with his king. In fact as in diag 23, there is *co-ordination between the kings* and White wins by using triangulation to break this co-ordination.

Black to play is in zugzwang,

e.g.

1 ...   ♚d5

Or 1 ... ♚f6 2 ♚e4 ♚e6 3 h3!.

2 ♚g3   ♚e5
3 h4   ♚f6

Or 3 ... gxh4+ 4 ♚xh4 ♚f6 5 ♚h5! and wins.

4 h5 and wins

But White to move cannot make any immediate progress.

If 1 ♚e3 ♚d5 2 ♚d3 ♚e5 3 ♚e3 ♚d5 etc.

Or 1 ♚g3 ♚f6 and 2 h4?? only draws: 2 ... gxh4+ 3 ♚xh4 ♚g6 etc.

Proceeding as in diag 23, we can make a co-ordinate square

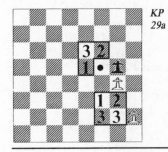

KP 29a

diagram: diag 29a.

Black's problem is that he must meet either ♔g2 or ♔f2 with ... ♔e6. For e6 is the only square adjacent to both e5 and f6. And he must always answer ♔f3 with ... ♔e5 and ♔g3 with ... ♔f6.

Now the solution is quite easy.

    1   ♔g3

But not 1 ♔g2? ♔f4! 2 h3 ♔e5. White has lost his reserve tempo of h2 - h3 and can only draw, e.g. 3 ♔f3 ♔f6! 4 ♔e4 ♔e6 5 ♔f3 ♔f6 etc.

1	...	♔f6
2	♔g2!	♔e6
3	♔f2!	♔f6

Or 3 ... ♔e5 4 ♔f3!.

4	♔g3!	♔f7

If 4 ... ♔e5 or 4 ... ♔e6 then 5 h4! wins. 4 ... ♔g6 5 ♔f3 is very similar to the main line.

5	♔f3	♔f6
6	♔e4	♔e6
7	h3 and wins	

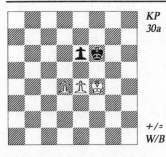

KP 30a

+/=
W/B

Black to play can force a draw with a typical combination. But, with space on both sides of the pawns, White to play wins easily.

Black to play:

1	...	e5+!
2	dxe5+	♔e6

Regaining the sacrificed pawn, Black forces a simple draw.

White to play:

1	♔e3	♔e7

Or 1 ... ♔g5 2 ♔d3 ♔f4 3 e5 ♔f5 4 ♔c4 ♔e4 5 ♔c5 ♔f5 6 ♔d6 and wins.

2	♔d3	♔d6
3	♔c4	♔c6
4	e5!	♔b6
5	d5	♔c7
6	d6+! and wins cf	

diag 19b.

KP 30b

+
W

Diagram 30b

Here 1 e5?? ♔c6 would lead to a draw, but White can win easily by going over to the kingside. As I emphasised before there is space on both sides of the pawns.

1	♔d3	

But not 1 d5? ♔c7! 2 ♔c5 exd5 3 ♔xd5 ♔d7=.

1	...	♔c6
2	♔e3	♔d6
3	♔f3	

But not 3 ♔f4?? e5+!.

3	...	♔e7
4	♔g4	

4 ♔f4 ♔f6 5 ♔e3 would also win.

4	...	♔f6
5	♔h5	

Again avoiding 5 ♔f4?? e5+.

5	...	♔f7
6	♔g5	♔g7
7	e5 and wins	

Pawn(s) v Pawn(s) ♙(♙) v ♟(♟)

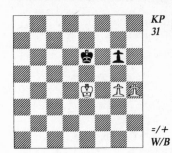

KP 31

=/+
W/B

In contrast to diag 30, there is now no room to break through on the kingside.

Black to play loses but White to play can only draw, i.e. *diag 31 is zugzwang*.

Black to play:
1	...	♚f6

Or 1 ... ♚d6 2 ♚f4 ♚e6 3 ♚g5 ♚f7 4 ♚h6 ♚f6 5 g5+ etc.

2	♚d5	

Not 2 ♚f4?? g5+.

2	...	♚e7
3	♚e5	♚f7
4	♚d6	

4 g5?? ♚e7= as Black has the opposition.

4	...	♚f6
5	g5+	♚f7

Or 5 ... ♚f5 6 ♚e7 etc.

6	♚d7 and wins	

White to play:
1	♚d4	♚d6
2	♚e4	

If 2 ♚c4 ♚e5!.

2	...	♚e6
3	♚f4	

3 g5 ♚d6 4 ♚d4 ♚e6 also achieves nothing.

3	...	♚f6
4	♚f3	♚f7!

Black must aim to *take the opposition as soon as the white king goes onto the e-file*. (Here if it were his move then ... ♚f6 would still be okay. The reason is that after ♚f4 the hackneyed trick ... g5+! comes to Black's rescue.)

5	♚e3	♚e7
6	♚d3	♚d7
7	♚c4	♚e6!
8	♚d4	♚d6

And there is no way to make progress.

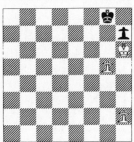

KP 32a

+/+
W/B

Tempo Moves

White must arrange to play g6 when the black king is on h8. Since the h-pawn has not moved, White can *choose* whether to play 1 h3 or 1 h4 and he therefore always wins.

Black to move:
1	...	♚h8
2	h4!	♚g8
3	h5	♚h8
4	g6	hxg6

Or 4 ... ♚g8 5 g7 etc.

5	hxg6	♚g8
6	g7 and wins.	

White to move:
1	h3!	

But not 1 h4? ♚h8 2 h5 ♚g8 3 g6 hxg6 4 hxg6 ♚h8=.

1	...	♚h8

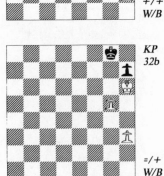

KP 32b

=/+
W/B

2	h4	♚g8
3	h5	♚h8
4	g6	etc.

Diagram 32b

Here White does not have a choice and, if it is his move, then it is a draw, viz.

1	h4	

1 ♚h5 does not help: 1 ... ♚g7 2 h4 ♚g8! 3 ♚g4 ♚g7 4 ♚f5 ♚f7 5 h5 and e.g. 5 ... h6 6 g6+ ♚g7= (see diag 19a).

1	...	♚h8
2	h5	♚g8=

But, of course, Black to move would lose:

1	...	♚h8
2	h4	♚g8
3	h5	♚h8
4	g6	etc.

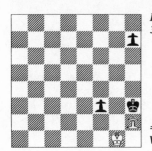

KP
33

=
W

Grigoriev 1920

Unless White takes drastic action, Black will win by forcing his king to e3. he will then play ... f2+ and have a *reserve tempo with the h-pawn* to force White into decisive zugzwang.

But White to move can force a draw by making Black *expend his reserve tempo prematurely.*

A. Incorrect Passive Defence

1	♔f2	♔g4
2	♔f1?	♔f4
3	♔f2	♔e4
4	♔e1	

Or 4 ♔f1 ♔e3 5 ♔e1 f2+ 6 ♔f1 ♔f3 7 h4 (7 h3 ♔g3 8 h4 h5) 7 ... ♔g3 8 h5 h6 and wins.

4	...	♔e3
5	♔f1	f2

6	h3	

Or 6 h4 h5.

6	...	h6
7	h4	h5

and wins.

B. Correct Active Defence

1	♔f2	♔g4
2	♔e3!	h6

Or 2 ... h5 3 ♔f2 ♔f4 4 ♔f1!.

3	♔f2	♔f4
4	♔e1!	

But not 4 ♔f1? ♔e3 5 ♔e1 h5 6 ♔f1 h4 7 ♔e1 f2+ 8 ♔f1 ♔f3 9 h3 ♔g3 and wins.

4	...	♔e3
5	♔f1	f2

5 ... h5 6 ♔e1 (but not 6 h3? - see diag 34) 6 ... h4 7 ♔f1 f2 8 h3=.

6	h3!	♔f3
7	h4=	

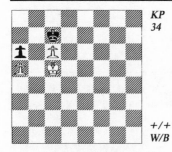

KP
34

+/+
W/B

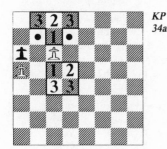

KP
34a

This is a position of zugzwang. White wins by triangulation (cf diag 23).

1	♔d5	♔c8

If 1 ... ♔b8 or 1 ... ♔d8 then 2 ♔d6 ♔c8 3 c7 wins immediately. Thus *d5 corresponds to c8.*

2	♔c4!	

As in diag 23, White moves backwards so as to put Black into zugzwang. 2 ♔d4 would do just as well.

2	...	♔d8
3	♔d4!	

Black is in zugzwang. If 3 ... ♔c7 4 ♔c5 so he must try:

3	...	♔c8

4	♔d5!	♔c7

Or 4 ... ♔d8/♔b8 5 ♔d6.

5	♔c5 and wins	

On his 2nd, 3rd and 4th moves the white king described a triangle ♔d5 - c4 - d4 - d5. Black was unable to do likewise and therefore lost the coordination.

Diagram 34a

This is a coordinate square diagram (similar to diag 23a). As we saw Black loses because he has nowhere to go from d8 since d7 is inaccessible to his king.

Pawn(s) v Pawn(s)   ♙(♙) v ♟(♟)

KP
35

=/+
W/B

Maizelis 1955
Rather surprisingly, this position is zugzwang. The solution combines elements from the last few examples.

Black to play:

1	...	♔c7
2	♔d5	♔d7
3	a5	♔c7
4	♔e6	♔c6
5	a6!	

This is a position of *mutual zugzwang*, i.e. White to play could only draw.

5	...	♔c7

Or 5 ... ♔c5 6 ♔d7 ♔xc4 7 ♔c6! (shouldering) and wins.

6	♔e7	♔c6

Or 6 ... ♔c8 7 ♔d6 ♔d8 8 ♔c6 ♔c8 9 c5 etc.

7	♔d8	♔d6
8	♔c8	♔c6
9	♔b8	♔b6
10	c5+ and wins	

White to play has various tries but nothing leads to a win, viz.

1	♔d5	♔c7
2	a5	♔d7
3	a6	♔c7
4	♔e6	♔c6

Here it is White to move and therefore drawn.

5	♔e7	♔c7!
6	♔e8	♔c8!

Or:

1	♔d5	♔c7
2	c5	♔d7
3	c6+	♔c7
4	♔c5	♔c8!

But not 4 ... ♔d8? 5 ♔d6 ♔c8 6 a5 ♔d8 7 c7+ ♔c8 8 ♔c6 (cf diag 33).

5	♔d6	♔d8
6	a5	♔c8
7	c7	a6=

Finally, if the white a-pawn is already on a5 then, of course, the black king must retreat to b8 or d8, viz.

1	♔d5	♔c7
2	c5	♔d7
3	c6+	♔c7
4	a5	♔d8!=

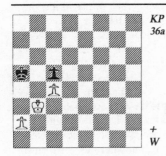

KP
36a

+
W

Walker 1841
White cannot make any headway on the queenside and must therefore aim to manoeuvre his king towards d5. With care, he is able to do this.
N.B. The position ♔d3 v ♔b4 is zugzwang.

1	♔a3!	♔b6
2	♔b2	♔a5
3	♔b3	

By triangulation White has gained a tempo.

3	...	♔b6
4	♔c3	♔a5
5	♔d2!	

But not 5 ♔d3? ♔b4 and White is in zugzwang.

5	...	♔a4

Or 5 ... ♔b4 6 ♔d3 and Black is in zugzwang.

6	♔e3!	♔a3
7	♔e4	♔xa2
8	♔d5 and wins	

Diagram 36b
Now the a-pawn is too exposed and White can only draw.

1	♔b2	♔a4
2	♔a2	♔a5
3	♔b3	♔b6
4	♔c2	♔a5
5	♔d3	♔a4
6	♔e4	♔xa3

And now both 7 ♔d5? ♔b4 and 7 ♔e5? ♔b3 lose (cf diag 11), so White must retreat with:

KP
36b

| 7 | ♔d3 | ♚b4 |
| 8 | ♔d2 | ♚xc4 |

| 9 | ♔c2= |

=
W

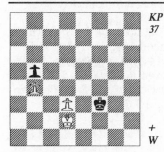

KP
37

Grigoriev 1920

In order to win, White must either penetrate with his king or get the d-pawn moving.

This position looks very simple but contains the fiendish trap 1 d4? ♚e4 2 ♔c3 ♚f5!=.

In fact it turns out to be another example of corresponding squares (see diags 23b and 37a).

+
W

1 ♔c2!

As mentioned above, if 1 d4? ♚e4 2 ♔c3 ♚f5! 3 ♔d3 ♚f4 4 ♔d2 ♚e4! and it is a draw.

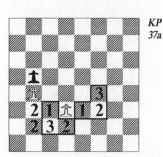

KP
37a

1 ... ♚f4

But not 1 ... ♚e3 2 ♔c3 and Black is in zugzwang and loses immediately. i.e. ♔c3 v ♚e3 is zugzwang.

Before proceeding further we should establish the other zugzwang positions:

♔d2 v ♚f3. Black must let the white king round with 1 ... ♚f4 2 ♔e2.

♔c2 v ♚f4. c2 is next to c3 and d2; f4 is next to e3 and f3.

What about the white king on b2 or b3? The black king must be next to e3 and f4, i.e. on f3.

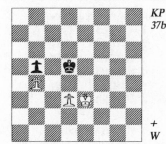

KP
37b

+
W

We thus obtain diagram 37a.

White continues:

| 2 | ♔b3 | ♚f3 |
| 3 | ♔b2! | |

Completing the triangulation begun on move 2. Of course ♔c2 - b2 - b3 - c2 would have been just as good.

3	...	♚f4
4	♔c2	♚f3
5	♔d2	♚f4
6	♔e2	♚e5
7	♔e3	♚d5 *(37b)*

White now wins with a very typical endgame combination. He forces a queen one tempo ahead of Black and then wins the black queen with a skewer.

8	d4!	♚c4
9	♔e4	♚xb4
10	d5	♚c5

Or 10 ... ♚a5 11 ♔e5 b4 12 d6 and White queens *with check*; if 12 ... ♚b6 13 ♔e6! does not help Black.

11	♔e5	b4
12	d6	♚c6
13	♔e6	b3
14	d7	b2
15	d8♕	b1♕
16	♕c8+	and
17	♕b8+	

Pawn(s) v Pawn(s) ♙(♙) v ♟(♟)

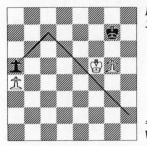

KP
38

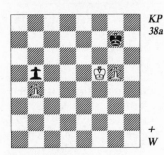

KP
38a

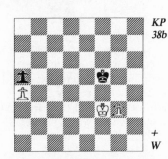

KP
38b

"Crossing the Line"

If the queenside pawns were on the b-file then White would win very easily by abandoning his passed pawn (see diag 38a).

In the diagram, however, White can only draw since he will reach king and a-pawn v king with the black king getting to c8.

As we shall see, White wins analogous positions so long as his pawn has not "crossed the line" (i.e. the frontier a5 - c7 - h2 as depicted on the diagram).

Diagram 38

1   ♔e5

1 g6 ♚g8! does not help White.

1	...	♚g6
2	♔d5	♚xg5
3	♔c5	♚f5
4	♔b5	♚e6
5	♔xa5	♚d7
6	♔b6	♚c8=

Diagram 38a

1	♔e5	♚g6
2	♔d5	♚xg5
3	♔c5	♚f6
4	♔xb5	♚e7
5	♔c6 and wins	

Diagram 38b

Here the white pawn is just on the line. White wins by abandoning it immediately.

1   ♔e3!

But not 1 g4+?? ♚g5 which only draws, e.g. 2 ♔g3 ♚f6 3 ♔f4 ♚g6 4 ♔e5 ♚g5 5 ♔d5 ♚xg4 6 ♔c5 ♚f5 7 ♔b5 ♚e6 8 ♔xa5 ♚d7 (just in time) 9 ♔b6 ♚c8=.

1	...	♚g4
2	♔d4	♚xg3

Now the black king is on the h2 - a7 diagonal and it will be shouldered off by the white king.

3	♔c5	♚f4
4	♔b5	♚e5
5	♔xa5	♚d6
6	♔b6!	♚d7
7	♔b7 and wins	

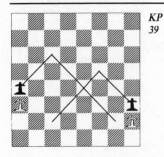

KP
39

By analogy with diag 38, there are also winning zones if the pair of rooks pawn's is further up (or indeed down) the board.

Note that it is to "White's" advantage to have his rook's pawn further advanced.

Diagram 39a

The white g-pawn is too far advanced, so it is a draw.

1	♔e3	♚g4
2	♔d4	♚xg3
3	♔c4	♚f4
4	♔b4	♚e5
5	♔xa4	♚d6
6	♔b5	♚c7=

Diagram 39b

Here the g-pawn is just on the line and White wins.

Pawn(s) v Pawn(s)   ♙(♙) v ♟(♟)

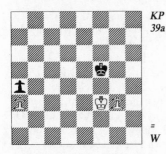

KP 39a		
1	♔e2	♔g3
2	♔d3	♔xg2
3	♔c4	♔f3
4	♔b4	♔e4
5	♔xa4	♔d5
6	♔b5	♔d6
7	♔b6	♔d7
8	♔b7 etc.	

= W

KP 39b		
1	♔d2	♔b3

+ W

KP 39c

= W

2	♔e2	♔xb2
3	♔f3	♔c3
4	♔g3	♔d4
5	♔xh3	♔e5
6	♔g4	♔f6=

Note that if we shift the white pawn from b2 to c2 (i.e. ♔d2, c2, h2 v ♔d4, h3) then White wins easily: 1 ♔e2 ♔c3 2 ♔f3 ♔xc2 3 ♔g3 ♔d3 4 ♔xh3 ♔e4 5 ♔g4 etc.

Diagram 39c

The b-pawn is outside the zone (it needs to be on b1!)

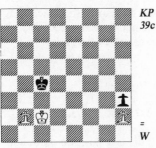

KP 40

A practical example:
White to play wins with 1 a5!.
But Black to play draws with 1 ... a5!.

+/=
W/B

N.B. The further advanced the white rook's pawn, the larger is the winning zone.

33

Pawn(s) v Pawn(s)   ♙(♙) v ♟(♟)

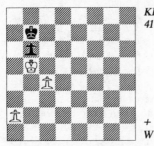

KP
41

*+
W*

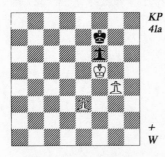

KP
41a

*+
W*

In both diagrams White wins by carefully hoarding tempi.

    1   a3!

    But not 1 a4? ♚c7! (1 ... ♚a7? 2 a5 wins) 2 ♚a6 (now both 2 c5 and 2 a5 are clearly hopeless) 2 ... ♚c6 3 ♚a7 ♚c7 4 ♚a8 ♚c8!=.

    1   ...   ♚c7

1 ... ♚a7 2 ♚c6 is no better.

    2   ♚a6   ♚c6
    3   a4   ♚c7
    4   ♚a7   ♚c6
    5   ♚b8!

and wins, viz. 5 ... ♚d6 6 ♚b7 ♚c5 7 ♚c7 ♚xc4 8 ♚xb6 ♚b4 9 a5.

    Diagram 41a

Here White wins with a reserve tempo less.

    1   e4

And if 1 ... ♚g7 2 g5! or 1 ... ♚e7 2 e5!. In each case White gains the opposition and wins easily (in contrast to diag 41 he does not have a rook's pawn to confuse matters).

Black to move also loses easily in diag 41a.

    1   ...   ♚e7
    2   ♚g6   ♚e6
    3   e4   ♚e7
    4   ♚g7 etc, as above.

KP
42

*+
W*

Grigoriev 1936

White has to decide which way to go with his king. It looks as if this should not be important. But in fact one way wins whilst the other only draws.

    The point is this:

a) In order to make progress, White has got to advance his forward f-pawn.

b) One of Black's main defensive tries will then be to block with ... f6 or ... f5.

c) White must then win by penetrating with his king.

d) Clearly this is easier via the queenside/centre.

e) But if Black's king is already well placed in the centre then the white king will get blocked.

Therefore, paradoxically White goes first to the less important side, the kingside. If Black then blocks the pawns, White will get his king to a good square on the queen-

side. Moreover, the black king will not operate effectively on the cramped kingside.

A.

    1   ♚e4?   ♚e6
    2   f4?

2 ♚f4 still won.

    2   ...   f6!

This is a position of mutual zugzwang - White to play is unable to win but Black to play would clearly lose, e.g.

If 3 f5+ ♚d6 4 ♚f4 ♚d5 5 ♚g3 ♚e5! 6 ♚g4 ♚e4 7 f3+ ♚e5 (zugzwang) =.

Or 3 ♚f3 f5! 4 ♚e3 ♚d5 5 ♚d3 ♚c5 6 ♚e3 ♚d5 7 ♚f3 ♚e6! (but not 7 ... ♚d4? 8 ♚g2! ♚d5 9 ♚h3! and White wins) 8 ♚g3 ♚f6 9 ♚h4 ♚g6=.

B.

    1   ♚g4!   ♚g6
    2   f4   f6

If 2 ... f5+ 3 ♚f3 ♚f6 (3 ... ♚h5 4 ♚e2!) 4 ♚e3 ♚e6 5

♔d4 ♚d6 6 f3 and wins.

Or 2 ... ♚f6 3 f5 ♚e5 4 ♔g5 ♚d5 5 f6 (5 ♚f6 ♚e4) 5 ... ♚e5 6 f3 ♚e6 7 f4 and wins.

| 3 | | f5+ |

3 ♔f3 ♚f7 4 f5 ♚e7! 5 ♔g4! transposes to the text.

| 3 | ... | ♚f7 |
| 4 | ♔h5 | ♚g7 |

| 5 | f3! | ♚h7 |
| 6 | ♔g4 | ♚g7 |

Or 6 ... ♚h6 7 ♔f4 ♚h5 8 ♔e3!.

| 7 | ♔f4 | ♚h6 |

7 ... ♚f7 8 ♚e4 ♚e7 9 ♚d5 ♚d7 10 f4!.

8	♚e3!	♚h5
9	♔d4	♚g5
10	♚e4 and wins.	

Technical Ideas and Procedures

In this short section, we examine some of the technical ideas which underlie all pawn endings.

KP 43

-/- W/B

KP 43a

± W

Reserve Tempi

It often happens that there is zugzwang on one side of the board, whilst both players strive to exhaust the opponent's moves on the other.

Diagram 43

White's king is nearer the kingside but it is his move. If Black plays correctly, then he will force his opponent into zugzwang, e.g.

| 1 | f3 |

1 h3 f6! would be similar.

Nor does 1 g3 help, e.g. 1 ... g6 2 f4 (2 h4 f5!, 2 f3 h6!, 2 h3 f6!) 2 ... h5 3 h3 f6 4 g4 h4 5 f5 g5 etc.

Black can try:

A.

1	...	f6?
2	f4	f5
3	h3	h6
4	g4!	

Of course not 4 h4? h5 5 g3 g6.

| 4 | ... | g6 |
| 5 | g5! | hxg5 |

Not 5 ... h5? 6 h4.

| 6 | fxg5 | f4 |

7	h4	f3
8	♔d3	f2
9	♔e2	♚xb3
10	h5	♚a3

Maybe 10 ... ♚c2.

11	hxg6	b3
12	g7	b2
13	g8♕	f1♕+
14	♔xf1	b1♕+

White has good winning chances unless there is immediate perpetual check.

B.

1	...	h6!
2	f4	h5
3	f5	h4
4	g4	hxg3

4 ... g5 is also good.

| 5 | hxg3 | g5! |
| 6 | f6 | |

6 g4 f6 is no better.

| 6 | ... | g4 |
| 7 | ♔d5 | ♚xb3 |

and wins by a tempo.

Diagram 43a

If we "move the queenside up a rank", however, then everything changes:

| 1 | f4 | h5 |

Black forces "zugzwang" but White has two extra tempi: his king is one move nearer the kingside, the black pawn one further from queening.

With the white king further advanced 1 ... f5 was not so bad, viz. 2 h3 h6 3 g4 g6 4 g5 hxg5 5 fxg5 f4 6 ⟨K⟩d4 f3 7 ⟨K⟩e3 ⟨K⟩xb4 8 h4 ⟨K⟩c5! 9 h5 b4 10 hxg6 b3 etc. But, of course, White is better in this line too.

2	f5	h4
3	g4	hxg3
4	hxg3	g5

5	f6	g4
6	⟨K⟩d6	⟨K⟩xb4
7	⟨K⟩e7	⟨K⟩c4
8	⟨K⟩xf7	b4
9	⟨K⟩e6	b3
10	f7	b2
11	f8♕±	

Diags 43 and 43a show clearly that:

Besides calculating the reserve tempi, we must also check when and if it could be zugzwang.

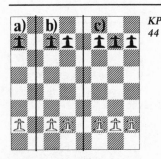

KP 44

Fine 1941

Assuming that the zugzwang really does exist, diag 44 shows correct play in three different cases.

A. 1 a3 a6 (but not 1 ... a5?? 2

a4) 2 a4 a5.

B. e.g. 1 c3 c6 2 d3 d6 3 c4 c5.

C. As we saw in diag 43a: 1 f3 h6! 2 f4 h5 3 f5 h4 4 g4 hxg3 5 hxg3 g5! 6 f6 g4.

The Opposition, Triangulation and Corresponding Squares

In king and pawn endings it often happens that the two kings exert an invisible but potent force on each other, both trying to force the other to give way. The most common instance of this is the opposition.

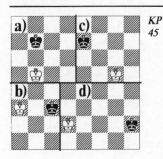

KP 45

The Opposition

We have already met this in many previous examples (e.g. diags 2-5, 9-10, 26-7 etc).

When the two kings face each other with one square in between, then whoever is to move will have to give way. The player not to move is then said to hold the opposition.

Diagram 45

In diag 45 we can see four different forms of the opposition

a) Vertical Opposition. This

is the most common form.

b) Horizontal Opposition.

c) Diagonal Opposition. This can easily lead to a) or b), e.g. if 1 ... ⟨K⟩f7 2 ⟨K⟩f5: a) or 1 ... ⟨K⟩e6 2 ⟨K⟩g6: b)

d) Distant Opposition. Here the kings *are an odd number of squares apart.* It is still a disadvantage to move first: With Black to move White can force his king to h1 or h3, e.g. 1 ... ⟨K⟩g1, g2, g3 2 ⟨K⟩e1, e2, e3: b) or 1 ... ⟨K⟩h3 2 ⟨K⟩e1! ⟨K⟩g2 3 ⟨K⟩e2 ⟨K⟩g3 4 ⟨K⟩f1 ⟨K⟩h2 5 ⟨K⟩f2.

In this "variation" Black

Pawn(s) v Pawn(s) ♟(♙) v ♟(♟)

could play instead 2 ... ♔g3 taking the diagonal opposition. But the white king can still *get past* with 3 ♔f1.

The preceding diagram means very little on its own. In diag 46 we can see the value of the opposition.

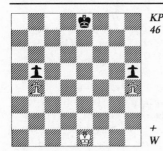

KP
46

Capablanca 1921
White wins by taking the distant opposition and converting it into "full" opposition.

A.

1	♔e2!	♔e7
2	♔e3	♔e6
3	♔e4	♔f6
4	♔f4!	

Not 4 ♔d5? ♔f5 5 ♔c5 ♔g4=.

| 4 | ... | ♔g6 |

Or 4 ... ♔e6 5 ♔g5 wins.

| 5 | ♔e5 | ♔g7 |

With the help of the opposition White has driven off the black king. Now both 6 ♔d5 and 6 ♔f5 ♔h6 7 ♔f6 ♔h7 8 ♔g5 win easily.

B.

| 1 | ♔e2! | ♔d8 |

A much more subtle defence. If now 2 ♔d3? ♔d7 or 2 ♔e3? ♔e7 Black takes the opposition and draws, e.g. 2 ♔e3? ♔e7 3 ♔e4 ♔e6 4 ♔f4 ♔f6! 5 ♔e4 ♔e6 6 ♔d4 ♔d6 etc.

Instead White plays:

| 2 | ♔f3! | |

A "bypass". Having given way with 1 ... ♔d8 the black king is unable to go to f7.

| 2 | ... | ♔e7 |
| 3 | ♔e3! | |

Distant opposition as in A.

| 3 | ... | ♔e6 |
| 4 | ♔e4 etc, as in A. | |

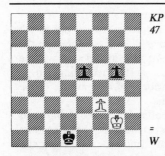

KP
47

Neustadtl
White can defend by taking the opposition with:

| 1 | ♔h1!! | |

But not 1 ♔f1? ♔d2 2 ♔f2 ♔d3 3 ♔g1 (it cannot go to f3) 3 ... ♔e3 4 ♔g2 ♔e2 5 ♔g3 ♔f1 6 ♔h3 ♔f2 7 ♔g4

♔g2 and wins.

| 1 | ... | ♔d2 |

1 ... g4 2 ♔g2! ♔d2 3 fxg4=.

2	♔h2	♔d3
3	♔h3	♔e3
4	♔g3	♔e2
5	♔g2=	

KP
48

Triangulation
We have already seen several examples of this: (cf diags 23, 29, 34, 37).

Triangulation occurs when one side's king moves *along a triangle* so as to lose a move. With his opponent unable to match him, he can transfer the move to his opponent thus gaining the opposition (or co-ordination).

Since diags 23, 29, 34 and 37 should explain this sufficiently, we have chosen a less static example here.

Diagram 48
Behting 1900
If 1 ♔e4? c5 2 ♔d3 ♔e8 3 ♔c4 ♔d7 and White can make no progress. He therefore plays the "tempo move":

| 1 | ♔f3! | c6 |

Pawn(s) v Pawn(s)   ♙(♙) v ♟(♟)

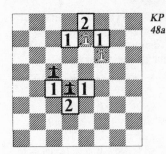

KP 48a

If 1 ... ♔e8 (1 ... c5 2 ♔e4! comes to the same thing) 2 ♔e4! c5 3 ♔d3 etc. White lost a move by playing ♔f4 - f3 - e4.

    2   ♔f4!   c5
    3   ♔e4

Actually, White's king did not describe a triangle in this case: ♔f4 - f3 - f4 - e4. The reason is that Black also had a tempo to lose ... c7 - c6 - c5.

The important thing is that Black's king is *totally restricted* - he cannot possibly lose a move since he has only a narrow walkway; whereas White's king can *choose* when to go to e4.

    3   ...   ♔e8

    4   ♔d3
Or 4 ♔d5 ♔d7 5 ♔c4 etc.
    4   ...   ♔d7
    5   ♔c4   ♔e8
    6   ♔xc5!   d3
    7   ♔d6   d2
7 ... ♔f7 8 ♔d7 d2 9 e8♕+.
    8   ♔e6   d1♕
    9   f7 mate

Diagram 48a
Diagram 48a shows the co-ordination between the kings once ... c5 has occurred. As we saw White was able to "take the coordination" by refusing to play his king to e4 until the right moment.

♔c4, e4 vs ♔d7, f7 are zugzwang, as is ♔d3 vs ♔e8.

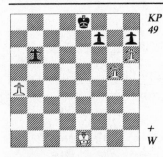

KP 49

Corresponding Squares
Occasionally the two kings will exert a strange force on each other at a great distance. We have already seen one example of this in the distant opposition, diag 46. But sometimes the opposition is not applicable. In that case the ending is difficult but there is a procedure which can always be used to attack it.

+ W

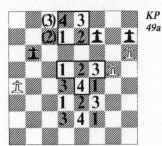

KP 49a

The Method of Corresponding Squares
  a) Find the fundamental zugzwang positions.
  b) Interpolate to find other positions of zugzwang.

This is not a topic which we can cover fully here - these positions are difficult and occur only very rarely.

But by working through one example we hope that we can provide a basis for the reader who is suddenly forced to tackle such a position. (See also diags 23, 29, 34, 37 where some simpler systems of corresponding squares occur.)

Diagram 49

Ebense 1935
White to move is able to advance his king far up the board. But in order to win he must play according to a number of zugzwang positions.

Following the Method of Corresponding Squares we first find the fundamental zugzwang positions.

♔d5 vs ♔d7. If 1 ... ♔c7 (or 1 ... ♔e7 2 ♔c6 etc.) 2 ♔e5 ♔d7 3 ♔f6 ♔e8 4 ♔g7 ♔e7 5 ♔xh7 ♔f8 6 g6 and wins.

♔e5 vs ♔e7. 1 ... ♔d7 2 ♔f6 as above, or 1 ... ♔e8 2 ♔d6.

♔f6 vs ♔f8. Obviously this is the only square for the black king.

With the white king on f5 Black must be able to answer 1 ♔f6 with 1 ... ♔f8 and 1 ♔e5

38

by 1 ... ♔e7!. Hence we have ♔f5 v ♔e8.

What about if the white king is on e4? Then Black can defend with his king on either e6 or d8. With the king on e6 if 1 ♔f4 ♔d7! or 1 ♔d4? ♔f5!.

♔e4 v ♔d8. The d8-square is next to e8, e7 and d7. If 1 ♔d5 ♔d7! or 1 ♔e5 ♔e7! or 1 ♔f5 ♔e8!.

We thus get the fundamental zugzwang positions

d5 v d7
e5 v e7
f5 v e8
e4 v d8
f6 v f8

It turns out that Black can always defend with his king on one of the four squares d7, e7, e8 and d8, only moving off there if the white king heads for b5 or goes to f6.

We can then extrapolate backwards, looking for which squares are next to which, to reach a set of zugzwang positions which can be recorded as in diag 49a.

For instance d4 is next to 1, 2 and 4 and is therefore a "3"

Diag 49a is a "corresponding square diagram" to record the information that we have discovered (obviously one could not use such a diagram during play; but it could be very useful during adjournment analysis!).

Note that diag 49a doesn't record *all the information* we have gleaned, e.g. the zugzwang positions f6 v f8; d4 v d6; e4 v e6 have been omitted for purposes of clarity.

c8 and c7 are labelled in brackets since they are good defensive squares against rear positions but not against forward ones.

E.g. ♔f5 v ♔c8 and ♔e5 v ♔c7 are *not* zugzwang: 1 ♔f6! in each case.

But ♔f3 v ♔c8 is zugzwang: 1 ♔e3 ♔c7 2 ♔e4 (or 2 ♔d4 ♔d6!) 2 ... ♔d8 etc.

Now the solution of diag 49:

Eberse 1935

1	♔d2!	♔d8
2	♔e2	♔e8
3	♔f3	♔e7
4	♔e3	♔d7
5	♔f4	♔d8
6	♔e4	♔e8
7	♔f5	♔e7
8	♔e5 etc	

White took the correspondence and held it according to diagram 49a.

This position is extremely difficult. But with the aid of diagram 49a it is not impossible!

Pawn(s) v Pawn(s) ♙(♙) v ♟(♟)

The Pawn Breakthrough

This is a vital weapon in all endings. But it is especially important in king and pawn endings. For without any other pieces to interfere, a sufficiently distant passed pawn will automatically become a queen.

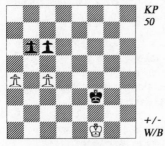

KP 50

+/-
W/B

Cozio 1766

White easily creates an un-stoppable passed pawn.

1	c5!	bxc5
2	a5	c4
3	a6	c3
4	♔e1!	

But not 4 a7?? c2 and wins.

4	...	c2
5	♔d2 and wins	

Black to move easily stops White with:

    1   ...   c5!

This wins easily but not 1 ... ♔e4?? (or 1 ... ♔e3??) 2 c5!.

Note that after 1 ... ♔e3?? 2 c5 bxc5 3 a5 c4 White must play 4 ♔e1! c3 5 ♔d1 etc, but not 4 a6?? c3 5 ♔e1 c2.

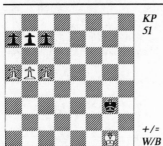

KP 51

+/=
W/B

This is a very famous exam-ple.

White to move forces a queen with:

1	b6	axb6

1 ... cxb6 2 a6!.

2	c6!	bxc6
3	a6	

Black to move defends with:

    1   ...   b6!

But not 1 ... a6? 2 c6! or 1 ... c6? 2 a6. And king moves could be met by 2 b6!.

2	axb6	axb6
3	cxb6	cxb6

and White saves the game by meeting ... ♔xb5 with ♔b3 taking the opposition (cf diag 4).

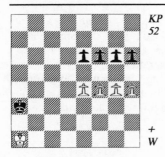

KP 52

+
W

White can easily force a queen. But this will help only if he can arrange to queen *with check* on f8 - otherwise Black will himself queen with *checkmate!*

    1   h5!

Not 1 g5? hxg5 2 f5 gxh4 - or 2 e5 fxe5.

Or if 1 f5? gxf5 2 e5 fxe5 3 g5 f4.

Or 1 e5? fxe5 (not 1 ... f5? 2 h5 gxh5 3 gxf5 exf5 4 e6).

    1   ...   gxh5

If 1 ... g5 2 e5! fxe5 3 f5.

2	e5	fxe5
3	f5 and wins	

Pawn(s) v Pawn(s)   ♙(♙) v ♟(♟)

Evaluating an Extra Pawn

An extra pawn should be enough to win in a pawn ending unless there is a good reason to the contrary.

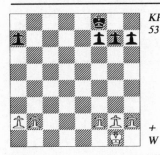

KP 53

+ W

Averbakh

This position is a very easy win:

First, White centralises his king. Then he sets up a passed pawn on the queenside to deflect the enemy monarch. Finally the white king has a tasty meal on the kingside.

1	♔f1	♚e7
2	♔e2	♚d6
3	♔d3	

3 b4 is also good of course.

3	...	♚c5
4	♔c3	

Completing the first stage.

4	...	f5

Black's moves are almost irrelevant. White simply carries out his plan.

5	b4+	♚b5
6	♔b3	g6
7	a4+	♚c6
8	♔c4	g5
9	b5+	♚b6
10	♔b4	f4
11	a5+	♚c7
12	♔c5	♚d7
13	b6	axb6+
14	axb6	

Completing the second stage.

14	...	♚c8

And now the third stage - the white king's feast.

15	♔d5	♚b7
16	♔e5	♚xb6
17	♔f5	♚c5
18	♔xg5	♚d5
19	♔xf4 and wins	

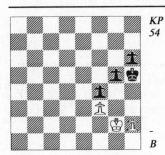

KP 54

- B

Zapata - Speelman
Mexico 1980

This position arose out of a queen ending. It is much harder than the previous example since with the pawns only on one side of the board there is no question of deflecting the white king.

Black is just able to win by *penetrating with his king*. He forces the enemy king back and then finally gets to the white pawns by seizing the opposition using a reserve tempo.

1	...	♚g6

Not 1 ... ♚h4? 2 h3 h5? 3 ♔h2 g4 4 hxg4 hxg4 5 fxg4 ♚xg4 6 ♔g2=.

2	♔f2	♚f5
3	♔e2	♚e5
4	♔d3	♚d5

Black has the opposition but for the moment he cannot force his way through.

5	h3	

5 ♔c3 h5 6 h3 (or 6 ♔d3 g4!) comes to the same thing.

5	...	h5
6	♔c3	♚c5
7	♔d3	♚b4!
8	♔d4	

If 8 ♔e4 ♚c4 9 ♔f5 (or 9 h4 gxh4 10 ♔xf4 ♚d4 and White is in zugzwang) 9 ... ♚d4 10 ♔xg5 (10 h4 gxh4 11 ♔xf4 ♚d3) 10 ... ♚e3 11 ♔xh5 ♚xf3 and wins by a tempo.

8	...	♚b3

But not 8 ... h4?? 9 ♔e4 ♚c4 10 ♔f5 ♚d4 11 ♔xg5 ♚e3 12 ♔g4! and wins. Black must keep control of g4 for the moment.

Pawn(s) v Pawn(s)   ♟(♟) v ♟(♟)

9   ♔d3   ♚b2!

Here White resigned. The point is that after 10 ♔d2. Black can now play 10 ... h4 since the white king cannot go to e3 and therefore loses a tempo, viz. 10 ... h4! 11 ♔d3 ♚c1! 12 ♔e4 ♚d2 13 ♔f5

♔e3 14 ♔g4 ♚f2 etc.

Passive defence also obviously fails since the f3-pawn will soon fall (cf diag 9), i.e. if 10 ♔d2 h4 11 ♔d3 ♚c1 12 ♔e2 ♚c2 13 ♔e1 ♚d3 14 ♔f2 ♚d2 15 ♔f1 ♚e3 16 ♔g2 ♚e2 etc.

Passed Pawns

Quite obviously, different passed pawns are more or less valuable. In general it is possible to say that:

A passed pawn gets more valuable the further it goes up the board - as long as it has adequate support.

"Outside passed pawns" are generally better than "inside passed pawns".

Protected passed pawns are usually better than either of the above.

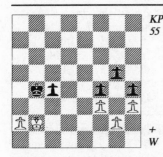

KP 55

+ W

Although the black king is further advanced, White's outside passed pawn gives him a very easy win.

1   a3+

1 ♔c2 would do just as well.

1   ...   ♚a4

1 ... ♚b5 or 1 ... ♚c5 would not help.

2   ♔c3   ♚xa3

3 ♔xc4 ♚b2 4 ♔d4 ♚c2 5 ♔e4 ♚d2 6 ♔f5 ♚e2 7 ♔xg5 ♚f2 8 ♔xf4 ♚xg2 9 ♔g4 etc.

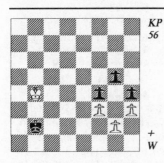

KP 56

+ W

Actually White would still win even with one tempo less: 1 ♔c4 ♚c2 2 ♔d4 ♚d2 3 ♔e4 ♚e2 4 ♔f5 ♚f2 5

♔xg5 ♚xg2 6 ♔g4! (zugzwang) and if 6 ... ♚f2 7 ♔xh4! or 6 ... ♚h2 7 ♔xf4!.

Pawn(s) v Pawn(s) ♙(♙) v ♟(♟)

KP
57

KP
57a

+
W

=/=
W/B

Philidor 1777

White's enormous protected passed pawn on c5 is invulnerable. Moreover, it seriously restricts Black's king which must stay in its square (cf diag 1).

White wins trivially by taking the h5-pawn: 1 ♔e3 ♔e5 2 ♔f3 ♔f5 3 ♔g3 ♔e5 (or 3 ... ♔g5 4 c6!) 4 ♔h4 ♔f5 5 ♔xh5 (cf diag 23) 5 ... ♔f6 6 ♔g4 ♔e5 7 ♔g5 ♔e6 8 ♔f4 ♔f6 9 ♔e4 ♔e6 10 ♔d4 ♔d7 11 ♔d5 etc.

Diagram 57a

The black passed pawn is now nearer to the square of the white c-pawn. The black king can therefore take part in the defence of the g-pawn. And with correct play he can now draw.

    1   ♔e3   ♔e5
    2   ♔f3   ♔f5
    3   ♔g3   ♔e5!

But not 3 ... ♔f6? 4 ♔g4! zugzwang and wins.

    4   ♔g4   ♔f6=

Black to move can still draw:

    1   ...   ♔e5
    2   ♔e3   ♔d5!

Not 2 ... ♔f5? 3 ♔d4 g4 (3 ... ♔e6 4 ♔e4 ♔f6 5 ♔d5 or 3 ... ♔f6 4 ♔d5) 4 ♔d5! g3 (4 ... ♔f6 5 ♔e4) 5 c6 g2 6 c7 g1♕ 7 c8♕+ ♔f4 8 ♕f8+! ♔g3 (8 ... ♔e3 9 ♕c5+) 9 ♕g8+ etc.

2 ... g4? also just loses: 3 ♔f2 ♔e6 4 ♔g3 ♔f5 5 ♔h4! ♔f4 6 c6 g3 7 ♔h3! ♔f3 8 c7 g2 9 c8♕ g1♕ 10 ♕f5+ ♔e2 11 ♕xb5+ ♔d2 (11 ... ♔f3 12 ♕f5+ ♔e2 13 ♕g4+) 12 ♕d5+ ♔e1 (12 ... ♔e2 13 ♕g2+; 12 ... ♔c-file 13 ♕c5+) 13 ♕e4+ ♔d2 14 ♕g2+.

This variation is a good example of the transposition from a pawn ending to a queen and pawn ending.

    3   ♔f3   ♔e5
    4   ♔g4   ♔f6=

White can win both black pawns with 5 c6 but should only reach a position such as diag 10, e.g. 5 ... ♔e6 6 ♔xg5 ♔d6 7 ♔f5 ♔xc6 8 ♔e5 ♔b6 9 ♔d5 ♔b7 10 ♔c5 ♔a6 11 ♔c6 ♔a7 12 ♔xb5 ♔b7! etc.

KP
58

+
W

Pawn Majorities and the Creation of Passed Pawns

Passed pawns do not just appear out of thin air. You have to work to create them. Sometimes a passed pawn can be manufactured by means of a combination - a pawn breakthrough cf diags 50-52 and diag 60 below etc.

But there is also a calmer procedure available. This is the *methodical creation of a passed pawn* through the evaluation of a "pawn majority".

Tal - Durasevic
Varna 1958

In diag 53, White won by creating an extra pawn on the queenside. In diag 58 the same sort of thing happens.

White has several important advantages:

a) His pawn majority of 3 v2 on the queenside will be easier to convert into a passed pawn than Black's more cumbersome 4 v 3.

Other things being equal, the nearer you are to creating

Pawn(s) v Pawn(s)   ♙(♙) v ♟(♟)

KP
58a

+
B

a passed pawn, the better. Therefore a pawn majority of 1 v 0 is better than 2 v 1 which is better than 3 v 2 etc. (see also notes to 8 ♔b5 and 10 ... g4). Moreover, the black queenside pawns have been weakened by ... b5 which means that White can quickly exchange off to 2 v 1.

b) On the move, White is able to get his king to an excellent square and commence operations before his opponent.

1   ♔d2   ♔d7

If 1 ... g5 2 fxg5 hxg5 3 h3! to be followed by g3 and h4 creating a passed h-pawn. Together with a passed c-pawn, this will easily force a queen.

2   ♔d3   ♔d6
3   c4!

Because of the weakening ... b5 White can quickly make a passed pawn.

3   ...   bxc4+

White was threatening 4 cxb5 axb5 5 b3 followed later by a4 creating a passed a-pawn, e.g. if 3 ... e5? 4 fxe5+ ♔xe5 5 cxb5 axb5 6 b3 ♔d5 7 a4 bxa4 8 bxa4 ♔c5 9 ♔e4 ♔b4 10 ♔e5 ♔xa4 11 ♔d6 wins easily.

Black might also try to defend by aiming to meet cxb5 with ... ♔xb5 but this would also be rather hopeless, e.g. 3 ... ♔c6 (if he wanted to play this then he should have done so on move 2) 4 ♔d4 f6 5 b4 e5+!? 6 fxe5 fxe5+ 7 ♔d3 e4+ (or 7 ... ♔d6 8 c5+ etc.) 8

♔xe4 bxc4 9 a4! wins easily.
4   ♔xc4   e5
5   fxe5+   ♔xe5
6   b4   f5
7   b5   axb5+
8   ♔xb5

White has completed the first part of his plan - he has a passed a-pawn.

Here we note a further advantage of a 'small' pawn majority: if you have such a majority, e.g. 2 v 1, then after the creation of the passed pawn there will be *no debris left*.

Black has *no pawns left on the queenside* so he can never defend by moving his king there and setting up his own passed pawn in that sector.

8   ...   f4
9   a4   g5
10   a5 (58a)
10   ...   g4

If 10 ... ♔d6 11 ♔c4 g4 (or 11 ... ♔c6 12 ♔d4 ♔b5 13 ♔e4 ♔xa5 14 ♔f5 ♔b5 15 h3!) 12 ♔d4 ♔c6 13 ♔e4 f3 14 gxf3 gxf3 15 ♔xf3 and White wins by several tempi.

Note that in this variation there was "black debris" left - the pawn on h6, and White therefore won by creating a passed pawn out of his minority.

11   ♔c4!

Now if 11 ... f3 12 gxf3 gxf3 13 ♔d3! stops the f-pawn and wins easily. Or 11 ... ♔e4 12 a6 f3 13 gxf3+ gxf3 14 a7 f2 15 a8♕ (CHECK).

Black therefore resigned.

Pawn(s) v Pawn(s)   ♙(♙) v ♟(♟)

Racing - The Struggle to Promote with Check

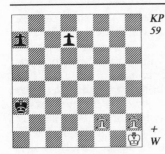

KP
59

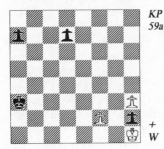

KP
59a

+
W

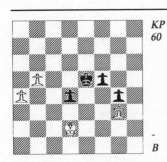

KP
60

-
B

In the previous example, diag 58, White finally won by forcing his opponent's king onto a square where he could promote with check. We have already seen other instances of this, e.g. diag 14. Later on, diag 70 will be another excellent example.

Diagram 59a
Grigoriev 1930
This is a famous study by Grigoriev. White wins by advancing his pawns in tandem.

    1   f4!
Not 1 ♔g2? ♔b3 or 1 ... d5 with a draw; nor 1 h4 d5!.
    1   ...   ♔b4
    2   h4!
Not 2 ♔g2?? a5! and Black wins!
    2   ...   d5
    3   f5   ♔c5
    4   h5

Stoltz - Nimzowitsch
Berlin 1928
Black seems to be in trouble. But with an excellent breakthrough he completely turns the tables.
    1   ...   f4!
    2   gxf4+
If 2 a5 ♔d6!.
    2   ...   ♔d6!!
On this square the king can

Not 4 ♔g2? ♔d6.
    4   ...   d4
    5   f6
Unfortunately, 5 ♔g2 also wins here, for if 5 ... ♔c4 6 f6 d3 7 f7 d2 8 f8♕ d1♕ 9 ♕f1+! etc.
    5   ...   ♔d6
    6   h6   d3
    7   f7   ♔e7
    8   h7   d2
    9   f8♕+   ♔xf8
    10   h8♕+ and wins

Diagram 59b
In *Pawn Endings*, Averbakh and Maizelis suggest several ways of correcting this study to eliminate the dual 5 ♔g2. None of them seems very satisfactory. It strikes me that the device employed in diag 59b, i.e. h2 - h3; add black pawn h2 will do very simply.

hold up the enemy passed pawns for just long enough, e.g.
    3   a5
3 f5 g3 4 f6 g2 5 f7 ♔e7 etc.
    3   ...   g3
    4   a6   ♔c7
    5   f5   g2
    and wins

Pawn(s) v Pawn(s)

More Positional Advantages

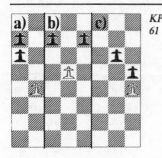

KP 61

Better Pawn Structure

Pawn structures can be deformed in a variety of ways: there are doubled pawns, isolated pawns and backward pawns.

A. Black's pawns are doubled.

B. Black's pawns are isolated.

C. Black's g-pawn is backward.

In each of the three cases A, B and C, Black is unable safely to create a passed pawn, i.e. *the weak pawns are not working properly.*

In a pawn ending the kings are obviously the most powerful single units. But one must also strive to make all of one's pawns work. Clearly it is a grave disadvantage if some of one's pawns are not working efficiently.

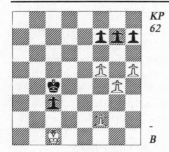

KP 62 - B

Doubled Pawns

Doubled pawns are usually okay defensively - as long as the enemy king cannot sit in front of them. But a pawn majority is often crippled by doubled pawns, i.e. it will be impossible to create a passed pawn.

*Ed. Lasker - Molle
Berlin 1904*

The game continued 1 ... h6? 2 f4? f6 3 g5 ♔d4 and White

resigned. But 1 ... h6? was a blunder since White should have played: 2 f6! gxf6 3 f4 ♔d4 4 g5 fxg5 5 fxg5 ♔e5 6 gxh6 ♔f6 7 ♔c2 (zugzwang) and wins.

The correct move was:

   1   ...   **f6!**
   2   **h6**

Otherwise Black plays 2 ... h6! with a complete blockade.

   2   ...   **gxh6**
   3   **f4**   **♔d5**

and wins easily.

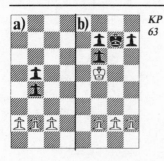

KP 63

A. Black's doubled pawns defend excellently. In the absence of the kings, White cannot create a passed pawn without giving Black one, further advanced, of his own.

E.g. after 1 c3 or 1 a3 Black takes and the two isolated pawns are restrained by the one black pawn on b5.

B. Here Black's pawn struc-

ture is disastrous. He quickly loses the f6-pawn and the game.

For example:

   1   **h3**

But not 1 g4?? ♔h6 2 ♔xf6? stalemate.

   1   ...   **h5**
   2   **h4**   **♔ moves**
   3   **♔xf6** etc.

Pawn(s) v Pawn(s)   ♙(♙) v ♟(♟)

KP 64

Black can easily defend by setting up a passed pawn on the queenside. But how should he start?

A.

The correct move is:

| | 1 | ... | a6! |

1 ... ♚f6 is also okay, but not 1 ... b6?? (see below).

2	f5+	♚f6
3	♚f4	b6
4	♚e4	a5
5	bxa5	bxa5=

B.
But:

| 1 | ... | b6?? |

... would be a terrible mistake.

| 2 | b5! |

The black a-pawn is backward and White has two different winning methods; viz:

| 2 | ... | ♚f6 |

a) 3 ♚d5 ♚f5 4 ♚c6 ♚xf4 5 ♚b7 ♚e5 6 ♚xa7 ♚d6 7 ♚xb6 etc.

b) 3 f5 ♚f7 4 ♚e5 ♚e7 5 f6+ ♚f7 6 ♚f5 ♚f8 7 ♚e6 ♚e8 8 f7+ ♚f8 9 ♚f6 a5 10 bxa6 b5 11 a7 b4 12 a8♕ mate.

KP 65

Botvinnik - Flohr
Moscow 1944
White's doubled b-pawns are perfectly good *defensively* on the queenside.

The most important features here are Black's kingside pawn majority and the white d-pawn.

On the move, White is able to *cripple* the black kingside majority and this gives a decisive advantage.

| 1 | g4! |

Now both ... f5 and ... h5 are effectively prevented. White's plan is to undermine the black pawn structure by playing h5. He will thus gain f5 for his king.

N.B. If the black h-pawn were on h7 then this plan could not succeed and Black would be at least equal.

Thus in the circumstances, the move ... h7 - h6 has drastically weakened Black's pawn structure!

1	...	♚e7
2	h4	♚d6
3	♚e4	b6
4	h5	gxh5

If 4 ... f5+ 5 gxf5 gxh5 6 f6, the white pawns protect each other (cf diag 7) and White wins trivially.

| 5 | gxh5 | a5 |
| 6 | ♚f5 |

6 bxa5 bxa5 7 b3 ♚c5 8 ♚f5 ♚xd5 9 ♚xf6 etc. also wins by a tempo.

6	...	axb4
7	♚xf6	♚xd5
8	♚g6	♚e6
9	♚xh6	♚f6
10	b3!	♚f7

Or 10 ... b5 11 ♚h7 ♚f7 12 h6 etc.

| 11 | ♚g5 | ♚g7 |

And White wins by one tempo: 12 ♚f5 ♚h6 13 ♚e5 ♚xh5 14 ♚d5 ♚g5 15 ♚c6 ♚f5 16 ♚xb6 ♚e6 17 ♚b5 ♚d7 18 ♚xb4 ♚c6 19 ♚a5! etc.

Pawn(s) v Pawn(s) ♙(♙) v ♟(♟)

+
W

+
W

KP 66 **Better King Position**
Given that your king has not got to defend against rampant passed pawns then it is always an advantage to have it in an active position further up the board than the opposing monarch. (The previous example, diag 65, was a good example of this.)

KP 66a *Botvinnik 1952*
White's only advantage is his active king; but it is sufficient for victory. His plan is to reach diag 66a on the move. First let us examine that position.

White to move wins easily with:

    1   f5!   g5

If 1 ... gxf5 2 gxf5 f6 (2 ... ♚g8 3 f6) 3 ♔e6.

    2   ♔e8!   ♚f6
    3   ♔f8 and wins

Note that since White is so much further advanced any Black "counterattack" is totally hopeless.

Black to move:

    1   ...   ♚g8
    2   ♔d8

Or 2 ♔d7, but not 2 f5?? gxf5 3 gxf5 ♚g7=.

    2   ...   ♚h7

If 2 ... ♚g7 3 ♔e8 ♚f6 (3 ... ♚g8 4 f5! ♚g7 5 ♔e7 etc.) 4

♔f8 ♚e6 5 ♔g7 ♚e7 6 f5! etc.

    3   ♔d7   ♚h8

3 ... ♚g8 4 ♔e7! or 3 ... ♚g7 4 ♔e8!; also if 3 ... ♚h6 4 ♔e8!

    4   f5!

This is now possible since the black king is very passive on h8.

    4   ...   ♚g7

Or 4 ... gxf5 5 gxf5 ♚h7 6 ♔e8!.

    5   ♔e7 and wins

We return to Botvinnik's position. In view of diag 66a, Black tries to defend by activating his king.

    1   ♔d5   ♚f8

If 1 ... ♚h6 2 ♔d6 ♚g7 3 ♔e7 ♚g8 4 ♔d8! etc, as above.

    2   ♔d6   ♚e8
    3   f5   g5
    4   ♔c7!

But not 4 f6? ♚d8 5 ♔e5 ♚d7 6 ♚f5 ♚d6 7 ♚xg5 ♚e6.

    4   ...   ♚e7
    5   ♔c8   ♚d6

If 5 ... f6 6 ♔c7 or 5 ... ♚e8 6 f6.

    6   ♔d8   ♚e5
    7   ♔e7   f6
    8   ♔f7

And White wins by a tempo because his pawn started *further up the board.*

+
W

KP 67 White's king is further advanced but he has yet to cause real damage. White wins with the following very typical plan:

a) He forces the enemy king to a passive position and his own to a very active one.

b) He undermines Black's

queenside pawn structure gaining access to some critical squares.

c) He penetrates with his king, wreaking havoc.

    1   ♔b5!

1 ♔d4? ♚e6 leads nowhere.

    1   ...   ♚c7

If 1 ... ♚e5 2 ♔a6 ♚f5 3

♔xa7 ♚xg5 etc, White queens too quickly.

2 ♔a6 ♚b8

The end of part a of the plan.

3 a5!

The second stage.

3 ... bxa5

If 3 ... ♚c7 4 axb6+ axb6 5 b3! and wins.

4 ♔xa5 ♚b7

If 4 ... ♚c7 then simplest is 5 ♔a6 ♚b8 6 b3! ♚c7 7 b4 ♚b8 8 b5 ♚a8 9 b6 and wins.

5 ♔b5 a6+

Or 5 ... ♚c7 6 ♔a6 ♚b8 7

b3! etc.

6 ♔a5

The simplest; 6 ♔c5 ♚c7 7 ♔d5 ♚d7 (7 ... ♚b6) 8 ♔e5 ♚e7 9 b4! also wins very easily.

6 ... ♚a7
7 b4! ♚b7
8 b5 axb5
9 ♔xb5

And White has the opposition (cf diag 9): 9 ... ♚c7 10 ♔c5 ♚d7 11 ♔d5 ♚e7 12 ♔e5 ♚f7 13 ♔d6 ♚f8 14 ♔e6 ♚g7 15 ♔e7 ♚g8 16 ♔f6 ♚h7 17 ♔f7 etc.

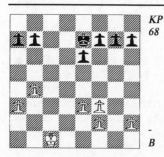

KP 68

KP 68a
- B

Cohn - Rubinstein
St. Petersburg 1909

This famous ending is an excellent example of better king position and pawn structure. Black wins with a plan very similar to White's in diag 67 above:

a) he forces his king to a very active position and White's to a very passive one.

b) He undermines White's kingside pawn structure gaining access to critical squares and weakening White's pawns.

c) He penetrates with the king and mops up.

1 ... ♚f6
2 ♔d2 ♚g5
3 ♔e2

The first point is that White does not have time to counterattack, i.e. if 3 ♔d3 ♚h4 4 ♔d4 ♚h3 5 ♔c5 ♚xh2 6 ♔d6 h5 7 ♔c7 b5! or 7 b5 h4 8 ♔c7 b6!.

We could also have verified this by counting: Black takes nine moves to queen ♚g5 - h4 - h3 x h2 - g2 and h7 - h1♛ plus one defensive move b7 - b6 = 10. White takes 13

moves: ♔d2 - d3 - d4 - c5 - d6 - c7 - b7 x a7 x b6 - c6, b4 - b5 - b6 - b7 - b8♕.

Thus although White starts first his pawn only reaches the sixth rank after Black has queened.

3 ... ♚h4
4 ♔f1 ♚h3
5 ♔g1

The completion of part a.

5 ... e5!

This excellent move practically paralyses White's kingside pawns by preventing 6 f4? exf4 7 exf4 ♚g4; nor is 6 e4 very enticing.

6 ♔h1?

6 b5 was better or 6 a4. Now Black gets a chance to fix the enemy queenside pawns and leave himself a reserve tempo there. He would still have been winning even without this but on principle it should not have been allowed.

6 ... b5!
7 ♔g1 f5

Black starts part b of his plan - undermining the white kingside pawns.

8 ♔h1 g5
9 ♔g1 h5

10　♔h1 (68a)
10　...　　g4

Another good plan is 10 ... h4 11 ♔g1 e4 12 fxe4 fxe4 13 ♔h1 (if 13 f3 exf3 14 e4 g4 and Black is much too fast) 13 ... ♔g4 14 ♔g2 h3+ 15 ♔g1 ♔f3 16 ♔f1 g4 and wins. Note that Black did not need his reserve tempo ... a7 - a6 in this variation.

11　fxg4

In the game Cohn tried 11 e4 fxe4! 12 fxe4 h4 13 ♔g1 g3 14 hxg3 hxg3 0-1 since if 15 f4 exf4 Black queens too soon and otherwise the e-pawn falls - see the column.

11　...　　fxg4

Several endgame books give the variation 11 ... hxg4? 12 ♔g1 f4 13 exf4 exf4 14 ♔h1 g3? (14 ... f3! still wins because of Black's reserve tempo, viz. 15 ♔g1 ♔h4 16 ♔f1 ♔h5 17 ♔g1 ♔g5 18 h3 gxh3 19 ♔h2 ♔g4 20 ♔h1 ♔f4 21 ♔h2 ♔e4 22 ♔xh3 ♔d3 23 ♔g4 ♔e2 24 ♔g3

a6!) 15 hxg3 fxg3 and the simplest is 16 ♔g1! though even 16 fxg3 draws: 16 ... ♔xg3 17 ♔g1 ♔f3 18 ♔f1 ♔e3 19 ♔e1 ♔d3 20 ♔d1 ♔c3 21 a4! a6 22 axb5 axb5 23 ♔c1 ♔xb4 24 ♔b2=.

Returning to our main line (only two moves from diag 68a). This can easily transpose back into the game, e.g.

12　e4

Or 12 ♔g1 e4 followed by ... h4, ... g3.

12　...　　h4
13　♔g1　　g3

This is the actual position where Cohn resigned.

14　hxg3　　hxg3
15　fxg3

If 15 f3 g2 16 ♔f2 ♔h2 or 15 f4 exf4 16 e5 f3 etc.

15　...　　♔xg3

And the e-pawn soon falls.

As we have seen there are several ways of carrying out part b of the plan - but some care is required.

Defensive Ideas

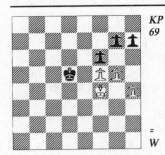

KP 69

= W

Stalemate
This is a very important defensive tool. Indeed diag 2 itself depends on stalemate. Sometimes the defender can find a stalemate defence in more complex positions.

Chigorin - Tarrasch
Ostend 1905

White played 1 gxf6? gxf6 2 ♔g4 ♔e4 but here he re-

signed. After 3 ♔h5 ♔xf5 4 ♔h6 ♔g4 5 ♔xh7 Black can play not 5 ... f5? 6 ♔g6!= but 5 ... ♔h5! and wins.

Maroczy pointed out that White does have a defence:

1　♔g4　　♔e4
2　g6!　　h6
3　♔h5!

And Black has no way of proceeding since 3 ... ♔xf5 would be stalemate!

Pawn(s) v Pawn(s)   ♟(♟) v ♟(♟)

KP
70
=
B

Theoretical Draw
Nimzowitsch - Chigorin
Carlsbad 1907
In this very interesting position Black played the weak 1 ... ♚e6? and lost quickly after 2 ♚c5 f5 3 h3 fxg4 4 hxg4 d4 5 ♚xd4 ♚d6 6 f5 1-0.

The main interest centres on the other move.

    1   **...**   **♚c6**

White is then very close to victory, but Black is able to hang on with one of the main lines ending in an important theoretical draw.

    2   **h3!**

Much the most dangerous. If 2 h4 ♚d6 3 h5 ♚e6! 4 ♚c5 f5 5 g5 hxg5 6 h6 ♚f7 7 fxg5 f4=. Both sets of pawns are invulnerable.

    2   **...**   **♚d6**
    3   **h4**   **♚c6**

But not 3 ... ♚e6? 4 ♚c5 f5 5 g5 etc. - on h4 the pawn supports this admirably.

There are now two lines:

A.
    4   **h5**   **♚d6**
    5   **g5**   **fxg5**
    6   **fxg5**   **♚e6**
    7   **g6**   **♚f6**
    8   **♚xd5**

Perhaps this is why Chigorin rejected 1 ... ♚c6. But of course it is a theoretical draw (diag 19a). For White can do

no better than give stalemate, e.g. 8 ... ♚g7 9 ♚e6 ♚g8 (9 ... ♚f8 10 ♚f6 ♚g8 11 g7 ♚h7 12 ♚f7) 10 ♚f6 ♚f8 11 g7+ ♚g8 12 ♚g6.

B.
    4   **g5**

This is more exciting. There now follows an extremely close race.

    4   **...**   **fxg5**

If 4 ... hxg5 5 fxg5! ♚d6? trying to avoid the race, then White wins: 6 h5 ♚e7 7 h6 ♚f7 8 h7 ♚g7 9 gxf6+ (or 9 g6) 9 ... ♚xh7 10 ♚xd5 ♚g8 11 ♚e6 ♚f8 12 f7.

    5   **fxg5**   **hxg5**
    6   **h5**   **g4**
    7   **♚e3!**

7 h6 g3 8 ♚e3 d4+ is a simple draw, i.e. 9 ♚f3 d3 10 h7 d2 11 ♚e2 g2=.

    7   **...**   **♚c5!**
    8   **♚f4**   **d4**
    9   **♚xg4**   **d3**
    10   **♚f3**   **♚c4**
    11   **h6**

Here Nimzowitsch concluded that White wins since if 11 ... ♚c3? White queens with check. But a Soviet player, I. Romanov, found instead:
    11   **...**   **♚b3!**
    12   **h7**

Or 12 ♚e3 ♚c2.
    12   **...**   **d2=**

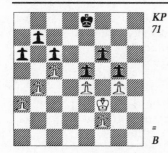

KP
71
=
B

The Blockade
Eliskases - Schmidt
Bad Oeynhausen 1938
Although the position is very blocked Black is in great danger. For White has a most dangerous plan.

a) Play the king to a5 answering ... ♚a7 with a4. In view of White's reserve tempo

f2 - f3, this will force the king to b6.

b) Undermine the black queenside pawn structure with a4, b5. Black must exchange twice on b5 and then answer ... ♚c7.

c) Using the reserve tempo f2 - f3 White can force ♚b6 and c6 after which the plan of

51

Pawn(s) v Pawn(s)   ♖(♙) v ♟(♟)

KP
71a

KP
71b

+
B

+
B

♔c6 - d6 - e6 x f6 will be un-stoppable.

A.
First let us observe this plan in action if Black does not re-act quickly enough.

| 1 | ... | ♔d7 |
| 2 | ♔e3 | ♔c7? |

This is already a losing move - see B.

| 3 | ♔d3 | ♔b8 |

If 3 ... a5 4 ♔c4 ♔b8 (4 ... a4 5 b5 wins easily or 4 ... axb4 5 ♔xb4!) 5 ♔b3 ♔a7 6 ♔a4 ♔a6 7 f3! axb4 8 ♔xb4 ♔a7 9 ♔a5 ♔a8 (if Black had not got the b7-pawn then he would draw with 9 ... ♔b7!) 10 ♔b6 and a4 - a5 - a6 wins eas-ily.

| 4 | ♔c4 | ♔a8 |

4 ... a5 transposes into the line above.

| 5 | ♔b3 | ♔a7 |
| 6 | ♔a4 | *(71a)* |

Black has two possibilities:
a) To submit to White's plan:

6	...	♔a8
7	♔a5	♔a7
8	a4	♔a8

We should note that if the white f-pawn were on f3 then this whole plan would be suicidal. Black could play 8 ... b6+ 9 cxb6+ ♔b7 10 b5 axb5 11 axb5 c5 and wins!

Here, of course, if 8 ... b6+ 9 cxb6+ ♔b7 then simply 10 f3.

| 9 | ♔b6 | ♔b8 |

Part a is completed.

10	b5	axb5
11	axb5	cxb5
12	♔xb5	♔c7

As envisaged under part b.

13	f3!	♔b8
14	♔b6	♔c8
15	c6	bxc6

16 ♔xc6 and wins

b) To seek counterplay:

| 6 | ... | b5+ |
| 7 | cxb6+ | |

Of course he must take. If 7 ♔b3? there is a total blockade and 7 ♔a5?? would even lose!

| 7 | ... | ♔xb6 |
| 8 | f3! | |

But not 8 ♔b3 c5!=.

| 8 | ... | ♔b7 |

If 8 ... c5 9 bxc5+ ♔xc5 10 ♔a5 White queens too soon, e.g. 10 ... ♔d4 11 ♔xa6 ♔e3 12 a4 ♔xf3 13 a5 ♔xg4 14 ♔b5! ♔f3 15 a6 g4 16 a7 g3 17 a8♕ g2 18 ♕a7?!. If Black instead chose 14 ... ♔h3 then White would play 19 ♕h8+ ♔g3 20 ♕xf6 g1♕ 21 ♕g7+ ♔h2 22 ♕xg1+ etc.

9	♔b3	♔c7
10	♔c4	♔b6
11	a4	♔c7!

Slightly better than 11 ... ♔b7 12 ♔c5 ♔c7 13 a5.

12	♔c5	♔b7
13	♔d6	♔b6
14	♔e6	

14 ♔d7 c5 15 bxc5+ ♔xc5 16 ♔e6 also wins - White gets a won queen ending.

| 14 | ... | a5 |

Now 14 ... c5 lost outright - White has an extra tempo on the above note.

15	bxa5+	♔xa5
16	♔d6!	♔b6
17	a5+ and wins	

Note in this line the con-stant possibility of White ob-taining a- v c-pawns cf di-ag 55.

B.
Returning to diag 71 Black can draw if he takes immedi-ate action.

| 1 | ... | ♔d7 |

Or 1 ... a5 immediately.

2 ♔e3 a5!

Now 3 bxa5 would merely block the position so White tries

3 ♔d3 axb4

4 a4

4 axb4 ♔c7 5 ♔c3 b5! 6 cxb6+ ♔xb6 7 ♔c4 ♔b7 8 ♔c5 ♔c7 9 f3 ♔d7=.

4 ... b6!

5 cxb6 c5

6 ♔c4 ♔c6

7 a5=

Both sets of pawns are in-vulnerable - after 7 ... ♔b7 8 ♔b5?? is too slow and would lose.

Diagram 71b

One further point. If the white a-pawn were on a2 then Black's defence line B would fail and he would be quite lost! E.g.

1 ... a5

2 ♔e3 axb4

3 ♔d3 b3

4 a4! and wins

Or 4 a3 and wins.

Some Final Examples

KP 72

= W

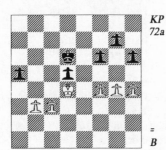

KP 72a

= B

Speelman - Cummings
Brighton 1980

Black has just recaptured on d5 with the e6-pawn - a difficult decision.

White has the advantage since he can force his king to d4.

However, Black should be able to hold the draw because:

a) He can control e5 with ... f6 thus preventing the position ♔d4 vs ♔d6 from being zugzwang.

b) The a-pawn is extremely valuable. In many variations Black can get counterplay by abandoning the kingside and playing ... ♔xb3 followed by the advance of the a-pawn.

Moreover, White cannot arrange to exchange the a-pawn since b4? will always be met by ... a4.

However, in time trouble I succeeded in extracting a win from the position.

1 c3

To stop ... d4 or ... ♔d4. However, e.g. 1 g4 was also in-teresting since both these moves would still be bad. White would be greatly helped later if he still had the reserve tempo c2 - c3.

1 ... ♔d6

This could be necessary eventually. But he could also consider playing on the king-side with 1 ... h5.

2 ♔d4 f6?

2 ... h5! was better. If then 3 f5 f6 and White can never un-dermine e5 or 3 h3 f5! and Black holds the opposition.

3 g4 ♔c6

4 h3!

If 4 h4 ♔d6 5 g5 hxg5 6 fxg5 fxg5 7 hxg5 g6 and Black draws easily.

4 ... ♔d6?

In time trouble Black fails to appreciate the danger. 4 ... g5! drew easily since if 5 f5 ♔d6 6 c4 dxc4 7 ♔xc4 ♔c6 Black has the opposition, or 5 fxg5 hxg5 (5 ... fxg5 6 ♔e5 ♔c5 7 b4+!! wins) 6 c4 dxc4 7 ♔xc4 ♔b6 8 ♔d4 (8 ♔d5 actually loses!) 8 ... ♔b5 9 ♔d3!=.

Pawn(s) v Pawn(s)   ♙(♙) v ♟(♟)

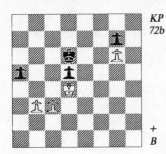

KP
72b

+
B

5 h4 (72a)

5 ... ♔c6?

This is the losing move. Black could still draw with 5 ... g6! (the only move): 6 c4 dxc4 7 ♔xc4 ♔c6 8 g5 fxg5 9 hxg5! hxg5! (9 ... h5 loses: 10 f5 ♔d6 11 fxg6 ♔e7 12 ♔d5 ♔f8 13 ♔e5 ♔g8 14 ♔f4 ♔f8 15 ♔g3 ♔g7 16 ♔h3! etc.) 10 fxg5 ♔b6 11 ♔d5 ♔b5= (Black queens first).

6 g5! hxg5

If 6 ... h5 7 g6 ♔d6 8 f5 ♔c6 9 c4 dxc4 10 ♔xc4 ♔d6 11 ♔b5 ♔e5 12 ♔xa5 ♔xf5 13 b4 ♔e6 14 b5 ♔d7 15 ♔a6! and wins.

Instead 6 ... ♔d6 7 g6! is very similar.

But 6 ... fxg5 would make White's task somewhat harder: 7 fxg5 ♔d6 8 gxh6 gxh6 9 h5 and:

a) 9 ... ♔c6 10 ♔e5 ♔c5 11 ♔f6 d4 12 cxd4+ ♔xd4 13 ♔g6 ♔c3 and White answers 17 ... a2 with 18 h8♕ winning.

b) 9 ... ♔e6 10 c4! (10 ♔c5 ♔e5 11 ♔b5 ♔e4 12 ♔xa5 ♔d3 13 ♔b4 ♔c2 is less clear) 10 ... dxc4 11 ♔xc4 ♔f5 12 ♔b5 White wins by a tempo.

7 fxg5!

Not 7 hxg5?? ♔d6 8 gxf6 (8 g6 f5) 8 ... gxf6 9 f5 ♔c6 10 c4 dxc4 11 ♔xc4 ♔b6 12 ♔d5 ♔b5=.

7 ... fxg5

This, Black's 41st move, was in fact sealed.

8 hxg5 ♔d6

9 g6 (72b)

By advancing the g-pawn, White has decisively improved his chances in the race which follows.

9 ... ♔c6

Or 9 ... ♔e6 10 ♔c5 ♔f6 (10 ... ♔e5 11 ♔b5 ♔e4 12 ♔xa5 ♔d3 13 ♔b4 ♔c2 14 ♔c5 wins easily - contrast the note to 6 ... hxg5. Now there are no rook's pawns) 11 ♔xd5 ♔xg6 12 ♔e6! ♔h7 (12 ... ♔h6/♔h5 13 c4 g5 ... 17 c8♕ g1♕ 18 ♕h8+ and 19 ♕g8+. This is a very typical variation.) 13 c4 g5 14 ♔f5 and wins.

10	♔e5	♔c5
11	♔e6	d4
12	cxd4+	♔xd4
13	♔f7	♔c3
14	♔xg7	♔xb3
15	♔f6	a4
16	g7	a3
17	g8♕+	**1-0**

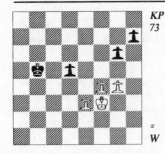

KP
73

=
W

This position arose in a county match and had to be adjudicated.

Clearly White is not worse; the question is merely whether he can force a win.

We can quickly eliminate 1 e4 since then Black can draw immediately: 1 ... dxe4+ 2 ♔xe4 ♔c6 3 ♔e5 ♔d7 4 ♔f6 h5!=.

1 f5? is dangerous only for White: 1 ... gxf5 2 gxf5 ♔c5 and:

a) 3 ♔f4 ♔d6 4 ♔g4 (4 e4=, but not 4 ♔g5? ♔e5 when White can only just force a draw: 5 f6! ♔e6 6 ♔f4 and if 6 ... ♔xf6 7 e4 d4 8 e5+; or 6 ... h5 7 ♔g5!; or 6 ... h6 7 f7! ♔xf7 8 ♔e5=) 4 ... ♔e7! (4 ... ♔e5?? 5 ♔g5 - zugzwang - 5 ... ♔d6 6 ♔f6) 5 ♔f4 ♔f6 6 e4=.

b) 3 ♔g4 ♔d6 4 ♔h5 (4 ♔f4 h6 5 e4!) 4 ... ♔e7 (4 ... ♔e5?? 5 ♔g5) 5 ♔g5 ♔f7 6 ♔f4 ♔f6 7 e4!=.

Pawn(s) v Pawn(s)   ♙(♙) v ♟(♟)

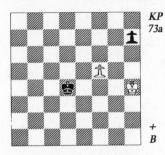

KP
73a

+
B

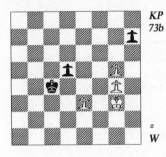

KP
73b

=
W

The *outside passed h-pawn* was a potent force in all these variations.

If 1 ♔e2 ♔c5 2 ♔d3 ♔d6 (2 ... h5? 3 f5!) 3 g5 (3 ♔d4? h5!) 3 ... ♔c5 4 ♔c3 ♔c6 5 ♔d4 ♔d6=.

That leaves:

    1   ♔g3

A.

    1   ...   ♔c5

This is the natural move but it loses. If 1 ... ♔c4 2 ♔h4 h6 (2 ... d4) 3 f5! wins.

    2   ♔h4   d4

If 2 ... h6 3 g5! wins easily.

    3   exd4+   ♔xd4
    4   f5   gxf5 *(73a)*

4 ... ♔e5 5 fxg6 hxg6 6 ♔g5 and wins.

    5   gxf5

Rather remarkably, this position is lost for Black. The problem is that ♔g5 vs ♔e5 is *decisive zugzwang* and Black cannot avoid this position on move.

    5   ...   ♔d5
    6   ♔h5   ♔d6
    7   ♔h6   ♔e5

Or 7 ... ♔e7 8 ♔g7!.

    8   ♔g5!   ♔d6

Black was in zugzwang - obviously White to move could only draw.

If 8 ... ♔d5 9 ♔f6 h5 10 ♔g5 (also 10 ♔g7 h4 ... 13 f8♕ and 14 ♕a8+!) 10 ... ♔e5 11 f6 etc.

Or 8 ... h6+ 9 ♔g6 h5 10 f6 etc.

    9   ♔f6   h5
    10   ♔g7   h4
    11   f6   h3
    12   f7   h2
    13   f8♕+ (CHECK)

B.

Returning to diag 73 after 1 ♔g3 Black does have another possibility:

    1   ...   g5!!

By sacrificing a pawn Black prevents 2 ♔h4. If White takes then he will lose his passed f-pawn and the black king is sufficiently active to just hold the draw.

    2   fxg5

2 ♔f3 ♔c4 3 ♔e2 (3 fxg5 ♔d3 see below: 3 f5 ♔c5 4 e4 ♔d6 5 ♔e3 ♔e5 6 exd5 ♔xd5 and ... ♔e5 ... h5=) 3 ... gxf4 4 exf4 ♔d4 5 ♔f3 ♔c3! 6 f5 (6 ♔e2 ♔d4) 6 ... d4=.

After 2 f5 ♔c5 is even less dangerous than after 2 ♔f3 ♔c4 3 f5.

    2   ...   ♔c4 *(73b)*

If Black is careful then he can draw this position, e.g.

    3   ♔f4

Not 3 ♔h4?? ♔d3 4 ♔h5 ♔xe3 5 ♔h6 ♔f4 6 ♔xh7 ♔xg5 and wins.

If 3 ♔f3 ♔d3 4 ♔f4 then Black can simply play 4 ... ♔e2 (also 4 ... ♔c3/4 ... ♔c4) 5 e4 dxe4 6 ♔xe4 ♔f2 7 ♔f4 ♔g2=.

    3   ...   ♔d3
    4   ♔f3

4 g6 hxg6 5 g5 d4=.

    4   ...   ♔c3

Or 4 ... ♔c4= but not 4 ... ♔d2? 5 e4 dxe4+?? 6 ♔xe4 ♔e2 7 g6 hxg6 8 g5 and wins.

    5   ♔f4

5 ♔e2 ♔c2 or even 5 ... d4.

    5   ...   ♔d3=

Thus diagram 73 really should be a draw with best play.

Knight v Pawn(s)

Knight v One Pawn

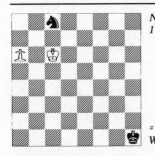

**NP
1**

1	♔b7	♞d6+
2	♔c7	♞b5+
3	♔b6	♞d6

A key motif that the knight must often use when combat-ting a passed pawn. The fork allows the knight an extra route to defence.

4	a7	♞c8+=

=
W

**NP
2**

1	a6

And the pawn queens. A graphic illustration of the knight's proverbial helpless-ness against rook's pawns. (This is also the point behind a thematic tactic; with ♞c5, Pa5 vs ♞d8, Pb7 - 1 ♞xb7!.)

+
W

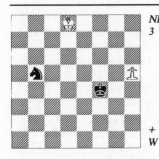

**NP
3**

Zelman Sila 1941

1	h6	♞d6
2	h7	♞f7+
3	♔e7	♞h8

4	♔f6+-

A basic win in which the king on f6 dominates both black pieces.

+
W

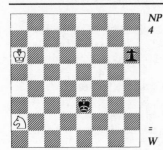

**NP
4**

Grigoriev 1932

1	♞b4	h5
2	♞c6	

Not 2 ♞d5+? ♔f3 (diagonal opposition).

2	...	♔e4

Or 2 ... h4 3 ♞e5 h3 (3 ... ♔f4 4 ♞g6+) 4 ♞g4+ and the knight succeeds in halting the pawn on the sixth rank.

3	♞a5!!	

Visually paradoxical, but since f1 is now the best square

for the knight, easy to unders-tand.

3	...	h4
4	♞c4!	

Black cannot prevent ♞d2-f1 or ♞e5-g4. (Not 4 ♞b3? ♔e3 erecting a king barrier. Similar to the diago-nal opposition, the king ne-gates the knight's two most active moves.)

4	...	h3
5	♞d2+	♔e3

=
W

56

Knight v Pawn(s)

♘ V ♟(♟)

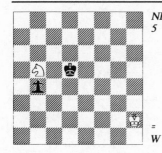

= W

6   ♘f1+=

Another example of how the knight, despite its inherent clumsiness, can prove agile if it can create a dual route to a key defensive square.

Grigoriev 1938

1   ♘c7+   ♚c4
2   ♘e8

Since the route via a3 is blocked, the knight heads for d2.

2   ...   ♚c5

Or 2 ... b3 3 ♘d6+! ♚b4 (to prevent ♘b5-a3) 4 ♘e4.

3   ♘f6   ♚d4

To prevent ♘e4-d2. This diagonal opposition to the knight is a key motif and must be noted. It forces the knight to travel to reenter the relevant zone of the board and places the king three moves away from a possible check.

4   ♘e8   ♚e5
5   ♘c7   ♚d6

6   ♘e8+!

Not 6 ♘b5+ ♚c5 7 ♘c7 b3 8 ♘e6+ ♚c4!-+.

6   ...   ♚c5
7   ♘f6   ♚d4
8   ♘e8   b3
9   ♘d6

White has finally achieved a square with access to both defensive routes.

9   ...   ♚c3
10   ♘e4+

Or 10 ♘b5+? ♚b4.

10   ...   ♚c2
11   ♘d6!   b2
12   ♘c4

Again the forking motif.

12   ...   b1♕
13   ♘a3+=

Knight v Two Pawns

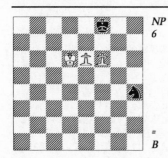

= B

Averbakh

At first sight the advanced connected pawns look very dangerous for Black, but he can still make a draw with accurate play.

1   ...   ♘g6!

The only way to draw. Not:

a) 1 ... ♚e8? 2 f7+ ♚f8 3 e7+ ♚xf7 4 ♚d7;

b) 1 ... ♘f3 2 f7 with e7+ and ♚d7 to follow (if 2 ...

♚g7 3 ♚e7);

c) 1 ... ♘f5+ 2 ♚d7.

2   ♚d7

Or 2 e7+ ♘xe7 3 fxe7+ ♚e8 4 ♚e6=.

2   ...   ♘e5+
3   ♚d8

3 ♚c7 is met by 3 ... ♘g4!.

3   ...   ♘c6+
4   ♚c7   ♘d4
5   ♚d7   ♘xe6!
6   ♚xe6   ♚e8=

Knight v Pawn(s)   ♘ V ♟(♟)

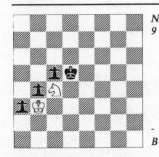

NP 7

Belenki 1955

1	♔d4	a3
2	♘e1+!	♔d2

If the king moves to the b-file then 3 ♔d3=.

3	♘f3+	♔c1

4	♔d3!	a2
5	♘d4	♔b1
6	♘c2	♔b2
7	♘a1!	♔xa1
8	♔c2=	

= W

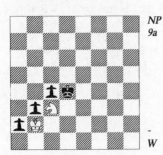

NP 8

Prokes 1963

1	♘h4	e5
2	♔e6	e4
3	♔f5	e3
4	♔g4	e2

5	♔h3	♔f1
6	♘g2	♔f2
7	♘f4	e1♘=

cf diag N14.

= W

Knight v Three Pawns

NP 9

Horwitz 1880, Averbakh 1954

1	...	♔c6!!

Alternatives let the win slip:

a) 1 ... a2? 2 ♘e3+ ♔e4 3 ♘c2 ♔d3 4 ♘a1 ♔d2 5 ♔xa2 c4 6 ♔b3+ ♔c2 7 ♘d4+ ♔d3 8 ♔b3=.

b) 1 ... ♔d4 2 ♘d6 ♔d3 3 ♘c4 ♔e2 4 ♘d6 ♔d1 5 ♘e4 c4+ 6 ♔xb4 a2 7 ♘c3+. 2 ♔c2 Or 2 ♘e3 ♔b5 3 ♘c4 a2 (see also diag 11).

2	...	♔b5
3	♘d6+	♔a4
4	♘c4	b3+
5	♔c3	a2
6	♔b2	♔b4
7	♘e3	c4
8	♘d5+	♔c5
9	♘c3	♔d4 (9a)

This is Horwitz's position (cf diag 11).

10	♘e2+	

Alternatively:

a) 10 ♔a1!? b2+ (10 ... ♔xc3??=) 11 ♔xb2 a1♕+ 12 ♔xa1 ♔xc3-+.

b) 10 ♘a4 c3+ 11 ♘xc3 a1♕+.

c) 10 ♘b5+ ♔d3 11 ♔a1 ♔c2 12 ♘d4+ (12 ♘a3+ ♔c3! 13 ♘b5+ ♔d3 14 ♔b2 c3+ 15 ♘xc3 a1♕+) 12 ... ♔d2! (12 ... ♔c3? 13 ♘xb3!=) 13 ♔b2 ♔d3 (13 ... c3+ 14 ♔a1 b2+ 15 ♔xa2 c2 JT) 14 ♘b5 c3+ 15 ♘xc3 a1♕+.

10	...	♔d3
11	♘c1+	♔d2
12	♔a1	b2+
13	♔xb2	a1♕+-+

Knight v Pawn(s)   ♘ V ♟(♟)

NP
10

Averbakh 1954
Here White manages to set up a blockade.

1	♘a2	♚d5
2	♘b4+	♚e4
3	♘a2	♚e3
4	♘b4	♚e2
5	♔c2	

Black can make no progress.

= W

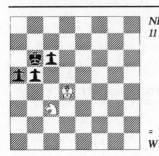

NP
11

Marble 1914

1	♘e4	a4
2	♘c5	

If the position were one rank up, this move would lose to ... a2. Without this possibility the pawns cannot be blockaded and Black wins.

2 ... ♚a5

Or 2 ... ♚c7 3 ♚e5 a3 4 ♘b3! a2 5 ♚d4 ♚d6 6 ♚c3 and the a-pawn falls.

3	♔c3	b4+
4	♔c4	b3

Or 4 ... a3 5 ♘b3+ ♚a4 6 ♘c5+=.

5 ♔c3!

A standard motif - a waiting move that allows the defender to transpose into a drawn pawn ending.

5	...	♚b5
6	♘xb3	axb3
7	♔xb3=	

= W

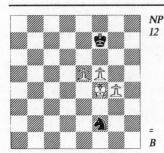

NP
12

**Möhring - Pribyl,
Hradec Kralove 1977**
A practical example of the Averbakh fix of the Fine rule. As Averbakh pointed out, all pawns need to reach the fifth rank to guarantee a win. Fine's rule of two pawns is not enough, as demonstrated by Averbakh and in this example from practical play.

58	...	♘d3+
59	♚e4	♘f2+
60	♚f4	♘d3+
61	♚e4	♘f2+
62	♚f3	♘h3!

Or 62 ... ♘d3 63 e6+ ♚e7 64 g5+-.

63	♚e3	♘g5
64	♚d4	♚e8
65	♚d3	♚f7
66	♚e3	♘h3
67	♚f3	♘g5+
68	♚g3	♚g7
69	♚f4	♘h3+

= B

70	♚e3	♚f7
71	♚d4	♚e7
72	♚d5	♘f4+
73	♚c4	♘h3!

Black defends in accordance with the rule.

74	♚d4	♘g5
75	♚d5	♘h7
76	♚e4	♘g5+
77	♚f4	♘h3+
78	♚f3	♘g5+
79	♚g3	♚f7
80	e6+	♚f6

Now the blockade suffices to hold.

81	♚h4	♘e4
82	♚h5	♘d6

To stop the e- and g-pawns (from e8) if White tries to break through with g5.

83	♚h6	♘e8
84	♚h5	♘d6
85	♚h4	♘e4

½-½

Knight v Pawn(s)   ♘ V ♟(♟)

NP 13
B

Skalkotas - T. Horvath
Athens 1983

1	...	♚g5
2	♚g2	e4

As we have seen, when the pawns reach the fifth rank they should win and this practical example provides no exception.

| 3 | ♘e7 |

Or 3 ♘d6 e3 4 ♚g3 f4+.

3	...	f4
4	♚f2	g3+
5	♚g2	♚h4?

Much better is 5 ... ♚g4 6 ♘d5 e3 7 ♚g1 ♚f3 winning immediately. White gets no checks or chances of a blockade.

| 6 | ♘f5+ | ♚g4 |

7	♘h6+	♚g5
8	♘f7+	♚f6
9	♘d8	♚e5
10	♘c6+	♚d5
11	♘e7+	♚d4
12	♘g6	♚e3
13	♘e5	♚d2!

Not 13 ... ♚e2 14 ♘g6 f3+ 15 ♚xg3 f2 16 ♘f4+=.

14	♘g6	f3+
15	♚xg3	e3
16	♘e5	f2
17	♘f3+	

Or 17 ♘c4+ ♚e2 18 ♘xe3 ♚xe3 19 ♚g2 ♚e2.

| 17 | ... | ♚e2 |

White resigned in view of 18 ♘d4+ ♚d1 19 ♚g2 (19 ♘f5 f1♘+ 20 ♚g2 e2) 19 ... e2.

Knight and One Pawn v King

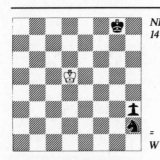

NP 14
W

Chekhover 1952

1	♚e4	♘g4
2	♚f3	♚g7
3	♚g3	h2

| 4 | ♚g2= |

White has forced a positional draw.

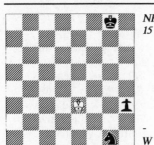

NP 15
W

| 1 | ♚f2 | ♘e2! |

Black has created a barrier that allows him to bring up his king and win. (Not 1 ... h2? 2 ♚g2 ♘f3 3 ♚h1=.).

Knight v Pawn(s)   ♘ V ♟(♟)

Knight and One Pawn v Pawn

NP 16

Kubbel 1914

1	h3	

Or 1 ♘g5+ ♚g4=.

1	...	♚g3
2	♘g5	♚f4
3	♘e4	♚f3
4	♔d4	♚f4

Or 4 ... ♚g2 5 ♘g5 ♚g3 6 ♔e5.

| 5 | ♔d5 | ♚f5 |
| 6 | ♘c3! | |

Not 6 ♘f2 ♚f4 7 ♔e6 (or 7 ♔d4 ♚f3 8 ♔e5 ♚xf2 9 ♔f4 ♚e2! 10 ♔g4 ♚e3 11 ♔xh4 ♚f4=) 7 ... ♚g3 8 ♔f5 ♚xf2

9 ♔g4 ♚e3 10 ♔xh4 ♚f4=.

6	...	♚f4
7	♘e2+	♚f3
8	♘g1+!	

Again the key square is the one that affords rearguard protection of the pawn.

8	...	♚g2
9	♔e4	♚xg1
10	♔f3!	

Or 10 ♔f4? ♚f2 11 ♔g4 ♚e3=.

10	...	♚f1
11	♔g4	♚f2
12	♔xh4	+–

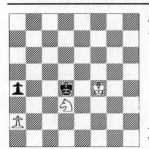

NP 17

Zatulovskaya - Ioseliani
Sochi 1981

A very similar example to diag 16.

| 1 | ♘c1 | ♚c3 |

After 1 ... ♚c4 2 ♔e4! White will lead play into the main note, i.e. 2 ... ♚c3 (2 ... a3 3 ♘e2+– or 2 ... ♚b4 3 ♔d4 ♚a3 4 ♔c4 ♚b2 5 ♔b4 a3 6 ♔a4 ♚xc1 7 ♚xa3 ♚c2 8 ♔b4+–) 3 ♔e3 transposing to the note to White's second move.

| 2 | ♔e4? | |

White should play 2 ♔e3 ♚c2 (2 ... ♚b2 3 ♔d2 a3 4 ♘d3+!! ♚xa2 5 ♔c2 (a position known even in the thir-

teenth century, and called the "Carvajal") 5 ... ♚a1 6 ♘c1 a2 7 ♘b3+) 3 ♘d3 ♚c3 4 ♔e4 ♚c4 5 ♘c1! (The king works forward and the knight works from the rear. The knight belongs behind passed pawns in such endings.) 5 ... ♚c3 6 ♔d5 ♚b2 7 ♔c4 ♚xc1 8 ♔b4+–.

2	...	♚b2
3	♔d3	♚xc1
4	♔c3	

White is a tempo down from the winning line.

4	...	a3
5	♔b3	♚d2
6	♚xa3	♚c3
½-½		

NP 18

Blackburne - Zukertort
Match 1881

| 1 | ♔f2! | g5 |

Or 1 ... ♚e4 2 ♘g2+–.

| 2 | ♚e2 | ♚e4 |
| 3 | ♚d2 | ♚f4 |

Or 3 ... ♚d4 4 ♘g2 ♚e4 5 ♚e2+–.

4	♚d3	♚f3
5	♚d4	♚f4
6	♚d5!	♚xe3

| 7 | ♚e5 | 1-0 |

With Black to move:

| 1 | ... | ♚g3! |
| 2 | ♚d1 | ♚f3! |

Not 2 ... ♚f2 3 ♚d2 ♚f3 4 ♚d3 ♚f4 5 ♚d4 ♚f3 6 ♚e5 ♚xe3 7 ♚f6+–.

3	♚d2	♚f2
4	♚d3	♚f3
5	♚d4	♚f4=

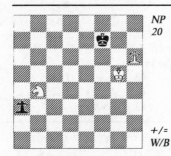

= W

NP 19

Plachetka - Hardicsay
Stary Smokovec 1982

49	♔e1	♔c2
50	♘d2	♔c1
51	♔e2	♔c2
	½-½	

Another example of this helpless knight formation with one pawn each. The transfer of the white king to the white pawn is impossible. One factor is that advancing the pawn puts it on one of the worst squares for the knight, which needs three moves to protect it there.

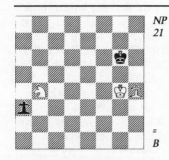

+/= W/B

NP 20

Grigoriev 1933
White to move wins:

1	♘a2!	♔g8
2	♔g6	♔h8
3	♘b4	♔g8
4	h7+	♔h8
5	♘c6	a2
6	♘d8	a1♕
7	♘f7+ and wins	

Black to move draws:

| 1 | ... | ♔g8! |

| 2 | ♔g6 | |

Or 2 ♔f6 ♔h7 3 ♔g5 ♔g8!=.

| 2 | ... | ♔h8 |
| 3 | ♘a2 | ♔g8= |

An illustration both of the typical winning method, and of the fact that the knight cannot win a tempo or triangulate by itself.

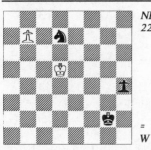

= B

NP 21

Gulko - Grigorian,
USSR ch 1974

A practical example of diag 20.

59	...	♔h6
60	h5	♔h7
61	♔g5	♔g7
62	h6+	♔h7
63	♘a2	♔h8
64	♔h5	♔h7
65	♘c3	♔g8
	½-½	

= W

NP 22

1	♔d6	♘b8
2	♔c7	♘a6+
3	♔b6	♘b8
4	♔c7	

Not 4 ♔a7?? ♘d7.

4	...	h3
5	♔xb8	h2
6	♔a7=	

Note that White only draws here because the knight has no squares to the left of the a-file.

With a c-pawn (w♔e5 v b♘e7) the knight could move to a7, and Black would win

Knight v Pawn(s)

♞ V ♟(♟)

NP
23

+
W

Averbakh 1955

1	♔g5	♔f7
2	♘b1	♔g7

Or 2 ... ♔e6 3 ♔g6 ♔e5 4 h4 ♔e4 5 h5 ♔d3 6 h6 ♔c2 7 h7 ♔xb1 8 h8♕+–.

3	♘d2!	♔h7
4	♔f5!	♔h6
5	♔e4	♔h5
6	♔d3	♔h4
7	♔c2	♔h3
8	♘f1!+–	

With the black pawn less advanced and White's pawn more advanced, White's winning method usually involves releasing the passed pawn and using the bishop to win a promotion race. (See also diag 24.)

NP
24

+
W

Gausel - Malishauskas 1992

73	♘b4	♔g5
74	♔g2	♔h4
75	♘c2	♔g5
76	♔g3	♔h5
77	h4	♔g6
78	♔g4	♔h6
79	h5	♔g7
80	♔g5	♔h7
81	h6	♔h8

Or 81 ... ♔g8 82 ♔g6 ♔h8

83 ♘d4 ♔g8 84 ♘f5 c2 85 h7+ ♔h8 86 ♘h6 c1♕ 87 ♘f7+.

82	♔g6	♔g8
83	♘d4	♔h8
84	♘f5	c2
85	♘d6	c1♕
86	♘f7+	♔g8
87	h7+	♔f8
88	h8♕+	1-0

For example, 88 ... ♔e7 89 ♕d8+ ♔e6 90 ♕d6+.

Knight and One Pawn v Two Pawns

NP
25

–
W

Pomar - Andersson Palma 1972

A clear example of the simplest knight and pawn against pawn winning process.

71 g4

Otherwise ... ♔f3 absorbs the kingside pawns.

71	...	hxg4
72	h5	♔e4
73	h6	♘f4+
74	♔g3	♔f5
75	h7	♘g6

The king works with the pawn, the knight deals with the passed pawn.

76	♔g2	♔f4
77	♔f2	g3+
78	♔g2	♔g4
79	♔g1	♔f3
80	♔f1	g2+
81	♔g1	♘h8

0-1

The knight is used as a source of tempi in what is a pawn ending at the other end of the board.

Knight v Pawn(s)

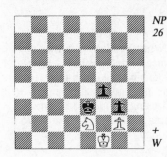

NP 26

Réti and Mandler 1924

1	♘g1	♔d2

If 1 ... ♔d3 2 ♘f3 ♔e3 3 ♘e1 ♔d2 4 ♘c2!! transposes.

2	♘f3+	♔d3!
3	♔e1	

Not 3 ♘e1+ ♔e3 4 ♘c2+ ♔d2 5 ♘b4 ♔e3 6 ♘d5+ ♔e4 7 ♘f6+ ♔e3 intending ... f3=.

3	...	♔e3
4	♔e5	♔e4

4 ... ♔d4 5 ♘g4 ♔d3 6 ♔d1 intending ♔e2, and if 6 ... f3 7 ♘e5+.

5	♘c4	♔d3

+ W

Or 5 ... ♔d4 6 ♔e2!.

6	♘d2	♔e3
7	♘f3	♔d3
8	♔f1!	

Zugzwang - White has reached the position after Black's second move, but now with Black to move.

8	...	♔e3
9	♘e1	♔d2
10	♘c2!!	♔d1

Or 10 ... ♔xc2 11 ♔e2 ♔c3 12 ♔f3 ♔d4 13 ♔xf4 ♔d5 14 ♔xg3+-.

11	♘b4	♔d2
12	♘d5+-	

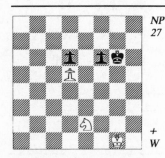

NP 27

Hasek 1951

1	♔f2	♔f5
2	♔e3	♔e5
3	♘c3	

Not 3 ♘f4 f5 4 ♔f3 ♔d4 and ... ♔e4=.

3	...	f5
4	♔d3	f4
5	♔c4	f3
6	♘d1	♔e4
7	♘f2+	♔e3

+ W

8	♘h1	♔e4
9	♘g3+	♔e5
10	♘f1	♔e4
11	♘h2	f2
12	♘f1	♔e5
13	♘d2+-	

This motif of forcing the passed pawn forward is slightly reminiscent of a line in Smyslov-Persitz (diag N71).

NP 28

Averbakh 1980

1	...	♘c4
2	♔g4	

Averbakh only gives this move but worth noting is 2 ♔g5 ♘d2 3 ♔g4 ♘b3 4 ♔g5

- B

(4 ♔h3 ♔d4+-) 4 ... ♘d4 5 ♔g4 ♘e2+- 6 a5 ♔d5 7 ♔f5 ♔c5 8 ♔e4 ♘b5 9 ♔d3 ♘g3.

2	...	♘e3+
3	♔g5	♘g2-+

NP 29

M Kovacs - Ftacnik 1979

1	♘d6	f2
2	♘f5+	♔f3!

Or 2 ... ♔f4? 3 ♘g3 ♔f3 4 ♘f1 ♔f4 5 ♘h2 ♔e3 6 ♔g2 ♔e2 7 ♘f1 ♔e1 8 ♘g3 (zugzwang) 8 ... h5 9 ♔f3! (again the technique of forcing

= W

the defending king far up the board, to create action in the opposite direction, is seen) 10 ... f1♕+ 11 ♘xf1 ♔xf1 12 ♔f4+-.

3	♘g3	♔f4
4	♘f1	♔f3
5	♘h2+	♔f4
6	♘f1	

Or 6 ♔g2 f1♕+ 7 ♔xf1 (7 ♘xf1 ♔g4=) 7 ... ♔g3 8 h5 ♔h4.

6	...	♔f3
7	h5	♔f4
8	♘g3	♔f3

9	♔h4	♔f4
10	♔h3	♔f3
11	♔h2	♔g4
12	♔g2	f1♕+
½-½		

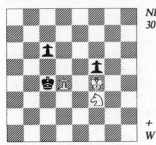

NP 30

Averbakh

1 ♔e5

Not 1 ♔xf5? c5=.

1 ... ♔d3

2 ♘e1+!

White must avoid:

a) 2 ♔xf5 ♔e3 3 ♔g4 ♔e4 intending ... c5, ... ♔d5=.

b) 2 ♔d6 ♔e3 3 ♔xc6 ♔xf3 4 d5 f4 5 d6 ♔g2 6 d7 f3 7 d8♕ f2=.

2 ... ♔c4

Or 2 ... ♔e3 (2 ... ♔d2 3 ♘g2) 3 ♘c2+ ♔d3 4 ♘b4+ ♔e3 5 ♘xc6 f4 6 ♔d5! f3 7 ♘e5+-.

3 ♘g2 ♔d3

4	♘f4+	♔c3
5	♘e6	♔c4
6	♔xf5	♔d5
7	♔f6	♔d6
8	♘f4	c5
9	d5	

White places the knight behind the pawn.

9	...	c4
10	♔f5	c3
11	♔e4	

Now the king relieves the knight.

| 11 | ... | c2 |
| 12 | ♘e2+- | |

The knight stops the pawn.

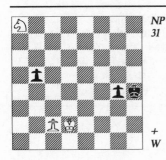

NP 31

Grünfeld - Rukavina
Belgrade GMA Open 1988

65	♔e2	♔h3
66	♘c7	g3
67	♘e6	g2
68	♘g5+	♔g3
69	♘f3	♔f4
70	♔f2	♔e4
71	♔xg2	♔e3
72	♔g3	b4
73	♔g4	♔e4

Alternatively:

a) 73 ... b3 74 cxb3 ♔d3 75 ♘d2;

b) 73 ... ♔e2 74 ♔f4 ♔d1 75 ♘d4 ♔d2 76 ♔e4 ♔c3 77 ♔d5 ♔b2 78 ♔c4 ♔a3 79 ♘c6.

| 74 | ♘d2+! | ♔d4 |
| 75 | ♘b1! | ♔e4 |

Or 75 ... ♔c4 76 ♔f3.

76	♔g5	♔e5
77	♔g6	♔e6
78	♔g7	♔e7
79	♔g8	♔e8
80	♘d2	♔e7
81	♘b3	♔e6
82	♔f8	♔d5
83	♔e7	♔c4
84	♔d6	♔c3
85	♘a1	

Very thematic - knight behind the pawn, king circling to the other side of the pawn(s).

1-0

Knight v Pawn(s)

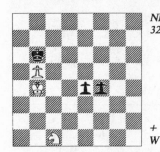

NP
32

Averbakh

Here the knight is well-placed to force a blockade of the pawns on its own.

| 1 | ♘b3 | f3 |

Or 1 ... e3 2 ♘d4.

| 2 | ♘d2 | f2 |
| 3 | ♘f1 and wins | |

+
W

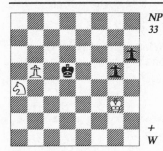

NP
33

Liberzon - Benzion
Israel 1974

White's task is to bring the king to the pawn, and blockade the kingside with the knight. This should not be possible with vigilant defence.

47	♔g4	♔d6
48	♔h5	♔d5
49	♔g4	♔d6
50	♘c3	♔c5

Liberzon suggests 50 ... ♔e5! 51 ♘e4 ♔e6! (51 ... ♔d5 52 ♔f5!+-) 52 ♔f3 (52 ♔h5 ♔d5) 52 ... ♔d5 53 ♔e3 g4=. Play might then continue 54 ♔f4 h5 55 ♔g3 (55 ♔f5 g3) 55 ... ♔e6 56 ♔h4 ♔d5 with mutual zugzwang.

| 51 | ♔f5 | ♔b6? |

+
W

Black should play 51 ... ♔d6! 52 ♔e4 (52 ♘e2 ♔c5 53 ♘d4 ♔d5 54 b6 ♔d6=) 52 ... ♔c5= (Liberzon).

| 52 | ♔e6 | ♔c5 |

Or 52 ... g4 53 ♔d5 g3 54 ♔c4 g2 55 ♘e2+- (Liberzon).

| 53 | ♔d7 | ♔b6 |

Or 53 ... g4 54 ♔c7 g3 55 b6 g2 56 ♘e2+-.

54	♔d6	h5
55	♔d5	h4
56	♔c4	g4
57	♘e2	1-0

After 57 ... h3 (57 ... g3 58 ♘g1 g2 59 ♘h3+-) 58 ♘g3 h2 59 ♘h1 ♔b7 60 ♔c5 ♔c7 61 b6+ ♔b7 62 ♔b5 ♔b8 63 ♔c6 ♔c8 64 b7+ ♔b8 65 ♘g3 White wins easily.

Knight and One Pawn v Three Pawns

NP
34

Rayner - Adams
London (Nat West) 1987

With the pawns paralysed, the knight has no difficulties despite the tenuous material balance.

56	...	♘c4+
57	♔d3	♘d6
58	♔e3	♘f5+
59	♔f2	

Or 59 ♔e2 ♔f4 60 ♔f2 ♘e3 61 ♔g1 ♔g3-+.

59	...	♔f4
60	♔g1	♔g3
61	♔h1	♘e3
62	f4	♔xf4
63	♔h2	♘f5
64	♔g1	♔g3
65	♔h1	♘e3
66	♔g1	♘xg2
67	♔h1	♘f4
68	♔g1	♘xh3+
69	♔f1	♘f2
	0-1	

-
B

Knight v Pawn(s) ♞ V ♟(♟)

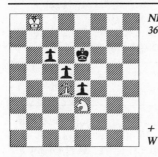

+
W

NP 35

Beliavsky - Eingorn
USSR ch, Lvov 1984
The knight is helpless against
the advance of the pawns.

59	h4	♚e5	
60	♚g6	♞e6	
61	g3	♞d4	
62	f4+	♚e6	
63	h5	♞f5	
64	g4	1-0	

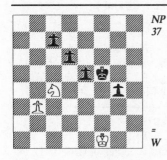

+
W

NP 36

Muñoz 1941

1 ♚a7!

The alternatives let the win
slip:

a) 1 ♚c7 c5 2 dxc5 d4 3
♞g2 ♚e5 4 c6 d3 5 ♞b7 d2 6
♞e3 ♚d4=;

b) 1 ♚b7 ♚d6 2 ♚b6 ♚d7 3
♞g4 ♚d6 4 ♞e5 e3 5 ♞f3 e2
6 ♞e1 ♚d7 7 ♚c5 ♚c7 8
♚b4 ♚b7 9 ♚c3 ♚b6=.

1 ... ♚e7

Also winning for White is 1

... ♚d6 2 ♚b7 ♚d7 3 ♚b6
♚d6 4 ♞g4 ♚d7 5 ♞e5+
♚d6 6 ♞xc6 e3 7 ♞b4.

2 ♞g4 ♚e6

Or 2 ... ♚d6 3 ♚b6 ♚d7 4
♞e5+.

3	♚b7	♚f5
4	♞e3+	♚f4
5	♞c2	e3
6	♚xc6	♚e4
7	♚c5	e2
8	♞e1	♚e3
9	♚xd5+-	

Knight and One Pawn v Four Pawns

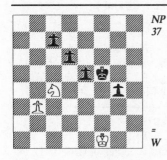

=
W

NP 37

Halasz - Borkowski
Porabka 1987

53 ♞e3+ ♚e4

Or 53 ... ♚f4 54 ♞d5+ ♚f3
55 ♞xc7 g3 56 b4 e4 57 ♞d5
e3 58 ♞xe3 ♚xe3 59 b5.

54 ♞xg4 ♚d3

Though the pawns look dangerous, the knight proves very
nimble.

55 ♞f6 c6
56 ♞g8!

This looks like the wrong direction but e7 is the best defensive square for the knight.

56 ... ♚c3

Alternatively:

a) 56 ... e4 57 ♚e1.

b) 56 ... ♚d2 57 ♞e7 c5 (57
... e4 58 ♞xc6 e3 59 ♞d4) 58

♞c8 d5 59 ♞b6 d4 60 ♞c4+
(60 ♞d7 e4 61 ♞xc5 e3 62
♞e4+ ♚d1 63 ♞g3 d3) 60 ...
♚c3 61 ♞xe5=.

57	♞e7	c5
58	♞c8	d5
59	♞b6	d4

Or 59 ... ♚d4 60 ♚e2 e4 61
♞d7=.

60	♞d7	d3
61	♞xc5	d2
62	♞e4+	♚c2
63	♞f2!	d1♛+
64	♞xd1	♚xd1
65	♚f2	♚d2
66	♚f3	♚d3
67	♚f2	e4
68	♚e1	♚c3
½-½		

Knight v Pawn(s)

NP 38

Vitolins - Gleizerov
Uzhgorod 1988
Black's position looks grim but the a-pawn paralyses White's forces.

41 d5

The white king cannot approach the a-pawn, and b5 is met by ♘d6 and ♘xb5.

41	...	♔f5
42	b5	♘d6+
43	♔b4	♘xb5
44	c4	

Or 44 ♔xa4 ♘c3+=.

44	...	a3
45	♔b3	♘d6
46	c5	a2
47	♔b2	

Or 47 ♔xa2 ♘e4 48 c6 ♘c3+=.

47	...	♘e4
48	c6	♔g4
49	c7	♘d6
50	♔xa2	♔xh4
51	♔b3	♔g5
52	♔b4	½-½

For example, 52 ... ♔f6 53 ♔c5 ♔e7 54 ♔c6 ♘c8=.

Knight and Two Pawns v Two Pawns

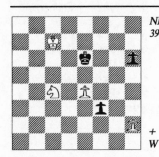

NP 39

Vainerman - Timoshchenko
Norilsk 1987

7 ♔c6?

Best is 7 ♔d8!! f2 8 ♘d2 h5 9 ♔e8 h4 10 h3! ♔e5 11 ♔f7 ♔f4 12 ♔g6 ♔e3 13 ♘f1+ ♔xe4 14 ♔g5+-.

7	...	f2
8	♘d2	♔e5
9	♔c5	h5!=
10	♔c4	f1♕+
11	♘xf1	♔xe4
12	♔c3	♔f3
13	♔d2?	

13 ♔d4! is not mentioned by Khuzman and Vainerman.

This looks analogous to diag 20: 13 ... ♔g2 (if instead 13 ... ♔f2 14 ♔e4 h4 15 ♔f4 h3 16 ♔g4 ♔g2 17 ♔h4+- or 13 ... ♔f4 14 ♘d2 h4 15 ♔d3 ♔g4 16 ♔e3 ♔h3 17 ♘f1 ♔g2 18 ♔e2 and wins, cf diag 17) 14 ♔e3 ♔xf1 15 ♔f4+- h4 16 ♔g4 ♔f2 17 ♔xh4.

13	...	♔f2
14	♘e3	♔g1
15	h4	½-½

In view of 15 ... ♔f2 16 ♔d3 ♔g3 17 ♘f5+ ♔f4 18 ♘e7 ♔g4 19 ♘g6 ♔f5=.

NP 40

Nunez - Valdes
Cuba 1990

1 ... ♘a7!

Not 1 ... g5 (1 ... ♔d7 2 ♔e5 repeats) 2 ♔e5 intending ♔f5, h4= (see also diags 20 and 21).

2 h3!

Alternatively:

a) 2 ♔e5 ♘c6+ 3 ♔e4 ♔e6-+;

b) 2 ♔c5 ♔d7 3 ♔d5 (3 ♔b6 ♘c6 4 ♔c5 ♔c7 5 ♔d5 ♘e7+ 6 ♔e6 ♘g8 7 ♔f7 g5-+) 3 ... ♘c6 4 h3 ♘e7+ 5 ♔e5 ♔c7-+;

2 ... ♘c8!

Or 2 ... g5 3 ♔e5 ♔f7 4 ♔f5 ♔g7 5 h4! gxh4 6 ♔g4=.

3 ♔e5

Or 3 ♔c6 ♔d8 4 ♔d5 (4 h4 g5-+ 5 hxg5 hxg5 6 ♔d5 ♔c7 7 ♔e5 ♘d6 and ... ♘f7) 4 ... ♔c7 5 ♔e6 g5 intending ... ♘e7-+.

3 ... h5?

Black goes wrong in time-trouble. Instead 3 ... ♘b6! 4 a7 (4 h4 ♘c8-+ 5 ♔d5 ♔d7 6

♔e5 ♚c7 7 ♔f6 ♘e7) 4 ... ♘a8! (4 ... ♚f7 5 ♔d4=) 5 ♔d5 ♘c7+ 6 ♔c6 (6 ♔e5 ♚f7-+ - note the knight barrier) 6 ... ♚d8 7 ♔d6 (7 h4 g5-+ 8 hxg5 hxg5 9 ♔c5 ♚c8 10 ♔d4 ♚b7 11 ♔e4 ♚xa7 12 ♔f5 ♘e6) 7 ... ♘b5+ 8 ♔e6 ♘xa7 9 ♔f6 g5 10 ♔g6 ♚e7-+.

4	h4	♘a7
5	♔d5	♔f7
6	♔c5?	

White misses his chance in the time scramble: 6 ♔e5!

♚g7 (6 ... ♘b5 7 ♔e4 ♚e6 8 ♔f4 ♚f6 9 ♔e4=) 7 ♔f4 ♚f6 8 ♔e4 g5 9 hxg5+ ♔xg5 10 ♔f3 h4 11 ♔g2 ♔g4 12 ♔h2 h3 13 ♔h1!= (see also diag 21).

6	...	g5
7	hxg5	h4
8	g6+	♔g8!!
9	♔b6	h3
10	♔xa7	h2
11	♔b8	h1♕
12	a7	♕b1+
	0-1	

cf QP12.

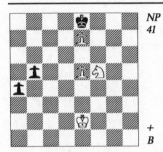

NP 41

+ B

Boudre - Plachetka
Paris 1989
A practical example of task switching. The white king must escort the pawn, and the knight must blockade the black pawns.

6	...	b4

Or 6 ... a3 7 ♘d4! a2 8 ♘b3 ♔xe7 9 ♔d3+-.

7	♔d3	b3
8	♔c3	♔d7
9	♘d4!	

Not 9 e6+?? ♔e8= when Black threatens to jettison his pawns and stalemate himself, and the white pawns are so far advanced that the knight is too tied to their defence to transfer to the blockade.

9	...	♔xe7
10	♘b5	b2
11	♘a3	♔e6
12	♔d4	

Mission accomplished.
1-0

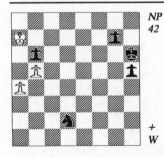

NP 42

+ W

Szabo - Groszpeter
Hungary 1984

1	a5	bxa5

Or 1 ... ♘c4 2 a6! ♘d6 3 ♔xb6 h4 4 ♔c5 h3 (4 ... ♘c8 5 b6+-) 5 a7 ♘b7+ 6 ♔b4 h2 7 a8♕ h1♕ 8 ♕h8++-.

2	b6	♘c4
3	b7	♘e5
4	♔b8!!	

An astonishing study-like move. Since the knight does not reach real control of b8 it loses. Not 4 ♔b6 ♘d7+ 5 ♔c7 (5 ♔c6 ♘b8+ 6 ♔c7 a4 7 ♔xb8 a3-+) 5 ... ♘c5-+.

5	...	♘c6+

Or 5 ... ♘d7+ 6 ♔c8! ♘b6+ 7 ♔d8.

6	♔c7	♘b4
7	♔b6	♘d5+
8	♔b5	♘c7+
9	♔xa5	1-0

Knight v Pawn(s)   ♞ V ♟(♟)

NP 43

+ W

Petrosian - Kurajica
Banja Luka 1979
White's h-pawn will prove a vital distraction.

45 ... c4?!/?

A better try is 45 ... a6!? (not 45 ... b5 46 ♘xa7 b4 47 a4 c4 48 ♘b5+-) 46 ♔g4 (46 a4 b5 47 a5 b4) 46 ... b5 47 ♔f5 and now:

a) 47 ... ♔f7 48 h4 c4 49 ♔e4 ♔g6 50 ♔d4 ♔h5 51 ♘b4 a5 (51 ... ♔xh4 52 ♘xa6 f5 53 ♘c7 f4 54 ♘xb5 f3 55 ♔e3 ♔g3 56 ♘c3 ♔g2 57 ♘e4 c3 58 ♔d3) 52 ♘c6 (52 ♘d5 b4 53 a4 c3 54 ♔d3 f5) 52 ... f5 (52 ... b4 53 ♘xb4 axb4 54 axb4 f5 55 ♔xc4 ♔g4 56 ♔d3 ♔g3 57 b5 f4 58 b6 f3 59 b7 f2 60 b8♛++-) 53 ♘xa5 ♔xh4 54 ♘c6 f4 55 ♔e4 ♔g3 56 ♘d4+-;

b) 47 ... ♔g7 48 ♘e7 c4 49 ♘d5 a5 50 ♔e4 ♔g6 51 ♔d4 and now:

b1) 51 ... f5 52 ♘e7+ ♔g5

53 ♘c6 b4 54 a4 b3 (54 ... c3 55 ♘xa5+-) 55 ♔c3+-;

b2) 51 ... ♔g5 52 ♘e7 ♔h4 53 ♘c6 ♔xh3 54 ♘xa5 f5 55 ♘c6 f4 56 ♘e4 c3 (56 ... ♔g3 57 ♘d4) 57 ♘d4 ♔g4 58 ♔d3! (58 ♘c2 f3 59 ♔d3 f2 60 ♘e3+ ♔f3) 58 ... f3 59 ♘xf3 ♔xf3 60 ♔xc3 ♔e4 61 ♔b4 ♔d5 62 ♔xb5+-;

b3) 51 ... b4 52 ♘xb4 axb4 53 axb4+-.

46 a4!
Black gets considerably more counterplay if he can achieve ... b5.

46 ... ♔f7

Or 46 ... a6 47 ♘b4 c3 48 ♔g4 a5 49 ♘c2 ♔g7 50 ♔f5+-.

47	♔g4	c3
48	♘b4	♔g6
49	h4	f5+
50	♔f4	a6
51	♔e5	♔h5
52	♔xf5	♔xh4
53	♔e4	1-0

Knight and Three Pawns v Pawns

NP 44

- B

Ghinda - Ionescu
Romanian ch 1985
A typical situation. Black has won material but this distant action has allowed the white king to become threateningly active.

50	...	♔d2
51	g3	♘c5+
52	♔e5	♔e3
53	♔f6	♔f3
54	♔xg6	♔g4-+

Black has returned his forces in good time.

55 ♔f6

To press e6 and keep the possibility of f5 alive. If instead 55 ♔h6 ♘e4 56 ♔g6

♘xg3 57 hxg3 ♔xg3-+.

55 ... ♔h3
56 f5

A better try was 56 ♔g5 ♔xh2 57 g4! (57 ♔xh5 ♔xg3 58 ♔g5 ♘e4+) 57 ... hxg4 58 ♔xg4 ♘d7! (58 ... ♔g2? 59 f5 e5 60 f6 ♘d7 61 f7 ♔f2 62 ♔f5 ♔e3 63 f8♛=) 59 ♔f3 (59 f5 e5 60 ♔g5 ♔g3-+) 59 ... ♔h3-+ (59 ... ♘f6!-+) 60 f5 e5 61 ♔e4 ♔g4 62 f6 ♔g5 63 f7 ♔f6.

56	...	♔xh2
57	fxe6	♘xe6
58	♔g6	♘g7!

Behind the pawn.

0-1

Knight v Pawn(s)   ♘ V ♟(♟)

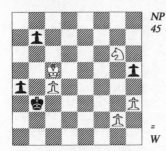

NP
45

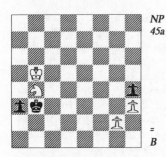

=
W

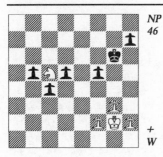

=
B

Kr. Georgiev - Zlatilov
Pleven 1987

9	♘f4	a3
10	♘d3	h4!
11	♔b5	♔c3
12	♘b4	

Or 12 ♘c1 ♔b2 13 ♔b4 ♔xc1 14 ♔xa3 ♔d2 15 ♔b4 ♔e2 16 ♔b5 ♔f2 17 ♔b6 ♔xg2 18 ♔xb7 ♔xh3 19 c5 ♔g2 20 c6=.

12	...	b6!
13	c5	

Or 13 ♔a4 ♔b2 14 ♘d3+ ♔c3 15 ♔xa3 ♔xd3 16 ♔b4 ♔e2 17 ♔b5 ♔f2 18 ♔xb6 ♔xg2 19 c5 ♔xh3 20 c6 ♔g2

21 c7 h3 22 c8♕ h2=.

13	...	bxc5
14	♔xc5	♔b3
15	♔b5	*(45a)*

The white king cannot deal with the a-pawn and return to safeguard the kingside. The knight alone has no solid post to defend either g2 or h3.

15	...	♔c3
16	♔a4	♔d4
17	♔xa3	♔e3
18	♘d5+	♔f2
19	♘f4	♔g3
20	♘g6	♔xg2

½-½

NP
46

+
W

Kharitonov - Chekhov
Irkutsk 1983

A good example of the battle to set up a blockade against a pawn mass.

1	♔f3	d4

Or 1 ... b4 (1 ... ♔f6 2 ♔e3 ♔e5 3 f4+ ♔d6 4 ♘a6 and ♔d4, ♘b4 +-) 2 ♔e3 b3 3 ♘a4 ♔f6 4 ♔d4 ♔e6 and now:

a) 5 f4!? ♔d6 and:

a1) 6 ♔c3!? ♔c6 (6 ... b2 7 ♔xb2 d4 8 ♘b6 ♔c5 9 ♘d7+ ♔b4 10 ♘e5 ♔c5 11 ♔c2 ♔d5 12 ♔d2 ♔c5 13 ♘d7+ ♔d6 14 ♘f6 h6 15 ♘g8+-) 7 ♔b4 ♔d6 (7 ... h6 8 h3 h5 9 h4 ♔d6 10 ♔b5) 8 ♔b5 h5 9 h4 c3 10 ♘xc3 d4 (10 ... b2 transposes) 11 ♘b1 ♔d5 12 ♘d2 b2 13 ♔b4 d3 (13 ... b1♕+ 14 ♘xb1 ♔e4 15 ♔c4 ♔f3 16 ♔xd4 ♔xg3 17 ♔e3 ♔xh4 18 ♔f3 ♔h3 19 ♘d2+-) 14 ♔c3 b1♕ 15 ♘xb1 ♔e4 16 ♘d2+ ♔e3 17 ♘c4+ ♔f3 18 ♘e5+ ♔xg3 19

♘g6+-;

a2) 6 ♘c3 b2 7 ♘b1 ♔c6 8 ♔c3 and:

a21) 8 ... ♔b5 9 ♘a3+ ♔a4 10 ♔xb2 ♔b4 (10 ... c3+ 11 ♔xc3+-) 11 ♘c2++-;

a22) 8 ... ♔c5 9 ♘a3 d4+ 10 ♔xb2 ♔d5 11 ♔c2 ♔c5 (11 ... ♔e4 12 ♘xc4+-) 12 ♘b1 (12 ♔d2 ♔d5 13 ♔e2 ♔c5 14 ♘b1 c3 15 ♔d3 ♔b4 16 ♔c2 ♔c4 17 ♘a3+ ♔b4 18 ♘b1 ♔c4=) 12 ... c3 (12 ... ♔d5 or 12 ... ♔b4) 13 ♔b3 (13 ♘xc3 dxc3 14 ♔xc3 ♔d5 15 ♔d3 ♔c5=) 13 ... ♔d5 14 ♘a3 ♔e4 15 ♔c2 (15 ♔c4 h5) 15 ... h5 16 ♘b5 ♔e3 (16 ... h4 17 ♘d6++-) 17 ♘d6 ♔e2 18 ♘xf5 d3+ 19 ♔xc3 d2 20 ♘d4++-;

b) 5 ♘c3 b2 6 ♔c5 f4 (6 ... ♔e5 7 f4+) 7 ♔d4 (with the idea of f3,♘b1,♔c3 +-) 7 ... f3 8 h3 ♔d6 9 ♘b1 ♔c6 10 ♔c3 ♔c5 11 ♘a3 d4+ 12 ♔xb2 ♔d5 13 ♔c2 ♔c5 14 ♘b1 ♔b4 15 ♘d2 d3+ 16 ♔d1 c3

71

Knight v Pawn(s)   ♞ V ♟(♟)

17 ♘xf3 ♚b3 18 ♘e5+-.

| 2 | ♘e6 | d3 |
| 3 | ♘d4 | c3 |

Or 3 ... b4 4 ♘c6 b3 5 ♘e5++-.

| 4 | ♚e3 | c2 |

Or 4 ... d2 5 ♚e2 b4 6 ♘c2 b3 7 ♘a3 b2 (7 ... f4 8 f3) 8 ♚d1 with the idea of ♘b1.

5	♘b3	♚g5
6	f3	f4+
7	♚xd3	h5
8	♚xc2	1-0

An excellent example of the knight's qualities.

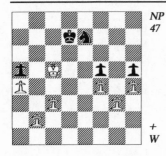

NP 47

Fischer - Taimanov
Vancouver (4) 1971
Black's remaining pawns are weak, White's king is active, and the knight has no decent squares: it is an easy win for the pawns.

65	b4	axb4
66	cxb4	♘c8
67	a5	♘d6

This is the only circuit with any future for the knight. (Not 67 ... ♚c7 68 b5 ♚b7 69 b6+-.)

| 68 | b5 | ♘e4+ |
| 69 | ♚b6 | ♚c8 |

Or 69 ... ♘xg3 70 a6+-.

| 70 | ♚c6 | ♚b8 |

70 ... ♘xg3 71 a6 ♚b8 transposes.

| 71 | b6 | 1-0 |

Since 71 ... ♘xg3 72 a6 ♘e4 73 a7+ ♚a8 74 b7+ ♚xa7 75 ♚c7 wins.

Further Examples from Practice

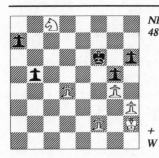

NP 48

A. Ivanov - Arkhipov
USSR 1985

| 1 | ... | a5 |

If instead 1 ... b4 2 ♘xa7 ♚e6 3 ♘b5 ♚d5 4 f4 gxf4 5 h4 ♚c4 6 g5 hxg5 7 hxg5 ♚d3 (7 ... ♚xb5 8 g6 b3 9 g7 b2 10 g8♕ b1♕ 11 ♕b8+) 8 d5 f3 9 d6 f2 10 ♚g2 ♚e2 11 ♘d4+ ♚e1 12 ♘f3+ ♚e2 13 ♘h2+- (A. Ivanov).

| 2 | ♘d6 | b4 |
| 3 | f4! | |

To create an outside passed pawn to restrain the black king.

3	...	gxf4
4	h4	a4
5	♘c4	a3(?!)

Slightly easing White's task by allowing a blockade. A better try was 5 ... ♚e6!? and now:

a) 6 ♚h3? and:

a1) 6 ... ♚d5?? 7 g5 hxg5 8 hxg5 a3 9 g6 a2 (9 ... ♚e6 10 ♘d2 a2 11 ♘b3 ♚f6 12 ♚g4+-) 10 g7 a1♕ 11 g8♕+ ♚e4 (11 ... ♚c6 12 ♘e5+ ♚c7 13 ♕f7+ ♚b6 14 ♕e6+ ♚b7 15 ♕e7++-) 12 ♕g6+ ♚xd4 (12 ... ♚f3 13 ♕g2+ or 12 ... ♚d5 13 ♘b6+) 13 ♕f6+;

a2) 6 ... a3 7 ♘d2 a2 8 ♘b3 ♚d5 9 g5 hxg5 10 hxg5 ♚c4 11 ♘a1 b3;

b) 6 ♚g2?! ♚d5 7 ♘b6+ ♚xd4 8 ♘xa4 ♚e4 and:

b1) 9 ♚f2 f3 10 g5 hxg5 11 h5 and now:

b11) 11 ... g4?? 12 h6 g3+ 13 ♚xg3 ♚e3 14 ♘b2 ♚e2 (14 ... f2 15 ♘d1+ ♚d2 16 ♚xf2 ♚xd1 17 h7) 15 ♘d3! ♚xd3 (15 ... f2 16 ♘xf2 b3 17 ♘d3) 16 ♚xf3 b3 17 h7 b2 18 h8♕ b1♕ 19 ♕h7+;

b12) 11 ... ♚f5= 12 ♚xf3 g4+ 13 ♚g3 ♚g5;

b2) 9 ♘c5+ ♚d4;

72

c) 6 Nd2! a3 (6 ... Kd5 7 g5 hxg5 8 hxg5 Ke6 9 Kh3 Kf5 10 g6 Kxg6 11 Kg4 Kf6 12 Kxf4 Ke6 13 Ke4 Kd6 14 Kd3 Kd5 15 Nc4 a3 16 Ne3+ Kc6 17 Kc4 a2 18 Nc2+-) 7 Nb3 transposing to the game.

6 Nd2   Ke6
7 Nb3   a2

Or 7 ... Kd5 8 g5 hxg5 9 hxg5 Kc4 (9 ... Ke6 10 Kh3 Kf5 11 g6 Kxg6 12 Kg4+-) 10 g6 Kxb3 11 g7 Kb2 12 g8Q b3 13 Qg2+ Kb1 14 Qf1+ Ka2 15 Qc4 Kb2 16 d5 a2 17 Qd4+ Kb1 18 Qd3+ Kb2 19 d6 a1Q 20 d7 (A. Ivanov).

	8	Na1!	Kd5
9	g5	hxg5
10	hxg5	Kxd4

Not 10 ... Ke6 11 Kh3 Kf5 12 g6! Kxg6 13 Kg4+-.

11	g6	b3
12	Nxb3+	Kc3
13	g7	Kxb3
14	g8Q++-	
14	...	Kb2
15	Qb8+	Kc1
16	Qa7	Kb1
17	Qb6+	Kc1
18	Qa5	Kb1
19	Qb4+	Kc1
20	Qa3+	Kb1
21	Qb3+	Ka1
22	Qc2	1-0

NP 49 — B

Zichichi - Hort
Venice 1969

Black has just played 8 ... Nxh3! (not 8 ... g4 9 hxg4+ Kxg4 10 Kg1 Kg3 11 Nf1= Maric) to which White obviously replied 9 Kxh3.

9 ...   Kf4
10 Kg2

Or 10 Ng2+ Kf3 11 Kh2 Ke2.

10 ...   Ke3

Black's advantage is obvious as the knight has no counter targets.

11 Nf3

After 11 Kf1 g4 the black king gains access to e2 or d3.

11 ...   Kxd3
12 Kf2

Instead 12 Nxg5 Kxc4 (12 ... Kc2?! 13 Nf3) 13 Kf3 Kb3 14 Ke4 Kxb2 15 Ne6 Kb3 (15 ... Kc3 16 Nf4 c4 17 Nd5+=) 16 Kd3 Kxa4 17 Kc4 Ka3 18 Nf4 a4 19 Nd5 Kb2 20 Nxb6 a3 21 Na4+ Kc2 22 Nxc5 a2 23 Nb3 Kb2! transposes to the game.

12	...	Kxc4
13	Ke2	Kb3
14	Nxg5	Kxb2

Or 14 ... Kxa4 15 Kd2 Kb3 16 Kc1.

15	Kd3	Kb3
16	Ne4	Kxa4
17	Kc4	Ka3
18	Nf6	a4
19	Nd5	Kb2
20	Nxb6	a3
21	Na4+	Kc2
22	Nxc5	a2
23	Nb3	Kb2!
	0-1	

Of course not 23 ... d3 24 Na1+ Kb2 25 Kxd3=.

Knight v Pawn(s)   ♘ V ♟(♟)

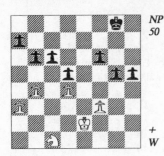

NP
50

+
W

Petursson - Ostenstad
Espoo Zt 1989

35 f4!

To create a wedge with f5, or to disrupt Black's kingside pawns. The rigidity of the black pawn structure gives the knight the advantage, despite three pawns.

35 ...   ♚f7

Or 35 ... g4 36 f5 h4 37 ♞e3 h3 38 ♞e2 h2 39 ♞g3 ♚f7 40 ♚f4 ♚e7 41 ♚xg4 ♚d6 42 ♚h3 c5 43 ♚xh2 cxb4 (43 ... c4 44 ♞e2+- or 43 ... cxd4 44 ♚g2 ♚e5 45 ♚f3 d3 46 ♚e3 d2 47 ♚xd2 ♚f4 48 ♞e2++-) 44 axb4 ♚c6 (44 ... a5 45 b5 a4 46 ♞e2 a3 47 ♞c3+-) 45 ♞h5 a5 46 bxa5 bxa5 47 ♞xf6 a4 48 ♞g4 a3 49 ♞e3 a2 50 ♞c2+-.

36 f5   ♚e7
37 ♚f3   ♚d6
38 ♞d3   b5?!

Alternatively, 38 ... ♚d7!? 39 a4 ♚d6 40 a5 ♚d7 41 a6 ♚d6 42 b5 cxb5 (42 ... c5?? 43 dxc5+ bxc5 44 b6+-) 43 ♞b4 h4 44 ♚g4 and now:

a) 44 ... ♚d7!? 45 ♞xd5 b4. This is a desperate attempt, and Black's various passed pawns do not seem enough to avoid a variety of similarly lost endings, e.g.

a1) 46 ♞xb4 is perhaps simplest: 46 ... ♚d6 47 ♚h3 b5 48 ♚g4 ♚d7 (48 ... ♚e7 49 ♞c6++-) 49 ♞d5 and now:

a11) 49 ... ♚d8 50 ♞xf6 b4 51 ♞e4 b3 52 f6 b2 53 ♞c3 ♚d7 54 d5 ♚d6 55 ♚f5 h3 56 f7 ♚e7 57 ♚g6 h2 (57 ... ♚f8 58 d6 h2 59 d7+-) 58 d6+ ♚d7 59 f8♕ h1♕ 60 ♕e7+ ♚c6 61 ♕b7+;

a12) 49 ... ♚d6 50 ♞xf6 b4 51 ♞e4+ ♚e7;

a2) 46 ♞xf6+;

a21) 46 ... ♚d6 47 ♞e4+ ♚e7 (47 ... ♚d7 48 d5 b3 49 f6 b2 50 ♞c3 ♚d6 51 ♚xg5 h3 52 f7 ♚e7 53 ♚g6 with the idea of d6 +-) 48 f6+ ♚f7 49 ♚f5 b3 50 ♞xg5+ ♚f8 51 f7 ♚e7 (51 ... ♚g7 52 ♚e6 b2 53 ♚e7 b1♕ 54 f8♕++-; 51 ... b2 52 ♚f6) 52 ♚g6 b2 53 ♚g7 b1♕ 54 f8♕+ ♚d7 55 ♕f7+ ♚d6 56 ♕e6+ ♚c7 57 ♕e7+ ♚c6 58 ♕b7+ ♚d6 59 ♞f7+ ♚e6 60 ♕c6+ ♚f5 61 ♕g6+;

a22) 46 ... ♚d8 47 ♞e4 b3 48 f6 b2 49 ♞c3 b5 50 d5 b4 51 ♞b1 ♚d7 52 ♞d2 ♚d6 53 ♚xg5 h3 54 f7 ♚e7 55 ♚g6 h2 56 d6+ ♚d7 (56 ... ♚f8 57 d7) 57 f8♕ h1♕ 58 ♕e7+ ♚c6 59 ♕b7+;

b) 44 ... ♚e7 45 ♞xd5+ ♚f7 46 ♞b4! (46 ♞xb6? b4 47 ♞c4 b3 48 d5 ♚e7=) 46 ... ♚e7 47 ♞c6+ ♚d7 48 ♞xa7 b4 49 ♞b5 ♚c8 50 a7 ♚b7 51 d5 b3 52 d6 b2 53 ♞c3+-.

39 ♞c5   ♚e7
40 ♞e6   ♚d6
41 ♞g7   h4
42 ♞e6   ♚e7
43 ♚g4   ♚d6
44 ♞c5   ♚e7
45 ♞d3   ♚f7
46 ♞c1   ♚e7
47 ♞b3   ♚e8
48 ♞d2   ♚f7
49 ♚h5   ♚g7
50 ♞f3   ♚h7
51 ♞h2   ♚g7
52 ♞g4!   a6?

Or 52 ... ♚f7 53 ♚h6 ♚e7 (53 ... h3 54 ♚h5 c5 55 dxc5 d4 56 ♞f2+- JT) 54 ♚g6! with the idea forcing of forcing a transposition to the above variation. This is more accurate than 54 ♚g7? h3 55 ♞h2 c5! 56 bxc5 a5 57 c6 b4 58 axb4 axb4 59 c7 ♚d7 60

Knight v Pawn(s)   ♞ V ♟(♟)

♔xf6 b3 61 ♔g7 b2 62 f6
b1♕ 63 f7 ♔xc7 64 f8♕
♕e4= (Hecht).

53	♘f2	♔h7
54	♘d3	

Instead 54 ♔g4 ♔h6 55
♘d3 h3 56 ♔xh3 ♔h5 57
♘f2+- (Hecht) is perhaps
simpler but Petursson has an
instructive technique planned.

54	...	h3
55	♘f2	h2
56	♘h1!	♔g7
57	♘g3	♔h7
58	♔g4	♔g7
59	♔f3!	

Not 59 ♔h3?! ♔h6 60
♔xh2 g4 and ... ♔f4.

59	...	♔h6

60	♔e3!	♔g7
61	♔f2	♔h6
62	♔f3!	♔g7
63	♔g2	♔h6
64	♔h3!	

White's clever manoeuvring
has forced Black to allow the
capture of the h2-pawn with
the black king on the seventh,
or to try the game continuation.

64	...	g4+
65	♔xg4	♔g7
66	♘h1!	♔h6
67	♘f2	♔g7
68	♔g3	♔h6
69	♔xh2	♔g5
70	♔g3	♔xf5
71	♔f3	1-0

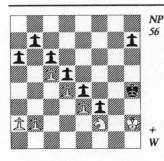

NP
56
+
W

Botvinnik - G Thomas
Nottingham 1936

40	b4

To play b5, undermining
the pawn chain and creating
pressure against c6.

40	...	♔g5
41	♔g3	♔f5
42	♘h3	♔f6
43	a4	♔f5
44	♘f4	♔f6
45	b5	axb5
46	axb5	

Intending ♘xd5, c6, b6 +-.

46	...	♔e7
47	b6	♔d7
48	♘h5!	♔d8
49	♘f6	h6
50	♘g4	h5
51	♘f2	

Blockading f3 - the white
king takes care of the h5-
pawn.

51	...	♔d7
52	♔h4	♔d8
53	♔xh5	♔e7
54	♔g4	♔e6
55	♔g3	♔d7
56	♘h3	♔d8
57	♘f4	

Perhaps better is 57 ♘g5!?
♔e7 58 ♘xf3 exf3 59 ♔xf3
♔f6 60 e4 dxe4+ 61 ♔xe4
♔e6 62 d5+ cxd5+ 63 ♔d4
♔d7 (63 ... ♔e7 64 c6!) 64
♔xd5 ♔c8 65 ♔e6! ♔d8 66
♔d6 ♔c8 67 ♔e7 ♔b8 68
♔d7 ♔a8 69 c6 bxc6 70
♔c7+- (Fine).

57	...	♔d7
58	♘h5	♔e6
59	♘g7+	♔d7
60	♘f5	♔c8
61	♘d6+	♔b8
62	♘f5!	

Now White aims to force ...
f2, loosening the pawn from
the chain.

62	...	♔c8
63	♔f4!	♔b8
64	♔e5	♔c8
65	♔e6	♔b8
66	♔d7	♔a8
67	♘g3!	♔b8
68	♘f1	♔a8
69	♔c8	1-0

After ... f2 the white king
comes and collects the
f-pawn, winning.

Knight v Knight

Knight and One Pawn v Knight

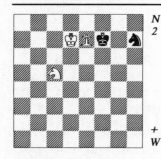

Averbakh
A basic drawing position.

| 1 | ... | ♘f8+ |
| 2 | ♔d8 | ♘e6+= |

Averbakh
A basic winning position.

1	...	♘f6+
2	♔d8	♘e8
3	♘e6	♘d6

Or 3 ... ♘f6 4 ♘g5+ ♔g7 5 ♘e4.

| 4 | ♔d7 | ♘e8 |
| 5 | ♘g5+ and wins |

Cheron 1926
Another basic win.

1	♘a5	♔f5
2	♘c4	♔g5
3	♘d6+	♔e5

| 4 | ♔c8 | ♘e6 |
| 5 | ♘e8 | |

With the idea of ♘c7 winning.

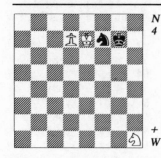

Cheron 1955

| 1 | ♔e6 | |

Not 1 ♘g3? ♘e5=.

| 1 | ... | ♘d8+ |
| 2 | ♔d6 | ♔f6 |

If 2 ... ♔f7 3 ♔c7 ♔e7 4 ♘f2 ♘e6+ 5 ♔c8 ♘d8 6 ♘d3 ♘b7 7 ♔c7 ♘d8 8 ♘e5.

3	♘f2	♘b7+
4	♔c7	♔e7
5	♘d3	♘d8

Or 5 ... ♔e6 6 ♘c5+.

6	♘e5	♘e6+
7	♔c8	♔d6
8	♘g6	♔c6
9	♘f4 and wins

Note the helplessness of the knight against an escorted pawn on the seventh (Fine's rule) - even the feeble white knight cannot save Black.

Knight v Knight

Dobrescu 1973

1	♘h4	g1♘
2	♘g2	e2
3	♘e1	♚e4
4	♔b3	♘f3

For 4 ... ♚e3 see the next diagram.

5	♔c2!	♚e3
6	♘g2+	♚f2
7	♘f4=	

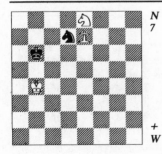

Tisdall/Dobrescu 1990

1   ♘g2+

Alternatively:

a) 1 ♘c2+ ♚d2 2 ♔b2 ♘f3 3 ♔b3 ♚d3 (3 ... ♘d4+? 4 ♘xd4 e1♕ 5 ♘f3+) 4 ♔b2 (4 ♘b4+ ♚e4 5 ♘c2 ♘d4+) 4 ... ♘d4 5 ♘e1+ ♚d2 6 ♘g2 ♘e6 7 ♔b3 (7 ♘h4 ♚e3) 7 ... ♘f4 8 ♘h4 ♚e3;

b) 1 ♔c3 ♘f3 and now:

b1) 2 ♘g2+? ♚f2 3 ♔d3 (3 ♘f4 e1♕+) 3 ... ♘e1+;

b2) 2 ♘d3 ♘e5 3 ♘e1 ♚f2 4 ♘c2 (4 ♔d2 ♘c4+) 4 ... ♘g4 5 ♔d4 ♘e3 6 ♘b4 ♚f1 7 ♘d3 ♘d1;

b3) 2 ♘c2+ ♚f2 3 ♔c4 (3 ♔b2 ♘d4 4 ♘b4 ♚f1 5 ♘d3 ♘e6) 3 ... ♘e5+ 4 ♔d5 ♘g4

5 ♔d4 ♘e3 6 ♘b4 ♚f1 7 ♘d3 ♘d1.

1	...	♚d2
2	♔c4	♘h3
3	♔d4	

If 3 ♘h4 ♚e3 and ... ♚f2 wins.

3	...	♘f4
4	♘h4	♚d1
5	♘f3	♘e6+
6	♔d3	♘g5

and wins

The key is getting the diagonal opposition to the knight, removing White's tactical defence. Fine's rule about escorted pawns triumphs (apparently) over the composer's idea.

Halberstadt 1938

An example of pure tactics and knight barriers.

1   ♔a3!!

Alternatively:

a) 1 ♘c7 ♘f6 2 ♘d5+ ♘xd5+;

b) 1 ♘c4 ♘e5+ 2 ♔d5 ♘g6;

c) 1 ♔a4 ♘c5+ 2 ♔a3 ♘e6;

d) 1 ♔c3 ♚c5 2 ♘d6 (2 ♔d2 ♚d4) 2 ... ♘f6 3 ♘e4+ ♘xe4+.

1	...	♚c6

Or:

a) 1 ... ♚a5 2 ♔b2 ♚a4 (2 ... ♚b4 3 ♘c7 ♘f6 4 ♘d5+) 3

♔a2 ♚a5 4 ♔a3 ♚b6 5 ♘c7 ♘f6 6 ♘d5+;

b) 1 ... ♚a7 2 ♔b2 ♚b8 3 ♔c2 ♚a7 4 ♔d2 ♚b8 5 ♔e2 ♚a7 6 ♔f2 ♚b8 7 ♔g3 ♚a7 8 ♔f4 ♚b6 9 ♔f5 ♚c6 10 ♘f6.

2	♔a2!!	

Not 2 ♔b2 ♘b6 3 ♘d6 (3 ♘f6 ♘c4+ 4 ♔c3 ♘d6 5 ♔d3 ♘e8) 3 ... ♘c4+ 4 ♘xc4 ♚d7.

2	...	♚b6

Or 2 ... ♚c5 3 ♘d6 ♘f6 4 ♘e4+.

3	♘c7	♘f6
4	♘d5+ and wins	

77

Knight v Knight

**N
8**

+
W

Kling 1867, Averbakh

    1 ♘e6

    1 ♘g6 was Kling's original solution, Averbakh's 1 ♘e6 is faster and simpler.

1	...	♔d5
2	♘f8!	♔e5
3	♔a8	

Not 3 b8♕? ♘c6+=.

3	...	♘c6
4	♘d7	♔e6

Or 4 ... ♔d6 5 ♘b6! ♔c7 (5 ... ♔c5 6 ♘c8 and ♘a7 winning) 6 ♘d5+ ♔d6 7 ♘b4+-.

5	♘b6	♔d6
6	♘c8+	♔c7
7	♘a7	♘b8
8	♘b5+ and wins	

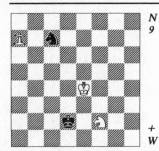

**N
9**

+
W

Hasek 1929

Knights are notoriously poor defenders against rook's pawns, as the next two examples demonstrate.

1	♘d1	♔c2

Or 1 ... ♔xd1 2 ♔d3 ♔c1 3 ♔c4.

2	♘e3+	♔b3
3	♘d5	♘a8
4	♔d4	♔a4
5	♔c5	♔a5
6	♘b4	♘b6
7	♔c6 and wins	

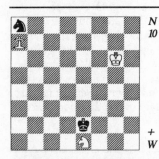

**N
10**

+
W

Halberstadt 1951

1	♔f5	♔e3

Or 1 ... ♔xe1 2 ♔e4 ♘c7 3 ♔d3!+-.

2	♔e6

Not 2 ♔e5 ♘b6=.

2	...	♘b6
3	♔e5! and wins	

**N
11**

+
W

Averbakh 1955

1	♘d3	♘g5
2	♘f4+	♔g4
3	♘e6	♘f3
4	♔d6!	♘h4
5	f7	

"Etc." - Averbakh, presumably following Fine's guideline that an escorted pawn on the seventh nearly always wins.. However, it is worth analyzing a little further, since the winning method is fundamental.

5	...	♘g6

6	♘c7	♔g5

Or 6 ... ♔f5 7 ♘d5 ♔g5 8 ♔e6 ♘f8+ 9 ♔e7 ♘g6+ 10 ♔e8 ♔h6 11 ♘e7.

7	♔e6	♔h6
8	♔f6	♔h7
9	♘e6	♔h6
10	♘f4	♘f8
11	♔e7	♘h7

11 ... ♔g7 is met by 12 ♘h5+.

12	♘d5	♔g7
13	♘f6 and wins	

N 12
+ W

Halberstadt 1939

1	c7	♘e7
2	♘d6	♔e2

If 2 ... ♔d2 3 ♔b2 ♔e2 4 ♔c2 or 2 ... ♔c2 3 ♔a3 ♔c3 4 ♔a4.

3	♔b3	

Not 3 ♔a3? ♔f3 4 ♔a4 ♘d5= or 3 ♔b2? ♔f3 4 ♔b3

♔f4 5 ♔c4 ♔e5 6 ♔c5 ♔e6=.

3	...	♔d3

Or 3 ... ♔f3 4 ♔c4 ♔e3 (4 ... ♔f4 5 ♔d4 ♔g5 6 ♔e5) 5 ♔c5 ♔f4 6 ♔d4+-.

4	♔a3	♔c3
5	♔a4 and wins	

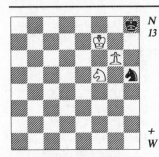

N 13
+ W

Horwitz and Kling 1851

1	♘d6	

Also winning is the neater 1 ♘h6 ♘g7 2 ♘e7 ♘h5 3 ♔f8 (Lommer).

1	...	♘g7
2	♘e4	♘e8

3	♔f8	♘g7
4	♔e7	♔g8
5	♘f6+	♔h8
6	♔f7	♘f5
7	♘e4	♘g7
8	♘d6	♘e8
9	♔f8 and wins	

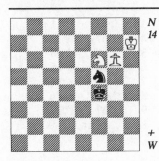

N 14
+ W

Bellin - Padevsky, 1979

1	♘d5+	♔e5
2	♘b4	♔e4

If 2 ... ♘d6 3 ♘c6+ and now:

a) 3 ... ♔e6 4 g7;

b) 3 ... ♔f4 4 ♘e7 ♘e8 5 ♔g8 ♔g5 6 ♔f8 ♘f6 7 g7;

c) 3 ... ♔f5 4 ♘e7+ ♔e4 (4 ... ♔e5 5 ♔g7 or 4 ... ♔f4 5 ♘d5+) 5 ♔g7;

d) 3 ... ♔f6 4 g7.

3	♘c6	♔d5
4	♘d8	♔e5

Or 4 ... ♘d6 5 ♔g7.

5	♘f7+	♔e6
6	♘h6	♘e7
7	g7	♔e5
8	♘g4+	♔f5
9	♘e3+	♔e6
10	♘g2	♔f7

Or 10 ... ♔f5 11 ♘h4+ ♔f6 12 ♘g6.

11	♘f4	1-0

Analysis by Minev.

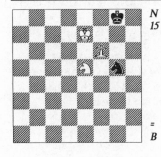

N 15
= B

Averbakh 1955

A very tricky example in which Black just manages to hold the balance.

1	...	♔h7
2	♘c4	♔g6!

Not 2 ... ♔h8 3 ♘d6 ♔g8 4 ♔e8 ♔h7 5 ♔d7 ♔h8 6 ♔d8 ♔h7 7 ♔e8 ♔g8 8 ♔e7 ♔h7 9 ♘e4 ♘f3 10 f7 ♘e5 11 ♘f6+.

3	♘d6	♔h5
4	♘e4	♘f3

5	♔e6	

Alternatively:

a) 5 f7 ♘e5 6 ♘f6+ ♔h4;

b) 5 ♘c5 (threatening 6 ♘d3 ♘g5 7 ♘f4+ ♔g4 8 ♘e6 ♘f3 9 ♔d6 ♘h4 10 f7) 5 ... ♔g4! 6 ♘e6 ♘e5 7 ♘d4 ♔f4 8 ♔e6 ♔e4=.

5	...	♔g6
6	f7	♘d4+
7	♔e7	♘f5+
8	♔e8	♘g7+
9	♔f8	♘f5=

N 16

Ulig 1970

1	♔g4	♞e5+
2	♔f5	♞f3
3	♞g6	g2

Or 3 ... ♔g2 4 ♞f4+ ♔h2 5 ♔g4 ♞e5+ 6 ♔h5 ♞d3 7

= W

♞g6 g2 8 ♞h4.

4	♞f4=	

See also diag 27 where this type of ending could be reached but is not analysed in study continuation.

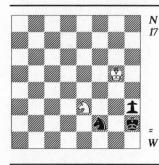

N 17

Réti 1929

1	♔h4	♔g1
2	♞g4	♔g2
3	♞e3+	♔h2
4	♞c2	

Or 4 ♞f1+ ♔g1 5 ♞g3 ♔g2 6 ♞f5 h2 7 ♞g3 ♞e4.

4	...	♞d3
5	♔g4	

Instead 5 ♞e3 ♞f4 6 ♞g4+

= W

♔g2 is the position after move one of Réti's other study (diag 18).

5	...	♞e5+
6	♔h4	♞f3+
7	♔g4	♞g5
8	♞e1	♔g1
9	♞f3+	♔g2
10	♞h4+	♔f2
11	♞f3 and draws	

N 18

Réti 1929

1	♔a7	

For 1 ♔b8 ♔b5 2 ♞b4 ♞c6+= see diag 17.

1	...	♔b5

Or 1 ... ♔c5 2 ♞d4! (2 ♞b4? ♔b5!=) 2 ... ♔xd4 3 ♔b6.

2	♞b4	♔a5

+ W

3	♔b8	♞c6+
4	♔b7	♞d8+
5	♔c7	♞e6+
6	♔b8	♞c5
7	a7	♞d7+
8	♔c7	♞b6
9	♔b7	♔b5
10	♞d5 and wins	

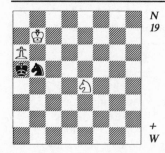

N 19

Réti 1929

The starting position is zugzwang: Black to move loses after 1 ... ♔b4 2 ♔b6 ♔c4 3 ♞c3! ♔d6 4 ♔c7 ♞e8+ 5 ♔c6+-. So White contrives to reach the diagram with Black to move, something not immediately obvious from the solution.

1	♞c5	♔b4

Instead 1 ... ♞d6+ 2 ♔c7 ♞b5+ 3 ♔c6 transposes to the text.

2	♔b6	♞d6

Or 2 ... ♔c4 3 ♞e4 ♔b4 4 ♞c3 ♞d6 5 ♔c7.

+ W

3	♞e4	

Not 3 ♔c6 ♞c8 4 ♞b7 (4 ♞e4 ♔a5 5 ♔b7 ♔b5= or 4 ♔c7 ♔xc5=) 4 ... ♞a7+ 5 ♔b6 ♞c8+ 6 ♔c7 ♔b5.

3	...	♞c8+
4	♔c7!!	♔b5

For 4 ... ♔a5 5 ♞c5 ♔b6 6 ♔c6 ♞c8 7 ♔b7 ♞d6+ 8 ♔c7 see the text.

5	♔b7	♔a5
6	♞c5	♞d6+
7	♔c7	♞b5+
8	♔c6	♞a7+
9	♔b7	♞b5
10	♞e4	♔a4
11	♞c3+ and wins	

Knight v Knight

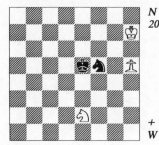

N
20

+
W

Cheron 1955
Yet again the knight struggles to prevent a rook's pawn from promoting.

   1   ♔g6   ♞e7+

   If 1 ... ♔e6 2 ♘g3 ♞xg3 3 h6 or 1 ... ♞h4+ 2 ♔g7 ♞f5+ 3 ♔f7 ♞h6+ 4 ♔g6 transposing to the text.

   2   ♔g7   ♞f5+

   3   ♔f7   ♞h6+

   4   ♔g6   ♞g4

   Or 4 ... ♞f5 5 ♞g3.

   5   ♔g5   ♞f6

   6   h6   ♞h7+

   7   ♔g6   ♞f8+

   8   ♔g7   ♔f5

   If 8 ... ♞e6+ 9 ♔f7 ♞g5+ 10 ♔g6 ♞e6 11 ♞c3 ♞f4+ 12 ♔g7 ♞e6+ 13 ♔f7 ♔f5 14 ♞e4.

   9   ♞g3+   ♔g5

  10   ♞e4+   ♔f5

  11   ♞d6+   ♔g5

  12   ♞f7+ and wins

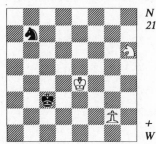

N
21

+
W

Voiya and Nestorescu 1951
Obviously if the extra pawn is still on its starting square the chances of a draw are significantly increased. Here is one winning position.

   1   ♔d5

   Not 1 g4 ♔c4 2 g5 ♞c5+ 3 ♔e5 ♞d7+ 4 ♔f5 ♞f8 5 ♞g4 ♔d5 6 ♞f6+ ♔d6 7 ♞h7 ♞e6= or 1 ♞f7 ♞c5+ 2 ♔f5 ♔d4 3 g4 ♔d5 4 g5 ♞e6=.

   1   ...   ♔d3

   2   g4

   If 2 ♞f5 ♞d8 3 ♔e5 ♞f7+ 4 ♔f6 ♔e4 5 ♞g3+ ♔e3.

   2   ...   ♔e3

   3   g5   ♔f4

   4   g6   ♞d6

   5   ♔xd6

   Or 5 g7 ♞e8.

   5   ...   ♔g5

   6   g7   ♔f6

   7   ♞f5! and wins

Immediate promotion only draws.

Knight and One Pawn v Knight and One Pawn

N
22

+
W

Vilela - Augustin
Prague 1980

   1   ♔c5!

   Not 1 a5 ♔d6 2 a6 ♞e5.

   1   ...   f5

   Or 1 ... ♞e5 2 a5 ♞d7+ 3 ♔c6.

   2   a5   f4

   3   a6   f3

   4   ♞c4   f2

   5   ♞d2   ♞f6

   6   ♔c6   ♞e4

   7   ♞f1   1-0

Knight and Two Pawns v Knight

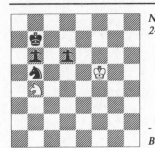

= W

Taimanov - Spassky
Leningrad 1952

1	♘f3	♔g4

Or 1 ... e5 2 ♘h4+ ♔g5 (2 ... ♔g4 3 ♔xf6 e4 4 ♘f5) 3 ♘f3+ ♔g4 4 ♔xf6 e4 5 ♘e5+ ♔g3 6 ♘c4= (Averbakh).

2	♘h2+	♔h3
3	♘f1	f5
4	♔f6	

Intending ♘e3xf5=.

Vitolins - Kochiev
USSR 1979

A good example of knights and two split pawns against knight.

63	...	♘c7
64	♔e4	b5
65	♔d4	♔b6
66	♔c3	♘e6
67	♘d5+	♔a5
68	♘e7	♔a4
69	♔b2	

Or 69 ♘d5 ♔a3 70 ♘b4 ♘d4! 71 ♘a6 ♘c6 72 ♘c7 b4+ 73 ♔c4 ♘e5+ 74 ♔d5 b3 75 ♘b5+ ♔b4.

69	...	♔b4!

Heading for c5 to accompany the d5-pawn forward, so that both pawns advance as a team.

70	♘d5+	♔c5
71	♘f6	d5
72	♔b3	♘d4+
73	♔c3	b4+
74	♔d3	♘c6
75	♘d7+	♔b5
76	♘f6	♘e7
77	♘d7	

Or 77 ♔d4 ♔a4.

77	...	♔a4
78	♘c5+	♔a3
79	♔c2	♘f5
80	♔b1	♘e3
81	♘e6	b3
82	♘c7	♘c4
83	♘b5+	♔b4
84	♘c7	d4

Again Black regroups so as to advance in tandem. The finish might be 85 ♔c1 b2+ 86 ♔c2 d3+.

0-1

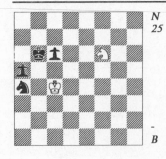

- B

Rogers - Sax
Adelaide 1986

Another double split pawn advantage. The rook's pawn makes it slightly more difficult to win.

48	...	♘c5
49	♘g4	♘e4
50	♘e3	♘d6+
51	♔c3	♔c5
52	♔b3	♔b5
53	♘c2	a4+
54	♔a3	♘c4+
55	♔a2	c5

Again *both* pawns are methodically advanced.

56	♘e1	♘e5
57	♘c2	♔c4!
58	♔a3	♔c3!
59	♘a1	

If 59 ♘e3 ♘c4+-+ or 59 ♘e1 ♔d2 intending ... c4-+.

59	...	c4
60	♔a2	♘d3
61	♔b1	♘b4

0-1

Knight v Knight

Paoli - M. Kovacs
Hungary 1971
A straightforward, but important, example.

1	...	♚e3
2	♘f3	h3
3	♘h2	♚f2

4 ♚xh3
Or 4 ♘f3 ♘h4! 5 ♘h2 ♚g2 (Maric).

4	...	♘e3
5	♚h4	♘g2
6	♚g5	♘g3

0-1

Prokes 1938

1 b7

If 1 e7 ♚f7 2 b7 ♘d6+ 3 ♚e5 ♘xb7=.

1	...	♘d6+
2	♚d4	

Or 2 ♚d5 ♘xb7 with zugzwang: 3 e7 ♚f7.

2	...	♘xb7

3 ♚d5 ♚g7
Or 3 ... ♘c5 4 e7 ♘e6 5 ♚d6 ♘g7 6 ♚d7 ♚f5 (6 ... ♚f7 7 ♚d8+ ♚f6 8 ♘e6) 7 ♘d4+ ♚e5 8 ♘e6 ♘h5 9 ♚d8.

4	♘d8	♘xd8
5	e7 and wins	

See also diag 16.

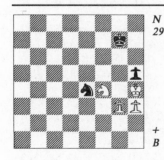

Pongrach 1887

1	♘e4	♚xh7
2	♘d2	♚g7
3	♘c4	♘b1

Or 3 ... ♘c2 4 b5 ♘e1 5 b6.

4 ♚d4
If 4 b5 ♘c3.

4	...	♚f7

5	b5	♚e7
6	b6	♚d7
7	♚c5	♘c3
8	♘e5+	♚c8
9	♚c6 and wins	

Use of the fortress position and knight domination forced a won position.

Knight and Two Pawns v Knight and One Pawn

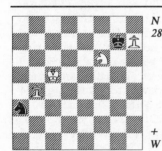

Tiller - D. Gurevich
Gausdal 1982

1	...	♚f6

Also possible is 1 ... ♚h7!? 2 ♘xh5 ♚h6 3 ♘f4! (3 g4 ♚g6=: e.g. 4 ♘f4+ ♚h6 5 ♘g2 ♚g6 6 ♘e1 ♚h6 7 ♘f3 ♚g6 8 g5 ♚f5 9 ♚h5 ♚f4 10 g6 ♘g3+ 11 ♚h6 ♘f5+ 12 ♚h7 ♚xf3=) 3 ... ♘f2 4 ♘e2 (intending ♘c3, g4, ♚g2) 4 ... ♘e4 5 ♘g1 ♘f2 6 ♘f3 ♘e4 7 ♘e5! ♚g7 8 ♘d3! ♚h6 9 ♚g4.

2 ♘xh5+ ♚f5
Or 2 ... ♚g6 3 g4 ♚h6 4 ♘f4 with zugzwang.

3	♘f4	♚f6
4	♘e2	♘e4
5	♚h5	♘f6+
6	♚h6	♘g8+
7	♚g7	♘f6
8	♘d4+	♚e5
9	♚g6	♘e4
10	♘e2	♘f2
11	h4	♘g4

12	h5	♔e6
13	h6	1-0

Analysis by D Gurevich.

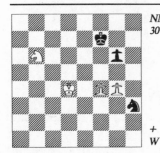

NN
30

Peretz - Domnitz
Netanya 1969
The misplaced knight on h3 renders Black's position critical.

42	♔e3	♔e6
43	♘a4!	♔d6

Black must try 43 ... g5!? now (this is really the main line, the game is tragic) 44 f5+ (intending ♘d3/e2 trapping the knight on h3. White seems to win the g5-pawn at the price of extricating the knight on h3, but Black has chances to create difficulties by erecting a blockade) and now:

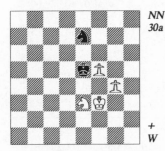

NN
30a

a) 44 ... ♔f6 45 ♘c3 ♔g7 (45 ... ♘f4!) 46 ♘e2+-;

b) 44 ... ♔e5 45 ♘c3 (45 ♘c5 ♔f6 46 ♘d3+-) 45 ... ♘g1 46 ♘e2+-;

c) 44 ... ♔d6 45 ♘c3 ♘f4 46 ♘e4+ ♔e5 47 ♘xg5 ♘d5+ 48 ♔f3 ♘e7 (incredibly, there is almost no theory on two pawns against none with a blockade - see also diags 29 and 53) 49 ♘f7+ ♔f6 50 ♘d6 ♔e5 (50 ... ♔g5 51 ♘e4+ ♔h4 52 ♔f4 ♘d5+ 53 ♔e5 (intending g5) 53 ... ♔xg4 54 ♘f6+) 51 ♘c4+ and now:

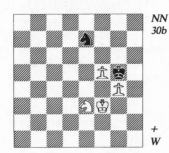

NN
30b

c1) 51 ... ♔d4 and:

c11) 52 f6! ♔g6 53 g5! ♔xc4 (53 ... ♔d5 54 ♔g4 ♔e6 55 ♔h5 ♘f4+ 56 ♔h6 ♘d5 57 ♔g7+-) 54 ♔e4 (54 ♔g4 transposes to the other note) 54 ... ♔c5 55 ♔f5 ♘h4+ 56 ♔e6+- intending f7, ♔f6;

c12) 52 ♘e3 ♔e5 transposing to the critical position discussed in c21 below.

c2) 51 ... ♔f6 52 ♘e3 and:

c21) 52 ... ♔e5 (a restraining move) *(30a)* 53 ♔g3 ♔e4 54 ♔h4! (White cannot mobilise his pawns by methodical means: 54 f6? ♘g6 55 ♘c4 ♔d5 56 g5 ♔xc4 57 ♔g4 ♔d5 58 ♔h5 ♘e5 59 g6 - 59 ♔h6 ♔e6 60 ♔g7 ♘d7 61 f7 ♔e7 62 g6 ♘f8 63 ♔h6 ♘xg6 64 ♔xg6 ♔f8= - 59 ... ♔e6 60 g7 - 60 ♔g5 ♘f7+= - 60 ... ♔f7=. However, he can exploit Black's active knight position by starting action behind it.) 54 ... ♔xe3 (55 g5 was threatened) 55 f6 ♘c6 56 g5 (56 f7 ♘e5) 56 ... ♘e5 57 ♔h5 ♔f4 58 g6+-;

c22) 52 ... ♔g5 *(30b)* Another critical position (see also diag 55). This is not a real blockade since the white king can get active and succeed - I believe - in getting around the blockade: 53 ♔e4 ♘g8 54 ♔e5 ♘f6 55 ♔e6 and now:

c221) 55 ... ♘e8 56 ♘d5 ♘g7+ (56 ... ♔h4 57 ♔e7 ♔xg4 58 ♘e3+) 57 ♔e5 ♔xg4 58 f6;

c222) 55 ... ♘e4 56 ♘d5 and:

c2221) 56 ... ♔xg4 57 ♘f6+;

c2222) 56 ... ♘c5+ 57 ♔e7 ♔xg4 (57 ... ♘e4 58 f6+-) 58 f6 ♘d3 59 ♔d6+-;

c2223) 56 ... ♔h4 57 ♔e5 (57 f6 ♔xg4=) and:

c22231) 57 ... ♘g5 58 ♘e3 ♔g3 (58 ... ♘f7+ 59 ♔f4 breaks the blockade) 59 f6 ♔f3 60 ♘f5+-;

c22232) 57 ... ♘f2 58 ♘e3 ♔g5 59 f6 ♘d3+ 60 ♔e6 ♘f4+ 61 ♔f7+-;

c22233) 57 ... ♘c5 58 f6

♔xg4 (58 ... ♘d7+ 59 ♔f5 or 58 ... ♔g5 59 ♔d6 ♘e4+ 60 ♔e7+-) 59 f7 ♘d7+ (59 ... ♔g5 60 ♔d6+-) 60 ♔e6 ♘f8+ 61 ♔e7 ♘g6+ (61 ... ♘h7 62 ♘f6+) 62 ♔e8 intending ♘e7 +-.

44 ♘c3 g5?

White threatened ♘e2 +-.

45	♘e4+	♔e6
46	♘xg5+	♘xg5
47	fxg5	♔e7
48	♔e4	♔f7
49	♔f5	♔g7
50	g6	♔h6
51	g7	1-0

N 31 — B

Mititelu - Stoica
Romanian Ch 1985

1	...	♔d6
2	♘d3	a5
3	♔f3	♘b4!

Not 3 ... ♘b6 4 ♘c1 ♔c5 (4 ... ♔d5 5 ♘b3 ♘c4 6 ♔f4 e5+ 7 ♔f5=) 5 ♘b3+ ♔b4 6 ♘d4 e5 (6 ... ♔xa4 7 ♔e4= or 6 ... ♘xa4 7 ♔xe6 ♘c3 8 ♔e3 a4 9 ♘d4=) 7 ♘c6+=.

4	♘f4	♘a6!
5	♘e2	

If 5 ♘d3 ♘c5 6 ♘b2 ♔d5 7 ♔e3 e5 8 ♔d2 ♔d4-+.

5	...	♔c5
6	♔e4	♔b4
7	♔d4	

Alternatively:

a) 7 ♔e5 ♘c5 8 ♔d6 ♔c4 and now:

a1) 9 ♘f4 ♘xa4 10 ♘xe6 ♘c3 11 ♘c5 ♔b5! 12 ♘d3 (12 ♘b3 a4 13 ♘a1 a3 14 ♔e5 ♔c4 15 ♔f4 ♘b5 16 ♔e3 ♔c3-+ or 12 ♘e6 a4 13 ♘d4+ ♔c4 14 ♘c2 ♔b3 15 ♘d4+ ♔b2) 12 ... a4 13 ♔e5 a3 14 ♘c1 ♔c4 and ... ♘e2 wins;

a2) 9 ♘c1 ♘xa4 10 ♔xe6 ♘c5+ 11 ♔d6 a4 12 ♔c6 ♘d3 13 ♘a2 ♔b3 14 ♔b5 a3.

b) 7 ♘f4 ♘c7 8 ♔e5 ♔xa4 9 ♔d6 ♘b3 10 ♔xc7 (10 ♘d3 a4 11 ♘c5+ ♔b4 12 ♘d3+ ♔c3-+) 10 ... a4 11 ♘d3 (11 ♘xe6 a3 12 ♘d4+ ♔b2) 11 ... ♔c3 12 ♘c1 e5 13 ♔d6 e4 14 ♔e5 ♔b2 15 ♘e2 a3-+.

7	...	♔xa4
8	♔c4	♘c7
9	♘c3+	♔a3
10	♘b1+	♔b2
11	♘c3	♘d5
12	♘a4+	♔c2
13	♘c5	♘b6+
14	♔b5	a4
15	♔b4	

If 15 ♘xa4 ♘xa4 16 ♔c6 ♔d3 17 ♔d6 ♘c5 18 ♔xc5 e5 or 15 ♔xb6 a3 16 ♘a6 ♔c3 or 15 ♘xe6 a3 16 ♔b4 a2 17 ♘d4+ ♔b1! 18 ♘b3 ♔b2 with zugzwang.

15	...	e5

0-1

Based on analysis by Stoica.

N 32 — + W

D. Gurevich - Dlugy
USA 1984

1 ♘h4!

Alternatively, 1 h4 ♘f3+ 2 ♔h5 ♔e3= or 1 ♘e5 ♘g2 or 1 ♔h4 ♔f3 2 ♔h5 ♔g3 3 h4 ♘f3=.

1	...	♘d3
2	♘g2!	♔f3
3	h4	♔xg2
4	h5	1-0

This important theme recurs often, e.g. see also diag 64.

Knight v Knight

Ulybin - Kontic
Tunja 1989

1   a5

Black cannot cope with threats to both flanks, despite the reduced material.

1   ...   ♘g3+

Alternatively, 1 ... ♔h7 2 ♘d4 and now:

a) 2 ... ♘g3+ 3 ♔g4 ♘e4 4 ♔f5 ♘d6+ (4 ... ♘g3+ 5 ♔f4 ♘f1 6 ♘f3 ♔g6 7 ♔e4 ♘g3+ 8 ♔d5 - JT) 5 ♔e5 ♘e8 (5 ... ♘c4+ 6 ♔f6) 6 ♔d5 ♔g6 7 ♘f3 ♔f5 8 ♔c6 ♔f4 9 ♔b6 ♔xf3 10 ♔xa6 ♔f4 11 ♔b6 ♔xg5 12 ♔c6;

b) 2 ... ♘d6 3 g6+ ♔g7 4 ♘e6+ ♔f6 (4 ... ♔g8 5 ♘c7 ♘c4 6 ♔h6 with the idea of ♘e8) 5 ♘c7 ♔g7 6 ♘xa6 ♘c4 7 ♘c7 ♘xa5 8 ♘e8+ ♔f8 (8 ... ♔g8 9 ♔h6) 9 g7+ ♔f7 10 ♔h6 ♘c6 11 ♔h7 ♘e7 12 ♘d6+ ♔f6 13 ♘c8.

2   ♔g4   ♘e4
3   ♘e7   ♔f7

Alternatively, 3 ... ♘c5 4 ♔f5 and now:

a) 4 ... ♘b7 5 g6 ♘d6+ (for 5 ... ♘c5 6 ♘c6 see 4 ... ♘b3 or 5 ... ♘xa5 6 ♔g5) 6 ♔g5 ♘e4+ 7 ♔f4 ♘c5 8 ♔f5 ♔f8 9 ♘d5 ♔g7 10 ♘c7 ♔g8 11 ♔g5 ♔g7 (11 ... ♘e4+ 12 ♔h6 ♘d6 13 ♘xa6 ♘c4 14 ♘c5 ♘xa5 15 ♘e4) 12 ♘e8+ ♔f8 13 ♔h6 ♘e6 14 ♘f6 ♔e7 15 ♘d5+ ♔f8 (15 ... ♔d6 16 ♘b4 ♔c5 17 ♘xa6+ ♔b5 18 ♘c7+ ♘xc7 19 g7) 16 ♘b4;

b) 4 ... ♘b3 5 ♘c6 ♘c5 6 g6 and:

b1) 6 ... ♔h6 7 ♔f6 ♘e4+ 8 ♔f7 and now:

b11) 8 ... ♘d6+ 9 ♔e7 ♘c4 10 ♔f6 ♘d6 11 ♘b4 ♘e8+ (11 ... ♘e4+ 12 ♔f7 ♘g5+ 13 ♔e7 is a tempo worse than 8

... ♘g5+) 12 ♔f7 ♘d6+ 13 ♔e6 ♘b7 14 ♔f6;

b12) 8 ... ♘g5+ 9 ♔e7 ♔xg6 10 ♘b4 ♘e4 11 ♘xa6 ♔f5 12 ♔d7 ♔e5 13 ♘c6 ♔d4 14 ♘c7 ♘c5 15 ♘e6+ ♘xe6 16 a6;

b2) 6 ... ♘b3 7 ♔g5 ♘c5 8 ♘d4 ♘e4+ 9 ♔f4 ♘c5 10 ♔f5 ♘b7 11 ♔g5 ♘xa5 12 ♔h5 (12 ♘f5+ ♔h8 13 ♔f6 ♘c6 14 ♔h6 ♘e7 15 g7+ ♔h7 16 ♘g4 ♘f5) 12 ... ♘c4 (12 ... ♘b7 13 ♘f5+) 13 ♘f5+ ♔f6 (13 ... ♔g8 14 ♔h6) 14 g7 ♔f7 15 ♔h6 ♘e5 16 ♔h7.

4   ♘d5   ♔g6
5   ♘f4+   ♔f7

Or 5 ... ♔g7 6 g6+-.

6   g6+

Not 6 ♔h5 ♔xg5 7 ♔xg5 ♘e7=.

6   ...   ♔g7
7   ♔f5   ♘d6+
8   ♔g5   ♘e4+
9   ♔g4   ♔h6

Alternatively:

a) 9 ... ♔g8 10 ♔h5 ♘g3+ 11 ♔g5 ♔f8 12 ♘h5 ♘e4+ 13 ♔h6 ♔g8 14 g7;

b) 9 ... ♔f6 10 ♔h5 ♔g7 11 ♘e6+ ♔f6 12 ♘c7 ♔g7 13 ♘xa6 ♘g3+ 14 ♔g4 ♘e4 15 ♔f4 ♘d6 16 ♘c7 ♔xg6 17 a6 ♘c8 18 ♔e5 ♔f7 19 ♔d5 ♔e7 20 ♔c6 ♔d8 21 ♘e6+ ♔e7 22 ♔c7 ♘d6 23 ♘d4;

c) 9 ... ♘d6 10 ♔h5 ♘c4 11 ♔g5 ♘xa5 12 ♘h5+ ♔f8 13 ♔h6 ♘c6 14 g7+ ♔f7 15 ♔h7 ♘e7 16 ♘f4 ♘g8 17 ♘d5 a5 18 ♘c3 ♘f6+ (18 ... ♘e7 19 ♘a4 ♘g8 20 ♘c5 ♘e7 21 ♘b7 a4 22 ♘d6+ ♔f6 23 ♘c8) 19 ♔h8 ♔g8 20 ♘e4 a4 21 ♘d6+ ♔e7 22 ♔xg8 a3 23 ♘f5+.

10   ♔f5   ♘d6+
11   ♔e6   ♘e4

Or 11 ... ♘c4 12 ♔f6 ♘d6

Knight v Knight

13 ♘e6.

12	♔d5	♘c3+
13	♔c6	♘a2

14 ♘c5 1-0

Notes largely based on those of Ulybin and Volovik.

N 34 — W

Hecht - Quinteros
Vrsac 1973

1	♔h2	♔g4
2	♘e6	♘b3

Black could also have tried 2 ... ♘f3+ 3 ♔h1 and now:

a) 3 ... ♔h4 4 ♘g7 ♔g3 5 ♘e6 ♔g4 6 ♘f4 ♔g5 7 ♘e2 ♔e6 8 ♔h2 ♔h4 9 ♘g3 ♔g4 10 ♘e2=;

b) 3 ... ♔f5 4 ♘f4 (4 ♘g7+ ♔f4 5 ♘e6+ ♔e3 6 ♘xd4!=) ♘g5 5 ♘e2 ♘e6 transposing to the previous variation;

c) 3 ... ♔g3 4 ♘f4! ♔f2 5 ♘e2!= ♔e3 6 ♘xd4!=.

N 34a — B

3	♘d8	♘a5

Not 3 ... ♘c5 4 ♘c6 ♘e6 5 ♘e5+.

4	♔g1

4 ♘f7 ♔c6 5 ♘h6+ ♔f4 6 ♔xh3 ♘e5 is dangerous but drawn.

4	...	♔g3

Also critical is 4 ... ♔f5 5 ♔h2 ♔f6 6 ♔xh3 ♔e7 7 ♔g4 ♔xd8 8 ♔f5 ♘c6 (8 ... ♘b3 9 ♔e4 ♔e7 10 ♔d5 ♔f6 11 ♔c4 ♔f5 12 ♔xb3 ♔f4 13 ♔b4) 9 ♔e4 *(34a)*.

Another key type of knight and pawn vs pawn position, (cf diags NP18-19) 9 ... ♔c7 10 ♔d5 ♔b6 11 ♔c4= (Hecht).

5	♔h1	♘b3
6	♘e6	♔h4
7	♔g1	♔g4
8	♔h2	♔h4
9	♘f4	♘d2
10	♘g6+	♔h5
11	♘e5	♔h4
12	♘g6+	♔g5
13	♘e5	♔f5
14	♘c6	½-½

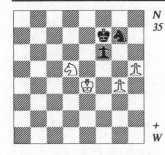

N 35 — W

Sanguinetti - Padevsky
Nice Ol 1974

1	♘f4	♘e8

Or 1 ... f5+ 2 gxf5 ♔f6 3 ♘d5+ ♔g5 4 f6 ♘e8 5 ♔e5!+-.

2	♔d5	♘c7+
3	♔c6	♘a6
4	♘d3!	♔g7
5	♔d6!	

Not 5 ♔b7 ♔h6 6 ♔xa6 f5= 7 gxf5 ♔xh5.

5	...	♔f7

Alternatively, 5 ... ♔h6 6 ♔e7 ♔g5 7 ♘f2 and now:

a) 7 ... ♘c5 8 ♔f7 f5 9 gxf5 ♔xh5 (9 ... ♔xf5 10 h6 ♘e6 11 ♘h3 ♘d8+ 12 ♔g7 ♘e6+ 13 ♔g8 ♘f8 14 ♘f4 ♔g5 15 ♔g7+-) 10 ♘e7 (The black king is boxed out. This is an optimal opposition of white king against knight, and the king is ideally posted as well.) 10 ... ♔g5 (10 ... ♘a6 11 f6 ♘c7 12 f7 ♘d5+ 13 ♔d6) 11 f6 ♔f5 (11 ... ♘d7 12 ♘e4+) 12 f7 ♔e6 13 ♘g4 (13 ♘d3);

b) 7 ... f5 8 ♘h3++-.

6	♔d7	♔g7

If 6 ... ♘b8+ 7 ♔c7 ♘a6+ 8 ♔b7 ♔g7 9 ♔xa6 ♔h6 10 ♘f4.

7	♔e7	♘c7

Or 7 ... ♘b8 8 ♘b4.

8	♘f4	♘a6
9	♘e6+	1-0

Knight v Knight

A. Zaitsev - Polugaevsky
Vladimir 1969
White has a strong single pawn. Black must abandon the

=
W

queenside to cope with the g-pawn and after ...

66 ♔g5

a draw was agreed.

Timoshchenko - Yusupov
USSR 1981
White is (should have been) thwarted by his bad knight position.

+
W

52	b4	♔b7
53	b5	♔c7
54	♔b4	♔b6
55	a5+	♔c7
56	♔c4	♔b7
57	♔d5	♘c7+
58	♔c5	♘e6+
59	♔c4	♔c7

Black should have played 59 ... ♔a7!! leaving c7 for the knight (Timoshchenko) e.g. 60 ♔d5 ♘c7+ 61 ♔c6 ♘e6 and now:

a) 62 a6 ♘d4+ 63 ♔c5 ♘e6+ 64 ♔d5 (64 ♔b4 ♔b6=) 64 ... ♘c7+ intending ♘xa6;

b) 62 b6+ ♔a6 and:

b1) 63 ♔d6 ♘d8= (63 ... ♔xa5?? 64 b7);

b2) 63 ♘g5 ♘d8+! 64 ♔c7 and:

b21) 64 ... ♘b7 65 ♘e6! (65 ♘e4 g6= with zugzwang, not 65 ... ♘xa5 66 ♘c5+ ♔b5 67

♘b3 ♘c6 68 b7 g5 69 ♘d4+) and now:

b211) 65 ... ♘xa5 66 ♘c5+ transposes to the previous note;

b212) 65 ... g5! 66 ♘xg5 ♘xa5 67 ♘e6 ♘b7 68 ♘d4 ♘d8! (68 ... ♘a5 69 ♘c6+-);

b213) 65 ... g6 66 ♘d4 g5 67 ♘c6 g4 68 ♘b4+ ♔xa5 (68 ... ♔b5 69 ♔xb7 g3 70 ♘c2 g2 71 ♘d4+) 69 ♔xb7 g3 70 ♘c6+ ♔a4 71 ♘e5;

b22) 64 ... ♔xa5 65 ♘f7 ♘e6+ 66 ♔b7 with an unclear position (Timoshchenko).

60	♔d5	♘f4+
61	♔e5	♘e2
62	♘g5	♘c3
63	♘e6+	♔b8

Or 63 ... ♔b7 64 ♘c5+ ♔c7 65 b6+ ♔c6 66 b7 ♔c7 67 a6 ♘b5 68 ♘d7.

64	b6	♘a4
65	♔d4	g5
66	♘c5	

Not 66 ♘xg5?? ♔b7=.
1-0

Knight v Knight

Kholmov - Hort
Leningrad 1967
The primary factor in this ending is the extent to which White is distracted by the b-pawn.

57	g5	♞h4
58	f5	♚g7
59	♞e6+	

Perhaps 59 ♚f4!?.

59	...	♚f7
60	♞d4	♚g7
61	♚f4	♞g2+
62	♚e5	♞h4
63	♚e4	

White could also try a direct approach: 63 ♚e6!? b3 and now:

a) 64 ♞xb3 ♞f3 65 g6 ♞h4 66 f6+ ♚xg6 67 ♞d4 (67 f7 ♚g7 68 ♞d4 ♞g6 69 ♞f5+ ♚f8=) and now:

a1) 67 ... ♚h6 68 ♞f5+ ♞xf5 69 ♚xf5 ♚h7 70 ♚e6;

a2) 67 ... ♚h7 68 f7 ♚g7 (68 ... ♞g6 69 ♞f5 ♞f8+ 70 ♚e7 ♞g6+ 71 ♚e8 ♚h8 72 ♞e7) 69 ♚e7 ♞g6+ 70 ♚e8 ♚f6 71 ♞f3 intending ♞h4+-;

a3) 67 ... ♞g2! 68 ♞e2 ♞h4 69 ♞f4+ (69 f7 ♚g7 70 ♞f4 ♞f5!=) 69 ... ♚h6 70 f7 ♚g7 71 ♞h5+ ♚f8 72 ♚f6 ♞g2 (72 ... ♞f5? 73 ♞f4) 73 ♚e6 ♞h4 74 ♞f4 ♚g7 75 ♞h5+ ♚f8 76 ♞f6 ♚g7 77 ♞d7 ♞g6=;

b) 64 f6+! and now:

b1) 64 ... ♚h7 65 ♞xb3 and:

b11) 65 ... ♚g6 and now:

b111) 66 f7 ♚g7 67 ♞d4 ♞g6 (this position with Black to move is easily won, see 64 ... ♚g6) 68 ♞e2 (68 ♞f5+ ♚f8 69 ♞d6 ♚g7) 68 ... ♞h8;

b112) 66 ♞d4! and:

b1121) 66 ... ♚h7 67 f7 ♚g7 (67 ... ♞g6 68 ♞f5 ♞f8+ 69 ♚e7 ♞g6+ 70 ♚e8) 68 ♚e7

♞g6+ 69 ♚e8+-;

b1122) 66 ... ♚xg5 67 ♞f3+ ♞xf3 68 f7;

b12) 65 ... ♞f3 66 ♚f5 ♞h4+ 67 ♚g4 ♞g2 68 ♞d4 ♚g6 69 ♞e6 ♞e3+ 70 ♚f3 ♞c4 (70 ... ♞d5 71 ♞f4+) 71 ♚f4 ♞d6 (71 ... ♞b6 72 ♚g4) 72 ♞f8+ ♚f7 73 ♞d7 (breaking the blockade) 73 ... ♚e6 74 g6;

b2) 64 ... ♚g6 65 f7 ♚g7 66 ♞xb3 ♞g6 67 ♞d4 and now:

b21) 67 ... ♞h8 68 ♞f5+ ♚f8 69 ♞d6 ♞g6 (69 ... ♚g7 70 ♚e7 ♞g6+ 71 ♚e8 ♞f8 72 ♞f5+);

b22) 67 ... ♞f4+ 68 ♚e7 ♞d5+ 69 ♚e8 ♞c7+ 70 ♚d7 ♞d5 (70 ... ♚xf7 71 ♚c7 ♚g6 72 ♞f3) 71 g6+-.

63	...	♞g2

Also possible was 63 ... ♚f7!? 64 ♚e5 ♞g2 (64 ... ♚g7 65 ♚e6 transposes to the above, and 64 ... ♚e7 loses to 65 g6+-) 65 g6+ ♚g7 66 ♞e6+ ♚h6 and now:

a) 67 g7 ♚h7 68 f6 ♚g8 69 ♞d4 ♚e3 (69 ... ♚f7 70 ♞f5) 70 ♞c6 ♚f7;

b) 67 ♚f6 ♞e3 68 g7 ♚g4+ 69 ♚f7 ♞e5+ 70 ♚f8 ♞d7+ 71 ♚e7 ♚h7 72 f6 (72 ♚xd7 b3 73 f6 b2 74 f7).

64	♞e6+	♚g8

64 ... ♚f7 65 ♞c5 ♞h4 66 ♚f4 ♞g2+ 67 ♚f3 ♞h4+ (67 ... ♞e1+ 68 ♚g4 and g6+ +-) 68 ♚g4 transposes.

65	♞c5	♞h4
66	♚f4	♚f7

Or 66 ... ♚g7 67 ♚g4 ♞g2 68 g6 ♞e3+ 69 ♚g5 ♞d5 70 ♞e6+ ♚g8 71 ♞d4 ♚g7 72 f6+ ♚xf6 73 ♞f5++- ♚h8 74 ♚xf6 b3 75 g7+ ♚h7 76 ♚f7.

67	♚g4	♞g2
68	g6+	♚f6

Or 68 ... ♔g7 69 ♔g5+-.
69 ♘d7+ ♔e7
Or 69 ... ♔g7 70 ♔g5 b3 71

f6+.

70 f6+ 1-0

Knight and Two Pawns v Knight and Two Pawns

N
39
-
B

N
40
=
B

Gines - Trias
corr 1981
With limites material, Black surprisingly embarks on a mating attack.

1 ... ♘g4!
2 ♘xg6

Not 2 ♘c6 ♔f2!.

2 ... ♔f2
3 ♘f4 ♔g1
4 ♘d3 ♔h1
0-1

Zugzwang and mate next move.

V. Kovacevic - Zlotnik
Belgrade 1988

1 ... ♘d7
2 ♔e4

Or 2 ♔g6 ♔d6 3 ♔xh6 ♔c5 4 ♘a2 ♔b6 5 g4 ♔a5 6 ♘c3 ♔b4=.

2 ... ♔d6
3 ♔d4 ♔c6!

Black must use the king against the a-pawn, the knight is best suited to fighting the other pawn. (Not 3 ... ♘e5 4 ♘e4+ ♔e6 5 ♘d2.)

4 ♔xc4 ♔b6
5 ♘d1

Or 5 ♔d5 ♔a5 6 ♔e6 ♘c5+ 7 ♔f5 ♔b4 8 ♘e4 ♘d3 9 g3 ♔xa4 10 ♔g6 ♔b5 11 ♔xh6 ♔c6=.

5 ... ♔a5
6 ♘b2 ♘b8
7 ♔b3 ♔b6
8 ♘c4+ ♔c5
9 ♘e3 h5
10 ♘f5 ♘d7
11 ♘g3 ♘f6
12 ♘f5 ♘e4

13 ♘g7 ♘f6
14 g3 ♔b6
15 ♔c4

If instead 15 ♔b4 ♔a6 16 a5 ♘d5+ 17 ♔c5 ♘e3= 18 ♘xh5 (18 ♔d4 ♘f1=) 18 ... ♔xa5 19 ♘g7 ♘g4 and Black will have no trouble in achieving the drawing method of the game.

15 ... ♔a5
16 ♔d4 ♔xa4
17 ♔e5 ♘g4+
18 ♔f4 ♔b5
19 ♘xh5 ♘h2?!

More accurate was 19 ... ♘h6.

20 ♘f6 ♔c5
21 ♘e4+ ♔d5
22 ♘d2 ♔e6
23 ♔g5 ♔e5
24 ♔h5 ♔f5
25 ♘c4 ♘f3
26 g4+ ♔f6
27 ♔h6 ♔f7
28 ♘d6+ ♔g8

Notes expanded on those by Zlotnik.

Knight v Knight

Horner - P. Littlewood
British Ch. 1981

1	...	♞d6

Not 1 ... a2 2 ♞xa2 d2+ 3 ♚c2 ♞e2 4 ♞c1+.

| 2 | g5 | ♞e4 |

| 3 | ♞d5+ |

Or 3 ♞xe4 ♚xe4 4 g6 a2 5 ♚b2 d2 6 g7 a1♛+.

| 3 | ... | ♚d4 |
| 4 | ♞b4 | ♚c3 |

0-1

Knight and Three Pawns v Knight and One Pawn

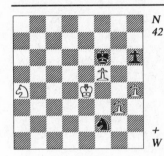

Rajkovic - Maric
Yugoslavia 1974

| 1 | ♚e3 |

Not 1 ♚f3 ♞d3 2 g4 (2 ♚g4 ♞e5+ 3 ♚h5 ♚xf5 4 ♚xh6 ♚g4=) 2 ... h5=.

| 1 | ... | ♞h3 |

If 1 ... ♞g4+ 2 ♚f4 or 1 ... ♞d1+ 2 ♚f4.

| 2 | ♚f3 |

Not 2 g4 h5 3 ♚f3 hxg4+ 4 ♚xg4 ♞f2+ 5 ♚f3 ♚xf5 6 ♚xf2 ♚g4.

| 2 | ... | ♚xf5 |
| 3 | ♞c3 |

Or 3 g4+ ♚f6 4 ♞c3 h5 5 gxh5 ♚f5 6 ♞e2+- (JT).

| 3 | ... | ♞g1+ |
| 4 | ♚f2! |

Not 4 ♚g2 ♚g4! 5 ♞e4 ♞e2= intending ... ♞xg3.

| 4 | ... | ♚g4 |
| 5 | ♞e4 | ♞f3 |

Or 5 ... ♚f5 6 ♞d2 ♚g4 7 ♞f1+-.

6	♞f6+	♚f5
7	♚xf3	♚xf6
8	♚e4	♚e6
9	g4	♚f6
10	♚d5	h5
11	g5+	♚e7
12	♚e5	♚f7
13	♚d6	**1-0**

Based on Rajkovic's analysis.

Knight and Three Pawns v Knight and Two Pawns

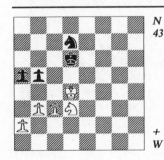

Prandstetter - Donchev
Prague Zt 1985

1	c4	bxc4
2	bxc4	♚c6
3	a3!

Not 3 c5 ♚b5 or 3 a4 ♞b6.

| 3 | ... | ♞f6 |

Or 3 ... ♚d6 4 c5+ ♚c6 5 a4! ♚c7 6 ♞e5 winning - White can penetrate with his king on b5 (Prandstetter).

4	♞e5+	♚b6
5	a4!	♚a6
6	c5	♞h5!
7	♚d5	♞f6+
8	♚d4

Not 8 ♚c6 ♞e4 9 ♞d7 ♞c3 10 ♞b6 ♚a7.

| 8 | ... | ♞h5 |
| 9 | ♞d3! |

Intending ♞-d5. If 9 ♞c4 ♞g3 10 c6 ♞e2+ 11 ♚c5 ♞c3 12 ♞b2 ♞e4+ (12 ... ♞a7 13 ♚c4 ♞e4 14 ♚b5+-) 13 ♚d5 ♞c3+ 14 ♚d6 ♞e4+ 15 ♚c7 ♞c5 16 ♚d6 (16 ♚b8 ♚b6 17

c7 ♘a6+) 16 ... ♘e4+ 17 ♔d7
♘c5+ 18 ♔c7 ♔a7 19 ♔c8
♔b6 20 c7 ♘a6 21 ♘c4+
♔c5 22 ♘xa5 ♘xc7.

    9   ...   **♘g3(?!)**

A better defence was 9 ...
♔b7 10 ♔c4 (10 ♔c3! ♘g3 11
♔c4 ♔a6 12 ♘f4 ♘e4 13
♘d5 - intending c6, as in the
note. Here it is Black to move,
but it is c6 that is threatened,
not any special zugzwang - 13
... ♘d2+ 14 ♔c3 ♘e4+ 15
♔d4 ♘g5 16 ♔c4 ♘e4 17 c6
transposing to the note 11 ...
♔a6 below) 10 ... ♔a6 11 ♔d5
♔b7 12 ♔d6 ♘f6 13 c6+
♔b6.

    10   **♘f4!**

If 10 ♔d5 ♘e2 11 ♔c6 ♘c3.

    10   ...   **♔b7**
    11   **♔c4**   **♘e4**

Or 11 ... ♔a6 12 ♘d5 ♘e4
13 c6 ♘d6+ 14 ♔d4! ♘c8 15
♔c5 ♔a7 (15 ... ♘a7 16

♘c7+) 16 ♔b5.

    12   **♔b5**   **♘c3+**
    13   **♔xa5**   **♘c6**
    14   **♘d3**   **♔d5**
    15   **♔b4**   **♘e2**

If 15 ... ♔d4 16 ♘f4! ♘a2+
(16 ... ♘xa4 17 ♘e6+) 17 ♔a3
♔xc5 18 ♘d3+.

    16   **a5**   **♘d4**
    17   **a6**   **♔c6**
    18   **♔c4**   **♘e6**
    19   **♘b4+**   **♔c7**
    20   **♔d5**   **♘f4+**
    21   **♔e5**   **♘g6+**
    22   **♔e4!**   **♔b8**
    23   **♔d5**   **1-0**

For example, 23 ... ♔c7 24
c6 ♘e7+ 25 ♔c5 ♘c8 26
♘d5+ ♔b8 27 ♘b6 ♘a7 (27
... ♘e7 28 c7+ ♔a7 29 ♔b5!)
28 ♔d6 ♘b5+ 29 ♔d7 ♔a7
30 ♘d5 ♔xa6 31 ♘c7+.

Notes based on those by
Prandstetter.

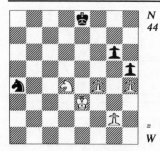

N 44

Zapata - Van der Wiel
Brussels SWIFT 1986

    1   **f5**   **♔f7!**

Not 1 ... gxf5 2 ♘f4! ♔f7 3
♔g5 f4 4 ♔xh5 ♔f6 5 ♔g4!
♔e5 6 ♘e2.

    2   **♔f4**   **♔f6**
    3   **fxg6**   **♔xg6**
    4   **♘e2!**

Aiming for f4 which will
force the black king out of
play.

    4   ...   **♘b2**
    5   **♔e4!**

White gradually improves
his pieces taking care that the
black knight is not allowed to
interfere with checks.

    5   ...   **♘d1**
    6   **♘f4+**   **♔h6**
    7   **♘d5!**

Restraining the knight on
d1.

    7   ...   **♘f2+**

7 ... ♔g6 8 ♔e5 should
transpose.

    8   **♔e5**   **♔g6**

Knight checks would be answered by ♔f5.

    9   **♘f4+**   **♔h6**
    10   **♔f5**   **♘g4**
    11   **♘d5**   **♘f2**

Or 11 ... ♘h2 12 ♔e3.

    12   **♔e3!**   **♘d3**
    13   **♔f6**   **♘e1?**

Alternatively:

a) 13 ... ♘f4 14 g3 ♘h3 15
♘f5+ ♔h7 16 ♘d6+-;

b) 13 ... ♘c5! (the best
square, to get on a checking
circuit and avoid zugzwang)
14 ♘f5+ ♔h7 and now:

b1) 15 ♔g5 ♘e6+;

b2) 15 g3 ♘e4+ 16 ♔f7
♘c3! 17 ♘d6 ♔h6 18 ♔f6
♘d5+ 19 ♔e5 ♘c3 (19 ...
♘b4!?) 20 ♘e4 ♘e2;

c2) 15 ♘d6 ♔h6 16 g3

♘d7+ 17 ♔e6 ♞c5+ and:

c21) 18 ♔f7 ♞d7! (18 ... ♞d3? 19 ♔f6+- or 18 ... ♞h7? 19 ♔f6 ♞h6 20 ♞f5++-) 19 ♞f5+ ♔h7 20 ♔e7 ♞c5 (20 ... ♔g6?? 21 ♔xd7 ♔xf5 22 ♔e7 ♔g4 23 ♔f6 ♔xg3 24 ♔g5+-) 21 ♔f6 ♞e4+=;

c22) 18 ♔f5 ♞d7! (Black must prevent ♔f6, other knight moves are too distant, e.g. 18 ... ♞b3 19 ♔f6+-) and now:

c221) 19 ♞e4 ♞b6 and White's knight is also distant from its optimal square(s). (Not 19 ... ♞f8 20 ♞f6+-.);

c222) 19 ♞f7+ ♔g7 20 ♞e5 and:

c2221) 20 ... ♞f6 21 ♞d3 ♔f7 (21 ... ♞h7!? 22 ♞c5 ♔f7) 22 ♞c5 ♔g7 and now:

c22211) 23 ♞e4 ♞h7 24 ♞g5 ♞f6 25 ♞e6+ ♔f7 26 ♞f4 ♔g7 27 ♞e2 ♞h7 (27 ... ♔f7 28 ♞g5 ♔g7);

c22212) 23 ♞g5 ♔f7 24 ♞h6 ♔f8 (24 ... ♔e7 25 ♔g6 with zugzwang or 24 ... ♔e8 25 ♔g7+-) 25 ♞e6+ ♔e7 26 ♞f4+-;

c2222) 20 ... ♞c5! 21 ♔g5 ♞e4+.

14	♞f5+	♔h7
15	g3	♞f3
16	♞d6	

Zugzwang, so White wins the h-pawn: 16 ... ♞d4 (16 ... ♔h6 17 ♞f7+ ♔h7 18 ♞g5+) 17 ♔g5 ♞e2 18 ♞f5.

1-0

Byrne - Padevsky
Monte Carlo 1968

43 ♔f4 ♞d7

A long three pawns vs two endgame. With no black weaknesses and no passed pawns Black should hold as long as passivity is avoided. Perhaps he could even try 43 ... h5!?

44 h4

Or 44 g4 g5+ 45 ♔e4 ♞c5+ 46 ♔e3 (46 ♔d5 ♞d3) 46 ... ♔g6=.

44		♞e5
45	♔e4	h5

Ensuring that there will be an exchange of pawns after any advance.

46	f3	♞f7
47	♞b5	♞h6

A good circuit. The black knight presses g3 and h4, and hinders any possibility of f4-f5 to isolate the h5-pawn.

48	♔f4	♞f5
49	g3	♞g7
50	♞c7	♞f5
51	♞d5+	♔g7
52	♞c3	

Instead 52 ♔g5 ♞xg3? (52 ... ♞d4!) 53 ♞f4 and both black pawns fall.

52	...	♞h6
53	g4	hxg4
54	fxg4	♞f7
55	♞e4	♞d8
56	♞c5	♔f6
57	g5+	♔g7
58	♔e5	♞c6+
59	♔d6	♞b4
60	♞e6+	♔f7
61	♞d8+	♔g7
62	♔e6	♞c2

Black creates counterplay against h4 just as his lack of space is becoming dangerous, e.g. 63 ♔e7 ♞e3 64 ♞e6+ ♔g8 65 ♔f6 (65 ♞d4? ♞f5+) 65 ... ♞g2=.

Knight v Knight

NN
46

Hecht - Gligoric
Busum 1969
Another safe three pawns v two pawns.

74	...	♔d6
75	♘b2	♔e5
76	♘d3+	♔d4

Or 76 ... ♔e4 77 ♘c5+ ♔e3 78 ♘d7.

| 77 | ♘f4 | ♘e7 |

See also diag 45.

78	g4!	hxg4+
79	♔xg4	♔e4
80	h5!	g5
81	♘h3	

Intending ♘xg5=. An efficient neutralisation by White.

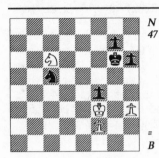

N
47

Anderssen - Steinitz
1866

| 1 | ... | ♘e6 |
| 2 | ♔g2 | ♔f5 |

It seems to me (JT) that this plan is too rigid. It is more logical to try to mount pressure against the white pawns. The h3-pawn is not as weak as it would be on h4, so this is not an easy task.

Another idea is 2 ... ♔h5!? and now:

a) 3 f3 ♔h4 4 ♘e7 ♔g5 5 ♘c6 ♔f5 6 ♔f2 ♔g5 7 ♔g2 (7 h4 looks very risky, the h-pawn being very vulnerable there) 7 ... ♔e6 8 ♘d4+ ♔d5 9 ♘e2 (9 ♘f5 ♘e6 10 ♔f2 ♔e5 11 ♘e7 ♔f6 12 ♘d5+ ♔g5 13 ♘e7 looks to be White's toughest attempt to break down) 9 ... ♘e6 10 ♔f2 ♔c4;

b) 3 ♘e7 ♘d4 4 ♘d5 ♔g5 (4 ... g5 5 ♘e7) 5 ♔h2 ♔f5 6

♔g2 ♔e4 7 ♘c3+ ♔d3 8 ♘d5 g5 9 ♘f6 (9 h4 f3+ 10 ♔g3 gxh4+ 11 ♔xh4 ♔e2 12 ♔g3 ♘f5+ 13 ♔g4 ♘d6) 9 ... ♔e2 and the d4-knight can move to f5 to guard h6, so the pawns remain flexible. Without f3, White has some problems guarding the invasion route via e4.

| 3 | f3 | g5(?) |

This is the rigid part. Surely it is better to try black king invasions towards e2/h3 and leave the g5 square open for pieces.

4	♔f2	♘c5
5	♘e7+	♔e6
6	♘c6	♔d5
7	♘e7+	♔c4
8	♘f5	h5
9	♘g7	h4
10	♔e2 drawing	

The main line is Fine's analysis; all else is new.

N
48

Sznapik - Romanishin
Caracas 1976

| 3 | ... | ♘d4 |
| 4 | ♘a4 | |

Intending ♘c5+.

4	...	♘f5
5	♔g4	♔f6
6	h5?!	

The pawn is even weaker on h5. White must consider passive defence with 6 ♘c5 h5+ 7

♔h3 ♔e5 8 ♘d3+ ♔e4 9 ♘e1 f6!? (9 ... ♘d4 is suggested by Bozic but it seems to me that h4 is weak enough to ensure that White's position should be critical or lost, certainly here where White is so passive) 10 ♘c2 ♔f3 11 ♘b4 ♘e7 12 ♘d3 and now:

a) 12 ... ♔e2? 13 ♘c5 ♔xf2 (13 ... ♘d5 14 ♔g3) 14 ♘e4+;

---

b) 12 ... ♞d5! 13 ♔h2 ♔g4-+.

6	...	g5
7	♘c5	♞g7
8	♘e4+	♚e5
9	♘xg5	

Or 9 ♘g3 f5+-+.

| 9 | ... | hxg5 |

| 10 | ♔xg5 | |

Or 10 h6 ♞e8.

10	...	♞e6+
11	♔h6	♚f6
12	♔h7	♞g7
13	h6	♞f5
14	f4	♚e6

0-1

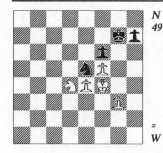

N 49

=

W

Gligoric - Levy
Hastings 1970

55	♘f3	♞f7
56	♔e3	♞h6
57	♔f4	♞f7
58	e5	

White is too tied down to the e4-pawn to do without this, which at least creates a passed pawn.

58	...	fxe5+
59	♘xe5	♞d6
60	♘g4	

Or 60 g4 h6 61 ♘d3 ♚f6 62 ♘f2 ♞f7 63 ♘e4+ ♚g7 64 ♘g3 ♚f6 65 ♘h5+ ♚e7 66 ♚e4 ♞g5+ 67 ♚d5 ♞f3 winning.

| 60 | ... | ♞f7 |
| 61 | ♔e4 | h5 |

It looks risky to expose the h-pawn, but the g4-knight makes it possible to threaten ♚e7.

62	♘f2	♔f6
63	♔f4	♚g7
64	♘e4	♚h6!
65	♘f6	♞d8
66	♘d7	♞f7
67	♘e5	♞d6
68	♘f3	♞f7
69	♘d2	♚g7
70	♘c4	♚f6
71	♘b6	♚g7
72	♘d7	♚h6
73	f6	♚g6
74	♚e4	

Or 74 ♘e5+ ♚xf6 75 ♘xf7 h4!= (75 ... ♚xf7? 76 ♚g5).

| 74 | ... | ♚g5 |

½-½

N 50

±

W

Gufeld - Grigorian
USSR 1980

| 1 | gxf5 | gxf5 |
| 2 | ♘f3 | ♞f6 |

Or 2 ... ♞d6 3 ♔d3 and:

a) 3 ... ♞b5 4 ♘g5 h6 5 ♘f3 ♞d6 6 ♘d4 h5 (6 ... ♚c5 transposes.) 7 ♘xf5;

b) 3 ... h6 4 ♘d4 ♚c5 5 ♘e6+ ♚d5 6 ♘g7 ♚c5 7 h3 with a zugzwang.

If 7 ... ♚d5 8 ♘xf5; otherwise the white king invades.

| 3 | ♘d4 | |

If 3 ♔d3 ♞d7 4 ♘d4 ♞c5+ 5 ♔e2 ♚e4 6 ♘b5 ♚d5 7 ♘c7+ ♚d6.

| 3 | ... | ♚e4 |
| 4 | ♘b5 | |

Intending ♘c3 mate.

| 4 | ... | ♚d5 |
| 5 | ♔f3 | |

Perhaps 5 ♔d3!? and now:

a) 5 ... ♞g4 6 ♘d4 ♞xh2 (6 ... ♞f2+ 7 ♚e2 ♞g4 8 h3 ♞h6 9 ♔d3 ♚c5 10 ♘e6+ ♚d5 11 ♘g5) 7 ♘xf5+-;

b) 5 ... ♞d7 6 ♘c7+ ♚d6 7 ♘e8+ ♚e7 (7 ... ♚d5 8 ♘g7 ♞c5+ 9 ♔e2 ♚e4 10 ♘h5+-) 8 ♘g7 ♚f6 9 ♘h5+ ♚e6 10 ♘g3 ♚f6 11 ♘e2 ♞c5+ 12 ♔c4 ♞e4 13 ♘d4 ♞d2+ 14 ♔d3 ♞e4 when White's king seems more active but f6 is a very solid defensive post for the black king. Not 14 ... ♞f1?? 15 ♘f3.

5 ... ♞g4
6 ♞d4

White has two other tries:

a) 6 h3 ♞h6 7 ♞d4 ♔d6 8 ♔g3 (8 e4 was suggested by Gufeld) and now:

a1) 8 ... ♔e7!? 9 ♔h4 (9 ♞f3 ♔f6 10 ♞g5 ♔g6) 9 ... ♔f6 10 ♔h5 (10 ♞f3 ♞f7) 10 ... ♞f7 11 ♞f3 ♞d6 12 ♞e5! ♔g7 13 ♔g5 h6+ 14 ♔h5 ♞e4;

a2) 8 ... ♔d5 (This was given by Gufeld but it looks dubious to me. The black king defends best from f6.) 9 ♔h4 ♔e4 10 ♔g5 ♞f7+ 11 ♔f6 ♞d6 12 h4 ♞e8+ 13 ♔g5!? (13 ♔f7 is inferior: 13 ... ♔xe3 14 ♞e6 ♞c7! - Gufeld) 13 ... ♔xe3 (Alternatively: 13 ... ♞d6 14 h5 h6+ 15 ♔g6+- or 13 ... h6+ 14 ♔xh6 ♔xe3 15 ♞e6 intending ♔g6 +-) 14 ♞xf5+ ♔e4 15 h5 ♞c7 16 ♞g7 ♞d5 17 f5 ♔e5 18 ♞e8 ♞f4 19 f6.

b) 6 e4+ ♔c5 7 exf5 ♞xh2+ 8 ♔g3 ♞f1+ 9 ♔g4 ♔c6 10 f6 ♔d7 11 ♞c7 ♞d2!= 12 ♔f5 ♞c4 13 ♞b5 ♞e3+=.

6	...	♞xh2+
7	♔g3	♞f1+
8	♔f2	♔e4!
9	♔xf1	♔xe3
10	♞e6	♔f3
11	♔g1	♔g3

½-½

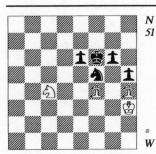

N 51

Bruinenberg - Muresan
Thessaloniki women's ol 1984

1	...	♔g7
2	♞e5	♞e3
3	♞d7	

White could also have played:

a) 3 ♞c6 ♔f6 and now:

a1) 4 ♔g3 ♞f5+ 5 ♔h3 ♞e7 6 ♞d4 ♞d5 7 ♔g3 (7 ♞e2 ♔f5 8 ♔g3 ♔e4) 7 ... ♞xf4 8 ♔xf4 e5+;

a2) 4 ♞d4 ♞d5 5 ♞e2 (5 ♔g3 ♞xf4) ♞f5 6 ♔g3 ♔e4.

b) 3 ♔g3!? ♔f6 4 ♞d7+ ♔f5 (4 ... ♔e7 5 ♞e5) and now:

b1) 5 ♞c5!? ♞d5 6 ♞d3 ♔e4 (6 ... ♞c3 7 ♔f3 ♞b5 8 ♞c5 ♞d4+ 9 ♔e3 ♞c2+ 10 ♔f3 ♞e1+ 11 ♔g3) 7 ♞c5+ when I (JT) do not see how Black wins against best defence. Pressure against e6 rather than g6 seems best;

b2) 5 ♞e5 ♔e4 6 ♞xg6 ♞d5 7 ♞f8 ♞xf4 8 ♞d7 e5 9 ♔f2 ♔d4 10 ♞f6 (10 ♔f3 ♞d5) 10 ... e4 11 ♔g3 e3 (Muresan, Stoica).

3	...	♔f7
4	♔g3	♔e7
5	♞c5?	

Instead:

a) 5 ♞b6 ♔d6 6 ♞c8+ ♔c7 7 ♞a7 ♞f5+ 8 ♔h3 ♞d4 trapping the a7-knight;

b) 5 ♞e5! ♞f5+ (5 ... ♔f6 6 ♞d7+ ♔f5 7 ♞c5 transposes to 3 ♔g3) 6 ♔h3 ♔d6 7 ♞xg6 ♔d5 8 ♞f8 ♞g7 9 ♔g3 ♔e4 10 ♞g6=;

5	...	♔d6
6	♞e4+	♔c6!
7	♞g5	♔d5
8	♞h7	♞f5+
9	♔h3	♞g7!
10	♞f8	♔e4
11	♔g3	

Or 11 ♞xg6 ♔f5 12 ♞e7+ ♔xf4 13 ♞g6+ ♔f5 14 ♞e7+ ♔e4-+.

11	...	♞f5+
12	♔h3	♞d4

Now 13 ♞xg6 ♞e2 transposes into note above.

0-1

Knight v Knight

♘ V ♞

NN
52

+
W

Serper - Suba
Hastings 1990

　　1　♘e1!

Intending 2 ♘f3 ♔g6 3 ♔d3-c4-c5-d6xe6.

　　1　...　　♘c3
　　2　♘f3　　♔g6

Not 2 ... ♘d5+ 3 ♔d4 ♘f4 4 ♘xg5+ ♔g6 5 h4+-.

　　3　♔d4　　♘d5
　　4　♔c5　　♘f4
　　5　♔d6　　♘xh3

If 5 ... ♔h6 6 ♔d7! ♔g6 7 ♔e7 (zugzwang) 7 ... ♔h6 8 ♔f6+-.

　　6　♔xe6　　♘f2
　　7　♘h2　　♘d3

If 7 ... ♘e4 8 ♔e7 intending e6+-. The presence of the g-pawns makes the e-pawn a potent force - it is easier for a knight to sacrifice itself for a pawn than to halt it, and here the knight cannot afford to be sacrificed.

　　8　♔d6　　♘f7
　　9　e6+　　♔e8
　10　♘f3　　♘f2
　11　♘xg5!

Not 11 ♘e5? ♘e4+=.

　11　...　　♔d8

Or 11 ... ♘xg4 12 ♘h7! ♔d8 13 e7+ ♔e8 14 ♔e6 intending ♘f6 mate.

　12　♘h7!　　♘e4+

Or 12 ... ♘xg4 13 e7+.

　13　♔e5　　♘f2
　14　♘f6　　♔e7
　15　♘d5+　　♔f8
　16　g5　　　1-0

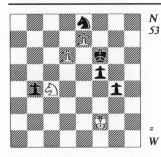

N
53

=
W

Arnaudov - Semkov
Bulgarian Ch. 1977

　　1　♘e3!

Not 1 ♔g3 b3 2 ♔f4 ♘xd6 3 ♘xd6 ♔xe7 4 ♘c4 ♔e6-+.

　　1　...　　♘xd6

If 1 ... b3 2 ♘xf5 draws.

　　2　♘d5+　　♔e6
　　3　♘xb4　　♔e7
　　4　♔g3

The blockade not only creates typical difficulties in advancing the pawns, but it is easy for the knight to threaten sacrifices liquidating both pawns.

　　4　...　　♔f6

If 4 ... ♘e4+ 5 ♔f4 ♔e6 (5 ... g3 6 ♘d5+ ♔e6 7 ♘e3= since both Black pieces are tied down to defending pawns) 6 ♘c2 ♔f6 7 ♘e3 ♘d6 8 ♘xg4+=.

　　5　♔f4　　♔g6

Alternatively:

a) 5 ... ♘c4 (intending a controlling ♘e3) 6 ♘d5+ ♔e6 7 ♘c7+ ♔d6 8 ♔xf5 g3 (8 ... ♘e3+ 9 ♔f4=) 9 ♘b5+ ♔c5 10 ♘c3 g2 11 ♘e2=.

b) 5 ... ♔e6 6 ♘c2! intending ♘d4xf5, ♘e3xg4.

　　6　♘d5　　♔h5
　　7　♘e3　　♔h4
　　8　♘f1　　♔h3

Or 8 ... ♘e4 9 ♘e3 ♘g3 (9 ... ♘d6 repeats) 10 ♘g2+ ♔h3 11 ♘e3 (= Mechkarov) 11 ... ♘e2+ 12 ♔xf5 g3 13 ♔g5! ♘c3 14 ♔h5= (see also diags 14 and 16).

　　9　♘g3　　♔g2
　10　♘xf5　　½-½

Knight v Knight

Knight and Three Pawns v Knight and Three Pawns

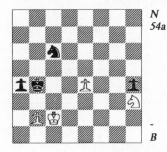

Em Lasker - Nimzowitsch
Zürich 1934

1 ... &f7

A classic example of the benefits of an outside pawn, but it must be noted that both of Black's pieces are superior as well. Still, White should hold with best defence.

2 &c1 &f6
3 &d2 &e5
4 &e3 h5
5 a3?!

White should activate the knight. Now Black has something to 'grip' on this flank. 5 &h3!? has two points: it begins to correct the pawns passivity and does not create any weakness on the queenside.

5 ... &c2+

More accurate is 5 ... &e6! 6 &g1 &g5.

6 &f3

Or 6 &d3 &b4+.

6 ... &b4
7 a3(?)

As pointed out by Fine, after 7 &f4! White should draw, e.g. 7 ... &d3 8 b4 &e1+ 9 &e2 &c2. This is just one obvious possible improvement for White and explains why Averbakh preferred to analyse this ending from Black's 23rd move.

5 ... a5!
6 &h3 &c2+
7 &d3 &e1+
8 &e2 &g2
9 &f3 &h4+
10 &e3 &g6
11 &g5 &f6
12 &h7+ &e7

13 &g5 &e5
14 &d4 &d6
15 &h3 a4
16 &f4 h4
17 &h3 b6!
18 &f4 b5
19 &h3

19 &c3 &c6 20 &d3 is better, making ... b4 and ... &xb4 problematic, i.e. 20 ... &c5 (20 ... &e5 21 &g6+) 21 &e6+ &d6 22 &f4.

19 ... &c6+
20 &e3

Or 20 &d3 &e5 21 &e3 &a5-+.

20 ... &c5
21 &d3 b4
22 axb4+ &xb4
23 &c2 *(54a)*

Averbakh starts his analysis from here. The whole ending is instructive, though from here it becomes technically correct.

23 ... &d4+
24 &b1

Or 24 &d3 &e6 25 &e3 (25 &c2 &c4-+) 25 ... &b3 26 &f4 &xb2 27 &xe6 a3.

24 ... &e6
25 &a2

Or 25 &c2 &c4-+.

25 ... &c4!
26 &a3 &d4
27 &xa4 &xe4
28 b4 &f3
29 b5 &g2

The finish might have been 30 b6 (30 &g5 &xg5 31 b6 &e6 32 &b5 &d8) 30 ... &xh3 31 b7 &c5+.

0-1

Knight v Knight

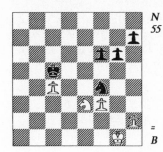

Stohl - Ilincic,
Vrnjacka Banja 1989

| | 38 | ... | ♘d3 |
| 39 | ♘d5?! | |

More accurate was 39 ♔f1 ♘e5 40 ♔e2 ♘xc4 41 ♘g4 (see also diags 49 and 61) 41 ... f5 42 ♘f6 h5 (42 ... h6 43 ♘g8 h5 44 ♘e7 ♘e5 45 f4 ♔d6 46 ♘c8+ ♔d7 47 ♘b6+ ♔c6 48 ♘c8 ♔d7 49 ♘b6+ ♔c7 50 ♘d5+ ♔d6 51 ♘b6) 43 ♘d7+. This ending "feels" tenable, for example:

a) 43 ... ♔d4 44 ♘f8 ♘e5 45 f4 (45 ♘e6+!?) 45 ... ♘g4 46 ♔f3 (or 46 h3 intending ♔f3, ♘xg6);

b) 43 ... ♔d6 44 ♘f8 and now:

b1) 44 ... g5 45 ♘h7 g4 46 fxg4 hxg4 47 h3 gxh3 48 ♔f3 f4 49 ♘g5 ♘e5+ (49 ... ♘d2+ 50 ♔f2) 50 ♔xf4 h2 51 ♘e4+ ♔d5 52 ♘f2 ♘d3+ 53 ♔g3=;

b2) 44 ... ♘e5 45 f4 ♔e7 45 f4 ♔e7 46 ♘h7 ♘f7 47 ♔f3.

39	...	f5
40	♘f6	h5
41	♘d7+	♔xc4
42	♘f8	♘f4-+

This is clearly an inferior version of this ending compared with the first note.

| 43 | ♔f2 | ♔d4 |

43 ... ♔d3!?.

| 44 | ♔g3 | |

An interesting try was 44 ♘d7!? ♔d3 45 ♘c5+ (45 ♘e5+) 45 ... ♔d2 46 ♘b3+ ♔c3.

| 44 | ... | ♔e3 |
| 45 | ♔h4 | |

Or 45 h4 ♘d3! (45 ... ♘e2+? 46 ♔g2 ♘d4 47 ♘xg6 ♘xf3 48 ♘e7!=) 46 ♘xg6 f4+ 47 ♔g2 ♘e1+-+.

45	...	♔xf3
46	♔g5	♔e4
47	♘d7	♘d5
48	♔xg6	f4
49	♘c5+	♔e3
50	♔f5	♘c3!
	0-1	

Dudkin - Gofman
USSR 1990

| 1 | ... | ♔d1 |

Immediate promotion only leads to a draw: 1 ... e1♕ 2 ♘xe1 ♔xe1 3 ♔c3 ♘d5+ (3 ... ♘xa4+ 4 ♔c4 ♘b6+ 5 ♔b5 ♘c8 6 ♔xa5 ♔e2 7 ♔b5 ♔e3 8 ♔c6 ♔f4 9 ♔d7 ♘a7 10 ♔e7=) 4 ♔c4 ♘xc7 5 ♔c5 ♔e2 (5 ... ♘e6+ 6 ♔b6 ♘xg5 7 ♔xa5 ♘e4 8 ♔b6 ♘d2 9 ♔c5= f5 10 a5 ♘b3+ 11 ♔d5) 6 ♔b6 ♘d5+ 7 ♔xa5 ♘c3 (7 ... ♔e3 8 ♔b5 ♘c3+ 9 ♔c6 ♘xa4 10 ♔d6 ♔f4 11 ♔e7) 8 ♔b6 ♘xa4+ 9 ♔c6 ♘c3 10 ♔d6 ♘e4+ 11 ♔e7 ♘xg5 12 ♔f6.

| 2 | ♘e3+ | ♔c1 |
| 3 | ♘g2 | ♔d2 |

| 4 | ♘h4 | ♔c1? |

4 ... ♔e1! 5 ♘g2+ (or 5 ♘f3+ ♔d1 with zugzwang whilst 5 ♔a3 clearly loses, as White will be at least a tempo - two usually - behind on the variations in the first note) 5 ... ♔f1 6 ♘e3+ ♔g1 7 ♘c2 ♔f2 8 ♔c3 ♘d5+ 9 ♔c4 ♘xc7 10 ♔c5 ♘e6+ 11 ♔b6 ♘d4.

5	♘g2	♔d1
6	♘e3+	♔e1?
7	♘d5!=	♘c8
8	♘f4	♘b6

Or 8 ... ♔d2 9 ♘xe2 ♔xe2 10 ♔c4 ♔e3 11 ♔b5 ♔d4 (11 ... ♔f4 12 ♔xa5 ♔xg5 13 ♔a6 f5 14 ♔b7=) 12 ♔c6! ♔e5 13 ♔d7 ♘a7 14 ♔e7=.

| 9 | ♘d5 | ½-½ |

Notes by Vladimirov.

Knight v Knight ♘ V ♞

Cook - Portisch,
Adelaide 1971

1	♘h5	♞e4

White had to play 2 bxc4 bxc4 3 ♔e3 ♞f7 4 a4 ♔g6 5 ♘g3 ♞xg3 6 ♔d4 (6 a5? ♞e4 7 a6 c3–+) 6 ... ♞e2+ 7 ♔xc4 ♞xf4 8 a5 ♞e6 9 a6 ♞c7 10 a7 ♔f6 (10 ... f4 11 ♔c5 f3 12 ♔c6 ♞a8 13 ♔b7 f2 14 ♔xa8 f1♕ 15 ♔b8=) 11 ♔c5 ♔e7 12 ♔c6 ♞d8 13 a8♕+! ♞xa8 14 ♔d5=.

2	...	♔f6
3	♞e8+	♔f7
4	♞c7	c3

0-1

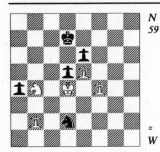

M. Gurevich - Bareev
Germany 1992

64	♞d3!	

Intending ♞c5 and ♔c3-b4.

64	...	♔c6
65	♔c3	♞f1
66	♔b4	♞e3
67	♔xa4	d4!?

Intending ♔d5-e4.

68	b4	♞d5
69	♔a5	♞c7
70	♞c5	♞b5
71	♔a4	♞c3+
72	♔a3!?	

More testing than 72 ♔b3 ♔d5 73 ♔c2 ♞e2 74 ♞d3 ♔c4 75 ♔d2 ♞g3=.

72	...	♔d5
73	♔b3	♞b5?

Black had to play 73 ... ♞e2! preventing the white king from having use of d3: 74 ♞d3 ♞c3 75 ♔c2 ♞e2 76 ♔d2 ♞c3=.

74	♔c2!	♞c3

If 74 ... ♔c4 75 ♞xe6 d3+ 76 ♔d2 ♞c3 77 ♞c5 ♞b1+ 78 ♔c1+–.

75	♔d3	♞d1!?

Or 75 ... ♞b5 76 ♞e4 intending ♞f6+–.

76	♞xe6!	

Not 76 ♞a6? ♞f2+ 77 ♔e2 ♞e4= intending 78 ♞c7+? ♔c4 79 ♞xe6 d3+ 80 ♔d1 ♔c3–+.

76	...	♞f2+

If 76 ... ♔xe6 77 ♔xd4 ♞b2 78 ♔e4! ♞c4 79 f5+ ♔e7 80 ♔d4+–.

77	♔e2	♞h3
78	f5!	

It was still possible to go wrong: 78 b5? ♔xe6 79 b6 ♞xf4+ 80 ♔f3 (80 ♔d2 ♔d7–+) 80 ... ♞g6 81 b7 ♞xe5+=.

78	...	♔xe5
79	b5	♞g1+
80	♔d1!	1-0

Notes by Gurevich.

Knight v Knight: More Pawns

N 59

± B

Fine 1941
1   ...   ♔f6
2 g3   ♔e5
3 ♘c6+   ♔e6
4 ♔e3   g5

Alternatively:

a) 4 ... ♔d7 5 ♘d4 f6 6 f4 ♔e7 7 h4 ♘f7?! (by analogy with Portisch's note to diag 75, 7 ... h5 (!) should be played) 8 g4 ♔d7 (if ... h6, h5 becomes a threat - see diag 75) 9 ♔d3 ♔e7 10 ♔c4 ♔d6 11 g5 fxg5 12 hxg5 and now:

a1) 12 ... h6 13 e5+ ♔e7 14 gxh6 ♘xh6 15 ♔d5 ♘g4 16 ♘c6+ ♔e8 (16 ... ♔d7 17 e6+ ♔e8 18 ♔d6 ♘f6 19 ♘b4 ♘e4+ 20 ♔e5 ♘f2 21 ♘d5 ♘g4+ 22 ♔d6+-) 17 ♔e6 ♘e3 18 ♘b4 ♘g2 19 ♘d5 and the g6-pawn is doomed;

a2) 12 ... ♔e7 13 e5 ♘d8 14 ♔d5 ♘f7 15 ♘c6+ ♔e8 16 e6

♘h8 17 ♔e5 ♔f8 18 ♔f6 ♔e8 19 ♔g7;

b) 4 ... f5 5 ♘d4+ (5 e5 ♘f7 6 f4 "is also good" - Fine)

b1) 5 ... ♔e7 6 e5 ♘c4+ 7 ♔f4 h6 8 h4 ♘b2 9 ♘xf5+ gxf5 10 ♔xf5 ♔f7 11 f4 (11 h5!? or 11 g4!?) 11 ... ♘d3 (11 ... ♘c4 looks to be a tougher defence) 12 h5 ♘f2 13 g4 ♘h3 14 g5+-;

b2) 5 ... ♔f6 6 exf5 gxf5 7 ♔f4 ♔g6 (7 ... h6 8 h3) 8 ♔e5 ♘f7+ 9 ♔e6 ♘d8+ 10 ♔e7 ♘b7 11 f4 ♘c5 12 ♘f3 ♘e4 (12 ... ♔h5 13 ♘e5 and ♔f6/e6) 13 ♘e5+ ♔g7 14 ♔e6;

After 4 ... g5, Fine continues 5 ♘d4+ ♔f6 6 f4 gxf4+ 7 gxf4 ♘c4+ 8 ♔f2 ♔g7 9 e5 ♔g6 10 ♔e2 ♘b2 11 ♔f3 ♘c4 12 ♔e4 ♘d2+ 13 ♔d5 ♘f1 14 f5+ ♔g5 15 e6 fxe6+ 16 ♔xe6 ♘xh2 17 f6 winning.

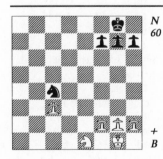

N 60

+ B

Keres - Reshevsky
Variation based on Fine's analysis, 1939
1   ...   ♔f8
2 ♔f1   ♔e7
3 ♔e2   ♔d6
4 ♘c2   ♔e5
5 ♘e3   ♘b2
6 ♘d1   ♘a4
7 ♔d3   ♔d5
8 ♘e3+   ♔c5
9 ♘f5   g6
10 ♘h6   f5
11 ♘f7   ♔d5
12 ♘g5   ♘c5+
13 ♔e3   h6
14 ♘f3   g5
15 g3   ♘e4

16 ♘d4   ♘xc3
17 ♘xf5   h5
18 f4

Not 18 ♘g7 h4 19 gxh4 gxh4 20 f4 h3 21 ♘f5 ♔e6 22 ♘g3 ♔d5 and Black's king position enables him to draw, according to Fine.

18   ...   gxf4+

Or 18 ... g4 19 ♘g7 ♔d6 20 ♘xh5.

19 ♔xf4   ♘e4
20 h4   ♘f6
21 ♘g7   ♔d6
22 ♔f5   ♔e7
23 ♔g6+-

See also diag 44.

Knight v Knight ♘ V ♞

Am Rodriguez -
Azmaiparashvili
Capablanca Memorial 1988

| 54 | ... | ♚c6 |

Here White has played h4, avoiding the stifling advance of the g-pawn (cf diag 59a).

| 55 | f3?! |

According to Hecht, who suggests the manoeuvre ♘b1-d2-f3-g5, this is dubious. Now the kingside pawn chain is weakened, though this (f3) is theoretically interesting since this structure could have arisen in diags 59 and 75.

55	...	♚c5
56	♘b1	♚d4
57	♘d2	♘c6
58	♘f1	

58 ♘b3+ transposes to the game.

58	...	♘b4
59	♘d2	♘c6
60	♘b3+	

60 f4 leads to a structure mentioned but not analysed by Fine. After 60 ... e4 it seems that White cannot prevent the gradual invasion of the black king:

a) 61 ♘f1 ♘a5 62 ♘d2 (62 ♘e3 ♘c4) ♚c3 63 ♘b1+ ♚b2 64 ♘d2 ♚c2 with zugzwang;

b) 61 ♘b3+ ♚c4 62 ♘d2+ ♚c3 63 ♚e3 (63 ♘b1+ ♚b2 64 ♘d2 ♘a5 65 ♚e3 ♚c3 66 ♘b1+ ♚b2 67 ♘d2 ♚c2 68 ♚e2 - Black wants to reach this position with White to move - 68 ... ♚c3 69 ♘b1+ ♚b2 70 ♘d2 ♚c2 with zugzwang) 63 ... ♚c2 and now:

b1) 64 ♘c4 (This pseudo-activity allows the black king around the back leading to a basic winning position. Passive play also seems doomed to meet death by zugzwang) 64 ... ♚d1 and:

b11) 65 ♚f2 ♘b4 66 ♘e3+ (66 ♘e5 ♘d5 transposes to the note) 66 ... ♚d2 67 ♘c4+ ♚c3 68 ♘b6 ♚d3-+. The black king always has a way of manoeuvring out of the knight's checks and reaching a position where the knight must take up an inferior circuit. For example, here the knight must go away from checking king on d2, or else the white king must yield vital turf;

b12) 65 ♘e5 ♘e7 66 ♚f2 ♘d5 67 ♘c4 (67 ♘xg6 e3+) e3+ 68 ♘xe3+ (68 ♚f3 e2 69 ♘b2+ ♚c2) 68 ... ♘xe3 69 ♚xe3 ♘e1 70 ♚f3 ♚f1-+;

b2) 64 ♚e2 ♘a5 (a key zugzwang position) 65 ♚e3 (65 ♘f1 ♘c4-+) 65 ... ♚d1-+.

60	...	♚d5!
61	♘d2	♘d4+
62	♚f2	

If 62 ♚e3 f4+ 63 gxf4 ♘f5+, ... exf4 and then wins the h-pawn.

| 62 | ... | f4! |

The h4-pawn falls now.

63	♘e4	♘f5
64	g4	hxg4
65	♘f6+	♚e6
66	♘xg4	♘xh4
67	♚e2	♘f5
68	♚d3	♘d6
69	♘f2	♚f5
	0-1	

N 62

Krezhov - Lukov
Bulgaria 1981

16	...	♘e2
17	♔f3	♘e1
18	♔g2?	

Incredibly passive. Better is 18 ♘f2 ♔f1 19 ♘d3 ♘g1+ (19 ... ♘d4+ 20 ♔e3 ♘b3 21 ♔f3 h5 22 ♘e5 ♘d2+ 23 ♔e3 ♘e4 24 ♔f3) 20 ♔e3 ♔g2 21 ♘c5 ♔xg3 22 ♘xe6 (22 h5 ♔g4 23 ♘xe6 ♘h3) 22 ... g6! (22 ... ♔xh4 23 ♘xg7 ♔g4 24 ♘e8) 23 ♘f8 ♘f3 24 ♘xg6 ♘xh4-+.

18	...	♘d4
19	♘g1	g6
20	♘h3	♔e2
21	♘g1+	♔e3
22	♘h3	♘f3
23	♔h1	

Or 23 ♘f2 ♘e1+ 24 ♔f1 ♘d3 25 ♘h3 ♔f3.

23	...	♘e1
24	♔h2	♔f3
25	♘g5+	

Also losing is 25 ♘g1+ ♔e3 26 ♘h3 ♘f3+ and now:

a) 27 ♔h1 ♔d2! 28 ♔g2 (28 ♘f2 ♔e2 29 ♔g2 ♘e1+ 30 ♔g1 ♔f3) 28 ... ♔e2;

b) 27 ♔g2 ♔e2 28 ♔h1 ♔f1.

25	...	hxg5
26	h5	gxh5
27	fxg5	♘c2
28	g4	

Or 28 g6 ♘e3 29 g7 ♘g4+.

28	...	hxg4
29	g6	g3+
30	♔g1	g2
31	g7	♘d4

0-1

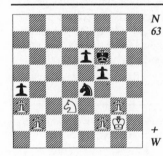

N 63

Korchnoi - Polugaevsky
Tilburg 1985

44	...	e5
45	f3	♘d2
46	♘c5	♘c4
47	♘xa4	♔g5
48	♘c5?	

White should play 48 ♔f1!! f4 49 ♔f2! ♔f5 (49 ... fxg3+ 50 ♔xg3 ♔f5 51 ♔f2 ♔f4 52 ♔e2 ♔g3 53 ♔d3 ♘d6 54 ♔e3+-) 50 g4+ ♔g6 51 ♘c3+- (Polugaevsky). Not, however, 48 ♔f2?! f4! 49 ♔g2 (49 gxf4+ exf4 50 ♔e2 ♔f5 51 ♔d3 ♘e5+ 52 ♔d4 ♘xf3+ 53 ♔d5 ♘e5 54 ♘c3 f3 55 ♘d1 ♘d3 56 b4 ♔f6 57 b5 ♔e7 58 a4 ♘b2=) 49 ... ♘e3+! 50 ♔h3 e4! 51 gxf4+ ♔xf4 52 fxe4 ♔xe4 53 ♘c3+ ♔d3 54 a4 ♘c4 55 ♘d1 ♔c2= (Polugaevsky).

48	...	♘xb2
49	a4	♘c4
50	♘b3	f4!
51	a5	

Or 51 g4 e4! (Polugaevsky) 52 a5 exf3+ 53 ♔xf3 ♘e5+ 54 ♔e4 ♘c6 55 a6 ♔xg4 56 ♘d4 ♘a7= (56 ... ♘xd4?? 57 a7).

51	...	fxg3
52	♔xg3	

Or 52 a6 e4! 53 fxe4 ♔f4 54 ♘d2 (54 a7 ♘b6 55 ♘c5 ♘a8 56 ♔g1 ♔e5=) 54 ... ♘b6 55 a7 ♘a8= (Polugaevsky).

52	...	♘d6
53	a6	♘b5
54	♘c5	♔f6!
55	♔g4	

Or 55 ♔f2 ♔e7 56 ♔e3 ♔d6 (Polugaevsky).

55	...	♘a7
56	♘e4+	♔g6
57	♔h4	♔f5
58	♔g3	♔e6
59	♔g4	♔d7
60	♔f5	♘c6
61	♘c5+	

Instead 61 ♘c3 ♔c7 62 ♘b5+ ♔b6 63 a7 ♔b7 64 ♔e4 ♘e7! 65 ♔xe5 ♘g6+ 66

♔f6 ♘f4 67 ♔f5 ♘e2 68 f4
♘xf4 with a positional draw
(Polugaevsky).

61	...	♔c7
62	♔e4	♔b6
63	♔d5	♘e7+

64	♔d6	♘g6
65	♘d7+	♔xa6
66	♘xe5	♘f4
67	♘c6	♔b7
68	♘e7	♘e2

½-½

N 64

Suba - Adorjan
Szirak 1986

A new structure. Here the
presence of a protected passed
e-pawn is balanced by the
rigidity of the rest of the
pawn structure. Black cannot
set his pawns in motion
without massive exchanges.

45	...	♘b7

If 45 ... ♔d6 46 ♘h1 ♔e7
47 ♘g3 ♔f7 48 h4 g6 49 h5!
g5 50 ♘e2 ♔e7 51 ♘c3 ♔d6
52 ♘b5+ ♔c6 (52 ... ♔d5 53
♘c7+) 53 ♘c3 ♘d7 54 ♘e4
♔d5 55 ♘c3+ = (Suba).

46	♘h1	h5
47	♘g3	hxg4
48	hxg4	♘d6
49	♘h5	♘e8
50	♘g3	♔d6
51	♔e4	♔e7

52	♔d5	♘c7+
53	♔c6	♘a6
54	♔b5	♘b8
55	♘h5	♔f7
56	♘g3	♘d7
57	♔c6	♘f8
58	♔d6	♘h7
59	♘e4	♔e8
60	♔e6	♔f8
61	♔d5	♔e7
62	♔c5	♔f7
63	♔d6	♘f8

Also drawing is 63 ... g6 64
fxg6+ ♔xg6 65 ♔e7!= (Suba).
After 63 ... ♘f8 the conclusion might be 64 ♔d5 g6 65
g5! gxf5 66 ♘xf6 ♘g6 67
♘d7 e4 68 ♔d4 (intending
♘c5xe4) 68 ... ♘f4 69 g6+!
intending ♘c5xe4=.

½-½

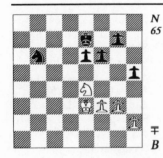

N 65

Tal - Sveshnikov
Leningrad 1991

51	...	♘c4+
52	♔d4	♘d6
53	♘c5	♘f5+
54	♔e4	♔d6
55	♘d3	g5
56	♘b4	♔c5
57	♘a6+	♔b6
58	♘b8	♔c7
59	♘a6+	♔c6!
60	♘b4+	

60 ♘b8+!? makes it harder
for Black to storm into the
kingside, though Black should
be able to transpose into a version of diags 61 or 80 after 60 ... ♔d6 61 ♘a6 ♘e7 (61
... h4!?) 62 ♘b4 f5+ 63 ♔d3
e5. Tal prefers a more active

continuation, but the pawn-
eating race favours Black.

60	...	♔b5
61	♘d3	♔c4
62	♘b2+	♔c3
63	♘a4+	

Or 63 ♘d3 ♔d2! (63 ...
♘d6+ 64 ♔e3) 64 ♘c5 transposing to the next note.

63	...	♔d2
64	f4	

Alternatively, 64 ♘c5 ♘d6+
65 ♔d4 e5+! (65 ... ♔e2? 66
♘xe6! ♔xf3 67 ♘g7 h4 68
gxh4 gxh4 69 ♔d5! ♘e4 70
h3!=) 66 ♔d5 ♘e8! 67 ♔e6
(67 ♘e4+ ♔e3 68 ♘xf6
♘xf6+ 69 ♔xe5 ♘h7! 70 f4
gxf4 71 gxf4 h4-+) 67 ... ♔e3
68 ♔e7 ♔xf3 69 ♔xe8 f5 70

♔f7 f4! 71 gxf4 exf4 72 ♔g6
♔e3! (72 ... g4 73 ♔xh5 g3 74
hxg3 fxg3 75 ♘d3=) 73 ♔f5
g4! (73 ... f3? 74 ♘e4 g4 75
♘g3 h4 76 ♘f1+ ♔f2 77
♔xg4=) 74 ♘e4 h4 and ...
g3-+ (Sveshnikov).

64	...	♘d6+
65	♔d4	gxf4!
66	gxf4	♔e2
67	♘c5	h4

68	♘xe6	♔f3-+
69	♔d5	♘f5
70	♘c5	♘e3+
71	♔d4	

Or 71 ♔e6 f5.

71	...	♘g4
72	h3	♘f2
73	f5	♘xh3
74	♘e4	♘f4
	0-1	

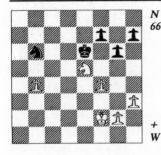

N
66

Ivkov - Filip,
Vrsac 1971
Conversion of an extra outside
pawn.

44	♔f3	f6
45	♘g4	♘d5

To make the b-pawn more
accessible to the king.

46	b5	♘b6
47	♘e3	♔d6
48	♔e4	

Intending ♔d4.

48	...	♔c5
49	f5	♔xb5

50	♘g4	♘d7

Or 50 ... gxf5+ 51 ♔xf5
♘d5 52 g3! and both black
pawns fall.

51	♘xf6!!	♘xf6+
52	♔e5	♘d7+
53	♔d6	♘f6
54	♔e6	♘h5
55	f6	♘f4+
56	♔d7	g5
57	f7	♘g6
58	g4	♔c5
59	♔e8	1-0

+
W

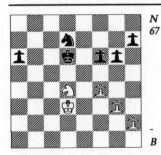

N
67

Seirawan - Byrne
Baden 1980
This is an example of a clean
exploitation of a pure extra
outside pawn.

41	...	♔d5
42	♘c2	♘c5+
43	♔c3	a5
44	♘e3+	♔e4
45	♘c4	♘b7

Black's king is already in, so
there is no reason to donate
the a-pawns and race.

46	♘b6	♘d6

Preventing ♘c4, and forcing
the white king to go and
round up the a-pawn.

47	♘d7	♔f5
48	♔b3	h5
49	♔a4	♘e4
50	♔xa5	♘d2
51	h3	♘e4!

Preventing g4+ by defend-
ing f6. Now the entire white
kingside falls.

0-1

-
B

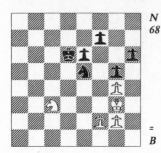

N
68

=
B

Ftacnik - Beliavsky
Wijk aan Zee 1985
White's doubled pawns are in now way a liability. Black must exchange a pawn early to gain space.

42	...	♘d7
43	f3	♘f6
44	♔f2	♔c5
45	♔e2	♔c4
46	♔d2	♘e8
47	♘e4	♔d4
48	g3	f5
49	gxf5	exf5
50	♘c3	♘f6
51	♘e2+	♔c4
52	♘c1	h5
53	♘d3	♔d4
54	♘e1	♘d5

55	♘c2+	♔c4

55 ... ♔e5 looks more dangerous?

56	♘a3+	♔c5
57	♘c2	f4

Or 57 ... h4 58 gxh4 gxh4 59 ♔e2 h3 60 ♔f2 f4 61 ♘g1 ♘e3 62 ♘a3! (62 ♘e1 ♔d4 63 ♔h2 ♔c3 64 ♔xh3 ♔d2 65 ♘g2 ♘xg2 66 ♔xg2 ♔e2-+) 62 ... ♔b4 63 ♘b1 ♔c4 64 ♔h2 ♔b3 65 ♔xh3 ♔b2 66 ♔g4= (Beliavsky).

58	gxf4	♘xf4
59	♔e3	½-½

Since 59 ... ♔c4 60 ♘a3+ ♔b4 61 ♘b1 intending ♘d2-e4 is drawn (Beliavsky).

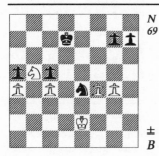

N
69

±
B

Godena - Seirawan
Lugano 1988
In this position, Black has a potential outside passed pawn - a tremendous bonus in a knight and pawn ending.

1	...	♔e7
2	♔e3	

2 ♘a7!? ♔d6 3 ♘b5+ ♔e6 4 ♔e3 (perhaps 4 ♘c7+!?) is similar to the game.

2	...	♘f6
3	♔f3	

Or 3 g5 ♘d7.

3	...	♘d7
4	♘c3	♘b6
5	♔e2	h6

Or 5 ... ♘xc4 6 ♘e4.

6	♔f3	♔e6
7	♔e4	♘xc4
8	f5+	♔f6?

A much clearer way to victory was 8 ... ♔d6 9 ♔f4 ♘b6 10 g5 hxg5+ (10 ... ♘d5+?? 11 ♘xd5 ♔xd5 12 g6+-) 11 ♔xg5 ♔e5 12 ♔g6 c4-+.

9	♔f4	

Not 9 ♔d5 ♘b6+ 10 ♔xc5 ♘xa4+ 11 ♘xa4 ♔g5-+.

9	...	♘d6
10	♘d5+	♔f7
11	♘e3	♘e8
12	♘c4	♘f6
13	♘d6+	

Much more resilient than 13 ♘xa5 ♘d5+ 14 ♔e5 ♘c3-+.

13	...	♔e7
14	♘b7	♘d7
15	g5	♔f8
16	♘xa5	♘b6
17	f6	h5
18	♔f5	g6+?
19	♔xg6	h4
20	♘b7	♘d7
21	a5	h3
22	a6	♘e5+

Not 22 ... h2 23 a7 ♘b6 24 ♘xc5 h1♛ 25 ♘e6+ ♔e8 26 f7+.

23	♔f5	♘c6
24	a7	♘xa7
25	♘xc5	h2??

Throwing the game away. Critical is 25 ... ♘c6 and now:

a) 26 ♘e6+!? ♔e8 27 g6 h2 28 f7+ (28 g7? ♔f7) ♔d7 29 f8♛ h1♛ 30 ♘c5+ ♔c7 31 ♛f7+ ♔b6 32 ♘d7+;

b) 26 ♘e4 (Seirawan) 26 ... h2 27 ♘f2 (27 ♘g3 ♘d4+ 28

♔e4 ♘e2 29 ♘h1 ♔f7=) 27 ... ♘d4+ 28 ♔e4 ♘e6 29 g6 leads to the interesting position of diag 73.

26 ♘d7+ ♔e8
27 ♔e6 h1♕
28 f7+ ♔d8

29 f8♕+ ♔c7
30 ♕b8+ 1-0

Notes based on those by Seirawan.

N 70 = B

Tisdall 1992

Analysis from Godena - Seirawan, Lugano 1988

White will try to get his king in on the h- or e-files, and can improve the knight to g3 to create tactical possibilities with the pawns. Black must try to create a blockade.

1 ... ♘g5+

The battle of two connected pawns v a rook's pawn is intriguing, and is seen here in its most extreme form (i.e. two pawns on the sixth, rook's pawn on the seventh; the pawns could not be more efficient.

2 ♔f5 ♘f3
3 ♘h1 ♔g8

Alternatively:

a) 3 ... ♘g1!? 4 f7 ♔g7 5 ♘g3 h1♕ (5 ... ♘f3 6 ♘h5+ ♔f8 7 ♔f6) 6 ♘xh1 ♘e2 7 ♘f2 ♘d4+ 8 ♔e5+-.

b) 3 ... ♘d4+ 4 ♔g5 ♘e6+ 5 ♔h6 ♔g8 6 ♘g3 and now:

b1) 6 ... ♘g7!? 7 ♔g5 (7 f7+ ♔f8 8 ♔g5 ♔e7 9 ♔g4 ♘e6 10 ♔f5 ♘d4+=) 7 ... ♘e6+ 8 ♔f5 ♘d8 9 ♘e5 ♔f8 10 ♔d5 ♔e8 (this looks to be one of the most critical positions, but black is still able to hold the balance) 11 g7 (11 ♔d6 ♔f8 12 ♔d7 ♘b7 13 g7+ ♔f7 14 g8♕+ ♔xg8 15 ♔e7 ♘d8= 16 ♔xd8 ♔f7) 11 ... ♔f7 12 ♔d6 and:

b11) 12 ... ♘b7+ 13 ♔c6 (13 ♔e5 ♘c5 14 ♔f5 ♘d7) ♘a5+ 14 ♔d7 ♘c4;

b12) 12 ... ♔g8?? 13 ♘f5 ♘f7+ 14 ♔c7;

b2) 6 ... ♘d8

4 ♘g3 ♔f8

Black should now be able to keep White at bay, but 4 ... ♘d4+ gives him chances to go wrong: 5 ♔e5 ♘e2?? (another example of why the black knight must never stray) 6 f7+ ♔g7 (6 ... ♔f8 7 ♔f6+-) 7 ♘f5+ ♔xg6 8 f8♕ h1♕ 9 ♕g7+ ♔h5 10 ♕h6+.

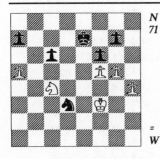

N 71 = W

Smyslov - Persitz

Hastings 1969

1 ♔e3

Or 1 g6 ♘e5+.

1 ... ♘e1
2 ♔e4 ♘c2

Also losing quickly is 2 ... fxg5 3 hxg5 ♘c2 (3 ... ♘d7 4 ♘e5+ ♔d6 5 f6 gxf6 6 g6) 4 ♘e5 ♘b4 (4 ... ♔d6 5 f6 gxf6 6 g6) 5 ♔d4 ♔d6 6 ♘c4+ ♔d7 7 g6+-.

More troublesome is 2 ... ♘g2! 3 g6 ♘xh4 4 ♘e3 and now (71a):

a) 4 ... ♔d6 5 ♔f4 and:

a1) 5 ... c5 6 a6 (6 ♔g4 ♔e5 7 ♔xh4 ♔e4 8 ♘c4 ♔xf5 9 ♘d6+ ♔xg6 10 a6 c4=) 6 ... c4 (6 ... ♔c6 7 ♔g4 ♔b6 8 ♔xh4 ♔xa6 9 ♘d5 c4 10 ♘xf6 c3 11 ♘d5+-) 7 ♘xc4+ ♔c5 8 ♘a5 ♔b5 9 ♘b7 ♔xa6 10 ♘d6 ♔b6 11 ♘e8

N 71a

= W

and now:

a11) 11 ... a5 12 ♘xg7 a4 13 ♘e6 a3 14 ♘d4;

a12) 11 ... ♔c6 12 ♘xg7 ♘g2+ (12 ... ♔d7 13 ♔g3) 13 ♔f3 ♘e1+ 14 ♔e2 with ♘e6 to follow, winning;

a13) 11 ... ♘g2+ 12 ♔f3 (12 ♔e4 ♔c6 13 ♘xg7 ♔d7 14 ♘h5 ♔e7 15 ♘f4 ♘h4 16 ♘d5+ ♔f8 17 ♘xf6 ♔g7 18 ♘h5+ ♔h6 19 ♘f4 a5=) 12 ... ♘e1+ 13 ♔g4! (13 ♔e4 ♔c6 14 ♘xg7 ♔d7 15 ♘h5 ♔e7) 13 ... ♔c6 14 ♘xg7 ♔d7 15 ♘e6 ♔e7 16 ♔h5 ♘g2 17 ♔h6 ♘e3 18 ♘d4;

a2) 5 ... ♔c5 6 ♘g4 and now:

a21) 6 ... ♔b4 7 ♘xf6 c5 8 ♘d5+ ♔xa5 9 ♔g5 ♘xf5 (9 ... ♘f3+ 10 ♔h5) 10 ♔xf5 ♔b5 11 ♔e6 a5 12 ♔f7 a4 13 ♔xg7 a3 14 ♘e3!+- (but not 14 ♘c3+? ♔c4 15 ♔f7 ♔xc3 16 g7 a2 17 g8♕ ♔b2!=;

a22) 6 ... ♔d6 7 ♘xf6 ♔e7 8 ♘h5 ♔f8 (8 ... c5 9 ♘xg7 c4 10 ♔e4 c3 11 ♔d3 ♔f6 12 ♘h5+) 9 ♔e5 and:

a221) 9 ... c5! 10 ♘g3 ♔e7 11 ♘e4 (11 a6 c4 12 ♔d4 ♔f6 13 ♔xc4 ♘xf5=) 11 ... c4 12 a6 ♘f3+ 13 ♔f4 (13 ♔d5 ♘h4=) 13 ... ♘e1=;

a222) 9 ... ♘f3+? 10 ♔d6 ♘d4 11 ♔g3 intending a6, ♔c5;

b) 4 ... a6 5 ♘f4 ♔d6 6 ♔g4 ♔e5 7 ♔xh4 ♔e4 8 ♘c2 c5 (8 ... ♔xf5 9 ♘b4 ♔e6 10 ♘xc6) 9 ♔g4 ♔d3 (9 ... c4 10 ♘b4 c3 11 ♘xa6 c2 12 ♘c5+ ♔d4 13 ♘b3+ ♔c4 14 ♘c1 ♔b5 15 ♔f4 ♔xa5 16 ♔e4) 10 ♘a3 c4 11 ♔f4 c3 (11 ... ♔d4 12 ♘c2+ ♔c3 13 ♘e3 ♔d4 14 ♘g4 c3 - or 14 ... ♔d3 15 ♘xf6 c3 16 ♘d5 - 15 ♘e3 ♔d3 16 ♔f3 ♔d4 17 ♘c2+ ♔e5 18 ♔e3 ♔xf5 19 ♘b4 winning) 12 ♔f3 ♔d4 (12 ... c2 13 ♘xc2 ♔xc2 14 ♔e4+-) 13 ♔e2 ♔c5 (13 ... ♔e4 14 ♘c2 ♔xf5 15 ♘b4) 14 ♔d3 ♔b4 15 ♘b1.

3	g6	♘b4
4	♘e3	♘a6
5	♔d4	♘c7
6	♔c5	♔d7
7	h5	♘e8
8	♘c4	1-0

With the idea of ♘d6!, h6. Notes based on those in *Informator*.

N 72

+ W

Ribli - Beliavsky
Reggio Emilia 1986

Black's king must stand and guard against the white king's entry. Black's kingside pawns are overextended and White can slowly exaggerate their weakness.

37	♔d4	♘h5
38	♘e2	♘g7

Or 38 ... ♘f6 39 ♘g3+- ♔e6 (39 ... f4 40 ♘e4+ ♘xe4 41 ♔xe4 ♔e6 42 f3 a6 43 ♔d4+- ♔d6 44 a4) 40 ♔c5.

39	♔c4	f4
40	♘d4+-	

Intending b5.

40	...	a6
41	f3	♘e8
42	♘e2!	♘f6
43	♘c3	g4
44	♔d4	

Intending ♔e4+-.

44	...	gxf3
45	gxf3	♘d7
46	♘e4+	♔c7

46 ... ♔e6 47 ♘c5++-.

47	♘c5	♘f6
48	♘xa6+	♔b6
49	♘c5	♘d5

Or 49 ... ♔b5 50 ♘e4.

50	♘a4+	♔a6

51	♘c3	♞e3	53	♘b1	1-0
52	♔e4	♞c2			

±
B

NN 73

Timman - Andersson
Tilburg 1987

1	...	h5

Playing to contain the white king.

2	g3	♞c3
3	♔g2	♞e4
4	♘b4	

If 4 ♔f3 ♞c3, but perhaps 4 ♔f1!?.

4	...	♞d2!
5	♘d3	g5
6	f3	♞c4
7	♔f2	♞d6
8	♘c5+	♔e7
9	♔e2	

9 e4 was suggested by Timman.

| 9 | ... | ♞f5 |

Note Black's handling of this ending. First, restricting the white king led to the creation of white pawn weaknesses. Now the black king uses these to force pawn exchanges to ease the defence. White helps by playing impatiently.

| 10 | g4?! |

Timman prefers 10 ♔f2 and then aiming for e4.

10	...	hxg4
11	hxg4	♞h6!
12	e4?	

White forces the position too quickly. He can wait and try to achieve a two connected against one passed pawn position with 12 ♔d3!?. For example:

a) 12 ... ♞f7;

b) 12 ... ♔d6!? 13 ♘a4 f5 (13 ... ♔e6 14 ♘c3 ♔d6) 14 gxf5 ♞xf5 15 e4 ♞h4 16 ♔e3 (16 e5+ ♔e6 17 ♘c5+ ♔f5 18 ♔e3 ♞g2+ 19 ♔f2 ♞f4) 16 ... dxe4 (16 ... ♞g2+ 17 ♔f2 ♞f4 18 ♘c3) 17 fxe4 g4 (17 ... ♞g2+ 18 ♔f2 ♞f4 19 ♘c3. I (JT) believe this structure should be very dangerous for Black since the g-pawn is not a major distraction. See also diags 37 and 69. It seems that centre pawns allow for maximum flexibility and the g-pawn could also be vulnerable.) 18 ♔f4! (18 e5+? ♔d5) 18 ... ♞f3 19 d5 ♞d2 20 ♘c3+-;

c) 12 ... f5 13 gxf5 ♞xf5 14 e4 ♞h4 15 ♔e3 transposing to the notes.

| 12 | ... | dxe4 |
| 13 | ♘xe4 | f5! |

Forced according to Timman. The implication is that three pawns against two with a passed d-pawn is winning.

| 14 | ♘f2 |

Or 14 gxf5 ♞xf5 15 ♔d3 ♔e6! 16 ♘xg5+ ♔d5=.

14	...	♔e6
15	♔e3	♞g8
16	♔d3	fxg4
17	♘xg4	♔f5
18	d5	♞e7
19	♔c4	♔f4

Intending 20 d6 ♞c8=.
½-½

Analysis by Timman.

Knight v Knight ♘ v ♞

Hübner - Larsen
Las Palmas 1976
A textbook exploitation of an extra outside pawn.

48	♔d4	♞d7
49	a4	♞f8

Or 49 ... e5+ 50 fxe5+ ♞xe5 51 ♞b5+ ♔e6 52 ♞c7+ ♔d6 53 ♞e8+ ♔e6 54 ♞g7+.

50	♞b5+	♔d7
51	a5	bxa5
52	bxa5	♔c6
53	♔c4	♞d7
54	♞d4+	♔d6
55	♔b5	♞c5
56	♞e2	

Not even allowing 56 a6 ♞xa6 57 ♔xa6 ♔d5 with chances to liquidate the pawns, though I believe it should still be winning, e.g. 58 ♞f3 ♔e4 59 ♞g5+ ♔xe3 60 ♞xe6 ♔f3 61 ♔b5 ♔g3 62 ♔c4 ♔xh3 63 ♔d5 ♔g4 64 ♔e5 h4 65 ♞g5.

56	...	♞d7
57	a6	♔c7
58	♞d4	e5
59	♞xf5	exf4
60	exf4	♞f6
61	♞e3	♞e4
62	♞d5+	

White's technique was excellent, though it was simplified by his having better pieces as well.

1-0

Portisch - Ljubojevic
Thessaloniki 1988

33	f4	f6
34	♔f3	♔f7
35	♔e3	♞c6
36	♞b3	g6
37	h4	♞b4

37 ... h5 was suggested by Polugaevsky. The four vs three structure (after an eventual d4 exd4) is of interest since it is also possible from diag 59 (though he, like Ljubojevic, omitted ... h5 and reached a crushing position for White.

38	d4	exd4+
39	♞xd4	♞a6

Perhaps 39 ... h5.

40	g4!+-	

Now White's space advantage is tremendous and the chances of being left with a weak h-pawn are very high (see also diag 59).

40	...	♞c7
41	♔d3	♔e7

Perhaps 41 ... h5!?.

42	♔c4	♔d7
43	h5!	gxh5
44	gxh5	♔e8

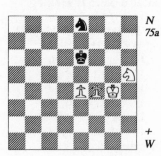

45	♔d3	♔f8
46	♞f5	♞e6
47	♔e3	♔e8
48	♔f3	♔d7
49	♞xh6	♞g7
50	♞g8	

Or 50 ♞f5 ♞e6 51 ♔g4 ♞f8 52 ♞d4 intending ♞f5 winning.

50	...	♞xh5
51	♔g4	♞g7
52	♞xf6+	♔e6
53	♞h5	♞e8 (75a)

A top-level example of two pawns v none. Perhaps due to time pressure Portisch does not really win cleanly, but as long as White avoids a blockade the win is simple.

54	♔f3	

More accurate was 54 e5 ♞c7 55 ♞g7+ ♔f7 56 ♞f5+-.

54	...	♞c7
55	♔e3	♞b5
56	♞g7+	♔d6
57	♞f5+	♔c5
58	♔d3	♞c7
59	♞d4	

Portisch takes his time.

More direct was 59 e5 ♘d5 60 ♔e4 ♘c3+ 61 ♔f3 ♔d5 62 ♔g4 ♔e6 63 ♘d4+ ♔d5 64 ♘f3+-.

59	...	♘e8
60	♘b3+	

Straightforward was 60 e5 intending ♘e4, f5, ♔d5, ♘f5+-.

60	...	♔b4
61	♘d2	♔c5
62	♘c4	♘g7
63	♘e5	♘h5

64	♔e3	♘f6
65	♘d3+	♔c4
66	♘f2	♔c5
67	e5	♘h5
68	♔e4	♘g3+
69	♔f3	♘f5
70	♔g4	♘d4
71	♘e4+	♔d5
72	♘g5	♔c6
73	♘f3	♔e4
74	f5!	1-0

Toth - Miles
Reggio Emilia 1984
Here White's fractured queen-side pawn structure, and weak c4-square give Black a positional advantage.

31	...	♔e7
32	♔c2	♔f6
33	g4?	

Better was 33 ♘h2 intending g3, f3 according to Miles.

33	...	g6!

Planning ... h5 creating more white weaknesses.

34	♔d3	

Alternatively:

a) 34 ♘d2 h5 35 ♘xc4 dxc4 36 f3 ♔e6! intending ... b5, ... g5!-+ (Miles);

b) 34 ♘h2 h5 35 f3 ♘e3+ intending ... ♘g2xh4; the knight is only temporarily out of play on h4.

34	...	h5
35	gxh5	gxh5
36	♘g5	♔f5
37	♘h7	♘d6
38	f3	♘f7
39	♔e3	♘h8!
40	♘g5	

Or:

a) 40 ♔f2 ♘g6 41 ♔g3 ♘f4 42 ♔f2 ♘e6 trapping the knight on h7.

b) 40 ♘f8 ♘g6 41 ♘xg6 ♔xg6 42 ♔f4 ♔f6-+. The white king will have to give ground and Black can combine a king advance with creating an outside passed pawn on the queenside.

40	...	♘g6-+
41	♘h3	c6!

Zugzwang.

42	♘f2	

Or 42 a4 a5.

42	...	♘xh4
43	♘d3	♘g6
44	♘b4	♘e7
45	♔f2	a5
46	♘d3	♘g6
47	♔g3	♘f4!
48	♘e5	

Or 48 ♘xf4 h4+-+.

48	...	♘e2+
49	♔h4	♘xc3
50	♘xc6	♘xa2
51	♘e7+	♔e6
	0-1	

Two Knights v Pawn(s)

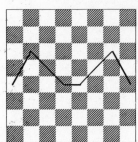

NNP
1

The 'Troitsky Line'

If the pawn is blockaded no further up then Black loses (ignoring the position of the knights).

NNP
2

A Cage

1   &f6

White cannot win immediately since the king on g6 is occupying a square that the e2-knight must use. But he is able to reset the cage with the guards on the 'other side' of the corner. First he must pass the move to Black:

```
1    ...    ♚h8
2    ♚g5    ♚h7
3    ♚h5    ♚h8
4    ♚h6    ♚g8
5    ♚g6
```

Now it is Black to move and the white king can force its way to f7.

```
5    ...    ♚h8
6    ♚f7    ♚h7
7    ♘g7!   ♚h6
8    ♚f6    ♚h7
```

9   ♘f5

Completing the transfer of the knight. But before the decisive action White must again manoeuvre to pass the move to Black.

```
9    ...    ♚h8
10   ♚e7!
```

Not 10 ♚f7? ♚h7 and White has got the tempi wrong.

```
10   ...    ♚g8
11   ♚e8    ♚h8
12   ♚f8    ♚h7
13   ♚f7    ♚h8
```

The rest is trivial.

```
14   ♘f4    e2
15   ♘g6+   ♚h7
16   ♘f8+   ♚h8
17   ♘e7    e1♛
18   ♘eg6 mate
```

NNP
3

A Second Cage

White to move wins easily:

```
1    ♘e4    d2
2    ♘f6+   ♚h8
3    ♘g5    d1♛
4    ♘f7 mate
```

Black to move draws.

```
1    ...    ♚h8
```

Of course if White could transfer the move to Black he would win trivially. But here that is not possible since he would have to triangulate with the black king on h7 or g8 at the edge of the cage - ready to run if given any air.

```
2    ♚f7    ♚h7
3    ♘g7    ♚h6
```

Not 3 ... ♚h8? 4 ♘f5 ♚h7 5 ♘e4 and wins.

```
4    ♚f6    ♚h7
5    ♘f5    ♚g8!
```

Again not 5 ... ♚h8? 6 ♚f7 ♚h7 7 ♘e4.

```
6    ♚e7    ♚h7!
```

And again not 6 ... ♚h8? 7 ♚f7 ♚h7 8 ♘e4.

```
7    ♚f7
```

Of course if 7 ♚f8 Black

+
W

+/=
W/B

can run with 7 ... ♔g6!.

| 7 | ... | ♔h8 |

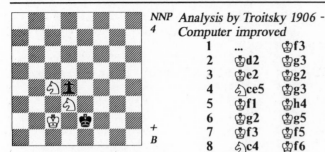

NNP 4 — *Analysis by Troitsky 1906 - Computer improved*

1	...	♔f3
2	♔d2	♔g3
3	♔e2	♔g2
4	♘ce5	♔g3
5	♔f1	♔h4
6	♔g2	♔g5
7	♔f3	♔f5
8	♘c4	♔f6
9	♔f4	♔e6

+ B

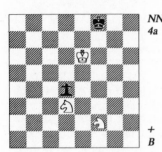

NNP 4a

10	♔e4	♔f6
11	♔d5	♔e7
12	♔e5	♔f7
13	♔d6	♔f6
14	♘d2	♔f5
15	♔e7	♔g6
16	♔e6	♔g7!

16 ... ♔g5? was analysed by Troitsky in 1906.

| 17 | ♘e4 | ♔g6 |

This is zugzwang and over the next few moves White threatens to 'lose a move'.

+ B

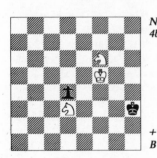

NNP 4b

18	♔e5	♔g7
19	♔d6	♔h6
20	♘ef2!	

Getting the knight out of the way so as to manoeuvre for the move.

| 20 | ... | ♔g7 |
| 21 | ♔e6 | ♔f8 (4a) |

21 ... ♔g6 22 ♘e4! is what White wants: 22 ... ♔g7 23 ♘d6 ♔g6 24 ♘f7 ♔g7 25 ♘fe5 ♔f8 26 ♔d7 and White is in control.

| 22 | ♘e4 | ♔e8 |
| 23 | ♘d6+ | ♔d8 |

Black is able to run to the queenside and avoid mate there. But eventually he will be driven back to the kingside in an unfavourable position with White in full control - see the note to 38 ... ♔f8.

| 24 | ♘f5 | ♔e8 |

+ B

25	♘g7+	♔d8
26	♔d6	♔c8
27	♘e6	♔b7
28	♔c5	♔a7
29	♔c6	♔a6
30	♘ec5+	♔a5
31	♘b3+!	♔a4

Not 31 ... ♔a6 32 ♘dc5+ ♔a7 33 ♔c7 d3 34 ♘d4 d2 35 ♘c6+ ♔a8 36 ♘d7 d1♕ 37 ♘b6 mate.

| 32 | ♘d2 | ♔a5 |

32 ... ♔a3 obviously leads to mate in the a1-corner: 33 ♔b5 ♔a2 34 ♔b4 ♔a1 35 ♘c4 ♔a2 36 ♔a4 ♔a1 37 ♔a3 ♔b1 38 ♔b3 ♔a1 39 ♔c2 ♔a2 40 ♘b4+ ♔a1 41 ♘a3 d3+ 42 ♔b3 d2 43 ♘bc2 mate.

33	♔c5	♔a6
34	♘c4	♔b7
35	♔d6	♔c8
36	♘a5	♔d8
37	♘b7+	♔e8
38	♔e6	♔f8

After Black's 21st move we had the same position except that the knight was on f2 rather than b7. Now White can confine the king as follows:

39	♘d6!	♔g7
40	♔f5	♔h6
41	♔f6!	

41 ♘e8? ♔h7! (41 ... ♔h5? 42 ♘g7+ and wins easily) 42 ♔f6 ♔g8 43 ♘d6 ♔f8 44 ♔e6 ♔g7 45 ♔f5 ♔h6! and White has made no progress (cf diag 5).

41	...	♔h5
42	♘f7	♔g4
43	♘g5!	♔h4
44	♔f5	♔g3
45	♔e4	♔g4
46	♘f7	♔h5

47	♔f5	♔h4
48	♘fe5	♔h5
49	♘g4	♔h4
50	♘f6	♔h3 *(4b)*
51	♔e5!	

Triangulating.

51	...	♔g3
52	♔e4	♔h3
53	♔f3	♔h4
54	♔f4	♔h3
55	♘h5	♔h4
56	♘g7	♔h3
57	♘f5	♔g2
58	♔g4	♔h2
59	♘g3!	

Troitsky continued naturally with 59 ♘h4 and forced a win as follows: 59 ... ♔g1 60 ♔g3 ♔f1 61 ♔f3 ♔g1 62 ♘g2 ♔h2 63 ♘gf4 ♔g1 64 ♔e2 ♔h2 65 ♔f2 ♔h1 66 ♘h3! ♔h2 67 ♘g5 ♔h1 68 ♘e1 d3 69 ♘ef3 d2 70 ♘e4 d1♘+ 71 ♔g3 ♘e3 72 ♘f2 mate. The database is five moves faster.

59	...	♔g2
60	♘e4	♔h2
61	♘d2	♔g2
62	♔h4	♔h2
63	♘f4	♔g1
64	♔g3	d3
65	♘h3+	♔h1
66	♘e4	d2
67	♘ef2 mate	

NNP 5

Motwani - I. Gurevich
Hastings Challengers 1991

73	♔c4	♘g7
74	♔c5	♘e8
75	♔c6	♘ec7
76	♔c5	♔d7
77	♔c4	♔c6
78	♔d3	♘e6
79	♔e4	♘e7
80	♔d3	♔d5
81	♔e3	♘f5+
82	♔d3	♘fxd4
83	♔e3	♘b3
84	♔d3	♘bc5+
85	♔e3	♔c4
86	♔e2	♔d4
87	♔d2	♘b3+
88	♔c2	♔c4
89	♔b2	♘bd4
90	♔a3	♘c2+
91	♔b2	♘e3
92	♔a3	♘d1

92 ... ♔c3! is correct - see diag 4.

93	♔a4?

Better was 93 ♔a2! after which Black should repeat with 93 ... ♘e3! 94 ♔a3 ♔c3! etc. (Not 93 ... ♔c3 94 ♔b1 ♘e3 - 94 ... ♔b2 95 ♔c1 - 95 ♔c1 ♔d3 96 ♔b2 ♔c4 97 ♔a3 ♘d1 98 ♔a2! etc. and Black makes no progress until he finds 98 ... ♘e3!.

93	...	♘b2+
94	♔a3?!	

Making it very trivial. However, 94 ♔a5 also loses rather easily: 94 ... ♔c5 95 ♔a6 ♘c4 96 ♔b7 ♔b5 97 ♔a7 ♘a5 98 ♔b8 ♔b6 99 ♔c8 ♔c6 100 ♔b8 ♘b3 101 ♔a7 ♘bc5 102 ♔b8 ♔d7 103 ♔a7 ♔c7 104 ♔a8 ♘a6 105 ♔a7 ♘b4 106 ♔a8 ♘d8 107 e6 ♘dc6 108 e7 ♘d5 109 e8♘+ ♔b6 110 ♘d6 ♘c7 mate.

94	...	♔c3
95	♔a2	♘c4
96	♔b1	♔d2
97	♔a1	♔c1
98	♔a2	♔c2
99	♔a1	♘d4
	0-1	

Two Knights v Pawn(s)   ♘♘ V ♟(♟)

+
B

A Special Feature of Rook's Pawns
Troitsky 1906

135 ...	♚a1
136 ♔b3	♚b1
137 ♘b2	♚c1
138 ♔c3	♚b1
139 ♘d3	♚a2
140 ♔b4	♚b1
141 ♔b3	♚a1
142 ♘e5	♚b1
143 ♘f3	♚a1

Not 143 ... ♚c1 144 ♔c3 ♚d1 145 ♘f4 ♚c1 146 ♘e2+ ♚d1 147 ♔d3 h3 148 ♘h2 etc.

144 ♘f4	h3
145 ♘h2	♚b1
146 ♘d3	♚a1
147 ♔c2	♚a2
148 ♘b2	♚a3
149 ♔c3	♚a2
150 ♘c4	♚b1
151 ♔d2	♚a2
152 ♔c2	♚a1
153 ♔b3	♚b1
154 ♘d2+	♚c1
155 ♔c3	♚d1
156 ♘b3	♚e2
157 ♔d4	♚f2
158 ♘c1	♚g3
159 ♔e3	♚h4

Alternatively:

a) 159 ... ♚xh2 160 ♔f2 ♚h1 161 ♘e2 ♚h2 162 ♘c3 ♚h1 163 ♘e4 ♚h2 164 ♘d2 ♚h1 165 ♘f1 h2 166 ♘g3 mate;

b) 159 ... ♚g2 160 ♘e2! ♚xh2 161 ♔f3! ♚h1 162 ♔f2 ♚h2 163 ♘c3 etc.

160 ♔f4	♚h5
161 ♔f5	♚h6
162 ♔f6	♚h7
163 ♘d3	♚g8
164 ♔e7	♚h7

Or 164 ... ♚g7 165 ♘e5.

165 ♔f7	♚h6
166 ♔f6	♚h7
167 ♘e5	♚g8
168 ♘g6	♚h7
169 ♘e7	♚h6
170 ♘f5+	♚h5
171 ♘e3	♚h6
172 ♘eg4+	♚h7
173 ♔f7	♚h8
174 ♘h6	♚h7
175 ♘f5	♚h8
176 ♔g6	♚g8
177 ♘g7	♚f8
178 ♔f6	♚g8
179 ♘e6	♚h7
180 ♔g5	♚g8
181 ♔g6	♚h8
182 ♔f7	♚h7
183 ♘g4	h2
184 ♘g5+	♚h8
185 ♘e5	h1♛
186 ♘g6 mate	

Bishop v Pawns

Bishop and One Pawn v King

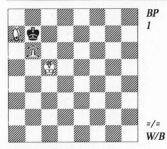

BP
1

Ponziani 1782

1   ♔b5   ♚a8

A fortress draw.

=/=
W/B

BP
2

1   a6   ♚a8

Another positional draw.

=/=
W/B

Bishop and One Pawn v One Pawn

BP
3

1   ♔e7 stalemate

Again no progress can be made.

=/=
W/B

BP
4

1	♔e7	♚b8
2	♔d8	♚a8
3	♗c6	♚b8
4	♗e4	♚a8

5   ♔c7=

No progress is possible - a positional draw.

=/=
W/B

116

BP 5

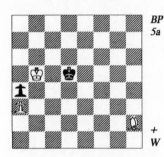

BP 5a

+W

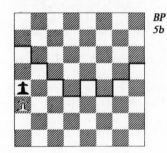

BP 5b

Rauzer 1928

1	♗c5	♔a5
2	♔b7	♔b5
3	♗b6	

Averbakh emphasises this as a key form of bishop and king vs king opposition which forces the black king back a rank.

3	...	♔c4
4	♔c6	♔b3

Or 4 ... ♔d3 5 ♔b5 ♔e4 6 ♔xa4 ♔d5 7 ♔b5 ♔d6 8 ♔a6 ♔c6 9 a4 ♔d7 10 ♔b7.

5	♗c5	♔c4
6	♗d6	

6 ♗e3 is given by Horwitz and Kling: 6 ... ♔b3 7 ♗c1 ♔c4 8 ♗b2 ♔b3 9 ♔b5!+− ♔xb2 10 ♔xa4 ♔c3 11 ♔b5.

6	...	♔d4
7	♔b5	♔d5
8	♗h2!	*(5a)*

This is the key diagonal

since it is the one most useful in keeping the black king out of the drawing corner. White also pulls the bishop out of the way of a possible gain of tempo by attack from the black king.

8	...	♔e6
9	♔xa4	♔d7
10	♔b5	♔c8
11	♔c6 and wins	

Averbakh's guidelines for this type of ending are:

a) Black doesn't draw just by being in the zone in diag 5b - he must also reach the corner in time;

b) When the bishop controls the h2/b8 (or corresponding) diagonal the black king *must be able* to answer ♔b5 with ♔d7. Here these conditions were not met.

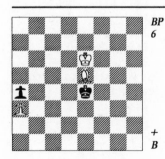

BP 6

+B

Rauzer 1928

1	...	♔f3!

Black prepares to run around to the right if White's king goes after the rook's pawn.

2	♔f5	♔e3
3	♗b2!	

The only winning move, found by Rauzer.

3	...	♔d3

Or 3 ... ♔f3 4 ♗c1 ♔g3 5 ♗g5 and now:

a) 5 ... ♔f3 6 ♗f4 ♔g2! (6 ...

♔f2 7 ♔e4 ♔g2 8 ♔d4 ♔f3 9 ♗h2 ♔g4 10 ♔c4 ♔f5 11 ♔b5 ♔e6 12 ♔xa4 ♔d7 13 ♔b5) 7 ♔g4! (7 ♔e4? ♔h3 8 ♔d4 ♔g4 and White's best is to reset with ♔e4) 7 ... ♔f2 8 ♗c1! (White is manoeuvring to reach ♔g4/♗g3 v ♔g2) 8 ... ♔e2 (8 ... ♔g2 9 ♗e3 transposes to the main line after White's 11th move) 9 ♔f4 ♔f2 10 ♗e3+ ♔g2 11 ♔g4 ♔h2 12 ♗f4+ ♔g2 13 ♗g3 (mission accomplished) 13 ...

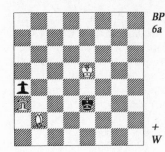

BP
6a

+
W

♔g1 14 ♔f3 ♔h1 15 ♗b8! (White removes his bishop from a possible tempo-gaining attack from the black king) 15 ... ♔g1 16 ♔e3 ♔g2 17 ♔d3 ♔f3 18 ♔c4 ♔e4 19 ♔b5 ♔d5 20 ♗h2! (zugzwang - Black must move away from the drawing corner) 20 ... ♔d4 21 ♔xa4 ♔c5 22 ♔a5 ♔c6 23 ♔a6 and Black does not reach a safe haven;

b) 5 ... ♔f2 6 ♔f4 ♔e2 7 ♔e4 ♔f2 (again Black tries to run this way; as the previous

example showed, being caught in the corner behind the pawns loses easily) 8 ♗f4 ♔g2 9 ♔d4 ♔f3 10 ♗h2 with a familiar winning set-up.

4   ♔e5   ♔e3 *(6a)*
4 ... ♔c4 5 ♗d4 ♔b3 6 ♗c5 leads to the previous example.

5   ♗c1+   ♔f3
6   ♔f5!   ♔g3
7   ♗g5!   ♔f3
8   ♗f4

And White wins as in note a above.

BP
7

=
W

Rauzer 1928
1   ♗d6

White must keep Black out of the corner.

1   ...   ♔d8
2   ♔b7   ♔d7
3   ♗c7   ♔e6

Making it more difficult to be driven right than after 3 ... ♔e7 4 ♔c6 ♔e6 5 ♗d6 (note again this type of opposition which is used to force the black king away).

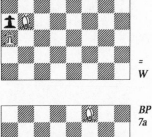

BP
7a

=
B

4   ♔c6   ♔e7
5   ♗b6   ♔e6
6   ♗c5   ♔e5
7   ♗f8 *(7a)*
7   ...   ♔d4?!

Rauzer and Averbakh both consider this to be a dangerous option. See diag 8 for an example where Black simply consents to being driven as far as the h8-corner, but refuses to move forwards. *This is a safer policy than the text.*

8   ♗g7+   ♔e4!

Not 8 ... ♔c4? 9 ♗e5 ♔d3 10 ♔d5 and Black's king is driven back, and he loses as in the first examples.

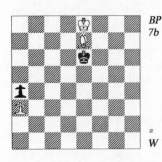

BP
7b

=
W

9   ♔d6   ♔f5
10   ♗e5   ♔g6
For 10 ... ♔e4? 11 ♔e6 see

diag 6.
11   ♔e6   ♔g5
For 11 ... ♔h7 see diag 8.
12   ♗d6   ♔g6

Not 12 ... ♔g4? 13 ♔f6 ♔h5 14 ♗f4 ♔g4 15 ♗c1 ♔h5 16 ♗g5 ♔g4 17 ♔g6 ♔f3 18 ♔f5 and Black has been driven out. *The inferior defences graphically illustrate the boundaries and safety of the zone.* Here White wins as in the previous example.

13   ♗e7   ♔g7
14   ♗b4   ♔g6
15   ♗c3   ♔g5
16   ♗e5   ♔g6
17   ♗f6   ♔h6
18   ♔f7   ♔h7
19   ♗e5   ♔h6
20   ♗g7+   ♔h7
21   ♔f8   ♔g6
22   ♔g8

This is now a direct transposition to diag 8.

22   ...   ♔f5
23   ♔f7   ♔g5!
24   ♗f8   ♔f5
25   ♗e7

For 25 ♗d6 see diag 8.

25   ...   ♔e5
26   ♔e8   ♔e6! *(7b)*

This time it is a minor zugzwang for White, who

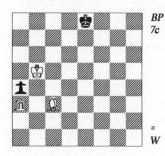

BP 7c

=
W

BP 8

=/=
W/B

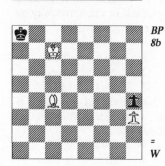

BP 8a

=
W

BP 8b

=
W

must lose his ideal shape.

27 &f8 &f6

White cannot win. He can only drive Black from corner to corner. As long as Black does not head out for open spaces he is safe. Rauzer continues further with:

28 &b4 &g7
29 &c3+ &g6
30 &e7 &f5
31 &d6 &g6

Lobron - Van der Wiel
Ter Apel 1987

Black is safely within the drawing zone.

72 &d4 &d6
73 &e4 &d7
74 &e5 &e7
75 &e6 &e8
76 &f6 &f8
77 &c4 &e8
78 &g7 &e7
79 &f7 &d6
80 &f6 &d7
81 &g6 &d8
82 &e6 &c7
83 &e8 &d8
84 &d7 &c7
85 &e7 &b8 (8a)

This game not only illustrates the drawing zone and method, it does so in most practical fashion. Van der Wiel avoids being driven forward like the plague, happily heading to the opposite corner, the safest policy.

86 &d6 &b7
87 &g4 &b8
88 &c6 &a7
89 &c7 &a8
90 &f3+ &a7
91 &c6 &a6
92 &b8 &b6

32 &c6 &f7
33 &b5 &e8 (7c)

Here Black does not reach d7 in time (see note re Averbakh's emphasis in diag 5a) but more importantly, since the bishop is not posted on the cutting diagonal h2-b8, he reaches the corner.

34 &xa4 &d7
35 &b5 &c7

93 &b7 &c5
94 &c7 &b5!

Best - staying in the width of the drawing zone rather than risking the front of it with 94 ... &d4 95 &d6.

95 &c8 &c5
96 &e6

Deviating from Rauzer's analysis which examined &d7, hoping to drive the king further back, but which allowed ... &d5 heading for the corner.

96 ... &b5
97 &d5 &a6
98 &c4+ &a7
99 &d3 &a8
100 &e2 &a7
101 &c4 &a8 (8b)

White has driven the black king as far as it will go, and his bishop is on the cutting diagonal - but Black is safe.

102 &d6 &b7
103 &e5 &c7
104 &f6 &d7
105 &g5 &e7
106 &xh4 &f6
107 &h5 &g7
108 &g5 &h8
109 h4 ½-½

Bishop v Pawns   ♗ V ♟(♟)

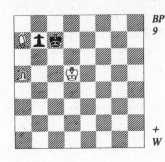

BP 9

+W

Paulsen - Metger
Nurenberg 1888

1 ♗d4!!

Not 1 ♔c5 b6+!= or 1 ♔c4 b5+!=.

1 ... ♔c6

Alternatively:

a) 1 ... b5 2 a6 ♔c6 3 ♔c3 ♔d6 4 ♔b4 ♔c6 5 ♔a5+-;

b) 1 ... b6 2 a6 ♔c6 3 ♔c4 ♔d6 4 ♔b4 ♔c6 5 ♗b8 b5 6 ♗a7!+-.

2 ♗b6!

Not 2 ♔c3? b6 3 a6 ♔b5=.

2 ... ♔d6

Or 2 ... ♔b5 3 ♔d5 ♔a6 4 ♔d6 ♔b5 5 ♔c7 ♔a6 6 ♔b8+-.

3	♔c4	♔c6
4	♔b4	♔d6
5	♔b5	♔d7
6	♔c5	♔c8
7	♗a7	♔c7
8	♔b5	♔d7
9	♗b8!	♔c8
10	♗h2	♔d7
11	♔b6	♔c8
12	♗c7	1-0

Bishop and One Pawn v Two Pawns

BP 10

-B

Tunik - Sorokin
Kuibyshev 1990

A simple illustration of how the bishop wins.

57 ... ♗d4
58 ♔f4 ♗f6

Preventing king entry.

59 ♔f3 ♔d3
60 ♔f4

Retreat is equally hopeless: 60 ♔g2 ♔e2 61 f3 ♔e3 62 f4 ♔e2 63 ♔h2 ♔f3 64 ♔h3 ♗e7 65 ♔h2 ♔g4 66 ♔g2 ♗c5 67 ♔h2 ♗f2.

60 ... ♔e2
61 f3 ♔d3
62 g4 ♔d4

Black has a limitless source of tempi, and waits for White's position to become rigid - White must either advance his pawns or retreat and allow the encroachment of the enemy king. All sub-variations show this dilemma.

63 ♔g3 ♔e3
64 f4 ♗e7
0-1

Due to 65 f5 (65 g5 ♗d6) 65 ... g5 66 ♔g2 ♔f4 67 ♔h3 ♔f3. *Black was aided by the inaccessibility of the g6-pawn.* This difference prevents the white king from becoming active in the same way as the next two examples.

BP 13

=B

"Averbakh's Barrier" 1972

1 ... f4!

Not 1 ... ♔f6? 2 ♔e2 ♔e5 3 ♔d3 ♔f6 4 ♔d4 ♔g6 5 ♔e5+-.

2 g4 ♔d4
3 ♔e2 ♔c3!

The black king creates a barrier.

4 ♗f5 ♔d4
5 ♔d2 ♔c4

6 ♗e4 ♔d4
7 ♗d3 ♔e5
8 ♔c3 f3!

Black must act quickly - if the white king reaches d3 White wins.

9	♔d2	♔f4
10	♗f5	♔g3
11	♔e1	♔g2
12	♗e4	♔g3
13	♗f5	♔g2=

Bishop v Pawns

♗ V ♙(♙)

BP
12

Speelman/Averbakh

1 &f3 &f7
2 &e3 &g7

3 &d4 &h6
and ... &g5/ ... f5=.

BP
13

end of Chekhover study

1 &b8 ♗f5
2 &c7 ♗e4
3 &d6 &g2
4 &e5 ♗f3
5 &f4 &h3
Or 5 ... &xh2 6 b7 ♗xb7 7
&xg4.

6 &g5 ♗b7
7 &h5 ♗c6
8 &g5 ♗f3
9 &f4!=
The bishop has no influence
on the game thanks to the
pawn on b7.

BP
14

Short - Kasparov
Belgrade 1989
Here White loses due to the
doubled pawns. Black's
weapon is to stalemate the
white king when he will be
obliged to play b5, transforming the wrong rook's pawn to
a winning knight's pawn.

93 ... &g2
94 &d1 &f3
95 &d2 &e4
96 &c3 &e3
97 &c2 &e2
98 &c1

98 &c3 ♗d3 99 &b3 &d2
100 &a3 &c2 101 &a2 ♗c4+

102 &a1 (102 b3 leads to the
game and if 102 &a3 ♗b3)
102 ... &c1 103 b3 ♗d3 104
&a2 ♗e4 105 &a3 &b1 106
&a4 ♗d3 107 &a3 &a1.
98 ... ♗d3
99 b3 &e1
100 &b2 &d2
101 &a1 &c2
102 &a2 &c1
103 &a1
White loses normally if he
flees the corner: 103 &a3 &b1
104 &a4 &b2 105 &a5 &a3
106 &b6 &xb4.
103 ... ♗b1
0-1

BP
15

Averbakh

1 ♗f2

White must prevent ... &g3.
Instead, 1 ♗h2!? is considered
dubious by Averbakh, who
claims that it seriously complicates White's task. I (JT)
believe it wins more quickly.
After all, this is the diagonal

White wants: 1 ... &h4 (1 ...
&f5 2 ♗c7 transposes to the
main line at White's fifth
move) 2 ♗c7 (2 ♗d6 &g4 3
&e3 c5 4 ♗f2 c4 5 ♗e5 &f5
6 ♗g7 &e4 and the black
pawns are very dangerous -
Averbakh) 2 ... &h5 (2 ... &g4
3 ♗d6 transposes into main

Bishop v Pawns

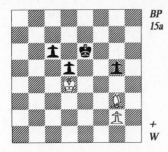

BP 15a

+ W

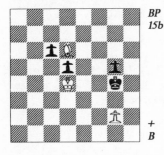

BP 15b

+ B

line at White's sixth move) 3 ♗g3! (Averbakh only gives 3 ♔e3 ♔g4! 4 ♔f2 c5 5 ♗b6 c4 6 ♗d4 ♔f4 and White can hardly win - Averbakh) 3 ... ♔g6 (3 ... ♔g4 4 ♗d6 transposes to the main line at White's sixth move, whilst 3 ... ♔h6 4 ♔e5 ♔g6 5 ♗f2 wins) 4 ♔e5 ♔h5 5 ♔f5 (intending ♗f2) 5 ... d4 6 ♗f2 c5 7 g4+ ♔h6 8 ♔e4 ♔g6 9 ♗g3 ♔f6 10 ♗d6.

| 1 | ... | ♔f4 |
| 2 | ♗e1 | ♔f5 |

Or 2 ... ♔g4 3 ♔e5 ♔h5 4 ♔f5 c5 5 g4+ ♔h6 6 ♗d2 (an ideal set-up - the bishop and g-pawn tie down Black to defence of g5 and prevent any invasion; here the g5-pawn falls and White copes easily with the other pawns).

3 ♗g3

After 3 ♔e3 ♔g4 4 ♔f2 c5 5 ♗a5 c4 6 ♗c3 ♔f4 7 ♗d2+ ♔g4 White is tied down to monitoring the c- and d-pawns. White wants to drive the black king to the sixth and then play g4, when he will be able to box in the black king, press g5, and switch tasks, e.g. ♗d4 and the king can invade.

3 ... ♔e6 (15a)

Averbakh says that Black must prevent ♗d6 but in fact that is a secondary concern. ♗d6 will be powerful when it simultaneously threatens g4!, allowing White to erect his ideal formation and then switch tasks (or free the white king to set-up g4).

| 4 | ♗b8 | ♔f5 |
| 5 | ♗c7! | |

Note that White does *not* play ^d6 - it is not an end in itself.

| 5 | ... | ♔g4 |

Preventing 5 ... g4, which can be met by 6 g3 ♔e6 7 ♗f4 ♔f5 (7 ... ♔e7 8 ♗c5 ♔d7 9 ♗b8 ♔c8 10 ♗e5 ♔d7 11 ♗f4) 8 ♗b8 (White must avoid lines where the black king gains activity, e.g. 8 ♗c5 ♔e4 9 ♗xc6 d4 10 ♔d6 d3 11 ♔e6 ♔f3 12 ♔f5 d2=; with care he can always bide time to keep the black king hemmed in) 8 ... ♔g5 9 ♔e5 ♔g6 10 ♗a7 and White will soon round up all the pawns.

6 ♗d6 (15b)

Now White frees the king from defence of c5. White has aimed for this position with Black to move. Now the white king can begin to drive Black back and then aim for g4.

6 ... ♔f5

Or 6 ... ♔h4 7 ♔e3 c5 8 ♔f3 c4 9 ♗e5 ♔h5 10 g4+ ♔h4 (10 ... ♔g6 11 ♔e3 ♔f7 12 ♗c3 ♔e6 13 ♔d4) 11 ♗f6.

7 ♔e3 ♔g4

Or 7 ... ♔e6 8 ♗c5 ♔f5 9 ♔f3 ♔e5 10 g4 d4 11 ♗e7.

8 ♔f2 ♔f5

Or 8 ... d4 9 ♔e2 ♔f5 10 ♔d3 ♔e6 11 ♗c5.

9	♔f3	d4
10	g4+	♔e6
11	♗c5	♔d5
12	♗e7	c5
13	♗xg5	c4
14	♗f6!	c3
15	♗g7!	

By waiting White forces the black king to the side, not yielding a route via, say, e4.

| 15 | ... | ♔c4 |

Not 15 ... c2 16 ♗h6 ♔c4 17 ♗c1 ♔c3 18 g5 d3 19 ♔e3.

16	♔e2	d3+
17	♔e3	d2
18	♔e2	♔b3
19	♔d1	♔c4
20	♔c2 and wins	

Bishop v Pawns ♗ V ♟(♟)

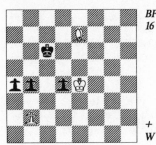

+
W

Batuyev 1940

1 ♗f6!

Not 1 ♗xb4? ♚b5 2 ♗f8 a3!! (an amazing resource; not 2 ... ♚c4 3 ♗a3! d3 4 ♚e3+-) 3 ♗xa3 ♚c4 with a positional draw: 4 ♗e7 ♚b3 5 ♗a3 ♚c4 6 ♚f3 ♚b3 7 ♚e2 ♚c2=.

1 ... ♚c5!

2 ♚d3!

Again we see the priority given to preventing activity of the enemy king. (Not 2 ♗xd4+? ♚c4 3 ♗e5 ♚b3=.)

2 ... b3

3 ♗g7!

Another common theme in bishop vs pawn endings is that waiting moves are often the most effective as the pawns are easily compromised. White must avoid 3 ♗xd4+ ♚b5! (3 ... ♚b4 4 ♗g7 and ♗f8+-) 4 ♚c3 a3!=.

3 ... ♚d5

4 ♗f8

Immobilising the pawn majority.

4 ... ♚e5

5 ♚c4!

Switching tasks. The bishop will monitor the d-pawn while the king mops up.

5 ... ♚e4

6 ♚b4 d3

7 ♗h6 and wins

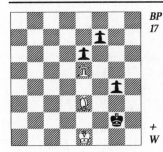

+
W

Walker 1841

1 ♚e2 ♚h3

2 ♗g5!

An excellent move that passes without comment in Averbakh's book. The point is seen in the straightforward continuation 2 ♚f2 ♚h4 3 ♚g2 (3 ♗c5 ♚g5 4 ♗e7+ ♚f4 5 ♗f6 g3+ 6 ♚g2 ♚g4=) 3 ... ♚h5 4 ♚g3 ♚g6 (with the idea of ... f6) 5 ♗d4 ♚g5=.

2 ... ♚g3

Or 2 ... g3 3 ♚f3 g2 4 ♗e3 ♚h2 5 ♚g4! g1♛+ 6 ♗xg1+ ♚xg1 7 ♚g5 ♚f2 8 ♚f6 winning.

3 ♚e3 ♚g2

4 ♗h4! ♚h3

5 ♗e1

White refuses the black king access to the fifth rank.

5 ... g3

Alternatively, 5 ... ♚h2 6 ♚f4 ♚h3 and:

a) 7 ♚g5 g3 8 ♚h5! wins as in main line. But not 8 ♚f6? g2 9 ♗f2 ♚g4! 10 ♚xf7 ♚f5=;

b) 7 ♗g3 f5 8 exf6 e5+ 9 ♚xe5 ♚xg3 10 f7.

6 ♚f4 g2

7 ♗f2 ♚h2

8 ♚g5

The beginning of a cute manoeuvre but 8 ♚g4! wins faster (JT).

8 ... ♚h3

9 ♚h5 ♚h2

10 ♚h6 ♚h3

11 ♚g5 ♚h2

12 ♚f6 and wins

BP
18

=
B

BP
18a

=
W

Westerinen - Arnason
Helsinki 1986
White is hard pressed to get his king into the safe corner. It seems that the best solution is to combine a route towards a1 with one to a5, which is also a drawing square thanks to the distraction of the h-pawn.

| 41 | ... | ♔c2 |
| 42 | b3 | |

After 42 ♔e5 ♔xb2 43 ♔d6 ♔a3! (not 43 ... ♔xa2 44 ♔c5 ♔b3 45 ♔b6 ♗b5 46 ♔a5! ♔c4 47 h4 ♔d5 48 h5 ♔c6 49 h6 ♗d3 50 h7=) the white king does not reach a5: 44 ♔c5 ♗b5 45 h4 ♗e2 46 h5 ♗xh5 47 b5 a5 48 b6 ♗f3 49 ♔b5 a4 50 ♔a5 ♗c6-+.

| 42 | ... | ♔c3 *(18a)* |
| 43 | ♔e5 | |

Better was 43 ♔e4! ♗g6+ (43 ... ♔xb4 44 ♔d3 ♔a3 45 ♔c4 a5 46 h4) 44 ♔e3 (44 ♔d5 ♔xb4 45 ♔c6 a5 transposes back to the game) and now:

a) 44 ... ♔b2?? 45 a4 ♔xb3 46 b5 axb5 47 axb5 ♗e8 48 b6 ♗c6 49 h4 ♔c4 50 h5 ♔c5 51 h6+-;

b) 44 ... ♗b1 45 b5!! axb5 46 a4! b4 47 a5 ♗a2 (47 ... ♗d3? 48 h4) 48 a6 ♗xb3 49 h4 ♗d5 50 h5 b3 51 h6 b2 52 h7=;

c) 44 ... ♔xb4 45 ♔d2 and:

c1) 45 ... ♗b1 46 ♔c1=;

c2) 45 ... a5 46 h4 ♔a3 47 ♔c3 ♗f7 (47 ... ♔xa2 48 ♔c4 ♗e8 49 h5=) 48 h5 and now:

c21) 48 ... ♔xa2 49 h6 ♗g8 50 b4= (50 ... a4?? 51 b5+-). White must avoid 50 h7? ♗xh7 51 ♔c4 ♗d3+!-+;

c22) 48 ... ♗xh5 49 ♔c4 ♗e2+ 50 ♔c5 ♗f1 (50 ...

♔xa2 51 ♔b6=) 51 ♔b6 ♔b4 52 a3+=;

c3) 45 ... ♔a3 46 ♔c3 ♗b1 47 ♔c4 ♗xa2 48 ♔c5 ♗xb3 49 ♔b6 ♔c4 50 ♔a5=.

| 43 | ... | ♔xb4 |
| 44 | ♔d6 | |

Not 44 ♔d4 ♗g6 45 h4 ♗b1 46 a3+ ♔xb3 47 ♔c5 a5-+.

| 44 | ... | ♔b5 |
| 45 | h4 | |

Again forced: 45 ♔d5 ♗g6 46 ♔d4 ♔b4 47 h4 ♗b1-+.

45	...	♗g6
46	♔c7	♗h5
47	♔b7	♗f3+
48	♔c7	

Or 48 ♔a7 a5 49 a3 (49 ♔b8 should transpose to the game) 49 ... ♗d1 50 b4 a4 51 ♔b7 ♗f3+ 52 ♔a7 ♔c4 53 ♔a6 ♔b3 54 b5 ♔xa3 55 b6 ♔b3 56 h5 a3 winning.

48	...	♗d1
49	♔b7	a5
50	♔c7	♔c5
51	♔b7	♔b5
52	♔c7	♗h5
53	♔b7	♗f7
54	♔c7	♗g6
55	♔b7	♗b1
56	a3	

56 h5 ♗xa2 57 h6 ♗b1 58 ♔a7 ♗e4 wins for Black.

56	...	♗g6
57	♔c7	♗f7
58	b4	a4
59	♔d6	♔c4
60	♔e7	

Or 60 ♔c6 ♗e8+.

60	...	♗h5
61	♔f6	♔b3
	0-1	

A surprisingly difficult ending.

Bishop v Pawns

BP 19

Bareev - King
Hastings 1990/91
The bishop has little chance against four pawns.

33	g4	♗c6
34	♔f2	♗d5
35	b4	♗c6
36	♔e3	♗a4
37	d5!	exd5
38	♔d4	♗d1

+ W

Black must make some gesture towards hobbling the kingside pawn mass but the advance of the b-pawn is also quickly decisive.

39	b5	♗xg4
40	b6	♗c8
41	♔xd5	1-0

41 ... ♔f5 42 ♔d6 ♔xf4 43 e6 wins easily.

Bishop and Two Pawns v Pawn(s)

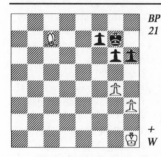

BP 20

Sveshnikov - Gulko
Moscow Ch 1983

75	♗h7!	1-0

An example of two wrong rook's pawns saving the win. Black cannot use the tactic ...

+ W

g5/ ... g6 to enter the corner as hxg6 wins thanks to the presence of the second h-pawn. (Not 75 ♗c4+ ♔f6 76 ♔f4? g5+=.)

BP 21

Mukhin - Polovets
Leningrad 1983
With the 'right' rook's pawn there are no technical difficulties.

42	...	f5

Or 42 ... ♔f6 43 ♔g2 and now:

a) 43 ... ♔g5 44 ♔g3 h5 45 ♗f4+ ♔f6 46 gxh5;

b) 43 ... ♔g7 44 ♔f3 ♔f6 45 ♔f4 ♔e6 (45 ... ♔g7 46

+ W

♔e5+-) 46 ♗a5 ♔f6 47 ♗c3+ ♔e6 48 ♗g7;

c) 43 ... h5 44 gxh5 gxh5 45 ♔g3 ♔g5 46 ♗f4+ ♔f5 47 ♗d2 ♔g6 48 ♔h4 f6 49 ♗e3 f5 50 ♗f4.

43	♗e5+	♔f7
44	gxf5	gxf5
45	♔g2	♔g6
46	♔g3	♔h5
47	♗f4	♔g6
48	♔h4	1-0

BP 22

Portisch - Stein
Sousse IZ 1967

49	♗e8!	♔e7
50	♗b5	f5

Alternatively, 50 ... ♔f6 51 ♗c4 or 50 ... ♔d6 51 ♗c4 f5? 52 ♗g8.

51	♔e3	♔f6
52	♔d4	h5

More testing was 52 ... ♔g5(!) 53 ♔e5 h5 54 h4+! (54 ♗e2 h4 55 g4 fxg4= 56

+ W

hxg4 h3) 54 ... ♔g4 55 ♔f6 ♔xg3 (55 ... f4 56 gxf4+- ♔xf4 57 ♗d7 ♔g3 58 ♔g5) 56 ♔g5+- (Portisch) 56 ... f4 57 ♗d3 f3 58 ♗xg6 f2 59 ♗d3.

53	♔e3!	h4
54	g4	♔e5
55	♗f1	♔f6
56	♔f4	g5+
57	♔e3	♔e5
58	♗a6	1-0

Bishop v Pawns

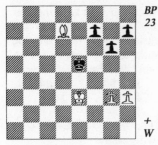

BP 23

+ W

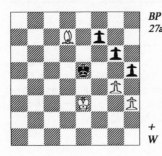

BP 27a

+ W

Speelman

1 g4!!

Not 1 ♗b5 f5 and:

a) 2 ♗d3 g5 3 ♔f3 f4! 4 g4 h6= is analogous to Averbakh's barrier - the addition of h-pawns does not hamper Black since h3 is a potential target. Also interesting is 4 ... h5!? 5 gxh5 ♔f6 6 h6 ♔f7 7 ♗h7 ♔f6 8 ♔g4 ♔f7 9 ♔xg5 f3 and the black king reaches the corner - Averbakh;

b) 2 ♗e8!? g5 3 g4 ♔f6! 4 ♗h5 (4 ♗b5 fxg4 5 hxg4 h5) 4 ... ♔e5 5 ♔d3 ♔f6 (not 5 ... ♔e6? 6 ♔d4! or 5 ... ♔f4? 6 ♔d4!+-) 6 ♔d4 ♔e6 arriving at a position of mutual zugzwang - Black to play would lose: ... ♔f6 - ♔d5; ... h6 - ♗g6. However, it is White to move: 7 ♔e3 (7 ♗e8 ♔e7 8 ♗h5 ♔e6! 9 ♗e8 ♔e7 10 ♗b5 fxg4 11 hxg4 h5) 7 ... ♔e5 8 ♔d3 ♔f6 and:

b1) 9 ♔c3 ♔e5 10 ♔c4 ♔e4! 11 ♔c5 (11 ♗e8 ♔f4!=) ♔e5! 12 ♔c6 f4!=;

b2) 9 ♔c4 ♔e5 10 ♔c5 f4! 11 ♔c4 (11 ♗e8 f3 12 ♗b5 h5=) 11 ... f3 12 ♔d3 ♔f4 13 ♗e8 ♔g3 14 ♔e3 f2 15 ♗b5 ♔xh3 16 ♔f3 ♔h4=.

Another attempt which is not quite good enough is 1 ♗a4 f5 2 ♗c2:

a) 2 ... g5 3 g4!! f4+ 4 ♔d3 and Black cannot achieve diag 13: 4 ... h5 5 ♗b1 hxg4 6 hxg4 ♔d5 7 ♗c2 ♔e5 8 ♗b3 ♔f6 (8 ... f3 9 ♔e3 f2 10 ♔xf2 ♔f4 11 ♗e6) 9 ♔e4+-;

b) 2 ... h5? 3 h4+-;

c) 2 ... h6!! and:

c1) 3 h4 ♔f6! (3 ... g5? 4

hxg5 hxg5 5 ♔d3!+- ♔d5 6 ♗a4 ♔e5 7 ♗d7 ♔f6 8 ♔d4) 4 ♔f3 (4 ♔d4 h5 and ... g5=) 4 ... g5 5 h5 (5 hxg5+ reaches diag 13) 5 ... f4! 6 g4 ♔e5= with a positional draw, by analogy to diag 13;

c2) 3 ♗d1 g5 4 ♔d3 g4! 5 hxg4 f4 6 gxf4+ ♔xf4 7 ♔d4 ♔g5 8 ♔e5 h5 9 gxh5 ♔h6=.

Both 1 ♗c6 f5 2 ♔f3 g5 3 ♔d3 g4! 4 hxg4 f4= as above and 1 ♗e8 f5 2 h4 ♔f6 3 ♔d4 ♔e7! (3 ... h5? 4 ♗xg6! ♔xg6 5 ♔e5+-) 4 ♗b5 ♔f6 5 ♗e2 h5 6 ♗xh5 gxh5 7 ♔d5 f4!= also fail to win.

1 ... h5 *(27a)*

Or 1 ... f6 2 h4 ♔d6 3 ♗c8 ♔e5 4 ♔f3 ♔d6 5 ♗a6 ♔e5 6 ♗d3 ♔e6 7 ♔f4 ♔e7 8 ♗c4 ♔f8 (8 ... h6 9 ♔e3) 9 ♔e3 ♔g7 10 ♔d4 ♔h6 11 ♗e2! ♔g7 12 ♔d5 ♔f7 13 ♔d6+-. The winning technique is to use the bishop to prevent ... h5 or ... f5, then invade with the king.

2 ♗c8!

2 ♔f3? (also not 2 g5? h4 and ..f6=) 2 ... hxg4+ 3 hxg4 ♔f6 4 ♔f4 (4 ♗e8 ♔g7 5 ♔e3 f6 6 ♔d4 ♔h6 is the fortress in diag 13) 4 ... ♔e7 5 ♗c8 f6 6 ♔e3 (6 ♔e4 f5+ 7 ♗xf5 gxf5+ 8 ♔xf5 ♔f7=) 6 ... ♔f7 7 ♔d4 ♔g7 again with the fortress from diag 13.

2 ... hxg4
3 hxg4 f6
4 ♗d7!

White still must take care to avoid diag 14.

4 ... ♔d6
5 ♗e8 and wins

Bishop v Pawns

$\text{\Large ♗ V ♟(♟)}$

BP 24

= W

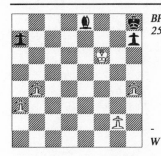

BP 25

- W

BP 25a

- W

BP 25b

- W

Anand - Dreev
Madras 1991
A remarkable twist on the corner fortress theme.

45	a6	♗b8
46	♔h1!	

White intends to jettison the g-pawn and then play a7, obliging Black to stalemate him.

46	...	♔g8
47	♔g1	

47 g5 transposes to the game.

47	...	♔f8
48	♔h1	♔g8
49	g5	f5
50	g6	f4
51	g7	♔f7

Or 51 ... f3 52 a7.

52	g8♕+	♔xg8
53	a7	♗xa7

½-½

Mestel - Speelman
London 1986

49	g4	

Or 49 ♔e7 ♗c6 50 g4 ♔g7.

49	...	♔g8
50	h5	♔f8

The ♗e8 does a remarkable job of pressuring both flanks from its humble post.

51	h6	

Removing much dynamic potential of the kingside pawns but other moves either lose a pawn or allow the black king to emerge. Also, the tactical possibility of g5-g6 keeps some pressure on this flank.

51	...	♗g6
52	b5	♔e8
53	♔e6	♔d8 (25a)

54	a4	

Or 54 ♔d6 a6! and now:

a) 55 bxa6 ♔c8 56 ♔c6 ♔b8 57 ♔b6 ♔a8 and White will lose both a-pawns through zugzwang;

b) 55 b6 ♔c8 56 ♔c6 ♗e8+ and wins, as in the game.

54	...	a6! (25b)
55	b6	a5
56	♔d6	♔c8
57	♔c5	♗e8
58	g5	♔b7
59	g6	♗xg6
60	♔b5	0-1

After 60 ... ♗d3+ 61 ♔xa5 ♔c6 62 ♔b4 ♔xb6 and White will soon lose both pawns.

127

Bishop v Pawns

Bishop v Pawns: Further Examples

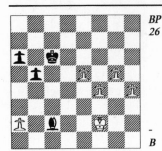

BP 26

B

Renet - Piket
Euro Junior Ch,
Groningen 1984

An example of the importance of blockade, and the strength of a passed pawn for the side with the bishop.

45 ... &g6

45 ... &f5 46 &e3 should transpose.

  46 &f3 &f5
  47 h5 &d5
  48 g6

Now White's pawn mass is neutralized. 48 h6 looks less logical, as zugzwang is easy then: 48 ... b4 49 &e3 a5 50 &d2 a4 51 &c1 a3-+. The white king cannot move because of ... b3, so the pawns drop.

  48 ... b4
  49 &e3 a5
  50 &d2 a4
  51 a3

White cannot prevent the harvesting of his pawn mass. No better is 51 &c1 &e6 (51 ...

a3? 52 g7 &h7 53 f5! &xe5 54 &c2 &g8 55 h6 &f6 56 h7=) 52 &d2 &e7 53 g7 &f7 54 h6 &g8 and wins as in the game.

  51 ... b3
  52 &c3 &e6
  53 g7

The pawns are no less vulnerable on h5/g6: 53 &b2 &e7 54 &c3 &f8 55 &b2 &g7 56 &c3 &e6 57 &b2 &h6 58 &c3 &xh5 59 g7 &g6-+.

  53 ... &f7
  54 h6 &g8
  55 &b2 &h7
  56 &c3 &e6
  57 &b2 &xh6
  58 f5 &g8!

Not 58 ... &xg7?? 59 fxe6 &f8 60 &b1 &e7 61 &b2 &xe6 62 &b1 &xe5 63 &b2=.

  59 e6 &xg7
  60 f6+ &xf6
  61 e7 &xe7
  62 &c3 &d6
     0-1

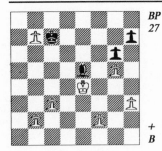

BP 27

+
B

Tringov - Peev
Plovdiv 1981

Black resigned without further play here. It would be interesting to see how he would fight against the mass of pawns:

  45 ... &h2
  46 f4 &xb7
  47 b4 (27a)

White does best not to hurry. Real drawing chances occur after the hasty 47 f5?! (this removes much of the worry of a white king invasion to the kingside) and:

a) 47 ... &c7 48 f6 &d6 49 b4 &e6 50 c4 &g3 51 c5 &e1

52 b5 &f2 53 c6 &b6 54 &d3 &c7 55 &d4 and now:

a1) 55 ... &b6+ 56 &c4 &f7 (56 ... &e3 57 c7 &d7 58 f7) 57 &d5 &c7 58 &c5;

a2) 55 ... &h2 56 &c4 &c7 57 &c5;

b) 47 ... gxf5+ 48 &xf5 &g3 and now:

b1) 49 c4 &c6 50 &g4 &f2 51 h4 &d6 52 h5 &e6 53 b4 &e1 54 b5 &f2 55 &f4 &c5 56 &e4 &f2 57 g6 (57 h6 &f7 58 &d5 &e3 59 c5 &xg5 60 c6 &e8).

b11) 57 ... h6? and:

b111) 58 g7?! &f7 59 &d5

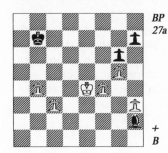

BP
27a

+
B

♔xg7 60 c5 ♔f6 61 b6 ♔e7
62 ♔c6 ♔d8 63 b7 ♗g3 64
♔b6 ♗f4! 65 c6 (65 ♔a7 ♔d7
66 b8♕ ♗xb8+ 67 ♔xb8
♔c6=) 65 ... ♗b8;

  b112) 58 ♔d3 ♗b6 59 ♔c3
♗c5 60 ♔b3 ♗d4 61 ♔b4
♔d6 62 c5+ ♔d5 (62 ...
♗xc5+ 63 ♔c4) 63 b6 ♔c6 64
♔a5+-;

  b12) 57 ... hxg6! 58 hxg6
♔f6 59 ♔d5 ♔xg6 60 c5
♔f7 61 c6 ♔e7=;

  b2) 49 ♔g4 ♗e5 50 h4 ♔c6
51 ♔f5 ♔d6 52 h5 ♗h8 53 h6
♔e7 54 g6 hxg6+ 55 ♔xg6
♔f8 56 h7 ♔e7 57 ♔f5 ♔f7
58 ♔e4 ♔g6 59 ♔d3 ♔xh7
60 b4 ♔g6 61 c4 ♔f5 62 c5
♔e6 63 ♔c4 ♔d7 64 b5 ♗f6

65 ♔d5=.

47	...	♗g3
48	c4	♗e1
49	b5	♗f2
50	♔e5	♗e3

Or 50 ... ♗g3 51 c5 ♗f2 52
♔d6 ♗e3 53 c6+ ♔b6 54 ♔e5
♗f2 55 ♔f6 ♗g3 56 ♔g7
♗xf4 57 h4 ♔xb5 58 ♔xh7
♔xc6 59 ♔xg6 ♔d7 60 ♔h7
♔e7 61 g6.

51	h4	♔b6
52	♔f6	♗xf4
53	♔g7	♔c5
54	♔xh7	♔xc4
55	b6	♔b5
56	b7	♔c6
57	h5	gxh5
58	g6 and wins	

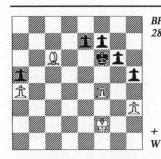

BP
28

+
W

Tompa - Schoeneberg
Leipzig 1977
    37   h4!
  Ideally fixing the kingside.
The presence of the a-pawns
makes this an easy win for
White.

37	...	e5
38	♔f3	♔f5

39	♗d7+	♔f6
40	♔e4	exf4
41	♔xf4	♔e7
42	♗b5	f6

Or 42 ... ♔f6 43 ♗c4.

43	♗c4	♔f8
44	♔e4	♔g7
45	♗e2	♔h6
46	♗d1	1-0

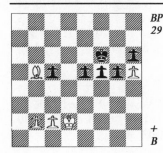

BP
29

+
B

Dolmatov - Shirov
Klaipeda 1988
    31   ...   e4
  Again the piece must work
patiently and aim to enforce a
blockade. After 31 ... g4 32 c3
the black king's attempt to
create play on the kingside is
shown to be misguided - the
b-pawn forces the black king
to watch the queenside.

32	♔e3	♔e5
33	♗d7	f4+
34	♔e2	♔d4
35	c3+	♔d5

Not 35 ... ♔c4 36 ♗e6+
♔b5 37 ♗d5.

36	b3	♔d6

37	♗c8	♔e5
38	♔f2	♔d5
39	♔f1	♔d6
40	♔g1	♔d5
41	♔f2	♔d6
42	♔g2	♔e5
43	♗g4!	

Not 43 ♔h3? e3 and Black
achieves ... ♔e4.

43	...	♔d5
44	♗f5	♔e5
45	♗c8!	

Zugzwang.

45	...	♔d5
46	♔h3	♔e5

Or 46 ... e3 47 ♗b7+ ♔e5
48 ♗f3 and here the pawns are
blockaded while keeping the

black king under control - the point of manoeuvring is to play ♔h3 with the black king on d5: 48 ... ♔f5 49 b4 cxb4 50 cxb4 ♔e6 51 b5 ♔d7 52 b6 ♔c8 53 ♔g4 e2 54 ♗xe2 ♔b7 55 ♔f5 ♔xb6 56 ♔g6 ♔c5 57 ♔xh6+-.

47 ♔g4 ♔d6

BP 30

= B

48 ♗b7

After 48 ... ♔e5 49 ♗c6 e3 (or 49 ... f3 50 ♗b7) 50 ♗f3 Black has no moves that do not worsen his position, and White wins as in the note to Black's 46th move.

1-0

Hartston - Ostermeyer
Reykjavik 1975

1 ... ♗b6

Not 1 ... ♔e6 2 ♔d2 ♔f5? (2 ... ♗b6!) 3 h4 ♔g4 4 f7 ♗e7 5 a4 ♔f3 6 ♔e1 ♗e4 (6 ... e4 7 a5 e3 8 a6 ♗d6 9 f8♕+! ♗xf8 10 a7+-) 7 a5 ♔d5 8 a6 ♔c6 9 h5 ♗f8 10 h6! 1-0 as in the game.

2 ♔d2 ♗f2!

Worse is 2 ... ♗d4?!, e.g.

a) 3 a4 ♗xb2 4 a5 (4 c3 ♗a3 5 ♔e3 ♗b2!) 4 ... ♗d4 5 a6 e4=;

b) 3 b4! cxb3 4 cxb3 with good chances for White, though possibly drawable:

b1) 4 ... e4 5 ♔e2! (5 b4? ♗b2! 6 a4 ♗a3 7 b5 ♗c5 8 ♔e2 ♗b6= or 5 a4 ♗c5!=) 5 ... ♔e6 6 b4 h6 7 h4 hxg5 8 hxg5 ♔f7 9 a4 ♔g6 10 a5 ♗c3 11 ♔e3! ♗xb4 12 a6+-;

b2) 4 ... ♔e6! and now:

b21) 5 a4 ♗c5 6 ♔c3 (6 ♔d3 ♔d5 7 ♔c3 ♗d4+ 8 ♔d2 ♗c5 9 ♔c3 ♗d4+ 10 ♔c2! ♗c5) 6 ... e4 7 b4 ♗e3 8 h4 (8 a5 ♗xg5 9 ♔d4 ♗xf6+=) 8 ... h6!= (8 ... ♗f2 9

a5 ♗xh4 10 ♔d4 e3 11 ♔d3!+-);

b22) 5 b4 h6 6 h4 ♗f2 7 ♔e2? (7 gxh6!) 7 ... ♗xh4 8 a4?? ♗xg5 9 a5 ♔d7! 10 f7 ♗e7-+.

However, 2 ... ♔e6! looks simplest of all: 3 ♔c3 (3 b4 cxb3 4 cxb3 h6 5 h4 ♗f2= or 3 ♔e2 ♗c5 4 ♔f3 ♔f5=) 3 ... ♗d4+ (3 ... ♔d5!?) 4 ♗xc4 ♗xb2 5 a4 e4=.

3 ♔c3 ♗h4
4 f7 ♔e7
5 ♔xc4 ♗xg5
6 a4 ♔xf7
7 ♔d5

Liberzon assesses this position as slightly better for White and it is probably drawn, e.g. 7 ... ♔e7 and:

a) 8 a5 ♔d7 9 ♔xe5 (9 c4 e4 10 ♔xe4 ♗d2 11 a6 ♔c6) 9 ... ♔c6 10 c3 ♔b5 11 b4 ♗d2 12 ♔d4 ♗e1 13 ♔d3 h5 14 h3 h4=;

b) 8 b4 ♗d2 9 b5 ♗a5 10 c4 e4 11 ♔xe4 ♔d6=;

c) 8 c4 e4! 9 ♔xe4 ♔d6 10 a5 (10 b4 ♗d2 11 b5 ♔c5=) 10 ... ♗d2! 11 a6 ♔c6=.

Bishop v Pawns

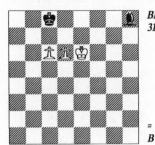

BP
31

Two Pawns
Averbakh 1972
    1   ...   ♗c3
    1 ... ♔d8? 2 c7+ ♔c8 3 ♔e7
wins.
    2   d7+
    Or 2 ♔e7 ♗b4=.

=
B

    2   ...   ♔d8
    3   c7+
    Or 3 ♔d6 ♗b4+.
    3   ...   ♔xc7
    4   ♔e7   ♗f6+!
    and draws

BP
32

Three Split Pawns
Kosten - Adorjan
Esbjerg 1988
Most dangerous for the bishop are separated passed pawns which can overload the bishop when it tries to restrain them both from afar. Again critical for the defence is the proximity of the king.
    56   ♗c4

-
W

BP
32a

    Or 56 ♔f3 f4 57 ♗f1 b3-+.
The f4-pawn is taboo since the bishop cannot restrain both knight's pawns.
    56   ...   ♔d6
    57   ♔f3   f4!

-
B

    58   ♗b3   ♔e5
    59   ♗d1
    Or 59 ♗c2 ♔d4 60 ♗e4 g2.
    59   ...   ♔d4
    60   ♗c2   ♔c3
    61   ♗e4   b3
    62   ♔xf4 *(32a)*
    62   ...   ♔d4!
    A tremendous blow, paralysing White. The bishop cannot move and restrain the pawns, and the white king cannot leave the bishop. Next will follow ... g2 overloading both pieces.
          0-1

BP
33

-
W

Hübner - Zuckerman
Students ol 1969
Here White is helpless against the pawns. The king is deflected to the queenside and the black king ushers the pawns in past the bishop.
    43   ♔c3
    White has no choice. If 43 ♗c3 Black can advance his kingside pawns and bring his king in on either side. The white king cannot cope with the connected pawns and the

bishop would be completely tied to guarding the b2-square.
    43   ...   h5
    44   ♔xb3
    Compare with diag 39.
    44   ...   h4
    45   ♗a5   h3
    46   ♗c7   ♔f5
    47   ♔c2   ♔e4
    48   ♔d2   ♔f3
    49   ♔e1   ♔g2
    With ... g4-g3 to follow
          0-1

Bishop v Pawns   ♗ V ♟(♟)

Bishop v Pawns: Three United Pawns

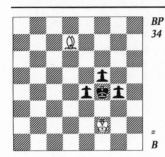

BP
34

=
B

Averbakh 1972, correcting
Cheron, Berger

    1   ...   ♔g5

After 1 ... ♔e5 2 ♗c8 the weakness of g4 forces Black to regroup to main line.

    2   ♗c6   ♔h4!
    3   ♔g2   e3

Alternatively, 3 ... g3 4 ♗d5 ♔g4 (4 ... e3 5 ♗f3 f4 6 ♗e2 ♔g5 7 ♔f3 is a drawing fortress, of type examined by Cheron and Averbakh: 7 ... ♔h4 8 ♔g2 ♔g5 9 ♔f3 ♔f5 10 ♗f1 ♔e5 11 ♗g2 ♔d4 12 ♔e2 and Black cannot invade) 5 ♗c6 ♔f4 6 ♗b7 (as Averbakh notes, White's defensive task consists largely of waiting) 6 ... ♔e3 7 ♔xg3 f4+ 8 ♔g2 f3+ 9 ♔f1=.

    4   ♗b5!

White cannot prevent ... f4 but can get into position to prevent ... f3.

    4   ...   ♔g5

After 4 ... f4 5 ♗e2 ♔g5 6 ♗d1 ♔f5 7 ♗e2 Black must play ... g3 to mount any threats, transposing into the fortress position we have already seen.

    5   ♗d3   ♔f4
    6   ♗e2

6 ♗b5 ♔e4 7 ♗d7! is also possible.

    6   ...   ♔e5
    7   ♔g3   ♔e4
    8   ♗f1   f4+
    9   ♔xg4   f3
    10   ♔g3   e2
    11   ♗xe2   fxe2
    12   ♔f2   ♔d3
    13   ♔e1   ♔e3=

A very instructive example, White's bishop managing to hinder the free movement of the pawn mass despite its apparent passivity.

BP
35

=
W

Streltsov, correcting
Averbakh 1962

    1   ♗b5   f3

Or 1 ... h3 2 ♗d7 h2+ 3 ♔h1 f3 and:

a) 4 ♗xg4? ♔xg4 5 ♔xh2 ♔f4 6 ♔g1 ♔e3+-;

b) 4 ♗c6? ♔f2 5 ♗b7 ♔e1! (5 ... g3? 6 ♗xf3) 6 ♗a6 (6 ♔xh2 ♔f2! or 6 ♗c6 f2 7 ♗b5 f1♕+ 8 ♗xf1 ♔xf1 9 ♔xh2 ♔f2 10 ♔h1 ♔g3 11 ♔g1 ♔h3 12 ♔h1 g3 13 ♔g1 g2) g3 7 ♗b7 g2+ 8 ♔xh2 ♔f2;

c) 4 ♗c8! f2 5 ♗a6.

    2   ♗d7   ♔f4
    3   ♗e6   g3

Or 3 ... h3 4 ♗d7 ♔g3 5 ♗e6 f2+ (or 5 ... h2+ 6 ♔h1 f2 7 ♗c4=. White is only sur-

viving this ending due the fact that one of Black's pawns is a rook's pawn, and the corner affords extra stalemate defences. Even with the pawn on g3 White can shuttle with the bishop - even ... ♔xf1 is stalemate) 6 ♔f1 h2 7 ♗d5=.

    4   ♗d7

4 ♗h3! is most accurate - see the main line.

    4   ...   ♔e3
    5   ♗e6   ♔e2
    6   ♗h3!

Streltsov. 6 ♗g4 g2 7 ♗h5 h3 8 ♗g4 h2+ 9 ♔xh2 ♔f2 winning was Averbakh's original solution.

    6   ...   ♔e1
    7   ♗f1   f2+
    8   ♔h1!=

Bishop v Bishop (Same)

♗ **v** ♗

Bishop and One Pawn v Bishop

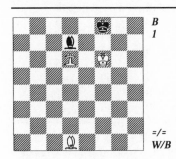

B 1

=/=
W/B

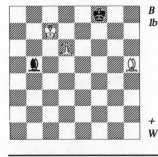

B 1a

=
W

B 1b

+
W

Averbakh
A basic position.

    1   ♗h5

Black to move draws with ... ♚e8-d8. Such a position with the weaker king in front of the pawn and "invulnerable to checks" is a basic drawing position.

    1   ...   ♗h3

1 ... ♗b5, 1 ... ♗c6, or 1 ... ♗a4 are safe. After 1 ... ♗h3 White has two tries:

A.

    2   ♚e5   ♗d7?

Passive defence loses. Instead 2 ... ♚g7! 3 ♚d5 ♚f6 4 ♚c6 ♚e5 5 ♚c7 ♚d4 6 ♗e8 ♚c5 reaches another basic drawing position - where the defending king cannot occupy the square in front but *can prevent* interception of his bishop's diagonal *(1a)*: 7 ♗d7

♗f1 8 ♗c6 ♗h3=.

    3   ♚d5   ♗a4
    4   ♚c5   ♗d7
    5   ♚b6   ♗a4

Or 5 ... ♗f5 6 ♚c7 ♗h3 7 ♗f3 and ♗b7-c8, clearing the advance of the d6-pawn.

    6   ♚c7   ♗b5 *(1b)*

A basic winning position: "Where the weaker side cannot sustain his king on an unassailable square in front of the pawn nor coordinate his king and bishop against a pawn advance" (Averbakh).

    7   ♗f3

And ♗c6 winning.

B.

    2   ♗g6   ♗d7!

Not 2 ... ♗g4? 3 ♗f5 ♗xf5 4 ♚xf5 ♚f7 5 ♚e5 ♚e8 6 ♚e6 ♚d8 7 d7.

    3   ♗f5   ♚e8!
with a draw

B 2

Centurini's Rule - kings in vertical opposition
A basic drawing position. This is also an illustration of the drawing zone for fighting passed pawns when the kings are in vertical opposition. This rule was observed by Centurini and can be diagrammed as in diag 2.

    1   ♗g4   ♗a4

Here the black bishop has two diagonals, and there is no diagonal of three squares or less, so he holds. (Note that a pawn on b6 or c7 would win since Black has one such diagonal then.) Centurini also observed two exceptions to the rule - diags 5 and 6.

Bishop v Bishop (Same)

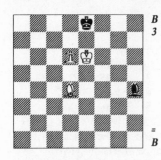

B
3

=
B

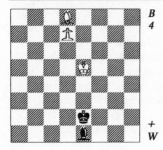

B
4

+
W

Averbakh 1954

1 ... ♗f8!

From examining Centurini's rule it is easy to deduce that centre pawns pose the least danger since they afford the longest diagonals for defence. But there is still danger:

a) 1 ... ♔d8? 2 d7;

b) 1 ... ♗d8? 2 ♗g7! ♗g5 3

Halberstadt 1939

1 ♔e4!!

We have seen the vital importance of controlling interception squares. Here we see the kings battle for this control. Although the pawn is still within the drawing zone Black is placed in zugzwang. Not 1 ♔d4? ♔f3!= or 1 ♔e6? ♔d3!= 2 ♔f7 (2 ♔d5 ♗d2!) 2 ... ♔e4 3 ♔e8 ♔f5 4 ♗b6 ♗h4 5 ♗c5 ♔e6 (mission accomplished - vertical opposition, controlling the interception square, with two long defensive diagonals within drawing zone).

1 ... ♗g3

Alternatively:

a) 1 ... ♗f2 amounts to the same as the main variation.

b) 1 ... ♗b4 and:

b1) 2 ♔d5? ♔d3= 3 ♔c6 (3 ♔e6 ♗e1! 4 ♔f7 ♔e4 5 ♔e8 ♔d5=) 3 ... ♔c4 4 ♔b7 ♔b5 5 ♔c8 ♔c6;

b2) 2 ♔d4! and:

b21) 2 ... ♗e1 3 ♔c5 ♔d3 (3 ... ♗f2+ 4 ♔c6 ♗e1 5 ♔b7 also as in main line) 4 ♔b6! transposing to the main line;

b22) 2 ... ♔f3 3 ♔c4 ♗e1 4 ♔b5 ♗g3 and:

b221) 5 ♔c6?! ♗e1 6 ♔b6! also wins, though less efficiently, but not 6 ♔b7? ♔e4 7 ♔c8 ♔d5 8 ♗g5 ♗a5 9 ♗f4 ♔c6=;

b222) 5 ♔b6!. Again this

d7+ ♔d8 4 ♗d4 ♔c7 5 ♗c5 ♗d8 6 ♗e7.

2	d7	♗d8
3	♗f6	♗a5
4	♗h4	♗b6
5	♔d6	♔f7
6	♔c6	♗a5
7	♔b7	♔e6
8	♔c8	♔d5
9	♗g3	♔c6=

move. Cheron notes that 5 ... ♗f2+ 6 ♔b7 ♗e1 and wins as in main line.

c) 1 ... ♗c3 (or 1 ... ♗d2) 2 ♔f5! (following the same routine on the other flank. White wins a tempo by threatening to move the ♗d8 to b6/c7) 2 ... ♗e1 (2 ... ♔b4 3 ♔c7 ♗e7 4 ♔e6 and White wins the necessary second tempo, with ♔e8, ♗d6-e7 to follow) 3 ♔g5! (again this motif - Black must waste a move to secure a square on the d8-h4 diagonal for the bishop) 3 ... ♗d2+ 4 ♔g6 ♗e1 5 ♔f7 ♔f3 6 ♔e8 ♔e4 7 ♗c7 ♗h4 8 ♗d6 and wins.

d) 1 ... ♔f1 and now:

d1) 2 ♔f5? ♔g2!= 3 ♔e4!? ♔h3 4 ♔f3 ♗d2! 5 ♔e2 ♗b4 6 ♔d3 ♔g4 7 ♔c4 ♗f5! 8 ♗b6 ♗e7 9 ♔d5 ♗g5 10 ♔d6 ♔e4 (or 10 ... ♗h4 11 ♔c7 ♔e6 12 ♔c8 ♔d5 13 ♗d8 ♗e1 14 ♗g5 ♗a5 15 ♗f4 ♔c6);

d2) 2 ♔d5! ♔e2 3 ♔c6 ♔d3 4 ♔b6!.

e) 1 ... ♔d1 and now:

e1) 2 ♔d5 ♔c2! and:

e11) 3 ♔c6 ♔b3 4 ♔b5 (4 ♔b7 ♗a4) 4 ... ♗g3;

e12) 3 ♔c4;

e2) 2 ♔f5! ♔e2 3 ♔g5! and again Black will have to invest a decisive tempo to get a square on the d8-h4 diagonal.

2 ♔d5!

Heading for c8.

```
2   ...      ♔d3
3   ♚c6
```

Winning a tempo since White threatens to play the ♗d8 along the h4-diagonal promoting the pawn.

```
3   ...      ♗e1
4   ♚b6      ♗f2+
5   ♚b7!
```

Gaining another tempo - not 5 ♚c7? ♔c4! 6 ♗g5 ♔b5! 7 ♚c8 (7 d8♕ ♗b6+ draws) 7 ... ♗b6 8 ♗f4 ♚c6=.

```
5   ...      ♗e1
```
Or 5 ... ♚c4 6 ♗e7.
```
6   ♚c8      ♗c4
7   ♗e7      ♗a5
8   ♗d6      ♚b5
9   ♗c7 and wins
```

The black king is a move too late. The paths of the kings are essential to understanding the fine points of bishop and pawns v bishop (see also diag 10). This is one of the most completely instructive positions.

B
5

=
W

Centurini 1856

This is the first exception to Centurini's rule (see diag 2). With his king on ♚g8 or g6 White would win easily with 1 ♗f8 to force the defending bishop to the h6-f8 diagonal. Then bishop to the a1-h8 diagonal when the black bishop is on h6. But with the white king on e8 the crossing of the

drawing zone does not help.

```
1   ♗f8      ♗e5
2   ♗c5      ♗g7
3   ♗e3      ♚d6
```

Here Black cannot be zugzwanged off the short diagonal since the white king is not participating.

```
4   ♗d4      ♗h6
    and draws
```

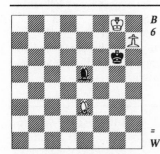

B
6

=
W

Centurini 1856

This is the second exception to Centurini's rule. Although the pawn on h7 has crossed the drawing zone and Black

has one diagonal it is still a draw.

```
1   ♗d2      ♗d4=
```

White cannot challenge the diagonal.

B
7

=
W

Averbakh 1954

```
1   ♗d2      ♚f8!
```

Black rushes to block the pawn. Averbakh uses this position to illustrate another type of defensive position - where White's interception of the vital diagonals leads to drawn pawn endings.

```
2   ♗g5      ♚g8
3   ♗f6      ♗f2
4   ♗c3      ♗h4
5   ♗d2      ♗e7
6   ♗g5      ♗xg5
```

Otherwise the pawn crosses the zone.

```
7   ♚xg5     ♚g7=
```

B 8

+ W

Horwitz 1880

1 Bg8+!

Or 1 Kf4 Bh6 2 Ke5 Bg5 3 Ke6 Kf4 4 Ke7 Ke5=.

1 ... Kh8!

Not 1 ... Kxg8 2 Bxg6+-.

2 Be6 Be8

Alternatively:

a) 2 ... Kh7 3 Bf5;

b) 2 ... Bd3 3 Kf4 Bb5 4 Ke5 Kh7 5 Kd6 and now:

b1) 5 ... Be8 6 Ke7 and:

b11) 6 ... Kg6 7 Bd7! Bf7 (7 ... Bxd7 8 f7) 8 Bf5+;

b12) 6 ... Bh5 7 Bf7 Be2 8 Be8 Bc4 9 Bd7 and Be6;

b2) 5 ... Kg6 6 f7 Kg7 7

Ke7.

3 Kf5

Or 3 Kh6 Bg6!.

3 ... Bh7

4 Bd5 Kh6

Also losing for Black are 4 ... Bd7+ 5 Ke5 Kg6 6 f7 Kg7 7 Kd6 and Ke7 or 4 ... Bh5 5 Ke6 Kg6 6 Ke7 Kf5 7 Bf7 Be2 8 Be6+.

5 Be6 Kg5

6 Ke7 Bh5

7 Bf7 Be2

8 Be8 Bc4

9 Bd7

And Be6 winning.

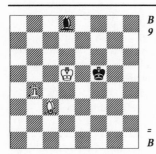

B 9

= B

Capablanca - Janowsky
New York 1916

This is the final position in which Janowsky resigned. However, Averbakh was subsequently able to demonstrate a draw by an ingenious pursuit of the standard drawing position:

1 ... Kf4

2 Bd4

Straightforward is 2 Be5+ Ke3 3 b5 Kd3 4 Kc6 Kc4=.

2 ... Kf3!!

3 b5

Or 3 Bc5 Ke2! 4 Kc6 Kd3 5 Kd7 Bg5 6 b5 Kc4=.

3 ... Ke2!

4 Kc6 Kd3

5 Bb6 Bg5

6 Kb7!

If 6 Bc7 Be3 7 Kd6 Kc4=.

6 ... Kc4

7 Ka6 Kb3!

8 Bf2 Bd8

9 Be1 Ka4!

And Black has managed to arrange the familiar defensive position.

B 10

+ W

Averbakh 1954

The small difference of the bishop on d2 rather than c3 (see diag 9) proves decisive since the black king must travel further to reach vertical opposition.

1 ... Kg4

2 b5 Kf3

3 Kc6 Ke4

Black would like to regain time lost by having to trek round the f4-square but if 3 ...

Ke2 4 Bf4! (4 Bb4? Kd3 5 Bd6 Kc4=) 4 ... Kd3 5 Bc7.

4 Kb7!! Kd3

5 Be1!

The bishop is aiming for a5.

5 ... Kc4

6 Ka6 Kb3

Now the king is one move late reaching a4.

7 Ba5 Bf6

8 b6 and wins

Now we reach diag 15.

Bishop v Bishop (Same)

B
11

+
W

Grigoriev

1 ♗d5

Not 1 ♔d4? ♔g5 2 ♗d5 ♔f6 3 ♗c4 ♗g4! 4 ♔c5 ♔e7 5 ♗a6 (5 b5 ♔d8 6 ♔b6 ♗d7 and ... ♗xb5) 5 ... ♗f3 6 ♔b6 ♔d8 7 ♔a7 ♗c6=.

1 ... ♔g5
2 ♗c4 ♗g4!

2 ... ♗f3 3 b5 ♔f6 4 ♗b4! ♔e7 5 ♔a5 and White achieves his main aim of b6 and ♔a7, reaching position seen in diag 14.

3 b5 ♔f6
4 b6 ♗c8

Or 4 ... ♗f3 5 ♔d4 ♔e7? (5 ... ♗b7 6 ♗d5 ♗a6 7 ♔c5 ♔e7 8 ♔c6 ♔d8 9 ♗e6 ♗c8 10 ♗c4 and the king invades.) 6 ♗d5 ♗xd5 7 ♔xd5 ♔d7 8 ♔c5 ♔d8 9 ♔d6+-.

5 ♔d4 ♔e7
6 ♔c5 ♔d7

Not 6 ... ♗b7 7 ♗d5 ♗c8 8 ♔c6+- (compare with diag 15) or 6 ... ♔d8 7 ♔d6 ♗b7 8 ♗e6 (see diag 14).

7 ♗b5+!

Not 7 ♗f1 ♗b7! 8 ♗h3+ ♔e7= or 7 ♗d5 ♗a6= and the black king reaches b8.

7 ... ♔d8
8 ♔c6!

Not 8 ♔d6 ♗b7 9 ♗d7 ♗f3 10 ♗e6 ♗b7! (see diag 13).

8 ... ♗d7+
9 ♔d6

Cheron stops here with the assessment +-.

9 ... ♗c8

9 ... ♗g4!? is not mentioned in other literature. The idea is 10 b7 ♗c8, but 11 b8♗! wins, e.g. 11 ... ♗b7 (11 ... ♗g4 12 ♗c7+ ♔c8 13 ♗a6 mate) 12 ♗c7+ ♔c8 13 ♗d7 mate.

10 ♗c4

10 ♗c6! ♗f5 11 b7 ♗c8! draws since the ♗c6 is not well placed after 12 b8♗.

10 ... ♗b7
11 ♗e6!

Reaching the winning position of diag 14.

B
12

+
W

Averbakh

Another basic winning position as the white pawn has crossed the drawing zone. Here the defending king supports the bishop but Black lacks adequate manoeuvring space along the diagonal, resulting in zugzwang.

1 ♗g4 ♔b5
2 ♗e2+ and wins

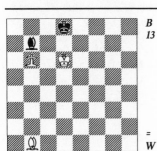

B
13

=
W

Dehler 1922

1 ♗f5

To prevent 1 ... ♔c8.

1 ... ♗f3
2 ♗e6 ♗b7!

The only move - Black must be ready to draw the pawn ending. This is a key position of mutual zugzwang. See diag 14 for the solution with Black to move here.

3 ♔c5

Or 3 ♗d5 ♔c8!.

3 ... ♗f3
4 ♗d5 ♗e2
5 ♗b7 ♔d7=

Black is saved by his king's proximity to the front of the pawn.

Bishop v Bishop (Same) ♗ V ♗

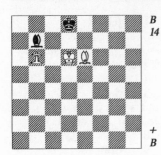

B 14

+
B

Dehler/Cheron 1922

This is identical to the position after Black's second move in diag 13 except that here it is Black to move.

| 1 | ... | ♗a6 |

A better try than 1 ... ♗f3?! 2 ♗d5 ♗xd5 3 ♔xd5 ♔d7 4 ♔c5 ♔d8 5 ♔d6 ♔c8 6 ♔c6 ♔b8 7 b7 ♔a7 8 ♔c7, or 1 ... ♗c8?! 2 ♗xc8 ♔xc8 3 ♔c6, or 1 ... ♔e8?! 2 ♔c7.

| 2 | ♔c6! | ♗e2 |

Alternatively:

a) 2 ... ♔e7 3 ♗c4 ♗xc4 (3 ... ♗c8 4 ♔c7) 4 b7;

b) 2 ... ♗c8 3 ♗c4 (3 ♗xc8?? ♔xc8=) 3 ... ♗f5 4 ♗b7 and ♔a7 winning as above (but not 4 b7?? ♗e4+).

3	♔b7	♗f3+
4	♔a7	♗e4
5	♗c4	♗f3
6	♗a6	♗d5
7	♗b7	♗e6
8	♗f3	♗c8
9	♗g4 and wins	

B 15

+
W

Savon - Am. Rodriguez
Erevan 1976

| 1 | ♔f6 | |

The vital difference between this and diag 13 is that White has the long diagonal.

| 1 | ... | ♗h6 |
| 2 | ♗b4 | |

Not 2 ♗d2?? ♗xd2 3 g7 ♗c3+.

| 2 | ... | ♗f8 |
| 3 | ♗d2 | ♗c5 |

Black can no longer prevent the king's entry.

| 4 | ♔g7 | ♗d4+ |
| 5 | ♔h7 | |

Now we have a basic winning position.

5	...	♗e5
6	♗h6	♗d4
7	♗g7	♗c5
8	♗e5	♗f8
9	♗d4 and wins	

B 16

+
W

Centurini 1847

| 1 | ♗h4 | |

White needs only to play ♗a7-b8 and win, but Black's king has time to run to a6 and prevent this. White wins via zugzwang since Black's bishop is now ideally placed.

1	...	♔b5
2	♗f2	♔a6
3	♗c5!	

Not 3 ♗e3 ♔d6! 4 ♗g5 ♔b5 5 ♗d8 ♔c6 6 ♗e7 ♗h2 and ♗c5-a7 manoeuvre is prevented by the black king.

| 3 | ... | ♗g3 |
| 4 | ♗e7 | |

Threatening to intercept the diagonal at c7.

4	...	♔b5
5	♗d8	♔c6
6	♗h4!	

Taking advantage of the bishop's exposed position to gain a vital tempo.

6	...	♗h2
7	♗f2	♔b5
8	♗a7	

And White reaches a7 ahead of the black king.

8	...	♔a6
9	♗b8	♗g1
10	♗f4	♗a7
11	♗e3 and wins	

Bishop v Bishop (Same)

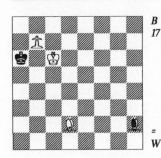

B 17

=
W

Centurini 1856

White to move:

1	♗e3	♗g3
2	♗b6	♗b8
3	♗d8	♗a7

All moves are met by ♗c7.

4 ♗c7 and wins

Black to move:

| 1 | ... | ♔a7 |
| 2 | ♗e3 | ♔b8 |

The king lodges in front of the pawn but is clearly not "invulnerable" to being shifted by checks.

3 ♗b6

Not 3 ♔b6? ♗g1!=.

| 3 | ... | ♗f4 |
| 4 | ♗d8 | ♗g3 |

5 ♔b6

Crossing safely and preparing ♗a7+.

5	...	♗f2+
6	♔a6	♗e3
7	♗h4	♗f4
8	♗f2	♔c7
9	♔a7!	

The second trip for the king, now preparing the manoeuvre ♗a7-b8.

| 9 | ... | ♔d7 |
| 10 | ♔a8 | |

Black is now helpless against ♗a7-b8.

10	...	♗e5
11	♗a7	♗f4
12	♗b8	♗e3
13	♗g3 and wins	

Bishop and Two Pawns v Bishop

B 18

=
W

Fine 1941

| 1 | ♔b2 | |

Or 1 ♔d1 ♔d3 2 b5 ♗d8 and ... ♔c4.

1	...	♗f4
2	♔a3	♗g5
3	♔a4	♗d8

4 b5 ♗b6=

White cannot profitably break the blockade. It is worth noting that even one file further up, Black cannot hold (see diag 19). He needs both the blockade and space.

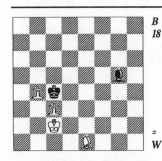

B 19

+
W

Fine 1941

1	♔b3	♗f5
2	♔a4	♗d7
3	♔a5	♗c8
4	b6	♗b7
5	♗f1	♗c8

After 5 ... ♔d6 6 ♔b5 ♗c6+

7 ♔a6 White reaches a winning knight's pawn position.

| 6 | ♗h3 | ♗b7 |
| 7 | ♗e6 and wins | |

Since ♗d5 breaks the blockade.

139

Bishop v Bishop (Same) ♗ V ♝

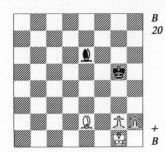

B
20

+
B

Berger 1921, Cheron 1945
With connected flank pawns problems may arise if the rook's pawn is the wrong colour.

  1 ... ♗h3

Illustrating White's difficulty - avoiding the bishop and wrong rook's pawn draw.

  2 g3 ♔f6

Pointed out by Cheron. Black tries to restrain the advance of the white king rather than wedge in between the pawns. Berger analyses 2 ... ♔h6 3 ♗f1 ♗g4 4 h4 ♗f5 5 ♔f2 ♗g4 6 ♔e3 ♗e6 7 ♔f4 ♗d7 8 ♗d3 ♗h3 9 ♗f5 ♗f1 10 g4 ♗e2 11 g5+ ♔h5 (11 ... ♔g7 12 ♗g4 and h5) 12 ♔g3 (12 g6? ♔h6 13 ♔e5 ♗h5=) 12 ... ♗d1 13 ♗e4 ♗b3 14 ♗f3+ ♔g6 15 ♔f4 and White achieves h5-h6 and wins as in the main line: 15 ... ♗f7 16 h5+ ♔g7 17 h6+ ♔h8 18 ♗f5 ♗e8 19 ♔f6 ♔g8 20 ♗d5+ ♔h8 21 ♗f7.

  3 ♗f1 ♗e6
  4 ♔f2 ♔e5

Or 4 ... ♔g5 5 h4+ ♔g4 6 ♗e2+ ♔h3 (retreating will transpose to the main line) 7 h5 ♗f5 8 h6 ♗g6 9 ♔f3 and wins easily.

  5 ♔e3 ♗d7
  6 h4 ♗g4
  7 ♗e2 ♗e6
  8 ♗d3!

Taking f5 from the black king. White must avoid 8 h5? (Berger) 8 ... ♔f5! and the win is gone:

a) 9 ♔d4 ♗f7 10 ♗d1 (10 ♔c5 ♔g5=) 10 ... ♗e8 11 ♔d5 ♗f7+ 12 ♔d6 ♗f6 13 g4 (13 ♔d7 ♔g5 or 13 ♗e2 ♗e8) 13 ... ♔g5 14 ♗e7 ♗xh5 15 gxh5 ♔h6=;

b) 9 ♗d3+ ♔g5! (9 ... ♔g4?

10 h6 ♗g8 11 ♔f2 ♔g5 12 h7+-) 10 ♗g6 ♗g4=;

c) 9 g4+ ♔g5 and ... ♗f7xh5!=.

  8 ... ♗f7

Alternatively, 8 ... ♗g4 9 ♗g6 ♗d1 (9 ... ♔f6 10 ♔f4) 10 h5 ♔f6 (Black must prevent h6) 11 ♔f4 ♗e2 12 ♗e8 ♔g7 (12 ... ♔e7 13 h6 ♔f6 14 g4! ♗xg4 15 ♔xg4 and the black king does not reach the corner +-) 13 ♔g5 ♗d3 14 ♗g6 ♗e2 15 h6+ ♔g8 16 ♔f4 ♗d1 17 ♗e4 ♗e2 18 ♗f3 ♗b5 19 g4 ♗h7 20 g5 and wins.

  9 g4 ♗e6
  10 g5 ♗f7

Or 10 ... ♗g4 11 ♗g6 and h5-h6.

  11 ♔f3 ♗h5+
  12 ♔g3

Zugzwang.

  12 ... ♔d4

After 12 ... ♗e8 (or 12 ... ♗d1 13 ♗g6) 13 ♔g4 ♗d7+ 14 ♔h5 White wins easily - he controls the corner.

  13 ♗b1 ♔e5
  14 ♗c2 ♔e6
  15 ♔f4 ♔f7
  16 ♗f5 ♗d1
  17 ♗g4 ♗c2
  18 h5 ♗d3
  19 ♗f5 ♗e2
  20 h6 ♗h5
  21 ♔e5 ♔f8
  22 ♔f6 ♔g8
  23 ♗e6+ ♔h8
  24 ♗f7 and wins

The end of a difficult process. Black had to keep the white king out of h5 or advancing in the centre, as well as preventing h4-h5-h6 or g3-g4-g5. By combining threats White was able to invade and advance his pawns while avoiding ♗xg5.

140

Bishop v Bishop (Same)

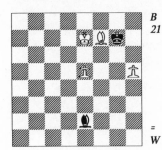

B
21
=
W

Goglidze - Kasparian
USSR 1929
(Analysis by Averbakh)
When the pawns are split wrong rook's pawns still present technical difficulties.

   1   ♗e8

Not 1 e6? ♗g4 and Black reaches a drawn bishop and rook's pawn position.

   1   ...   ♗g4
   2   ♔d8

Or 2 ♔d6 ♔h6 3 ♗d7 ♗xh5 4 e6 ♔g7 5 e7 ♔f6=.

   2   ...   ♔h6

Averbakh's 2 ... ♗e6 is also possible: 3 ♗d7 ♗f7 4 ♔e7 ♗c4 5 ♔d6 ♗b3 6 ♗c6 ♗f7 7 ♗d5 ♗xh5! 8 e6 ♔f6 9 e7 ♗e8=.

   3   ♗d7   ♗xh5
   4   e6   ♔g7
   5   e7   ♔f6

Not 5 ... ♗g6? 6 ♗e8 ♗e4 7 ♗h5 ♗c6 8 ♗g4 and wins.

   6   ♗e8   ♗e2
   7   ♗g6   ♗b5=

This position is Horwitz and Kling (1851). White can try ...

   8   ♗e8   ♗e2!

The only move! The danger is seen after 8 ... ♗d3? 9 ♗h5 ♗b5 10 ♗g4 and White reaches this diagonal too soon for Black to defend.

   9   ♗f7   ♗b5
  10   ♗h5   ♔e5
  11   ♗g4   ♔d6=

A well-known basic draw.

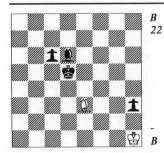

B
22
-
B

Sokolsky - Lipnitsky
USSR 1950
(Analysis by Averbakh)
In this example Black is able to use the h-pawn as a diversionary tactic to reach a won bishop and one pawn position.

   1   ...   ♗e5
   2   ♗b6   ♗d4
   3   ♗a5   c5
   4   ♔h2   c4
   5   ♔xh3   ♔e4
   6   ♔g2

Or 6 ♔g4 ♔d3 7 ♔f5 ♗e3 8 ♔e6 ♗d2 and White's king does not arrive in time.

   6   ...   ♔d3
   7   ♔f1   ♗c3
   8   ♗d8   ♗b4
   9   ♗f6   ♔c2!

The king heads for the ideal b1-square. White is helpless once the pawn crosses c3, and

this cannot be prevented.

  10   ♔e2   ♔b3!

Black intends to interrupt the enemy bishop on b2 but first maximises his position by getting out of the way of his pawn. The white king cannot reach c1.

  11   ♗e5   ♗a3
  12   ♗f6   ♗b2
  13   ♗g5   c3
  14   ♗h6   c2
  15   ♔d3   ♗a3
  16   ♗g5   ♔b2
  17   ♔c4   ♔b1
  18   ♔b3

The vertical opposition does not help as the b-pawn has crossed the drawing zone.

  18   ...   ♗c1
  19   ♗f6   ♗h6
  20   ♗b2   ♗f8
         0-1

Bishop v Bishop (Same)

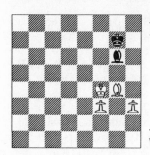

B
23
+
W

Fischer - Keres
Zürich 1959
This is a good example of exploiting a split two-pawn advantage.

67	♔g5	♗d3
68	f4	♗e4
69	h4	♗d3
70	h5	♗e4
71	h6+	♔h8
72	♗f5	♗d5
73	♗g6	♗e6
74	♔f6	

A probe. 74 ♗h5 is more direct.

74	...	♗c4

After 74 ... ♗d7 White can still regroup with ♔g5/♗g4 as in the game.

75	♔g5	♗e6
76	♗h5	♔h7
77	♗g4	♗c4
78	f5	♗f7
79	♗h5	♗c4
80	♗g6+	♔g8
81	f6	

Black resigned. He is helpless against 81 ... ♗b3 82 ♔f4 ♗c4 83 ♔e5 ♗b3 84 ♔d6 ♗c4 85 ♔e7 ♗b3 86 ♗f5.

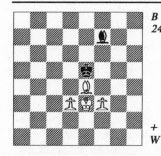

B
24
+
W

Fine 1941
A more straightforward conversion of the two pawn advantage.

1	f4+	♔d6
2	f5	♔e5
3	d4+	♔f6
4	♔f4	♗b3
5	♗c6	♗c2
6	♗d7	♗b3
7	♔e4	♗c4

8	d5	♗b3
9	♗e6	♗c4
10	♔d4	♗e2

Or 10 ... ♗a2 11 ♔c5 and d6.

11	d6	♗b5
12	d7	♔e7
13	f6+	♔d8
14	f7	♔e7
15	f8♛+	♔xf8
16	d8♛+ and wins	

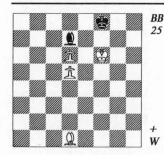

BB
25
+
W

Averbakh 1954
An instructive example with doubled pawns.

1	♗h5	♗h3

Or 1 ... ♗b5 2 ♔e6 ♗e8 3 d7.

2	♗f7	♗d7
3	♗g6!	

Not 3 ♗e6? ♔e8!.

3	...	♗b5

Or 3 ... ♗g4 4 ♗f5+-.

4	♔e6	

And d7 will win the bishop. Basically, *unless Black's king can securely block the pawns*, the first pawn will win the bishop and the remaining pawn will win the game.

Bishop v Bishop (Same)

Bishop and Three Pawns v Bishop and Two Pawns

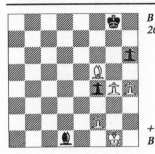

B
26

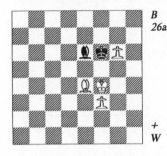

B
26a

Tukmakov - Timoshchenko
USSR 1968

| | 45 | ... | ♔g7 |
| | 46 | g5! | |

Creating a barrier around the f4-pawn. White's winning chances are based on this pawn's frailty.

46	...	hxg5
47	hxg5	♗h5
48	♔g2	♗g6
49	♗g4	♗e4+
50	♔h3	♔g6
51	♔h4	♗c6
52	♗d1	♗d7

Or 52 ... f3 53 ♔g4 ♗d7+ 54 ♔f4 ♗c6 55 ♗xf3 ♗xf3 56 ♔xf3 ♔f5 57 ♔e3 ♔xg5 58 ♔e4+-.

53	♗c2+	♔g7
54	♗e4	♗e6
55	♔h5	♗d7
56	f3	♗h3
57	g6	♗d7
58	♔g5	♗e6

Or 58 ... ♗b5 59 ♔xf4 ♔f6 60 ♔g4+-.

| 59 | ♔xf4 | ♔f6 (26a) |

White has been able to surround the f4-pawn, but at the cost of poorly placed pawns, advanced against Philidor's rule (they should go forward in tandem, on the black squares, to complement the white bishop). This does not save Black here.

| 60 | ♔g3 | |

Compare with diags 18 and 19. The black king cannot maintain the blockade of the pawn and keep the white king out.

| 60 | ... | ♔g5 |
| 61 | f4+ | ♔h5 |

After 61 ... ♔h6 62 f5 ♗c4 63 f6+-, or 61 ... ♔f6 62 ♔h4 and White will either achieve ♔h6 or ♔h7 when the g-pawn alone wins, or if ... ♔g7 then ♔g5 guarantees the smooth advance of the pawns. If the black bishop were on c4 instead of e6, he could reply ... ♗e2, but he needs to guard g4 against ♔g4-h5.

62	f5	♗b3
63	f6	♔h6
64	♔f4 and wins	

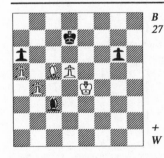

B
27

+
W

Larsen - Stein
Belgrade 1970

| | 61 | b5! | |

"In this position White's passed pawns supported by the bishop completely block Black's forces, so that White's king manages to remove from the board both of Black's pawns" (Larsen).

| 61 | ... | axb5 |
| 62 | a6 | |

Remarkably, this position might have been considered under bishop and two pawns against bishop. Even the wrong h-pawn (and two black pawns) cannot prevent White from winning!

| 62 | ... | ♔c8 |
| 63 | d6 | ♔b8 |

The difference between this ending and diag 21 is that the pawns have reached the sixth rank. The h-pawn and bishop form a barrier around the black king, allowing White to win with the d-pawn. The irrelevance of the rest of the board becomes clear as Black

Bishop v Bishop (Same)

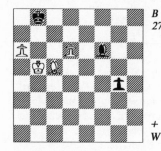

B
27a

B
27b

+
W

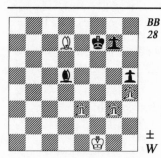

+
W

can only watch help-
lessly (63 ... b4 would be met
by 64 d7+).

    64   ♔d5   ♗f6

Or 64 ... b4 65 ♔c4
(Larsen) 65 ... g5 66 ♗xb4
♗xb4 67 ♔xb4 g4 68 d7 ♔c7
69 a7.

    65   ♔c6   g5
    66   ♔xb5   g4 (27a)
    67   ♔c4   ♔a8

Or 67 ... g3 68 ♔d3 g2 69
♔e2 ♗e5 70 d7 ♗f6 71 ♔f2.

    68   ♔d3   ♗e5
    69   d7   ♗c7
    70   ♔e4   g3

    71   ♔f3   ♗d8

Or 71 ... ♔b8 72 ♗d6.

    72   ♔xg3   ♗a5 (27b)
    73   ♔g4   ♗d8
    74   ♔f5   ♗a5
    75   ♔e6   ♗c7
    76   ♔f7   ♗a5
    77   ♔e8   ♗c7
    78   ♗e7   ♗a5
    79   ♗d8   ♗d2
    80   ♗b6   ♗g5
    81   ♗c5   1-0

The a-pawn carried its
weight by keeping the black
king totally occupied.

BB
28

Dizdarevic - Short
Germany 1988
    1   ♔e2   ♔f6?

Better was 1 ... ♗e4! 2 ♔d2
♔f6 3 ♔c3 ♔e5! 4 ♗e8 ♗f3 5
♔d3±.

    2   ♗e8!   g6
    3   ♔d3   ♔f5
    4   ♔d4+-   ♗e6
    5   e4+   ♔f6

Or 5 ... ♔g4 6 ♔e5 ♗f5 (6
... ♗b3 7 ♔f6 ♔xg3 8 ♔g5+-)
7 exf5 gxf5 8 ♔f6 ♔xg3 9
♔g5+-.

    6   ♔c5

In the game Dizdarevic -
Short, White blundered with 6
♔e3?? (time-trouble) 6 ... g5 7
♗xh5 gxh4 8 gxh4 ♗f5! ½-½.

    6   ...   ♔e5
    7   ♗xg6   ♗g4

Or 7 ... ♗g8 8 ♗xh5 ♔xe4 9
♔d6 ♔f5 10 ♔e7 winning.

    8   ♔c4   ♔f6

The alternative is also unpleasant: 8 ... ♗e2+ 9 ♔c3
♗b5 10 ♔d2 ♔d4 11 ♗e1
♔e3 12 ♗xh5 ♔xe4 13 ♔f2+-

e.g. 13 ... ♗d7 (13 ... ♔f5 14
♔e3 ♔e5 15 ♔f3) 14 ♗g6+
♔e5 15 ♔f3 ♗c8 16 ♗c2 ♗d7
17 h5! ♗e6 18 g4 ♔f6 19 h6
etc.

    9   ♗e8   ♔e5
    10   ♔d3   ♗f3
    11   ♔e3

Or even 11 ♗g6 ♗g4 12
♔e3 ♔f6 13 ♗e8 ♔e5 etc. as
in the main line.

    11   ...   ♗g4

Not 11 ... ♗xe4 12 ♗xh5+-.

    12   ♗f7!   ♔f6

Alternatively, 12 ... ♗d1 13
♗g6 ♗g4 14 ♗e8.

    13   ♗c4   ♔e5
    14   ♗b3   ♗d7
    15   ♗f7   ♗g4
    16   ♗e8   ♗d1
    17   ♗d7   ♗b3
    18   ♗f5   ♗d1

Or 18 ... ♗f7 19 ♔f3 ♗b3 20
g4 ♗c2 21 g5+-.

    19   g4!   hxg4
    20   h5   ♗c2
    21   h6   ♔f6
    22   e5+! and wins

±
W

Bishop v Bishop (Opposite)

Bishop and Two Pawns v Bishop

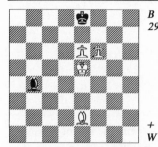

B
29

+
W

Tarrasch 1921
> 1 &b5+ &f8
> 2 &d5

And White wins by &d7 and e7+. The &b4 must stay on its present diagonal pre

venting e7+. Ideally the bishop should attack the f6-pawn *and* prevent e7. This is only possible from d8, and after &f5 the bishop on d8 is driven away by zugzwang.

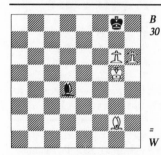

B
30

=
W

Salvioli 1887
> 1 &d5+ &f8!=

Note that with the bishops controlling different coloured squares (i.e. white bishop on f2/black bishop on d5), White

would win by posting the bishop on the long diagonal and playing h7. The control over the corner *nearest* the pawns is an important consideration.

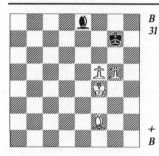

B
31

+
B

Tarrasch 1921
> 1 ... &h5
> 2 &d4+ &h7

Or 2 ... &f7 3 &c3 zugzwang - 4 g6 is achieved next move. Between this zugzwang motif and the idea

of &f6 Black is helpless.
> 3 &e5 &g7
> 4 &e6+ &h7
> 5 &f6 and wins

The pawns must go through.

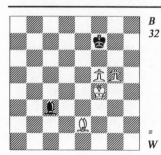

B
32

=
W

Henneberger 1916
> 1 &g4

Alternatively, 1 &h5+ &e7! 2 &g6 &b2 3 &g4 &c3 4 &h5 &g7! (preventing the king's entry) 5 &h7 &f7! and White's king is rebuffed.
> 1 ... &b2
> 2 &h5 &g7!

Not 2 ... &g7? 3 &c4+ &e7 4 &g6+- or 2 ... &c3 3 &h6! &g7+ 4 &h7 followed by bishop check and &g6.

> 3 &b5 &c3
> 4 &e8 &b2
> 5 &g6 &c3
> 6 &g4

White seems to have achieved his aim. Now the threat is &h5 followed by walking the king to e6 to finally force through f6.
> 6 ... &a5!

This must be now while the loose bishop disallows f6+.
> 7 &h5 &d8!=

145

Bishop v Bishop (Opposite) ♗ V ♝

B
32a

=
W

With a familiar drawing position (32a). The bishop hits one pawn and prevents the advance of the other (Berger/ Averbakh). A critical ending that fully illustrates the ideas for both sides.

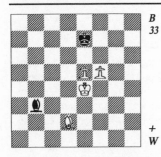

B
33

+
W

Henneberger 1916

　1　　　　♗g5+!

　Not 1 ♗b4+ ♔f7! 2 ♔d4 ♗c2 3 e6+ ♔f6=. The text move prevents 1 ... ♔f6.

　1　　　...　　　♔d7

　Or 1 ... ♔f7 2 ♔d4 ♗a2 3 ♔c5 ♗b3 (3 ... ♗b1 4 e6+ ♔e8 5 f6 ♗g6 6 ♔h6 ♗h5 7 ♔d6 ♗g6 8 ♔e5 ♗h5 9 ♔f5)

4 ♔d6 and the pawns advance to the sixth.

　2　　♔f4　　♗a2
　3　　♗h4　　♗f7
　4　　♔g5　　♔e7
　5　　♔h6+　♔d7
　6　　♔g7　　♗c4
　7　　♔f6 and wins

Again the pawns advance safely to the sixth rank.

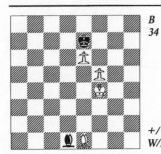

B
34

+/+
W/B

Tarrasch 1921

　1　　　...　　　♔d6

　If White were to move in the starting position he would win easily by playing ♔e5 and f6. Black prevents this.

　2　　♔g5

　Again success will depend on whether White can "bypass" round and invade with his king to successfully support the pawn advance.

　2　　　...　　　♗e2

　2 ... ♗b3 looks like a tougher defence than Tarrasch's solution, e.g. 3 ♗g3+? ♔e7 and ... ♗xe6= (Nor 3 ♗b4+ ♔e5 4 e7 ♗f7 5 ♗c3+ ♔d6 6 ♔f6 ♗h5 and ... ♔d7-e8=. But the logical 3 ♔f6! ♗d1 4 ♗g3+ wins as the king gets to either e5 or e7, guaranteeing the advance of the pawns.)

To me (JT) this method is more technical than Tarrasch's.

　3　　♗g3+

　3 ♔f6 wins simply, with a bishop check forcing white king access to e5 (or e7).

　3　　　...　　　♔d5

　Or 3 ... ♔e7 4 ♔f4 ♔d6 5 ♔e3+ and wins.

　4　　e7　　　♗b5
　5　　♔g6　　♗e8+
　6　　♔g7

Now Black loses a piece.

　6　　　...　　　♔c6
　7　　f6　　　♔d7
　8　　f7 and wins

Note that the start position would be drawn if moved two files to the right (Averbakh). Then there would be no room for the king to circle and invade (by-pass) and thus no way to progress.

Bishop v Bishop (Opposite)

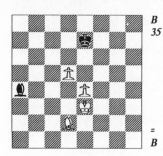

B
35

Averbakh

| | 1 | ... | ♗e8! |
| | 2 | ♗b4+ | ♔d7! |

Black aims for the drawing array of bishop attacks the pawn and cooperates to prevent advance seen before.

| | 3 | ♔d4 |

Not 3 e5 ♗f7=.

| | 3 | ... | ♗f7 |
| | 4 | ♔e5 | ♔e8 |

This move is not necessary, but demonstrates the difference between this example

=
B

and the position shifted one file to the right (see next diag). Black can also demonstrate the advantages of his extra space with 4 ... ♗g6 5 ♗a3 ♗h7 and Black has nothing to fear - this diagonal is long enough to avoid zugzwang.

	5	♔f6	♗g8
	6	♔g7	♗f7
	7	♗a3	♗h5
	8	e5	♗f3
	9	d6	♗g4
	10	♔f6	♔d7=

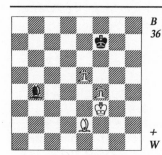

B
36

Tarrasch 1921

	1	...	♗f8
	2	♗c4+	♔e7
	3	♔e4

3 f5? ♗g7!= is a draw.

	3	...	♗g7
	4	♔f5	♗h6
	5	♔g4!

Zugzwang.

| | 5 | ... | ♗f8 |

In the previous example Black could maintain bishop pressure against the back

+
W

pawn but here he is driven back.

| | 6 | ♔g5 | ♗g7 |
| | 7 | ♔g6 | ♔f8 |

Alternatively, 7 ... ♗f8 8 f5 or 7 ... ♗h8 8 ♔h7.

| | 8 | ♔h7 and wins |

A final reminder of Black's restricted space - now there is one less square on the short diagonal (in the previous example ... ♗h5 was possible) - this is a fatal difference.

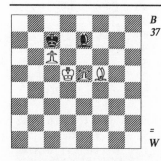

B
37

Salvioli 1887

	1	♔e6	♗b4
	2	♗e4	♔d8
	3	♔f7	♗a3
	4	e6	♗b4=

White cannot make pro

=
W

gress. The king on d8 stops both pawns. The ability for the king to act against both pawns is the determining factor for a successful defence.

B
38

Salvioli 1887

	1	♗f3	♔d8
	2	♔e6	♗b4
	3	f6	♗c5
	4	f7	

Or 4 ♔f7 ♗b4 5 ♔g6 ♗c5

+
W

6 f7 leading to the main line.

	4	...	♗b4
	5	♔f6	♗c3+
	6	♔g6	♗b4
	7	♔g7 and wins

Bishop v Bishop (Opposite) ♗ V ♝

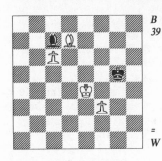

B
39

=
W

Averbakh 1950

1 ♔d5   ♚f6

"If Black can post his bishop where it simultaneously restrains both pawns while the king successfully holds off the enemy king, the game ends in a draw" (Averbakh).

2 ♔c5   ♚e7
3 ♔b5   ♚d8

4 ♔a6   ♝f4
5 ♔b7   ♝c7=

White cannot progress - he is shadowed by his counterpart, and there is no point at which the black forces cannot cooperate against the advance of one of the pawns. It is this factor which determines the outcome of the game.

B
40

=
W

Averbakh 1950

1 ♔c5   ♚e6
2 ♔b5   ♚f5
3 ♔c5   ♚e6
4 ♝b8   ♝g2

5 ♔b5   ♝b7=

The white king cannot get round thanks to the obstruction on the b-file.

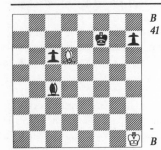

B
41

-
B

**Forintos - Taimanov
Skopje 1970**

Here is a typical example of the strength of widely separated pawns.

37 ...   ♚e6
38 ♝f8   ♚d5
39 ♔g2   c5
40 ♔f2   h5
41 ♝e7   ♝d3
42 ♔e3   c4
43 ♝h4   ♚e5
44 ♝e1   ♚f5
45 ♔f3   ♝e4+

White confronts a dilemma - the king must choose which pawn to combat; he cannot fight both.

46 ♔e3

Or 46 ♔g3 ♝d5 47 ♔h4 ♝f3 48 ♔g3 ♚e4 and ... ♝g4, ... ♚d3, escorting the c-pawn.

46 ...   ♝d5
47 ♝g3   ♚g4
48 ♝d6   h4
49 ♝e5   ♝f7
50 ♝c3   ♝g6
51 ♝e5   ♝e8
52 ♝c3   ♝b5
53 ♝d2   h3
54 ♔f2   ♝c6

0-1

After 55 ♔g1 ♚f3 56 ♔h2 ♚e2 57 ♝b4 ♝g2 the c-pawn will cost White the bishop. White could not avoid the division of his forces.

Bishop v Bishop (Opposite) ♗ V ♝

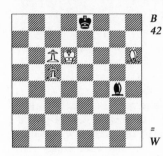

B
42

Berger 1899, Averbakh

    1   ♗g5

White cannot allow ... ♚d8 drawing easily.

    1   ...   ♗f5
    2   c7

2 ♚c7 ♗e4! 3 ♚b7 ♗f3 4 ♚b6 ♗e4 5 c7 ♚d7=.

    2   ...   ♗h3
    3   c6

Not 3 ♚c6 ♗g2+! (3 ... ♗c8? 4 ♚b6 ♚d7 5 ♗f4 ♚e6

6 ♚a7 ♚d5 (or 6 ... ♚d7 7 ♚b8 ♗a6 8 ♗d6+-) 7 ♚b8 ♗f5 8 ♗d6+-) 4 ♚b6 ♚d7=.

    3   ...   ♗c8
    4   ♚c5   ♚f7!

Passive defence loses, e.g. 4 ... ♗h3 5 ♚b6 ♗c8 6 ♚a7 and Black will have to surrender the bishop for the c7-pawn.

    5   ♚b6   ♚e6
    6   ♚a7   ♚d5
    7   ♚b8   ♗a6=

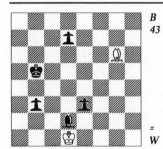

B
43

Chekhover 1950

    1   ♗e8   ♚c6
    2   ♚e2   ♗c1

The centre pawns alone do not pose a danger to White - the b-pawn is critical. Black has to worry that if advanced too quickly to b2 it will become an obstacle to its own king trying to invade on that flank.

    3   ♚d1   ♗b2
    4   ♚e2   ♗d4
    5   ♚d1   ♚d6
    6   ♗f7!

Now that ... d5 is not possi

ble, White forces the b-pawn forward.

    6   ...   b2
    7   ♗g6   ♚c5
    8   ♚e2   d5
    9   ♗f5   ♚b4
    10   ♗g6   ♚a3
    11   ♗b1

The same kind of fortress seen in diag 39.

    11   ...   ♚b3
    12   ♚d1   ♚c3
    13   ♚e2   ♗c5
    14   ♚d1   d4
    15   ♚e2   ♚b3
    16   ♚d3=

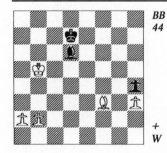

BB
44

Walther - Fischer
Zurich 1959

    54   a4?

Now Black draws according to Fischer. Instead he should play 1 b4! (Fontana) 1 ... ♚c7 55 ♚a5! ♚b8 56 b5 ♗a3 57 b6 ♚c8 58 ♚a6 ♚b8 59 ♗g2 ♚c8 60 ♚a7 ♗c5 61 a4 and a5, ♚a8 with the promotion of the b-pawn.

    54   ...   ♚c7
    55   b4   ♚b8
    56   a5

Without this move White cannot arrange to play b6.

    56   ...   ♚a7

    57   ♚c4

Black can sacrifice his bishop on b6, leaving White with the wrong rook's pawn (though he then has to worry about the "Rauzer" ending - see diags BP6-10).

    57   ...   ♗g3
    58   b5   ♗f2
    59   ♗e2   ♗e3
    60   ♚b3   ♗d2
    61   b6+   ♚b7
    62   ♚a4   ♚c6
    63   ♗b5+   ♚c5
          ½-½

64 b7 ♗f4 65 a6 ♚b6= (Fischer).

B
45

=
W

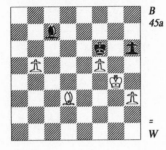

B
45a

=
W

Csom - Vaganian
Buenos Aires ol 1978
I see no reason why Csom (and "Bukic") drew this ending.

47	♘d5+	♔d6
48	♘c4	♔c5
49	♘f1	♗c7
50	h4	

This removes a king route via h5 but makes bishop and wrong rook's pawn endings more dangerous for Black. Bukic gives 50 f5!? ♔d6=. Really? He leaves much unsaid if this is true. For example, 51 ♘c4 ♗d8 52 ♘d5 (this is like a mirror of zugzwang in diag 57 - will the wrong rook's pawn save Black?) 52 ... ♔c5 53 ♔e5 ♔xb5 54 f6 ♔c5 55 f7 ♗e7 56 ♔e6 ♗f8 57 ♘f3 (57 ♘h1 ♔d4 58 ♔d7 h5 does not change the type of ending) 57 ... ♔d4 58 ♔d7 ♔e3 59 ♗g4 ♔f4 60 ♔e8 ♗b4 61 f8♕+ ♗xf8 62 ♔xf8 h5 63 ♘d7 h4 and black should be able to get his king back into the drawing zone via the e-file. (See also diags BP5-9).

Bukic also gives 50 ♔f5 ♔d4 51 ♔g4 ♔d5! 52 f5 ♔e5 53 ♘d3 ♔f6 *(45a)*=. Let us take this a little further: 54 ♗c2 ("zugzwang") 54 ... ♘d6 55 ♔f3 ♔e5 56 b6 ♘c5! 57 b7 ♘d6 58 ♔g4 ♔f6 59 ♗h5 ♘f4 60 ♘d3 ♔f7 61 ♗b1 ♔f6 62 ♗c2 ♔f7 63 ♘b3+ ♔f6 64 ♗e6 ♔g7 65 ♔g4 ♘b8 66

♔f3 ♔f6 67 ♔e4 ♔e7 68 ♘c4 ♔f6 69 ♘d3 ♔e7=. It looks as if Bukic is right here.

50	...	♘d8
51	h5	♗c7
52	f5	

Necessary to free the king from defence of the f4-pawn, though there are few invasion routes for the white king.

52	...	♔d6
53	♗h3	

Why not 53 ♘c4 here? Again this is very reminiscent of diag 50:

a) 53 ... ♘d8 54 ♘d5 ♔c5 (54 ... ♗f6 55 b6+- or 54 ... ♗b6 55 f6+-) 55 ♔e5 ♗xb5 56 f6 ♔c5 57 f7 ♗e7 58 ♔e6 ♗f8 59 ♘f3 ♔d4 60 ♔d7 and White wins since he will win the bishop for the f-pawn, and then has no difficulty winning the h-pawn whilst keeping the black king out of the corner;

b) 53 ... ♔c5 54 f6 ♔xc4 55 f7 ♘d6 56 b6+-.

53	...	♘d8
54	♗g4	♘f6
55	b6	♔c6
56	b7	♔xb7
57	♔d5	♔c7
58	♔e6	♗c3
59	f6	♔d8
60	f7	♗b4
61	♗e2	♗a3
62	♗c4	♗b4
63	♔f6	♗c3+
	½-½	

Bishop v Bishop (Opposite)

Opposite Bishops: More Pawns

B
46

+
W

Gheorghiu - Garcia
Buenos Aires 1970
An interesting duel between pawn masses. The extra pawn proves decisive.

    44   ♗b3+!

Forcing the black king to choose.

    44 ...   ♔d7

Black chooses to monitor the white pawn mass.

    45 ♔c2   e4
    46 ♗d5

In effect paralysing Black's pawns. If they advance they will become blockaded.

    46 ...   ♔c7
    47 a4   ♔b8

    48 ♔b3   ♔a7
    49 ♗e6

Forcing a blockade of the black pawns. Since White also has the advantage that his bishop controls the appropriate corner, (see also diags 36 and 51) Black has no hope of defending.

    49 ...   e3
    50 ♗c4   ♗h4
    51 ♗e2   f4
    52 ♔c4   ♗e1
    53 b5   ♗a5
    54 ♔d5   ♔b7
    55 ♔d6   ♗c7+
    56 ♔d7   1-0

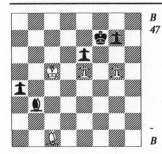

B
47

-
B

Tal - Polugaevsky
USSR Ch 1974

    1 ...   ♗c2

Also winning is 1 ... ♔g6 2 ♔d6 ♔f5 (zugzwang) 3 ♔e7 g6 4 ♔f7 ♗c2-+ (Polugaevsky) 5 ♗b2 ♗d3 (5 ... ♔xg5? 6 ♗xe6 ♔h4 7 ♔d5 g5 8 ♔c4 g4 9 ♔b4=) 6 ♔e7 ♗c4.

    2 ♔d6   ♗f5
    3 ♗a3   ♔g6
    4 ♗c1   ♔h5

4 ... ♗g4 and ... ♔f5, ... g6 wins more easily according to Polugaevsky.

    5 ♔e7   g6
    6 ♔d7   ♔g4

Or 6 ... a3 7 ♗xa3 ♔xg5-+ (Polugaevsky).

    7 ♔d6   ♔g3
    8 ♔c5   ♔f3
    9 ♔d4?!

A better try was 9 ♔c6! ♔g4 10 ♔d6 a3 11 ♗xa3 ♔xg5 12 ♗c1+ ♔h4 13 ♔c5 g5 14 ♔d4 g4 15 ♔e3 ♔g3 16 ♗d2 ♔h2-+.

    9 ...   ♔g4
           0-1

White resigned in view of ... ♗b1, ... ♔f5 when he will soon be forced to surrender a second pawn due to zugzwang.

Suetin - Matanovic
Titovo Uzice 1966

64	...	h5
65	♗c8	♗f6
66	♗d7	♗e5
67	♗e6	g4
68	fxg4	fxg4
69	hxg4	hxg4
70	♔f2	

+
B

This position is given as drawn in *Informator*. Is this really the case? It looks very much like Salvioli's split win (diag 38). Did Suetin resign, and this is an old typographical error?

Our analysis runs 70 ♔f2 g3+ 71 ♔g2 (71 ♔e2 d3+ 72 ♔f1 d2 73 ♗b3 ♔e3 74 ♗d1 ♔d3 75 ♔g2 ♔c3 76 ♔f1 ♔b2 77 ♗a4 ♔c1 78 ♔e2 ♗d4-+) 71 ... ♔e3-+.

Uhlmann - Jansson
Raach 1969

48	h4	gxh4
49	gxh4	♗e1
50	h5	♗d2

Or 50 ... ♔g5 51 ♗g6 ♗b4 52 ♔e4 ♗d6 (52 ... ♔f6 53 ♔d3 ♗f8 would still transpose into the game - JT) 53 ♔d3+-. The white king reaching c6 is decisive.

51	♗g6	♗b4

Alternatively, 51 ... ♗f4 52 ♔e4 ♗h6 53 ♗h7 (53 ♗f5 ♗f8 reaches the key position but unfortunately with White to move) 53 ... ♗g7 (53 ... ♗d2 54 ♗f5 ♗b4 55 h6 or 53 ... ♗f4 54 ♗g8 ♔e7 55 ♔f5) 54 ♗g8 ♔e7 55 ♔f5+-. These variations illustrate Black's desperation against the split pawns. He must prevent them from advancing, and he must prevent the white king from invading either flank. Also, trading the e-pawn for the h-pawn loses.

+
W

52	♔e4	♗d6 *(49a)*
53	♔d3	♗f8
54	♔c4	♔e7
55	♗e4	♔d6
56	♗f3!	

Not 56 ♔b5 ♔c7 57 ♔a6 ♗g7 58 d6+ ♔xd6 59 ♔xb6 ♗h6 60 a5 ♗e3+ 61 ♔b7 ♔e7 62 a6 ♔f7= (JT).

56	...	♗h6
57	♔d3	♔e7
58	♔e4	♔f6
59	♗g4	

Threatening d6.

59	...	♗f8
60	♗f5!	

Zugzwang - the position that White has been aiming to reach.

60	...	♔g5

Instead, 60 ... ♗h6 61 d6+- or 60 ... ♗d6 61 h6+-.

61	♔xe5	♔xh5
62	d6	

The d-pawn wins the bishop on f8.

1-0

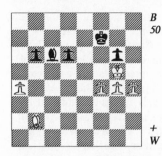

B
50

+
W

BB
51

=
B

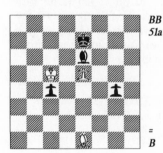

BB
51a

=
B

Korchnoi - Botvinnik
Moscow 1960

38 h5

White does not even deign to thin out the queenside with ♘d4.

38	...	gxh5
39	♔xh5	♗xa4
40	f5	♗d1
41	♔g5	b5
42	♘c3	

It is noteworthy that Black resigned here. His pawns are meaningless - they cannot even distract the bishop from the long diagonal (see also diag 3).

Ostenstad - H. Olafsson
Espoo Zt 1989

46	...	♔f3!
47	♔xa4	♔g2
48	e4!	

This pawn is White's hope for a draw - it must be used later to distract the black bishop. Not 48 ♗f6? ♔xh2 49 ♗h4 c3 50 ♔a3 ♔h3 51 e4 ♗e6 52 e5 ♔g2-+ (zugzwang!).

| 48 | ... | ♗g8 |

Or 48 ... ♗xe4 49 ♔b4 ♗d3 50 ♗f6 ♔xh2 51 ♗h4 ♔g2 52 ♔c3 ♔f2 53 ♔d2=.

| 49 | ♔b4 | ♔xh2 |
| 50 | ♗e1 | ♔g2 |

Not 50 ... h4?? 51 gxh4 g3 52 h5 g2 53 ♗f2 g1♕ 54 ♗xg1+ ♔xg1 55 h6 ♔f2 56 e5 ♔e3 57 e6+-.

51	♔c3	♗f1
52	♗d2	♔f2
53	♗f4	♔f3
54	♗d6	♔g2!

Obviously not 54 ... ♔xe4 55 ♗e7 ♔f3 56 ♗h4=.

55	♔d2	♔h3
56	♔e3	h4
57	gxh4	♔xh4
58	♔f2	♗h7

Alternatively, 58 ... c3 59 ♔e2 ♗c4+ 60 ♔d1 ♗b3+ 61 ♔c1 g3 62 e5 ♔h3 63 e6 g2 64 ♗c5 ♔h2 65 e7 ♗a4 66 e8♕ ♗xe8 67 ♔c2=.

59	♗g3+	♔h3
60	e5	♗g8
61	♗f4	♗d5

Or 61 ... c3 62 ♔e2 ♗c4+ 63 ♔d1 ♗b3+ 64 ♔c1 and draws as in the previous note.

62	♗g3	♗f7
63	♗f4	♗d5
64	♗g3	♗e6
65	♗f4	♔h4
66	♗g3+	♔g5
67	♔e3	♔g6
68	♔d4	♔f7
69	♗e1!	♔e7
70	♔c5!	(52a)

The king can barricade the queenside so that Black cannot mobilise his pawns without allowing the e-pawn to advance.

70	...	♔d7
71	♔b5	♔c7
72	♔c5	♗g8
73	♗a5+	♔b7
74	♗e1	♔a6
75	♔d6!	

The black king gets through now but White attains the advance of the e-pawn, which can be used to distract the black bishop and so be swapped for the g-pawn.

75	...	♔b5
76	e6	♔a4
77	e7	♗f7
78	♔e5	½-½

Due to 78 ... ♔b3 79 ♔f4 ♗h5 80 e8♕=.

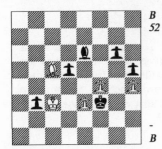

B
52

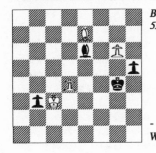

B
52a

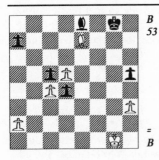

B
53

Kotov - Botvinnik
Moscow 1955

1	...	g5!!
2	fxg5	

Or 2 hxg5 h4 3 f5 (3 ♗d6 ♗f5! 4 g6 ♗xg6 5 f5 ♗xf5 6 ♔xb3 ♔g2 and the h-pawn wins the bishop) 3 ... ♗xf5 4 ♔xb3 h3 5 ♗d6 and now:

a) 5 ... ♔g2? 6 ♔c3 h2 7 ♗xh2 ♔xh2 8 ♔d4 ♗e4 (8 ... ♗e6 9 e4=) 9 g6= (another example of the deflecting pawn motif);

b) 5 ... ♔xe3! and ... ♔g2, (... ♗e6) wins.

2	...	d4+!

Preserving the dangerous distant b-pawn.

3	exd4	

Or 3 ♗xd4 ♔g3 4 g6 ♔xh4 5 ♔d2 ♔h3 6 ♔e2 ♔g2 7 ♗f6 h4 and wins.

3	...	♔g3!-+

Not 3 ... ♔g4? 4 d5! ♗xd5 5 ♗f2=.

4	♗a3	

To free the king to fight the h-pawn. Also hopeless is 4 ♗e7 ♔xh4 5 g6+ ♔g4 (52a)

An excellent illustration of the ingredients for a successful opposite bishops ending: White's forces are divided by Black's dangerous pawns: whilst White's pawns are harmless, unable to deflect the ♗e6 which can monitor both while guarding b3.

4	...	♔xh4
5	♔d3	♔xg5
6	♔e4	h4
7	♔f3	

Or 7 d5 ♗xd5+ 8 ♔xd5 h3-+.

7	...	♗d5+
	0-1	

Since 8 ♔f2 ♔g4 9 ♔g1 ♔f3 10 ♔h2 ♗e6 11 d5 ♗d7 and the black king escorts the b-pawn home. (Most of the above annotations stem from Botvinnik.

Piskov - Nunn
Germany 1992

1	...	♗g6
2	♗xc5	♔f7
3	♗xd4	

Instead 3 ♗xa7 is an interesting try: 3 ... ♗d3! (3 ... ♗b1? 4 a4 ♗a2 5 ♗xd4 ♗xc4 6 d6 ♔e6 7 ♗c5 gives White winning chances) 4 c5 ♗c4 5 d6 and now:

a) 5 ... ♔e6! 6 a4?! (6 ♔f2 ♗xa2=) 6 ... d3= 7 d7 ♔xd7 8

c6+ ♔xc6 9 ♗e3;

b) 5 ... ♗xa2? 6 c6+-.

3	...	a6
4	a3	♗d3
5	c5	♗c4
6	d6	♔e6

The blockade renders the extra pawns harmless.

7	♔f2	♔d7
8	♔g3	♗e6
9	h4	♔c6
	½-½	

Bishop v Bishop (Opposite) ♗ V ♗

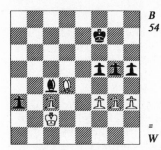

B
54

=
W

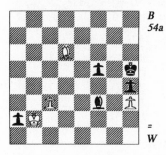

B
54a

=
W

Unzicker - Botvinnik
Varna Ol 1962
(Analysis by Speelman)

    1   ♗e5!?

Suggested by Speelman as an improvement on the game. Not:

a) 1 f4? h4! 2 ♗f2 (2 gxh4 gxf4) 2 ... g4!-+; or

b) 1 h4? f4! 2 ♗e5 (2 ♗f2 gxh4 3 gxh4 ♔e6 intending ... ♗d5xf3 -+) 2 ... ♔e6! 3 ♗c7 gxh4 4 ♗xf4 (4 gxh4 ♔f5-+) 4 ... h3 5 g4 h4 6 ♗h2 ♗e2 0-1 was the game Unzicker - Botvinnik, viz. 7 ♔b3 ♗xf3 8 ♔xa3 ♗xg4 9 ♔b4 ♔d5 10 c4+ ♔e4-+.

But also possible are:

c) 1 ♗b6 ♗d5 (1 ... ♔g6?! 2 ♗c7! h3 3 gxh4 gxh4= as after 1 ♗e5) 2 ♗c7! (2 h4 f4 3 ♗c7 g4! 4 fxg4 f3 5 ♗b6 hxg4-+ e.g. 6 ♗e3 ♔g6 7 ♗d4 ♗f7 8 ♗e3 ♔f5 9 h5 ♗xh5 10 ♔b3 ♔e4) 2 ... ♗xf3 (2 ... ♔g6 3 f4=) 3 ♔b3 ♗g2 4 ♔xa3 ♗xh3 5 ♔b2 f4 6 gxf4 g4 7 ♔c1 g3 8 f5 h4 9 ♔d2 (9 ♗d8 g2 10 ♗b6=) 9 ... ♔f6 10 ♔e3 ♔xf5 11 ♔f3=;

d) 1 g4!? (I suspect that White can also make a draw with this):

d1) 1 ... f4? 2 gxh5 ♗d5 3 h4=;

d2) 1 ... ♗f1? 2 gxh5 ♗xh3 3 f4! gxf4 (3 ... g4 4 ♗f2=) 4 ♔b3 ♔g8 5 ♔xa3 ♔h7 6 ♔b2 ♔h6 7 ♔c1 ♔xh5 8 ♔d2=;

d3) 1 ... ♔g6? 2 ♗e5 h4 (2 ... f4 3 h4!=) 3 f4 and now:

d31) 3 ... ♗e2 4 gxf5+ (4 fxg5 ♗xg4!?) forcing a draw: 4 ... ♔xf5 5 ♗d6 g4 6 hxg4+ ♗xg4 7 ♗c5 h3 8 ♗g1 ♔e4 9 f5=;

d32) 3 ... fxg4 4 hxg4=;

d4) 1 ... h4 2 gxf5 ♗e2 3

♗b6! (3 f4? g4! 4 hxg4 ♗xg4 5 f6 ♗f5+ 6 ♔b3 h3 7 ♗g1 ♔xf6 8 c4 ♔g6 9 c5 ♔h5 10 c6 ♔g4 11 c7 ♗f3-+) 3 ... ♔f6 (3 ... ♔e7 4 f6+ ♔xf6 5 f4 g4 6 hxg4 h3 7 ♗g1 ♗xg4 8 f5=) 4 f4 g4 5 hxg4 h3 6 g5+ ♔xf5 (6 ... ♔f7 7 ♗g1 ♗d3+ 8 ♔b3 ♗xf5 9 ♔xa3 ♗g6 10 ♗h2 ♔h5 11 c4 ♔g4 12 g6 ♗xg6 13 f5=) 7 ♗g1 ♔g4 8 f5 ♔g3 9 ♗c5!=.

d5) 1 ... ♗d5!? 2 gxf5! ♗xf3 3 ♔b3! h4 4 ♔xa3 ♗g2! (4 ... ♗e4 5 f6) 5 ♔b2 ♗xh3 6 ♔c1! (6 f6? - this does not work if the bishop on e6 can hold both pawns - 6 ... ♗e6 7 ♔c1 g4 8 ♔d2 g3 9 ♗e5 ♔g6 10 ♔e3 ♔g5-+ - 10 ... ♔f5? 11 ♗xg3!= - 6 ... ♔f5 7 ♔d2=.

    1   ...   h4

The only move; not 1 ... ♔e6? 2 f4 ♗f1 (2 ... h4 3 gxh4 gxh4 4 ♗d4=) 3 ♗c7! (3 h4 g4 4 c4).

	2	gxh4	gxh4
	3	♗c7	♔g6
	4	♗d6	a2
	5	♔b2	♔h5
	6	♗c7	♗d5
	7	♗d6	♗xf3

(54a)

Or 7 ... ♗c4 8 ♔a1 ♗f1 9 ♔xa2 ♗xh3 10 ♔b2 ♗g2 11 ♔c1 ♗xf3 12 ♔d2 ♔g4 13 ♔e3=.

	8	♔xa2	♗g2
	9	♔b2	♗xh3
	10	♔c1	♔g4
	11	♔d2	f4

Alternatively, 11 ... ♔f3 12 ♔e1 and now:

a) 12 ... ♗g2 13 ♗h2 (13 c4!? f4 14 ♗c5 ♔g3 15 ♗f2+ ♔g4 16 ♗c5 ♔f3 17 ♗f2 h3 18 ♗g1 ♔g3 19 ♗f2+ ♔h2 20 ♗d4=) 13 ... ♗h3 14 ♗d6 transposes to b below;

b) 12 ... ♔g2 13 ♗e7 (13

Bishop v Bishop (Opposite)

♔e2? ♗g4+ 14 ♔e3 h3 15 c4
♗h5 16 c5 ♗e8-+) 13 ... ♔g3
14 ♗c5 ♗g2 15 ♗f2+ ♔g4 16
♗c5 ♔f3 17 ♗f2 ♔g4 18 ♗c5
♔f3 19 ♗f2 h3 20 ♗g1 ♗h1
(20 ... ♔g3 21 ♗f2+ ♔h2 22
♗c5 ♗d5 23 ♔f2=) 21 ♔f1 f4
(21 ... ♔g3 22 ♗f2+ ♔h2 23
♗g1+!=) 22 ♗h2 ♗g2+ 23
♔e1 ♔e3 24 ♗g1+ ♔f3 25
♗h2=.

12 ♔e1!

Not 12 ♔e2?? ♗g3 13 ♗c5
♔g2 winning for Black.

12	...	♔f3
13	♗e7	♔g3
14	♗c5	♗g2

Or 14 ... ♗g4 15 ♗f2+ ♔h3
16 ♔f1=.

15 ♗f2+ ♔g4

16 ♗g1

Or 16 c4 h3 17 ♗g1 ♔g3 18
♗f2+ ♔h2 19 ♗d4 ♗c6 20
♔f2=.

| 16 | ... | ♗d5 |
| 17 | ♗h2 | |

Not 17 ♔f2?? ♗h3 18 ♔f1
♗c4+ 19 ♔f2 ♗e2 20 c4 (20
♔xe2 ♗g2 21 c4 f3+ 22 ♔e3
♔xg1 23 ♔xf3 h3-+) 20 ...
♗xc4 21 ♔f3 ♗d5+ 22 ♔f2
(22 ♔xf4 ♗g2 23 ♔g4 h3 24
♔h4 ♗e6-+) 22 ... ♗c6 23
♔f1 ♗b5+ 24 ♔f2 ♗e2-+.

17	...	♔f3
18	♔d2	♗c4
19	♔e1	♔e3
20	♗g1+	♔f3
21	♗h2=	

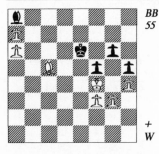

BB
55

Averbakh 1951

1 ♔g5 ♔f7

Or 1 ... ♗xf3 2 ♔xg6 ♔e5 3
♗e3 ♔e6 4 ♗f4 and Black
loses a second pawn through
zugzwang.

2 f4!!

An incredible move which
would seem to remove any
chance of winning. Not 2 g4
hxg4! 3 fxg4 fxg4 4 ♔xg4
♔e6 5 ♔g5 ♔e4 6 a8♕ ♗xa8
7 ♔xg6 ♔d7= (White cannot
avoid a bishop and wrong
rook's pawn ending).

2 ... ♗e4!

3 ♗f2!

Not 3 ♗d4 ♗f3 4 g4 hxg4! 5
h5 gxh5 6 ♔xf5 h4= (Aver-
bakh) 7 a8♕ ♗xa8 8 ♔xg4 h3
9 ♔xh3 ♔e6 10 ♔g4 ♔d7 11
f5 ♔c7=.

3 ... ♔g7

Or 3 ... ♗f3 4 g4!! hxg4 (4 ...
fxg4 5 ♗g3! ♔g7 6 f5 gxf5 7
♔xh5 f4 8 ♗xf4 g3+ 9 ♔g5
g2 10 ♗e3 and White wins
easily by transferring the king
to the queenside) 5 h5! gxh5 6

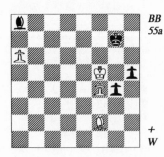

BB
55a

♔xf5 is an inferior version of
the game for Black.

4 g4!! hxg4

No better is 4 ... fxg4 5 f5
gxf5 6 ♔xh5 ♔f6 7 ♗g3 ♗f3
8 ♔h6 ♗e4 9 h5 ♗f3 10 ♗h4+
♔f7 11 ♔g5 ♗e4 12 ♗g3 ♔g7
13 ♗e5+ ♔f7 14 h6+- e.g. 14
... ♔g8 15 a8♕+ ♗xa8 16
♔g6.

5	h5	gxh5
6	a8♕!	♗xa8
7	♔xf5 (65a)	

This position is worth a diagram due to the graphic difference between the forces, especially the easily blockaded
black pawns. Even the wrong
rook's pawn cannot save
Black.

7	...	♔f7
8	♔g5	♗f3
9	a7	♗a8

Better seems 9 ... ♔g7,
when Averbakh's given solution is more relevant.

10 ♗h4

Given by Averbakh, but I
(JT) see no reason to avoid the

straightforward 10 ♔xh5 ♔e6 11 ♔xg4 ♗e4 (or 11 ... ♔d7 12 f5 ♔c8 13 f6+-) 12 f5+ ♗xf5+ 13 ♔f4.

10   ...   ♗f3
11   f5

Not 11 ♔xh5? g3+ 12 ♔g5 g2= (Averbakh). The difference is that the g-pawn will be used to distract the bishop from defence of the f-pawn if White transfers his king to the queenside.

11   ...   ♔g7
12   ♗g3   ♔f7
13   ♗e5   ♗e4
14   ♔xh5!   g3
15   ♗xg3   ♔f6
16   ♔g4   ♗xf5+
17   ♔f4 and wins

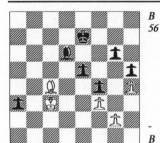

B 56

Welin - Tisdall
Gausdal Young Masters 1983
Black works to create a second, distant, passed pawn.

57   ...   ♔f6
58   ♗b5   ♔g7!

Black guards h5 before playing ... g5.

59   ♗e8   ♔h6
60   ♗f7   g5
61   ♔d3

Capturing on g5 makes it easier for Black's king to invade, e.g. 61 hxg5+ ♔xg5 62 ♔c2 ♔h4 63 ♗g6 ♔g3 64 ♗xh5 ♔xg2 65 ♗g4 e4 66 fxe4 f3 67 ♔b3 f2 68 ♗e2 f1♕ 69 ♗xf1+ ♔xf1 70 e5 ♗e7.

61   ...   gxh4

62   ♔e2   ♔g5
63   ♗e6   ♗c5
64   ♔f1   ♗d4
65   ♗d5   h3!

Opening a path for the king and undermining f3.

66   gxh3   e4!

Creating a second passed pawn.

67   fxe4   f3

White faces perpetual zugzwang and the loss of all pawns - another example of dynamic creation of passed pawns over material considerations. The finish might be 68 ♗e6 (or 68 e5 ♗xe5 69 ♔f2 ♔f4 70 ♗f7 ♗d4+ 71 ♔f1 ♔g3) 68 ... ♔f4 69 ♗d5 ♔g3 70 ♗e6 h4.

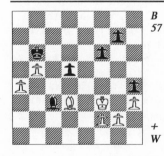

B 57

Palacios - Pilnik
Argentine Ch 1975

1   ♔g4

This position is winning since White can set up a passed pawn on the h-file.

1   ...   ♗e1

After 1 ... g5 2 g3 hxg3 (2 ... ♗e1 3 gxh4 gxh4 4 ♔xh4 ♗xf2+ 5 ♔g4+-) 3 fxg3 the h-pawn will be decisive.

2   ♔xh4   ♗xf2+
3   ♔h5   g5

Alternatively:
a) 3 ... ♗e3 4 ♔g6 ♗h6 5 h4 ♔a5 6 g4+-;
b) 3 ... ♔c5 4 ♔g6 ♔b4 5 ♔xg7 ♔c3 6 ♗f1 d4 7 b6 d3 8

b7 ♗a7 9 ♗xd3 ♔xd3 10 h4+-;
c) 3 ... ♔a5 4 ♔g6 ♗xa4 5 ♔xg7 f5 6 ♔g6 f4 7 ♔f5 ♗e3 8 ♔e5+-.

4   ♔g6   ♗d4
5   g3   ♗e5
6   h4!+-   ♗xg3
7   h5   ♗e5
8   ♔f5!?   ♗d6
9   h6   ♗f8
10   h7   ♗g7
11   ♔g4   d4
12   ♔h5   ♗h8
13   ♗f5   ♔c5
14   ♔g6   g4
15   ♗xg4   d3
16   ♔f7   d2
17   ♔g8   f5

18	♗h5	♗e5		20	♔xh8	f4
19	h8♕	♗xh8		21	♗d1	1-0

BB 58

Yusupov - Frias
Lone Pine 1981
(Analysis by Yusupov)

36 ♔b5

Planning c5, ♔c4 isolating and attacking d4.

36 ... g5

To create a target for counterplay on f4. If White exchanges on g5 then Black gains the f6-square from which to defend d4.

37	c5	bxc5
38	bxc5	gxf4
39	gxf4	♗f8
40	h4!	

Now White can combine threats against d4 or h7 to create a second passed pawn. Not 40 ♔c4 ♗h6 41 f5 ♗e3= or 40 h3 h5!=.

| 40 | ... | h5 |

Or 40 ... ♗h6 41 ♗e4!.

41	♗f3	f5
42	♔c4!	♗e7
43	♔xd4	♗xh4
44	♔e5!	♗f2
45	c6	h4
46	♔xf5	h3
47	♔g6	♗g3
48	f5	♔d6
49	f6	♗e5
50	f7	♔e7
51	c7	1-0

51 ... ♗xc7 52 ♔g7.

BB 59

Vaganian - Anikaev
USSR Ch 1979

White has more trumps than meets the eye: the h-pawn as a decoy/passed pawn: the a3-pawn as a target; and f7 as the base of a chain fully edible to the bishop.

40	h5	♔e7
41	♗a4	♔f6
42	♔e2	♔g7
43	♗e8	♔f6

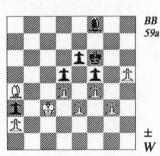

BB 59a

If the black bishop tries to create counterplay with ♗b4-e1 then h6-h7 will distract the black king from defence of the kingside pawn chain.

44	♔d3	♔e7
45	♗a4	♔f6
46	♔c3 (59a)	

Now the black bishop is locked out and the a3-pawn is about to become a target.

46	...	♔g7
47	♗e8	

Again this move, which preserves the h-pawn.

47	...	♔f6
48	♔b3	♔e7
49	♗b5	♔f6
50	♗e8	♔e7
51	♗c6	♔f6

Or 51 ... ♔d8 52 ♗b5 ♔c7 53 ♗e8 f6 54 ♗f7 ♔d7 55 ♗g8+- (Vaganian).

| 52 | h6! | |

Now White cashes in the h-pawn to create a passed a-pawn which costs Black his bishop.

52	...	♗xh6
53	♔xa3	♗f8+

Or 53 ... ♔g6 54 ♗e8 ♔h5 55 ♔b3! ♔g4 56 ♔c3+- (Vaganian).

54	♔b3	♗d6
55	a4	♗c7
56	♔b4	♗d6+?

Black could continue to resist with the much tougher 56 ... ♔e7 57 a5 (57 ♔b5 ♔d6) 57 ... ♔d6 58 ♗e8 (58 ♔b5 ♗xa5) 58 ... ♔e7 (58 ... f6 59 ♔b5+-) and now:

a) 59 a6 ♗b8 60 ♗xf7 (60

♗a4 ♗a7 61 ♗d1 ♔d6 62 ♗h5 f6 63 ♗f7 ♗b6 64 ♔b5 ♗a7 65 ♗g8 e1♕) 60 ... ♔xf7 61 ♔c5 and:

a1) 61 ... ♔e7 62 ♔b6 (62 ♔c6 ♔d8=) 62 ... ♗d7 63 a7 (63 ♔b7 ♗a7!= 64 ♔xa7 ♔c7 65 ♔a8 ♔c8) 63 ... ♗xa7+ 64 ♔xa7 ♔c7=;

a2) 61 ... ♗a7+ 62 ♔d6 ♔f6;

b) 59 ♗a4 (it is better to reserve a6, which makes it more difficult for the white king to invade) 59 ... ♔d6 60 ♔b5 ♗b8 61 ♗d1 f6 (Black cannot avoid this) 62 ♗h5 e5 63 ♔b4 (63 ♔b6 ♗c7+ 64 ♔b5 ♗b8) 63 ... ♗a7 64 ♔c3 ♔c6 65 ♗e2 and:

b1) 65 ... ♔d6 66 ♗a6 ♔d7 (66 ... ♔c7 67 ♗d3) 67 ♗b7 ♔d6 68 ♗c8 ♔c6 (68 ... exd4+ 69 exd4 ♔c6 70 ♗a6 ♔d6 71 ♗d3 ♔e6 72 ♗c2 ♗b8 73 ♔b4 ♗a7);

b2) 65 ... exd4+ (not 65 ... e4 66 ♔e4 and White can win the f5-pawn since Black must prevent ♔b5 JT) 66 exd4

♔d6 (66 ... ♔b7? 67 ♗d3+- zugzwang but perhaps 66 ... ♗b8!?) 67 ♗d3 ♔e6 (67 ... ♔c6 68 ♗xf5 ♔b5 69 ♗e6 ♔xa5 70 ♗xd5 ♔b6 71 ♔d3 ♔c7 72 ♔e4 ♔d6 73 ♗c4 (this ending is critical - White's win is problematic since:

b21) 68 ♗a6 ♔d6 69 ♗c8 ♔c6 70 ♔d3 ♗b8 71 ♔e3 ♔b5 72 a6 ♗a7 73 ♗xf5 ♔xa6 74 g4 ♗b6 75 g5 (75 ♗e6 ♗d8 76 ♗xd5 ♔b6 77 ♔e4 ♔c7 78 ♔f5 ♔d6 79 ♗c4 ♔e7 and I see no way to avoid the ending 80 g5 fxg5 81 fxg5 ♗b6 82 d5 ♗d4 83 ♔g6 ♗e3 and White cannot progress without allowing the known position 84 ♔h5 ♗d4 85 g6 ♗g7 when the g6-pawn makes it impossible for White to invade round the right flank) 75 ... fxg5 76 fxg5 ♗d8 77 ♔f4 ♔b5 78 ♗d3+ ♔b4=;

b22) 68 ♗c2 ♗b8 69 ♔b4 ♗a7 70 ♔b5 ♔d6 71 ♗xf5 ♗xd4 72 ♗d3 ♗f2=.

57   ♔b5   1-0

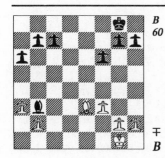

B 60

Ljubojevic - Karpov
Milan 1975

1	...	♔f7
2	♗f4	c6
3	♗d6	

White could consider immediately centralising the king.

3	...	♔e6
4	♗f8	g6
5	♔f2	a5
6	♔e3	b6
7	h4	c5
8	g4?!	

This also gives the white king distracting weaknesses to defend. 8 ♗h6 with the idea of ♗c7 looks better - White should try to force Black's pawns onto white squares.

8	...	♗d1
9	♔e4	a4
10	h5	gxh5
11	gxh5	f5+
12	♔e3	♔d5
13	h6	

White now must waste time removing the kingside pawns from danger, and Black's king takes up a dominant post.

13	...	♔c4
14	f4	♔b3
15	♗g7	

Or 15 ♔d2!? ♔xb2! 16 ♔xd1 c4 (16 ... ♔xa3 17 ♔c2 ♔b4 18 ♔b2= Matanovic) 17 ♗e7 (17 ♗g7+ c3 18 ♔e2 ♔c2 19 ♗e5 b5 20 ♗d6 ♔b1-+) 17 ... b5 18 ♗f8 c3 19

♗g7 b4!-+.

15	...	♚c2
16	♗e5	♝h5
17	♗f6	♝f7
18	♗e5	♝b3
19	♗g7	b5
20	♗f8	c4
21	♗g7	b4!
22	♔d4	

Or 22 axb4 c3 23 bxc3 (23 ♗xc3 a3) 23 ... ♝c4 24 b5 a3 25 b6 a2 26 b7 a1♛ 27 b8♛

♛g1+ 28 ♔f3 ♝d5+ 29 ♔e2 ♛g2+ 30 ♔e3 ♛e4+ 31 ♔f2 ♛f3+ 32 ♔e1 ♛g3+ 33 ♔e2 ♝c4+.

22	...	c3
23	bxc3	bxa3-+

For the record, the game concluded 24 c4 a2 25 ♔c5 ♔b1 26 ♔b4 a1♛ 27 ♗xa1 ♔xa1 28 c5 ♔b2 29 c6 a3 30 c7 ♝e6 31 ♔c5 a2 32 ♔d6 ♝c8 0-1.

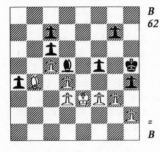

B 62

= B

Kurajica - Karpov
Skopje 1976

1	...	g5
2	♔f2!	

Not 2 ♗a3?! f4+! 3 gxf4 g4! 4 fxg4+ ♔xg4 (Karpov).

2	...	♝a2
3	♗a3	♝b1
4	♔e2	♝a2
5	♗c1	♝e6
6	♔f2	♝c8
7	d5?	

A bad reaction. White fears an eventual occupation of d5 by the black king, but it was better to wait: 7 ♔e2 ♝a6 and now:

a) 8 ♗b2 hxg3 9 hxg3 f4 10 gxf4 (10 g4+ ♔h4 11 ♔f2 ♔h3 intending ♝xd3-c4-e6xg4-+) 10 ... gxf4 11 ♗c1 ♔g5 12 ♗b2 ♔h4 13 ♔f2 ♝xd3;

b) 8 ♔e3 f4+ 9 gxf4 g4 10 f5!=.

7	...	cxd5
8	d4	f4!
9	gxf4	

Or 9 g4+ ♔g6-+ intending ... ♔c4, ... ♝d3.

9	...	g4
10	♔g2	♝f5

11	♔f2	gxf3
12	♔xf3	♝e4+
13	♔f2	♔g4
14	♗b2	♔xf4
15	♗c1+	♔g4
16	♗b2	c6
17	♗c1	♔h3
18	♔g1	♝g6
19	♔h1	

Or 19 ♗b2 ♔g4 20 ♔f2 ♔f4 21 ♔e2 ♔e4 22 ♗c3 ♝h5+ and wins (JT).

19	...	♝h5!

19 ... ♔g4 20 ♔g2 ♔f5 21 ♔f3 ♝h5+ 22 ♔e3 does not make progress - f3 must be denied to the white king (Karpov).

20	♔g1	♝d1!
	0-1	

Due to the variations:

a) 21 ♗b2 ♔g4 22 ♔g2 ♝f3+ (22 ... h3+?? 23 ♔f2 ♔f4 24 ♔e1 ♝h5 25 ♔d2 ♔f3 26 ♔d3 ♔g2 27 ♔e3 ♔xh2 28 ♔f2 drawing - another example of self-obstruction by pawns) 23 ♔f2 ♔f4 and again the king crosses to the queenside (Karpov);

b) 21 ♔h1 ♔g4 22 ♔g2 ♔f5 23 ♔f2 ♔e4 and wins.

Bishop v Knight

Bishop and One Pawn v Knight

BN 1

A basic win

1	♗b4	♘c7
2	♗c3	♘a8
3	♗a5	

The bishop takes up this square on principle - this is the method that wins against pawns in positions shifted to the right (when the knight must be fully dominated).

+ W

Here the white king could go to b6 earlier.

3	...	♘c7
4	♔b6!	♘a8+
5	♔a6 and	
6	♔b7 winning	

This is an important method, and applies to start positions shifted to the right.

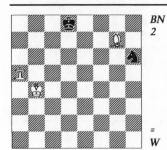

BN 2

Sevitov 1937, corrected by Shakhmatny v SSSR reader

1 ♗e5! ♘f7!

Instead:

a) 1 ... ♘f5? 2 a6 ♘e7 3 ♔c5 ♘c8 4 ♔c6 ♘a7+ 5 ♔b7 ♘c8 (5 ... ♘b5 6 ♔b6) 6 ♗f6+ ♔d7 7 ♗e7!! is an excellent illustration of White's weaponry. The bishop dominates both pieces, overloading them thanks to the pressure exerted by the white king;

b) 1 ... ♘g4 2 ♗g3 ♘f6 3 a6 ♔c8 4 ♔c5 ♘d7+ 5 ♔b5! ♘f6 6 ♔c6 ♘e8 7 a7 ♘c7 8 ♔b6 and wins as in the previous example.

2 ♗f4 ♔d7!

Preparing the c6-square for the knight.

3 ♔b5 ♘d8

= W

4	a6	♘c6
5	♔b6	♘e7
6	♔b7	♘c6
7	♗c7	

We have reached a 1958 position of Averbakh's (Cheron overlooks this possibility and considers Sevitov's position to be a win for White).

7	...	♘a7!
8	♗f4	♘c6!

Not 8 ... ♘b5 9 ♔b6 or 8 ... ♘c8 9 ♗g3 ♔d8 10 ♗h4+ ♔d7 11 ♗e7!.

9	♔b6	♘e7
10	♗g3	

Or 10 ♗c1 ♘c8+! 11 ♔b7 ♘d6+ 12 ♔b8 ♘b5!.

10	...	♘c6
11	♗e1	♔c8
12	♗g3	♔d7

and draws

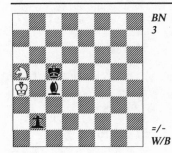

BN 3

Prokes 1946

1 ♘b3+ ♗xb3+

2 ♔a3!! and draws

Black cannot promote meaningfully without stalemate. A common yet practical study theme. But there is another useful theme hidden here: 1 ... ♔d5 (JT) 2 ♘d2

=/- W/B

♔d4 and now:

a) 3 ♘b1! ♔d3 4 ♘a3 (4 ♘a3 ♔c2 transposes into the next note) 4 ... ♗a2 5 ♘b1!! ♔c2 6 ♘a3+ ♔c3 7 ♘b5+ ♔c4 8 ♘a3+ ♔c5 9 ♘b1!;

b) 3 ♔a3 ♔c3 4 ♘b1+ ♔c2 5 ♘d2 ♗g8 and wins.

Bishop v Knight

BN 4

+/+
W/B

A key position

　　1　...　　♞e8

White to move would win with 1 ♗d7. This is the position he seeks to reach. Again Black is hampered by the edge of the board; shifted one file to the left, this position would be drawn.

2	♗d7	♞g7
3	♔h7	♞h5
4	♗g4	♞g7
5	♗h3	♞h5
6	♔h6	♞g7

Or 6 ... ♞f4 7 g7 ♔f7 8 ♔h7.

7	♗d7 and wins

BN 5

+
W

Haik - Vaiser
Sochi 1985

74	...	♞c5
75	♔a3	♔g5
76	♔b4	♞d7

Or 76 ... ♞d3+ 77 ♔b5.

77	b7	♔f5
78	♔b5	♔e6

79	♗c1	♔d6
80	♗f4+	♔e7
81	♔c6	♔d8
82	♗g3	♔e7
83	♔c7	♞c5

On any king move, 84 ♗d6.

84	♗d6+	1-0

BN 6

+
W

Averbakh

　　1　♗d4

As often happens, Black will suffer due to the knight's lack of squares near the edge of the board. Even shifted just one file to the right, Black would draw.

1	...	♔c4
2	♔a5	♔b3

One file to the right ... ♞a2 would draw, re-entering play with the threat of ... ♞c3+.

3	♗f6	♔a3
4	♗g5	♔b3
5	♗c1	♞c5
6	b6	♔c4
7	♗a3	♞d7
8	b7	♔d4
9	♔b5	♔d5
10	♗c1	♔d6
11	♗f4+	♔d5
12	♗g3	♔e6
13	♔c6	

And wins as in diag 5.

BN 7

+
W

Krogdahl - Wolf
Hamburg Ol 1930
Without the king's help a knight is helpless against a bishop and pawn.

　　52　♗e4

Preventing the knight from getting back.

52	...	♔b6
53	♔f5	♞e2
54	g5	♞g3+
55	♔e5	♔c7

Or 55 ... ♞h5 56 ♗f3 ♞g7 57 ♔f6 ♞e8+ 58 ♔e7 ♞g7 59 ♗g4.

　　56　♗f3

56 g6 also wins easily: 56 ... ♞h5 57 ♗f3 ♞g7 58 ♔f6 ♞e8+ 59 ♔e7 ♞d6 (59 ... ♞g7 60 ♗g4) 60 ♗g4.

56	...	♔d8
57	♔f6	♔e8
58	g6	1-0

Bishop v Knight

BN
8

+/+
W/B

Chess Player's Chronicle 1856

| 1 | ... | ♚b6 |

This is diag 11 one file to the left. Black loses here since the bishop has more squares on the d8-h4 diagonal! This allows him to arrange zugzwang. If White were to move, he reaches the solution with 1 ♗c3.

2	♗e5	♚c5
3	♗c3	♚b6
4	♗a5+!	♚b5
5	♗d8	♚c5
6	♗h4	♚b5
7	♗g5!	

The difference here is that White can wait on this diagonal and force the transfer to d4.

7	...	♚c5
8	♗e3+	♚d5
9	♗d4	♞d6
10	c7 and wins	

BN
9

=
W

A basic draw

| 1 | ♗b4+ | |

This position is clearly drawn. The ♞e6 is inviolate - the white king has no hope of dislodging it. White's other weapon in such endings, dominating the king with the bishop to create a zugzwang position, fails due to the impo

tent white king position.

1	...	♚c6
2	♗a5	♚d6
3	♗b6	♚c6
4	♗c7	♚d5
5	♚b7	♞c5+
	and draws	

White is prevented from re-grouping.

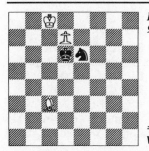

BN
10

+
W

A basic win

| 1 | ♗b4+ | |

Black threatened ... ♞e7-c6+. If the white king were on e8, ... ♚e6 is a version of the basic draw.

| 1 | ... | ♚e6 |
| 2 | ♚c7 | |

The first danger to the weaker side: pressure against the knight from the white king.

| 2 | ... | ♚d5 |
| 3 | ♗a3 and wins | |

Zugzwang through bishop domination.

BN
11

=
B

Mandeleilyu 1938

| 1 | ... | ♚c6! |

This is one of an interesting set of positions. Black's task is to avoid the bishop arriving on e4 with zugzwang, so he takes care that ♗e4 arrives with check. (Not 1 ... ♚c5 2 ♗e4 or 1 ... ♚e5 2 ♗e4 ♞e6 3 d7 which is still zugzwang.)

| 2 | ♗a4+ | ♚c5 |
| 3 | ♗e8 | |

The bishop is restricted by the need to prevent ... ♞g6+.

3	...	♚d5
4	♗f7+	♚c6
5	♗h5	♚c5!
	and draws	

Not 5 ... ♚d5 6 ♗f3+ and ♗e4 next.

Bishop v Knight

BN 12

+
W

Bron 1955

1 ♗b3+

Although the knight on f8 looked vulnerable in the previous example, it served an important extra duty in guarding the e6-square. Here the "more active" knight on f6 loses.

1 ... ♔c5

Or 1 ... ♔e5 2 ♗e6.

2 ♗e6 ♔c6
3 ♗c4 ♔c5

4 ♗b3 ♔c6
5 ♔e6 ♘h7

5 ... ♔c5 6 ♗d5! ♘h7 transposes.

6 ♗d5+ ♔c5
7 ♔e7

Not 7 d7?? ♘f8+.

7 ... ♘f6

Or 7 ... ♘f8 8 ♗e4.

8 ♗f3 ♘g8+
9 ♔e6 ♘f6
10 ♗e4! and wins

BN 13

=
W

Kasparian 1974

1 ♔b7 ♗d3
2 ♘c3+

Not 2 ♘c7+? ♔d6 3 ♘e8+ ♔e7 4 ♘c7 ♗c4-+.

2 ... ♔d4

Immediately drawing is 2 ... ♗c4 3 ♘d1!=.

3 ♘a2!

Losing is 3 ♘d1? ♗f5! 4 ♔c6 e4 5 ♔d6 ♗g4 6 ♘f2 e3 7 ♘xg4 e2-+.

3 ... e4

Or 3 ... ♔c4 4 ♔c6 e4 5 ♘c1! ♔c3 (5 ... e3 6 ♔d6 ♔c3 7 ♔e5 should transpose to main line) 6 ♔d5 ♔b2 7 ♘e2=.

4 ♔c6 ♗c4
5 ♘c1 ♔c3
6 ♔d6!

Zugzwang arises after 6 ♔c5? e3-+.

6 ... ♔d2
7 ♔e5 e3
8 ♔e4!

Not 8 ♔d4 or 8 ♔f4? ♗d5!.

8 ... ♗f7
9 ♔f3 ♗d5+
10 ♔f4

A position of mutual zugzwang is reached (cf diag 11).

10 ... ♗e6
11 ♔f3 ♗f7
12 ♔e4 ♗g6+
13 ♔f4!

Not 13 ♔f3? ♗c2 14 ♔f4 ♗a4 15 ♔e4 ♗c6+ and ... ♗d5-+ next.

13 ... ♗c2
14 ♔f3 ♗d1+
15 ♔e4 ♗c2+
16 ♔f3! ♗a4
17 ♔f4!=

Bishop and One Pawn v Knight and Two Pawns

BN 14

-
B

Tukmakov - G. Agzamov
USSR Ch 1983

With pawns restricted to one side of the board, the knight's stock rises against the bishop.

64 ... ♘e6
65 ♗b6

Or 65 ♗a5 g6 66 h5 f5+ 67 ♔h4 g5+ 68 ♔g3 ♘f8 69

♗d8 ♘h7 and wins.

65 ... g6
66 ♗a5

Or 66 h5 f5+ 67 ♔h4 g5+ 68 ♔g3 ♔e5-+.

66 ... f5+
67 ♔g3 ♘f4
68 ♗d2 ♘h5+
69 ♔f2

Bishop v Knight

After 69 ♔h3 Black plays
69 ... ♔f3 intending ... ♞f4+
and ... ♔g4.

| 69 | ... | ♞f6 |

The last white pawn proves
too vulnerable.

70	♗g5	♞d5
71	♔g3	f4+
72	♔f2	♞e3

73	♗d8	♞c4
74	♗c7	♔f5
75	♔f3	♞d2+
76	♔e2	♞b3
77	♗b6	♔g4

White cannot prevent the
knight from attacking and
winning the h4-pawn.

0-1

Bishop and Two Pawns v Knight

BN
15

Cheron 1956

| 1 | ... | ♞g6 |
| 2 | ♔g2? | |

White should play 2 ♗d3!
♞f4 (2 ... ♞h4 3 ♗e4!) 3 ♗c2
♞h5 4 h4+ ♔h6 5 g4 ♞f6 6
g5+ ♔g7 7 ♔g3 and wins as
in diag 16.

| 2 | ... | ♞h4+!! |

An instructive trap men-
tioned by Cheron.

3	♔f2	♞f5
4	g4	♔f4!!
5	♗d3	♞h4
6	♗c2	♞f3
7	♗d1	♞h4
8	♗e2	♞g6
9	♗f1	♞e5
10	♗e2	♞g6=

With a blockade.

BN
16

Fine/Averbakh/Cheron 1941

| 1 | g4! | |

A violation of Philidor's
rule (advance pawns onto
squares of the opposite colour
of your own bishop) but
White can use zugzwang to
foil blockading attempts. With
the wrong rook's pawn, Fine
contends that it is safer to advance the knight's pawn first,
taking care to avoid real
blockades, in order to make it
harder for the knight to arrange a drawing sacrifice.
Also of great interest is the
stereotyped dark-square push
1 h4 ♔h6 (This position is
also considered by Fine, and
judged a draw by him, since
the threat of sacrificing the
knight to reach a wrong rook's
pawn ending is so troublesome. Averbakh and Cheron
point out that it is not the idea

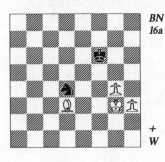

BN
16a

h4 at fault but Fine's idea
♔f2.) 2 ♔g2 (2 g4?? ♞xg4+)
2 ... ♔g7 3 ♗d1! (3 ♔f2? -
Fine - 3 ... ♞g6! 4 h5 ♞e5 5
♔e3 ♔h6 6 ♔f4 ♞f7=) 3 ...
♞g6 4 ♔h3! (the crucial difference) 4 ... ♞e5 5 ♗c2 ♞c4
6 ♗d3 ♞e3 7 ♔h2 ♔f6 8 ♔g1
♔e5 9 ♔f2 ♞g4+ 10 ♔f3
♞h2+ 11 ♔e2 ♞g4 12 ♗a6
♔e4 13 ♗b7+ ♔e5 14 ♗c8
♞f6 15 ♔f3 ♔d6 16 ♗f5!
♔e5?! (This slightly eases
White's task. It is better to
wait with the king, playing
♔e5 in response to ♗g6,
when White does not achieve
♔f4 so easily. For this possibility see diag 17.) 17 ♗g6 (So
that ... ♞h5+ does not foil
♔f4) 17 ... ♔e6 18 ♔f4
♞d5+ 19 ♔g5 ♞f6 20 h5 and
wins. So both g4 and h4 are
possible to begin the advance,
but h4 is much more difficult

to win.

1	...	♘c6

Or 1 ... ♔g5 2 ♔g3 ♘g6 3 ♗d3 ♘h4 4 ♗e4.

2	♔g3	♘d4
3	♗d3+	♔f6 *(16a)*
4	h4	♘e6
5	♗c4	♘c5
6	♔f4	♘d7
7	♗d3	♔g7
8	g5	♘f6!?
9	♗e4	♘h5+
10	♔g4	♘f6+
11	♔f5	♘h5
12	♗f3	♘g3+
13	♔f4	♘f1
14	h5	

And the pawns go through with a win for White.

BN 17

Smagin - Naumkin
Palma open 1989

An example illustrating the method with wrong rook's pawn ahead of knight's pawn.

93	...	♘g8
94	♔e3	♘f6
95	♗g6	♘g4+
96	♔f3	♘h2+
97	♔e2	♘g4
98	♗c2	

The bishop must drive the knight back.

98	...	♘h2
99	♗d1	

Averbakh manoeuvred the bishop to c8, but this makes no difference.

99	...	♘g4
100	♔f3	♘f6
101	♗c2	♔e6!
102	♗d3	♔d6!

Black waits for ♗g6. He intends to reply ... ♔e5, keeping the white king out of f4.

103	♗g6	♔e5
104	h5	♘d5 *(17a)*

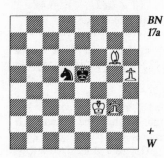

BN 17a

Or 104 ... ♘g8 105 g4 ♔f6 106 ♔f4 ♘h6 107 g5+ ♔g7 108 ♗e8 and now:

a) 108 ... ♘g8 109 ♗b5 ♘h6 (109 ... ♘f6 110 h6+ ♔g6 111 ♗d3+ ♔f7 112 gxf6 ♔xf6 113 ♗h7 winning) 110 ♗c4 ♔h7 111 g6+ ♔g7 112 ♔g5 ♔h8 113 ♗d5 (113 ♔f6 ♘g4+ 114 ♔f7 ♘e5+ 115 ♔f8? ♘xg6+) 113 ... ♔g7 114 ♗e6 transpos-

ing to the note above;

b) 108 ... ♔h7 109 g6+ ♔g7 110 ♔g5 ♘g8 111 ♗d7 ♘h6 112 ♗e6 ♔h8 113 ♔f6.

105	h6	♔f6
106	♗f5	♘e7
107	g4	♔f7
108	♗e4	♔g8
109	♗f5	♔h8

109 ... ♔f7 cannot keep the white king out for long: 110 ♔f4 ♘d5+ 111 ♔e5.

110	♗e6	♘g6

After 110 ... ♔h7 111 g5 ♔h8 112 ♔f4 White must only be wary of combinations involving stalemate and ... ♘xh6/g5. For example:

a) 112 ... ♘g6+ 113 ♔f5 and now:

a1) 113 ... ♘f8 114 ♔e5 and:

a11) 114 ... ♘g6+ 115 ♔f6 ♘f8 (115 ... ♘h4 116 ♗f5 ♔g8 117 ♗e4) 116 ♗f5 transposes;

a12) 114 ... ♔h7 115 ♗f5+ ♔h8 116 ♔f6 ♔g8 117 ♔e7 ♔h8 118 ♔f7;

a2) 113 ... ♘e7+ 114 ♔f6 ♘g6 115 ♗f5 ♘h4 116 ♗e4 ♔g8 117 ♔e5 ♔f7 118 ♔f4;

b) 112 ... ♔h7 113 ♗f5+ ♔g8 114 ♔e5 ♔f7 115 ♗e4 ♔g8 116 ♔f6.

111	♔e4	♘f8
112	♗f5	♔g8
113	♔d5	♔f7
114	♔e5	♔g8
115	♔f6	1-0

Bishop v Knight

BN 18 *Cuijpers - van Mil*
Dieren open 1988

=/=
W/B

A positional draw; White has not a hope of winning.

BN 19 *Torre - Gheorghiu*
Wijk aan Zee 1981
White's hopes are based on the wrong rook's pawn, but the helplessness of the lone knight is seen.

75	...	a5
76	♔d4	a4
77	♔c3	♗c6
78	♔b4	♗d7
79	♔a3	♔d6

Intending ... ♗e6 trapping the knight on h6.

| 80 | ♘g8 | f5 |

B

| 81 | ♘f6 | ♗c6 |
| 82 | ♘h5 | ♔e5 |

Preventing the knight from taking up a circuit directly in front of the f-pawn.

83	♔b4	♗e8
84	♘g3	f4
85	♘f1	♔d4
86	♘h2	♗h5

White resigned due to 87 ♔xa4 (87 ♘f1 ♔d3) 87 ... ♔e3 88 ♔b4 ♔f2 89 ♔c4 ♔g2.

Bishop and Two Pawns v Knight and One Pawn

BN 20 *Petrovic - Averbakh*
Graz open 1987
Averbakh in practice. The knight is helpless against bishop and pawn without the aid of its king.

| 51 | ... | ♗e2! |

First driving the knight further away.

| 52 | ♘b6 |

Or 52 ♘d6 ♗xg4+ 53 ♔xf6 ♗d7 54 ♘e4 g4 55 ♘f2 g3 56 ♘d3+ ♔e3 57 ♘e1 ♗c6 58 ♔g5 ♗e4 59 ♔g4 (59 ♔h4 ♔f2 60 ♔h3 transposes) 59 ... ♔f2 60 ♔h3! (by analogy to diag 13, not 60 ♔h4 ♗f5 or 60 ♔f4 ♗f5! 61 ♘f3 g2-+) 60 ... ♗c2 61 ♔g4 (61 ♔h4? ♗f5) 61 ... ♗d1+ 62 ♔h3 (62 ♔f4? ♗e2 or 62 ♔h4 ♗e2 63 ♔h3

B

♗c4 64 ♔h4 ♗b5! and Black wins because the a6-f1 diagonal is longer than the analogous diagonal in diag 13, so that Black can force a zugzwang position: 65 ♔g4 ♗d7+ and ... ♗f5-+) 62 ... ♗e2 63 ♔h4 ♗c4 64 ♔g4 ♗e6+ and ... ♗f5 wins.

52	...	♗xg4+
53	♔xf6	♗f3
54	♘d7	♗e4!

Not 54 ... g4 55 ♘e5 g3 56 ♘g6+ ♔e3 57 ♘h4 ♗e4 58 ♔e5=.

| 55 | ♘e5 | ♗f5! |
| 56 | ♘c6 |

Or 56 ♘f3 g4 57 ♘d4 (57 ♘h4?! ♗e4-+) 57 ... ♗c8! transposing (not 57 ... ♗d3? 58 ♘e6+ ♔e3 59 ♔g5 g3 60

167

♞f4 ♗e2 61 ♞h3=).

| 56 | ... | g4 |
| 57 | ♞d4 | ♗c8 |

And White resigned due to 58 ♞e2+ (... ♔e3-f2 is coming in any event) 58 ... ♔f3 59 ♞d4+ ♔f2.

BN 21

+ W

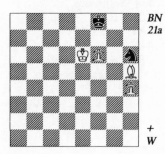

BN 21a

+ W

Khasin - Mariasin
USSR 1970

1 ♗a2

Intending ♔e6-f5-g5xh5. This is better than 1 ♔f5 ♞e3+ 2 ♔e5 ♞g4+ 3 ♔e6 and now:

a) 3 ... ♔e8?! 4 ♗f3 ♔f8 (4 ... ♞xf6 5 ♔xf6 ♔f8 6 ♗d5) 5 ♗xg4 hxg4 6 h5+-;

b) 3 ... ♞h6! 4 ♗b3 (4 ♗f3 ♞g8! 5 ♗xh5 ♞xf6=) 4 ... ♔g8 (4 ... ♞g4 5 ♔f5+-) 5 ♔e7+ (5 ♔e5+ ♔h7 6 ♗c2+ ♔h8 7 ♔e6 ♞g8! 8 f7 ♔g7=) 5 ... ♔h8 6 ♔e8 ♔h7 7 ♗c2+ ♔h8 8 ♗g6 (8 ♗d7 ♞g8 9 f7 ♔g7!=) 8 ... ♔g8 9 ♗xh5 ♔h7 10 ♗f7 ♞g4 11 ♗g8+ ♔h8 12 f7 ♞f6+ 13 ♔f8 ♞d7+ 14 ♔e7 ♞e5!=;

c) 3 ... ♞e3?! 4 ♗f3 transposes to the main line.

1 ... ♞e3!

Not 1 ... ♞h2 2 ♔f5 ♞f3 3 ♗d5! ♞xh4+ 4 ♔g5 or 1 ... ♔g8 2 ♔e7+ ♔h7 3 f7 ♞e5 4 ♗b1+ and wins.

2 ♗b3 ♔e8!

A better defence than 2 ... ♞g2 3 ♗d5 ♞e3 (3 ... ♞f4+ 4 ♔e5 ♞g6+ 5 ♔f5 ♞xh4+ 6 ♔g5+- or 3 ... ♞xh4 4 ♗e4+-) 4 ♗f3 ♞c2 5 ♗xh5 ♞d4+ 6 ♔e5 ♞c6+ 7 ♔d6 ♞d4 8 ♗g6 ♞e2 9 ♔e5+-.

3 ♗d5

3 ♔e5 ♞g2 4 ♗d5 ♞xh4 5 ♗e4 ♔f7= (JS).

3 ... ♞g4!?

3 ... ♞f1!?, intending ♞g3, protecting h5 and eyeing e4 if the bishop leaves the a2-g8 diagonal, also looks a tough defence. From g3 the knight also has the ♞e2-f4 circuit. But 4 ♗f3 (4 ♔f5 ♞e3+ 5 ♔e5 ♔f8) 4 ... ♞g3 5 ♔e5 (5 ♗d1 ♞e4 6 ♗xh5+ ♔f8 7 f7 ♞f6 8 ♗g6 ♔g7 9 h5 ♞g8 and ♞h6=) 5 ... ♔f7 6 ♗d5+ ♔f8 and now:

a) 7 ♗c4! (JS). Again a waiting move by the bishop destroys Black's coordination: 7 ... ♞h1 8 ♔f4 ♞f2 9 ♗d5 (9 ♔g5 ♞e4+ 10 ♔g6 ♞g3) 9 ... ♞d1 (9 ... ♞g4 10 ♔g5 or 9 ... ♞d3+ 10 ♔g5) 10 ♔g5 ♞c3 (10 ... ♞e3 11 ♗e6 ♞g2 12 ♗b3) 11 ♗f3+- (JS);

b) 7 ♗f4 ♞f1 8 ♔g5 ♞g3 9 ♔g6 ♞e2.

However, 3 ... ♔f8 loses immediately to 4 ♗f3+- (JS). The knight is very unfortunately placed.

4 ♗f3 ♞h6

Not 4 ... ♞xf6?? 5 ♔xf6 ♔f8 6 ♗d5.

5 ♗xh5+ ♔f8 (21a)

This ending, with the pawn possibly on h5 or h6 and the knight on this circuit, is critical. Perhaps it is also of theoretical interest since it differs from Averbakh and the endings which he cites.

6 ♗g6!

Not 6 ♗d1? ♔g8 (6 ... ♞g8? 7 ♗b3 ♞h6 8 ♔e5 ♞g4+ 9 ♔f5+-) 7 ♗b3 ♔h7 8 ♔e7 ♞f5+ 9 ♔f8 (9 ♔e8 ♔g6 10 f7 ♞d6+ or 9 ♔e6 ♞h6 repeats, with the idea of ♞g8, ♔g7, ♞h6=) 9 ... ♔g6!= (not 9 ... ♞xh4?? 10 ♗c2+ winning).

6 ... ♞g8

Or 6 ... ♔g8 intending ... ♔h8, ... ♞g8, ... ♔g7, ... ♞h6.

For example, 7 ♔e7 ♚h8 8 ♔e8 ♘g4 9 f7 ♘f6+ and now:

a) 10 ♔e7 ♘g8+ 11 ♔f8 ♘h6;

b) 10 ♔f8 ♘d7+ 11 ♔e7 ♘f8 12 h5 ♚g7 13 ♗f5 ♚h8 14 ♗h7! (this manoeuvre is known from a study of Behting in 1892, quoted by Averbakh) 14 ... ♘xh7 (14 ... ♚g7 15 h6+!+-) 15 h6+- zugzwang.

    7   ♗h7   ♘h6

White's win is problematic. The h6-circuit is powerful.

    8   h5   ♘g4
    9   ♔f5   ♘h6+

Or 9 ... ♘e3+ 10 ♔g5 ♘d5 11 h6 ♔f7 12 ♗g6+ ♚g8 13 f7+ ♚f8 14 h7.

    10   **♔f4!** (JS)

Not 10 ♔g6 ♘g4 11 h6 ♘e5+ 12 ♚h5 ♘d7 13 ♚g5 ♘e5 14 ♗g6 ♚g8 15 ♚f5 ♘d7 (intending ... ♘xf6=) 16 f7+ ♚h8= 17 ♚g5 ♘f8 18 ♗f5 ♘g6 19 ♚f6 ♘f8 20 ♔e7 ♘g6+ 21 ♚e8 ♘f8 22 h7 ♚g7 23 ♚e7 ♚h8=.

    10   **...**   **♘f7**

Or 10 ... ♚f7 11 ♚g5 ♘g4 12 ♗g8+.

    11   **♗c2**   **1-0**

With the idea of ♗b3. (See also diag 22.)

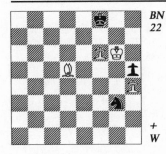

BN 22

    + W

*Speelman 1992
(after Khasin - Mariasin)*

    1   ♔g5   ♚e8!

Not 1 ... ♘e2? 2 ♗c4 ♘g3 3 ♚f4 ♘h1 4 ♚f3+-.

    2   ♚h6   ♚f8

Or 2 ... ♘f5+ 3 ♚g6 ♘e3 4 ♚g7 ♘f5+ 5 ♚g8 ♘h6+ 6 ♚h7 ♘f5 7 ♗e4+-.

    3   ♚g6   ♘e2
    4   ♗c4   ♘g3
    5   ♗d3   ♚g8
    6   ♚g5

Not 6 ♚h6 ♚f7! 7 ♚g5 ♚f8.

    6   ...   ♚f8

Black is in zugzwang.

    7   ♚f4   ♚f7
    8   ♚e5   ♚f8

Or 8 ... ♘h1 9 ♗c4+ ♚f8 10 ♚f4 ♘f2 transposing to the main line.

    9   ♗c4   ♘h1!

    10   ♚f4   ♘f2
    11   ♗d5   ♘h3+!

Alternatively:

a) 11 ... ♘g4 12 ♚g5 ♘e3 13 ♗b3 ♘g4 14 ♚g6+- (zugzwang);

b) 11 ... ♘d3+ 12 ♚g5 ♘b4 13 ♗c4 ♘c6 14 ♚xh5+-.

    12   **♚f5**

Not 12 ♚g3?! ♘g1 13 ♗c4 ♘e2+ (13 ... ♚e8!? intending 14 ♚g2 ♘e2).

    12   **...**   **♘g1!**
    13   **♚g5!**

Not 13 ♚g6 ♘e2! (13 ... ♘h3? 14 ♚h6! ♘f4 15 ♗c4+-) 14 ♗c4 ♘g3 etc.

    13   **...**   **♘h3+**

Or 13 ... ♘e2 14 ♗c4 ♘g3 15 ♚f4 etc.

    14   **♚h6!**   **♘f4**
    15   **♗c4 and wins**

Bishop v Knight

Barlov - Eingorn
Zagreb IZ 1987

68	b6+	♔d6
69	b7	♔c7
70	♔a6	♔b8
71	♗f7	♘e4
72	♗xh5	♘c5+
73	♔b6	♘xb7

Another example that the "wrong" rook's pawn can be just as dangerous as the "right". The knight has problems with both.

74 ♗g4

The first priority: keeping the black king from approaching the corner.

74	...	♘d8
75	h5	♘f7
76	♗e6	♘g5

Or 76 ... ♘h6 77 ♔c6 ♔a7 78 ♔d6 ♔b6 79 ♔e7 ♔c7 80 ♔f6 ♔d6 81 ♗h3 ♘g8+ 82 ♔g7 ♘e7 83 h6.

77	h6	♘h7
78	♔c6	♘f6
79	♔b6	♔a8
80	♔a6	

Also winning is 80 ♔c7 ♔a7 81 ♔d6 ♔b6 82 ♔e7 ♘h7 83 ♗f5 ♘g5 84 ♔f6.

80	...	♔b8
81	♔b6	1-0

Vaganian - Mikhalchishin
Lvov 1984

1 ♗f3!

Not 1 ♗g6 ♘b7! 2 ♗xh5 ♘d6 3 c5 ♘f5+=.

1	...	♘a4
2	♗xh5	♘b6
3	c5	♘d7

Or 3 ... ♘d5+ 4 ♔d2 ♔d4 5 c6 ♔c5 6 ♗e8 ♔d6 7 h5 ♘f6 8 h6.

4	c6	♔d6
5	♗f3	

Not 5 cxd7 ♔xd7 6 ♔f4 ♔e7 7 ♔g5 ♔f8 8 ♔h6 ♔g8=.

5	...	♘e5
6	h5	♘xc6
7	h6!	♘e7

Or 7 ... ♘e5 8 ♗h5.

| 8 | ♗e4 | 1-0 |

Bishop and Two Pawns v Knight and Two Pawns

Novikov - Kiss
Budapest 1989

Minimal material does not save the knight when the action is spread over the entire board.

43 ♔e3 ♘b3

Or 43 ... ♘f5+ 44 ♔f4 ♘d6 45 ♔e5 ♔e7 46 ♔d5 ♘c8 47 a5 ♔d8 48 a6 ♔c7 49 ♔e5+– ♘d6 (49 ... ♔b6 50 ♗d3) 50 a7.

44	♔d3	♔e7
45	♔c4	♘a5+
46	♔b4	♘b7
47	♗c6	♘d6
48	♔c5!	

Hindering ... ♔d8.

48	...	♘c8
49	a5	♔d8
50	♗b7	♘e7
51	♔b6	

Black could resign here.

51	...	♘g6
52	a6	♘f8
53	a7	♘d7+
54	♔b5	♔c7
55	a8♕	1-0

Bishop v Knight

**BN
26**
*Geller - Suba
Moscow 1986*
A graphic illustration of how king and knight can shoulder aside defence with reduced material.

43	♗f4	♚e2
44	♗e5	♞c2
45	♗f4	♞e3+

B

And White resigned without waiting to see 46 ♔g1 (46 ♗xe3 ♚xe3 47 ♔g1 ♚f3 48 ♔h2 ♚f2-+) 46 ... ♚f3 47 ♗c7 ♞f5 48 ♔h2 ♚f2 49 ♗e5 ♞e3 50 ♗d4 ♚f3 51 ♗xe3 (51 ♔g1 ♞f5-+) 51 ... ♚xe3 52 ♔g2 ♚e2-+.

0-1

**BN
27**
*Gaprindashvili - Tuzovsky
Tbilisi 1974*
White's positional trumps give him practical chances, but Black should be able to prevent the invasion ♔c5.

57 ♞d3

Or 57 ♞e6+ ♗xe6 58 ♔xe6 c5 59 bxc5 b4 60 a6 b3 61 a7 ♔b7 62 c6+ ♚xa7 63 c7 b2 64 c8♕ b1♕=.

W

**BN
27a**
57 ... ♗f7
Also playable is 57 ... ♗h7.

58	♔d4	♔d6
59	♞c5	♔c7
60	♔e5	

Or 60 ♞e4 ♗g6!.

60 ... ♗g8

*+
W*

61	♞d3	♗f7
62	♔d4	♗g6??

Black should play 62 ... ♔d6 63 a6 (63 ♞c5 ♔c7 64 ♞e4 ♗g6!) 63 ... ♔c7 64 ♞c5 ♗e6 65 ♞e5 ♗c8 66 a7 ♔b7 67 ♞xc6 ♗d7=.

63	♞e5	♗f5
64	♔c5	

Posting the king here is decisive.

64 ... ♗e4 *(27a)*

Black resigned without waiting for a move due to 65 ♞f7 ♗d5 66 ♞d6 ♗f3 67 a6 ♔b8 68 ♔b6 ♗h5 69 a7+ ♔a8 70 ♔a6 ♗g4 71 ♞e8.

1-0

Bishop and Two Pawns v Knight and Three Pawns

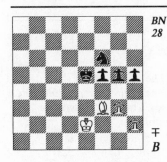

**BN
28**
*Suetin - Stein
Kislovodsk 1972*

59 ... ♞g4
60 h3(?!)

Alternatively:

a) 60 h4 gxh4 61 gxh4 ♔f4 and wins;

b) 60 ♔d3 ♞xh2 61 ♗xh5 ♞f1 62 g4 ♞g3 63 ♗g6 fxg4 64 ♔e3 ♞f5+ 65 ♔f2 g3+ and wins;

c) 60 ♔e1!?, to avoid the weakness at h3, may be best.

*∓
B*

60	...	♞f6
61	♔f2	h4
62	♔g2	♔d4
63	gxh4	gxh4
64	♔f2	♔e5
65	♗c6?	

65 ♔e3 must be best. Preventing a king invasion is more important than losing a second pawn. After 65 ... ♞e4 White can try 66 ♗e2!? with the idea of reaching diag 32. White is better off without the

h3-pawn.

65	...	♔f4
66	♗b7	♘e4+
67	♔g2	

By comparison to diag 57, here the presence of the h3-pawn renders counterplay against the h4-pawn impossible, so White cannot prevent Black from maximising his position before winning a second pawn.

67	...	♔e3
68	♗c8	f4

69	♗a6	♘d2
70	♗b5	f3+
71	♔g1	♔f4
72	♔h2	♘e4
73	♗a6	♘c3
74	♔g1	

Or 74 ♗c4 ♘e2 75 ♗a6 ♔e3 76 ♗b7 ♔g3 77 ♗a6 ♔d2 78 ♔g1 ♔e1.

74	...	♔g3

Black wins the h-pawn with his knight.

0-1

See also diags 29, 30 and 37.

BN 29

= W

Zuckerman - Ostojic
Wijk aan Zee 1968

Here Black faces little danger since his pawn structure is sound and complements the bishop.

59	♘e2	♔e6
60	♘g3	♗f6
61	♔f3	♔f7
62	♘e4	♗a1
63	h4	♔g7
64	♘g3	♗b2
65	h5	♗c3

Black defends passively. Keeping the pawns on white squares avoids the problems we have seen in similar endings. Black also refrains from pawn exchanges that would produce a passed pawn for White.

66	g5	♗b2
67	f5	gxf5
68	♘xf5+	♔f7
69	♔g4	♗c1
70	♘d4	♗b2
71	♘e2	♗a3
72	♔f5	♗b2
73	♘f4	♔g7
74	♘d5	

White is further handicapped by the fact that playing h6 gives Black the possibility of ... ♗xg5, sacrificing the bishop to reach a known fortress draw.

74	...	♗c1
75	h6+	♔h8
76	♘f6	

Admitting the truth.

76	...	♗xg5
77	♔xg5	½-½

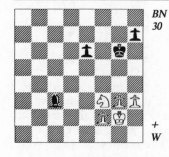

BN 30

+ W

Korchnoi - Hübner
Johannesburg 1981

39	♔f1	♗b4
40	♔e2	♗c5
41	♘d2	♔f5
42	♔f3	h6
43	♘c4	♔f6
44	♘b2	♔f5
45	♘d3	♗b6
46	h4	♗d8
47	g4+	♔g6
48	h5+	♔f6

48 ... ♔g5 49 ♘e5 forces Black back.

49	♔e4	

The first phase is over: White has driven back the black king and fixed the h6-pawn.

49	...	♗b6
50	f3	♗g1
51	♘e5	♔g7
52	f4	♗c5

52 ... ♗b6 53 ♘f3 (53 g5!

transposes to the main line) 53 ... ♘d8 was suggested by Marjanovic, with the idea of 54 g5? hxg5 55 fxg5 ♗xg5 56 ♘xg5 ♔h6.

| 53 | ♘f3 | ♗d6 |
| 54 | g5 | ♗e7 |

Not 54 ... hxg5 55 fxg5 ♗e7 56 ♔f4+-.

55	g6	♔f6
56	♘e5	♔g7
57	♔d4	♗b4
58	♔c4	♗d2
59	♘d3	♗e3
60	♔b5	♔f6
61	♔c6	♔e7

62 g7!

White forces the ending of diag 31.

62	...	♔f7
63	♔d7	♔xg7
64	♔xe6	♗d2
65	f5	♗c3
66	♘f2	♗b2
67	♘g4	♗c1
68	f6+	♔g8

Or 68 ... ♔f8 69 ♔f5 ♔f7 70 ♘e5+ ♔g8 71 ♔g6 as in diag 28.

69	♔e7	♗a3+
70	♔e8	♔h7
71	♘e3	1-0

BN 31

Popchev - Cvitan
Dubrovnik 1990

1	...	f6
2	♗d5	♘b5
3	♗c6	♘c3

Threatening ... ♘d1+ and ... ♔e3.

4	♗b7	♘d1+
5	♔g2	♔e3
6	♔g3	♘c3
7	♗c6?!	

Allowing a tactical finish, but sterner defence loses methodically: 7 ♔g2 ♘e2 8 ♗e4 (8 ♗c6 ♘d4 transposes to the game, but not 8 ♗d5?? ♘f4+)

8 ... ♘d4 9 ♔g3 ♔e2 (9 ... ♘xf3? 10 ♗xf3 e4 11 ♗g2) 10 ♔g2 ♘e6 11 ♗c6 ♘f4+ 12 ♔g1 (12 ♔g3 ♔f1 and ... ♘e2+, ... ♔f2) 12 ... ♘d3 13 ♔g2 (13 ♗b5 ♔e3 and ... ♘e1) 13 ... ♘e1+ 14 ♔g3 ♔f1 15 ♗b5+ ♔g1 16 ♗c4 ♘g2 17 ♗b5 ♘e3 and ... ♘f1+, ... ♔f2 and the f-pawn falls.

7	...	♘e2+
8	♔g2	♘d4
9	♗b7	♘xf3!
10	♗xf3	e4
11	♗d1	♔d2
	0-1	

Bishop and Three Pawns v Knight and Two Pawns

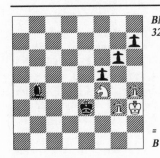

BN 32

Nimzowitsch - Davidson
Semmering 1926

| 1 | ... | ♗d6 |
| 2 | ♘d5+ | |

Another interesting defensive try is 2 ♘e6!? ♔f2 3 ♘g5 h6 4 ♘f7 ♗xg3 5 ♘xh6 and now:

a) 5 ... ♗f4 6 ♘f7 ♗c7 7 ♘h8 (7 h5!? gxh5 8 ♘h8) 7 ... f4 and:

a1) 8 h5! f3 9 hxg6 ♔e1 (9 ... ♔e3 10 g7 f2 11 g8♕ f1♕+ 12 ♕g2 ♕f5+ 13 ♕g4 ♕h7+ 14 ♕h4) 10 g7 f2 11 g8♕ f1♕+ 12 ♕g2 ♕d3+ 13 ♔g4 ♕d7+ 14 ♔g5;

a2) 8 ♘f7 f3 9 ♘g5 (9 h5 ♔e2) 9 ... ♔e2 10 ♘xf3 ♔xf3 11 h5 g5-+;

b) 5 ... ♗c7! 6 ♘f7 (6 h5 ♗f4 7 ♘g4+ ♔f3!-+) 6 ... ♔e2 and:

b1) 7 ♘h8? f4;

b2) 7 h5!? (I think that White must try this while the g5-square is under control) 7 ... gxh5 8 ♔g2 (8 ♘g5!? intending ♔g2, ♘e6) 8 ... ♗f4 9 ♘d8?! (9 ♔h3!? with the idea of ♔h4) 9 ... ♗e5 10 ♘f7 and White has excellent drawing chances;

b3) 7 ♘g5 ♗e5 8 ♔g2 ♗f6 9 ♘f3 ♔e3 (9 ... f4 10 ♘g1+ ♔e3 11 ♘f3 is analogous to the main line - White to move is in zugzwang) 10 ♔g3 ♗e7 11 ♔g2 f4 12 ♘e5 ♔e2 13 ♘f3 ♗d8 14 ♘d4+ (14 ♘e5 ♗f6 15 ♘f3 ♔e3-+) 14 ... ♔e3 15 ♘c2+ ♔e4 16 h5 (16 ♔h3? f3-+) 16 ... gxh5 (16 ... g5! 17 h6 g4 18 h7 ♗f6 19 ♘b4 ♗e5 20 ♘c6 f3+ 21 ♔f1 ♗c3-+ 22 ♔f2 ♔f4) 17 ♘e1 ♗b6 18 ♘f3 ♔e3 19 ♘g5 ♔e2 20

♘f3 ♗f2 21 ♘e5 h4 (see also diag 21) 22 ♔h1 ♗d4 23 ♘g6!? f3 24 ♘f4+ looks like a successful version of the defence in (diag 21): 24 ... ♔f1 25 ♘h3 ♗e3 26 ♔h2 ♔e2 27 ♔h1.

| 2 | ... | ♔f3 |
| 3 | ♘f6 | h5? |

Black should play 3 ... h6!-+ (Kmoch) 4 ♘g8 (4 g4 f4-+) 4 ... g5 5 ♘xh6 (5 hxg5 hxg5 6 ♘h6 ♗xg3 7 ♘xf5 g4+) 5 ... g4+ 6 ♔h2 ♗xg3+ 7 ♔h1 (7 ♔g1 ♗f2+ 8 ♔h1 g3) 7 ... ♔f4! 8 h5 ♔g5 and wins.

| 4 | ♘d5 | ♔f2 |

Or 4 ... ♗xg3 5 ♘e7.

| 5 | ♘f6 | ♗xg3 |
| 6 | ♘e4+! | fxe4 |
| ½-½ |

Notes based on analysis by Speelman.

BN 33

Sveshnikov - Tukmakov
USSR 1984

40	♔g2	g5
41	fxg5	♗xg5
42	♘f3	♗h6
43	♔g3	♔e7
44	♔g4	♗e3
45	♘e5	♔f6
46	♘c4	♗d4
47	h4	♔g7
48	h5	f6
49	♘d6	♗e5

49 ... ♗c5! is an improvement suggested by Sveshnikov.

50	♘b7!	f5+
51	♔g5	♗f6+
52	♔f4	♗c3
53	h6+	♔g6

Or 53 ... ♔f6 54 h7 ♗d2+ 55 ♔f3 ♔g7 56 h8♕+ ♔xh8 57 ♘d8 e5 58 ♘f7+= (Sveshnikov).

54 ♘d6!

Not 54 h7? e5+ 55 ♔f3 ♔xh7-+.

| 54 | ... | ♔f6 |
| 55 | ♘c4 | ♔g6 |

Or 55 ... e5+ 56 ♔f3 ♔g6 (56 ... e4+ 57 ♔f4 ♔g6 58 h7=) 57 ♘d6= (Sveshnikov).

56	♘d6	♗b2
57	h7	♗f6
58	♘e8!	♗b2
59	♘d6	♗g7
60	♘c8!	♔f6

Or 60 ... ♔xh7 61 ♘e7=.

| 61 | ♘d6 | ♔g6 |

Also drawing is 61 ... e5+ 62 ♔f3 ♔e6 63 ♘c4 e4+ 64 ♔f4 ♔f6 65 ♘e3 ♗h6+ 66 ♔g3 f4+ 67 ♔g4 ♔g7 68 ♘f5+ ♔xh7 69 ♘xh6 e3 70 ♘f7 e2 71 ♘g5+ ♔g6 72 ♘f3= (Sveshnikov).

| 62 | ♘c8 | ½-½ |

Bishop v Knight

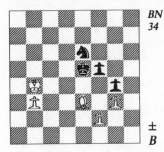

BN
34

±
B

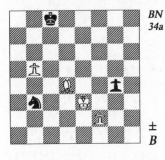

BN
34a

±
B

Yusupov - Anand
Linares 1992
The bishop has an extra pawn with play on both sides of the board. Only the reduced material gives Black hope.

	44 ...	f4

Forcing simplification.

45	gxf4+	♘xf4
46	♔c4	♘h5
47	♗a7!	

Preventing ... g3.

47	...	♔e6
48	♗b8	♘f6
49	♔d4	♘d5
50	♗g3	♘b4
51	♔c5	♘d3+
52	♔c4	♘e1
53	b4	♘c2
54	b5	♔d7

Black could not prevent the pawn's advance to b5, but now must make a stand on b7.

55	♗e5	♘e1
56	♔d5	♘d3
57	♗d4	

Or 57 ♗g3 ♘b4+ 58 ♔c5 ♘d3+ 59 ♔b6 ♔c8 60 ♔a7 ♘c5 61 b6 ♘b7 62 ♗h4 ♘a5 63 ♔a6 ♘b7 64 ♗e7 ♔b8 and White does not seem able to zugzwang Black on the queenside (see also diag 4). Here the king in the corner would lose (there is no stalemate with the g-pawn) but c8 seems safe.

57	...	♘f4+
58	♔e4	♘e2
59	♗e5	♔c8
60	♔e3	♘c1
61	♗b2	

Playing to dominate the knight.

61	...	♘b3
62	♗d4 *(34a)*	
62	...	♘c1

62 ... ♔b7!? is very similar to the critical line considered later: 63 ♔d3 ♘c1+ 64 ♔d2 ♘b3+ 65 ♔c3 ♘c1 66 ♗e3 g3

67 f4 g2 68 f5 ♘e2+ 69 ♔b4 (not 69 ♔c4 g1♕ 70 ♗xg1 ♘xg1 71 f6 ♘f3=) 69 ... ♘f4 70 ♔c5+.

| 63 | ♔d2 | ♘b3+ |
| 64 | ♔c3 | ♘a5?! |

A better try is 64 ... ♘c1! and now:

a) 65 ♗e3!? and:

a1) 65 ... ♘e2+ 66 ♔d3 ♘g1 67 f4 ♘f3 (67 ... ♘h3 68 f5 g3 69 f6 ♔d7 70 b6 g2 71 b7 ♔c7 72 f7) 68 ♔e4! (intending to escort the f-pawn and attack the g-pawn) 68 ... ♘h4 (68 ... ♘h2 69 f5 g3 70 ♔f4 g2 71 f6 ♘f1 72 ♗g1 ♔d7 73 f7 ♔e7 74 b6) 69 ♗f2! ♘g6 70 f5 ♘f8 71 ♔f4+;

a2) 65 ... g3 66 f4 (66 fxg3 ♘e2+=) 66 ... g2 67 f5 ♘e2+ (67 ... g1♕ 68 ♗xg1 ♘e2+ 69 ♔b4! ♘xg1 70 f6 ♔d7 71 f7 ♔e7 72 b6 ♘f3 73 b7 ♘e5 74 f8♕+) 68 ♔b4 ♔d7 69 b6 ♔c6 and:

a21) 70 f6 ♘f4 intending ... ♘d5=;

a22) 70 ♔a5! ♔b7 71 f6 ♘f4 72 f7 ♘e6 73 ♔b5 ♘f8 (73 ... ♔b8 74 ♔a6!) 74 ♔c5! winning as the f-pawn will claim the knight (but not 74 ♔c4? ♔c6 75 ♔d3 ♔d6 76 ♔e2 ♘d7 77 ♔f2 ♔e7=);

b) 65 ♔c2 ♘e2 (65 ... ♘a2 66 ♗c5) 66 ♔d3 (66 ♗e3 g3 67 f4 g2 68 f5 g1♕ 69 ♗xg1 ♘xg1 70 f6 ♘f3 71 f7 ♘d4+ 72 ♔d3 ♘e6=) 66 ... ♘f4+ 67 ♔e4 ♘e2 and White has not made progress.

65	♗e5	♔d7
66	♗f4!	♔c8
67	♔d4	♔b7
68	♔c5	♔a7
69	♔b4	♔b7
70	♗c7	

And Black resigned due to 70 ... ♔a8 71 b6.

Bishop v Knight

Bishop v Knight: Many Pawns

BN 35

+ W

Szabo - R.Byrne
Havana Ol 1966
1   ♘d2

Not 1 d6+? ♗xd6 2 ♘xd6 ♔xd6 3 ♔b6 ♔d7 4 ♔b7 ♔d6! (4 ... ♔d8? 5 ♔c6 ♔e7 6 ♔c7 ♔e8 7 ♔d6 ♔f7 8 ♔d7 ♔f8 9 ♔e6 ♔g7 10 ♔e7 ♔g6 11 ♔f8+-) 5 ♔c8 ♔c5 6 ♔d7 ♔c4 7 ♔e6 ♔d3 8 ♔xf6 ♔xe4 9 ♔xg5 (9 ♔e6 ♔f3!=) 9 ... ♔xe3 10 ♔f5 e4=.

1	...	♗a3
2	♘f1	♗d6
3	♘g3	♗e7
4	♘h5	♔d7
5	♔b6	♗d8+
6	♔b7	♗e7
7	♘g7	♗b4
8	♘f5	♗c5
9	♘h6	♗f8

Or 9 ... ♗xe3 10 ♘g8.

| 10 | ♘f5 | ♗c5 |
| 11 | ♘h6 | ♗f8 |

Or 11 ... ♗e7 12 ♘g8 ♗d8 13 ♔b8 ♗c7+ 14 ♔a7 ♗d8 15 ♔b7+- (zugzwang).

12	♘g8!	♗g7
13	♔b8	♔d8
14	♔b7	♔d7
15	♔a6!	

In the game Szabo actually let the win slip: 15 ♔b6 ♔d6 16 ♘e7 ♔d7 17 ♘c6 ♗f8 18 ♘a5 ♗b4 19 ♘c4 ♗f8 20 ♘d2 ♗e7 21 ♘b3 ♗d8+ 22 ♔b5 ♗e7 23 ♘c5+ ♔c7 24 ♘e6+ ♔d7 25 ♔c6 ♗b4 26 ♘g7 ♗e7 27 ♘f5 ♗f8 28 ♘g3 ♗e7 29 ♘h5 ♗d8+ 30 ♔c5 ♗e7+ 31 ♔b5 ♗d6 32 ♘g7 ♔c7 33 ♔a6 ♔c8 34 ♔a5 ♔b7 35 ♘e8 ♔c8 36 ♔a6 ♔d7 37 ♘g7 ♔c8 38 ♘f5 ♗f8 39 ♔b6 ♔d7 40 ♔b7 ♗b4 ½-½.

| 15 | ... | ♔d6 |

Alternatively:

a) 15 ... ♔e8 16 ♔b6 (16 ♔b7?! ♔d7!) 16 ... ♔f7 17 d6+-;

b) 15 ... ♘h8 16 ♔b6 ♗g7 17 ♔b7;

c) 15 ... ♔c7 16 ♔b5 ♔d7 17 ♘c5 ♗f8+ 18 ♔b6 ♗g7 19 ♔b7 with a zugzwang: 19 ... ♘h8 (19 ... ♔d6 20 ♘e7 or 19 ... ♔d6 20 ♔c8!? f5 21 exf5 e4 22 f6+-) 20 ♘e7 ♗g7 21 ♘c8 ♗f8 22 ♘b6+ ♔d6 23 ♔c8+-.

| 16 | ♔b6 | f5! |
| 17 | exf5 | ♔xd5 |

Or 17 ... e4 18 f6 ♘h8 (18 ... ♗f8 19 ♘e7) 19 ♔b7 ♔xd5 20 ♔c7 ♔e6 21 ♔d8 ♗f7 22 ♔d7 ♔xg8 23 ♔e7 ♔h7 24 f7 ♗g7 25 f8♕ ♗xf8+ 26 ♔xf8 ♔g6 27 ♔e7+-.

| 18 | f6! | |

Not 18 ♔c7? ♗e4 19 f6 ♗xf6 20 ♘xf6+ ♔xe3 21 ♔d6 ♔f4 22 ♔d5 e4=.

| 18 | ... | ♗f8 |

Also losing is 18 ... ♘h8 19 ♔c7 ♔e4 20 f7 ♗g7 21 ♘e7 ♗f3 22 ♘f5 ♗f8 23 ♔d7 ♔xg4 24 ♔e8+-.

| 19 | ♔c7 | ♔e6 |

Or 19 ... ♔e4 20 ♔d7 ♔xe3 21 ♔e8 ♗a3 22 f7 e4 23 ♘e7.

20	e4!	♔f7
21	♘e7	♔xf6
22	♘d5+	♔e6
23	♔c6 and wins	

For example: 23 ... ♗a3 24 ♘c7+ ♔e7 25 ♔d5 ♗b2 26 ♘a6 ♗c3 27 ♘c5 ♗d4 28 ♘d3 ♔f6 29 ♔d6 ♗c3 (29 ... ♗a7 30 ♘c5 ♗b8+ 31 ♔d5 ♔e7 32 ♘d3 ♔f6 33 ♘b4 ♗c7 34 ♘c6) 30 ♘c5 ♗b4 31 ♔d5 ♔e7 32 ♘d3+-.

BN 36

BN 36a

+W

+W

Novikov - Mikhalchishin
Lvov 1987

44 f3

White mobilises his pawn majority. The control of g4 and the ability to generate a protected passed e-pawn seem to make White's pawn structure more dangerous than an unblemished one.

44 ... ♔e7
45 ♔e1 ♞a4
46 ♔d2 ♞b6
47 ♔d3 ♞c8

Or 47 ... ♞d7 48 ♔d4 ♔d6 49 ♗b5 ♞f6 50 e4 fxe4 51 fxe4 ♔e7 52 e5 ♞g4 53 ♗d3 ♔f7 54 ♔d5 and ♔d6, e6 winning - Mikhalchishin.

48 ♔d4 ♞a7
49 ♔c5 ♞c8
50 e4 fxe4 *(36a)*

Or 50 ... ♞d6 51 e5 ♞e8 (51 ... ♞b7+ 52 ♔b6 ♞d8 53 ♔c7 ♔e8 54 ♗b3 ♔e7 55 ♗d5 ♔e8 56 ♔d6) 52 ♔c6 ♞g7 53 ♔c7 ♞e8+ 54 ♔c8 ♞g7 55 ♗d5 ♞e8 56 ♗c6 ♞g7 57 ♗d7 ♔f8 58 ♔d8 ♔f7 59 ♗c8 ♞e8 60 e6+ ♔f8 61 e7+ ♔f7 62 ♗e6+.

51 fxe4 ♞d6
52 ♔d4 ♞e8

Alternatively, 52 ... ♞c8!? 53 e5 ♔d7 (53 ... ♔f8 54 ♔c5 ♞e7 55 ♗e6 ♔e8 56 ♔d6 ♔d8 57 ♗d7 ♞g8 58 ♗c6 ♞e7 59 ♗e4 ♔e8 60 ♔e6+-) 54 ♔c5 ♞e7 55 ♗f7 ♔c7 56 e6 ♔d8 57 ♔d6 ♞f5+ 58 ♔e5 ♞e7 (58 ... ♞xh4 59 ♔f6+-) 59 ♔f6 ♞d5+ 60 ♔xg6 ♞xf4+ 61 ♔g5 ♞d5 (61 ... ♞xe6+ 62 ♗xe6 ♔e7 63 ♗c4 ♔f8 64 ♔g6+-) 62

♔xh5 ♔e7 63 ♔g6 and now:

a) 63 ... ♔f8 (the toughest defence) 64 h5 ♞f4+ 65 ♔f6 (65 ♔g5? ♞xe6+ 66 ♗xe6 ♔g7=) 65 ... ♞d5+ 66 ♔e5 ♞e3 67 h6 ♞g4+ 68 ♔d6 ♞f6 (68 ... ♞xh6 69 e7+ ♔xf7 70 ♔d7) 69 ♗g6 ♔g8 70 e7 ♞h8 71 ♗f7 (71 ♔e6? ♞g8!) 71 ... ♞h7 72 ♔e6;

b) 63 ... ♞f4+ 64 ♔g7 winning by zugzwang.

53 e5 ♞g7

Or 53 ... ♞c7 54 ♔c5 ♞e8 55 ♗f1 ♞c7 56 ♗h3 ♞a6+ 57 ♔b5 ♞c7+ 58 ♔c6 and now:

a) 58 ... ♞a6 59 ♗f1 ♞b4+ (59 ... ♞b8+ 60 ♔d5 ♞d7 61 ♗d3 ♞f8 62 f5 transposes) 60 ♔c5 ♞c2 61 ♗d3+-;

b) 58 ... ♞e8 59 ♗d7 ♞g7 60 ♔c7 ♔f7 61 ♔d6 ♔f8 62 ♗h3 ♞e8+ (62 ... ♔e8 63 e6+-) 63 ♔d7 ♞g7 64 e6+-.

54 ♗d3 ♞e6+

Also losing is 54 ... ♔f7 55 ♔d5 ♞e8 56 ♔c6 ♞g7 57 ♔d7+-.

55 ♔e3 ♞f8
56 ♗c2!

Zugzwang (not 56 f5?? ♞d7! 57 ♔d4 gxf5 58 ♗xf5 ♞xe5=).

56 ... ♔e6

Alternatively:

a) 56 ... ♔f7 57 f5+-;

b) 56 ... ♔e8 57 f5 ♞d7 58 ♗a4.

57 ♔d4 ♔e7
58 f5 gxf5
59 ♗xf5 ♔f7
60 ♔e4 ♔g7
61 ♔f3! ♔h6
62 ♔f4 ♔g7
63 ♔g5 1-0

Bishop v Knight

♗ V ♞

Bishop and Four Pawns v Knight and Four Pawns

BN
37

- B

Gulko - Romanishin
Lvov 1978
This ending vividly illustrates the superiority of knight v bishop with action on one flank. White's pawn weaknesses make life very difficult. Though I believe White should draw, his practical task is difficult.

38	...	♔g6

Romanishin later suggested 38 ... ♔e6!? planning to bring the king to c4 as an alternative method.

39	♔g3	f5!?
40	exf5+	

White could consider passive play like ♔g3-g2 etc, trying to make Black force this capture.

40	...	♔xf5
41	♗e3	♘e1
42	♗d2	♘c2
43	♗c1	♘d4
44	♗e3	♘e2+
45	♔g2	h5
46	h4?	

The decisive error; the pawn proves to be accessible here. White must defend passively. Mikhalchishin considers allowing ... h4 to be winning for Black as well but his analysis is unconvincing. After 46 ♗d2 h4 Mikhalchishin claims that Black wins by putting his king on d5 and knight on f4 (see diag 43): 47 ♔h2 ♘f4 48 ♗c3 (or 48 ♗e3 ♘d3 and ... ♘e1-+) 48 ... ♔e6 49 ♗d2! with drawing chances.

46	...	♔e6
47	♗g5	♔d5
48	♗e7	♘d4
49	♗d8	♘f5
50	♔f1	♘d4

51	♔g2	♘e6
52	♗e7	♔c4
53	♗d6	♔d4
54	♗e7	♔d5
55	♔g3	♘d4
56	♗d8	

56 ♗a3 is given as stronger by Romanishin but Black seems to win after:

a) 56 ... ♔c4?! (Mikhalchishin) 57 ♗b2 creates difficulties and perhaps even better is 57 f4!? ♘e2+ 58 ♔f3 ♘xf4 59 ♔e4 ♘g6 60 ♗b2 ♘xh4 61 ♗xe5 and White should draw easily;

b) 56 ... ♘f5+! and after 57 ♔h3 e4 Black transposes to the game structure.

56	...	♘f5+
57	♔h3	♔d4
58	♗c7	e4
59	fxe4	

Clearly 59 f4 would only increase the number of pawns White is likely to lose, without any positive effect on the position.

59	...	♔xe4
60	♗b6	♔f3
61	♗c5	g6
62	♗b6	♘d6

Preparing to attack f2.

63	♔h2	♘c4!

Here d2 is the ideal square for the knight.

64	♗d4	♘d2
65	♗b6	♔g4

White is unable to guard both weaknesses.

66	♗d8	♘f3+
67	♔g2	♘xh4+
68	♔h2	♘f3+
69	♔g2	h4
70	♗c7	h3+
71	♔f1	g5
72	♗d8	♔f5

73	♗c7	g4		77	♗c7	♘e2
74	♗b8	♔e4		Intending ... g3, ... h2.		
75	♗c7	♘d4		78	♗h2	♘c3

Yielding the f3-square to the king.

				79	♗b8	♘e4
76	♗b8	♔f3		80	♔g1	♘xf2
					0-1	

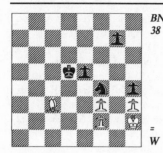

BN 38   = W

Mikhalchishin 1978

1	...	♘d3
2	♔g2	♔c4
3	♗d2	

Here Mikhalchishin again defends cooperatively with 3 ♗a5 ♘f4+ 4 ♔h2 ♔d3 (now the black king has come too far) 5 ♗c7 ♘g6 6 ♔g2 ♔e2 7 ♗d6 ♘f4+ 8 ♔h2 ♘d3 9 ♗e7 ♔xf3 10 ♗xh4 ♘xf2 and the e-pawn wins - Mikhalchishin. Nevertheless, as the main line

shows, the key defensive diagonal is c1-h6, and even if Black can achieve this position (which I do not believe) Mikhalchishin's winning method does not consider the best defence.

3	...	♔d4

3 ... ♘f4+ 4 ♗xf4 exf4 5 ♔f1 ♔d3 6 ♔e1=.

4	♔f1	

And ♗g5 with good drawing chances.

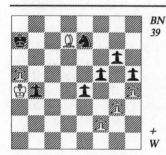

BN 39   + W

Ivanchuk - Ribli
Reggio Emilia 1988

White is winning due to action on both flanks and a black kingside exposed to invasion.

56	♗e8	

Also possible is 56 ♔xb4!? e3 57 fxe3 ♘d5+ 58 ♔c5 ♘xe3 59 ♗b5 f4 60 gxf4 ♘g2 61 ♔d6 ♘xh4 (61 ... ♘xf4? 62 ♗f1+-) 62 ♔e5 (62 ♗f1 ♘f5+ 63 ♔e5 h4=) 62 ... ♘g2= 63 ♗f1 ♘xf4 64 ♔xf4 h4 65 ♔g4 g5 66 ♗e2 ♔b7 67 ♗f1 ♔a7 68 ♔xg5 h3 69 ♗xh3 ♔a6.

56	...	e3

56 ... ♔b7 does not help: 57 ♔xb4 e3 58 fxe3 ♘d5+ 59 ♔a4 ♘xe3 60 ♗xg6 ♘f1 61 ♗xh5 ♘xg3 62 ♗f3+ ♔a7 63 h5.

57	fxe3	♘d5
58	♗xg6	♘xe3
59	♗xh5	♘f1
60	♗d1!	

Not 60 ♗f3 b3.

60	...	♘xg3
61	h5	♘e4
62	h6	♘g5
63	♗c2	f4
64	h7	♘f7
65	♗g6	♘h8
66	♗h5	**1-0**

cf diag BBNN1a

Bishop v Knight

♗ **V** ♞

BN
40

±
W

BN
40a

+
W

Rodriguez - Eingorn
Havana 1986
1 ♔c4

Not 1 ♔e4 ♘g8 2 ♔f4
♘h6 3 ♗e4 ♘g8 4 f3 ♘h6 5
g4 hxg4! 6 fxg4 ♘g8 7 ♔g5
♘h6 8 h5!? gxh5 9 gxh5 (9
♔xh5 ♘g8 looks drawn to
me - JS) 9 ... ♘g8=.
1 ...   ♔f8
2 ♔c5   ♘f5?!

Better was 2 ... ♔e8.
3 ♗e4

Alternatively: 3 ♗c8 ♘h6 4
d5 exd5 5 ♔xd5 ♔e7 6 ♗h3
♘g8 7 f3 f6! 8 ♗e6 ♘h6 and
now:

a) 9 exf6+ ♔xf6 10 ♔d6
(10 f4 ♘f5! 11 ♗xf5 ♔xf5 12
♔d6 ♔g4 13 ♔e5 ♔xg3 14
f5=) 10 ... g5 11 hxg5+ (11
♔d7 gxh4 12 gxh4 ♘f5 13
♗xf5 ♔xf5 14 ♔e7 ♔f4 15
♔f6 ♔xf3 16 ♔g5 ♔e4 17
♔xh5 ♔f5=) 11 ... ♔xg5 12
♔e5 h4 13 f4+ ♔h5 14 gxh4
♔xh4 15 ♔f6 ♔g3 16 ♔g5
♔f3 17 ♗a2 ♔g3 18 ♗d5
♔h3! 19 ♗c4 ♔g3 20 ♗b3
♔f3 21 ♗d1+ ♔e3! (21 ...
♔g3?? 22 ♗h5 ♘g8 23 f5+-)
22 ♗h5 ♔e4=;

b) 9 g4 hxg4 10 fxg4 ♘xg4!
11 ♗xg4 fxe5 12 ♔xe5 ♔f7 13
♔f4 ♔f6 14 ♗d1 ♔f7 15 ♔g5
♔g7 16 ♗c2 as in the game
Rodriguez - Eingorn.
3 ...   ♘e7 (40a)

Not 3 ... ♘h6? 4 ♔d6 (in-
tending ♗xg6) and now:

a) 4 ... ♔g7 5 f3 ♘g8 6 ♔d7
♘h6 7 ♔e8 ♔g8 8 d5 exd5 9
♗xd5 ♔g7 10 ♗b3 (zugzwang)
10 ... ♘f5 (10 ... ♔g8 11 e6!
fxe6 12 ♗xe6+ ♔g7 13
♔e7+-) 11 ♗xf7 ♘xg3 (11 ...
g5 12 hxg5 ♘xg3 13 e6 ♘f5
14 ♔d7 h4 15 e7 ♘xe7 16
♔xe7 h3 17 f4 h2 18 ♗d5) 12
♔d7! ♘f5 13 e6 ♔f6 14 ♗xg6

♔xg6 15 e7 ♘xe7 16 ♔xe7
♔f5 17 ♔f7 ♔f4 18 ♔g6
♔xf3 19 ♔xh5 ♔f4 20
♔g6+-;

b) 4 ... ♘g4 and:

b1) 5 f4!? ♔g7! (5 ... ♘h6?
6 ♗xg6 fxg6 7 ♔xe6 ♘f5 8
d5+- since White is a tempo
up on the main line);

b2) 5 f3 ♘h6 (5 ... ♘h2 6
d5 exd5 7 ♗xd5 ♘f1 8 ♗xf7!
♔xf7 9 ♔d7+- or 5 ... ♘e3 6
♗xg6 fxg6 7 ♔xe6 will transpose to the main line) 6 ♗xg6
fxg6 7 ♔xe6 ♘f5 8 d5 ♘xg3
9 d6 ♔e8 10 ♔f6 ♘f5 11 f4
and now:

b21) 11 ... ♔d7 12 ♔xg6
♘xh4+ 13 ♔f6! (13 ♔xh5?
♘f5 with a blockade and
drawing chances) 13 ... ♘g2 14
e6+ and wins;

b22) 11 ... ♘xh4 12 e6 ♘f5
13 d7+ ♔d8 14 ♔xg6 and:

b221) 14 ... h4 15 ♔xf5 h3
16 ♔e5! h2 (16 ... ♔c7 17 ♔f6
h2 18 ♔e7 h1♕ 19 d8♕+
winning or 16 ... ♔e7 17 f5 h2
18 f6+) 17 ♔d6 h1♕ 18 e7+;

b222) 14 ... ♘e7+ 15
♔xh5+-;

b223) 14 ... ♘g3 15 f5+-;

b224) 14 ... ♘d4! and:

b2241) 15 ♔f6? ♘c6 16 f5
h4 17 ♔f7 (17 ♔g7 ♘d4 18
♔f6 ♘xf5!=) 17 ... h3 18 f6
♘e5+ 19 ♔g7 h2 20 f7
♘xd7! 21 exd7 h1♕ 22 f8♕+
♔xd7=;

b2242) 15 ♔f7! ♘f5 (15 ...
♘c6 16 f5 h4 17 f6 ♘e5+ 18
♔g7 and White is a tempo up
on the line above) 16 ♔f6!
♘e7 (16 ... ♘d6 17 ♔g5 ♘b5
18 f5 ♘d4 19 ♔f6 transposes
to the main line) 17 ♔g5 ♘c6
18 f5! (18 ♔xh5?? ♘d4=) 18 ...
♘d4 19 ♔f6 ♘c6 20 ♔f7 h4
21 f6 ♘e5+ 22 ♔g7+- etc.
4 ♔d6   ♔e8

5 f3

This is probably winning. Also 5 ♔c7 ♘g8 6 f3 and now:

a) 6 ... ♘e7 7 g4 hxg4 8 fxg4 ♘g8 9 ♗c6+! (after 9 g5? ♘e7 White is in zugzwang) 9 ... ♔f8 (9 ... ♔e7 10 g5 ♔f8 11 ♔d7 ♘e7 12 ♗e4) 10 ♔d7 ♘h6 11 ♗f3 (zugzwang) 11 ... ♘g8 (11 ... ♔g8 12 ♔e7 ♔g7 13 ♔e8 ♔g8 14 d5 exd5 15 g5 ♘f5 16 ♗xd5 ♔g7 17 ♗xf7 ♘xh4 18 ♗d5 ♘f5 19 e6+-) 12 g5 ♘e7 13 ♗e4 ♘g8 (13 ... ♘f5 14 ♗xf5 gxf5 15 g6 f4 16 gxf7 f3 17 d5 f2 18 dxe6 f1♕ 19 e7+ ♔xf7 20 e8♕+ and wins) 14 ♗xg6 fxg6 15 ♔xe6 ♘e7 16 d5 ♘f5 17 d6 ♔e8 18 h5! ♘g7+ 19 ♔f6 ♘xh5+ 20 ♔xg6+-;

b) 6 ... ♔e7! and:

b1) 7 ♗c2 ♘h6 8 ♗d3 ♘g8 9 ♗f1 ♘h6 10 ♗h3 ♘g8 11 g4 hxg4 12 fxg4 ♔e8 and:

b11) 13 g5 ♘e7 14 ♔d6 (14 ♗g4 ♘d5+ 15 ♔d6 ♘e3 16 ♗h3) 14 ... ♘c8+ 15 ♔c5 ♘e7;

b12) 13 ♗g2 ♘h6! 14 ♗f3 ♔e7;

b2) 7 g4!? hxg4 8 fxg4 ♘h6 and now:

b21) 9 g5! and:

b211) 9 ... ♘f5 10 ♗xf5 gxf5 11 h5 f4 12 h6 ♔f8 13 g6 fxg6 (13 ... f3 14 h7 ♔g7 15 gxf7) 14 d5 f3 15 d6 f2 16 d7 f1♕ 17 d8♕+ winning, e.g. 17 ... ♔f7 18 ♕d7+ ♔f8 19 ♕g7+ ♔e8 20 ♕xg6+ ♔e7 21 ♕g7+ ♔e8 22 ♕d7+ ♔f8 23 ♕xe6 ♕c1+ 24 ♕c6 etc;

b212) 9 ... ♘g4!;

b22) 9 ♗f3 ♔e8 10 ♔d6 ♔d8 should hold.

5 ... ♔d8

Not 5 ... ♘c8+ 6 ♔c7 ♘e7

7 g4+- or 5 ... ♘g8 6 ♗xg6 fxg6 7 ♔xe6 ♘e7 8 d5 ♘f5 9 ♔f6 ♘xg3 10 ♔xg6+-.

6 g4 hxg4

Also possible is 6 ... ♘c8+!? 7 ♔c5 ♘e7.

7 fxg4 ♘c8+
8 ♔c5 ♘e7
9 d5

Or 9 h5 gxh5 10 gxh5 ♘g8 11 ♔d6 ♘h6.

9 ... exd5
10 ♗xd5 ♔e8
11 ♔d6 ♘c8+
12 ♔c7 ♘e7
13 ♗c4 ♘g8
14 ♔d6

Not 14 g5? ♘e7 15 ♗d3 ♘d5+ (15 ... ♘f5? 16 ♗xf5 gxf5 17 h5 f4 18 h6 ♔f8 19 g6 fxg6 20 e6 f3 21 h7 ♔g7 22 e7) 16 ♔d6 ♘f4 17 ♗e4 ♔f8.

14 ... ♘h6
15 ♗e2 ♔d8!

Alternatively:

a) 15 ... ♔f8? 16 ♔d7 and now:

a1) 16 ... ♘g8 17 ♗f3 ♘e7 (17 ... f6 18 e6+-) 18 ♗e4 ♘g8 19 g5 ♘e7 20 e6 fxe6 21 ♔xe6+-;

a2) 16 ... ♔g7 17 ♔e8 ♔g8 18 g5! ♘f5 19 ♗c4 ♘xh4 (19 ... ♘g7+ 20 ♔e7 ♘f5+ 21 ♔f6+-) 20 ♗xf7+ ♔g7 21 ♗d5+-;

b) 15 ... ♘g8 16 g5 ♘e7 17 ♗g4 ♘g8 18 e6 fxe6 19 ♗xe6 ♘e7 20 ♔e5+- e.g. 20 ... ♔f8 21 ♔f6 ♔e8 22 ♗f7+ ♔f8 23 ♗xg6 ♘d5+ 24 ♔e5+-.

16 ♗d1!

Not 16 e6? fxe6 17 ♔xe6 ♔e8 18 ♔f6 (18 g5 ♘f5 19 h5 ♘g7+ 20 ♔f6 ♘xh5+=) 18 ... ♔f8 (18 ... ♘xg4+? 19 ♗xg4 ♔f8 20 ♗e6+-) 19 g5 ♘f5 20 h5 ♘g3 21 h6+- ♘e4+ 22 ♔xg6 ♔g8!= (22 ... ♘xg5? 23 ♗c4!).

16	...	♔e8	23 ♗d5+	♔h8
17	♗f3	♔d8	24 ♕e4	♞d6
18	e6	fxe6	25 ♗xg6	♔g8
19	♔xe6	♔e8	26 h6	♔h8
20	♔f6	♔f8	27 ♔e6! and wins	
21	g5	♞f5		
22	h5	♔g8		

Alternatively, 22 ... ♞d4 23 ♗d5! gxh5 24 g6 or 22 ... ♞h4 23 h6 ♔g8 24 ♗e4+-.

Bishop v Knight and One Pawn

BN 41

=/+ W/B

Key position 1

White to move draws:

1   ♔xa8   ♔c8

And draws. See knight endings, fortresses/positional draws. The start position is critical as it is mutual zugzwang.

Black to move loses:

1   ...   ♔c6
2   ♔xa8   ♔c7
3   ♞d6! and wins.

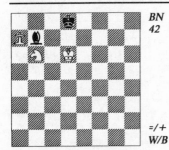

BN 42

=/+ W/B

Key position 2

1   ♞d5

Mutual zugzwang. Black to move in the starting position loses since the black king must allow ♔c7, when White gradually achieves key position 1, as demonstrated in the next example.

1   ...   ♔c8
and draws

BN 43

+ W

Prokop 1930

1   ♔e5!!   ♗a8

Black cannot really prevent White from achieving the critical position:

a) 1 ... ♗b7 2 ♔d6 ♔d8 (2 ... ♗g2 3 ♞b6 ♗b7 4 ♔c7 ♗g2 5 ♞c8! transposes) 3 ♞b6 transposes;

b) 1 ... ♗f3 2 ♞b6 (with the idea of ♞d5) 2 ... ♗b7 3 ♔e6!.

2   ♞b6   ♗b7
3   ♔e6!   ♔d8

4   ♔d6

Now we have arrived at key position 2.

4   ...   ♔e8
5   ♔c7   ♗g2
6   ♞c8!   ♗a8
7   ♔b8   ♔d8
8   ♞d6!   ♔d7
9   ♞b7

Reaching key position 1.

9   ...   ♔c6
10   ♔xa8   ♔c7
11   ♞d6 and wins

182

BN
44

1 ♘c7 ♘a6.

Black's extra diagonal is so short that he still cannot cope with the dangerous pawn. The only salvation is an excellent king position, on a5 or a4.

1	...	♚b4

Or 1 ... ♗b8 2 ♚b6 and

2	♘b5	♗b8
3	♚b6	♚b3
4	♘c7	♚a4
5	♘a6	♗g3
6	♘c7	♗f2+
7	♚a6	1-0

+
W

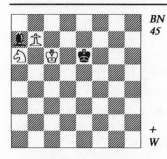

BN
45

1	♚c7	♚d5

Or 1 ... ♗f2 2 ♚c8 ♗a7 3 ♘c7+ and ♘b5 as illustrated in diag 52.

2	♘b4+	♚e6

Not 2 ... ♚c4 3 ♘c6 ♗e3 4

♘e5+! or 2 ... ♚e4 3 ♚c8! and ♘c6.

3	♘c6	♗c5
4	♚c8	♗d6
5	♘b4 and wins	

Now ♘a6-c7 is unstoppable.

+
W

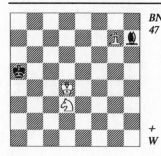

BN
46

Cheron/Averbakh

1	♘c7	♚a5
2	♘b5	♗b8

and draws

Here the presence of the black king prevents White from making any progress.

=
W

BN
47

Suetin - Korchnoi
Leningrad 1951
A practical example of the previous two diagrams.

66	♚c5	♚a4
67	♘e5	♚b3
68	♘f3	♚c3
69	♚d6	1-0

+
W

Bishop v Knight

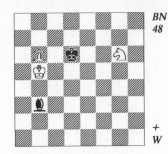

BN
48

Yakimchik 1958

    1   ♞e7!

A vivid example of the knight's potential for domination when centralised. Even the proximity of his king does not save Black. (Not 1 ♞f4? ♗d1= 2 ♞d5 ♗e2+ 3 ♔a5 ♔c6.)

    1   ...   ♗d1

Or 1 ... ♗c2 2 ♞d5! ♗d3+ 3 ♔a5 ♔c6 4 ♞b4+.

+
W

    2   ♞f5+!   ♔d7
    3   ♞d4

The knight now guards the majority of the bishop's useful squares.

    3   ...   ♗g4

Or 3 ... ♔c8 4 ♔a6 and ♔a7.

    4   ♔a6   ♔d8
    5   ♞c6+

And the b-pawn queens. (Not 5 b7?? ♗c8.)

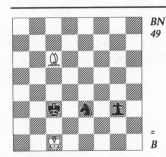

BN
49

Bellon - Anand
Biel 1988

    71   ...   ♔d3
    72   ♗f3   ♞f5

Or 72 ... ♞g4 73 ♔d1 ♔e3 74 ♗b7 ♔f2 75 ♔d2 ♞e5 76 ♗h1 ♞f3+ 77 ♔d3 ♞h4 78

=
B

♔e4 ♞g2 79 ♔f5 ♔g1 80 ♔g4 ♔h2 81 ♔f3=.

    73   ♔d1   ♔e3
    74   ♗h1   ½-½

White's king is too close for the bishop on the long diagonal to be threatened.

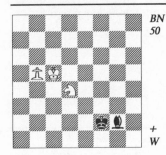

BN
50

Kosek 1910

    1   ♞c6!

A realistic study that illustrates the winning method with a knight's pawn on the sixth rank. Black's second diagonal (a6-c8) is very short and his only hope is that his king will arrive in time to assist in defence. White must avoid:

a) 1 b6? ♗a8 and draws as in 1 ♔d6?;

b) 1 ♔d6? ♗a8! 2 ♞c6 ♔e3 3 ♔c7 ♔d3 4 ♔b8 ♔c4 5 ♞a7 ♗f3 6 b6 ♔c5 7 ♔c7

+
W

♗g2= (the diagonal can no longer be blocked).

    1   ...   ♗f1

1 ... ♗h3 2 b6 ♗c8 3 ♔d6 ♗b7 4 ♔c7 transposes.

    2   b6   ♗a6
    3   ♔d6   ♗b7

Not 3 ... ♔e3 4 ♔c7 and ♞b4 winning.

    4   ♔c7   ♗a8
    5   ♞a5   ♔e3
    6   ♞b7   ♔d4
    7   ♔b8

And the black king is one move too late: unable to attack b6, Black loses.

BN 51

= W

Cheron 1950

1 ♗c5+!

White has just enough time to bring his king back and draw. Critical is his ability to reach a square that prevents ♘f5, a move which drives the bishop off h4-e1 as well as preparing diagonal blocks ♘e3/g3. Black's threats are instructive. (Not 1 ♗h4+ ♔g2 2 ♔c7 ♘e4 - intending ♘g3 - 3 ♗e1 ♘c5 and ... ♘d3, ... ♔h3 drives the bishop off the diagonal.)

1 ... ♔e2
2 ♗g1!

The only move to draw. Alternatively:

a) 2 ♔c7 ♘d5+ 3 ♔d6 ♘e3;

b) 2 ♔b7 ♘d1 (intending ... ♘e3) 3 ♗g1 ♘f2 4 ♔c6 (4 ♗h2 ♘h3!! 5 ♗g3 ♘f4 6 ♔c6 ♘h5 7 ♗h4 ♘g7! and ... ♘f5 wins the diagonal) 4 ... ♔f1 5 ♗h2 ♘g4! 6 ♗g3 (6 ♗c7 ♔e2 7 ♗g3 ♘e3 and ... ♘f5) 6 ... ♘e3! 7 ♔d7 ♘f5 8 ♗c7 ♔e2 9 ♗b6 ♘e3.

2 ... ♘d1
3 ♔c7!

Not 3 ♔c8? ♘f2 4 ♔d7 (4 ♗h2 ♘h3 5 ♗g3 ♘f4 and again ... ♘h5-g7-f5 occurs in time to win) 4 ... ♔f1 5 ♗h2 ♘g4 6 ♗g3 (6 ♗c7 ♘e3 7 ♗g3 ♘f5 8 ♗c7 ♔e2) 6 ... ♔g2 7 ♗h4 (7 ♗e1 ♘e5+ 8 ♔e6 ♘d3 9 ♗h4 ♔h3) 7 ... ♔h3 8 ♗e1 ♘e5+ and ... ♘d3.

3 ... ♘f2
4 ♗h2! ♔f1

Or 4 ... ♘h3 5 ♗g3 ♘f4 6 ♔d6 ♘h5 7 ♗h4 ♔g7 8 ♔e5!.

5 ♗e5!

Not 5 ♔c6? or 5 ♗f4? ♘g4 6 ♗g3 ♘e3-+.

5 ... ♘g4
6 ♗d4 ♔e2
7 ♗g1 ♘f2
8 ♗h2!

With a draw (by repetition).

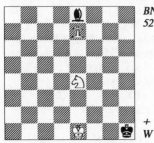

BN 52

+ W

Kosek

1 ♘f6!

The right way. The bishop must now take up the shorter diagonal. Otherwise White's king marches up to d6 and cuts the diagonal with ♘d7 (see note).

1 ... ♗g6

Or:

a) 1 ... ♗a4 2 ♔d2! ♗g2 3 ♔c3 ♗f3 4 ♔b4 ♗c6 5 ♔c5 ♗a4 6 ♔d6;

b) 1 ... ♗f7 2 ♔f2 ♔h2 3 ♔f3 ♔h3 4 ♔f4 ♔h4 5 ♔f5 ♔g3 6 ♔g5 ♔f3 7 ♔h6 ♔f4 8 ♔g7.

2 ♔f1! ♔h2
3 ♔f2 ♔h3
4 ♔f3 ♔h4
5 ♔f4 and wins

The king invades. A simple study but one that illustrates maximal use of the white pieces.

Bishop v Knight

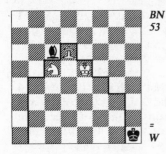

BN 53

Averbakh 1958

An illustrative position from one of Averbakh's many excellent drawing "charts". He notes that a bishop draws against pawns, (other than rook's pawns) that have not crossed the diagonals controlled from ♘d7/♗e7 (light/dark), without the help of the black king.

1	♔e6	♗b5
2	♔e7	♗c6
3	♔d8	♗b5
4	♔c7	♗g1
5	♘d3	♔h1
6	♘e5	♗e8
7	♘d7	♗g1
8	♔d8	♗g6
9	♔e7	♗f5
10	♘c5	♗c8
11	♘d7	♔h1
12	♔d8	♗a6
13	♔c7	♗b5
14	♘e5	♗e8

and draws

White's task is obviously hopeless.

Bishop v Knight and Two Pawns

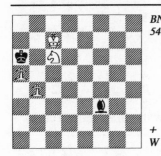

BN 54

Horwitz 1885

1   ♘b8+

A drastic solution but there is no way to make simple progress.

1   ...   ♔b5

Not 1 ... ♔a7 2 b5.

2   a6   ♗a8

Instead 2 ... ♔xb4 leads to a position analysed by Cheron: 3 ♔b6 ♗a8 4 ♘c6+ ♔c4 5 ♘d8 ♔b4 (5 ... ♔d4 6 ♔a7 ♗f3 7 ♘b7 ♔c4 8 ♔b6) 6 ♘b7 ♔c4 7 ♔c6 ♔d4 (7 ... ♔b4 8 a7 ♔c4 9 ♔c7 leads to the previous diag, i.e. 9 ... ♔b5 10 ♔b8 ♔c6 11 ♔xa8 ♔c7 12 ♘d6) 8 ♔c7 ♔d5 9 ♔b8 ♔c6 10 ♔xa8 ♔c7 11 ♘c5.

3   a7   ♔xb4

Here 3 ... ♗f3 4 ♘d7 ♔xb4 5 ♔b6 ♔c4 6 ♘c5 ♗a8 7 ♘b7 ♔d5 8 ♔c7 transposes.

4   ♔b6!

It is vital to shoulder out the black king.

4   ...   ♔c4
5   ♘a6   ♔d4

Or 5 ... ♗g2 6 ♘c5 ♗a8 7 ♘b7 ♔d5! 8 ♔c7 transposing.

6   ♘c7   ♗g2
7   ♘e6+   ♔e5
8   ♘d8

Intending ♘b7.

8   ...   ♗a8
9   ♔c7   ♔d5!
10   ♘b7!

Not 10 ♔b8 ♔d6 11 ♘b7+ (11 ♔c8!? ♔c5 12 ♔c7 ♔b5 13 ♔b8 ♔b6 14 ♘f7 ♗f3 15 ♘d6 ♗g2 16 ♘c4+ ♔a6= as White can no longer block the diagonal) 11 ... ♔d7 (see the previous diagram) 12 ♘a5 ♔d8 13 ♔xa8 ♔c7!=.

10   ...   ♔e6
11   ♘a5!   ♔e7

Or 11 ... ♔e5 12 ♔b8 ♔d6 13 ♘c4+ ♔c6 (13 ... ♔d7 14 ♘b6+) 14 ♔xa8 ♔c7 15 ♘d6.

12   ♔c8!   ♔e8

For 12 ... ♔d6 13 ♔b8 ♔d7 14 ♘b7 see diag 47.

13   ♘c4!   ♔e7
14   ♔b8   ♔d8
15   ♘a5!   ♔d7
16   ♘b7 and wins

Mission accomplished - diag 39 is reached with the right person to move.

Bishop v Knight

BN
55

=
B

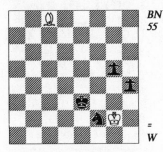

BN
55

=
W

BN
55b

=
B

Horwitz/Averbakh/Cheron

1 ... ♘d3

Despite the knight's ability to "change colours" it still experiences tremendous difficulties in breaking a bishop's blockade. Here the bishop succeeds in stopping the pawns which have been 'misplaced' (Philidor's rule - advance pawns on the colour of the enemy's bishop). Note that Black must avoid 1 ... ♔f3 2 ♗d5+ ♔f2 3 ♗b7 ♘f3 4 ♔g4 ♘g1 5 ♔xg5= (Cheron). Black is several tempi away from reaching a winning Horwitz position: 5 ... ♔g3 (5 ... h3 6 ♔h4 h2 7 ♗h1 ♘e2 8 ♔h3 ♔g1 9 ♗b7) 6 ♗c8.

2 ♗c8!!

The only move according to Cheron:

a) 2 ♗d7? ♘f2+ (I - JT - do not see why Cheron inserts this repetition. Black should play 2 ... ♔f3! and get on with it) 3 ♔g2 ♘d3 4 ♔h3 ♔f3 and now:

a1) 5 ♗c6+ ♔f2 6 ♔g4 ♘e5+ 7 ♔xg5 ♔g3 8 ♗g2! (8 ♗h1 h3 9 ♔f5 ♘g4 10 ♔g5 ♘e3 11 ♔h5 ♘g2-+ - Cheron - 12 ♔g5 h2 13 ♔h5 ♔f2 14 ♔g4 ♔g1 15 ♔f3 ♔xh1 16 ♔f2 ♘e3) 8 ... ♘g4 9 ♔h5 ♘e3 10 ♗h1 h3 11 ♔g5 h2 12 ♔h5 ♘g2 etc;

a2) 5 ♗g4+ ♔f2 6 ♗d1 (6 ♗d7 ♘f4+ 7 ♔g4 h3 8 ♔xg5 h2 9 ♗c6 ♘g2) 6 ... ♘f4+ 7 ♔h2 ♘e2 8 ♔h3 ♔f3 9 ♗a4 ♘f4+ 10 ♔h2 g4 lifting the blockade and winning;

b) 2 ♗c4 (or other bishop moves along this diagonal) 2 ... ♘f2+ 3 ♔g2 ♘e3 4 ♗e6 ♘d3 5 ♗c8 ♘f4+ 6 ♔h2 ♔f3 7 ♗b7+ ♔g4 (with the idea of ... h3, ... ♔h4, ... g4) 8

♗c8+ ♔h5 and ... g4.

2 ... ♘f2+

Not 2 ... ♔f3 3 ♗b7+ ♔f2 4 ♔g4 ♘e5+ 5 ♔xg5 h3 6 ♔h4 h2 7 ♔h3=.

3 ♔g2 ♔e3 (55a)

Or 3 ... ♘g4 4 ♔h3 ♘e3 5 ♗a6 and now:

a) 5 ... g4+. This deserves a look (JT). Again White will be saved because his light-squared bishop copes better in these endings than the dark-squared one could in the ending one rank back (see diag 56): 6 ♔xh4 ♘f5+ 7 ♔h5 ♘d6 8 ♗f1 g3 (8 ... ♔f3 9 ♗e2+) 9 ♔h4 ♔f3 10 ♔h3 ♔f2 11 ♗g2 ♘f5 12 ♗b7 ♘d4 13 ♔g4;

b) 5 ... ♘f5 6 ♗e2 ♘d4 ♗g4 ♘f3 8 ♗c8=.

4 ♗f5!

4 ♗d7? ♘d3 5 ♔h3 ♔f3! transposes to 2 ♗d7?.

4 ... ♘d3

Not 4 ... g4 5 ♗xg4 ♘xg4 6 ♔h3.

5 ♔h3 ♘e5

For some reason, neither Cheron nor Averbakh analyse this move, which is analogous to the winning method with the pieces one rank back (see diag 63). They only give 5 ... ♘f4+ 6 ♔g4 h3 7 ♔g3! drawing.

6	♗e6	♔f4
7	♗c8	♘f3
8	♗d7 (55b)	

This position (Horwitz 1880) is analysed by Cheron who gives it as equal, but Black's next, analogous to diag 57, is not considered.

8	...	♘g1+
9	♔g2	♘e2
10	♔h3	♔f3
11	♗c6+	♔f2

Intending ... ♘g1+ reaching

Bishop v Knight

♗ V ♘

diag 54.

12	♔g4	♘f4
13	♔xg5	♔g3

14 ♗d7!=

This last move is not possible in diag 57.

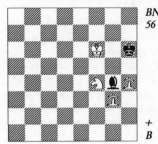

BN 56

+ B

Averbakh/Geller 1954

1 ... ♗d7

Here the excellent white piece placement allows a win - most critical is that Black must wait before taking up the ideal king position on h5, allowing White time to break the blockade or create a decisive passed pawn. (Also 1 ... ♗d1 2 ♔f5 ♗c2+ 3 ♔g4 - intending h5, ♔h4, g4 - 3 ... ♗d1+ 4 ♔h3 and g4+-.)

2	♔e5	♗g4
3	♔e4	♗c8

Or 3 ... ♔g7 4 ♘d5 ♔h6 5 ♔f4 ♗e6 6 ♘e3 ♔h5 7 ♘f5 and g4.

4	♘d5	♔h5
5	♔e5!	♔g4

Alternatively, 5 ... ♔h6 6 ♔f4 ♔h5 7 ♘e3 ♗a6 (7 ... ♗h3 8 ♘f5) 8 g4+! ♔xh4 9 ♘f5+ ♔h3 10 g5 ♗c4 11 g6 ♗b3 12 ♔g5 ♗c4 13 g7 ♗g8 14 ♔g6 ♗c4 15 ♘d6 ♗g8 16 ♘f7 ♔h4 17 ♘h6 ♗b3 18 ♘f7 ♗c2+ 19 ♔h6.

6	♘f6+	♔xg3
7	h5	♗a6
8	h6	♗d3
9	♘e4+ and wins	

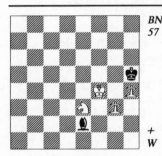

BN 57

+ W

Cheron, correcting Averbakh 1964

1 ♘d5

This exact version of Horwitz's study, one rank back, shows that White's extra manoeuvring room for the knight (e.g. g8) and the restricted space for the bishop on the d1-h5 diagonal, are decisive differences, though it appears drawn by analogy.

1 ... ♗d1

Alternatively:

a) 1 ... ♗a6 2 ♘f6+ ♔g6 3 ♘e8 ♔h5 4 ♘g7+ ♔g6 5 ♘f5 shows the extra room for the knight proving vital;

b) 1 ... ♗b5 2 ♘f6+ ♔g6 3 ♔e5 ♗e2 4 ♘d5 and White will reach diag 62.

2	♘f6+	♔g6
3	♔e5	♗f3
4	♘d5	♔h5
5	♘e3	♗e2
6	♔f4	♗b5

Or 6 ... ♗a6 7 g4+ ♔xh4 8 ♘f5+ ♔h3 9 g5 ♗c4 10 g6+-.

7	♘f5	♗e2
8	♘g7+	♔g6
9	♘e6	♔h5
10	♔f5	♗d3+
11	♔f6	♔g4
12	♘f4	♔xg3
13	♔g5	♗h7
14	h5	♔f3
15	♘g6	♔g3
16	h6	♗g8
17	♔f6	♔g4
18	♔g7	♔g5
19	♘e7 and wins	

BN
58

+/+
W/B

Averbakh 1958

1 ... ♗f1+

With White to play: 1 ♘e6+ ♔d7 2 ♘f4.

2 ♔a5 ♗g2
3 ♔b4!! ♗f1

Alternatively:

a) 3 ... ♗e4 4 ♘b5+ ♔d7 (4 ... ♔c6 5 a7 ♔d7 6 ♔a5) 5 ♔d6 ♗a8 (5 ... ♗g2 6 ♔b5 ♔c7 7 ♘e8+ ♔d7 8 ♔b6 ♔xe8 9 c6 or 5 ... ♔c6 6 ♔a5 ♔c7 7 ♘b5+) 6 ♘c4 ♔c7 7

♘b6 and the bishop falls to the a-pawn;

b) 3 ... ♗d5 4 ♔b5 ♗e4 5 ♘e6+ (5 c6? ♗d3+ 6 ♔a5 ♗e4 7 a7 ♗xc6 8 ♘xc6 ♔b7) 5 ... ♔d7 6 ♘g5! and ♔b6.

4 ♘b5+ ♔c6
5 a7 ♔b7
6 c6+ ♔a8
7 ♔a5 ♗xb5
8 ♔xb5 ♔xa7
9 ♔c5 and wins

BN
59

=
B

BN
59a

=
W

H. Olafsson - Ivanchuk
Reykjavik 1990

White's bishop is less active than in Averbakh's examples (diags 58 and 60), but the critical factor is that *here it is problematic for the black king to find an invasion route.* In Averbakh's studies the white king always enjoyed a dominant position, and the real difficulty of this kind of ending is somewhat overlooked because of this.

77 ... ♘g6
78 ♔f3 ♔f6

Since the h4-pawn occupies a square Black would rather have for his king, he regroups. 78 ... ♘f4 is met by 79 ♗f1 and Black has not achieved king entry.

79 ♗f1 ♔e5
80 ♗b5 ♘f4
81 ♗d7 ♘e6!*(59a)*
82 ♗c8 ♘g5+

82 ... ♘d4+ is also threatening, but leads to no clear win:

a) 83 ♔g2 ♔f4 84 ♔h3 ♔g5 85 ♗a6 ♘e6 86 ♗c8 ♘f4+ 87 ♔h2 ♔g4 88 ♗a6?! (88 ♗d7 ♘e2 89 ♗c8 ♘d4 90 ♗d7 is better, when Black's progress is impeded) 88 ... ♘e6 89 ♗e2+ ♔g5 90 ♗d1?

(90 ♗f3 ♔f4 followed by ♘g5, ♔e3, f5-f4-f3; but still 90 ♗a6!? is best) 90 ... ♘d4 91 ♗a4 (91 ♔g2 f4 92 ♔f2 h3 93 ♗a4 ♔h4 94 ♗d7 f3) 91 ... f4 92 ♔h3 f3 93 ♗d7 ♘e2 94 ♗b5 ♘f4+ 95 ♔h2 f2 and the march ... ♔e1 wins. An example of what White must avoid;

b) 83 ♔e3 h3 (83 ... f4+ 84 ♔f2 ♘f5 85 ♔f3 h3 86 ♗d7 ♘h4+ 87 ♔f2 h2 88 ♗c6 ♔f5 89 ♗d7+ ♔e5 90 ♗c6 and Black cannot progress) 84 ♗b7 ♘e6 85 ♔f3.

83 ♔e3 ♘e4
84 ♔f3 ♘g5+
85 ♔e3 h3

Not 85 ... f4+ 86 ♔f2 ♔e4 87 ♗b7+ ♔f5 88 ♗c8+ ♔g6 89 ♗d7 h3 90 ♗g4.

86 ♗b7 f4+

Or 86 ... ♘e4 87 ♔f3 f4 88 ♗c8! (88 ♗xe4 h2) 88 ... ♘d2+ (88 ... ♘g5+ 89 ♔f2 could transpose to the game) 89 ♔f2 h2 90 ♗b7 f3 91 ♗xf3 ♘xf3 92 ♔g2=. This is White's main defensive trump; Black's greatest hurdle.

87 ♔f2 ♔d4

After 87 ... ♔f6 88 ♗c8 Black cannot reach diags 66 or 68.

88 ♗a8?

Losing immediately. A better try was 88 ♗c6!? (Or 88 ♗c8!? and I - JT - do not see how Black can make progress - his king cannot approach, the knight is tied to h3, and ... h2 or ... f3 cannot be arranged without allowing a liquidating combo) 88 ... ♞e4+ 89 ♔f3 h2 90 ♔g2 f3+ 91 ♔xh2 ♔e3

92 ♗b5 (not 92 ♔g1? ♔e2 93 ♗b5+ ♔e1 94 ♔h2 ♞c3 95 ♔g3 f2 96 ♗a6 ♞e2+) 92 ... ♔d2 93 ♔h3 ♞c3 94 ♔g4 f2 95 ♔f3 ♔e1 96 ♗a6=.

88	...	♞e4+
89	♔f3	♔e5
90	♗b7	♞g3
	0-1	

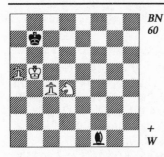

BN 60   + W

Averbakh 1958

1	♞c2!

A material situation investigated by Averbakh. The knight wins if White avoids advancing the pawns too quickly (i.e. without full support of his pieces), and can penetrate with his king. The start position is virtually identical to diag 67, the difference being White's (i.e. the side with the pawns) king position.

1	...	♗d3

Or 1 ... ♗h3 2 a6+ ♔a7 (2 ...

♔c7 3 ♞a3 ♗d7+ 4 ♔c5 and as in main line) 3 ♔a5 ♗c8 (3 ... ♗f1 4 ♞a3) 4 ♞b4 ♗d7 5 c5 (5 ♞d5 ♔e6) 5 ... ♗e8 (5 ... ♗c8 6 ♞c6+ ♔a8 7 ♞d4 and ♞b5) 6 ♞d5 and ♞c3-b5.

2	♞a3	♗e2
3	a6+	♔a7

Not 3 ... ♔c7 4 ♔c5 ♗f3 5 ♞b5+ and ♔b6.

4	♔a5	♗f3
5	♞b5+	♔b8
6	♔b6	♔c8
7	a7 and ♞c7
	1-0	

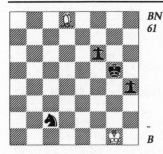

BN 61   - B

Cohn - Lowitzky 1912

1	...	♞d4
2	♔f2	♞c6
3	♗b6	♔g4
4	♗c7	f5
5	♗d6	f4
6	♗c7	♞d4
7	♗d6	♔f5

Also possible is 7 ... h3 - Averbakh points out that this straightforward approach also works: 8 ♗c5 (8 ♔g1 ♔g3 9 ♗c5 ♞f3+ 10 ♔h1 ♞e5 11 ♔g1 ♞d3 transposes) 8 ... ♞f3 9 ♗b6 ♞e1! 10 ♔g1 ♞d3 11 ♔h2 f3 12 ♔g1 ♔g3 13 ♗a7 (13 ♗c7+ ♞f4 14 ♗b6 ♞e2+ 15 ♔h1 f2) 13 ... h2+ 14 ♔h1 f2.

8	♗c7

As the notes show, there is nothing to be gained by try-

ing to prod the pawn forward quickly, as in the analogous ending with a white-squared bishop defending. *When the bishop does not control the queening squares, the win is easier, as both pawns are more dangerous.*

8	...	♔e4
9	♔g2	♞f5
10	♔h3	

Or 10 ♗b6 ♞e3+ 11 ♔g1 f3 12 ♗c7 h3 13 ♗d6 ♞g4 14 ♗g3 (14 ♗c7 f2+ 15 ♔f1 ♔f3) 14 ... ♔e3 15 ♗h4 ♔e2 16 ♗g3 f2+.

10	...	♔e3
11	♔g4	f3
12	♔xf5	h3
13	♔g4	h2
14	♗xh2	f2
	0-1	

Two Bishops v Knight

BBN 1 — The Fortress

Black's best chance of holding this endgame is to attempt to construct the Horwitz and Kling fortress and hope to last out for fifty moves. However, even the fortress position is not sufficient to force a theoretical draw.

BBN 2 — Horwitz and Kling 1851

There are four ways to break the Horwitz and Kling fortress:

1 In the diagram Black to move loses in 38 moves.

2 With white bishops on a4 and g3 Black to move loses in 38.

3 With white bishops on g2 and g3 Black to move loses in 40.

4 Put the black king on c7 and the bishops on a4 and f2. Black to move loses in 39.

_W_

BBN 3 — Botvinnik - Tal

World Ch, Moscow 1961

In this example Black never quite manages to establish the fortress.

   77   &xa6

77 ♘c5+ ♔d6 78 ♘xa6 also fails to reach Horwitz and Kling viz. 78 ... ♗d2 79 ♘b8 ♗g5 80 ♘a6 ♗d8+ 81 ♔a7 ♔c6.

77	...	♗f1+
78	♔b6	♔d6
79	♘a5	♗c5+!
80	♔b7	♗e2
81	♘b3	♗e3
82	♘a5	♔c5
83	♔c7	♗f4+

White resigned in view of 84 ♔d7 ♔b6 85 ♘b3 ♗e3 etc.

0-1

+ _W_

BBN 4 — The Longest Win

This position demonstrates a longest win:

1 ♗f8 ♔g3 2 ♗d6+ ♔f3 3 ♔a7 ♔f2 4 ♗h2 ♔f1 5 ♔b7 ♔f2 6 ♔c6 ♔f1 7 ♔d6 ♔f2 8 ♔e6 ♔f3 9 ♔f5 ♔f2 10 ♔g4 ♘e3+ 11 ♔h3 ♘c4 12 ♗g2 ♘a3 13 ♗f4 ♘c4 14 ♔e4 ♔e2 15 ♔h4 ♘d2 16 ♗g6 ♘f1 17 ♔g5 ♔f3 18 ♗d6 ♔e3 19 ♗c5+ ♔f3 20 ♔f5 ♘e3+ 21 ♔e5 ♘g2 22 ♗h5+ ♔g3 23 ♗b6 ♘f4 24 ♗d1 ♘g2 25 ♔d4 ♘e1 26 ♔e3 ♘g2+ 27 ♔d2 ♔f4 28 ♔e2 ♔f5 29 ♗c2+ ♔e6 30 ♗b3+ ♔d6 31 ♗f2 ♘f4+ 32 ♔e3 ♘e6 33 ♗g3+ ♔e7 34 ♔e5 ♘c5 35 ♗d5 ♘e6 36 ♔e4 ♘c5+ 37 ♔f5 ♘d7 38 ♗f4 ♘b6 39 ♗f3 ♘c4 40 ♔e4 ♘d6+ 41 ♔d5 ♘f7 42 ♗d1 ♔f6 43 ♗c2 ♘g5 44 ♗e5+ ♔e7 45 ♗g3 ♘e6 46 ♔e5 ♘d8 47 ♗e1 ♘f7+ 48 ♔d5 ♘h8 49 ♗h4+ ♔f7 50 ♔d6 ♘g6 51 ♗b3+ ♔f8 52 ♗f6 ♔e8 53 ♗c3 ♘f4 54 ♗d4 ♘g6 55 ♗d1 ♔f8 56 ♗c3 ♘e7 57 ♗h5 ♘f5+ 58

♔e5 ♘h6 59 ♔e6 ♘g8 60
♗d4 ♘h6 61 ♔f6 ♘g8+ 62
♔g6 ♘e7+ 63 ♔h7 ♘d5 64
♗c5+ ♘e7 65 ♔h6 ♔g8 66
♗xe7 ♔h8 67 ♗g4 ♔g8 68
♗e6+ ♔h8 69 ♗f6 mate.

John Roycroft has broken the process down approximately as follows:

a) Bring up the king - 11 or 12 moves.

b) Drive the defender into a corner where he will set up Horwitz and Kling - 14 or 15 moves.

c) Force the defender out into the open - by starting from one of the known winning positions above one can in principle prevent him from re-

setting in another corner.

d) Contain the enemy. He must also be prevented in practice from reaching Horwitz and Kling while the pieces gradually assume better positions.

e) Catch him in a corner - the rest is relatively straight-forward.

Obviously this description (which I have summarised) is rather tenuous; and stage four in particular is extremely difficult. I have included diagram diag 4 only for the explanation above and its curiosity value. We will see a practical example of man's frailty in diag 5 below.

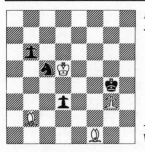

BBN 5

+ W

A Practical Example
Timman - Speelman
Linares 1992

This was the adjourned position. And since I had just missed a forced draw with 60 ... ♔f3! instead of the asinine 60 ... b6 I was not best pleased! Both of us had a chance to appeal to the silicon monsters for help overnight. But in fact while Jan received a great sheaf of information from Jan van der Herik of the University of Lindburg, my stuff somehow went astray. Still, I feel that it is much more important for the attacker to have proper information on such a position rather than the defender. And I was certainly extremely feeble in any attempt to see the grim truth in black and white.

The analysis below is based on an article by Professor van der Herik in the ICCA (International Computer Chess Association) Journal (Volume 15,

March 1992).

61	♗e5	♔f3
62	♗f4	d2
63	♗xd2	♘e4
64	♗h6	

Not 64 ♗e2+?? ♔xe2 65 ♔xe4 b5 66 ♔d4 b4 67 ♔c4 ♔c2! 68 ♔xb4 ♔d3=.

64	...	♘xg3
65	♗d3	b5
66	♗xb5	

Actually, at the time of the game I was not convinced that this was correct since now I can reach the Horwitz and Kling position. But having studied the fortress, Jan was happy to allow me to reach it.

66	...	♘f5
67	♗f8?!	♘e3+

67 ... ♔f4! is slightly better, setting up a 'pseudo-fortress'.

68	♔d4	♘g2
69	♔d3?	

A mistake since Black can now make a break for freedom. White should play 69 ♗c6+! (also 69 ♗f8-e7, and d6 c5 or b4).

BBN 5a

+B

BBN 5b

+W

BBN 5a

69 ... ♞f4+
70 ♚d2 (5a)
70 ... ♞g2??

A cardinal error. By insisting on maintaining the Horwitz and Kling position for as long as possible, I made his task immeasurably easier as now when Black is forced to abandon it his opponent is already well coordinated. 70 ... ♚e4! was correct: 71 ♗g7 ♚d5 72 ♗b2 ♚c5 73 ♗f1 ♞e6 74 ♚e3 ♚d5 75 ♗g2+ ♚c4 76 ♗f6 ♞c5 reaching a 'pseudo-fortress'.

71 ♗c6+ ♚f2
72 ♗d6 ♞h4!

The best.

73 ♗c5+ ♚g3 (5b)

73 ... ♚f1? obviously loses quickly and no human player would consider playing it. The database demonstrates the win with 74 ♗d5 ♞f3+ (74 ... ♞f5 75 ♗e6 ♞h4 76 ♗h3+ ♞g2 77 ♚d3 or 74 ... ♞g6 75 ♚e3 ♚e1 76 ♗c4 ♞h4 77 ♗b4+ ♚d1 78 ♗e2+ ♚c2 79 ♗d3+ ♚b3 80 ♗d2) 75 ♚e3 ♞g1 76 ♗b4 ♞h3 77 ♗e7 ♞g1 78 ♗h4 ♞h3 79 ♚f3 ♞g1+ 80 ♚g3 ♞e2+ 81 ♚h2 ♞f4 82 ♗c4+ ♞e2 83 ♚h3.

74 ♗b6

A serious inaccuracy. After 74 ♚d3! ♞g2 (or 74 ... ♚f4 75 ♗d6+ ♚g5 - 75 ... ♚f5 76 ♗d7+ - 76 ♚e4) 75 ♗b6 transposes back into the game, without allowing Black to play 74 ... ♚f4.

74 ... ♞g2?

This was the last chance to run with 74 ... ♚f4! 75 ♗c7+ ♚f5 76 ♚e3 ♚e6 77 ♚e4 ♞f5 78 ♗d5+ ♚f6 79 ♗d8+ ♚g6 80 ♚e5 ♞g7 reaching the Horwitz and Kling position again.

75 ♗d5 ♞h4
76 ♚e2 ♚f4

Black has been forced out of the Horwitz and Kling position in unfavourable circumstances and can never set up another.

77 ♗b3 ♞f5
78 ♗c7+ ♚g5
79 ♗e5!

This excellent move controls g7, thus preventing Black from resetting with ... ♞g7 and ... ♚g6.

79 ... ♚g4

If 79 ... ♚g6 80 ♗c2!.

80 ♗c2 ♞g3+
81 ♚f2 ♞f5
82 ♗d1+ ♚g5!

If 82 ... ♚h4? 83 ♗f6+ ♚h3 84 ♗d8 ♞g3 85 ♚f3 and White wins easily.

83 ♚f3 ♞h4+
84 ♚e4 ♞f5
85 ♗a4

85 ♗c2 is slightly more accurate since 85 ... ♚g6 is prevented.

85 ... ♞e7

85 ... ♚g6! makes life very slightly harder for White: 86 ♗e8+ ♚g5 87 ♗d7 ♞e7 88 ♗e6 ♞g6 89 ♗c3.

86 ♗d7 ♞g8
87 ♗f4+!

Obviously this is best. After any other move Black could reset Horwitz and Kling which, the computer informs us, would add at least 22 moves to the winning process.

87 ... ♚g6?!

87 ... ♚f6 is slightly better to control e5 for the moment.

88 ♚e5 ♞f6
89 ♗b5 ♚f7
90 ♗c4+! ♚g6
91 ♚e6 1-0

Here I resigned. I suppose it was a little early but it was

quite clear to me that I was going to lose in the end.

The database gives:

a) 91 ... ♞e8 92 ♗d3+ ♚h5 93 ♚e7 ♚g4 94 ♗e5;

b) 91 ... ♞g4 92 ♗e2 ♞h6! (92 ... ♞f6? 93 ♗d3+ ♚g7 94 ♗e5) 93 ♗d2 ♞g8 94 ♗e3 ♞h6 95 ♗b5 ♞g8 96 ♗d4 ♞h6 97 ♗e8+ ♚h7 98 ♗h5 ♞g8 99 ♚f7 ♞h6+ 100 ♚f6 ♞g8+ 101 ♚g5 ♞e7 102 ♗f3 ♚g8 103 ♚f6 ♞c8 104 ♗c5;

c) 91 ... ♞h5 92 ♗d3+ ♚g7 93 ♗d6 ♚h6 94 ♚f5 ♞g7+ 95 ♚g4 ♞e8 96 ♗f8+ ♞g7 97 ♚f4.

It is evident from this analysis that human beings cannot play the ending as well as databases. This should hardly be a surprise to us and personally I am happy to be fallible but carbon-based. Actually, I did not defend this ending very well.

But apart from some minor (in human terms) slips, Jan played excellently. With 75 moves to play with - as was the case here - 'White' should have fine winning chances. However under a re-instituted 50 move mercy rule, the defender should have every chance to draw, especially if he cuts and runs early: even if the position is technically winnable in less than 50 moves.

±
W

BBNB *Ye Rongguang - Nunn*
1 *Lucerne 1989*

A good example of the power of two bishops with reduced pawns.

44 ♔f4 ♘c4
45 ♗c5

Not 45 ♔g5? ♘xa3 46 ♔h6 ♘c4 47 ♗xh7+ ♔f7 48 ♗g6+ ♔g8 49 h4 ♘d6! and ... ♘f7=.

45 ... ♔g7
46 h4! ♔g8?!

A better defence was 46 ... h6.

47 ♔g5!

Now the weakness at h7 is fixed.

47 ... ♘e5
48 ♔f6 ♘f3
49 ♗f2!

White wants to avoid advancing the pawn to h6 when Black would have additional chances of reaching a fortress draw, e.g. 49 h5? ♗f7 50 h6 ♗b3 and ♘d2=. Black can sacrifice the knight for the a-pawn, with a fortress.

49 ... ♘b3
50 ♗g4 ♘d5
51 a4! ♘d2

Or 51 ... a5 52 ♗b6! ♘xh4 53 ♗xa5 ♘b3 54 ♗c3! and if 54 ... ♘xa4 55 ♗e6+ ♔f8 56 ♗f7 and ♗b4 mate.

52 ♗e1 ♘f3
53 ♗g3 ♘d2
54 a5! ♘c4

Not 54 ... ♘e4+?! 55 ♔e5 ♘xg3 56 ♔xd5 and the a-pawn will queen.

55 ♗e1 ♘b3
56 ♔c3 ♘c5
57 ♔e5 ♘b3
58 ♔d6 ♔f7
59 ♗h5+ ♔g8
60 ♔c6 ♔f8
61 ♗b4+ ♔g7
62 ♔b6+- ♔f6
63 ♗g4 ♘c1

Or 63 ... ♔g6 64 ♗c8 ♔h5 65 ♗e1 ♘c1 66 ♗xa6 ♘xa6 67 ♔xa6 ♘d3 68 ♔b6+-.

64 ♗c8 ♘d3
65 ♗a3 1-0

Notes from Ye Rongguang.

W

BBNB *Timoshchenko - Khalifman*
2 *USSR 1987*

1 ... ♗c5+
2 ♔g2

Or 2 ♔e2 ♗b5+ and Black wins.

2 ... ♗c6
3 ♗d1 a4!

Not 3 ... ♔g4? 4 a4! ♗e3 5 h5! ♔xh5 (5 ... ♗xg5 6 ♔f2=) 6 ♔g3 ♗d5 7 ♗c2=.

4 h5

Or 4 ♗e2 a3 and ... ♗d5-+.

4 ... a3
5 g6 hxg6

A catastrophic error would be 5 ... h6?? 6 g7 ♗d5 7 ♗b3+-.

6 hxg6 ♗d5!

Not 6 ... ♗d4 7 ♔f1! ♗xf3 8 ♗xf3 ♔xf3 9 ♗e1=.

7 ♔f1

Alternatively:

a) 7 g7 ♗xa2 8 ♘e1 ♗d5+! 9 ♗f3 ♗g8 10 ♘d3+ ♔e3-+;

b) 7 ♔h3 ♗xa2 and ... ♗e6-+;

c) 7 ♔h2 ♗xa2 8 ♘d2 (intending ... ♗b3) 8 ... ♗g8! 9 ♗b3 (9 ♘b3 a2 10 ♘a1 ♗d4 11 ♗b3 ♗xb3 12 ♘xb3 ♗g7 and ... ♔e4-d5-c4 is even worse than the game.) 9 ... a2 10 ♗xa2 ♗xa2-+ 9cf diag BBN1-2).

7 ... ♗xa2
8 ♘e1

Or 8 ♘d2 ♗c4+ 9 ♘xc4 a2 10 g7 a1♕ 11 g8♕ ♕xd1+ 12 ♔g2 ♕g1+ 13 ♔h3 ♕xg8.

8	...	♗c4+
9	♕e2	a2
10	♘c2	♗b3
11	♘a1	♗d5-+
12	♕d1	♗d4
13	♕b3	♗xb3
14	♘xb3	♔e4

15	♔e2	♔d5
16	♔d3	♗g7
17	♔c2	♔c4

And White resigned due to 18 ♘a5+ ♔b4 19 ♘b3 ♔a3. (Analysis based on notes by Khalifman.)

BBNB *Kasparov - Gligoric*
3
Lucerne Ol 1982
White must overcome considerable obstacles before capitalising on his extra pawn.

41 ♔b4!

Not 41 gxf4? ♗xf3!! 42 ♗xf3 ♘xb5+ 43 ♔d3 ♘xd4 44 ♔xd4 gxf4= or 41 g4 h5!! 42 gxh5 (42 h3 hxg4 43 hxg4 ♘xb5+! 44 ♗xb5 ♗xf3 45 ♗a6 ♔d7=) 42 ... ♗xf3! 43 ♗xf3 ♘xb5+ 44 ♔d3 ♘xd4=.

41 ... fxg3

Or 41 ... ♘f5 42 ♗f2 ♘e3 43 ♔c5 ♔e5 44 g4+-.

42 hxg3 h5
43 ♗f2 ♘f5
44 f4! gxf4

The alternatives are no better:

a) 44 ... h4 45 gxh4 gxf4 46 ♗g4 ♔e5 47 ♗xf5 ♔xf5 48 ♔c5 ♔e6 49 ♔b6+-;

b) 44 ... g4 45 ♔c5 ♘d6 46 ♗d3 and:

b1) 46 ... ♗e4 47 ♗xe4 ♘xe4+ 48 ♔c6 h4 49 b6 h3 50 ♗g1 ♘d6 and now:

b11) 51 b7! ♘xb7 52 ♔xb7 ♔f5 53 ♔c6 ♔e4 54 f5! ♔f3

55 f6 ♔g2 56 f7 ♔xg1 57 f8♕ h2 58 ♕c5+ ♔g2 59 ♕c2+ ♔g1 (59 ... ♔xg3 60 ♕e4 ♔f2 61 ♕h1 g3 62 ♔d5) 60 ♕d1+ ♔g2 61 ♕xg4 h1♕ 62 ♕e4++-;

b12) 51 f5+ ♔e5 52 f6 ♔e6 53 ♗h2 (53 f7 ♘xf7) 53 ... ♘c4;

b2) 46 ... ♘e4+ 47 ♗xe4 ♗xe4 48 b6 ♗b7 49 ♗d4 ♗e4 50 ♗e5 ♗b7 51 ♗c7 ♗e4 (51 ... h4 52 gxh4 ♔f5 53 h5 g3 54 ♗e5 g2 55 ♗d4+-) 52 ♗d8 ♗b7 53 ♗h4 ♗e4 54 f5+!+-.

45 gxf4 ♘g7

Or 45 ... h4 46 ♗g4 ♔f6 47 ♔c5 ♗g2 48 b6 ♘g3 49 ♗e1!+-.

46	♔c5	♗g2
47	♗d4	h4
48	♗xg7	h3
49	♗g4+	♔e7
50	♗xh3	♗xh3
51	♔b6!	**1-0**

The conclusion might have been 51 ... ♗f1 52 ♔c6 ♔d8 53 b6 ♗g2+ 54 ♔d6. (Notes based on those of Garry Kasparov.)

BBNB *Beliavsky - Karpov*
4
Reykjavik 1991
An interesting material balance. Black's defences hold thanks to his greater space, particularly his active king. He also has the weapon of reaching drawn a opposite-coloured bishops endings.

45 ... ♗c6?!

More accurate was 45 ... h5 intending ... h4=.

46	♗f7	♗b7
47	♔d3	♗g2
48	♗g6	f4

Perhaps 48 ... ♔e6!?.

49	♔e2	♗d5
50	♗e4	♗c4+
51	♔f3	♗f7

Or 51 ... g4+ 52 ♔xg4 fxe3

53 fxe3 ♗xe3 54 ♘h7! (54 ♗g6 ♔e6 55 ♘e4 ♗e2+=) 54 ... ♗f7!? (54 ... ♔e7 55 ♘e4 ♗e6+ 56 ♔h5) with good chances of a successful defence.

    52 ♘a4   ♗a7?

Or 52 ... ♗c7! 53 gxf4 (53 b5 ♗b3 54 b6 ♗d1+! 55 ♔g2 ♗xa4=) 53 ... gxf4 54 exf4 exf4 55 ♔xf4 ♔e7+! and ... ♗xh2=.

53	b5	♗h5+
54	g4	♗f7
55	b6	♗b8
56	♔e2	♗b3
57	♘c3	♔c5
58	b7	♗e6
59	♔f3	

Perhaps 59 h3!?.

59	...	♔c4
60	♘e2	♗d7

Or 60 ... ♔c5!?.

61	♘c1	♗e6
62	h3	♔b5!
63	♔e2?	

Although the position is drawn, better chances were offered by 63 ♔g2 ♗c7 and now:

a) 64 ♘d3 ♗c4 65 ♘e1 ♔b4 66 ♘f3 ♗e2! (66 ... ♔c3? 67 h4 ♗e2 68 h5! ♗xf3+ 69 ♔xf3 ♔d2 70 exf4 exf4 71 ♗b1 ♔e1 72 ♗d3 ♔b8 73 ♗b5 intending ♔e4-f5-g6-h6+-) 67 ♘g1 ♗c4;

b) 64 ♘e2 ♗c4 65 ♘g1 ♔c5 66 h4 (66 ♘f3 ♗e2 67 ♘d2 ♗b5!) gxh4 67 ♔h3 ♗e6 68 ♔xh4 ♗f7 69 ♘f3 fxe3 70 fxe3 ♔b6.

63	...	♔b6!
64	♔d3	♔c5
65	♔c3	♗c4=
66	♗f3	♗c7
67	♘d3+	♗xd3
68	♔xd3	♔d6
69	♔e4	♔e6

½-½

Notes by Anatoly Karpov.

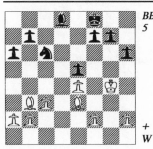

BBNB *Stein - Blau*
5 *Havana Ol 1966*

A smooth demonstration of advantages - active king, queenside majority - from a master of the bishop pair.

    25 ♗d5!

Centralisation and restraint of the black queenside.

25	...	♗c7
26	h4!	

Creating a bind on the opposite flank.

26	...	♔e8
27	h5	♗d6
28	b4	♗c7

Or 28 ... ♘d8 29 ♗b6.

    29 a4

Simply mobilising the pawn majority.

29	...	♘d8
30	c4	b6
31	♔f5	♔e7
32	b5	axb5
33	axb5	♘e6?

A better defence was 33 ... ♔d6 34 ♗c1 ♔d7 (34 ... ♔c5 35 ♗a3+ ♔d4 36 ♗b2++-) 35 ♗b2+-.

34	♗xe6	fxe6+
35	♔g6	♔f8
36	c5	1-0

B

+
W

BBNB *Sosonko - Karpov*
6   *Waddinxveen 1979*

Another graphic demonstration of two bishops with targets to attack. Besides the tra-
ditionally weak queenside, the
e5-pawn is exposed.

28	...	♗c8
29	♗e4	♗d4
30	♘d3	a5
31	♔g2	f5

The beginning of a re-
morseless process. Black undermines the ♘d3 by driving
the ♗e4 back.

32	exf6	gxf6
33	g4	♔f8
34	b3	♔e7

35	♔g3	♔d6
36	♔f4	♗d7
37	h3	♗b5
38	f3	♗d7
39	♔g3	

White is in zugzwang: 39
♘c1 ♗f2 and ... e5+.

39	...	f5

Now the bishop goes ...

40	gxf5	exf5
41	♗b7	♗b5

and now the knight ...

42	♘e1	♗c3
43	♘c2	

Or 43 ♔f2 ♔e5.

43	...	♗d3

Finally the a-pawn drops.

0-1

BBNB *Polugaevsky - Ostojic*
7   *Belgrade 1969*

Another execution by the
bishop pair with queenside
pressure.

20	♔c2	♔f8

Or 20 ... ♘c4 21 ♗xa7
♘xb2 22 ♗c8 b5 23 ♗a6 ♘c4
(23 ... b4 24 ♗b5 +-) 24 a4.

21	b3	♔e8
22	a4	♔d8
23	a5	♘c8
24	♗xc8	♔xc8
25	♗xa7	

The bishop ending poses
few problems.

25	...	e6
26	♔d3	exd5
27	exd5	♗b2
28	♔c4	♗c1
29	♔b5	♔c7
30	♗b6+	♔d7
31	a6	bxa6+
32	♔xa6	♗d2
33	♗a5	

White plays ♔b7 and the b-
pawn goes in.

1-0

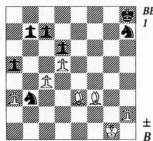

BBNN **Naumkin - A. Kuzmin**
1 *Moscow ch 1987*

Naumkin assesses this position as winning. The outside passed pawn and feeble knights are a typical example of a bad two knights v two bishops ending, but this assessment seems simplistic. The advantage is substantial, but Black can still fight.

36	...	♔g7
37	♔f2	♘f6
38	♔g3	♘d7
39	♔f4	♘e5
40	♗e2	♔f6
41	h4	♘g6+
42	♔g3	c6

Black tries to liquidate. The problem with two knights v two bishops is that even with reduced pawns the defensive problems persist due to the increasing power of the bishops as the board clears. Instead 42 ... ♘c5 43 h5 ♘e5 44 ♔f4 b6 (44 ... ♘ed3+ 45 ♗xd3 ♘xd3+ 46 ♔e4+-) 45 ♗d4 ♘cd7 46 ♗g4 is clearly too passive for Black.

43	dxc6	bxc6
44	h5	♘e5
45	♔f4	a4

Now Black aims to create counterplay against c4.

46	♔e4	♘f7
47	♗d1	♘a5
48	♗d4+	♔g5
49	♗e3+	♔f6
50	♗d4+	♔g5
51	♔d3	♘e5+

Or 51 ... c5 52 ♗e3+ ♔f6 53 ♗f4!.

52	♗xe5	dxe5
53	c5!	

We now get a good bishop v

knight.

53	...	♘b3
54	♔c4	e4
55	♔b4	

Not 55 ♗xb3? axb3 56 ♔xb3 ♔xh5 57 a4 (57 ♔c2 ♔g4 58 ♔d2 ♔f3 59 ♔e1 ♔e3-+) 57 ... ♔g4 58 a5 e3 59 a6 e2 60 a7 e1♕ 61 a8♕ ♕e3+ 62 ♔c4 ♕e4+ 63 ♔c3 ♕e5+.

55	...	e3
56	♔xa4	♘xc5+

Or 56 ... ♘d4 57 ♔a5 (+- Naumkin) 57 ... ♘b5 58 ♔b4! (58 a4? ♘c3 59 ♗f3 ♔f4) 58 ... ♘d4 59 a4 e2 60 ♗xe2 ♘xe2 61 a5 ♘d4 62 a6 ♘b5 63 ♔a5+-.

| 57 | ♔b4 | ♘e6?! |

Naumkin gives 57 ... ♘d3+ 58 ♔c3 ♘f4 59 ♗f3! (Black seems to hold after 59 a4 e2 60 ♗xe2 ♘xe2+ 61 ♔c4 ♘g3! 62 a5 - the only route to the c8 circuit - 62 ... ♘f5 63 a6 ♘d6+ 64 ♔c5 ♘b5 and Black succeeds in stopping the a-pawn on the seventh: 65 ♔xc6 ♘a7+=) 59 ... ♘xh5! and now:

a) 60 ♗xh5 ♔xh5 61 a4 (61 ♔d3 ♔g4 62 ♔xe3 ♔f5=) 61 ... ♔g4 62 a5 ♔f3;

b) 60 a4 ♘f4 61 a5 ♘e6 62 ♗xc6 (62 a6 ♘c7= or 62 ♔d3 ♔f4 63 ♗xc6 e2=) 62 ... ♘d4 63 ♗a4 (63 ♗d5 ♔f4= 64 a6 e2 65 ♔d2 ♘b5 66 ♔xe2 ♔e5 67 ♗c4 ♘a7 intending ... ♔b6 =) 63 ... ♔f4 64 a6 e2 65 ♔d2 ♔f3=.

58	a4	♘d4
59	a5	e2
60	♗xe2	c5+
61	♔c4!	1-0

Two Bishops v Two Minor

+
W

BBNN **Botvinnik - Bronstein**
2
World ch (23) Moscow 1951
This was the adjourned position, a decisive one for the title match.

42 ♗d6?!

42 ♗b1 was the other method of the basic plan: to bring the bishop to a2 and mount pressure against d5. It would probably have been better. Botvinnik gives 42 ... ♘c6 (42 ... ♘c4 43 ♗f4! and next ♗a2 or 42 ... fxe4 43 fxe4 dxe4 44 ♗xe4+ ♔g7 45 ♗xb7! - Flohr - 45 ... ♘xb7 46 ♔c4 and ♔-b5xa6xb6+-) 43 exd5 exd5 44 ♗a2 ♘ab4 (44 ... ♘e7 45 ♗h4) 45 ♗b3 and White will win the d-pawn (with ♗d6 next).

42 ... ♘c6
43 ♗b1 ♔f6?!

A better try was 43 ... ♘a7 44 exd5 exd5 45 ♗a2 b5 46 a5 b4+! 47 ♔d3 ♘b5 48 ♗e5 ♘ac7 49 ♔c2 ♔f7 50 ♔b3 ♘a6 when Botvinnik assesses the position as drawn. If 51 ♗b1 ♔e6 52 ♗d3 ♘a7!.

44 ♗g3!!

Zugzwang. Not 44 ♗f4 ♘e7!.

44 ... fxe4

Alternatively:

a) 44 ... ♘ab4 45 ♗e5+! (45 ♗c7? dxe4 46 fxe4 fxe4 47 ♗xe4 ♘d5+=) 45 ... ♔g6 46 ♗d6 ♘a6 47 exd5 exd5 48 ♗a2+-;

b) 44 ... ♔g6 45 exf5+ exf5

46 ♗a2 transposing to 42 ♗b1.

c) 44 ... ♘e7 45 ♗h4+ ♔f7 46 ♗xe7 ♔xe7 47 exd5 exd5 48 ♗xf5 h6 49 ♗c8.

45 fxe4 h6
46 ♗f4 h5
47 exd5

Otherwise ... ♘e7 and Black gets to use d5.

47 ... exd5
48 h4 ♘ab8
49 ♗g5+ ♔f7
50 ♗f5

Preventing ... ♘d7. This position is an excellent illustration of bishop domination.

50 ... ♘a7

Instead 50 ... ♘e7 51 ♗xe7 (51 ♗h3 ♘bc6 52 ♗g2 ♔g7 53 ♗xe7 ♘xe7 54 ♔b4 ♘c6+ 55 ♔b5 ♘xd4+ 56 ♔xb6 should also win - Botvinnik) 51 ... ♔xe7 52 ♗g6 ♘c6 53 ♗xh5 ♘a7 54 ♔b4! wins.

51 ♗f4 ♘bc6
52 ♗d3 ♘c8
53 ♗e2 ♔g6
54 ♗d3+ ♔f6
55 ♗e2 ♔g6
56 ♗f3 ♘6e7

Or 56 ... ♘8e7 57 ♗g5 (57 ♗c7!? ♘f5 58 ♗xd5 ♘fxd4 59 ♗xb6 is also good - Botvinnik) 57 ... ♘f5 58 ♗xd5 ♘fxd4 59 ♗e4+ ♔f7 60 ♔c4.

57 ♗g5 1-0

A possible variation is 57 ... ♘c6 58 ♗xd5 ♘d6 59 ♗f3 ♔f5 60 ♗c1! (Smyslov) 60 ... b5 61 ♗xc6 bxc6 62 a5.

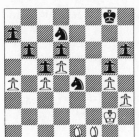

BBNN
3

- B

Portisch - Nunn
London 1982

Black has a material advantage but also a good knight pair as White is handicapped by a bad white-squared bishop. In fairly 'crowded' positions the bishops may often find that only one can be good at a time.

38	...	♘e5
39	♗e2	♔f7
40	♗f3	♘f6!

40 ... ♘xf3? 41 ♔xf3 is assessed by Nunn as equal. White is left with the best bishop and can protect his pawns from attack while d6 and h6 are exposed.

41	♗e2	♘g6
42	♗f1	

Or 42 ♔f3 ♘h4+ 43 ♔f2 ♘e4+ 44 ♔e3 (if 44 ♔g1 the black king advances into the white position via e5) 44 ... ♘g2+ 45 ♔xe4 ♘xe1 and Black wins easily since he has left White with the bad bishop.

42	...	h5!
43	gxh5	

Creates another entry route for the black king via f5 but White had little choice, e.g. 43 ♔g3 hxg4 44 hxg4 ♘e5 45 ♗e2 ♘e4+ 46 ♔g2 ♔f6 47 ♗f3 ♘xf3 48 ♔xf3 ♔e5 49 ♔e3 a5! and the black king enters due to zugzwang (Nunn).

43	...	♘xh5
44	♔f3	♘e5+

45	♔e4	♔g6
46	♗e2	♘f6+
47	♔e3	♔f5
48	♗c3	a6
49	♗e1?!	

Nunn recommends waiting with ♗b2 when Black makes progress with ... ♘e8-c7 and ... b5.

49	...	g4!

Now Black invades further with the king. The fact that all pawns are now on one flank also favours the knights.

50	hxg4+	♘fxg4+
51	♔d2	

Or 51 ♗xg4+ ♔xg4 and c4 falls.

51	...	♔e4
52	♔c3	♔e3
53	♗d1	

Also unsuccessful is 53 ♗xg4 ♘xg4 54 ♗g3 (54 ♗h4 ♘f2 55 ♗d8 ♘e4+ 56 ♔b3 ♔d3-+) 54 ... ♘f2.

53	...	♘f3!
54	♗g3	

Or 54 ♗xf3 ♔xf3 55 ♗h4 ♔e2 56 ♗d8 ♘f2 57 ♗xb6 ♘e4+ 58 ♔c2 ♔e3 59 ♗a5 ♔d4 60 ♔b3 ♔d3 and ... ♘d2+ wins.

54	...	♘f2
55	♗c2	♘g5
56	♔b2	♘ge4
57	♗h4	♔d4
58	♗b3	♘d3+
59	♔a3	♘e5
	0-1	

Notes based on Nunn's analysis.

Two Bishops v Two Minor

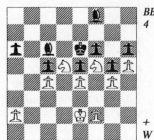

BBNNGeller - Ivkov
4   Budva 1967

A typical good position for the knights, with many pawns and a blocked structure that leaves one of the bishops bad. This in turn handicaps the good bishop which cannot be exchanged, removing the usually powerful option of reaching good bishop vs knight.

48	♔d2	♗a4
49	f3	♗c6
50	♘c3	

Preventing possible counterplay with ... ♗a4.

50	...	♗d7
51	♔c2	♗e8
52	♔b3	♗d7
53	♘d5	♗c6
54	♔a3	

Black is, not surprisingly, in zugzwang. Of course not 54 ♘c7+ ♔d7 55 ♘xa6?? when 55 ... ♗b7 traps the knight.

54	...	a5

Also insufficient are 54 ... ♗d7 55 ♘c7++-; 54 ... ♗e8 55 ♘c7++-; and 54 ... ♗b7 55 ♔a4+-.

55	♔b3	♔d7

Or 55 ... ♗d7 56 ♘c7+ ♔f7 57 ♘b5+-.

56	♘xf6+	♔e6
57	♘d5	

57 ♘g8 or 57 ♘h7 are also possible.

57	...	♔d7
58	♘c3	1-0

After 58 ... ♔c7 59 ♘b5+ ♔b6 60 ♘bd6 and ♘f7 White wins more material.

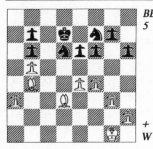

BBNNKorchnoi - Matanovic
5   Palma 1968

Again we see the power of the bishops with a fluid pawn structure, and that pawn exchanges do not simplify the defence as they also increase the range of the bishops.

32	♔f2	g6

Or 32 ... e5 33 f5 and the white king heads for g6.

33	e5!	

Not 33 ♔e3?! e5 34 f5 gxf5 35 exf5 h5! and ... ♘h6.

33	...	fxe5
34	♗xg6	exf4
35	gxf4	e5
36	♔f3	♔e6
37	a4	♔d5
38	h4	♔e6

Or 38 ... ♔d4 39 f5 e4+ 40 ♔f4 e3 41 f6 e2 42 ♔f3 ♘e5+ (42 ... ♔e5 43 ♗c3+ ♔e6 44 ♔xe2 ♘e8 45 ♗d4) 43 ♔xe2 ♘xg6 44 ♗xd6 ♘h8 45 ♗f4.

39	♗c2!	

Better than 39 ♗c3 e4+!? 40

♗xe4 ♘xe4 41 ♔xe4 ♘d6+ 42 ♔f3 h5 43 ♗d4.

39	...	♘f5
40	♗b3+	♔f6
41	fxe5+!	♘xe5+
42	♔e4	♘xh4
43	♗c3	♘hg6
44	♗d4	h5
45	♗xb6	♘d7

Or 45 ... h4 46 ♗d8+ (46 a5!? h3 47 ♗g1) 46 ... ♔g7 47 ♗xh4 ♘xh4 48 ♔xe5+-.

46	♗d4+	♔e7
47	a5	h4
48	♗d5	h3
49	♗xb7	♔d6
50	♗g1	♘c5+

White also wins after 50 ... ♔c7 51 ♗c6 ♘f6+ 52 ♔f5 ♘e7+ 53 ♔xf6 ♘xc6 54 a6 h2 (54 ... ♘d4 55 ♗xd4 h2 56 ♗e5+ or 54 ... ♘a7 55 b6+ ♔b8 56 ♗h2+) 55 b6+!+-.

51	♔f3	♘e5+
52	♔g3	h2
53	♔xh2	♘xb7
54	a6	♘f3+
55	♔h1	1-0

Two Bishops v Two Minor

BBNN *Botvinnik - Furman*
6 *Training game 1961*

1	...	♔f8

Or 1 ... ♘c7 2 a4 a6 3 a5 bxa5 (3 ... ♘d7 4 bxa6 ♘xa6 5 ♗xd5) 4 b6 ♘b5 5 b7 ♘d7 6 ♗xd5.

2	a4	♔e7
3	♗a3+	♔d7
4	f3	♘c7
5	♗f8	g6
6	♔f2	♔e6
7	♔g3	♘d7
8	♗h6	f5
9	♗f4	♘e8

10	fxe4	fxe4
11	♔h4	♘d6
12	♗xd6	♔xd6
13	♔g5	♔e6
14	h3	♘f6
15	♔h6	♘h5

Planning counterplay starting with ... ♘f4!

16	♗b3!	♘g3
17	♔xh7	♔f5
18	♗xd5	g5
19	♔g7	g4
20	hxg4+	♔xg4
21	♗e6+	1-0

+
B

BBNN *Flohr - Botvinnik*
7 *Leningrad match (6) 1933*

Black's pawn structure is better than in diag 6, since his pawns are less advanced, and therefore less exposed to the bishops. Also there is no obvious pawn weakness on the queenside.

26	♗e3	♔d8
27	♔e1	♔c7
28	♔d2	♘c5
29	b4	♘cd7

Shereshevsky considers that Black should try ... ♘a4 and ... b5 as a superior method of defence. White could have prefaced b4 with ♗-c2.

30	g3	

Shereshevsky considers 30 a4 more accurate, which seems true as it limits Black's options.

30	...	♘b6
31	♔c2	♘bd7
32	a4!	♘b6
33	a5	♘bd7
34	♗c1	♔d8
35	♗b2	♘e8
36	♔d2	♘c7
37	♔e3	♔e7
38	♗f1	♘b5
39	h4	♘c7
40	♗h3	

±
W

White methodically improves his position. Now the ♗h3 eyes c8, and he can increase the pressure by advancing the kingside pawns.

40	...	♘e8
41	f4	f6
42	♗f5	

A typical device. White provokes weaknesses. As the black pawn structure advances, it becomes more accessible to White, and creates more space for the bishops to work in (cf 5 ♗f8 in diag 6).

42	...	g6
43	♗h3	h6

Black sees that he needs the possibility of ... g5 in reply to the thrust f5 by White: 43 ... ♘g7 44 f5 g5 45 hxg5 fxg5 46 f6+! and wins, since the bishop swoops into c8 (Botvinnik).

44	♗c1!	

White takes aim at the new target in the enemy camp.

44	...	♘g7
45	fxe5	dxe5

45 ... fxe5 46 ♔f3 h5 47 ♗g5+ completely paralyses Black.

46	♔f3	h5
47	♗e3	♔d6

Preventing ♗c5.

48	♗h6	♞e8
49	g4	hxg4+
50	♗xg4	♞c7
51	♗e3	♞b5
52	♔e2!	

The final finesse. White centralises the king and restricts the prospects of the knight on b5.

52	...	♞c7
53	♔d3	f5!

Desperate but if 53 ... ♞b5 54 ♗e6 ♔e7 55 ♗c5+ ♔e8 56 d6 the weaknesses on b7 and g6 prove fatal.

54	exf5	gxf5
55	♗xf5	♞xd5
56	♗d2	♞7f6
57	♔c4	♔c6
58	♗g6	b5+
59	♔d3	♞e7
60	♗e4+	♞ed5

Or 60 ... ♞xe4 61 ♔xe4

♔d6 62 h5 ♔e6 63 h6 ♔f6 64 h7 and the h-pawn will cost Black all of his pawns.

61	♗g5	♞h5
62	♗f3	♞g3
63	♗d2	♔d6
64	♗g4	♞f6
65	♗c8	♔c6
66	♗e1!	

Instead 66 ♗xa6 ♞f5 threatens the h4-pawn and prepares counterplay with the e-pawn.

66	...	e4+?!

Now the e-pawn becomes weak and the knights lose all coordination. Better was 66 ... ♞ge4 67 ♗f5 (67 ♗xa6 ♞d6 with counterplay against the trapped bishop on a6) 67 ... ♞d6 68 ♗g6 ♔d5.

67	♔d4	♞gh5
68	♗f5	♔d6
69	♗d2	1-0

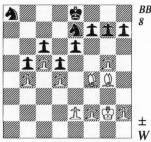

BBNN
8
±
W

Miles - Gonda
Buenos Aires Ol 1978

The rigid pawn formation gives the knights counter chances.

32 ♗e5

A thematic probe - compare with 5 ♗f8 in diag 6.

32 ... g6?

Alternatively:

a) 32 ... ♞f5? 33 ♗xf5 exf5 34 ♔f3!+-. The knight is pathetic. (But not 34 ♗xg7? ♞c7 and b4 falls.)

b) 32 ... ♔d7! planning ... ♞c7-a6 with unclear play (Miles).

33	♔f3	♔d7
34	♔f4	♞c7?

A better defence was 34 ... ♞g8 35 h4 ♞c7 36 ♗xc7 ♔xc7 37 ♔e5 ♔d7 38 h5 with a large advantage to White -

Miles.

35	♗xc7	♔xc7
36	♔e5	♞g8
37	♗xe6!	fxe6
38	♔xe6	♔d8
39	♔d6	♞e7
40	e3	♞e8
41	♔c7	♔f7
42	♔d7	♔f8
43	f3	♞f5

Or 43 ... ♔f7 44 e4 dxe4 45 fxe4 ♔f8 46 h3 ♔f7 47 e5! ♔f8 48 e6 ♞d5 49 ♔xc6 ♞xb4+ 50 ♔xb5+-.

44	♔xc6	♞xe3
45	♔d7	♞c4
46	c6	♞b6+
47	♔d8	1-0

Due to 47 ... ♔f7 48 c7 ♔e6 49 c8♕+ ♞xc8 50 ♔xc8 ♔f5 51 ♔d7+-.

Notes based on those of Miles.

Rook v Pawn(s)   ♖ v ♟(♙)

Endings with rook against pawn(s) arise very frequently out of single rook endings - one of the players has to sacrifice his rook for a passed pawn. They are therefore extremely important for the practical player.

Rook v One Pawn

Usually, of course, the player with the pawn will be trying to draw. However, there are some exceptional position and here we examine some of these.

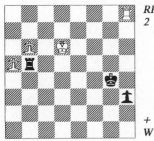

RP 1

Saavedra 1895

    1   c7

The black rook is now so badly placed that it simply cannot stop the pawn.

    1   ...   ♖d6+

    2   ♔b5

But not 2 ♔b7? ♖d7=; nor 2 ♔c5? ♖d1.

    2   ...   ♖d5+

    3   ♔b4

Again White must avoid going to the c-file 3 ♔c4? ♖d1!=.

+ W

    3   ...   ♖d4+

    4   ♔b3

Now 4 ♔c3 ♖d1 5 ♔c2! comes to the same thing.

    4   ...   ♖d3+

    5   ♔c2   ♖d4!

If 6 c8♕? ♖c4+! 7 ♕xc4 is stalemate. But with the black king trapped in the corner White can underpromote.

    6   c8♖!!   ♖a4

    7   ♔b3 and wins

RP 2

Fenton - Potter
1875

This is how a position like diag 1 can arise. The game continued:

    1   ♖xh3   ♔xh3

    2   ♔c6   ♖xa5

    3   b7   ♖a6+

And here a draw was agreed! Although White wins by force with 4 ♔c5 ♖a5+ 5

+ W

♔c4 ♖a4+ 6 ♔c3 ♖a3+ 7 ♔b2 etc.

(Twenty years later a newspaper columnist, G. Barbier, published diag 1, based on diag 2, as a draw. But then a reader, the now immortal F Saavedra, noticed the winning underpromotion and thus the famous diag 1 was born.)

RP 3

Maizelis (based on a study by Troitsky) 1895

Here the white king has to take a different route to escape the checks.

    1   f7   ♖c6+

    2   ♔e5!

But not 2 ♔e7? ♖c1 3 f8♕ ♖e1+ 4 ♔f7 ♖f1+=.

+ W

    2   ...   ♖c5+

    3   ♔e4   ♖c4+

    4   ♔e3   ♖c3+

    5   ♔f2   ♖c2+

    6   ♔g3   ♖c3+

    7   ♔g4   ♖c4+

    8   ♔g5   ♖c5+

    9   ♔g6   ♖c6+

   10   ♔g7 and wins

Rook v Pawn(s)

♖ V ♟(♟)

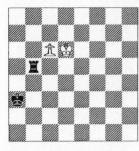

RP
4

=
W

Finally, here is an example of a successful stalemate defence.

1	c7	♖b6+
2	♔d5	♖b5+
3	♔d4	♖b4+
4	♔d3	♖b3+
5	♔c2	♖b2+
6	♔c1	♖b4!
7	c8♕	

Obviously the underpromotion 7 c8♖ achieves nothing here.

7	...	♖c4+
8	♕xc4 stalemate	

Apart from exceptional cases like those examined on the previous pages, only the player with the rook can hope to win. There are essentially three ways in which he can hope to do so:

A. Racing
White aims to control the pawn's queening square with his king and rook before his opponent can safely promote it.

As we shall see this is much easier if the black king does not interfere with his counterpart's approach. And therefore *shouldering off* is one of Black's main defensive weapons in this case.

B. Cutting off the enemy king
If the black king starts on a bad square then it may be possible to cut him off from his pawn permanently. In that case White will have all the time in the world to bring up his king.

Cutting is one of the most powerful tools in this ending.

C. Allowing the pawn to underpromote and then winning
i) This is quite possible when the defender had a *rook's pawn* since the resultant ending of rook v knight is won (see diag 13).

However, with other pawns the analogous rook v knight ending is drawn and this method is therefore inoperative.

ii) When the defender does have a *rook's pawn* there is an additional possibility of confining the king in front of the rook's pawn. This will gain several tempi (see diag 14).

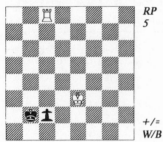

RP
5

+/=
W/B

Racing
Diag 5 is the end of a typical race. The white rook is ideally placed behind the passed pawn, controlling the queen ing square through it.

Obviously here the result depends on the move. White to play wins with 1 ♔d2, Black to play draws with 1 ... c1♕+.

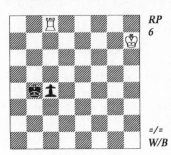

RP 6

=/=
W/B

In the previous position the result was obvious, but here it requires rather more thought.

First let's consider diag 6 with Black to move. Here we can use the method of *counting* to ease calculation.

It would take Black *five moves* unopposed to queen his pawn (i.e. ♔b4-b3-b2; c4-c3-c2-c1♕).

The white king will also take *five moves* to control c1 - the queening square (i.e. ♔h7-g6-f5-e4-d3-d2).

Therefore Black to move can draw simply by pushing his pawn. Let's verify that.

1	...	c3
2	♔g6	♔b3
3	♔f5	c2
4	♔e4	♔b2
5	♔d3	c1♕=

What about if White is to move?

Now if Black simply pushes his pawn then we know from counting that the white king will seize control of the queening square one vital move before the pawn can promote, i.e.

1 ♔g6

And if now 1 ... c3? 2 ♔f5 ♔b3 3 ♔e4 c2 4 ♔d3 ♔b2 5 ♖xc2+ (or 5 ♔d2) and wins.

However, Black has time to switch to an alternative method of defence - *shouldering off*.

1	...	♔c3!
2	♔f5	♔d3
3	♔f4	

If 3 ♖d8+ ♔e3! does not help White. The rook is already ideally placed behind the pawn.

| 3 | ... | c3 |
| 4 | ♔f3 | |

Or 4 ♖d8+ ♔e2!=.

| 4 | ... | c2 |

4 ... ♔d2 5 ♖d8+ ♔e1 also draws.

| 5 | ♔f2 | ♔d2 |
| 6 | ♖d8+ | ♔c3= |

Going back to the position after 4 ♔f3. This is so important that it deserves a diagram of its own: see diag 7.

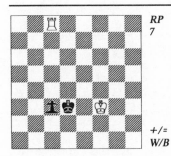

RP 7

+/=
W/B

As we saw above, Black to move draws in this position. But White to move wins by driving the enemy king out of the way, thus allowing his own king to take part in the struggle.

1 ♖d8+

1 ♔f2 ♔d2 (or 1 ... c2 2 ♔e1) 2 ♖d8+ ♔c1 3 ♔e2 c2 4 ♖c8 ♔b1 5 ♔d2 also wins.

1	...	♔c2
2	♔e2	♔b2
3	♖c8	c2
4	♔d2 and wins	

Diag 7 is so fundamental that we can also use it for counting.

Diagram 7a
Note that White's rook could also start on h8. He still wins with 1 ♖d8+!. Let's return to diag 6 and see what happens with the white king on other squares.

Diagram 7b
Here the white king is only three moves from f3. White to move wins with:

1 ♔g5

If now 1 ... c3 then Black loses by a tempo as before, or if he tries to shoulder off the white king with

1 ... ♔c3

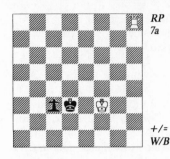

RP
7a

+/=
W/B

RP
7b

+/=
W/B

KP
7c

+/+
W/B

then it is easy to see that we reach diag 7 with *White to move.*

But Black to move draws with 1 ... ♚c3. He reaches the formation of diag 7 in three moves - so does White. Therefore it will be *Black to move* in diag 7.

Diagram 7c

Here Black loses even with the move since White's king is only two squares from f3. It will be White to move in diag 7.

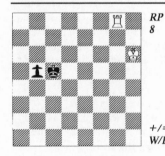

RP
8

+/=
W/B

Here the white rook is not quite so well placed. Nevertheless White to move wins easily since his king reaches e3 in only three moves.

Black to move can draw *as long as he pushes his pawn first.*

| | 1 | ... | b4 |
| | 2 | ♚g5 | ♚d4 |

On principle it is right to shoulder off the enemy king. But 2 ... b3 3 ♚f4 ♚c4 4 ♚e3 b2! (not 4 ... ♚c3 5 ♖c8+! wins analogous to diag 7) 5 ♖b8 ♚c3 6 ♚e2 ♚c2 7 ♖c8+

♚b3! also draws.

| | 3 | ♚f4 | b3 |
| | 4 | ♖h8 | |

Or 4 ♚f3 b2 5 ♖b8 ♚c3 6 ♚e2 ♚c2= as above.

| | 4 | ... | ♚c3 |
| | 5 | ♚e3 | |

And as this position is analogous to diag 7 with Black to move it is therefore a draw.

We could have derived this result in advance by *counting.*

Black takes four moves to get his king to c3 and pawn to b3. White takes four moves to get his king to e3 and rook to

Rook v Pawn(s)   ♖ v ♟(♙)

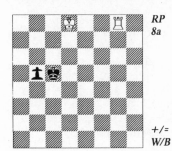

RP 8a

+/= W/B

b8.

Thus as long as Black does not allow White to *win a tempo* in some way, White can do no better than reach diag 7 (one file to the left) with Black to move.

However, if Black *pushes his king too soon* then White does have a "trick".

| 1 | ... | ♚c4? |
| 2 | ♖c8+! | ♚b3 |

If 2 ... ♚d3 3 ♖b8! ♚c4 White has won a tempo and a simple count reveals that he therefore wins.

| 3 | ♚g5 | b4 |
| 4 | ♚f4 | ♚a2 |

In order to push the pawn as fast as possible, Black again has to put his king in front of the pawn.

| 5 | ♚e3 | b3 |
| 6 | ♚d2 | |

6 ♖a8+ leads to the same thing.

6	...	b2
7	♖a8+!	♚b1/♚b3
8	♖b8(+)	♚a2
9	♚c2 and wins	

From this example we can see that *once the black king* has reached the fourth rank it is usually wrong *to advance it further forward* than the pawn since then White may get the chance to *win a tempo* tactically.

We shall see the reason for the qualification that the king must have reached the fourth rank in diag 10.

Diagram 8a

Here the white king is too far away from e3. But instead it can aim to outflank Black coming down the a-file. For as we know:

It is always to the attacker's advantage for his king to be on the opposite side of the pawn to the opponent's king.

Counting again, we can see that it takes White seven moves to control b1 with both king and rook (i.e. ♚d8-c7-b6--a4-a3-a2, ♖b8) and Black seven moves to escort his pawn home (i.e. ♚c5-c4-c3-c2, b5-b4-b3-b2-b1♛).

Therefore, other things being equal, White to move wins, Black to move draws, and this is indeed the case.

Note the similarity to diag 5 which despite appearances is essentially exactly the same as the final position White is aiming for.

White to move:

| 1 | ♚c7 | b4 |
| 2 | ♖b8! | |

But not 2 ♖g5+ ♚c4 3 ♚c6 b3 4 ♖g4+ ♚c3 5 ♚c5 b2 and Black draws by two tempi.

2	...	♚c4
3	♚b6	b3
4	♚a5	♚c3
5	♚a4	b2
6	♚a3	♚c2
7	♖xb2+	

(or indeed 7 ♚a2) and wins

But with Black to move after 1 ... b4 2 ♚c7 b3 3 ♖b8 ♚c4 4 ♚b6 b2 (or indeed 4 ... ♚b4) 5 ♚a5 ♚c3 6 ♚a4 ♚c2 7 ♚a3 White has arrived a move too late: 7 ... b1♛=.

209

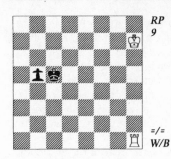

RP 9

=/=
W/B

Black to move draws rather easily. With White to move the position is also drawn but Black must be a little careful.

   1   ♔g6   b4

Not 1 ... ♔d4? 2 ♖b1 ♔c4 3 ♔f5 and wins - see B below.

   2   ♔f5

A.

   2   ...   ♔d4!

Shouldering off the white king.

   3   ♔f4

If 3 ♖h3 ♔c4 4 ♔e4 b3 or 3 ♖b1 ♔c3 4 ♔e4 b3 = in each case.

   3   ...   b3
   4   ♖b1   ♔c3
   5   ♔e3   b2=

B.

   2   ...   ♔c4?

2 ... b3? 3 ♔e4 ♔c4 4 ♖c1+ is even simpler for White.

   3   ♔e4   ♔c3
   4   ♔e3   b3

If 4 ... ♔c2 hoping for 5 ♖h8? b3 6 ♖c8+ ♔d1!= White plays 5 ♖h2+ ♔c3 6 ♖h8 b3 7 ♖c8+ transposing into diag 7 with White to move.

   5   ♖c1+   ♔b2

Or 5 ... ♔b4 6 ♔d3 b2 7 ♖b1 ♔b3 8 ♔d2 ♔moves 9 ♔c2 etc.

   6   ♔d2

6 ♖c8 also wins.

   6   ...   ♔a2

And here White must avoid the *stalemate trap* 7 ♔c3? b2 8 ♖c2 ♔a1! 9 ♖xb2, but instead 7 ♖c8 b2 8 ♖a8+ and 9 ♖b8! or indeed 7 ♖h1 both win very easily.

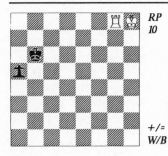

RP 10

+/=
W/B

Cutting off the enemy king
White's king is a very long way off from the action and a count reveals that the normal racing technique will draw by a tempo.

White must play ♖a8 to stop the black king from shouldering off his own and ♔h8-d3, i.e. six moves, while Black takes only five to reach the dispositions of diag 7 (see also diag 12).

But White to move wins *on the spot* with

   1   ♖g5!

Now Black's king is *cut off on the third rank.*

   1   ...   a4
   2   ♔g7

And Black is completely helpless since if ...

   2   ...   a3
   3   ♖g3

Or indeed 3 ♔h6 a2 4 ♖g1 - a1xa2.

   3   ...   a2
   4   ♖a3 and wins

Black to play in diag 10 must give first priority to getting his king beyond the third rank.

   1   ...   ♔b5!

Not 1 ... a4?? 2 ♖g5!. But now he draws easily. Note that if

   2   ♖g4   a4
   3   ♔g7   a3
   4   ♔f6   a2
   5   ♖g1   ♔b4=

i.e. Cutting off only works if the black king is on the third rank or further back.

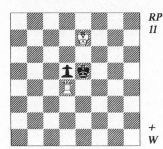

RP
11

+
W

Zugzwang

This is not a very frequent motif in these endings. But it can occur when the *rook is on the pawn's queening square.*

Réti 1928

White must retreat his rook. If 1 ♖h4 d4 2 ♖h5+ ♔e4 3 ♔d6 d3 Black draws by a tempo - White requires five moves to control d1 twice. Black needs only four to escort his pawn home. That leaves:

A.

    1   ♖d1

The most "natural" move, but incorrect.

    1   ...   d4
    2   ♔d7   ♔d5!

White is in zugzwang! If 3 ♔e7 ♔e5 or 3 ♔c5 ♔c7 doesn't help, and if the rook leaves the d-file Black plays simply 3 ... d3. So

    3   ♖d2   ♔e4

Or 3 ... ♔c4
    4   ♔c6   d3
    5   ♔c5   ♔e3
Gaining an invaluable tempo on the rook
    6   ♖moves d2
    and draws

B.

    1   ♖d2!!
1 ♖d3! has the same effect.
    1   ...   d4
    2   ♖d1!
Now it is Black who is in zugzwang
    2   ...   ♔d5
    3   ♔d7!   ♔e4
Or 3 ... ♔c4 4 ♔e6! etc. White must always attack with his king on the opposite side of the pawn to Black's if possible.
    4   ♔c6   d3
    5   ♔c5   ♔e3
    6   ♔c4   d2
    7   ♔c3 and wins

RP
12

+/=
W/B

Special Cases with a Rook's Pawn

Although this position is very similar to diag 7 there is one important difference.

White to play still wins very easily viz. 1 ♖b8+ ♔a2 2 ♔c2 ♔a1 3 ♔b3 a2 4 ♖h8 ♔b1 5 ♖h1 mate!

Black to move:

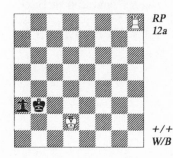

RP
12a

+/+
W/B

    1   ...   ♔b2!
In diag 7 Black could also simply push the pawn, but here that loses: 1 ... a2? 2 ♖b8+ ♔a3 3 ♔c2 a1♘+ 4 ♔c3 ♔a2 5 ♖b7 and wins.
    2   ♖b8+
If 2 ♖h2+ ♔b3!=.
    2   ...   ♔c1!
But not 2 ... ♔a1? 3 ♔c2 a2

4 ♔b3 ♔b1 5 ♖h8 a1♘+ 6 ♔c3 ♔a2 7 ♖b8 and wins.
    3   ♖a8
If 3 ♖c8+ ♔b1 draws; or 3 ... ♔b2 4 ♖c2+ ♔b3!= - but not 4 ... ♔b1?? 5 ♔c3 a2 6 ♖b2+ and wins.
And 3 ♔c3 a2 does not help either.
    3   ...   ♔b2
    4   ♔d2   a2
    5   ♖b8+   ♔a1!=

Diagram 12a

Here Black loses even with the move: 1 ... ♔b2 (or 1 ... a2 2 ♖b8+ ♔a3 3 ♔c2! a1♘+ 4 ♔c3 ♔a2 5 ♖b7 wins) 2 ♖b8+ ♔a1 3 ♔c2 a2 4 ♔b3 etc.

RP 13

+/=
W/B

Attacking from behind

White to play wins easily with 1 ♔d6 - 4 ♔d3 and, exactly as in diag 12, 5 ♖b8+. Black cannot oppose this since the pawn is not far enough advanced for him to shoulder off the white king.

Black to move must choose between 1 ... ♔b4 and 1 ... a4.

A.

  1   ...   a4!

This draws fairly comfortably, viz:

  2   ♔d6

If 2 ♖h5+ ♔c4 3 ♔c6 a3 4 ♖h4+ ♔b3 5 ♔b5 a2= the white king is too far behind the pawn.

  2   ...   a3!

But not 2 ... ♔c4? 3 ♖h4+ ♔b3 4 ♔c5 a3 5 ♖h3+ and wins as in variation B.

  3   ♔d5   ♔b4
  4   ♔d4   a2

Or 4 ... ♔b3 5 ♖h3+ (5 ♔d3 ♔b2! in diag 12) 5 ... ♔b2 6 ♔c4 a2 7 ♖h2+ ♔a3!=

  5   ♖a8   ♔b3
  6   ♔d3   ♔b2=

B.

  1   ...   ♔b4?

As usual it is wrong to push the king before the pawn. Now White could gain a tempo with 2 ♖b8+? ♔c3 3 ♖a8 ♔b4 but this merely reaches diag 12 with Black to move. Instead there is another way of playing.

  2   ♔c6!   a4
  3   ♖h4+   ♔b3
  4   ♔b5   a3
  5   ♖h3+   ♔b2
  6   ♔b4   a2
  7   ♖h2+   ♔b1
  8   ♔b3

And not 8 ♔a3?? a1♕+ 9 ♔b3 ♕a8! and wins.

  8   ...   a1♘+
  9   ♔c3 and wins

This method of attacking from behind and then forcing underpromotion works *only against a rook's pawn.*

For if we move the final position one file to the right (ignoring the rook) then the knight has sufficient room to draw (see diag RN1) - it can go to a3.

Finally note that with White to move his king must be only two ranks behind the black pawn.

RP 14

+
W

Imprisoning the black king

White to move wins with:

  1   ♖b8!

As a result, despite his bad king position he wins by a tempo: 1 ... ♔a3 2 ♔g7 a4 3 ♔f6 ♔a2 4 ♔e5 a3 5 ♔d4

♔a1 6 ♔c3 a2 7 ♔b3 ♔b1 8 ♖h8 a1♘+ 9 ♔c3 ♔a2 10 ♖b8 etc.

Diag R97 and R98 variation B show this appalling black king position arising in practice.

Rook v Pawn(s)

Rook v Two Pawns

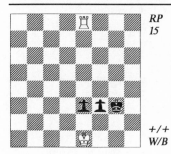

RP 15

+/+
W/B

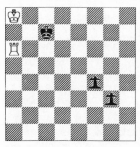

RP 16

+/-
W/B

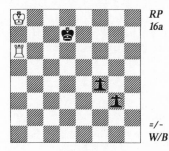

RP 16a

=/-
W/B

Connected Pawns

a) If the "white" king can get in front of the two pawns then he will win easily, e.g. diag 15.

Here White to move must avoid the trap 1 ♖xe3? ♔g2!= but he simply plays

    1   ♔f1!   ♔f4

Or 1 ... e2+ 2 ♔e1 ♔g2 3 ♖g8+ ♔h3 4 ♔f2 ♔h4 5 ♖e8 (or 5 ♖g1) 5 ... ♔g4 6 ♖f8 zugzwang and wins.

    2   ♖e7

Zugzwang.

    2   ...   e2+

Or 2 ... f2 3 ♔g2 zugzwang and wins at once.

    3   ♔f2   ♔g4
    4   ♖f7

Zugzwang and wins.

Black to move obviously cannot achieve much, e.g. if 1 ... ♔f4 2 ♔f1 or 1 ... ♔g2 2 ♖g8+ ♔ moves 3 ♔f1 and 4 ♖e8 etc.

b) *In the absence of both kings, two connected passed pawns beat a rook if they are both on the sixth rank. However, if the rook can prevent them both reaching the sixth rank then it wins.*

In diag 16 Black to move wins easily with either 1 ... g2 or 1 ... f3, i.e. 1 ... g2 2 ♖g6 f3 followed by 3 ... f2. Or:

    1   ...   f3

This is the fundamental type of position.

    2   ♖g6

If 2 ♖f6 g2! or 2 ♖a3 f2/g2 wins.

    2   ...   f2
    3   ♖f6   g2
    and wins

But White to move wins with:

    1   ♖g6!

Immobilising both pawns.

Black must bring up his king to try to help.

    1   ...   ♔d7
    2   ♖g4!   g2

Or 2 ... ♔e6 3 ♖xf4 and 4 ♖g4 etc.

    3   ♖xg2   ♔e6
    4   ♖g5! and wins

Diagram 16a

Here Black draws even when White is to move (of course, Black to move still wins easily).

    1   ♖g6   ♔e7
    2   ♔b7

If 2 ♖g4 g2 or 2 ... ♔f6 both draw.

    2   ...   ♔f7

2 ... g2 3 ♖xg2 ♔f6! 4 ♔c6 ♔e5 also draws.

    3   ♖g4   ♔f6
    4   ♖xf4+   ♔g5=

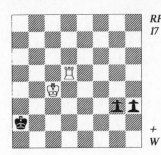

RP 17

Shapiro 1914

Despite the two pawns on the sixth, White actually wins here since he can create *threats* against the black king and sometimes win a pawn *with check*.

1	♖d2+	♔b1

If 1 ... ♔a3 2 ♖d3+ and ♖xg3, or 1 ... ♔a1 2 ♔b3 and ♖d1 mate!

2	♔c3!	♔c1

If 2 ... h2 3 ♖d1+ ♔a2 4 ♖h1! or 2 ... g2 3 ♖d1+ ♔a2 4 ♖g1! in each case with decisive zugzwang.

3	♖a2	♔d1

3 ... ♔b1 4 ♖e2 h2/g2 5 ♖e1+ ♔a2 6 ♖h1/♖g1 and wins.

4	♔d3	♔c1
5	♔e3!	h2

Or 5 ... g2 6 ♔f2 etc.

6	♖a1+	♔c2
7	♖h1!	♔c3
8	♔f3 and wins	

RP 18

Defence by Perpetual Attack
Keres - Eliskases
Nordwijk 1938

Black to play would obviously like to win easily with 1 ... ♔c5. But with White to move the pawns are unstoppable. Nevertheless Eliskases was able to draw by a very typical manoeuvre. Black pursues the white king round the board always by *threatening mate and checking*. As a result, White simply has not got time to promote his pawns.

A.

The game continued:

1	a7	♖a2
2	b6	♔c3!
3	♔b1	

The only way to make progress. If 3 ♔d1 Black follows the white king with his own 3 ... ♔d3 4 ♔e1 ♔e3 5 ♔f1 ♔f3 6 ♔e1 ♔e3 etc.

3	...	♖a6
4	b7	♖b6+!
5	♔c1	

Or 5 ♔a1 ♖a6+.

5	...	♖h6!

And here the draw was agreed. For if 6 ♔d1 ♔d3 7 ♔e1 ♔e3 8 ♔f1 ♔f3 9 ♔g1 ♖g6+! 10 ♔h2 ♖h6+ 11 ♔g1 ♖g6+ 12 ♔f1 ♖h6! 13 ♔e1 ♔e3 etc.

B.

White could also have tried:

1	b6	

... but Black can still draw:

1	...	♔c3
2	♔d1	♔d3
3	♔e1	♔e3
4	b7	

4 a7 ♖a2 would soon transpose back into A above.

4	...	♖h2!
5	♔f1	

If 5 ♔d1 ♔d3 6 ♔c1 ♔c3 7 ♔b1 ♖h1+! 8 ♔a2 ♖h2+ 9 ♔a3 (9 ♔b1=) 9 ... ♖h6 (or 9 ... ♖h1=) 10 ♔a4 ♖xa6+ 11 ♔b5 ♖a1=.

5	...	♔f3
6	♔g1	♖h8!

But not 6 ... ♖b2? 7 a7 ♖b1+ 8 ♔h2 ♖b2+ 9 ♔h3 ♖b1 10 b8♕ and wins.

7	a7	♖g8+
8	♔h2	♖h8+
9	♔g1	♖g8+
10	♔f1	♖h8
11	♔e1	♔e3
12	♔d1	♔d3
13	♔c1	♔c3
14	♔b1	♖h1+
15	♔a2	♖h2+
16	♔a3	♖h1
17	♔a4	♔c4
18	♔a5	♔c5=

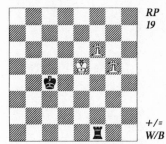

RP 19

+/=
W/B

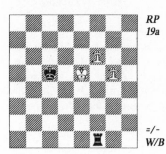

RP 19a

=/-
W/B

c) The "white" king is much better placed than the black king.

Tarrasch - Janowski
Ostend 1907

Here White's king is supporting his pawns whilst the black king is rather badly placed. Obviously only White can hope to win. Tarrasch played:

A.

    1   g6

Although this looks natural, White could have won more simply with 1 ♔e6 ♖e1+ 2 ♔f7 ♔d5 3 g6 ♖g1 (or 3 ... ♔e5 4 ♔g7! ♔f5 5 f7 ♖e7 6 ♔g8) 4 ♔g7! (not 4 g7 ♔e5=) 4 ... ♔e6 5 f7 and wins.

    1   ...   ♖e1+
    2   ♔d6   ♖g1!

In the game, Janowski played 2... ♖d1+? 3 ♔e7 ♖e1+ 4 ♔f7 1-0 in view of 4 ... ♔d5 5 g7 ♖g1 6 g8♕ etc.

    3   g7

If 3 f7? ♖xg6+ 4 ♔e5 ♖g5+ 5 ♔e4 ♖g1!= as in B(i) below.

    3   ...   ♔d4!
    4   ♔c6!

Not 4 f7 ♖g6+!=; and if 4 ♔e6 ♔e4 5 ♔e7? (5 ♔d6!) 5 ... ♔e5=.

    4   ...   ♔c4
    5   ♔d7!   ♔d5
    6   ♔e8!   ♔e6
    7   f7   ♖a1
    8   f8♘+! and
    9   g8♕ wins

B.

In diag 19 Black has two ways to draw:

i)

    1   ...   ♖g1!
    2   f7

If 2 ♔f5? ♔d5 is already almost winning for Black! (see

the note to 3 ... ♖g1! in diag 19a).

    2   ...   ♖xg5+
    3   ♔e4

Or 3 ♔e6 ♖g6+ 4 ♔e7 ♖g7!=.

    3   ...   ♖g1

And now White must acquiesce in a draw with 4 ♔e5 since if 4 f8♕? ♖e1+ and 5 ... ♖f1+ wins for Black!

ii)

    1   ...   ♔c5
    2   ♔e6

Or 2 g6 ♖e1+ 3 ♔f5 ♔d5! (but not 3 ... ♔d6? 4 g7 ♖f1+ 5 ♔e4!) 4 g7 ♖f1+ 5 ♔g6 ♖g1+ 6 ♔f7 ♔e5 7 ♔e7 ♖g2= since White can make no progress.

    2   ...   ♖e1+
    3   ♔f7

This is forced eventually. If 3 ♔d7 ♖f1 (or 3 ... ♖d1+) 4 ♔e7 ♖e1+ 5 ♔f8? (5 ♔f7) 5 ... ♖g1!=.

    3   ...   ♖g1
    4   g6   ♔d6
    5   ♔g7

Or 5 g7 ♔e5= (as in the note to 2 ♔e6).

    5   ...   ♖f1!
    6   f7   ♔e7=

Diagram 19a

With White to move this is variation B(ii) directly above. But Black to move wins:

    1   ...   ♖e1+
    2   ♔f5   ♔d6
    3   ♔g6

Or 3 g6 ♖f1+ 4 ♔g5 ♔e6 etc.

    3   ...   ♖g1!

But not 3 ... ♔e6 4 ♔g7 ♖f1 5 g6! ♖xf6 6 ♔h7 ♖f1 7 g7 ♖h1+ (7 ... ♔f6 8 g8♘+) 8 ♔g8! ♖g1 (or 8 ... ♔f6 9 ♔f8 ♖a1 10 g8♘+!=) 9 ♔f8!=.

Rook v Pawn(s)   ♖ V ♟(♟)

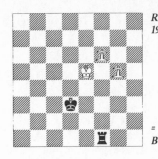

RP
19c

=
B

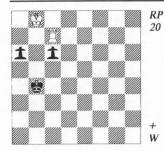

RP
20

+
W

4	♔f5

Or 4 f7 ♔e7 and wins.

4	...	♔d7
5	g6	♔e8

and wins
(cf diag 15).

Diagram 19c

Black to play just manages to draw with

1	...	♖e1+
2	♔d6	♖f1

3	♔e6	♖e1+
4	♔f7	♔e4
5	g6	

Or 5 ♔g7 ♖a1! 6 f7 ♖a8 7 g6 (7 ♔f6 ♖a6+! 8 ♔g7 ♖a8) 7 ... ♔f5=.

5	...	♔f5
6	♔g7	

Or 6 g7 ♖g1=.

6	...	♔g5
7	f7	♖f1=

Isolated Pawns

a) The rook trying to win

This will usually be the case unless the pawns are very far advanced. White must concentrate on the more dangerous of the enemy pawns since one passed pawn unsupported by the king is not very dangerous.

Benko 1980

Here White must get his rook back into play as fast as possible so:

1	♖b7+!

If 1 ♖xc6? a5 2 ♖b6+ ♔c3 3 ♖a6 ♔b4=. It takes Black only three moves to get ♔b3, a3 and White five to get his king to d3 - hence Black even has a spare move, cf diag 12.

1	...	♔c3
2	♔c7	a5
3	♖a7!	

Gaining a vital tempo (cf diag 8).

3	...	♔b4
4	♔d6!	

It is vital to leave Black with his c-pawn! If 4 ♔xc6? we merely reach diag 12 with Black to move when he defends with *stalemate*.

4	...	a4
5	♔e5	a3
6	♔d4	♔b3
7	♔d3	♔b2
8	♔d2	a2
9	♖b7+	♔a3

With the black c-pawn still alive 9 ... ♔a1 fails trivially to 10 ♔c2 c5 11 ♖h7 c4 12 ♖h1 mate.

10	♔c2	a1♘+
11	♔c3	♔a2
12	♖b2+	♔a3
13	♖b6	♔a2
14	♖xc6	♔b1
15	♖b6+	♔c1
16	♖b2 and wins	

(Indeed a game - Sultan Khan - Michell, Scarborough 1930, ended in Black's resignation in this position - play was identical from 12 ♖b2+ onwards.)

Rook v Pawn(s)   ♖ V ♙(♙)

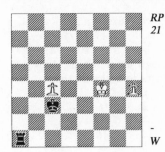

RP
21

Leal - Filguth
Mexico 1978
This is another example of avoiding a stalemate and also of the order of priorities in this sort of ending. Black's main task here is to *get his king into a decent position* - not to take "irrelevant" material.

W

A.

The game continued:
    1   h5
Black now wrongly took on c4: 1 ... ♚xc4? and a simple count shows that Black can now do no better than to reach diag 12 (with colours reversed) but with the opponent to move. Rather incredibly however, Black did succeed in winning: 1 ... ♚xc4? 2 h6 ♚d5 3 ♚f5 ♖f1+ 4 ♚g6 ♚e6 5 ♚g7 ♖g1+ 6 ♚f8 ♖f1+ 7 ♚g7 ♖f7+ 8 ♚g8?? (8 ♚g6=) 8 ... ♚f6 9 h7 ♖g7+ 0-1

But the right move wins:
    1   ...   ♖h1
Or 1 ... ♚d4 2 h6 ♖h1.
    2   ♚g5   ♚d4!
    3   ♚g6
3 h6 ♚e5 transposes back to the text. Or if 3 c5 ♚xc5! wins by a tempo - the king reaches e7 in only two more moves.
    3   ...   ♚e5
    4   h6
Or 4 c5 ♚e6 5 c6 ♖g1+ 6 ♚h7 ♚f7 and wins.
    4   ...   ♚e6
    5   h7
If 5 c5 ♖g1+ 6 ♚h7 ♚f7 etc, and 5 ♚g7 ♚e7 6 h7 ♖g1+ 7 ♚h8 (7 ♚h6 ♚f7 is the main line) loses due to the extra c-pawn.
    5   ...   ♖g1+
    6   ♚h6   ♚f7

    7   h8♘+   ♚f6
    8   ♚h7   ♖c1
    9   ♚g8
Or 9 ♘g6 ♖h1+.
    9   ...   ♖xc4
    and wins

B.

White can also try:
    1   c5   ♚d4!
He must attend to his king first. If 1 ... ♖f1+? 2 ♚e5! ♚b4 3 c6! ♖c1 (or 3 ... ♖f8 4 h5 ♚b5 5 c7 ♚c6 6 c8♛=) 4 ♚f6 (also 4 h5= but not 4 ♚d6? ♚b5 and wins) 4 ... ♖xc6+ 5 ♚g7+ (or even 5 ♚g5=).
Or if 1 ... ♖h1 either 2 ♚e5 or 2 c6 draws.
    2   c6   ♖f1+!
Driving away the enemy king to make room for his own. Not 2 ... ♖h1? 3 c7 ♖xh4+ 4 ♚f5 ♖h8 5 ♚e6=; nor 2 ... ♖c1 3 h5 ♖xc6 4 ♚g5 ♚e5 5 h6= And 2 ... ♚d5 is the right idea but is inefficient viz. 3 c7 ♖c1 4 ♚f5 ♖xc7 5 h5 ♖f7+ 6 ♚g6 ♚e6 7 h6 ♖f1 8 ♚g7!= (cf diag 12).
    3   ♚g5   ♚e5
    4   c7
Or 4 h5 ♖g1+ 5 ♚h6 ♚f6!.
    4   ...   ♖g1+!
Forcing White to obstruct his own pawn. Not 4 ... ♖c1 5 h5 ♖xc7 6 h6=.
    5   ♚h6   ♖c1
Also 5 ... ♖g8 wins.
    6   ♚g6   ♖c6+!
Gaining yet another tempo - though 6 ... ♖xc7 7 h5 ♖c6+ also wins.
    7   ♚g5   ♖xc7
    and wins
I reiterate: The most important thing about this example is that Black *must attend to his king first.*

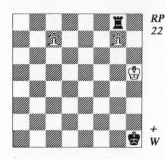

RP
22

+
W

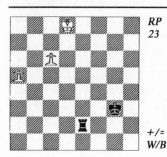

RP
22a

=
W

b) The pawns are trying to win

White wins easily after:

　1　♔g6　♖c8
　2　♔f6

Of course not 2 ♔h7?? ♖xc7=.

　2　...　♔g2
　3　♔e6

And the black rook has no-where to go. White threatens 4 ♔d7 and if 3 ... ♖g8 4 ♔f7! wins.

Diagram 22a
(i.e. c7 - b7)

But here the pawns are far enough apart for the rook to be able to deal with them:

　1　♔g6　♖b8
　2　♔f6　♔g2
　3　♔e6　♔f3
　4　♔d6　♖g8!
　5　♔e6　♖b8!=

Since White cannot threaten both ♔c7 and ♔f7 simultan-eously it's only a draw.

RP
23

+/=
W/B

Berger and Kocklehorn 1888
Obviously with pawns so close together there is no hope in putting the rook on the first rank.

But Black to move can force the draw by a policy of har-assment:

　1　...　♖d2+
　2　♔c7　♖a2
　3　♔b6　♖b2+

Whenever the white king emerges onto an open file, Black checks it. If it hides in front of a pawn he attacks the other one with his rook.

　4　♔a7　♖c2=

But White to move wins:

　1　a6

1 c7 ♖d2+ 2 ♔c8 ♖a2 3 a6! transposes into the main line.

　1　...　♖d2+
　2　♔c8　♖a2
　3　c7

Actually 3 ♔b7 wins slightly more simply: 3 ...

♖b2+ 4 ♔a8 ♖c2 5 a7 ♔f4 6 ♔b7 ♖b2+ 7 ♔a6 ♖a2+ 8 ♔b6 ♖b2+ 9 ♔c5 ♖a2 10 c7 ♔e5 11 ♔b4! etc (not 11 ♔c4?? ♔d6). That was the composers' original intention. The text was found by Se-lezniev in 1921.

　3　...　♔f4

If 3 ... ♖xa6 4 ♔b7 wins.

　4　♔b7　♖b2+
　5　♔c6　♖c2+
　6　♔b6　♔e5

Or 6 ... ♖b2+ 7 ♔a5 ♖c2 8 a7!. But now the black king can shelter on the e-file.

　7　♔b7!!

But not 7 a7? ♔d6 8 ♔b5 (8 a8♕ ♖b2+=) 8 ... ♖b2+ 9 ♔c4 ♖a2 10 ♔b3 ♔xc7 11 ♔xa2 ♔b7=.

　7　...　♖b2+
　8　♔c6　♖c2+
　9　♔d7　♖d2+
　10　♔e8　♖c2

Or if 10 ... ♖h2 simply 11 c8♕ wins.

　11　a7 and wins

Rook v Pawn(s)   ♖ V ♟(♟)

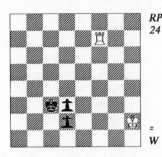

RP
24

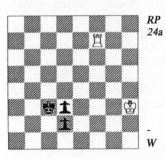

RP
24a

Doubled Pawns

These are pretty unlikely in practice.

Tarrasch 1911
White to play draws since his rook can get to the first rank with his king sufficiently near the pawns.

  1   ♖c7+   ♚d4

If 1 ... ♚b4 2 ♖b7+ ♚c5 3 ♖b1 ♚d4 4 ♔g2 ♚c3 5 ♔f2 ♚c2 6 ♔e3!=.

  2   ♖d7+   ♚e4
  3   ♖e7+   ♚f5
  4   ♖f7+   ♚e5!

Not 4 ... ♚e6?? and Black actually loses: 5 ♖f1 ♚e5 6 ♔g2 ♚d4 7 ♔f2 ♚c3 8 ♔e3 ♚c2 9 ♖f2! etc.

  5   ♖f1   ♚e4

If 5 ... ♚d4 6 ♔g2 ♚c3 7

♔f2 ♚c2 8 ♔e3!= as above in the note to 1 ... ♚d4.

  6   ♔g3

Also 6 ♔g2 ♚e3 7 ♖f3+ ♚e2 8 ♖f2+ ♚d1 9 ♖f8! draws (Cheron).

  6   ...   ♚e3
  7   ♖h1   ♚e2
  8   ♖h2+   ♚d1
  9   ♖h8   ♚e2
 10   ♖h2+!=

But not 10 ♖e8+? when the black king can hide on g1.

Diagram 24a
Berger
Here, however, Black wins easily by hiding his king on h1: 1 ♖c7+ ♚d4 2 ♖d7+ ♚e3 3 ♖e7+ ♚f2 4 ♖f7+ ♚g1 5 ♖g7+ ♚h1! etc.

= W

= W

Rook v Three or More Pawns

Since there are several possible pawn structures, many positions with this material balance are "un-theoretical". We can distinguish the following three cases:

A. Rook vs Three connected passed pawns. There is a considerable body of theory on this; see diags 25-29.

B. Two of the pawns are connected, the third is isolated. Normally the rook should try to deal with the more dangerous connected pawn first, see diag 30.

C. All pawns isolated (or doubled). Often a third isolated pawn *unsupported by its king* will make little difference. If his king is well placed, then the player with the rook can often hope to win. See diag 31.

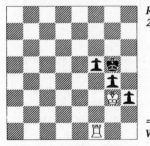

RP
25

Rook vs Three Connected Passed Pawns

Black has an ideal pawn structure with *only one weakness - the base pawn on f5*. Against the correct defence, White can only "win" this pawn at the cost of freeing the g- and h-pawns, in which case Black will win!

= W

Diag 25 is therefore drawn:

Van der Lasa 1943
  1   ♖f2   ♚g6
  2   ♔f4   ♚f6
  3   ♖e2   ♚f7
  4   ♖e5

Not 4 ♔xf5?? g3 and Black wins!

  4   ...   ♚g6

5	♖a5	♔h6
6	♖a6+	♔g7
7	♖e6	♔f7
8	♖h6	♔g7
9	♖h5	

Not 9 ♔g5? f4 10 ♖h4 f3! (10 ... g3? 11 ♔xf4 g2 12 ♖g4+ wins) and now Black wins.

9	...	♔g6
10	♖g5+	

10 ♖xf5? h2.

10	...	♔h6
11	♖g8	

11 ♖xf5? h2 12 ♖f8 ♔g7! wins.

11	...	♔h7
12	♖d8	♔g7!

But not 12 ... ♔g6? 13 ♖f8 (zugzwang) 13 ... ♔h6 14 ♖f6+! and wins (cf diag 26).

13	♖d6	♔f7!

Not 13 ... ♔h7? 14 ♔g5 ♔g7 (14 ... h2 15 ♖h6+) 15 ♖d7+ ♔g8 16 ♔f4! followed by ♖d5xf5 and wins.

14	♖h6	♔g7
15	♖h5	♔g6=

White is merely going round in circles. This position has already arisen after Black's ninth move.

Diag 25 is a fundamental position for Black to aim for. This type of position is also drawn if the position is "moved over" one or more files (e.g. ♔e3, ♖d1 v ♔e5, d5, e4, f3 is also a draw).

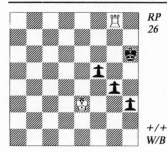

RP 26

+/+
W/B

Lehner 1887, Kopaev 1958
In this position, however, the white rook has penetrated to an ideal post *behind the black pawns*. (The reader can check through diag 25 again to verify that starting from that less favourable position the rook can never reach such a good square.)

Black to move *is in zugzwang* and loses quickly:

1	...	♔h7

Or 1 ... ♔h5 2 ♔f4 ♔h6 3 ♔xf5.

2	♖g5	♔h6
3	♖xf5	h2
4	♖f1	g3
5	♔f3 and wins	

But with White to move, the position is much more difficult. (This position used to be thought drawn in this case, but Kopaev found the win.)

1	♔e2!

If 1 ♔f4? ♔h7 is a position from diag 25 (after 11 ... ♔h7). After 2 ♖g5 ♔h6 3 ♖g8 ♔h7 4 ♖d8 ♔g7!, as we saw, White can never again manoeuvre his rook to a sufficiently favourable square.

1	...	♔h5

Now, however, Black cannot disturb the rook since if 1 ... ♔h7 2 ♖g5 ♔h6 3 ♖xf5 wins - the white king is much better *defensively* on e2 than f4.

2	♔f2	♔h4

If 2 ... ♔h6 3 ♔e3! zugzwang and wins. And 2 ... f4 leads to the main line.

3	♖g7	f4

Forced since if 3 ... ♔h5 4 ♔e3 ♔h6 5 ♖g8 (zugzwang) etc; or 3 ... g3+ 4 ♔xg3 h2 5 ♖g8 wins.

4	♖h7+	♔g5
5	♔g1!	

Although Black's pawns are slightly further advanced they are now much less secure - *both the g- and f-pawns are loose*. White now forces the win by transferring his king to h2 in front of the most dangerous pawn.

  5   ...   ♔f5

If 5 ... f3 6 ♔f2 ♔f4 7 ♖f7+ and 8 ♔g3 wins easily.

  6   ♔h2   ♔e4

If 6 ... ♔e5 7 ♖g7 ♔f5 8 ♖g8, or 6 ... ♔g5 7 ♖f7 forcing the fatally weakening ... f3 in each case.

  7   ♖g7   ♔f3

Or 7 ... ♔e3 8 ♖xg4 f3 9 ♔xh3 f2 10 ♔g2 wins.

  8   ♖g8   ♔e2

8 ... g3+ 9 ♔xh3 ♔f2 10 ♖a8!.

  9   ♖xg4   f3

 10 ♖e4+   ♔f1

 11 ♔g3!

11 ♔xh3? f2 would be a draw since if 12 ♖f4 ♔g1!.

 11 ...   f2

Or 11 ... h2 12 ♔xh2 f2 13 ♖f4 and 14 ♔g2 etc.

 12 ♖f4 and wins

Once Black was forced to *break ranks* with ... f4, the *extra weakness* of the g5-pawn proved fatal.

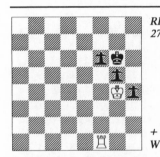

RP 27

+
W

Given the critical nature of the play in diags 25 and 26 it is hardly surprising that here White wins easily.

  1   ♖f2   ♔f7

  2   ♔f5   ♔g7

  3   ♖a2   ♔f7

Or 3 ... ♔h6 4 ♖a7 h3 5 ♖a3.

  4   ♖a7+   and

  5   ♔xf6

wins trivially.

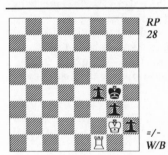

RP 28

=/-
W/B

After A. Sahni 1634

Here only Black has winning chances.

Black to play wins with:

  1   ...   f3+

  2   ♔h1

Or 2 ♖xf3 h1♕+ 3 ♔xh1 ♔xf3 and wins.

  2   ...   g2+

  3   ♔xh2   gxf1♘+

            or ♗!

and wins (not 3 ... gxf1♕?? or ♖?? stalemate).

White to play draws with:

  1   ♔h1!

Not 1 ♖a1? f3+ 2 ♔h1 ♔h3 and wins.

  1   ...   f3

Or 1 ... ♔h3 2 ♖f3 ♔g4 3 ♖a3=. White waits for ... f3 and then takes it.

  2   ♖xf3!   ♔xf3

            stalemate

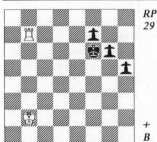

RP 29

+
B

Hollis - Florian

Corr. 1974 (variation)

In this practical position Black's only real chance is to aim for diag 25. For if he abandons the f-pawn then White's king will simply be too close. However, I think that White can just manage to frustrate this plan, e.g.

  1   ...   h4

  2   ♔c2   g5

If 2 ... ♔g5 simply 3 ♖xf7 wins: 3 ... ♔g4 4 ♔d2 h3 5 ♔e2 ♔g3 6 ♔f1 ♔h2 (6 ... h2 7 ♖h7 is simple) 7 ♔f2 g5 8 ♖g7 ♔h1 9 ♔g3 h2 10 ♖a7 or 10 ♖h7 and wins.

Rook v Pawn(s)

RP
29a

+
W

| 3 | ♔d3 | ♔g6 |
| 4 | ♖b6+ | |

He must embarrass the black king. If 4 ♔e3 f5 5 ♖b8 ♔g7! and White cannot prevent Black from reaching diag 25.

Or 4 ♔e4 f5+ 5 ♔e5 h3! (not 5 ... g4? 6 ♖b6+ ♔g5 7 ♖b8! and wins) 6 ♖b6+ ♔h5 7 ♔xf5 h2 8 ♖b1 (or 8 ♖b8 ♔h4) 8 ... ♔h4=.

Maybe White can also play 4 ♖b8 aiming at once for the g8- or h8-square. But then the check seems more forcing.

| 4 | ... | ♔f5 |

If 4 ... f6 5 ♔e4! ♔h5 6 ♔f3! f5 7 ♖f6 wins easily. And 4 ... ♔h5 5 ♔e3 ♔g4! transposes to the main line - 5 ... f5? 6 ♔f3 is much worse for Black. While of course if the black king retreats, 4 ... ♔g7, then 5 ♔e4! wins.

| 5 | ♔e3 | ♔g4 (29a) |

If 5 ... g4? 6 ♖b5+; or 5 ... h3 6 ♔f3 g4+ 7 ♔g3 ♔g5 8 ♖b8! f5 9 ♖f8 ♔g6 10 ♔f4 zugzwang and wins.

| 6 | ♔f2! | |

As usual, it is correct to improve the king's position first.

If 6 ♖f6? White wins the f-pawn but Black's king gets very active. As a result it would appear to me that Black draws, viz. 6 ... ♔g3 7 ♔e2 and:

a) 7 ... h3? 8 ♔f1 h2 (8 ... ♔h2 9 ♖f2+! ♔h1 10 ♖xf7 wins) 9 ♖h6 (now the pawn is doomed and Black soon runs out of moves) 9 ... g4 10 ♖h8 f5 11 ♖h7 f4 12 ♖h8 f3 13 ♖h7 f2 (else White reaches a position like diag 15) 14 ♖h8 ♔f3 15 ♖xh2 g3 16 ♖h3! (interestingly this position is zugzwang - White to move

would draw with the only move 16 ♖h2!) 16 ... ♔g4 17 ♖h8 ♔f3 18 ♖f8+ ♔e3 19 ♔g2 ♔e2 20 ♖e8+ ♔d2 21 ♔f1! and 22 ♖g8, 23 ♖xg3 etc.

b) 7 ... ♔g2! *shouldering off* the white king: 8 ♖f2+ ♔g1 9 ♖f5 (if 9 ♔f3? g4+; or 9 ♖xf7 h3 10 ♖f1+ ♔g2 11 ♖f2+ ♔g3! draws similarly to diag 12 - but not 11 ... ♔g1?? 12 ♔f3) 9 ... g4 10 ♖f4 f5! 11 ♖xf5 h3 12 ♖g5 h2 13 ♖xg4+ ♔h1=.

| 6 | ... | f5 |

But now if 6 ... ♔h3 7 ♖f6 does win: 7 ... ♔h2 8 ♔xf7 g4 9 ♖g7 g3+ 10 ♔f3 ♔g1 (10 ... ♔h3 11 ♖g4 g2 12 ♖g8! or 10 ... ♔h1 11 ♖g4 ♔g1 12 ♖xh4 etc.) 11 ♖g4 ♔f1 12 ♖a4! ♔g1 13 ♖xh4 g2 14 ♖g4?! ♔h1 15 ♖h4+! ♔g1 16 ♔g3 ♔f1 17 ♖f4+ ♔g1 18 ♖f8 ♔h1 19 ♖h8+ ♔g1 20 ♖h2 and wins cf the end of diag 26.

And prevarication by 6 ... ♔f5 does not help at all, e.g. 7 ♖h6 ♔e5 8 ♔g2 f5 9 ♔h3 etc, similar to the main line.

| 7 | ♔g2 | ♔h5 |

If 7 ... f4 8 ♖b5 ♔h5 9 ♔f3 h3 10 ♖b8 etc. Or 7 ... ♔f4 8 ♔h3 ♔e3 9 ♖g6 f4 10 ♔g4! ♔f2 11 ♖a6 wins.

8	♖f6	♔g4
9	♖f8	♔f4
10	♔h3	♔e4
11	♖g8	♔f4
12	♖g7	

zugzwang and wins

Although the detail of diag 29 is rather complex, in essence White's plan is very simple.

He forces the black king to make a choice, either:

a) It retreats, in which case it cannot support its pawns

and so White wins easily.

b) It advances. In that case the king, although quite active, is not really dangerous to White. But being so far advanced it *cannot easily guard the first rank.* Therefore White can force his rook to the favourable squares *behind the pawns* and thus win.

RP 30

= W

Two pawns Connected, The Third One Isolated

Réti 1929

Obviously, White is on the defensive. Black is threatening 1 ... g3 after which it would be impossible to deal with all the pawns - or indeed 1 ... f3.

So White's move must be a choice between 1 ♖f8 and 1 ♖g8, but which one? The answer is provided by diag 22. There we can see that White will draw if Black is left with b- and g-pawns, but b- and f-pawns would win. Therefore:

    1   ♖g8!

But not 1 ♖f8? f3 2 ♖f4 b4 3 ♖xg4 b3 4 ♖g1 (checks don't help - the black king simply approaches the rook) 4 ... f2 5 ♖f1 b2 6 ♔g7 ♔d4 7 ♔f6 ♔d3 and wins.

    1   ...   g3
    2   ♖g4   b4

If 2 ... ♔d4 3 ♖xf4+ ♔e3 4 ♖b4 g2 5 ♖b3+! and White keeps on checking until the black king hides on h2, but then comes "1" ♖xb5! g1♕ 2 ♖h5+ and 3 ♖g5+=.

    3   ♖xf4   b3
    4   ♖f1   g2
    5   ♖g1   b2=

as in diag 22a.

RP 31

= W

Isolated Pawns

Tartakower - Anon 1933

Although he has three pawns, Black is lost since White can *dominate Black's king with his own king.* Eventually Black will be forced to abandon the f-pawn. But if White is careful, even then the black king will remain out of play.

    1   ♖b1   ♔g4
    2   ♔d2   ♔f3
    3   ♖a1   c4

If 3 ... ♔g2 4 ♔e2 and obviously he should advance the queenside pawns before trying to support them with his king. Not 3 ... ♔e4 4 ♔e2 and 5 ♖xa5 winning easily.

    4   ♖c1   a4
    5   ♖a1   c3+

This abandons d3 to the white king thus making it harder for the black king to reach the queenside. However, 5 ... a3 does also lose, e.g. 6 ♖c1 a2 7 ♖a1 ♔e4 8 ♔e2 c3 9 ♖xa2 f1♕+ 10 ♔xf1 ♔d3 11 ♔e1 c2 12 ♖a3+ and 13 ♔d2 etc.

    6   ♔d3   c2
    7   ♔d2?!

There was no point in relinquishing this excellent square. Simply 7 ♖c1 was better.

    7   ...   a3
    8   ♖f1   a2
    9   ♖c1??

9 ♔d3! was correct: 9 ... ♔g2 10 ♔e2 ♔g3 11 ♖a1 ♔g2 12 ♖c1 ♔g3 13 ♖f1 zugzwang and wins as in the game.

    9   ...   ♔e4!

Now is the time to transfer the king towards queenside. With three strings to his bow, Black can just draw. Instead in the game he played 9 ... ♔g2?? 10 ♔e2 ♔g3 11 ♖f1 ♔f4 (or 11 ... ♔g2 12 ♖xf2+

and 13 ♖f1) 12 ♔xf2 ♔e4 13 ♔e2 1-0.

    10 ♔e2

If 10 ♔xc2 ♔e3 draws easily - the a-pawn is already superfluous. Or 10 ♖f1 ♔d4= (not 10 ... ♔f3?? 11 ♔d3).

    10 ...   ♔d4
    11 ♔d2

11 ♔xf2 ♔c3 and 12 ... ♔b2=.

    11 ...   ♔e4=

White cannot take either the c- or the f-pawn without allowing the black king to support the other pawn effectively.

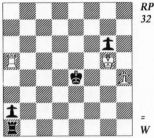

RP 32

= W

Practical Examples
Steinitz - Gunsburg
9th Match Game 1890

The white king cannot hide from the black rook for if 1 ♔h6 g5!. White is therefore definitely going to lose his rook. And, since he can win the g-pawn he will get an ending of rook vs pawn.

But which particular ending of rook v pawn should White aim for? And conversely, what should Black try to get?

This is a very difficult practical question. It's all very well analysing an ending of rook vs pawn on a board during the adjournment or even at home later. But during a game one may have to make snap decisions as to which ending is drawn and which is won or lost (depending on which side you are playing).

In order to facilitate these decisions, it's helpful to have some knowledge of *theoretical positions* (diags 5 and 7-12 are especially important); and then *counting* as explained in the text there may well ease calculation.

White played:

    1   ♖a4+

If 1 ♔xg6 ♖g1+ 2 ♔f6 a1♕+ 3 ♖xa1 ♖xa1 4 h5. Now the attempt to reach diag 12 fails by a tempo - it will be White to move (after 4 ... ♖h1 5 ♔g6 ♔e5 6 h6 ♔e6). But Black can use another approach effective only against rook's pawns (cf diag 13). He will *attack from behind*: 4 ... ♔f4 5 h6 ♖a6+ 6 ♔g7 ♔g5 7 h7 ♖a7+ 8 ♔g8 ♔g6 9 h8♘+ ♔f6 and wins. 1 ♔h6 g5 2 hxg5 (if 2 h5 g4 is too quick) 2 ... ♖h1+ is also clearly lost.

Steinitz therefore decided to give some checks, hoping that his opponent would move his king in the wrong direction - this was clearly the best practical chance.

A.
And in the game it paid off. Black played:

    1   ...   ♔f3?
    2   ♖a3+

If 2 ♔xg6 ♖g1+ 3 ♔f7 a1♕ 4 ♖xa1 ♖xa1 5 h5 ♔g4 6 h6 ♔g5 7 h7 ♖a7+ 8 ♔g8 ♔g6 still wins.

    2   ...   ♔f2??

2 ... ♔e4 still won followed by a transposition into B.

    3   ♔xg6   ♖g1+
    4   ♔f7   a1♕
    5   ♖xa1   ♖xa1

And with the black king so far away it is completely drawn.

B.
Instead the black king should have run towards the rook. From the side it is well posted

to reach a position like diagrams 7 and 12 quickly. Thus:

1 ... ♔d5!
2 ♖a5+ ♔c6
3 ♔xg6

If 3 ♖a6+ ♔b7 4 ♖xa2 ♖xa2 5 ♔xg6 ♖g2+ 6 ♔f6 ♖h2 7 ♔g5 ♔c7 and Black is a tempo ahead of the text.

Or 3 ♔h6 g5! 4 hxg5 (4 ♖a6+ ♔b7 5 ♖xa2 ♖xa2 6 hxg5 ♖h2+! 7 ♔g7 ♔c7 transposes back in effect) 4 ... ♖h1+ 5 ♔g7 a1♕+ 6 ♖xa1 ♖xa1 7 g6 ♔d7 8 ♔f7 (or 8 ♔h7 ♔e7 9 g7 ♖h1+ etc) 8 ... ♖f1+ and wins as in diag 7.

Note that when fighting against a g-pawn it is sometimes useful to give a check on the h-file. This will drive the king in *front of the pawn.* (If instead White had had an f-pawn then 1 ... ♖ - g-file+ would be met by ♔ - h-file *not blocking the pawn*).

3 ... ♖g1+
4 ♔f7 a1♕
5 ♖xa1 ♖xa1
6 h5 ♖h1!
7 ♔g6 ♔d7
8 h6 ♔e7!
and wins

But not 6 ... ♔e6? 7 ♔g7!= see diag 12.

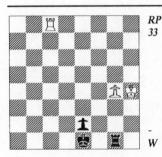

RP 33

Nunn - Smejkal
Lucerne Ol 1982
Clearly White is going to lose his rook for the e-pawn. Here he must choose between 1 ♔g5 activating the king first and 1 g5. In fact both lose.

A.

1 ♔g5 ♔f2
2 ♖e8 e1♕

But not 2 ... ♖g3 (threatening 3 ... ♖e3) 3 ♖xe2+ ♔xe2 4 ♔f5 and now the attempt to play for diag 7 fails - the black king takes four moves to reach d6. White takes only three to play g5 - g6 - ♔f6. Whilst if 4 ... ♔f3 5 g5, the rook interferes with the king - if it were on g2 or g1 then 5 ... ♔g3! would win.

3 ♖xe1 ♔xe1!
Not 3 ... ♖xe1 4 ♔f6!=.
4 ♔f4

Trying to hold off the enemy king. If 4 ♔f5 ♔f2 5 g5 ♔g3 etc.

4 ... ♔f2
5 g5 ♖g2!
Zugzwang.

6 ♔f5 ♔g3
7 g6 ♔h4
8 ♔f6 ♔h5
and wins by a tempo.

B.

1 g5
This was the game continuation.

1 ... ♔f2
2 ♖f8+ ♔e3

Not 2 ... ♔g2? 3 ♖e8 e1♕+ 4 ♖xe1 ♖xe1 5 g6 ♔f3 6 ♔g5=.

3 ♖e8+ ♔d3
If 3 ... ♔f4 4 ♖f8+ forces 4 ... ♔e3 again.
4 ♔h5

Clearly it cannot help to drive the black king towards f7.

4 ... e1♕!
A vital choice. Not 4 ... ♖g3? 5 ♖xe2 ♔xe2 6 ♔g6! ♔f3 7 ♔f5!=. As in the note to 2 ... e1♕ in variation A, the black rook interferes with its king.

5 ♖xe1 ♖xe1
6 ♔g6
If 6 g6 ♖g1 7 ♔h6 ♔e4 8

g7 ♔f5 9 ♔h7 ♖h1+! etc. as in the main line.

But now Black must find just one more good move. If the obvious 6 ... ♔e4, 7 ♔f6 shoulders the king off and White can do no better than reach a drawn position of rook vs knight: 7 ... ♖f1+ 8 ♔e6! ♖a1 9 g6 ♖a6+ 10 ♔f7 ♔f5 11 g7 ♖a7+ 12 ♔f8 ♔f6 13 g8♘+!=. Remember that attacking from behind only works against a rook's pawns.

Instead Smejkal played:

    6   ...   ♖f1‼

Preventing the white king from shouldering off.

    7   ♔h7   ♔e4
    8   g6   ♔f5
    9   g7   ♖h1+

The h-file again as in diag 32 variation B above.

    10   ♔g8   ♔g6
    11   ♔f8   ♖f1+
    12   ♔g8   ♖a1!

But not 12 ... ♖f7?? 13 ♔h8 ♖xg7 stalemate.

    0-1

In view of 13 ♔h8 ♖h1+ 14 ♔g8 ♖h7 and 15 ♖xg7 etc.

RP 36

-B

Marco - Maroczy
Vienna 1903
Here White's pawns are very dangerous. But Black managed to create one passed pawn. And that *one pawn, supported by the rook,* was sufficient to decide the game in his favour.

The game continued:

    1   ...   ♔d7
    2   ♔e3   ♖c8
    3   b3

If 3 c5 b6 is also good for Black. But this move loses clearly - if a trifle dramatically.

    3   ...   b5!
    4   c5   a5
    5   ♔d3   a4
    6   bxa4

Obviously White must use his king actively. If, for example, 6 ♔c2 a3 7 ♔b1 ♔c6 8 ♔a2 ♖a8 White soon runs out of moves and loses all his beautiful passed pawns.

    6   ...   bxa4
    7   ♔c4   ♖b8

Allowing a little drama. Of course 7 ... a3 8 ♔b3 ♖a8 9 ♔a2 ♔c6 also wins easily.

    8   d5   a3
    9   c6+   ♔c7
    10   ♔c5   a2
    11   d6+   ♔c8
    12   e6   a1♕
    0-1

True, Black won by 'only one tempo'. But really that was his choice rather than his opponent's.

Rook v Rook

♖ V ♜

Rook and Pawn v Rook

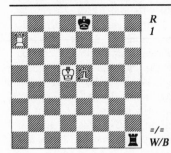

R
1

=/=
W/B

Philidor 1777

If the defending king is in front of the pawn and *cannot be displaced* then the position is of course drawn.

In diag 1 White threatens to advance his king with 1 ♔d6. Philidor found an excellent recipe to avoid this:

1 ... - ♖h6! -

The white king is cut off from the sixth rank. White cannot drive the black rook away since any exchange of rooks will lead to a drawn pawn ending, e.g. 2 ♖c7 ♖g6 3 ♖c6 ♖xc6 4 ♔xc6 ♔e7=.

Therefore White advances his pawn.

2 e6

Now 3 ♔d6 is a terrible threat, but 2 e6 removed the king's *shelter* from "checks from behind".

2 ... ♖h1!
3 ♔d6 ♖d1+
4 ♔e5 ♖e1+=

The king has no reasonable shelter from the checks so it is quite drawn.

Now let's assume that it is White to move in diag 1.

1 — ♔d6! —

If 1 ♔e6? ♖h6+.

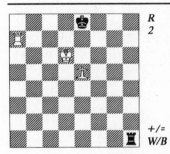

R
2

+/=
W/B

Lasker

White is threatening to win with 2 ♖a8+ ♔f7 3 e6+ ♔f6 4 ♖f8+ ♔g7 5 e7 etc. There is in fact only one good defence.

1 ... — ♖e1!! —

This move stops the e-pawn's advance after 2 ♖a8+ ♔f7.

Alternatively:

a) 1 ... ♖h6+? 2 e6 and wins;

b) 1 ... ♖d1+? (this seems plausible but in fact the rook is misplaced on d1) 2 ♔e6 and:

b1) 2 ... ♔f8 3 ♖a8+ ♔g7 4 ♔e7 ♖d2 5 e6 (see diag 6).

b2) 2 ... ♔d8 3 ♖a8+ ♔c7 4 ♔e7 ♖h2 5 e6 (cf diag 7).

2 ♔e6

As mentioned above 2 ♖a8+ ♔f7 gets nowhere since the back rook indirectly controls e6. Now the black king faces a vital choice. Which way should he run? Dr Lasker pointed out that the black king should always go to the "short side of the pawn".

There is a very important general principle here. Think of the board as cut into two by the file of White's pawn. Then there is a "long side" consisting of the a, b, c, d files, and a "short side" consisting of the f, g, h files.

As we shall see in a moment, Black is going to have to defend by *checking from the side* with his rook. As always in rook endings, the rook requires some *space* in which to operate.

Therefore Black's king goes to the short side leaving the rook the long side for its checks.

2 ... ♔f8!
3 ♖a8+ ♔g7
4 ♖e8

If 4 ♔d6 ♔f7!.

4 ... ♖a1!

Threatening flank checks.

5 ♖d8

Or 5 ♔d7 ♖a7+ 6 ♔c6

♖a6+ 7 ♔b7 ♖a1=.

    5   ...   ♖e1!
    6   ♖e8   ♖a1=

Actually, with the rook operating on the long side 6 ... ♖a1 is not forced. 6 ... ♖e2 7 ♔d7 ♖a2 would still be good enough (cf diag 5). But of course 6 ... ♖a1 is best.

As we shall see later, Black could have just got away with sending his king to the long side, i.e. from diag 2: 1 ... ♖e1

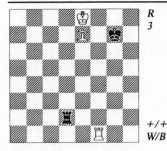

R 3

R 3b

+/+
W/B

+/+
W/B

Lucena

English-speaking chess players always refer to this and similar positions as the "Lucena position" and it is spuriously supposed to have been included by him in his manual in 1497! Actually it was first published by Salvio in 1634 and he attributed it to a certain Scipione Genovino.

No matter! In everyday chess parlance this is certainly the Lucena position and it, together with diag 1 - the Philidor position - form the fundamental theory of rook and pawn against rook.

After:

    1   ♖g1+   ♔h7

Or 1 ... ♔f6 2 ♔f8. White now has two different winning methods:

A.

He can bring his rook to d8:

    2   ♖a1   ♔g7
    3   ♖a8   ♖d1

Or 3 ... ♔f6 4 ♔f8 ♖h2 5 ♖a6+ (not 5 e8♕?? ♖h8 mate)

    4   ♖d8   ♖e1
    5   ♔d7   ♖d1+
    6   ♔c6 etc.

B.

He can "build a bridge":

2 ♔e6 ♔d8(?) 3 ♖a8+ ♔c7 4 ♖e8 ♖h1!= see diag 7 by Horwitz and Kling.

Diag 2 is rather difficult. We included it here since it arises naturally in the context of the Philidor position and is moreover fundamental in its own right. If the reader were to find it confusing, then he might find it less so if it is seen in the context of the following positions, diags 3-7.

    2   ♖g4!

White wishes to interpose the rook in order to terminate Black's checks. 2 ♔f7 at once gets nowhere, e.g. 2 ... ♖f2+ 3 ♔e6 ♖e2+ 4 ♔f6 ♖f2+ 5 ♔e5 ♖e2+ 6 ♔d6 ♖d2+ 7 ♔c5 ♖e2 8 ♔d6 ♖d2+ and the king must take shelter in front of the pawn: 9 ♔e6 ♖e2+ 10 ♔f7 ♖f2+ 11 ♔e8 ♖d2 etc.

    2   ...   ♖d1
    3   ♔f7   ♖f1+
    4   ♔e6   ♖e1+
    5   ♔f6   ♖f1+

If 5 ... ♖e2 6 ♖g5 ♖e1 7 ♖e5.

    6   ♔e5   ♖e1+
    7   ♖e4 and wins

By playing the rook to the fourth rank White successfully "built his bridge", i.e. arranged to interpose the rook.

Diag 3b

We should note here that method A only works because the rook has got room to get to d8.

In diag 3a only method B will work:

    1   ♖d1+   ♔e7
    2   ♖d4!   etc.

Rook v Rook

R
4

=
B

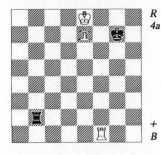

R
4a

+
B

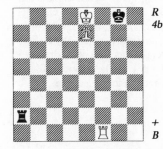

R
4b

+
B

Flank Checks

A rook needs sufficient room
- *checking distance* - in order
to operate effectively.

A.

1	...	♖a8+
2	♔d7	♖a7+
3	♔d6	♖a6+
4	♔d5	♖a5+
5	♔c6	♖a6+
6	♔b7	♖e6=

B.

Diagram 4a

Here the rook has insufficient
room.

| 1 | ... | ♖b8+ |

If 1 ... ♖a2 2 ♖g1+ wins easily as in diag 3.

| 2 | ♔d7 | ♖b7+ |
| 3 | ♔d6 | ♖b8 |

3 ... ♖b6+ 4 ♔c7 ♖e6 5
♔d7 wins.

| 4 | ♔c7 | ♖a8 |

Black seems to be safe since
if 5 ♔d7? ♖a7+ transposes
into diag 4. But White plays:

| 5 | ♖a1! |

And wins easily since if 5 ...
♖e8 or 5 ... ♖h8 6 ♔d7 etc.
For the ending of queen vs
rook which would arise after 5
♖xa1 6 e8♕ see diag QR2.

C.

Diagram 4b

The black king is misplaced
and White therefore wins despite the good position of the
black rook.

| 1 | ... | ♖a8+ |
| 2 | ♔d7 | ♖a7+ |

White even has two ways to
win!

a) 3 ♔d6 ♖a6+ 4 ♔c5 ♖a8
(or 4 ... ♖e6 5 ♖f8+ shows the
problem of the king on g8) 5
♔c6! ♔g7 6 ♖a1 ♖b8 7 ♔c7
and wins;

b) 3 ♔e6 ♖a6+ 4 ♔e5
♖a5+ 5 ♔f6 ♖a6+ 6 ♔g5
♖a5+ 7 ♔g6 ♖a8 8 ♖f6 and
wins.

The second method, B, is
somewhat better since Black
cannot even reach queen v
rook.

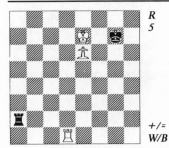

R
5

+/=
W/B

White is threatening to win at
once with 1 ♖g1+ after which
he would quickly reach the
"Lucena Position" (cf diag 3).

Black to move is able to draw
precisely because his rook is
on the vital a-file

| 1 | ... | ♖a7+ |
| 2 | ♖d7 |

Not 2 ♔e8 ♔f6; nor 2 ♔d6
♔f8.

Now Black must choose a
square on the a-file. In fact
any move will draw except for
2 ... ♖a6?? e.g.

| 2 | ... | ♖a1 |

Now White has several tries

A.

| 3 | ♔e8+ | ♔f6 |
| 4 | e7 | ♔e6! (5a) |

↙ White can make no progress
since if 5 ♔d8 ♖a8+ or 5
♔f8 ♖f1+! 6 ♔e8 ♖a1!.

Note that if the black rook
were on a6 then 5 ♔f8 would
have won - that's why 2 ...
♖a6?? would have been a
gross blunder.

B.

229

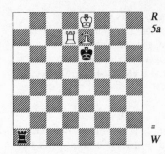

R
5a

=
W

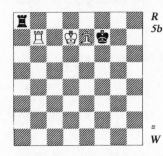

R
5b

=
W

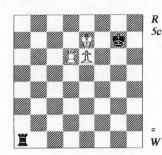

R
5c

=
W

3	♔d6+	♔f6
4	♖f7+	♔g6

Black is threatening to start flank checks with 5 ... ♖a6+ - note the power of the a-file. Hence White has nothing better than:

5	♖c7	♔f6=

C.

3	♖b7 (or 3 ♖c7)	

This does not threaten anything so Black can simply pass with, e.g.

3	...	♖a2
4	♔d8+	

4 ♔e8+ ♔f6 5 e7 ♖a8+ is the same as this column. Or 4 ♔d6+ ♔f6 5 ♖f7+ ♔g6 in B above. Finally if 4 ♔d7 ♖a8! 5 e7 ♔f6 also leads to the column.

4	...	♔f6
5	e7	♖a8+
6	♔d7	♔f7 (5b)

Clearly this is quite drawn. Black must only take care to avoid 7 ♖b1 ♖a7+ 8 ♔d8

♖xe7?? (8 ... ♖a8+=) 9 ♖f1+ ♔e6 10 ♖e1+.

D.

3	♖d6 (5c)	

This is White's most cunning move. If Black now passes with 3 ... ♖a2? then there comes 4 ♔e8! and if 4 ... ♔f6 5 e7+ or 4 ... ♖a8+ 5 ♖d8 and 6 e7; in both cases White reaches the Lucena position. The only defence is:

3	...	♖a8!

Preventing 4 ♔e8.

4	♖d1	

If 4 ♔d7 ♔f6 (not 4 ... ♖a7+? 5 ♔e8! wins), or 4 ♖d8 ♖a7+.

4	...	♖a7+
5	♖d7	♖a1=

Diag 5 can often arise from more complex rook endings and is thus rather important.

It is fiddly, since White has several tries, but it is drawn - the vital a-file provides Black with sufficient resources.

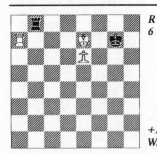

R
6

+/+
W/B

In contrast to diag 5, here White controls the a-file. This enables him to win but only with some difficulty. It turns out that Black to move would be zugzwang!

A.

1	...	♖c8

Here the rook is too close to White's king.

2	♖a1	♖c7+
3	♔d6	and
4	e7	etc.

B.

1	...	♖b1
2	♖a8!	

Here the rook controls the queening square so that the flank checks lose their significance.

2	...	♖b7+
3	♔d6	♖b6+
4	♔d7	♖b7+
5	♔c6	♖e7

Or 5 ... ♖b1 6 e7.

6	♔d6 and wins	

C.

1	...	♔g8
2	♔f6	♖f8+

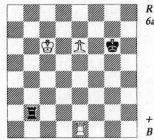

R 6a

+ B

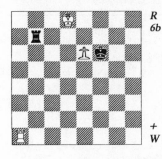

R 6b

+ W

3	♖f7	♜a8
4	♖g7+	♚h8

Or 4 ... ♚f8 5 e7+.

5	♖g1	

And White soon reaches the Lucena position.

D.

1	...	♚g6

This seems most natural, but the king is badly placed on g6 since it cannot go to f8.

2	♖a1!	♜b7+
3	♚d6	♜b6+
4	♚d7	♜b7+
5	♚c6	♜b2

If 5 ... ♜e7 6 ♚d6 etc; or 5 ... ♜b8 6 ♚c7 ♜b2 7 ♜e1! etc, as in the column.

6	♖e1!	*(6a)*

Here we can clearly see why the king is worse on g6 than g7. Unfortunately 6 ... ♚f7 is illegal so:

6	...	♜b8
7	♚d7!	♜b7+
8	♚c8	♜e7

Or 8 ... ♜a7 9 e7 etc.

9	♚d8	

and wins, for if 9 ... ♚f6 10 ♖f1+ ♚xe6 11 ♖e1+.

After 1 ... ♚g6 in diag 6,

White has also got another winning method - though this does allow queen v rook, viz: 2 ♖a1 ♜b7+ 3 ♚d8 (instead of 3 ♚d6) 3 ... ♚f6 *(6b)* 4 e7! ♜b8+ 5 ♚c7 ♜e8 6 ♚d6 ♜b8 7 ♖f1+ ♚g7 8 ♚c7 ♜a8 9 ♖a1! and wins (cf diag 4b).

Now what about diag 6 with White to move?

If 1 ♖a1? ♜b7+ 2 ♚d6 ♜b6+ 3 ♚d7 ♜b7+ 4 ♚d8 ♜b8+ 5 ♚c7 ♜b2 6 ♖f1 ♜a2! and draws as in diag 5.

But instead White can use zugzwang:

1	♚d6+	♚f6

1 ... ♚g6 2 ♖a1! as in D above, or 1 ... ♚f8 2 ♚d7 ♜e8 (2 ... ♚g7 3 ♚e7!) 3 ♖a1 etc.

2	♚d7!	

This is mutual zugzwang, i.e. White to move could only draw.

2	...	♚g7
3	♚e7!	

White has managed to "lose a move" by triangulation (cf the section on pawn endings) and so it is Black to move. As we saw above he is in zugzwang and must lose.

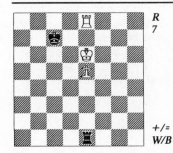

R 7

+/= W/B

Horwitz and Kling

Although the black king is on the *long* side of the pawn (cf diag 2) he can still draw with exact defence.

1	...	♜h1!

As we shall see, White threatened to win with 2 ♚f7 so passing with 1 ... ♜e2? would have lost.

2	♖f8	

Or 2 ♚f7 ♜h7+ 3 ♚g6 ♜h1=.

2	...	♜e1!

The only move, returning the rook to its former post. If,

for example, 2 ... ♜h6+? 3 ♚e7 ♜h7+ 4 ♚f7 ♜h1 5 e6 would win.

3	♖e8	

Or 3 ♚f6 ♚d7.

3	...	♜h1!=

White to move:

1	♚f7!	♜h1

If 1 ... ♚d7 2 e6+; or 1 ... ♖f1+ 2 ♚e7 ♜h1 3 ♖f8.

2	♖g8	

Not 2 e6? ♜h7+ 3 ♚g6 ♜h1.

2	...	♜h7+
3	♖g7	♜h8

Rook v Rook ♖ V ♜

4 ♔e7!

Now that e6 is assured, the king returns to e7. Not 4 e6? ♔d6 5 e7 ♔d7 6 ♖g1 ♖h7+ 7 ♔f8 ♖h8+!=.

4	...	**♔c6**
5	**e6**	**♔c7**

Black had no way of improving his position.

6 ♖g1

There are also other winning moves. The black rook is simply not effective on the short side.

6	...	**♖h7+**
7	**♔f8**	**♖h8+**

Or 7 ... ♔d6 8 e7 ♖h8+ 9 ♔g7 ♖e8 10 ♔f6 and wins.

8	**♔g7**	**♖h2**
9	**♖d1!**	

And White soon reaches the Lucena position.

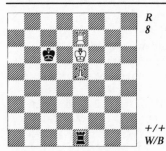

R 8
+/+
W/B

Kopaev

Here Black's king is worse than in diagram 7 and he loses even with the move:

1	...	**♖h1**
2	**♖g7**	**♖h6+**
3	**♔f5**	**♖h5+**
4	**♔f6**	**♖h6+**
5	**♖g6** *(8a)*	

A.

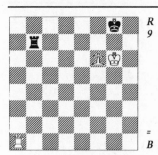

R 8a
+
B

5	...	**♖h7**

Not 5 ... ♖h8 6 ♔g7+!.

6 ♖g8!

6 e6? ♔d6=.

6 ... ♖h6+

White was threatening 7 ♖d8. If 6 ... ♔d7 7 e6+ ♔d6 8 ♖d8+; or 6 ... ♔c7 7 ♖g7+.

7	**♔g5**	**♖e6**
8	**♔f5**	**♖e7**

If 8 ... ♔d7 9 ♖d6+!.

9 ♖d8 and wins

B.

5	...	**♖h1**
6	**♔e7+**	**♔c7**

6 ... ♔d5 7 e6 ♖h7+ 8 ♔f8 ♖h8+ 9 ♔g7 wins.

7	**e6**	**♖h7+**
8	**♔e8**	**♖h8+**

With the rook on g6 8 ... ♔d6 fails to 9 e7+.

9	**♔f7**	**♔d6/♔d8**

9 ... ♖h7+ 10 ♖g7 ♖h8 11 ♖g8 etc.

10	**e7+**	**♔d7**
11	**♖h6! and wins**	

R 9
=
B

Stalemate Defence

If Black defends passively then he loses quickly: 1 ... ♖b8? 2 ♖a7 ♖c8 3 ♖g7+ ♔f8 4 ♖h7 ♔g8 5 f7+ ♔f8 6 ♖h8+.

Instead he can use stalemate to save himself:

1	...	**♖g7+**
2	**♔f5**	**♖g2**

And draws easily.

Rook v Rook

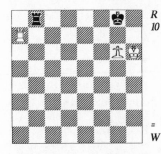

R 10

=
W

Here, despite the fact that his rook is passive, Black is perfectly safe. In the absence of the "i-file" White can do absolutely nothing, e.g.

| 1 | ♖g7+ | ♔h8 |

But not 1 ... ♔f8?? 2 ♔h7! ♖b1 3 ♖f7+ ♔e8 4 ♖f2 and wins.

| 2 | ♖h7+ | ♔g8= |

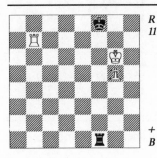

R 11

+
B

White again has a g-pawn but here that is actually a help. Of course Black would draw if he had time for 1 ... ♔g8 and 2 ... ♖f8 but unfortunately he doesn't.

| 1 | ... | ♖g1 |

Trying to defend as in the Horwitz and Kling position (diag 7). Of course if 1 ... ♔g8 2 ♖b8+ ♖f8 3 ♖xf8+ ♔xf8 4 ♔h7 and wins.

| 2 | ♖b8+ | ♔e7 |
| 3 | ♖g8! | |

The Black king is on the long side - almost the only side - of the pawn. Since flank checks are totally impracticable, White wins trivially:

3	...	♖g2
4	♔h7	♔f7
5	g6+	♔e7
6	♖a8	♖h2+
7	♔g8	♔f6
8	g7	♔e7

And we have the old favourite, the Lucena position (cf diag 3b).

R 12

+/=
W/B

Frontal Defence and the "Combined Method"

Black's king is cut off from the pawn. Flank checks are quite useless here since the black king is on the *long side*. But with the pawn only on the fourth rank there is an additional defensive resource - pressure from the rook in front of the pawn.

White to play:
The black king is misplaced on e7 - as we shall see e6 would be much better. White to play is able to win by a technical procedure discovered by Grigoriev, which is named the "Combined Method".

In *Step 1* White advances his king as far as possible: this turns out to be two squares diagonally in front of the pawn.

| 1 | ♔b4! | |

Not 1 c5? ♖d8=; or 1 ... ♖h4 2 ♔b3 ♖g4 3 c6 ♖g6=.

| 1 | ... | ♖b8+ |

If 1 ... ♖d8 2 ♖xd8 ♔xd8 3 ♔b5! wins.

| 2 | ♔a5 | ♖c8 |

2 ... ♖a8+ 3 ♔b6 ♖b8+ 4 ♔c7 etc.

| 3 | ♔b5 | ♖b8+ |
| 4 | ♔a6 | |

Step 1 is completed.

| 4 | ... | ♖c8 |

Step 2 now consists of routing the enemy since his king is on such an inactive square.

| 5 | ♖d4! | ♔e6 |

Now we can see why e7 was bad square for the black king - it is too far away from e5.

| 6 | ♔b7 | ♖c5 |

If 6 ... ♔e5 7 ♖d5+.

233

7	♔b6	♜c8
8	c5 and wins.	

Black to play:

With Black to play there are even two good defences:

A.

1	...	♜d8
2	♖xd8	♔xd8
3	♔b4	♔c8!=

B.

1	...	♔e6

Although this is less forcing it is important because it also draws.

2	♔b4	

If 2 c5 ♔e7! 3 ♔c4 ♜d8!=.

2	...	♜b8+
3	♔a5	♜c8
4	♔b5	♜b8+
5	♔a6	♜c8
6	♖d4	♔e5!

This is the difference.

7	♖d5+	♔e6
8	♔b5	♜b8+
9	♔a4	♜c8
10	♔b4	♜b8+
11	♖b5	♜h8
12	♖b7	♔d6
13	♔b5	♜h5+
14	♔b6	♜c5
15	♖d7+	♔xd7
16	♔xc5	♔c7!=

R 13

+/= W/B

R 13a

+ B

We should also note that frontal defence only works when the pawn is on the *fourth rank or further back*.

White to move wins easily in diag 13 with:

1	♔b5	♜b8+
2	♔a6	♜c8
3	♔b6	♜b8+
4	♔c7	etc.

The black rook has insufficient checking distance.

Black to move draws with:

1	...	♜d8!
2	♖xd8	♔xd8
3	♔b5	♔c7=

Diag 13a

1	...	♜d8
2	c6!	♜xd5
3	♔xd5	♔e8
4	♔e6!	etc.

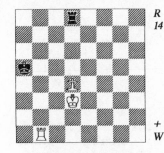

R
14

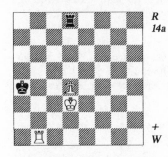

R
14a

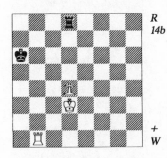

R
14b

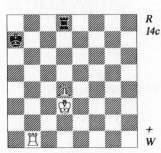

R
14c

Cheron 1926

Black's king is on the short side of the pawn. This means that the "Combined Method" *per se* does not work, e.g. 1 ♔e4 ♖e8+ 2 ♔f5 ♖d8 3 ♔e5 ♖e8+ 4 ♔f6 ♖d8 5 ♖d1 ♔b6 6 ♔e7 ♖d5 7 ♔e6 ♖h5 8 ♖c1 ♖h6+=.

But the black king, whilst well placed from one point of view, is on the rook's file. And this means that White can use *mating threats*.

First, let's examine what happens with the black king on other squares.

Diag 14a
1   d5!   ♖xd5+
2   ♔c4 and wins

Of course if Black didn't play 1 ... ♖xd5+, then he would lose checking distance (cf diag 13).

Diag 14b
1 ♔e4 ♖e8+ 2 ♔f5 ♖d8 3 ♔e5 ♖e8+ 4 ♔d6 ♖d8+ 5 ♔c6! and wins.

Diag 14c
1 ♔e4 ♖e8+ 2 ♔f5 ♖d8 3

♔e5 ♖e8+ 4 ♔d6 ♖d8+ 5 ♔c7!.

In fact a5 is the best square for Black's king. And since it is the *only* one, we should not be too surprised to find that White can put Black into *zugzwang*:

1   ♖b2   ♔a4
2   ♖b7

But not 2 d5?? ♖xd5+ 3 ♔c4 ♔a3.

2   ...   ♔a5
3   ♖b1!

Now 3 ... ♔a4 leads to diag 14a or 3 ... ♔a6 to diag 14b. If 3 ... ♖d7 the rook loses checking distance and 4 ♔e4 wins easily. That leaves only:

3   ...   ♖h8
4   d5   ♖h4
5   d6!   ♔a6

If 5 ... ♖h6 6 ♔d4 ♖xd6+ 7 ♔c5, or 5 ... ♔a4 6 d7 ♖h8 7 ♔c4. Finally if 5 ... ♖g4 6 d7 ♖g8 7 ♔d4 ♖d8 8 ♔c5.

6   d7   ♖h8
7   ♔d4   ♖d8
8   ♔d5   ♖xd7+
9   ♔c6 and wins

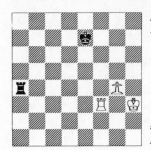

R
15

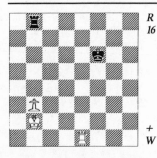

R
16

R
16a

Fischer - Sherwin
Portoroz 1958
The black rook is doing nothing on a4 and must be regrouped immediately to deliver frontal checks:

A.
The correct defence is therefore:

1	...	♖a8!
2	♔h4	

If 2 g5 ♖f8=, or 2 ♖f5 ♖f8 3 ♖xf8 ♔xf8 4 ♔h4 ♔g8=.

Note that if the white rook were on f4 protecting the pawn then he would win with 2 ♔h4 ♖h8+ 3 ♔g5! ♖g8+ 4 ♔h6. Here however it is drawn.

2	...	♖h8+
3	♔g3	♖f8!=

The Combined and Zugzwang Method
The extremely difficult position in diag 16 was first analysed by Grigoriev. Believing, it now appears mistakenly, that the simple combined method was insufficient he was forced to employ the extra weapon of *zugzwang*.

First let's see what happens with the black king on other squares.

Diagram 16a

1	♔c3	♖c8+
2	♔d4	♖b8

2 ... ♖d8+ 3 ♔c5 ♖c8+ 4 ♔d6 ♖b8 5 ♖b1 ♔e4 6 b4 ♔d3 7 b5 ♔c2 8 ♔c7! wins.

3	♖b1!	

Not 3 ♔c4 ♖c8+ 4 ♔d5 ♖b8 5 ♖b1? (5 ♔c4!) 5 ... ♔e3! 6 b4 ♔d3 7 b5 ♔c2=. However, 3 ♖f1+ ♔g5 4 ♔c3 would also be good.

3	...	♔f5

B.
In the game, however, Black lost an invaluable tempo with:

1	...	♔e6?
2	♔h4	♖a8

If 2 ... ♖a7 not 3 g5? ♖f7= but 3 ♔h5!.

3	g5	

Black's rook now has insufficient checking distance. Since he also lacks time to contest the f-file he is lost.

3	...	♖h8+
4	♔g4	♔e7

Of course 4 ... ♖g8 5 ♔h5 ♖h8+ 6 ♔g6 ♖g8+ 7 ♔h6 is hopeless (cf diag 13).

5	g6	♖f8
6	♖f5!	♖h8

If 6 ... ♖xf5 7 ♔xf5 ♔e8 8 ♔e6; or 6 ... ♖f6 7 ♔g5.

7	♔g5 and wins.	

4	♔d5	♔f6
5	b4	♔e7
6	♔c6 and wins	

Diagram 16b

1	♔c3	♖c8+
2	♔d4	♖b8
3	♔c4	♖c8+
4	♔d5	♖b8

4 ... ♖d8+ 5 ♔c6 ♖c8+ 6 ♔d6 ♖b8 7 ♖b1 ♔e4 8 b4 ♔d3 9 b5 ♔c2 10 ♔c7! as in diag 16a above (note to 2 ... ♖b8).

5	♖b1	

Transposing into diag 16a.

Diagram 16c
1 ♖e3 ♔f6 2 ♔c3 will transpose into the main line (see below). With the king still further back on f8, 1 ♖e4 is also possible.

Diagram 16d
With the king on f3 or further up (i.e. on f2 or f1).

=
B

+
W

+
W

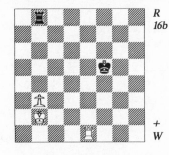

R
16b

1	♖e6	♔f4
2	♔a3	♔f5

2 ... ♖a8+ 3 ♔b4 ♔f5 4 ♖c6 ♔e5 5 ♔c4 and 6 b4.

3	♖a6	♔e5
4	b4	♔d5
5	♔a4	♔c4
6	♖c6+ and wins	

Returning to
Diagram 16

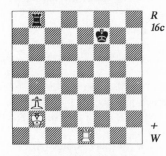

R
16c

1   ♖e4

If 1 ♔c3 ♖c8+ 2 ♔d4 ♖b8! 3 ♔c4 ♖c8+ 4 ♔d5 ♖b8. Now White can try 5 ♖b1 or 5 ♖e3. Grigoriev thought that both lead to a draw - hence his solution. Later analysis has shown that in fact both should win. However, Grigoriev's solution is very pleasing, and in any case one solution is quite sufficient.

1   ...   ♔f5

If 1 ... ♔f7 2 ♔c3 forces b4, or 1 ... ♖h8 2 ♖e3! ♔f6 3 ♔c3 is the main line.

2   ♖e3   ♔f6

2 ... ♔f4 3 ♖e1 ♔f5 is diag 16b or 3 ... ♔f3 is diag 16f. For 2 ... ♖h8 3 b4 ♔f4! 4 ♖e1 ♖h3 see diag 16c.

3   ♔c3

Not 3 ♖e1 ♖h8 4 b4? (4 ♖e3) 4 ... ♖h3! see diag 16f.

3	...	♖c8+
4	♔d4	♖b8
5	♔c5	♖c8+
6	♔d6	♖b8
7	♖f3+	♔g5
8	♔c5! (16e)	

8 ♔c7 ♖b4 9 ♔c6 ♖b8!.

8   ...   ♖c8+

8 ... ♔g4 9 ♖d3! ♖c8+ 10 ♔b6 ♖b8+ 11 ♔c7 ♖b4 12 ♔c6 ♔f4 (12 ... ♖b8 13 ♖d4+ ♔f5 14 b4 ♔e5 15 ♖h4) 13 ♔c5 ♖b8 14 b4 ♖c8+ 15 ♔d5 ♖d8+ 16 ♔c4 ♖c8+ 17 ♔b3

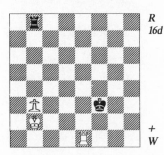

R
16d

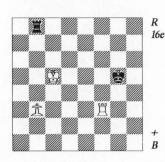

R
16e

+
W

+
W

+
W

+
B

♔e4 (17 ... ♖b8 18 ♖d5, or 17 ... ♔e5 18 b5) 18 ♖d6 ♔e5 19 ♖a6 and wins.

9	♔d4	♖b8
10	♔c3	♖c8+
11	♔b2	♖b8

The black king is now cut off an extra file - cf diag 16 and White therefore wins straightforwardly.

12	♖f1!	♔g6
13	♔c3	♖c8+
14	♔d4	♖b8
15	♔c4	♖c8+
16	♔d5	♖b8
17	♖b1	♔f7
18	b4	♔e7
19	♔c6 etc	

Diagram 16f

This position can arise from the main line - note to 2 ... ♔f6.

White to play

1   ♔c2!

Not 1 b5? ♖h5.

1   ...   ♔f5

1 ... ♖g3 2 b5 ♖g5 3 b6 ♖c5+ 4 ♔d3 ♖b5 5 ♖e6 wins.

2   b5   ♔f6

2 ... ♖g3 3 b6 ♖g7 4 ♔c3 ♖b7 5 ♖b1 ♔e6 6 ♔c4 ♔d7 7 ♔b5 ♖c8 8 ♔a6 ♖d7 9 ♖h1 ♖d8 10 ♔a7 wins.

3   b6   ♔f7

If 3 ... ♖h8 4 ♔c3 ♖b8 5 ♖b1 ♔e6 6 ♔c4 ♔d7 7 ♔b5 ♔c8 8 ♖c1+! ♔b7 9 ♖c7+ ♔a8 10 ♖a7+ mate!; or 3 ... ♖h7 4 ♔c3 ♖b7 5 ♖b1 (see last note).

4   ♖b1!

4 b7? would only draw.

4	...	♖h8
5	♔c3	♔e6
6	♔b4	♔d7
7	♖c1!	♖c8
8	♖c5! etc.	

cf diag 15, variation B.

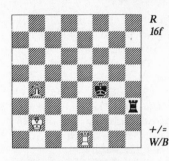

R
16f

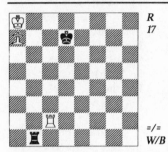

+/=
W/B

Black to play
With an extra tempo, Black can draw:

| 1 | ... | ♔f5! |
| 2 | b5 | |

Or 2 ♔c2 ♔f6 3 b5 ♖h5 4 ♖b1 ♔e6 5 b6 ♖h8=.

| 2 | ... | ♖d3! |

The only move - 2 ... ♔f6 loses.

3	♔c2	♖d5
4	♖b1	♖c5+!
5	♔d3	♔e5
6	b6	♖c8=

R
17

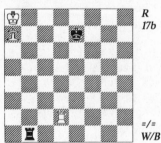

=/=
W/B

R
17a

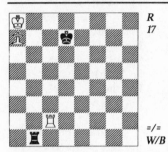

+/=
W/B

R
17b

=/=
W/B

Rook's Pawns
Rook's pawns are usually weaker than other pawns since:

a) Their king can easily get hemmed in on the rook's file (cf diag 17);

b) Whilst they provide the usual protection from checks from behind, these pawns *cannot help* in the case of *flank checks* cf diag 21.

In contrast to the Lucena position, diag 3, here White can do nothing since his king is hemmed in on the a-file,

e.g.

1	♖h2	♔c7
2	♖h8	♖b2
3	♖b8	♖c2=

Diagram 17a
Here White gets in 1 ♖c8! and, as we shall see under diag 18, this wins.

Black to play would draw easily with 1 ... ♔d7.

Diagram 17b

| 1 | ♖h2 | ♔d7 |
| 2 | ♖h8 | ♔c7= |

R
18

Here the black king is sufficiently far from the action for White to win.

    1   ♖h2

1 ♖c2 would amount to the same thing.

1	...	♔e7
2	♖h8	♔d6

+/+
W/B

A little better than 2 ... ♔d7 - see the note to 5 ♔c8.

3	♖b8	♖a1
4	♔b7	♖b1+
5	♔c8	

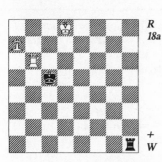

R
18a

If 5 ♔a6 ♖a1+ 6 ♔b6 ♖b1+ 7 ♔a5 ♖a1+ and the king must escape via c8. But if Black had played 2 ... ♔d7 then 7 ♔c5! would have won easily.

+
W

5	...	♖c1+
6	♔d8	♖h1
7	♖b6+!	

7 ♔e8? ♖h8+ 8 ♔f7 ♖h7+=.

7	...	♔c5 (18a)
8	♖c6+!	

Not 8 ♖e6? ♖a1 9 ♔e7 ♔b6=; nor 8 ♖a6 ♖h8+ 9 ♔c7 ♖h7+ 10 ♔d8 ♖h8+ 11 ♔e7 ♖h7+ 12 ♔f8 (12 ♔f6?? ♖h6+) 12 ... ♖h8+ 13 ♔g7 ♖a8=.

8	...	♔b5

Or 8 ... ♔d5 9 ♔a6 wins.

9	♖c8!	♖h8+
10	♔c7	♖h7+
11	♔b8 and wins	

R
19

White can gain a decisive tempo with:

1	♖d8	♔e7
2	♖b8!	♖a1
3	♔b7	♖b1+
4	♔a8	♖a1
5	a7	

+/=
W/B

Also 5 ♖b6 ♔d7 6 ♔b7 etc.

5	...	♔d6
6	♔b7	

Transposing into diag 18 (of course Black to play draws easily with 1 ... ♔e7 - leading to diag 17b).

R
20

White to move wins with a typical combination:

1	♖h8!	♖xa7
2	♖h7+	

Black to move can defend with the single move:

1	...	♔g7!

+/=
W/B

Or some checks and then ... ♔g7.

He must avoid 1 ... "♔ 3rd rank" which, whilst preventing the skewer, allows an immediate check, i.e. if 1 ... ♔e6?/f6?/g6? 2 ♖e8+/f8+/g8+ wins.

After 1 ... ♔g7! White can make no progress. Black waits for the enemy king to reach b6 and then checks it away, returning at once with his rook to the a-file, e.g.

2 ♔f3 ... ... 6 ♔b6 ♖b1+ 7 ♔c7 ♖a1 8 ♔b7 ♖b1+ 9 ♔c6 ♖a1=.

Diagram 20a

Here Black is defenceless. The e-file is "mined" and the king has nowhere to hide.

If 1 ... ♔f7 or 1 ... ♔d7 then 2 ♖h8!; and if 1 ... ♔d6 or 1 ...

R
20a

+/+
W/B

♔e6 or 1 ... ♔f6 then 2 ♖checks.

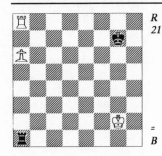

R
21

=
B

R
21a

=
B

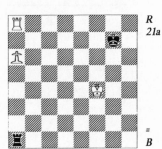

R
21b

+
B

White plans to bring his king to the queenside freeing his rook. Since the pawn is only on a6 this will work against passive defence. Dr Tarrasch rather naturally considered the position won but later the analysis revealed a better defence.

First here is Tarrasch's solution:

| 1 | ... | ♔f7 |
| 2 | ♔f3 | |

But not 2 a7?? ♔g7!=.

| 2 | ... | ♖a4 |

As we saw in diag 20 the king cannot cross the e-file - if 2 ... ♔e7 3 a7! wins.

3	♔e3	♔g7
4	♔d3	♔f7
5	♔c3	♔g7
6	♔b3	♖a1
7	♔b4	♔f7
8	♔b5	

Now White threatens to free his rook

8	...	♖b1+
9	♔c6	♖c1+
10	♔b6	♖b1+
11	♔a7	♔e7
12	♖b8	

And wins as in diag 19, viz:

12	...	♖a1
13	♔b7	♖b1+
14	♔a8	♖a1
15	a7	♔d6
16	♔b7	etc.

But the Soviet analysts Rauzer and Rabinovich noted

that the rook's pawn *does not defend against the flank check.*

Hence:

1	...	♖a5!
2	♔f3	♖f5+
3	♔e4	♖f6

Now White cannot free his rook:

4	♔d5	♔h7
5	♔c5	♖g6
6	♔b5	

Or 6 a7 ♖a6!=.

| 6 | ... | ♖g5+ |
| 7 | ♔b4 | ♖g6= |

Diag 21 has been analysed with Black to move for various positions of the white king, e.g.

Diagram 21a

| 1 | ... | ♖a5! |

1 ... ♖f1+ loses immediately to 2 ♔e5 ♖f6 3 ♖g8+!; but 1 ... ♖c1 is also sufficient to draw:

a) 2 ♖b8 ♖a1 3 ♖b6 ♖a5! (3 ... ♔f7 4 ♔e5 ♔e7 5 ♖b7+ and 6 a7) 4 ♔e4 ♔f7 5 ♔d4 ♔e7 6 ♔c4 ♔d7 7 ♔b4 ♖a1;

b) 2 ♖a7+ ♔g6! is the only move for reasons similar to those in the note to 3 ... ♔g6! below.

| 2 | ♔e4 | ♖b5 |
| 3 | ♖a7+ | ♔g6!! |

This is the only square. The king must remain as near as possible to the a-file. But at

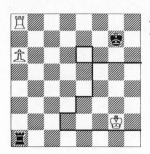

R
21c

the same time he must threaten to set up the draw with ... ♖b6; and this is not possible with the king on f6 in view of a later ♖h7.

Thus if 3 ... ♔f6? 4 ♔d4 ♖b6 (or 4 ... ♖a5 5 ♖a8!) 5 ♔c5 ♖e6 6 ♖h7!+-; or 3 ... ♔h6? 4 ♖b7 ♖a5 5 a7 ♔g6 6 ♔d4 ♔f6 7 ♔c4 ♔e6 8 ♔b4 ♖a1 9 ♔c5 wins simply.

4   ♖b7   ♖a5
5   a7   ♔f6
6   ♖h7   ♔g6!

Not 6 ... ♔e6? 7 ♖h6+! ♔d7 8 ♖h8!+-.

7   ♖b7   ♔f6=

Diagram 21b

If 1 ... ♖a5 2 ♔b3 ♖b5+ 3 ♔a4 ♖b6 4 ♔a5! wins.

Or 1 ... ♖e1 2 ♖a7+! ♔f6 3 ♖h7 ♔e6 4 a7 ♖a1 5 ♔b2 ♖a5 6 ♔b3 etc.

Or 1 ... ♖h1 2 ♖a7+! ♔f6 3 ♔b3 ♖h8 (3 ... ♔e6 4 a7) 4 ♖b7 ♔e6 5 a7 and wins.

Rather than get involved in a huge amount of detail in this complex ending, here is a diagram which summarises the information which the analysts have discovered.

Diagram 21c

Black to play draws if the white king is in the zone - otherwise he loses.

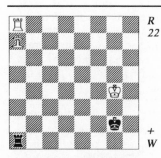

R
22

+
W

Troitsky
Black's king is hiding behind his opposite number. White wins by moving his king to a position from which he can deliver a murderous discovered check:

1   ♔f4   ♔f2
2   ♔e4   ♔e2
3   ♔d4   ♔d2
4   ♔c5   ♔c3

Or 4 ... ♖c1+ 5 ♔b4 ♖b1+ 6 ♔a3 and wins.

5   ♖c8!   ♖xa7
6   ♔b6+ and wins

Diagram 22a

White to move wins with:

1 ♔f6! (not 1 ♔f7? ♔f5=) 1 ... ♔f4 2 ♔e6 ♔e4 3 ♔d6 ♔d4 4 ♔c6 ♔c4 (4 ... ♖c1+ is still hopeless) 5 ♖c8!.

But Black can draw with:

1   ...   ♔g5!

viz: 2 ♔f7 ♔f5 3 ♔e7 ♔e5 4 ♔d7 ♔d5 5 ♔c7 ♔c5 6 ♖c8 (or 6 ♔b7 ♖b1+) 6 ... ♖xa7+ 7 ♔b8+ ♔b6=.

R
22a

+/=
W/B

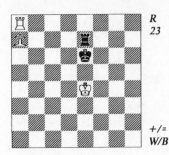

R
23

+/=
W/B

Cheron 1923
White to move would win easily by bringing his king to b6:
1 ♔d4 ♖d7+ 2 ♔c5 ♖e7 3 ♔b6 etc.

Black to play must decide which way to move his king.

A.

1	...	♔d6+?
2	♔d4	♔e6

2 ... ♖d7 3 ♔c4 ♖c7+ 4 ♔b5 ♖d7 5 ♔b6.

3	♔c5	♔e5
4	♔c6!	

This is zugzwang, viz: if 4 ... ♔e6 5 ♔b6, or 4 ... ♔e4 5 ♔d6, or 4 ... ♖e6+ 5 ♔d7 ♖d6+ 6 ♔c7.

Thus 1 ... ♔d6+? loses. Driven back onto the *e-file*, *which is generally a bad file to be on*, he fell into zugzwang.

B.

1	...	♔f6+
2	♔d4	♖f7!

Black sets up his defence on the safer f-file: If 2 ... ♖e7 3 ♔c5 wins as in A; or 2 ... ♖d7+ 3 ♔c5 is hopeless.

3	♔d5	

If 3 ♔c5 ♔f5 4 ♔b6 ♖f6+ and 5 ... ♖f7 draws. There is no zugzwang since the f-file is far enough away from the pawn.

3	...	♔f5
4	♔d6	♔f6!
5	♔c6	♔f5
6	♔c5	♔f4!
7	♔b6	♖f6+
8	♔c7	♖f7+
9	♔c6	♔f5=

White cannot make any progress since it is impossible simultaneously to threaten ♔b6 and ♔e6. Thus there is no zugzwang since the *f-file is sufficiently far from the pawn.*

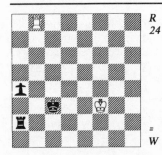

R
24

=
W

Euwe - Alekhine
World Championship 1935
This is a very difficult position which arose in the 1935 World Championship Match. White has two plausible continuations: A. 1 ♔e3 and B. 1 ♖c8+.

A.

1	♔e3	

This is the move which Euwe actually chose.

1	...	♖h2?

1 ... a3! leads to a win after 2 ♖c8+ ♔b2 3 ♔d2 (or 3 ♔d3 ♔b1 4 ♖b8+ ♔b2 5 ♖h8 ♖c2!) 3 ... ♔b1+ 4 ♔d1 ♖h2! 5 ♖b8+ ♖b2 6 ♖c8 ♖b4! etc.

2	♖c8+	

This is also a mistake. 2 ♖a8! (Romanovsky) draws: 2

R
24a

-
W

... ♖a2 (if 2 ... ♖h4 White checks the black king to the a-file since if he interposes ... ♖b4/... ♔c4 White can take) 3 ♖c8+ ♔b2 4 ♔d2 ♔b1+ 5 ♔d1 ♖b2 (5 ... ♔h2 6 ♖a8+!) 6 ♖c4! a3 7 ♖c3 and draws since if 7 ... a2?? 8 ♖c1 mate.

2	...	♔b2
3	♖b8+	♔c1
4	♖c8+	

Or 4 ♖a8 a3!.

4	...	♔b1
5	♖b8+	♖b2
6	♖a8	♖b3+
7	♔d4	a3
8	♔c4	♔b2
9	♖h8	♖c3+
	0-1	

B.

1	♖c8+	♔d2

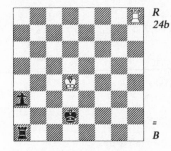

R
24b

=
B

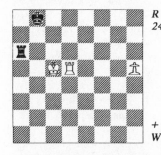

R
24c

+
W

R
24d

=/-
W/B

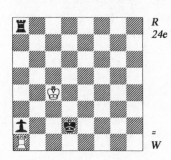

R
24e

=
W

If he brings the king to-wards the rook, i.e. 1 ... ♔b4 2 ♖b8+ ♔c5 3 ♖c8+ ♔b6 4 ♖b8+ ♔c7, then 5 ♖b1! draws.

2 ♖h8

If 2 ♖d8+ ♔c1 3 ♖c8+ ♔b1 4 ♖b8+ ♖b2 5 ♖a8 ♖b4 wins easily. In this sequence it would be better to break off the checks and resume observation of the a-pawn; but this also seems to lose, e.g. 2 ♖d8+ ♔c1 3 ♖a8 a3 4 ♔e4 ♖e2+ 5 ♔f3 ♖h2 6 ♔g3 ♖a2 7 ♔f3 ♖a1 8 ♔e3 ♖c2! (24a). Now if 9 ♔d4 ♖d1+ 10 ♔c4 ♖d3 and wins.

Or if White starts checking he may reach a lost position like diag 23 variation A, e.g. 9 ♖c8+ ♔b3 10 ♖b8+ ♔c4 11 ♖c8+ ♔b5 12 ♖b8+ ♔c6 (12 ... ♔a6! is even simpler) 13 ♖c8+ ♔b7 14 ♖c2 a2 15 ♖e2 ♔c6 16 ♔e4 ♔c5 17 ♔e3 ♔c4 18 ♔e4 ♔c3 zugzwang and wins.

2 ... ♖a1

The idea of this move is that if White starts checking then he won't have ♖b1 at the end, i.e. if 3 ♖d8+ ♔c3 4 ♖c8+ ♔b4 5 ♖b8+ ♔c5 6 ♖c8+ ♔b6 7 ♖b8+ ♔c7 would now win. But instead White plays:

3 ♔e4! a3

If f3 ... ♔c3 4 ♖c8+ draws; or if 3 ... ♖b1 4 ♔d4 is also sufficient.

4 ♔d4! (24b)

This seems to us to be suffi-cient to draw viz:

i)

4	...	a2??
5	♖h2+	♔d1
6	♔d3	

And White wins!

ii)

| 4 | ... | ♔c2 |
| 5 | ♔c4 | |

5 ♖c8+ also draws.

| 5 | ... | ♖d1 |

If 5 ... ♖e1 6 ♖h2+ ♔b1 7 ♔b3 ♖e3+ 8 ♔b4 a2 9 ♖h1+=.

| 6 | ♖h2+ | ♔b1 |

Or 6 ... ♖d2 7 ♖xd2+! ♔xd2 8 ♔b3.

| 7 | ♔b3 | ♖d3+ |
| 8 | ♔c4! | |

But not 8 ♔b4?, when 8 ... a2 wins with the rook on the d-file.

| 8 | ... | ♖e3 |
| 9 | ♖h1+= | |

iii)

4 ... ♖d1 transposes into (ii) above: 5 ♖h2+ ♔c1+ 6 ♔c3 ♔b1 7 ♔b3 ♖d3+ 8 ♔c4! etc.

iv)

| 4 | ... | ♖e1 |
| 5 | ♖a8! | ♖e3 |

Or 5 ... ♖a1 6 ♖h8!.

| 6 | ♖h8! | |

But not 6 ♔c4? ♔c2 which wins since the king can now *protect* the pawn.

Now, however, Black cannot make progress, e.g.

| 6 | ... | ♖d3+ |

If 6 ... ♖e1 7 ♖a8 repeats; or 6 ... a2 7 ♖a8 wins the pawn.

7	♔c4	♔c2
8	♖h2+	♔d2
9	♖xd2+!=	

Thus it seems that line B leads to a draw.

Diagram 24c

This extremely difficult po-sition comes from diag 41b. Until I consulted John Nunn's database, I believed that there was only a single path to victory.

A.

    1   Kd4

I had believed that this led to a draw.

    1   ...   Re6!

If 1 ... Kc7 2 Ke5 Rh6 3 Kf4 Kc6 4 Ra5 Kd7 5 Kg5 is simple.

    2   Re5

2 Rg5 Kc7 3 Rg6 Kd6!=.

    2   ...   Rh6!

    3   Rc5!!

This is what I'd missed. If 3 Ke4 Kc7 4 Kf4 Kd6 5 Ra5 Ke7=.

    3   ...   Kb7

    4   Ke4   Kb6

    5   Rf5   Kc6

    6   Kf4   Kd7

    7   Kg5   Rh8

    8   h6

Not 8 Rf7+? Ke6 9 Rg7 Ra8 10 h6 Ra1 11 Kg6 Rg1+=.

    8   ...   Ke7

8 ... Ke6 9 Rf6+ Ke7 10 Ra6 is no better.

    9   Ra5 and wins

For example: 9 ... Rg8+ 10 Kh5+- Rg1 11 h7 Kf7 12 Ra7+ Ke6 13 Kh6 etc.

B.

    1   Rd6!

If the rook started on d5 then this would indeed be the unique winning move.

    1   ...   Ra1

If 1 ... Ra5+? 2 Kb6; or 1 ... Ra7 2 Kb6 Rb7+ 3 Kc6 Rc7+ 4 Kd5 Rh7 5 h6 Kc7 6 Ra6! Rh8 (6 ... Kb7 7 Rg6!) 7 Ke5 Kd7 8 Ra7+ Kc7 9 h7 and wins.

    2   Rf6!!

The database confirms that this is the only winning move.

If 2 h6? Kc7; or 2 Kc6 Kc8 3 h6 Rh1! 4 Kd5 Rh5+ 5 Ke4 Kc7 6 Ra6 Kb7! (6 ... Kd7? 7 h7!) 7 Rg6 Kc7 8 Kf4 Kd7 9 Kg4 Rh1 10 Kg5 Ke7; or finally, if 2 Rg6? Kc8! 3 Kd6 Ra5!!= - that is why the rook must go to f6 rather than g6.

    2   ...   Rh1

If 2 ... Kc7 3 Rf7+ Kd8 4 h6 Ke8 5 h7!; or 2 ... Kc8 3 Kd6 Ra5 4 h6.

    3   h6   Kc8

Or 3 ... Kc7 4 Rf7+ Kd8 5 h7 Ke8 6 Rg7 and 7 Rg8+.

    4   Kd6

And since his king has been shouldered off, Black loses.

Diagram 24d

Here the result depends on the move.

Black to move wins easily, viz: 1 ... Kg3 2 Ke5 Kf3 3 Kd5 Ke3 4 Kc5 Kd3 5 Kb5 Ra8 6 Kb4 Kc2 and wins.

With White to move the position is more interesting:

    1   Ke5   Kg3

    2   Kd5   Kf3

    3   Kc5   Ke3

    4   Kb5   Ra8

    5   Kc4!

Not 5 Kb4? Kd3 6 Kb3 Rb8+ and if 7 Kxa2/7 Ka3 Kc2! wins or 7 Ka4 Kc3!.

    5   ...   Kd2 *(24e)*

    6   Kb3   Rb8+

    7   Kc4!

But not 7 Kxa2 Kc2!; or 7 Ka4 Kc3! as above.

    7   ...   Rb2

Or 7 ... Ra8 8 Kb3=.

    8   Rh1   Ke3

If 8 ... Kc2 9 Ra1, or 8 ... Ke2 9 Kc3 Rb1 10 Rh2+.

    9   Ra1

Threatening 10 Kc3.

    9   ...   Kd2

    10   Rh1=

Rook v Rook

Rook and Two Pawns v Rook

This will generally be a win unless there is a good reason why not. However, there are quite a number of exceptional positions. First we shall look at connected pawns.

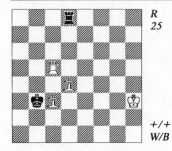

R 25

+/+
W/B

Connected Pawns

These should easily win unless:

a) There is a blockade or

b) The attacking king is cut off from the pawns.

Even if a), b) or both apply the position may well be won.

White is threatening to win almost automatically by advancing his queenside formation up the board, i.e. 1 d5 2 c4 3 ♖c6 4 d6 5 c5 6 ♖c7 7 d7 8 c6 9 ♖c8. Black can interfere with this plan but White nevertheless wins easily:

1	...	♔c2
2	d5	♔d3
3	c4	♔d4

4	♖c6	♔e5

Now White threatens to win by bringing his king to either c5 or f7, e.g. 5 ♔g3 - f3 - ... - 11 ♔c5. Black cannot really interfere with this since he must play ... ♖d8 - d7 - d8 in order to prevent d6.

He can decide to allow d6 but that is also rather hopeless, e.g.

5	♔g4	♖f8
6	d6	♔e6
7	c5	♔d7
8	♖c7+	♔d8
9	♖a7	♖f6

Else White plays 10 c6.

10	♔g5	♖e6
11	♔f5 and wins.	

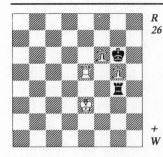

R 26

+
W

Ornstein - Spiridonov
Albena 1976

Black has a *blockade* but White is able to break it with the help of his king.

1	♖d5	♖g1

If 1 ... ♖a4 2 ♖d8! gets the rook to a much more active position since if 2 ... ♔xg5 3 f7. Once the rook gets active White will win easily, e.g. 2 ... ♖g4 3 ♖g8+ ♔f7 4 ♖g7+ ♔f8 5 ♔f3 ♖a4 6 ♖b7 ♖a6 (else 7g6) 7 ♔g4 etc.

2	♔d4	♖c1

White is trying to get his king to the pawns so he must go round the rook. Black is trying to prevent this.

3	♖e5	♖d1+
4	♔c5	♖d7
5	♖d5!	

Avoiding the trap: 5 ♖e7? ♖xe7 6 fxe7 ♔f7 7 ♔d6 ♔e8!=.

5	...	♖a7
6	♔d6	♖a6+
7	♔e7	♖a1
8	♖d6	♖a7+
9	♖d7	♖a6
10	f7	1-0

Rook v Rook

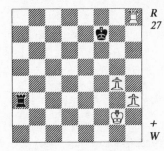

R 27

+ W

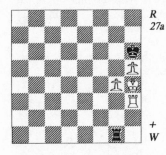

R 27a

+ W

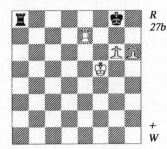

R 27b

+ W

Zukertort - Steinitz
London 1883

Here White has rook and knight's pawns which tend to be harder to win than other pawn pairs. The reason is that there is no natural shelter from flank checks, i.e. if 1 h4? ♖a2+ the king cannot shelter on "h4" beside the h-pawn.

This position should be an easy win if White arranges to advance his pieces in close formation, always taking care to *keep a good square free for his king.*

Through neglecting this principle, Zukertort came very close to drawing this won position.

1	♖b8	♔g6
2	♖b5	♖c3
3	♖e5	

3 ♖f5 would be better and then 4 ♖f3, 5 ♔g3 advancing the pawns only after the king has found a good post.

3	...	♖a3
4	h4?!	

As before, better was 4 ♖f5, e.g. 4 ... ♖b3 5 ♖f3 ♖b1 6 ♔g3 ♖g1+ 7 ♔h4 ♖a1 8 ♖b3 ♖a6 9 ♖b4 ♖c6 10 g5 and 11 ♔g4 12 h4 etc. (assuming the black rook stays on its third rank).

4	...	♖b3
5	h5+	

But not 5 g5?? ♔h5 and the *perfect blockade* is sufficient to draw, e.g. 6 ♖e4 ♖a3 7 ♖f4 ♖b3 8 ♖f3 ♖b4 9 ♖f8 ♖xh4=.

5	...	♔h6
6	♖f5	♖a3
7	♖f3	♖a1

If 7 ... ♖a5 not 8 ♔g3? ♔g5!= but 8 ♖f6+! ♔g5 9 ♖g6+ ♔f4 10 h6 and wins (see next note).

8		♔g3?

8 ♖f6+! ♔g5 (8 ... ♔g7 9 ♖g6+ ♔h7 10 ♔g3 and the king is in play again) 9 ♖g6+ ♔f4 10 h6 ♖a2+ 11 ♔f1 ♔f3 (11 ... ♖h2 12 g5 ♔f5 13 ♖g7 and wins automatically - cf intro to diag 26) 12 ♔e1 ♔e3 13 ♔d1 ♔d3 14 ♖d6+ ♔e3 15 g5 ♖h2 16 ♔c1 and wins, e.g. 16 ... ♖h5 17 ♖g6 ♔d3 18 ♖g7 ♔c3 19 ♖c7+ ♔d3 20 h7 etc.

8	...	♖g1+
9	♔h4	♖h1+
10	♖h3	♖g1 *(27a)*
11	♖h2!	

This is zugzwang, but White should not have needed this weapon.

11	...	♖a1
12	g5+	♔g7
13	♖f2	♖h1+

Or 13 ... ♖a4+! 14 ♔g3 ♖b4 15 ♖f4 ♖b1 16 ♔g4 etc.

14	♔g4	♖g1+
15	♔f5	♖h1?!
16	h6+	♔h7

Now 17 g6+! ♔xh6 18 ♔f6 would win at once - therefore 15 ... ♖a1! would have been better than 15 ... ♖h1?!.

Zukertort actually played 17 ♔f6 ♖g1! and won after further (mis)adventures in eight more moves. The text line, given by him after the game as an improvement, is very instructive.

17	♖f4	♖g1
18	♖e4	♖f1+
19	♔g4	♖g1+
20	♔h5	♖h1+
21	♖h4	♖g1
22	♖h2!	

Zugzwang (cf diag 27a).

22	...	♖g3
23	♖e2	♖h3+
24	♔g4	♖a3
25	♖e7+	♔g8
26	g6	♖a4+

27 ♔f5   ♜a8 *(27b)*
Now White must avoid stalemate after 28 h7+ ♔h8 29
♔g5?? (29 ♖e5!) 29 ... ♜a5+
30 ♔h6 ♜h5+!, but he can
easily win by either:
a) 28 ♖d7 ♜b8 29 ♔e6
♜b6+ (29 ... ♜a8 30 ♔e7 and

31 ♖d8+, or 29 ... ♜f8 30 ♔e7
etc:) 30 ♖d6 ♜b8 31 ♔e7
♜b7+ 32 ♖d7 ♜b8 33 ♖d8+
or;
b) 28 ♖e5 (also 28 h7+ and
29 ♖e5!) 28 ... ♔h8 29 ♔g5
followed by h7 and ♔h6.

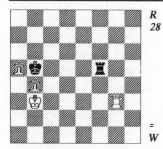

R
28

More Blockades
White can do absolutely nothing here, for example: 1 ♖c3
♜h5 2 ♖c5+ ♜xc5 3 bxc5
♔xc5!=; or 1 ♖g8 ♜f3+ and 2
... ♔xb4 draws easily; or 1
♖g4 ♜f3+ 2 ♔c2 ♜h3 3 ♖d4
♜g3 4 ♖d3 ♜g4=.

=
W

Diagram 28a
However, if we move the position one file to the left White
wins trivially:
1   ♖d3   ♜h5
2   ♖d5+   ♜xd5
3   cxd5
and if 3 ... ♔xb5 4 ♔d4 or 3
... ♔xb5 4 ♔d4.

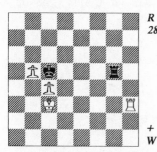

R
28a

+
W

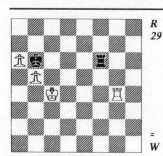

R
29

Horwitz and Kling
Here Black must be much
more careful than in diag 28.
But with correct play it is still
drawn.
1   ♖e4   ♜h6
2   ♖e8!   ♜h4+
3   ♔d5   ♜h7!
Of course not 3 ... ♔xb5? 4
a7. And 3 ... ♜b4? fails to 4
♖b8+ ♔a7 5 ♔c5! (not 5
♖b7+ ♔a8 since Black can
then sacrifice his rook to force
stalemate) 5 ... ♜b1 6 ♖b7+

=
W

♔a8 7 ♜h7 etc.
Now however Black threat-
ens 4 ... ♔xb5.
4   ♖b8+   ♔a7
5   ♖e8   ♔b6
6   ♔c4   ♜h4+
7   ♔d3   ♜h7=

Diagram 29a
Obviously if we move diag 29
up a rank then White wins
trivially.
1   ♖g8! etc.

Rook v Rook

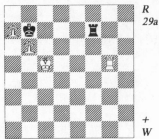

R
29a

+
W

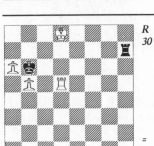

R
30

=
W

Cheron 1926
The white king hopes to break the blockade. But it just holds.

1	♔c8	♖g7
2	♖d7	♖g8+
3	♖d8	♖g7
4	♔b8	

If 4 ♖d6+ ♔xb5 5 ♔b8 ♖g8+=.

| 4 | ... | ♖h7 |

Now if 5 a7 ♖b7+!, or 5 ♖e8 ♖g7 6 ♖e6+ ♔xb5 7 a7 ♖g8+=. Therefore White plays:

| 5 | ♖d6+ | ♔c5! |

But not 5 ... ♔xb5 6 a7 ♖h8+ 7 ♔c7 ♖h7+ 8 ♖d7 etc.

| 6 | b6 | |

If 6 ♖e6 ♔xb5 7 a7 ♖h8+=

since the white rook is too far from its king. (We can note, by the way, the similarity of this position to variation arising from diag 24b.)

Or 6 a7 ♔xd6 7 a8♕ (7 b6 ♔c5) 7 ... ♖h8+ 8 ♔b7 ♖xa8 9 ♔xa8 ♔c5=.

Finally if 6 ♖d8 ♔b6! repeating.

| 6 | ... | ♔xd6 |
| 7 | ♔a8 | |

Or 7 a7 ♔c5 8 a8♕!=.

7	...	♖h8+!
8	♔a7	♔c6
9	b7	♔c7
10	b8♕+	♖xb8

Stalemate

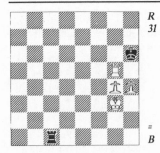

R
31

=
B

**Freeing the rook -
"Triangular Positions"**
Kasparian 1946
The Soviet study composer and analyst Kasparian analysed a considerable number of positions similar to this in great detail. He named them "triangular positions" in view of the configuration of White's rook and two pawns.

Black's plan is to check the white king away from the pawns and then attack them along the fourth rank:

1	...	♖c3+
2	♔f4	♖c4+
3	♔f5	

Or 3 ♔f3 ♖c3+ 4 ♔e2 ♖c4!.

3	...	♖c5+
4	♔f6	♖c6+
5	♔f7	♖c7+
6	♔e6	♖c4!=

White cannot free his rook since if 7 ♖g8 ♔h7!. The black rook keeps observing the pawns and checks the white king if it strays to the f-file.

Diagram 31a
Here the black rook lacks *checking distance* and so he loses.

| 1 | ... | ♖d3+ |

248

Rook v Rook   ♖ v ♜

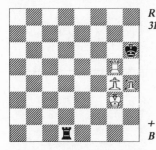

R
31a

+
B

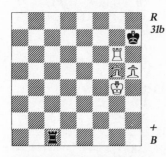

R
31b

+
B

2	♔f4	♜d4+
3	♔f5	♜d5+
4	♔f6	♜d6+
5	♔e5	

Disrupting Black's defensive plan.

| 5 | ... | ♜a6 |
| 6 | ♖f5 | |

And White soon unravels, for example: 6 ... ♜a5+ 7 ♔f4 ♜a4+ 8 ♔g3 ♜a3+ 9 ♔f3; or 6 ... ♜a4 7 ♖f6+ ♔g7 8 ♖f4 ♜a5+ 9 ♔e4 ♜a3 10 ♖f5 ♔g6 11 ♖e5 etc.

Diagram 31b

Flank checks fail as in diag 31a. Here Black can also try checking from behind but that fails too:

1	...	♜g1+
2	♔f5	♜f1+
3	♔e6	♜h1
4	♔f7!	

And wins since if 4 ... ♜xh5 5 ♖g7+ ♔h8 6 ♖g8+ ♔h7 7 g6+ ♔h6 8 ♖h8+ etc.

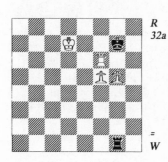

R
32

=
B

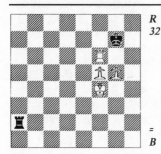

R
32a

=
W

Kasparian 1946

It is really rather remarkable that this position is drawn. The reason is that in contrast to diag 31b, here the black king is not on the edge of the board. The ending of rook and pawn against rook which results, therefore, turns out to be drawn.

| 1 | ... | ♖f2+ |

Here, checking from the side would be silly since the king could go to h5.

| 2 | ♔e3 | |

The only way to make progress. If, for example, 2 ♔g3 ♖f1 3 ♔g2 ♖f4 4 ♔g3 ♖f1 5 ♔g4 ♖g1+ 6 ♔f4 ♖f1+ 7 ♔e3 ♖g1 8 ♖g6+ ♔f7 9 ♔f2 ♖g4 etc.

White can free his rook only by advancing the king to d7.

2	...	♖g2
3	♖g6+	♔f7
4	♔f3	♖g1!
5	♔e4	♖g2
6	♔d5	♖g1
7	♔d6	♖g2
8	♔d7	♖g1
9	♖f6+	♔g7 *(32a)*

Now White must sacrifice the g-pawn, e.g.

10	♖d6	♖xg5
11	♔e6	♖g1
12	♔e7	

If 12 f6+ ♔g6 13 ♔e7 ♖f1 14 ♖e6 ♖f2 15 ♖e1 ♖a2! 16 ♖g1+ ♔h7 17 f7 ♖a7+=.

Or 12 ♖d7+ ♔h6! (not 12 ... ♔g8? 13 ♖d8+ ♔h7 14 f6 ♖e1+ 15 ♔f7 ♖e2 16 ♔f8 and the good position of the rook on d8 gives White a win) 13 f6 ♖a1 14 ♖d8 ♖a6+ 15 ♔e7 ♖a7+ 16 ♖d7 ♖a8!= cf diags 4 and 5. This position is somewhat better for Black than those since his rook has an "extra file".

12	...	♖f1!
13	♖g6+	♔h7
14	♔f6	♖a1!=

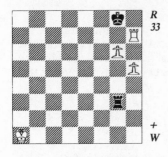

R
33

+
W

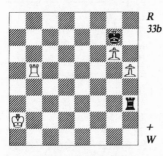

R
33a

=/+
W/B

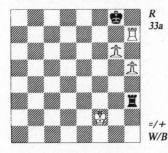

R
33b

+
W

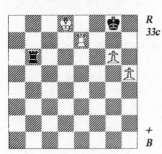

R
33c

+
B

Kasparian 1946
This remarkable position was also discovered by Kasparian. It looks as though White should win easily but there is a snag.

If 1 ♔b2 ♖h3 2 ♔c2 ♖g3 3 ♔d2 ♖h3 4 ♔e2 ♖g3 5 ♔f2 ♖h3 *(33a)*. White wants to free his rook. But if 6 ♔g2 ♖a3 7 ♖b7 ♖a5! forces his rook back since if 8 h6 ♖g5+.

Or 6 ♔g2 ♖a3 7 ♔h2 ♖b3 8 ♖a7 ♖b5 9 h6 ♖h5+.

Finally if 6 h6 ♖h5 7 ♔f3 ♖g5! 8 ♖g7+ ♔h8 9 ♔f4 ♖f5+! etc. with stalemate or perpetual check.

The white king is misplaced on the g- or h-file since the pawns are then loose.

Black to move in diag 33a, however, would be in zugzwang for if 1 ... ♖a3 (numbering from the diagram) 2 ♖b7 ♖a5 (or 2 ... ♖h3 3 ♖b5! see the main line) 3 h6 wins easily; or 1 ... ♔f8 2 ♔g2 ♖a3 3 ♖f7+ ♔g8 4 h6; or 1 ... ♖h4 2 ♔g3 etc.

White cannot lose a move in diag 33a since if 1 ♔f1 ♖f3+! (1 ... ♖g3? 2 ♔e2!) 2 ♔e2 (2 ♔e1 ♖e3+!; 2 ♔g1/g2 ♖a3) 2 ... ♖g3 3 ♔f2 ♖h3 etc.

Working from the fact that diag 33a is zugzwang Kasparian found the following solution to diag 33.

1　　♔a2!!

Not 1 ♔b2? ♖h3 as above: nor 1 ♔b1 ♖b3+! 2 ♔c2 (2 ♔c1 ♖c3+) 2 ... ♖g3!=.

Now Black has two reasonable defences:

A. Passive Defence

1	...	♖h3
2	♔b2	♖g3
3	♔c2	♖h3
4	♔d2	♖g3
5	♔e2	♖h3
6	♔f2	

Diag 33a but with Black to move.

6	...	♖a3
7	♖b7	♖h3
8	♖b5	♔g7
9	♔g2	♖h4
10	♔g3	♖h1

Or 10 ... ♖a4 11 ♖b7+ ♔g8 12 h6.

11	♖b7+	♔g8
12	♔g4 etc.	

B. Active Defence

1	♔a2	♖c3
2	♖b7	♖h3

If 2 ... ♖g3 3 ♔b2 ♖g5 4 ♖h7 ♖g3 5 ♔c2 "White has the co-ordination" (cf various pawn endings, e.g. diag P49). Black is now in zugzwang and will reach diag 33a on the move.

3	♖b5	♔g7 *(33b)*
4	♖g5!	

He must prevent 4 ... ♔h6 wedging the king between the pawns.

4	...	♖h4

If 4 ... ♔g8 5 ♔b2 ♖e3 6 ♔c2! (but not 6 h6? ♖h3 7 h7+ ♔g7) 6 ... ♖a3 7 ♔d2 ♖b3 8 ♔e2 ♖a3 9 ♔f2 ♖b3 10 ♖d5 ♖b6 (10 ... ♔g7 11 ♖d7+; 10 ... ♖h3 11 ♔g2) 11 ♔f3 ♔g7 12 ♖d7+ wins.

Or if 4 ... ♔h6 5 g7!; or 4 ... ♖c3 5 h6+!.

5	♔b3	♖h1
6	♔c4	♖c1+
7	♔d5	♖d1+
8	♔c6	♖c1+
9	♔d6	♖d1+
10	♖d5	♖a1
11	♔e7	♖a6

11 ... ♖e1+ 12 ♔d8! ♔h6 13 ♖d7! ♔xh5 14 g7 ♖g1 15 ♔e8

etc.

12	♖d7	♖b6
13	♔d8+	♔g8
14	♖e7 *(33c)*	
14	...	♖a6

Or 14 ... ♔f8 15 ♖f7+ ♔g8 16 ♔e7 ♖a6 17 ♖f6 ♖a7+ 18

♔e6 ♖a6+ 19 ♔f5 ♖a5+ 20 ♔g4 ♔g7 21 ♖f7+ etc.

15	♔d7	♖b6
16	♖e6	
17	♔d6	♖b7+
18	♔e5	♖b6+
19	♔f6 and wins.	♖b5+

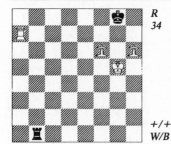

R 34

+/+ W/B

Isolated Pawns

Rook and two isolated pawns should usually win against a rook, but there are some exceptional positions. By far the most important class of these is:

"Rook, RP+BP vs Rook"

Although many positions are theoretically drawn, the defender has to play *extremely accurately* in order to attain this result.

Before examining correct defence we should first look at various positions which the defender must *avoid*:

Belavenets

The black king is cut off on the back rank. This almost always leads to a loss.

White is threatening to win immediately with, e.g. 1 h7+ ♔h8 2 ♖a8 ♔xh7 3 f7 etc. Black to play must therefore

start checking:

1	...	♖g1+
2	♔f5	♖f1+
3	♔e6	♖e1+
4	♔d6	♖d1+

Or 4 ... ♖h1 5 ♖a8+ ♔f7 6 h7! ♖xh7 7 ♖a7+ etc.

5	♔e7	♖e1+
6	♔d8	♖f1

If 6 ... ♔f8 7 ♖g7 followed by h7 and ♖g8+.

7	h7+	♔h8
8	♔e7	

But not 8 f7? ♖xf7! 9 ♖xf7 stalemate.

8	...	♖e1+

Now if 8 ... ♖xf6 9 ♖a8+!, or 8 ... ♔xh7 9 f7 ♔g7 10 ♔e8 etc.

9	♔f7!	

But not 9 ♔f8? ♖e8+! 10 ♔f7 ♖f8+ and Black forces a draw.

9	...	♖b1
10	♖a8+	♔xh7
11	♔f8	♔g6
12	f7 and wins	

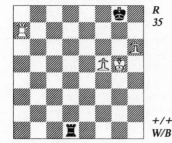

R 35

+/+ W/B

White threatens 1 f6 reaching diag 34, so Black must start:

1	...	♖g1+
2	♔f6	

Now there are two main defensive ideas:

A. To keep the rook flexible with 2 ... ♖b1

B. To attack the h-pawn with 2 ... ♖h1.

A third idea, observation of the f-pawn with 2 ... ♖f1, leads to diag 36b, viz: 3 ♖g7+ ♔h8 4 ♖e7! ♔g8 5 ♖e8+ ♔h7 6 ♔e6 ♖a1 7 f6 ♖a6+ 8 ♔f5 ♖a5+ 9 ♖e5 ♖a1 10 f7 ♖f1+ 11 ♔e6 ♔g6 12 ♖g5+!.

A.

2	...	♖b1
3	♖e7!	♖a1
4	♔e5	

If 4 h7+ ♔h8 5 ♔f7 ♖a5!! (5 ... ♔xh7 6 ♔f8+ ♔h6 7 ♖e6+! see diag 35a) 6 f6 ♔xh7=, e.g. 7 ♔f8+ ♔g6 8 f7 ♔f6!.

4	...	♖e1+

R
35a

+
W

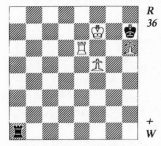

R
36

+
W

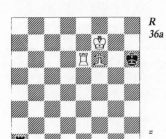

R
36a

=
W

5	♔d6	♖d1+
6	♔e6	♖e1+
7	♔d7	♖d1+

Or 7 ... ♖f1 8 ♖e8+ ♔h7 9 ♔e6 ♖a1 10 f6 ♖a6+.

8	♔e8	♖f1
9	♖e5	♔h7
10	♔f7!	♔xh6 *(35a)*
11	♖e6+!	

11 f6 ♖a1! is only a draw (cf diag 5 etc).

| 11 | ... | ♔h7 |
| 12 | f6 | ♖a1 |

The rook cannot get to its first rank and so Black loses (cf diag 5c).

| 13 | ♔f8 | ♖a8+ |
| 14 | ♖e8 and wins. | |

B.

| 2 | ... | ♖h1 |

Although Black's king is better here than in previous examples, White's monarch is also very effective. On f7 it is well placed to support the f-pawn; and as we shall see White is therefore winning.

In order to understand diag 36 we should first look at diag 36a.

Maizelis 1939

The position is very similar to diag 5c. Actually it is slightly better for Black since his rook has "an extra file".

White is threatening to reach the Lucena position with 1 ♔f8! and if 1 ... ♔g6 2 f7+.

Black to play can defend with the only move 1 ... ♖a8. For White's various winning attempts, all of which lead to a draw see (by analogy) diag 5.

Returning to diag 36, White is threatening 1 f6. Thus if,

| 3 | ♖g7+ | ♔f8 |

3 ... ♔h8 4 ♖e7 ♖xh6+ (or 4 ... ♔g8 5 ♖e8+ ♔h7 6 ♔e6 etc.) 5 ♔f7 ♖a6 6 f6 ♔h7 7 ♔f8+ ♔g6 8 f7 ♔f6 9 ♔g8! and wins.

| 4 | ♔g6! | |

Kopaev showed that this is the only move to win.

4	...	♖g1+
5	♔h7	♖f1
6	♖a7	♖g1

If 6 ... ♖xf5 7 ♔g6 and 8 ♖a8+, 9 h7.

7	f6	♖g2
8	♖g7	♖f2
9	♔g6	

And the plan of h7 and ♖g8+ is unstoppable.

A.

| 1 | ... | ♖a2 |
| 2 | f6! | ♖a8 |

If 2 ... ♔xh6 3 ♔f8! as above.

| 3 | ♖e8 | ♖a7+ |
| 4 | ♔e6! | |

But not 4 ♔f8 ♔g6 5 ♔g8 ♔xf6 6 h7 ♖g7+ 7 ♔h8 ♖a7! (not 7 ... ♖g1? 8 ♖f8+ ♔e6 9 ♖g8 - cf diag 18).

4	...	♖a6+
5	♔f5	♖a5+
6	♖e5	♖a1
7	f7	♖f1+
8	♔e6	♔g6 *(36b)*

Now if 9 h7 ♖f6+!=, but White has:

| 9 | ♖g5+!! | ♔xg5 |
| 10 | h7 | |

And the king hides on f8.

10	...	♖e1+
11	♔d7	♖d1+
12	♔e8	♖e1+
13	♔f8	♖h1
14	♔g7 and wins	

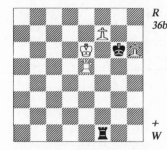

R
36b

+
W

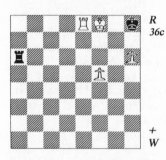

R
36c

+
W

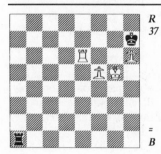

R
37

=
B

B.

1	...	♖a7+
2	♔f8	♖a8+
3	♖e8	♖a6

Else 4 f6; or 3 ... ♖a7 4 ♖e7+.

4	♖e7+	♔h8
5	♖e6	♖a8+
6	♖e8	♖a6 (36c)
7	f6!	♖xf6+
8	♔e7+ and wins	

We should note that if White's rook were on d6 then 1 ... ♖a7+ would have drawn: 2 ♔e8 ♖a8+ 3 ♔e7 (or 3 ♔d8 ♖a6!) 3 ... ♖a7+ 4 ♔d7 ♖a8 5 ♖d8 (5 f6 ♔xh6= cf diag 5) 5 ... ♖a7+ 6 ♔f6 ♖a1 7 ♖e8 ♖a2 8 ♔f7 ♔xh6!.

Defensible Positions

"Black's" defence consists essentially in preventing the various lost positions which we have already examined.

Maizelis 1939

White is threatening 1 ♖e7+. If 1 ... ♖a7? 2 ♖e5 and 3 f6 wins easily, so:

1	...	♖g1+
2	♔f6	

Now if 2 ... ♔xh6 3 ♔e7+ ♔h7 4 f6 and wins; or 2 ... ♖a1 3 ♔f7 in diag 36.

So Black must play:

2	...	♖f1!

Now White can try:

A.

3	♖e8	

If 3 ♖e7+ or 3 ♖e5 ♔xh6!.

3 ♖e3 would be met as in the main line with 3 ... ♖a1!.

3	...	♖a1!

Preparing for the flank checks. If 3 ... ♖f2? 4 ♔e6 ♖a2 5 f6 ♖a6+ 6 ♔f5 etc.

C.

1	...	♖a8

This prevents 2 f6? ♔xh6!= as in diag 36a.

2	♖e8	♖a7+

If 2 ... ♖a6 3 ♖e1 ♖a7+ (3 ... ♔xh6 4 ♖e6+) 4 ♔f8 ♔xh6 (4 ... ♖a8+ 5 ♖e8) 5 ♖e6+.

Or 2 ... ♖a6 3 ♖e1 ♖b6 4 f6 ♖b8 5 ♖e8 etc. as in A.

3	♔f8	♔xh6

3 ... ♖a6 4 ♖e7+ ♔h8 5 ♖e6! etc as in B

4	♖e6+!	

See also diag 35a.

4	...	♔g5

Or 4 ... ♔h7 5 f6 etc (cf diag 36a).

5	f6	♔f5
6	♖b6 and wins	

(see diag 36 variation A).

4	♔f7	

Or 4 ♖e6 ♔xh6 (also 4 ... ♖f1 repeating) 5 ♔e7+ ♔h7 6 f6 ♖a8!=.

4	...	♔xh6
5	♖e6+	♔h7
6	♔f8!?	

Or 6 f6 ♖a8!=.

6	...	♖a8+

7 ♖e8 ♖a6 8 ♖e7+ ♔h8 9 ♖e6 ♖a8+ 10 ♔f7 ♔h7=.

B.

3	♔e5	♖a1

Also 3 ... ♖e1+ 4 ♔d6 ♖f1!=.

4	♔d6	♖a5
5	f6	♔g6

5 ... ♔xh6 was also sufficient.

6	♖e8	♖a6+
7	♔e7	♖xf6
8	♖g8+	♔h7
9	♖g7+	♔h8
10	♔xf6 stalemate	

This finish (from 3 ... ♖a2) occurred in Bondarevsky - Keres, 1939.

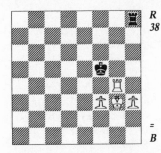

R
38

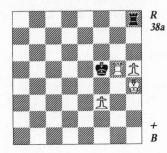

R
38a

Keres - Sokolsky
Moscow 1947
As we shall see in the next examples (diags 39, 39a) "Black's" correct defensive plan is to put his rook on or near a1, *once White has advanced his h-pawn.*

Here Black is lost through adopting this plan too early, thus allowing White to *run the h-pawn* and support it from *behind* with his rook:

1   ...   ♖a8

He could also play 1 ... ♔f6 2 h4 ♖h5.

2   h4   ♖a1?

The losing move! Correct was 2 ... ♖h8 3 ♖g5+ ♔f6 4 ♔g4 ♖a8 5 h5 and only now 5 ... ♖a1! when 6 ♖g6+ ♔f7 7 f4 is very similar to diag 39 variation A.

3   h5   ♖a6

This is forced for if 3 ... ♖h1 4 ♖h4; or 3 ... ♖g1+ 4 ♔h2 ♖f1 5 h6!.

4   ♖h4   ♖h6
5   ♖f4+!   ♔g5
6   ♖g4+   ♔f5

Of course if 6 ... ♔xh5 7 ♖h4+ and 8 ♖xh6+ wins, or 6 ... ♔f6 7 ♖g6+!.

7   ♔h4   ♖h8

If 7 ... ♖a6 8 ♖g5+ ♔f4 9 ♖g6 ♖a1 10 ♖f6+ ♔e5 11 ♖f8 ♖h1+ 12 ♔g5 ♖g1+ 13 ♔h6 and White wins easily by playing ♔h8, h7 and then ♖f4 - g4 freeing the king.

8   ♖g5+ *(38a)*
8   ...   ♔f6

If 8 ... ♔f4 9 ♖g7 ♔f5! (9 ... ♔xf3 10 ♔g5 is simple) 10 ♖g6! (zugzwang) 10 ... ♖a8 (10 ... ♖h7 11 ♖g8!) 11 ♖g5+ ♔f6 12 h6 ♖a1 13 ♖g3 ♖a4+ 14 ♖g4 ♖a1 15 ♔g3 and wins.

9   ♔g4   ♔f7
10   ♖f5+!

Disrupting Black's defence.

10   ...   ♔g7
11   ♔g5   ♖g8
12   ♖f6   ♔h7+

The king finally reaches the h-file, but meanwhile White's pieces have become very active - and the black rook is three moves from g1 where it can disturb White.

13   ♖g6   ♖a8
14   f4   ♖a1
15   ♖e6

But not 15 f5? ♖g1+= (see diag 39 variation B).

15   ...   ♖g1+
16   ♔f6

This position is winning since the pawn on h5 controls g6. Black is quite unable to organise a reasonable defence.

16   ...   ♖f1

Or 16 ... ♖h1 17 f5 ♖xh5 18 ♖e7+ ♔h6 19 ♖e8 ♔h7 20 ♔e6 wins.

17   f5   ♖f2

18 ♖e5 ♖h2 19 ♖e7+ ♔h6 20 ♖e8 ♔h7 21 ♔e6 ♖e2+ 22 ♔f7 ♖a2 23 f6 ♖a6 24 ♔e7 ♖a7+ 25 ♔f8 ♖a6 (note that the h-pawn prevents 25 ... ♔g6) 26 f7 ♖a7 27 ♖c8 ♖a1 28 ♔e7 1-0.

Rook v Rook

R
39

=
B

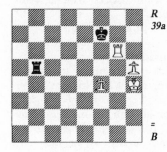

R
39a

=
B

Gligoric - Smyslov
Moscow 1947

Diag 39 is the normal defensive position. Black keeps his rook an a1 so as to be able to check on the fifth rank or the g-file as required.

1 ... ♖b5!?

He can simply pass with 1 ... ♖c1 and if 2 ♔g5 ♖g1+ 3 ♔f5 ♖b1 etc. as in Gligoric - Smyslov.

2 ♖g6+

Now both obvious retreats draw.

A.

2 ... ♔f7

This is what Smyslov played:

3 ♖g5

Another idea is 3 ♔h4 (Kopaev) *(39a)*. White now threatens to *cut* the enemy king decisively with 4 ♖g3, i.e. if 3 ... ♖a5? 4 ♖g3 ♖a1 (4 ... ♖b6 5 ♔g5 ♔g7 6 ♖a3) 5 h6 ♖h1+ 6 ♔g5? ♖a1 7 f5 ♖b1 8 ♖g4! ♖a1 9 ♖h4 ♖g1+ 10 ♔f4 ♖f1+ 11 ♔g4 ♖g1+ 12 ♔f3 ♖g8 13 h7 and wins.

Black lost here since his king was stranded on f7. Instead after 3 ♔h4 ♖b1! is just in time, e.g. 4 ♔g5 ♖g1+ 5 ♔f5 ♖h1 6 ♔g5 ♖g1+ 7 ♔h6 ♖f1 8 ♖g7+ ♔f6! 9 ♖g8 ♔f7 10 ♖g4 ♖h1=; after 11 ♔g5 ♔g7 12 f5 the black king isn't cut off in contrast to the line above.

3 ... ♖b1
4 ♖c5

If 4 h6 ♖a1! 5 ♖h5 (5 ♔f5 ♖a5+; 5 h7 ♖g1+! 6 ♔f5 ♖h1 7 ♖a5 ♔g7!=) 5 ... ♔g8 6 f5 ♔h7= and the black king is very good against the h6-pawn, e.g. if 7 f6 ♖a4+ 8 ♔f5 ♖a5+ 9 ♔e6 ♖a6+!=.

4 ... ♔f6
5 ♖c6+ ♔g7
6 ♔g5 ♖g1+
7 ♔f5 ♖a1

And the game was drawn after a further 27 moves: 8 ♖c7+ ♔h6 9 ♖e7 ♖b1 10 ♖e8 ♔g7 11 ♖e5 ♖a1 12 ♖d5 ♖f1 13 ♖d4 ♖a1 14 ♖d6 ♖a5+ 15 ♔g4 ♖a1 16 ♖e6 ♖g1+ 17 ♔f5 ♖a1 18 h6+ ♔h7 19 ♖d6 ♖a2 20 ♔g5 ♖g2+ 21 ♔f6 ♔xh6! 22 ♔e7+ ♔h7 23 f5 ♖e2+ 24 ♖e6 ♖a2 25 f6 ♖a8!= (diag 36a).

B.

2 ... ♔h7

Perhaps this is even easier: Black doesn't have to worry about diag 39a.

3 f5

The only way to make progress. It doesn't help to have the black king cut off on the h-file, so e.g. 3 ♔h4 and 4 ♖g3 would be ridiculous here.

3 ... ♖b1
4 ♔g5

If 4 f6 ♖b6! 5 ♔h4 ♖a6 6 f7 (6 ♖g7+ ♔h8 7 ♔g5 ♖xf6!) 6 ... ♖a4+ 7 ♖g4 ♖xg4+!=.

4 ... ♖g1+
5 ♔f6 ♖a1
6 ♖g2

If 6 ♔e6 ♖a6+ 7 ♔e5 ♖a5+ 8 ♔f4 ♖a1! 9 ♖e6 ♔g7!=.

Or 6 ♖g7+ ♔h6 7 ♖e7 ♖a6+ 8 ♖e6 ♖a7! as in the main line.

6 ... ♔h6
7 ♖e2 ♖a6+!

And not 7 ... ♔xh5? 8 ♖h2+ ♔g4 9 ♔g6 wins.

8 ♖e6 ♖a7!=

Black is threatening 9 ... ♔xh5 and if 9 ♖e7/e8/e1 9 ... ♖a6+ 10 ♔f7 ♔g5!=.

Summary

This ending is usually defensible. "White" will have to sacrifice his h-pawn to win with the f-pawn. But the ending of rook and pawn against rook with the defending king on the short side will be drawn.

"Black" usually loses if:

a) His king is cut off on the back rank (diags 34, 35);

b) He allows the enemy king to safely reach f7 (see diag 36);

c) He allows the h-pawn to run with his king cut off on the f-file (cf diags 38, 39a).

The correct drawing plan is:

a) To wait, with the rook able to go to h8, until White advances his forces (Diag 38; 2 ... ♜h8!);

b) As soon as White advances his men and is thus unable to put his rook behind the h-pawn. Black should switch his rook to the a1 corner. We are now talking about a position like diag 39.

c) The rook will now be based on a1. Its function is to harry the white king, preventing it from establishing itself on dangerous squares, e.g. g5.

The black king sits on g7, Black answers rook to the seventh checks with ... ♚h6 and ♜g6+ with either ... ♚f7 or ... ♚h7. The latter is perhaps simpler (cf diag 39, variation B).

d) In order to make progress, White must either

d1) Play f5. This is not dangerous with the black king on f7. If it is on h7, Black still defends easily as in diag 37, variation B.

d2) Try h6+. In this case the black king must go to h7 and he can then defend as in diag 37, taking care not to allow the white king to reach f7 i.e. diag 36.

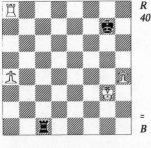

R 40

= B

Problems with Rook's Pawns

White's rook is passively placed *in front of the a-pawn*. Black keeps it there permanently with:

1 ... ♜c4!

Now he can defend precisely as in diag 21. The extra pawn is almost irrelevant, e.g.

2 a5 ♜c5
3 a6 ♜c6
4 ♔f4 ♚h7
5 ♔e5 ♚g7
6 ♔d5 ♜f6
7 ♔c5 ♚h7
8 h5

Of course if 8 ♔b5 ♜f5+! driving the king away from the a-pawn.

8 ... ♚g7

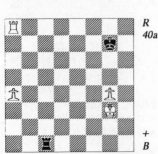

R 40a

+ B

9 h6+ ♚h7!

But not 9 ... ♚xh6? 10 a7 ♜a6 11 ♜h8+; nor 9 ... ♜xh6? 10 ♔b5 ♜h5+ 11 ♔b6 ♜h6+ 12 ♔b7 and wins.

10 ♔b5 ♜f5+
11 ♔c4 ♜f6=

The position is dead since White simply cannot free his rook.

Diagram 40a

Now White can win since his king will find shelter on h5, viz:

1 ... ♜c4
2 ♔h4 ♜d4
3 ♔h5 ♜d5+
4 g5 and wins

R
41

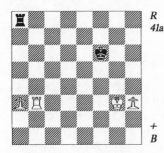

R
41a

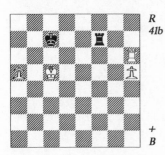

R
41b

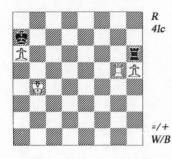

R
41c

=
B

+
B

+
B

=/+
W/B

Gothenburg v Stockholm corr.

Black played:

1 ... ♖a4!

Now White can free his king only at the cost of the h-pawn.

2 ♖f3+ ♔g6
3 ♔f2

The only way to make progress.

3 ... ♖xh4
4 ♔e2 ♖a4
5 ♔d2 ♖a6
6 ♔c2 ♖f6!
7 ♖d3 ♔f7
8 ♔b3 ♔e7
9 ♔b4 ♖d6!=

Diagram 41a

Kopaev 1958

Now White's rook can defend both pawns whilst he activates the king. He is therefore able to win.

1 ... ♖a4
2 ♖f3+ ♔g6

If 2 ... ♔e6 White wins by pushing the h-pawn.

3 ♔f2 ♖e4

Trying to cut off the king from the a-pawn.

4 ♖g3+! ♔f5
5 ♖g4 ♖e6
6 a4 ♖b6
7 ♔g3 ♖b3+
8 ♔h4 ♖a3
9 a5! ♔f6
10 ♖g5 ♖a1
11 ♔h5 ♖a3
12 h4 ♖a4
13 a6!

Again he uses the skewer as after 8 ... ♖a3. Black had to allow this since if his king were on f7 White would play 13 ♖f5+!.

13 ... ♔f7
14 ♖g6 and wins

Diagram 41b

If the black king were on a7 then the position would be completely drawn. But here White is able to free his rook.

1 ... ♖f5+
2 ♔b4 ♖e5

Not 2 ... ♖f4+ 3 ♔b5 ♖f5+ 4 ♔a6, nor 2 ... ♔b7 3 ♖b6+ and 4 ♖b5 or 4 h6.

3 a6 ♔b8

3 ... ♖e4+? 4 ♔c3 ♖e5 5 a7 ♔b7 (or 5 ... ♖a5 6 ♖h8) 6 ♖a6!.

4 ♖b6+ ♔a7
5 ♖b5 ♖e6!

If 5 ... ♖e1 6 ♖f5 ♔xa6 7 ♔c5 ♔b7 8 ♔d6 and White wins since the black king is completely shut out; or 5 ... ♖e4+? 6 ♔a5 ♖e6 7 ♖b7+ ♔a8 8 ♖b6 ♖e5+ 9 ♖b5 etc. (Note that if Black had played 2 ... ♖d5 instead of 2 ... ♖e5 then 5 ... ♖d1 here would still be hopeless after 6 ♖f5 ♔xa6 7 ♔c5 ♔b7 8 ♖d5! and wins.)

6 ♖g5 ♖h6 *(41c)*

For 6 ... ♖xa6? see diag 41b, variation Ai.

When I first looked at this position, I suspected that it might be zugzwang! The point is that:

a) Black cannot take the a-pawn if in answer to ♖g6 he cannot then play ... ♖a5;

b) White is prepared to abandon the a-pawn but only if his king is sufficiently far "east" of Black's.

A.

Thus with Black to move (numbering from diag 41c) i)

1 ... ♖xa6

This fails miserably to

2 ♖a5!

Whilst it is important

generically that 2 Rg6 also wins when Black cannot reply 2 ... Ra5, viz. 2 ... Ra1 3 Kb5! Rh1 (if 3 ... Kb7 4 Rg7+ Kc8 5 h6 etc; or 3 ... Rb1+ 4 Kc6 Rb2 5 Kd7) 4 h6 Kb7 5 Rg7+ Kc8 6 h7 etc.

ii)

1	... Ka8
2	Ra5! Rc6

2 ... Ka7 3 Kc4 Kb6 4 a7!.

3	Kb5 Rh6

Or 3 ... Rc1 4 Kb6.

4	Kc4 Ka7
5	Kd4 etc.

iii)

1	... Kb8
2	Kc5

Zugzwang.

2	... Ka7

If 2 ... Kc8 3 Rg6! Rxh5+ 4 Kb6; or 2 ... Rxa6 3 Rg6! as in Ai.

3	Kd5 Rxa6
4	Ke5 Kb7
5	Kf5 Kc7
6	Rg6 Ra5+
7	Kg4 Kd7
8	h6

and wins by a tempo.

B.

With White to play, simplistic

play fails since Black ends up a vital tempo ahead of Aiii, for example:

i)

1	Kc5 Kb8
2	Kd5 Rxa6
3	Ke5 Kc8
4	Kf5 Kd7
5	Rg6 Ra5+
6	Kg4 Ke7
7	h6 Ra1=

ii)

But White can improve with:

1	Kc5 Kb8
2	Rd5! Rxa6

If 2 ... Ra7 3 Kd4 Kxa6 4 Ke4 Kb6 5 Kf4 Kc6 6 Ra5 Kd7 7 Kg5 and wins cf diag 24c; or 2 ... Re6? 3 Rd6!; or 2 ... Kc7 3 a7 Ra6 (3 ... Kb7 4 Kd4) 4 Rg5 Kb7 5 Rg7+ Ka8 6 Rg8+! Kxa7 7 Rg7+ Kb8 8 Rg6 see var Ai.

And White can now win with:

3	Rd6 Ra1
4	Rf6!!

While 3 Kd4 Re6 4 Re5 Rh6 5 Rc5!! also wins; for both lines see diag 24c.

R 42

Fischer - Geller
Curaçao 1962
Although most normal positions with rook and two pawns v rook are won, there can be some technical problems.

Here Black must be careful not to advance his g-pawn too quickly (see diag 43). But Geller was able to force the win by advancing his e-pawn with the rook *behind* it. This deflected White's forces and Black reached a won position

of rook and g-pawn v rook.

1	Rf8+ Ke6
2	Re8+ Kd5
3	Ra8 Rf7!
4	Kg4 Re7

Now White must blockade the e-pawn.

5	Ra5+ Ke6
6	Ra6+ Kf7
7	Kf3 Re6 (42a)

But not 7 ... e4+? 8 Ke3 Re6 9 Rxe6! Kxe6 10 Kxe4=.

A.

8	Ra8

R
42a

-
W

This is what Fischer actually played.

8 ...	e4+
9 ♔e3	g5
10 ♖a1	♔g6
11 ♖b1	♖e5

Black plans to advance his king and therefore defends his g-pawn to prepare this.

12 ♔d4

If 12 ♖a1 ♔f5 13 ♖f1+ ♔g4 14 ♔d4 ♖a5 15 ♔xe4 ♔g3 and the g-pawn can't be stopped.

12 ...	♔f6
13 ♖e1	

Black threatened 13 ... e3, and if 13 ♔e3 ♔f5 etc. as above.

13 ...	♖a5!
14 ♖xe4	

14 ♔xe4? ♖e5+; 14 ♖f1+ ♖f5 and 15 ... ♖f4.

14 ...	♔f5
15 ♖e8	♔g4
16 ♔e3	♔g3
	0-1

(cf diag 11).

B.

In diag 42a, White could also try:

8 ♖a7+	♔f6
9 ♔e4	

But Black should win by driving White's forces slowly backwards, constantly offering to sacrifice the e-pawn, e.g. 9 ... ♖d6 10 ♖a8 ♖d4+ 11 ♔f3 ♖b4 12 ♖f8+ ♔g5 13 ♖g8 ♖b7 14 ♖e8 ♖b3+ 15 ♔f2 (or 15 ♔e4 ♔g4! 16 ♖xe5 g5 wins) 15 ... ♔f4 16 ♖f8+ ♔g4 17 ♖e8 ♖b2+ 18 ♔e3 g5 19 ♖xe5 ♔h4 20 ♔f3 g4+ etc.

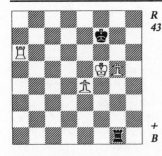

R
43

+
B

Dvoretsky - Filipowicz
Polanica Zdroj 1973

White's g-pawn is too far advanced. Since his king cannot go to g5 he must play with the e-pawn. This makes the win much harder, but not impossible.

1 ...	♖f1+
2 ♔e5	♖e1
3 ♖f6+!	

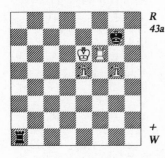

R
43a

+
W

In the game, Dvoretsky played 3 g6+? ♔g7 4 ♔d5 ♖d1+ 5 ♔e6 ♖g1 6 ♖a7+ (if 6 ♔d7 ♖e1 7 ♖e6 ♖e2 8 e5 ♖e1 9 ♖e8 ♖a1!=) 6 ... ♔xg6 7 e5 ♖b1?? (7 ... ♖e1! 8 ♔d6 ♔f5 9 ♖f7+ ♔g6 10 e6 ♖a1!= see diag 5) 8 ♔e7 ♖b6 and White won as in diag 6, viz. 9 e6 ♖b8 10 ♖a1 ♖b7+ 11 ♔d8 ♖b8+ 12 ♔c7 ♖b2 13 ♖e1! ♖c2+ 14 ♔d7 ♖d2+ 15 ♔e8 1-0.

3 ...	♔g7
4 ♔f5	♖f1+

5 ♔e6	♖g1
6 e5	♖a1 (43a)

A.

7 ♖f2?	♔g6
8 ♖d2	

White now threatens 9 ♔e7, e.g. if 8 ... ♖a6+? 9 ♔e7 ♔f5 10 ♖f2+! ♔xg5 11 e6 ♔g6 12 ♖g2+ ♔f5 13 ♔f7 wins.

Black can defend by preventing this with either 8 ... ♖a7 or 8 ... ♖a5, e.g.

8 ...	♖a7
9 ♖d1	♖a5!
10 ♖d2	♖a7
11 ♖d8	♖a6+
12 ♖d6	♖a7
13 ♖d8	♖a6+
14 ♔e7	♔xg5
15 e6	♔g6!

And the position is a theoretical draw (cf diag 5).

B.

7 ♔d5	♖a5+

Alternatively:

a) If 7 ... ♖d1+ 8 ♔c6 ♖c1+ 9 ♔d7 ♖a1 then White can win with either 10 e6 or move simply 10 ♖d6!;

b) or if 7 ... ♖d1+ 8 ♔c6 ♖a1 9 e6 ♖a6+ 10 ♔b7 ♖d6 11 ♔c7 ♖a6 12 e7 ♖a7+ 13 ♔d6 ♖a6+ 14 ♔d5 ♖a5+ 15 ♔c6 ♖a8 (15 ... ♖a6+ 16 ♔b7) 16 ♖e6 ♔f7 17 ♖e5 ♔e8 18 ♔d5 wins easily - White soon forces ♔g6 or if 18 ... ♖a5+ 19 ♔e4 ♖xe5+ 20 ♔xe5 ♔xe7 21 g6 ♔e8 22 ♔e6!

c) or 7 ... ♖g1 8 ♔d6 ♖xg5 9 ♖f1 ♖h5 10 ♖a1! and wins.

    8   ♔d6

8 ♔e4 also wins: 8 ... ♖a1 (8 ... ♖a4+ 9 ♔f5 ♖a1 10 ♖d6) 9 ♖d6 ♔f7 10 e6+! ♔e7 11 ♖b6 and the white king soon reaches g6.

    8   ...   ♖a6+
    9   ♔c7   ♖a7+

Or if 9 ... ♖a5 10 e6 ♖xg5 (10 ... ♖a6 see b) above) 11

♖f7+! ♔g8 (or 11 ... ♔g6 12 ♖f8!) 12 ♖f1 ♖a5 13 e7 and White wins easily because of the bad position of Black's king on g8 - see diag 4c.

    10   ♔b6   ♖a1
    11   e6   ♖c1
    12   ♖f7+   ♔g6

Here Minev gives 13 ♖c7? ♖e1 14 ♖c6 ♔f5!=, but White plays instead:

    13   ♖d7!   ♖c8

13 ... ♖e1 14 e7! ♔xg5 (or 14 ... ♔f7 15 g6+ ♔e8 16 g7 ♖g1 17 ♖d8+) 15 ♔c7 (possible with the rook on d7) 15 ... ♔f6 16 ♔d8.

    14   ♖d5!

But not 14 e7? ♖e8 15 ♔c6 ♔xg5 16 ♔d6 ♔f6 17 ♖a7 ♔f7=.

    14   ...   ♔g7
    15   ♖e5   ♔f8
    16   e7+   ♔e8
    17   g6   ♖c1
    18   ♖g5! and wins

R
44

Doubled Pawns
Suetin - Kholmov
Kiev 1954

This position is drawn, but Black must be much more careful than in the Philidor position, diag 1.

    1   ♖d7+

=
W

A.

    1   ...   ♔f8

This is what Kholmov played.

    2   ♖d6   ♖a7!

The only move. If 2 ... ♖a1 3 ♔f6 ♔g8 4 ♖d8+ ♔h7 5 ♔e7 ♖a7+ (or 5 ... ♖e1+ 6 ♔f7 ♖e4 7 f6 ♖xf4 8 ♔e6 wins) 6 ♖d7 ♖a8 7 f6 ♔g6 8 f7 ♔g7 9 f5.

Or 2 ... ♖a4 3 ♔f6 ♔g8 (3 ... ♔e8 4 ♖e6+ ♔f8 5 ♖b6!) 4

♔g6! wins.

    3   ♔f6   ♖f7+
    4   ♔g5   ♖g7+

And White played on for a few moves, but of course it is quite drawn.

    5   ♖g6   ♖a7
    6   ♖f6+   ♔g7
    7   ♖b6   ♖c7
    8   ♖b8   ♖a7
    9   ♖e8

Threatening 10 ♖e7+!.

    9   ...   ♔f7
    10   ♖h8   ♔g7
    11   ♖h6   ♔f8

Or 11 ... ♖b7 12 f6+ ♔g8 13 ♔g6 ♖g7+!= - but not 13 ... ♖a7?? 14 f7+!.

    12   f6   ♖a1!

The extra pawn is now almost irrelevant.

    13   ♖h8+   ♔f7

Rook v Rook

14	♖h7+	♔f8
15	♔f5	♖b1
16	♖d7	♖a1
17	f7	♖a6
18	♔g5	♖g6+!
	½-½	

B.

Black can also play:

1	♖d7+	♔g8
2	♖d6	♖a4!

This attack on the black pawn is a typical defensive manoeuvre.

3	♖d8+	♔f7
4	♖d7+	♔g8
5	♔e6	

If 5 ♖d4 ♖a6; or 5 f6 ♖a1; or 5 ♔f6 still 5 ... ♖xf4.

5	...	♖xf4
6	♖d8+	♔g7!
7	♖d7+	♔g8
8	♔f6	♖f1
9	♖d8+	♔h7
10	♖f8	♖a1=

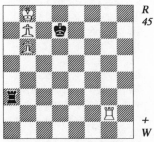

R 45 *Duras 1902*

White cannot win by the normal method of building a bridge (cf diag 3 - the Lucena position) since the b6 pawn obstructs his king. But there is a way:

1	♖d2+	♔e7
2	♖d6!!	

The only way to win. If 2 ♖d5 ♖a1 3 ♔c7 ♖c1+ and the king must go back.

2	...	♖c3

If 2 ... ♔xd6 3 ♔c8 ♖c3+ 4 ♔d8 and wins; or 2 ... ♖a1 3 ♔c7 ♖c1+ 4 ♖c6.

3	♖c6!	♖xc6

Or if 3 ... ♖d3 4 ♖c5 etc.

4	♔a7 and wins	

Rook and Pawn v Rook and Pawn

Although material equality tends to lead to a draw there are many positions in which one side has sufficient positional advantage to force a win.

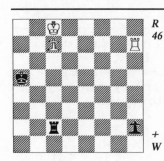

R 46 *Lasker 1890*

White's pawn is supported by his king but Black's is essentially alone. White cannot win immediately since if he brings his king into the open Black will check it away from the pawn. But there is a way:

1	♔b7	♖b2+
2	♔a7	♖c2
3	♖h5+	♔a4
4	♔b6	

Threatening ♖xh2 again.

4	...	♖b2+
5	♔a6	♖c2
6	♖h4+	♔a3
7	♔b6	♖b2+
8	♔a5	♖c2
9	♖h3+	♔a2
10	♖xh2! and wins	

This manoeuvre occurs surprisingly often in actual games.

Rook v Rook

R
47

+
W

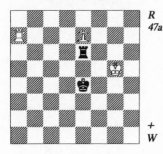

R
47a

+
W

Keres

This is Keres' excellent elaboration of Lasker's theme. (Actually there is even some introductory play. Initial position: ♔b7, ♖a6, e6, h6 v ♔g8, ♖a1, a5, e7: 1 ♔c8! a4 2 ♔d7 a3 3 ♔xe7 a2 4 ♖a7! ♔h8 5 h7 ♔xh7 reaching diag 47.)

| 1 | ♖e8+ | ♔g6 |

The king should go forward. If 1 ... ♔g8/h8 2 e7 ♔g7 3 ♖a3 and 4 ♖+, 5 ♖ 2nd rank wins more easily.

| 2 | e7 | ♔h5 |

If 2 ... ♔g7 3 ♖a3 ♖b1 4 ♖xa2 ♖b8+ 5 ♔d7 White wins since the black rook is only on the b-file.

Or 2 ... ♔h6 3 ♖a3 ♔g5 4 ♖g3+ ♔f4 5 ♖g2 ♔f3 (or 5 ... ♔e3 6 ♖b2!) 6 ♖b2 ♔g3 7 ♖d2 ♔f3 8 ♔d7 ♔e3 9 ♖b2 ♖d1+ 10 ♔c7 ♖c1+ 11 ♔b7 and wins easily since he *queens with check*.

| 3 | ♖a3 | ♔h4! |

If 3 ... ♔g5 4 ♖g3+ and 5 ♖g2 as above; and if 3 ... ♔g4 4 ♔f7 at once - see the main line.

| 4 | ♖a5! |

Now 4 ♔f7? ♖f1+ 5 ♔g6 ♖g1+ 6 ♔h6 ♖e1 does not work - he must wait for the black king to go onto the g-file or the sixth rank.

After 4 ♖a5! Black is in *zugzwang!* If 4 ... ♔h3/♔g3 we will reach the main line a couple of tempi faster.

4	...	♔g4
5	♔f7	♖f1+
6	♔g6	♖e1
7	♖a4+	♔h3!
8	♔f6	♖f1+
9	♔g5	♖g1+
10	♔h5	♖e1
11	♖a3+	♔g2
12	♖xa2+	♔f3
13	♖a7	♖e6!
14	♔g5	♔e4 *(47a)*

Now if 15 ♖d7? ♔e5, White would be in zugzwang so he "loses a move".

15	♖b7!	♔e5
16	♖d7	♔e4
17	♖d1	♔f3
18	♖f1+	♔e2
19	♖f7	♔e3
20	♔f5 and wins

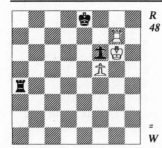

R
48

=
W

Bukic - Muller
Varna 1975

Although Black must obviously lose his pawn, correct defence would still hold the draw.

| 1 | ♖b7 |

If 1 ♔xf6? ♖a6+ 2 ♔g5 ♔f8 would be a simple draw.

| 1 | ... | ♖a6? |

This already loses. 1 ... ♔f8! was correct, trying to get the king to the *short side* of the white f-pawn, e.g. 2 ♖b6 (if 2 ♖f7+ ♔g8! does not help White at all) 2 ... ♖g4+ 3 ♔xf6 ♔g8 4 ♖b8+ ♔h7 5

♔e7 ♖a4= cf diag 5 etc.

| 2 | ♔g7! |

Now the black king will be driven away from the pawns to the *long side*.

2	...	♖c6
3	♖b8+	♔e7
4	♖b1	♖a6
5	♖e1+	♔d8
6	♔f7	♔d7
7	♖d1+	

7 ♖e6 would also win.

| 7 | ... | ♔c7 |
| 8 | ♔e7 | 1-0 |

There's no defence to the threat of 9 ♖d7+ and 10 ♖d6.

Rook v Rook

R
49

=
B

Gligoric - Fischer
Belgrade Ct 1959
Even very strong players can
make mistakes in these apparently simple positions.

1   ...   ♖h3
2   ♖c1   ♖h8?

2 ... ♖h5! drew easily since
even if 3 ♖c5 ♖xc5!= or if 3
♔b7 ♖h4!.

3   ♖c7+!

In the game, Gligoric played
3 ♔xb5? ♖b8+ 4 ♔a4 ♖a8+
5 ♔b3 ♖c8! 6 ♖xc8 ♔xc8 7
♔c4 ♔b8!=, but this move
should win.

3   ...   ♔d8

Or 3 ... ♔d6 4 ♖c6+ ♔d7 5
♔xb5 ♖b8+ 6 ♖b6 ♖h8 7
♖b7+ ♔c8 8 ♔a6 ♖h6+ 9
♔a7 and wins.

4   ♖c5   ♔d7
5   ♔b7!   ♔d6
6   ♖xb5   ♖h7+

If 6 ... ♖h4 White can untangle with 7 ♔a6 or 7 ♔a7.
Black's king can never reach
b8.

7   ♔a6   ♖h8
8   ♖c5   ♖b8
9   ♖c4!

But not 9 ♔a5 ♖a8+ 10
♔b5 ♖b8+ and if 11 ♔a4
♖a8+ 12 ♔b3 ♔d7 13 b5
♖c8!=; or 11 ♔c4 ♖h8! (not
now 11 ... ♔d7? 12 b5 ♖c8 13
b6 winning) 12 ♔b3 ♔d7 13
b5 ♖c8!=.

9   ...   ♔d5
10   ♖h4   ♔c6
11   b5+! and wins

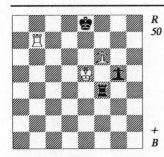

R
50

+
B

"Artificial Shelter"
Kotov - Eliskases
Stockholm 1952
Were it not for the g-pawn,
Black would draw easily. But
he is quite lost, since that
pawn gives the white king
shelter.

1   ...   ♖f2
2   ♔e6!   ♖e2+
3   ♔f5   g4
4   ♔g6!   ♖f2

Or 4 ... g3 5 f7+.

5   f7+   ♔f8
6   ♖b8+   ♔e7
7   ♖e8+   1-0

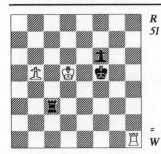

R
51

=
W

Racing
Races with rook and pawn
each occur quite frequently.
Usually they lead to an ending
of rook vs pawn:

Alekhine - Bogoljubow
World Ch 1929
Although White is far ahead
in the race, correct defence
should still lead to a draw:

1   ♖b1

Putting it where it belongs -
behind the passed pawn 1
♖f1+? would merely give
Black a vital tempo.

1   ...   ♖d3+
2   ♔c6   ♖d8
3   b6

A.

3   ...   ♔g4?

This natural looking move,
which Bogolyubow actually
played, leads to a loss.

4   b7   f5

Or 4 ... ♖b8 5 ♔c7 ♖xb7+
6 ♔xb7 f5 7 ♔c6 and wins.

5   b8♕   ♖xb8
6   ♖xb8   f4
7   ♔d5   f3
8   ♔e4   f2

263

9	Rf8	Kg3
10	Ke3	1-0

B.

3	...	Ke4!

This way he will impede the white king on its return journey.

4	b7	

Or 4 Re1+ Kf4 5 Rf1+ Ke5 6 b7 f5 7 Kc7 Rf8 8 b8Q Rxb8 9 Kxb8 f4 10 Kc7 Ke4 11 Kd6 f3=.

We should note here that White can *never force a queen*. If in the last line he played Rd1 - d8, Black would reply ... Rf7+ and ... Rxb7

4	...	f5
5	b8Q	

Or if 5 Ra1 Rb8!.

5	...	Rxb8
6	Rxb8	f4
7	Rb4+	

Or 7 Re8+ Kd4 8 Rf8 Ke3=.

7	...	Ke3
8	Kd5	f3
9	Rb3+	Ke2

But not 9 ... Kf4? 10 Kd4 f2 11 Rb1 and wins.

10	Ke4	f2
11	Rb2+	Ke1
12	Ke3	f1N+

And draws cf diag RN1.

R 52 – B

Gilg - Tartakower
Semmering 1929

Here Black is able to "cheat" by preventing his opponent from racing at all.

1	...	Rg1!

But not 1 ... e1Q? 2 Rxe1 Kxe1 3 Kh7 Kf2 4 h6 Kf3 5 Kh8 Kf4 6 h7 and draws by a tempo.

2	Ra2	Kf3

Now if 3 Rxe2, Black having an extra tempo would win, viz: 3 ... Kxe2 4 Kh7 Kf3 5 h6 Kf4 6 Kh8 Kf5 7 h7 Kg6 8 Kg8 Ra1 9 h8N+ Kf6 etc. (cf diag RP13).

3	Ra3+	Kf4
4	Ra4+	Kg3!
5	Ra3+	

If 5 Re4 e1Q the black king is once again too close.

5	...	Kh4
6	Ra4+	Kg4
7	Ra1	Re4
8	Rh1+	

Or 8 Re1 Re6+.

8	...	Kg4
9	Rg1+	Kf5
10	Re1	Kf6

But not 10 ... Re7? 11 Rf1+!.

11	Kh7	Kg5
12	h6	Re7+
	0-1	

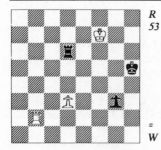

R 53 – W

Korchnoi - Kasparov
London 1983

This very difficult position played a crucial role in the Candidates semi-final match.

1	Rd2	Kg4

1 ... Rd4 to blockade the d-pawn is too slow, viz: 2 Ke6 Rg4 3 Rg2 Kh4 4 Ke5=.

2	d4!	

Not 2 Ke7 Rd4! 3 Ke6 Kf4! shouldering off the white king and winning easily.

2	...	Kf5!

Black's first aim must be to attack the white d-pawn - if he simply ran his own pawn then it would be a simple draw. Black therefore tries to exclude the white king from the struggle, prior to attacking the d-pawn.

If 2 ... Kf3? 3 Ke7 Rd5 (or 3 ... Rg6 4 d5 etc.) 4 Ke6

R
53a
=
B

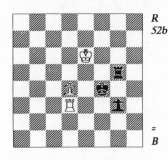

R
52b
=
B

draws easily.

2 ... ♔f4 is a possible compromise move. But after 3 ♔e7 ♖g6 4 ♖g2! ♔e4 5 ♔f7 ♖g4 6 ♔f6 ♔f3 7 ♖xg3+! leads to a draw (see variation Aii below).

In this variation, instead of 4 ♖g2, 4 d5 is also just possible - see Ai below.

    3   ♔e7 *(53a)*

A.

    3   ...   ♖g6

i)

    4   d5?   g2
        and wins

However if the black king were on f4, Black would have to try to win another way:

    4   ...   ♔e5
    5   d6

If 5 ♔f7 ♖f6+ 6 ♔e7 ♖f2 7 ♖d1 g2 8 d6 ♖f1 wins.

    5   ...   ♖g7+
    6   ♔f8

6 ♔e8? ♔e6 7 ♔f8 g2!.

    6   ...   ♖d7
    7   ♖d3!

7 ♖g2? ♔f4 8 ♖d2 ♔e3 9 ♖g2 ♔f3 10 ♖d2 g2 and wins.

    7   ...   ♔f4
    8   ♔e8   g2
    9   ♖d4+!

A good illustration of the power of disruptive checks in rook endings in particular. 9 ♔xd7? g1♕ and now, e.g. 10 ♖d5 would give White excellent drawing chances but this move actually forces a draw.

    9   ...   ♔f5

If the king goes to the e-file then ... ♖g-file will draw, e.g. 9 ... ♔e3 10 ♖g4=.

Black could also try to run his king to h2 but then White draws with a skewer, e.g. 9 ...

♔g5 10 ♖d5+ ♔h4 11 ♖d4+ ♔h3 12 ♖d1 ♖xd6 13 ♖xd6 g1♕ 14 ♖h6+ and 15 ♖g6+=.

    10   ♖d5+   ♔f6

10 ... ♔e6 11 ♖g5 and if 11 ... ♖h7?? 12 ♖g6+.

    11   ♖d1   ♖g7

Or 11 ... ♖h7 12 ♖g1 ♔e6 13 ♔f8=.

    12   ♖g1!

Not 12 ♔f8? ♖h7 and wins; nor 12 d7?? ♖g8 mate!

    12   ...   ♔e6
    13   ♔f8   ♖g3
    14   d7!   ♔xd7
    15   ♔f7=

ii)

    4   ♖g2!   ♔e4

Or 4 ... ♖g7+ 5 ♔f8 ♖g4 6 ♔f7 ♔e4 7 ♔f6 transposes to the text.

    5   ♔f7   ♖g4
    6   ♔f6   ♔f3

Or 6 ... ♔xd4 7 ♔f5.

    7   ♖xg3+!

And White just draws, e.g. 7 ... ♖xg3 8 d5 ♔e4 9 d6 ♖d3 10 ♔e7 (or indeed 10 ♔e6) 10 ... ♔d5 11 d7=.

B.

    3   ...   ♖d5

This is what Kasparov actually played.

    4   ♖d3!!

Luring the black king to a bad square. Not 4 ♖d1 ♔e4 5 ♖g1 ♔f3 6 ♖d1 g2 7 ♔e6 ♖xd4!.

    4   ...   ♔f4
    5   ♔e6   ♖g5! *(53b)*

With the black king on the fifth rank, 5 ... g2 6 ♖d1 ♖xd4 fails to 7 ♖xd4 check.

i)

    6   d5?

The losing move which Korchnoi actually played:

6   ...   ♖g6+!
But not 6 ... g2? 7 ♖d4+!
♔e3 8 ♖d1 and draws.

7   ♔e7
Or 7 ♔f7 g2 8 ♖d1 ♖d6 etc.

7	...	g2
8	♖d1	♔e5
9	d6	♖e6+
10	♔d7	♖xd6+
11	♖xd6	g1♕

and Black soon won.

ii)
But there was still a draw

with:

6	♖d1!	g2

Or 6 ... ♔e4 7 d5 ♖g6+ 8 ♔e7 ♔e5 9 d6 and White is a precise tempo ahead of the game variation Bi above, i.e. if 9 ... ♖e6+ 10 ♔d7 g2 11 ♖e1+= or if 9 ... g2 simply 10 d7=.

7	♖g1	♖g6+
8	♔f7	♖g3
9	d5	♔e5
10	d6!	♔xd6
11	♔f6=	

Rook and Two Pawns v Rook and Pawn

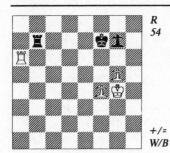

R
54

+/=
W/B

"Bunched Pawns"

Although most positions with the pawns all together are drawn, they require very accurate defence.

Black to play would draw easily with 1 ... g6!, or even 1 ... ♖b4. But with White to play the position is already winning.

    1   **f5!**   **♖b1**

If Black remains passive, White wins as follows: 1 ... ♖c7 2 ♔h5 ♖b7 3 ♖a8 ♖c7 (3 ... ♖b6 transposes to the main line) 4 g6+ ♔f6 5 ♖f8+ ♔e5 6 f6! gxf6 7 ♔h6 ♖c1 8 g7 ♖h1+ 9 ♔g6 ♖g1+ 10 ♔f7. In this position Black resigned in Chekhover - Kazakevic, Odessa 1949; after 10 ... f5 11 g8♕ ♖xg8 12 ♔xg8 the f-pawn is too slow.

Or if 1 ... ♖c7 2 ♔h5 g6+ 3 ♔h6 gxf5 4 g6+ ♔f6 5

♖a6+! leads to a win.

2	♖a7+	♔f8
3	♔h5	♖b6

He must prevent 4 ♔g6.

4	♖a8+	♔f7

If 4 ... ♔e7 5 f6+ gxf6 6 g6 ♖b1 7 g7 ♖h1+ 8 ♔g6 ♖g1+ 9 ♔h7 ♖h1+ 10 ♔g8 f5 11 ♖a7+ ♔e6 12 ♔f8 and wins.

5	g6+	♔e7
6	♖g8	♔f6
7	♖f8+	♔e5
8	f6!!	

8 ♔g5 ♖b1! would only be a draw.

8	...	♖xf6
9	♖f7!	

Black is remarkably helpless.

9	...	♖f5+

Or 9 ... ♔e6 10 ♖xg7 ♖f8 11 ♔h6 ♔f6 12 ♔h7 and wins.

10	♔g4	♖f6
11	♔g5	♖a6
12	♖xg7 and wins	

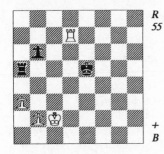

R
55

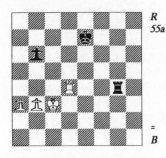

+
B

=
B

Flohr - Szabo
Budapest 1950
With the king badly cut off, White should win quite easily

1	...	♚e6
2	♖d2	♖h5
3	♔b3	♖h4
4	♖d8!?	

By threatening 5 ♖b8 he forces the black king to retreat.

4	...	♚e7
5	♖d5!	♖g4

Black has to wait since if 5 ... ♚e6? 6 ♖b5.

6	♔c3	♖h4
7	b3?	

This is a mistake since White needs b3 for his king and if he makes too many pawn moves White risks some pawn endings being drawn. After 7 b3? I can see no win for White!

The correct plan was 7 ♖d4! ♖h3+ 8 ♔b4 ♖h5 9 ♔b3 ♖g5 (or 9 ... ♖h3+ 10 ♔a4) 10 ♖b4! ♖g6 11 ♔a4 ♔d7 12 ♔b5 ♔c7 13 ♔a6+- as in L. A. Schneider - Romanishin, Buenos Aires Ol 1978, but with flanks reversed.

7	...	♖g4
8	♖d4	*(55a)*

If 8 a4 ♖h4 9 ♖d4 ♖h5 10 ♖b4 ♖c5+ 11 ♔c4 ♔d6!= as in the main line.

| 8 | ... | ♖g5! |

In Flohr - Szabo White won easily after 8 ... ♖g3+? 9 ♔c4 ♖g5 10 ♖d5+- ♖g4+ (or 10 ... ♖g3 11 a4 ♖h3 12 b4 ♖g3 13 ♔b5 ♖g4 14 ♖h5) 11 ♔b5 ♖g3 12 b4 ♖g6 (12 ... ♖xa3 13 ♔xb6) 13 ♔a6 ♖h6 14 b5 1-0.

| 9 | ♔c4 | |

If 9 ♖b4 ♖c5+ (not 9 ... ♖g6? 10 ♔c4) 10 ♖c4 (10 ♔d4 ♖c6 also holds) 10 ... ♖a5! (not 10 ... ♖h5? 11 ♖c6 when White wins) and if 11 ♖c6 ♔d7! 12 ♖xb6 ♔c7=.

9	...	♖c5+!
10	♔b4	

Or 10 ♔d3 ♖a5 11 a4 ♖h5.

10	...	♖h5
11	a4	♖g5
12	♔c3	♖c5+!
13	♖c4	♔d6!!
14	♖xc5	♔xc5
15	b4+	♔c6

And the pawn ending is drawn cf diag P31.

R
56

In this typical position Black can draw if he is sufficiently careful; but there is definitely some play left in the position.

| 1 | ♔g5 | |

A.

| 1 | ... | ♖c5! |

Although this is the only move, it draws relatively simply:

| 2 | ♖b7+ | ♔f8! |

But not 2 ... ♔e6 3 f5+ ♔xe5 4 ♖e7+ ♔d6 5 ♖xf7 and wins.

| 3 | f5 | |

If 3 ♔f6 ♖c6+; or 3 ♔h6 ♖c6+ 4 ♔h7 f6!=.

3	...	♖xe5
4	♔f6	♖e1
5	♖xf7+	♔g8!

Of course it must go to the *short side.*

6	♖g7+	♔f8
7	♖a7	♔g8
8	♖a8+	♔h7
9	♔f7	♖b1=

B.

1	...	♖c1?
2	♖b7+	♔f8
3	f5	♖h1 *(56a)*

Rook v Rook ♖ V ♜

R
56a

+
W

i)

Now if he forces events immediately White will only draw.

    4   ♖b8+   ♔e7

Not 4 ... ♔g7 5 f6+ ♔h7 6 e6! and wins.

    5   f6+?   ♔d7!

    6   ♖b7+   ♔e8!

But not 6 ... ♔e6 7 ♖e7+ ♔d5 8 ♖e8! and the threat of 9 e6 is decisive.

    7   ♖b8+   ♔d7

    8   ♖f8   ♖g1+

    9   ♔h6

Or if 9 ♔f4 ♖f1+ 10 ♔g3 ♔e6=.

    9   ...   ♔e6

    10   ♖e8+   ♔f5

    11   ♔h7   ♖g2

    12   ♖g8

This position arose with colours reversed in a clock simultaneous game Karpov - King. Black played 12 ... ♖h2+ and lost quickly. Instead, correct is:

    12   ...   ♖a2!

    13   ♔g7

White cannot improve on this - if 13 ♖e8 ♖g2!.

    13   ...   ♔xe5

    14   ♔xf7

If 14 ♖e8+ ♔f5 15 ♖e1 ♖a7 16 ♖e7 ♖a6!=; or 14 ♖f8 ♔f5; 15 ♖xf7 ♖g2+!=.

    14   ...   ♔f5!

    15   ♖f8   ♖a7+

    16   ♔g8   ♔g6

    17   f7   ♖b7=

This drawing variation is quite significant. If White contrived, in a position like diag 56, to advance his f-pawn to f6 early on then we might well transpose into it eventu-

ally.

ii)

Instead in diag 56a, White should quietly "pass":

    4   ♖a7!!

This is zugzwang!

    4   ...   ♖h2

a) If 4 ... ♔e8 5 ♔f6 ♖h6+ 6 ♔g7 ♖h5 7 ♖xf7 ♖g5+ 8 ♔h6! wins;

b) 4 ... ♔g8 5 ♖a8+ ♔g7 (or 5 ... ♔h7 6 ♔f6 etc.) 6 f6+ ♔h7 7 e6! and wins;

c) 4 ... ♖h7 5 f6 (but not 5 e6?? f6+) 5 ... ♔e8 6 e6!.

d) Finally if the rook moves from the h-file then 5 ♔f6 will win at once.

    5   ♖a8+   ♔e7

    6   f6+   ♔d7

    7   ♖f8   ♖g2+

If 7 ... ♔e6 8 ♖e8+ ♔d5 9 e6; or 7 ... ♔h7 8 ♔g4 ♔e6 (8 ... ♔c7 9 ♖e8 ♔d7 10 ♖e7+ and 11 e6) 9 ♖e8+ ♔d5 10 ♔g5 ♖h1 11 e6 and wins.

    8   ♔f4!

With the rook a rank further away as in variation Bi, this achieved nothing, but here it wins since Black cannot afford to give another check.

    8   ...   ♔e6

Or 8 ... ♖f2+ 9 ♔e3 and 10 ♖xf7+ etc.

    9   ♖e8+   ♔d5

    10   ♖d8+

Only not 10 e6? fxe6 11 f7 ♖f2+ etc.

    10   ...   ♔c6

Or 10 ... ♔e6 11 ♖d6 mate!

    11   ♖f8 and wins

R 57

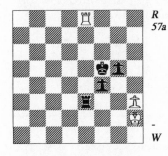

R 57a

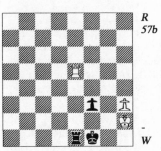

R 57b

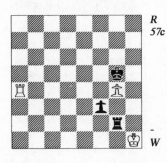

R 57c

Wedberg - Speelman
Gothenburg 1982
This position is drawn. Black has only got two real winning tries and both fail after the natural:

   1   ♖b2!

A.
To play the king to e3 and then exchange rooks.

White can allow this since the resulting pawn ending is drawn, e.g. 1 ... ♚e4 2 ♖c2 ♚e3 3 ♖b2 ♚d3 4 ♖a2 ♖d2+ (4 ... f3+ 5 ♚g3 does not help Black) 5 ♖xd2 ♚xd2 6 ♚f3 ♚d3 7 h4! gxh4 8 ♚xf4=.

B.
To play ... ♚h4 (this must be prevented but that is not too difficult): 1 ... ♚g6 2 ♖c2 ♚h5 3 ♖c8! (forced: if he allowed 3 ... ♚h4 he would be lost) 3 ... ♖a2+ 4 ♚f3! ♖a3+ (or 4 ... ♖h2 5 ♖h8+ ♚g6 6 ♖g8+ ♚f6 7 ♖h8=) 5 ♚g2 ♖g3+ 6 ♚h2. Now Black can try but there's really nothing much to do, e.g. 6 ... ♖e3 7 ♚g2 ♚g6 8 ♖f8 ♖e2+ 9 ♚f3 ♖h2 10 ♖h8 ♚g7 11 ♖h5 ♚f6 12 ♖h8 ♖h1 13 ♚g2 ♖d1 14 ♖f8+ ♚g7 15 ♖f5 ♖d2+ 16 ♚f3 ♖d3+ 17 ♚g2 ♚g6 ½-½ (Smyslov - Keres, 1949).

However my opponent, who was extremely tired, blundered with:

   1   ♖e8?   ♖g3+
   2   ♚h2   ♖e3 *(57a)*

This position is lost since Black has gained a vital tempo to advance his king.

A.

   3   ♖f8+

This was played in the game.

   3   ...   ♚e4
   4   ♖g8

Or 4 ♖e8+ ♚f3 5 ♖g8 ♖e2+ and:

a) 6 ♚g1 ♖g2+ 7 ♚f1 (7 ♚h1 g4!) 7 ... ♚h2 8 ♚g1 ♖xh3 9 ♖xg5 ♖g3+!;

b) 6 ♚h1 ♚e3 7 ♖e8+ ♚f2 8 ♖g8 f3 9 ♚h2 (9 ♖xg5 ♖e1+ transposes to the game) 9 ... ♚e3+ 10 ♚g3 ♖g2+ mate!

   4   ...   ♖e2+
   5   ♚g1   ♚e3!
   6   ♖xg5   ♖e1+
   7   ♚h2   f3
   8   ♖e5+   ♚d2

Not 8 ... ♚f2? 9 ♖a5= (cf diag 5 etc).

   9   ♖f5   ♚e2
   10   ♖e5+   ♚f1 *(57b)*
   11   ♖a5

If 11 ♖f5 f2 12 ♚g3 ♖e3+ 13 ♚g4 (or 13 ♚h2 ♚e1 14 ♚g2 ♖e2) 13 ... ♚g2 14 h4 ♖g3+! wins.

Or 11 ♖d5 (to control the d-file but it is too near the black king) 11 ... f2 12 ♖d2 ♖e8 13 ♖a2 (or 13 ♚g3 ♖e3+ 14 ♚g4 ♚g1! as in the game) 13 ... ♚e1 14 ♚g3 f1♕ 15 ♖a1+ ♚e2 16 ♖xf1 ♚xf1 17 h4 (or 17 ♚g4 ♚g2 etc) 17 ... ♖e4! and wins (cf diag RO10).

   11   ...   f2
   12   ♖a2   ♖d1!

The only move to win.

   13   ♚g3   ♖d3+
   14   ♚g4   ♚e1!
             0-1

But not 14 ... ♚g1? 15 ♖a1+! f1♕ 16 ♖xf1+ ♚xf1 17 h4 and White draws by a tempo. Now however White must take at once - if 15 ♖a1+ ♚d1; and so Black wins by a tempo (cf diags RP5-14).

B.

3	♖a8	♖e2+
4	♔g1	f3
5	♖a4	♖g2+!

But not 5 ... ♖e4? 6 ♖a2 ♔f4 7 ♔f2 ♖e2+ 8 ♖xe2 fxe2 9 h4! and draws.

6	♔h1	

If 6 ♔f1 ♖h2 Black wins easily, e.g. 7 ♖a5+ ♔g6 8 ♖a3 ♖xh3 9 ♔f2 ♔h5 etc.

6	...	g4
7	hxg4+	

Or 7 ♖xg4 ♖xg4 8 hxg4+ ♔xg4 etc.

7	...	♔g5! *(57c)*

Black must preserve the pawn to provide shelter for his king and avoid stalemate.

8	♖a1	♖e2!

But not 8 ... ♔h4? 9 ♖f1! ♔g3 10 ♖g1 ♔f2 11 ♖a1= since Black has to take the g-pawn: 11 ... ♔xg4 12 ♖a2+ ♔g3 13 ♔g1 ♖b4 14 ♖g2+! etc.

9	♖f1	

If 9 ♔g1 ♔f4 10 g5 ♔g3 11 g6 ♖g2+ and wins; or 9 ♖g1 ♔f4 10 g5 f2 etc.

9	...	♔f4
10	g5	♔g3
11	♖g1+	♔h3
12	♖f1	f2
	and wins	

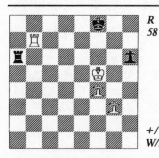

*R
58*

*+/=
W/B*

Smyslov and Levenfish analysis by Minev
With his pawns further back it is easier for White to man-oeuvre his king to h5. More-over, the black king is badly cut off on the back rank.

A.
White to play wins since he can get his king safely to h5

1	♔g4!	♖a3

If 1 ... ♖g6+ 2 ♔h4 ♖f6 (or 2 ... ♔g8 3 g4 and 4 ♔h5 etc) 3 ♔h5 ♔g8 4 ♖b5 ♔g7 5 f5 ♔h7 6 g4 ♔g7 7 ♖b7+ ♔g8 8 ♖e7 and 9 ♖e6 follows.

*R
58a*

*=
B*

2	♖h7	♖a6
3	♔h5	♖a3
4	♔h4	♖a6
5	g4	♔g8
6	♖b7	♖g6
7	♔h5!	

But not 7 f5? ♖g5= when White cannot evict the rook.

7	...	♖a6
8	f5	

And there is no defence to the threat of ♖e7 - e6; or if 8 ... ♔f8 9 ♖h7.

B.
Black to play seems just able to draw:

1	...	♖a3

If 1 ... ♔g8 2 ♖e7 ♖a3 3 ♔g4 transposes to the main line; or if 3 g4 ♖g3! 4 ♖e6 ♔h7! seems to draw - but not 3 ... ♖a4 4 ♖e4 ♖a6 5 ♖e6 etc.

2	♔g4	

2 g4, cutting the king's path to h5, simplifies the defence considerably: 2 ... ♖a6 3 ♖d7 ♖b6 4 ♔e5 ♖g6! 5 g5 hxg5 6 f5 ♖g7!=.

2	...	♔g8
3	f5	

If 3 ♔h4 ♖f3 stops both pawns from advancing but 4 ♖e7! (zugzwang) 4 ... ♖f1! (not 4 ... ♖a3? 5 g4, nor 4 ... ♔f8 5 ♖h7; and 4 ... ♔h8 is also bad: 5 ♔g4 ♖a3 6 f5! ♖a5 - or 6 ... ♔g8 7 ♔h4! - 7 f6! and White wins - see the note after diag 58a) 5 ♔g4 (or 5 ♔h5 ♖f3!) 5 ... ♖f2 6 ♖e6 ♔h7! 7 ♔f5 ♖g2 just holds.

3	...	♖a5!
4	♖e7	

If 4 f6 Rg5+! 5 Kf4 Rg6 6 Kf5 Rxg3=.

Or if 4 Rd7 Rb5 5 Kf4 Rb4+! 6 Ke5 Rb3! 7 g4 (7 Ke6 Re3+= as in the main line) 7 ... Rb4 8 Rd4 (if 8 g5 hxg5 9 f6 g4 10 Ke6 Rb8! just draws - cf diag 50 - here Black's a vital tempo up) 8 ... Rb7 9 Ke6 Kg7= cf diag 57, variation A.

4 ... Rb5
5 Kf4 (58a)

Now White is threatening 6 f6. If Black remains passive with 5 ... Ra5? he will lose: 6 f6 Rb5 (if 6 ... Rg5 7 g4 anyway) 7 g4 Rg5 8 Ra7 (zugzwang) 8 ... Rb5 (if 8 ... Kf8 9 Rh7, or 8 ... Kh8 9 Ra8+ and 10 f7; or 8 ... Rg6 9 Kf5) 9 Rg7+ Kh8 (9 ... Kf8 10 Rh7 etc.) 10 g5! hxg5+ 11 Kg4 and we have diag 57c with colours reversed.

Instead Black can now play:
5 ... Rb4+!
6 Ke5 Rb3!
7 Kf4

If 7 Ke6 Re3+! 8 Kf6 Rxg3=; but not 7 Ke6 Rxg3? 8 Re8+ Kh7 9 f6 and wins (see diag 57b but with colours reversed).

Or if 7 g4 Rb4 8 Ke6 Re4+!=.

7 ... Rb4+!
8 Ke4 Rb5!

Much the simplest. If 8 ... Rb7? 9 f6 Kf7 10 Kf5 h5! 11 Re5 (11 Re7+ Rxe7 12 fxe7 h4!=) 11 ... Ra7 12 Kg5 h4! 13 gxh4 Ra1 then the ending of rook, f- and h-pawn against rook appears to be drawn since the f-pawn is too far advanced; but that would be a ludicrous way to defend in practice.

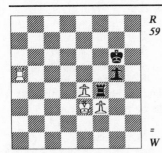

R 59

Although the e-pawn looks a little dangerous, Black is able to defend successfully. Note that his king is on the *short* side of the e- pawn, e.g.
1 Rb5
Or 1 Ra6+ Kg7 2 e5 Rf5 3 Ke4 Rf4+ 4 Kd5 Rxf3=.

1	...	Rf8
2	Rb3	Rf4!
3	Kd4	g4!
4	fxg4	Rxg4
5	Rf3	Rg1
6	e5	Ra1=

=
W

RP 60

Kotov - Pachman
Venice 1950
Black avoided diag 60 since it seems hopeless. But there is a nice resource
1 ... Rc6!!
If 1 ... Kf5? 2 Rf7+ Ke6 3 Rf6+ is indeed the end.
2 Rxg6+
If 2 Ke4 Rc4+ 3 Ke3 Kf5 4 Rf7+ Kg4 5 Rf6 Ra4=.
Or 2 Kg4 Kd5 3 Rf7 (3 f5 Rc4+) 3 ... Ra6 4 Rf6 Rxf6 5 gxf6 Ke6 6 Kg5 Kf7=.
2 ... Kf5
3 Rxc6 stalemate
White could try 3 Rh6/g7/g8. But 3 ... Rc3+ and 4 ... Kxf4 draws easily in all cases.

=
B

Rook v Rook

Rook and Connected Passed Pawns v Rook and Pawn

Although connected passed pawns are immeasurably more valuable than a single one, the player with material disadvantage can sometimes draw if his pawn is far advanced – or, in some circumstances, even win!

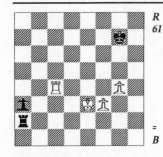

R
61

=
B

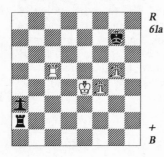

R
61a

+
B

In diag 61 Black has to make the big decision of where to put his rook.

A.

1	...	♖h2?
2	♖a4	a2

This loses since he cannot effectively impede the advance of the white pawns, e.g.

3	♖a6	♔f7
4	g5	♔g7
5	♔e4	♔f7
6	f4	♔g7
7	f5	♖e2+
8	♔f3	♖b2
9	♖a7+	♔f8
10	♔f4	♖c2
11	f6 and wins

B.

1	...	♖a1!

This is effective since the rook maintains the ability to "go sniping" at the right moment.

2	♔f4	a2
3	♖a4	

If 3 ♖c2 ♔f6 4 g5+ ♔g6 5

♖f2 (5 ♖c6+ ♔g7 6 ♖a6 ♔f7 transposes back to the column) 5 ... ♖b1! 6 ♖xa2 ♖b4+ 7 ♔e5 ♔xg5 (or indeed 7 ... ♖b5+!) 8 ♔g2+ ♔h6 9 f4 ♖b5+=.

3	...	♔f6
4	♖a6+	♔g7
5	g5	♔f7

White now has no useful move e.g.

6	♔f5	♖f1
7	♖a7+	♔g8!
8	♖xa2	♖xf3+
9	♔g6	♖f8=

Diagram 61a

If however we move White's forces up a rank, then Black is lost, viz.

1	...	♖a1
2	♔f5	a2
3	♖a5	♔f7
4	♖a7+	♔f8
5	♔f6	

And the threat of mate gives White a priceless tempo.

5	...	♔e8
6	f5 etc	

R
62

=
W

Maroczy - Tarrasch
San Sebastian 1911

Here we are involved in a pure race. Black will win the white rook for his h-pawn and then try to get his king back in time to draw. This, rather, is what *ought* to happen. But Maroczy blundered with:

1	♔c6?

1 ♖xh2! was correct, winning by a tempo: 1 ... ♔xh2 2 ♔a6 ♔g3 3 b5 ♔f4 4 b6 ♔e5

5 b7 ♖b1 6 ♔a7 ♔d6 7 b8♕+ ♖xb8 8 ♔xb8 etc.

1 ♔a6 is also sufficient to win; though White must take some care after 1 ... ♖a4! 2 ♖xh2! ♖xb4! 3 ♖h5 etc.

1	...	♖c1+!
2	♔b6	

Now if 2 ♔b5 h1♕ 3 ♖xh1 ♖xh1 Black with an *extra tempo* can hold the draw.

2	...	♖c4!

Threatening to interpose

with 3 ... ♖h4.

    3   ♖xh2   ♖xb4+

    4   ♔c5   ♖a4!
         ½-½

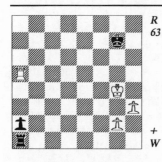

R
63

+
W

In contrast to diag 61, here the black rook is totally ineffective. The reason is simple: as long as White leaves his g-pawn *on the second rank* it will provide perfect shelter for his king. And if the black rook moves then ♖xa2 will *defend* the g-pawn.

Therefore White wins automatically e.g.

    1   h4   ♔g6
    2   ♖a6+   ♔f7
    3   ♔g5 etc.

Diagram 63a
Of course if neither of

White's pawns were on the second rank then it would be drawn.

    1   h4   ♔g6
    2   ♖a6+   ♔g7
    3   ♔g5   ♖g1=

cf diag 61 variation B.

But White's shelter could equally well be on the h-file:

Diagram 62b

    1   ♔h5   ♔f7
    2   g4   ♔g7
    3   g5   ♔f7
    4   ♔h6 etc.

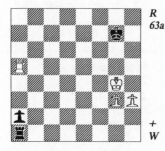

R
63a

+
W

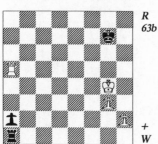

R
63b

+
W

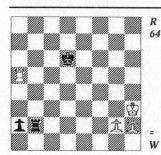

R
64

=
W

Reshevsky - Alekhine
AVRO 1938

The black rook is much better here than in the previous diagram. It both exerts pressure along the seventh rank, thus slowing down White's advance; and threatens to build a bridge on the a-file gaining, the vital tempo with a flank check.

These possibilities are sufficient for Black to achieve a

draw:

    1   g4   ♔c6!

But not 1 ... ♔e6? 2 ♔g3 ♔f6 3 h3 ♔g6 4 ♔h4 ♖h2 5 ♖a6+ ♔g7 6 g5 ♔h7 7 ♔g4 intending 8 h4, 9 ♔h5 etc.

With his rook on the seventh rank Black has no way of opposing the slow advance of White's kingside in a close phalanx. Therefore he must seek counterplay:

    2   ♔g3

Or 2 g5 ♖b5=.

2	...	♚b6
3	♖a8	♚b5
4	h3	

White's advance is of necessity extremely slow. If 4 g5 ♖b3+ and the king cannot cross the fourth rank, i.e. if 5 ♔f4?? ♖b4+ and 6 ... ♖a4.

| 4 | ... | ♚b4 |
| 5 | ♔f4(?) | |

5 ♔h4 gives Black slightly more trouble. But with the white king blocking his own pawns, Black actually has time to promote the a-pawn, e.g. 5 ... ♚b3 6 g5 ♖b1 7 g6 a1♕ 8 ♖xa1 ♖xa1 9 ♔h5 (or 9 ♔g5 ♖g1+ 10 ♔f6 ♖f1+ 11 ♔e7 ♖e1+ 12 ♔f7 ♖f1+ 13 ♔g8 ♖h1=) 9 ... ♚c4 10 g7 ♖g1 11 ♔h6 ♚d5 12 ♔h7 ♔e6 13 g8♕+ ♖xg8 14 ♔xg8 ♔f6=.

| 5 | ... | ♖c2! |

Threatening to win by building a bridge with ... ♖c4+ and either 7 ... ♖c3+ - a3 or 7 ... ♖c5+ - a5 depending on the white king.

| 6 | ♖b8+! | ♚c3 |
| 7 | ♖a8 | ♚b4! |

½-½

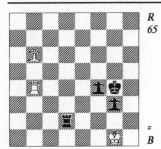

R 65
=
B

Kostic - Réti
Gothenburg 1920

Although Black's pawns are extremely menacing, the powerful b-pawn ought to have saved the day:

| 1 | ... | ♚g5! |

If 1 ... ♔h3 2 ♖xf4 ♖d1+ 3 ♖f1 ♖xf1+ 4 ♔xf1 ♔h2 5 b7 g2+ 6 ♔e2 g1♕ 7 b8♕+=.

Or 1 ... ♔f3 2 ♖b3+ ♚e4 (2 ... ♔e2 3 ♔g2!) 3 ♖b4+ ♚f5 4 b7 f3 5 ♖f4+!=.

Or 1 ... ♔f5 2 b7 f3 3 ♖f4+!= as above.

| 2 | b7? | |

Allowing 2 ... f3 after which Black is winning. 2 ♖b5+ or 2 ♖b3 would have drawn.

| 2 | ... | f3 |
| 3 | ♖b1 | |

With the black king on g5 3 ♖f4+ is of course impossible.

3	...	♖g2+
4	♔f1	♖h2
5	♖b5+	

Or 5 ♔g1 (5 ♔e1 ♖h1+ x b1) 5 ... f2+ and 6 ... ♖h1+.

5	...	♚g4
6	♔e1	♖e2+!
7	♔d1	g2

0-1

White can only give one more check: 8 ♖b4+ ♚h3, end.

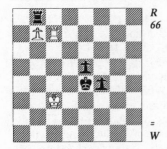

R 66
=
W

Matanovic - Velimirovic
Skopje 1975

Obviously any attempt to queen the b-pawn by advancing the king would be much too slow. So White is forced to defend with his king in front of the black pawns. Normally this would lose rather easily but here, due to a minor miracle, White succeeded in holding the draw - and indeed the position does appear to be drawn.

1	♔d2	♚f3
2	♔e1	e4
3	♖h7!	e3

If 3 ... ♔e3 4 ♖c7 f3 5 ♖c3+ ♔f4 6 ♖c7 will hold. We should note that if Black advances his f-pawn then the king's most convenient refuge on f4 will be on a square where White can queen b8♕

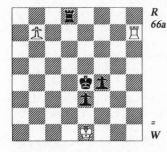

R 66a

= W

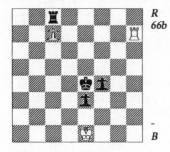

R 66b

- B

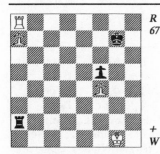

R 67

+ W

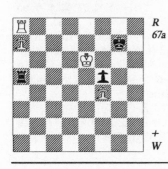

R 67a

+ W

with *check*. Therefore, on general grounds it ought to be better to advance the pawns the other way round.

4 &h3+ &e4
5 &h7 &d8 (66a)

If 5 ... &f8 6 &f1! (not 6 &e2? f3+ and queens by force; nor 6 &e7+ &f3 7 &h7 &g8; nor when if 6 ... f3 7 &e7+ &d4 8 &d7+ &c5 9 &e7 (or 9 &f7 e2+ 10 &f2! &e8 11 &e1!=) 9... e2+ 10 &f2=.

6 &h4!!

The only move, pinning the f-pawn.

If 6 &h6? &g8 7 &f1 f3 8 &e6+ &d4 9 &d6+ &e5 10 &b6 &b8 and Black wins by playing ... &f5 to stop b8& being check and then activating his king, e.g. 11 &b4 &f5 12 &f1 &h8 13 &b5+ &e6 14 &b6+ &d7 15 &g1 f2+ etc.

6 ... &g8
7 &f1 &d3
8 &h7!

Only not 8 &xf4? e2+ 9 &f2 &g1!.

8 ... &e4
9 &g7 &h8
10 &h7 &b8
11 &e1 ½-½

We have returned to diag 66a. As demonstrated, Black has no good way to proceed.

We should note that White was only able to draw because he had a "b-pawn" which controlled the whole queenside!

Diagram 66b
Black wins very easily with:
1 ... &a8!

After which White has no conceivable defence.

If the pawn were instead on the a-file then with the king on e4 exposed to a8& check, White would be alright. But in that case, Black ought to have arranged to play f3 instead of ... e3 when the extra possibility of ... &c8 at the right moment must win.

"R + 2 v R + 1" Isolated Pawns

If White can win the black f-pawn then he will win automatically by advancing his own. On f6, Black will face a hopeless choice (cf diag 20):

a) He can play 1 ... &xf6 allowing 2 &f8+;

b) He can play 1 ... &f7 allowing 2 &h8 &xa7 3 &h7+;

c) He can play 1 ... &h7 allowing 2 f7 and 3 f8&.

Therefore the position turns on whether White can win the black pawn. This he is easily able to do using zugzwang:

The king easily advances past the black rook, e.g.

1 &f1 &h7
2 &e1 &g7

3 &d1 &h7
4 &c1 &g7
5 &b1 &a6
6 &b2 &h7
7 &b3 &g7
8 &b4 &h7
9 &c5 &a1
10 &d6

Of course if 10 &b6 &b1+.

10 ... &a5
11 &e6?!

11 &e7 would win a little faster.

11 ... &g7 (67a)

This is a position of *zugzwang* - obviously Black to move would lose more quickly. With the precise pawn structure White is able to "lose a move".

12 &d6! &h7

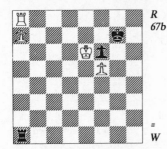

R
67b
=
W

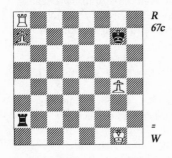

R
67c
=
W

If 12 ... ♖a6+ 13 ♔e5 ♖a5+ 14 ♔e6 etc.

13	♔e7	♖a6

Or 13 ... ♔g7 14 ♔e6.

14	♔f7	♖a4
15	♔e6!	♖a5
16	♔f6	

And wins as noted above by simply advancing the f-pawn.

Diagram 67b

Here White cannot win the black pawn and so it's drawn, i.e. he reaches ♔e6 with the black king on g7 and the rook somewhere, e.g. a1.

Now if

1	...	♖a2?
2	♖d8!	♖a6+
3	♖d6	♖xa7
4	♖d7+	♖xd7
5	♔xd7	♔h6
6	♔e7! and wins	

But Black can draw with either 1 ... ♖a6+ or 1 ... ♖e1+. Perhaps the latter is simpler. Black gives a large number of checks and then returns ... ♖a1 when the white king is safely off the sixth rank.

c) With f3 v f4 the position is also drawn (as is f2 v f3).

White can force his king to f5, but on f5 it does not interfere with the black king which can happily shuffle ... ♔g7 - h7=.

Note that in contrast in diag 67a the king *on f6* prevented ... ♔g7.

With f6 v f7 White wins automatically by forcing his king to e7 and then taking the f-pawn. Black is completely powerless to prevent this.

Diagram 67c

Despite the fact that Black has no pawns this is completely drawn:

1	g5	♖a3
2	g6	♖a2!

(Of course not 2 ... ♔xg6?? 3 ♖g8+.) And White can do nothing.

This would equally apply if we moved the g-pawn to the h-file:

1	h5	♖a3
2	h6+	♔h7!=

cf also diag 20.

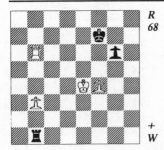

R
68
+
W

Levenfish - Botvinnik
Leningrad 1937

In diag 67 and its offshoots the white "a-pawn" was already on the seventh rank. This meant that the plan of supporting the pawn with the king was completely doomed. And so White had to play on the kingside.

Here, in contrast, the b-pawn is far back. White is therefore able to undertake the active plan of sacrificing his kingside to queen the b-pawn. With the white pieces already active this led to a win.

1	b4	♖e1+
2	♔d4	♖f1
3	♔e5	♖e1+
4	♔d6	♖e4?!

This loses rather tamely. It seems to me that Black would complicate White's task with 4 ... ♖d1+ 5 ♔c7 ♖d4 6 b5 ♖b4!. Now if 7 ♖b8? ♖xf4 the white rook is misplaced. But instead he could play simply 7 ♔d6! and if 7 ... ♖xf4 8 ♖c6 transposes back into the game.

5	b5	♖xf4

Or if 5 ... ♖b4 6 ♖b7+ ♔f6 7 ♖b8 ♔g7 8 b6 ♖xf4 9 ♖c8

♖b4 10 ♖c6 ♔h6 11 ♔c7 ♔h5 12 b7 ♖xb7+ (White threatened 13 ♖b6) 13 ♔xb7 g5 14 ♔b6 and White wins by a tempo, e.g. 14 ... ♔g4 15 ♔c5 ♔f3 16 ♔d4 g4 17 ♔d3 g3 18 ♖f6+ etc; or 14 ...g4 15 ♔c5 g3 16 ♔d4 g2 17 ♖c1 etc. All the same that would have been closer than what actually occurred:

6　♖c6　1-0

Black resigned in view of 6 ... ♖b4 7 b6 g5 (if 7 ... ♔f6 8 ♔c5+) 8 ♔c7 g4 9 b7 g3 10 b8♕ ♖xb8 11 ♔xb8. Here there is no way for Black to support his pawn and so White can simply go and win it with his rook.

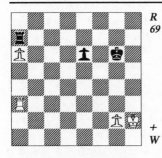

R 69

Capablanca - Marshall
St. Petersburg 1914
Here the white rook is *actively placed behind the passed pawn.* As a result the position is a trivial win.

1	♖a5!	♔f6
2	g4	♔e7
3	♔g3	♔d6
4	♔f4	♔c7
5	♔e5	♔d7
6	g5	♔e7
7	g6	♔f8
8	♔xe6	♔e8
9	g7	♖xg7
10	a7	♖g6+
11	♔f5	1-0

Black could equally well have resigned in the diagram position.

+ W

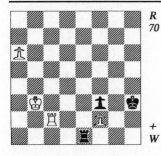

R 70

Alatortsev - Chekhover
Tbilisi 1937
Although White's pawn is far advanced, Black has counterplay against the f2-pawn. White can win the black rook for his passed pawn; but he must act with great care in order to win the rook in a position where his king is sufficiently near the kingside.

1	a7	♖e8
2	♖a2	♖a8
3	♔c4	♔g2
4	♔c5!	

But not 4 ♔b5? ♖xa7 5 ♖xa7 ♔xf2 6 ♔c4 ♔e2! 7 ♖a2+ ♔e3! 8 ♖a3+ ♔e2 9 ♔d4 f2 10 ♖a2+ ♔e1 11 ♔e3 f1♘+!= cf diag RN1.

4　　　♖c8+

4 ... ♔f1 5 ♔b6 ♖e8 transposes to the main line. Now with the white king one tempo nearer the kingside 4 ... ♖xa7 fails by a tempo.

5　♔b6　♖e8 *(72a)*

White now faces a problem.

+ W

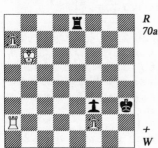

R 70a

If 6 a8♕? ♖xa8 7 ♖xa8 ♔xf2 is drawn, or 6 ♔b7 ♖e7+ 7 ♔b6 ♖e8!

White would like to play 6 ♖c2 so as to threaten 7 ♔b7 ♖e7+ 8 ♔b8!, but then Black has 6 ... ♖e6+! 7 ♔b7 (or 7 ♔c7 ♖e8! 8 ♔b7 ♖e2!) 7 ... ♖e2!! 8 ♖xe2 fxe2 9 a8♕ *(not check)* 9 ... e1♕; or 8 a8♕ ♖xc2 is also clearly drawn.

Given that 6 ♖c2 is not yet feasible White finds another move:

6　♔c6!!

This is zugzwang!

6　...　♔f1

If 6 ... ♖a8 7 ♔b7, or 6 ... ♖e6+ 7 ♔d7! winning at once in each case. Or 6 ... ♖h8 7 ♔b7 ♖h7+ 8 ♔b6 ♖h8 (8 ... ♖h6+ 9 ♔c5 ♖h8 10 a8♕! wins with the king on c5) 9 ♖c2 ♖e8 10 ♔c7! transposes back to the main line.

7	♔b7	♖e7+
8	♔b6	♖e8
9	♖c2!	

+ W

Now with the black king on the eighth rank if 9 ... ♖e6+ 10 ♔b7 ♖e2 11 ♖c1+! wins, so:

    9   ...   **♔g2**

    10   **♔c7!**

Another zugzwang.

    10   ...   **♖e7+**

If 10 ... ♔moves 11 ♔b7 wins; or 10 ... ♖a8 11 ♔b7; or

10 ... ♖h8 still 11 ♔b7 ♖h7+ 12 ♔b8 wins.

    11   **♔b8**   **♖e8+**

Or 11 ... ♖e2 12 ♖xe2 fxe2 13 a8♕ *check* and wins (cf diag QP2).

    12   **♖c8**   **♖xc8+**

    13   **♔xc8**   **♔xf2**

    14   **a8♕**

And Black soon resigned.

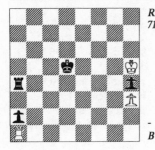

RP 71

Yukhtman - Chistiakov
USSR 1956

This position is easily won. Black can use zugzwang to force his king across the fifth rank without losing his h-pawn.

    1   ...   **♔e6!**

    2   **♔h6**

If 2 ♖e1+ ♔f6! 3 ♖f1+ ♔e5 4 ♖a1 ♔f5!, or 2 ♔g5 ♔e5, or 2 ♔g6 ♖a5! winning easily in all cases.

    2   ...   **♔f5?**

This was the game continuation, but 2 ... ♔f6! 3 ♔h5 ♔f5 zugzwang would win on the spot.

    3   **♔h5**   **♔f4?**

3 ... ♔f6! 4 ♖f1+ (4 ♔h6 ♖a5) 4 ... ♔e5 5 ♖a1 ♔f5!.

    4   **♔xh4**

And even now Black can still win with:

    4   ...   **♖a5!**

The game staggered on 4 ... ♔f3+?? 5 ♔g5 ♔g3 6 ♔f5 ♔xh3 7 ♔e5 ♔g3 8 ♔d5 ♔f3 9 ♔c5 ♔e3 10 ♔b5 ♖a8 11 ♔c4! ♔d2 12 ♔b3 ♖b8+ 13 ♔a3?? (13 ♔c4! ♖b2 14 ♖h1=) 13 ... ♔c2! 0-1. Rook endings are difficult!

    5   **♖f1+**   **♔e3**

    6   **♖a1**   **♔f3!**

    7   **♖f1+**   **♔g2**

    8   **♖a1**   **♖a4+**

    9   **♔g5**   **♔xh3**

And Black, a tempo ahead of the note above, wins easily, viz. 10 ♔f5 ♔g3 11 ♔e5 ♔f3 12 ♔d5 ♔e3 13 ♔c5 ♔d3 14 ♔b5 ♖a8 15 ♔b4 ♔c2 etc. (See also diag 24d).

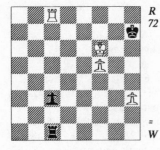

R 72

Petrosian - Karpov
USSR Ch 1976

This position is very intimately bound up with the theory of rook, f- and h-pawn against rook (cf diags 34 - 39a).

By sacrificing the c-pawn at the right moment Karpov just succeeded in drawing.

    1   **h4**

If 1 ♔f7 ♖f1! 2 f6 ♖a1 3 ♖xc3 (or 3 ♖c7 c2) 3 ... ♖a7+ and Black draws since the white rook can't interpose on

the c-file, i.e. if 4 ♔e6 ♖a6+ 5 ♔e7 ♖a7+ 6 ♔d6 ♖a6+ 7 ♖c6 ♖xc6+! 8 ♔xc6 ♔g6=.

Note how Black first lured the f-pawn to f6 before activating his rook.

    1   ...   **♖c2!**

Much the safest but I suspect that 1 ... c2 would also just hold, viz: if 2 h5 ♖a1 3 ♖xc2 ♔h6 threatens to start checking and if, e.g. 4 ♖e2 ♖a6+! 5 ♔e6 ♖a7!= (see diag 39a variation B after 8 ... ♖a7).

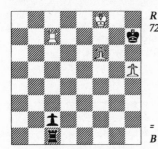

R
72a

=
B

2	h5	♜c1
3	♔f7	♜c2
4	f6	♜c1
5	♔e7	c2

Now that the f-pawn has advanced to f6 it is far more vulnerable to the black king and so c2 is both necessary and possible.

6	♔f7	♔h6
7	♜c5	♔h7
8	♜c6	♔h6
9	♔f8	♔h7!
10	♜c7+	*(72a)*

If 10 f7 ♜a1! 11 ♜xc2 ♜a8+= since again he cannot interpose on the c-file.

| 10 | ... | ♔h8! |

But not 10 ... ♔h6? 11 f7 ♔h7 (11 ... ♜a1 12 ♔g8!) 12 h6 ♔xh6 13 ♔g8 ♜g1+ 14 ♔h8 ♜f1 15 ♜c6+ ♔h5 16 ♔g7 ♜g1+ 17 ♔h7 ♜f1 18 ♜c5+ ♔h4 19 ♔g6 ♜g1+ 20 ♔h6 ♜f1 21 ♜c4+ ♔h3 22 ♔g6 ♜g1+ 23 ♔h5 ♜f1 24 ♜c3+.

This is an old Lasker manoeuvre (cf diags 46, 47).

11	f7	♜a1!
12	♜xc2	

If 12 ♔e7 ♜e1+ 13 ♔f6 ♜f1+ 14 ♔g6 ♜g1+ 15 ♔h6, Black has an exquisite draw: 15 ... c1♛+! 16 ♜xc1 ♜g6+! forcing stalemate.

12	...	♜a8+
13	♔e7	♜a7+

And Karpov drew easily though he had to take a modicum of care:

14	♔f6	♜a6+
15	♔g5	♜a5+
16	♔g4	♜a4+
17	♔g3	♜a3+
18	♔g2	♔g7
19	♜f2	♔f8
20	♜f5	

Or 20 ♜f6 ♜a5 21 h6 ♜h5=.

| 20 | ... | ♜a6! |

Only not 20 ... ♜a7? 21 h6 ♜xf7 22 h7.

| 21 | ♔g3 | ♜h6 |

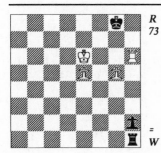

R
73

=
W

Capablanca - Spielmann
Berlin 1938

Here Black draws much more easily than in the previous position. The main reason for this is the position of Black's pawn. Since it is on the h-file when White takes it, his rook will never be able to interpose against flank checks.

1	♜g6+	♔h7
2	♜f6	♔g7

But not 2 ... ♜g1? 3 ♜h6+ ♔g7 4 ♜xh2 ♜xg5 5 ♜f2! and wins (cf diags 43, 43a).

3	♜f2	♔g6
4	♜g2	♔h7

4 ... ♜a1 would also draw: 5 ♜xh2 ♜a6+ 6 ♔d5 ♜a5+ 7 ♔d6 ♜a6+ 8 ♔c7 ♔xg5=, but Black has no reason to force events.

5	♔e7	♔g7
6	e6	♔g6

But not now 6 ... ♜a1? 7 ♜xh2 ♜a7+ 8 ♔d8 ♜a8+ 9 ♔c7 ♜a7+ 10 ♔b6 ♜e7 11 ♜e2 and wins.

| 7 | ♜f2 | ♔g7 |

Or 7 ... ♜a1 transposing to the game with the king on g6. This is playable.

8	♜d2	♔g6
9	♔d7	♜a1!
10	♜xh2	♜a7+
11	♔c8	

The best try: otherwise it will have to go to the b-file to stop the checks.

| 11 | ... | ♜e7 |

Or 11 ... ♔xg5 12 ♔d8 ♔f6 13 ♜h6+ ♔g7=.

12	♜e2	♔f5!
13	g6	♜xe6=

Rook v Rook

♖ V ♜

More Pawns - "Theoretical Positions"

"Theoretical positions" with a larger number of pawns generally fall into two types.

a) All the pawns on one side of the board - "White" has an extra pawn or two;

b) There are an equal number of pawns on one side of the board - "White" has an extra passed pawn on the other side.

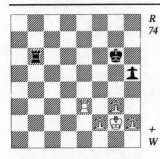

R 74

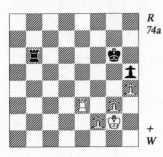

R 74a

+ W

This is a very simple technical win. White's plan, which is unstoppable, is to create two connected passed pawns, e.g.

1   ♖e5   ♖a6
2   h3   ♖a4

White threatened 3 g4.

3   ♖d5   ♖b4
4   ♖d6+ ♔g7

If 4 ... ♔f5 5 h4! (threatening 6 ♖h6) 5 ... ♖b5 6 ♖h6 ♔e4 7 ♖g6 ♖b8 8 ♖g5 ♖h8 9 f3+ and White wins easily.

5   ♖e6   ♖a4
6   ♔f3   ♖a3+

Or 6 ... ♖b4 7 ♖e5 ♔g6 8 g4 etc.

7   ♔f4   h4

If 7 ... ♖a2 8 ♔g5 is simplest; or 7 ... ♖a4+ 8 ♔g5 ♖a5+ 9 ♔h4.

8   ♔g4! and wins

Note that White won with absolutely no "mess" whatsoever.

Diagram 74a

Now the plan of h3 and g4 does not exist, but White still wins without fuss e.g.

1   f3

Now he has to play to obtain h- and g-pawns which involves a little more care. Of course 1 ♔f3 is also good.

1   ...   ♖b2+
2   ♔h3   ♔f5
3   ♖a3   ♖b6!

If 3 ... ♖b5 or 3 ...♖f2 then 4 ♖a6! wins easily.

4   ♖d3!

But not 4 ♖a5+ ♔g6 5 g4? hxg4+ 6 fxg4 ♖b3+ (5 ♖e5 ♖b3! 6 ♔g2! ♖a3 etc).

4   ...   ♖a6

If 4 ... ♖f6 5 ♖d5+ ♔g6 6 ♔g2 and 7 g4; or 4 ... ♔e5 5 ♖d8 ♔f6 6 ♖g8 and wins.

5   ♖d5+   ♔g6
6   g4   hxg4+

If 6 ... ♖a3 7 ♖xh5 ♖xf3+ 8 ♔g2 etc.

7   fxg4

And with the rook on d5 ready to interpose, White wins easily.

7   ...   ♖a3+
8   ♔g2   ♖a2+

Or 8 ... ♖b3 9 ♖f5 -f3 etc.

9   ♔f3   ♖a3+
10 ♔e4   ♖a4+
11 ♖d4   ♖a6
12 ♔e5 etc.

cf diags 27-31.

Perhaps White has some even easier way to win diag 74a but we can see already how a weakening of White's pawn structure complicates the win.

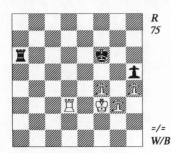

R
75

=/=
W/B

Speelman 1984

Now White has no viable pawn break since if 1 g4 hxg4+ 2 ♔xg4 we get the notorious ♖f+h v ♖.

It would appear that this position is drawn - certainly if there is a win it is extremely difficult, e.g.

A.

1	♖d5	♖a3+
2	♔g2	♖a2+
3	♔h3	♔g6
4	f5+	♔f6
5	♖d6+	

Or 5 ♖d8 ♖a5!.

5 ... ♔g7!

Now 5 ... ♔xf5? 6 ♖h6 wins.

6 ♖d7+

Or 6 f6+ ♔g6=.

6 ... ♔h6!

Again the only move. If 6 ... ♔f6 7 ♖h7; or 6 ... ♔g8 7 f6 and ♖g7+ -g5 or 6 ... ♔h8 7 f6 (threatening 8 ♖d8+, 9 f7) 7 ... ♖f2 8 ♖d5!.

But now White has no way of exchanging the f- for Black's h-pawn and so the position is drawn.

B.

1	♔e4	♖e6+!
2	♔d5	♖a6

2 ... ♖e1 is also good.

3 ♖c3 ♖a5+

And now:

a) 4 ♔c6 ♖a6+ 5 ♔b5 ♖a1 6 ♖c6+ ♔g7! 7 ♖c5 (7 f5 ♖f1) 7 ... ♔h6! 8 f5 ♖a3 9 ♔c6 (9 f6 ♖f3 10 ♖c6 ♔h7!) 9 ... ♖xg3 10 ♔d6 ♔g7 11 ♔e6 ♖e3+ 12 ♔e5 ♖a3 13 f6+ ♔g6! 14 ♖g5+ ♔h6 15 ♖d5 ♔g6!= (cf diag 5) etc;

b) 4 ♔d4 ♖a4+ 5 ♖c4 (or 5 ♔e3 ♖a6) 5 ... ♖a3 6 ♖c6+ ♔f7 7 ♖c3 ♖a4+ 8 ♔d5 (8

♔e3 ♖a6! 9 ♖d3 ♔f6!) 8 ... ♖a5+ 9 ♔d6 ♖a6+ 10 ♖c6 ♖a3 11 ♔e5 ♖xg3!? (or simply 11 ... ♖a5+) 12 ♖c7+ ♔g8! 13 f5 ♖g4 14 ♔e6 ♖e4+! 15 ♔f6 ♖xh4 16 ♖g7+ ♔f8 17 ♖d7 (or ♖a7) 17 ... ♔g8 18 ♖d8+ ♔h7 19 ♔e7 ♖e4+ 20 ♔f7 ♖a4 21 f6 ♖a7+ 22 ♔e6 ♖a6+ 23 ♖d6 ♖a1 24 ♖d7+ ♔g6= (cf diag 5 - note that here Black has an extra file to check on).

Black to move should simply wait with 1 ... ♖b6 and if 2 ♖a3 ♔g6 is now possible. With the white rook on d3 he must avoid:

1	...	♔g6?
2	♖d5	♖a3+

If 2 ... ♖a4 3 ♖d6+ ♔f7/g7/h7 4 f5! or 3 ... ♔f5 4 ♖h6 wins.

Or 2 ... ♖b6 3 ♔e4!.

3 ♔e4

Now White has a tempo since if 3 ... ♖xg3 4 ♖g5+.

3 ... ♔h6

If 3 ... ♔f6 4 ♖g5! followed by f5, ♔f4 - f3 - g2 - h3 and White finally wins the h-pawn whilst defending his g-pawn.

Or 3 ... ♖a4+ 4 ♔e5 ♖a3 5 f5+! is clearly no worse for White than the main line.

4	♖d3	♖a4+
5	♔e5	♖a5+
6	♔e6	♖a6+

Or 6 ... ♔g6 7 ♖d5 ♖a6+ 8 ♔e5 etc.

7	♖d6	♖a3
8	f5	♖xg3

8 ... ♔g7 9 f6+ ♔g6 10 ♔e7 ♖a7+ 11 ♖d7 ♖xd7+ 12 ♔xd7 ♔f7 13 ♔c6 ♔e6 14 f7 ♔xf7 15 ♔d7 ♔f6 16 ♔d6 ♔f5 17 ♔e7 ♔g4 18 ♔f6 ♔xg3 19 ♔g5 and wins.

9	♔e7+!	♔h7	
10	f6	♖f3!	

Or 10 ... ♖e3+ 11 ♖e6 ♖f3
12 ♔f8! ♖a3 13 f7 ♖a8+ 14
♖e8 ♖a7 15 ♖d8 ♔g6 16
♖d6+ ♔h7 17 ♔e8 wins.

11	♖d8!	♖e3+
12	♔f8	♔g6
13	f7	♖f3

14	♖d6+	♔h7
15	♖d5!	

15 ♔e7?? ♔g7=; 15 ♔e8
♖e3+! 16 ♔f8! ♖f3 17 ♖d5.

15	...	♔g6
16	♖g5+	♔f6
17	♔g8	♔e7
18	♖g7 and wins	

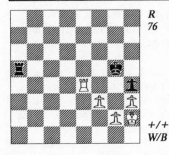

R 76

+/+ W/B

Speelman 1984
Somewhat paradoxically, this is a rather easy win. The reason is that White's rook can now operate on the eighth rank.

A.

White to move:

1	♖e8!	♖a4

If 1 ... ♖b5 2 ♖g8+ ♔f6 (or 2 ... ♔h5 3 ♖h8+ ♔g5 4 f4+!) 3 ♖g4 ♖h5 and with the rook so passive White wins easily: 4 ♔g1 ♔f5 5 ♔f2 ♖h8 6 ♔e3 ♖e8+ (White threatened 7 f4) 7 ♖e4 ♖g8 (7 ... ♖h8 8 f4 ♖a8 9 ♖e5+ ♔g6 10 ♖g5+ ♔h6 11 ♔f3 ♖a2 12 ♖g8 ♖a3+ 13 ♔f2 ♖a2+ 14 ♔g1 and wins) 8 ♖f4+! ♔e5 9 ♖g4 ♖h8 10 f4+ ♔f5 11 ♔f3 and wins.

2	♖e5+	♔f6

Or 2 ... ♔f4 3 ♖h5 ♔e3 4 ♖g5 ♖a8 5 ♖g4 ♖h8 6 ♔g1 ♖h5 7 ♖e4+ ♔d3 8 ♔f2 ♖h8 9 ♖a4 ♖h7 10 f4 ♖f7 11 ♔f3 etc.

3	♖e4	♖xe4
4	fxe4	♔e5
5	g4!	♔f4

If 5 ... hxg3+ 6 ♔xg3 ♔xe4

7 ♔g4! wins, or 5 ... ♔xe4 6 ♔g2 etc.

6	♔g2	

Also 6 ♔g1!.

6	...	♔xe4
7	♔f2	♔f4
8	♔f1!	♔e5
9	♔e1	

And the pawn ending is winning, viz: 9 ... ♔d4 10 ♔f2 ♔e4 11 ♔e2 ♔f4 12 ♔d3 ♔e5 13 ♔e3 ♔f6 14 ♔f4 ♔g6 15 ♔e4! (15 g5? ♔h5=) 15 ... ♔f6 16 ♔d5 ♔g5 17 ♔e5 ♔g6 18 ♔f4 and wins (cf diag P23).

B.

Black to move:

1	...	♖a8
2	♔g1	♖b8
3	♔f2	♖b2+
4	♖e2	♖b8
5	♖e5+	♔g6

5 ... ♔f4 6 ♖h5 ♖b2+ 7 ♔g1 ♔g3 8 ♖g5+ wins.

6	♖e4	♔g5

If 6 ... ♖b2+ 7 ♔g1 ♖b1+ 8 ♔h2 ♔g5 9 ♖e8!; or if 6 ... ♔h5 still 7 f4.

| 7 | f4+ | ♔f5 |
| 8 | ♔f3 and wins | |

R 78

+ B

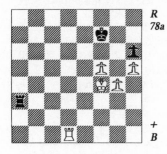

R 78a

+ B

Speelman 1984

If White can get his king out then he will win fairly easily (see diag 77a). This isn't surprising since diag 75 is only just drawn.

   1   ...   **♔h7**

1 ... ♖f3 2 ♖d7+ ♔g8 (2 ... ♔f6 3 ♖h7 ♔e5 4 ♖xh6 ♔f4 5 ♖a6) 3 ♖d1 ♔g7 4 ♖g1 practically transposes. But not e.g. 1 ... ♖b3? 2 f6+! ♔f7 3 ♖d7+ ♔xf6 (or 3 ... ♔g8 4 ♖d8+!) 4 ♖h7 and wins easily.

   2   **♖d1**   **♔g7**
   3   **♖g1**   **♔f6**
   4   **♖g3**   **♖a1**
   5   **♖e3**   **♖h1+**
   6   **♔g3**   **♔g5**

If 6 ... ♖g1+ 7 ♔f3 ♔g5 8 ♖e7! transposes; or 7 ... ♖f1+ 8 ♔g2 ♖f4 9 ♖e6+ ♔g5 10 ♖g6+ ♔h4 11 f6 ♖a4 12 ♔f3 and wins.

   7   **♖e7!**   **♖g1+**
   8   **♔f3**   **♖xg4!**
   9   **♖g7+**   **♔xh5**
   10   **f6**

This is why the rook went to e7 and not e8.

   10   ...   **♖g6**

If 10 ... ♖a4 11 f7 White wins comfortably, viz. 11 ... ♖a3+ 12 ♔e4 ♖a4+ 13 ♔d5 ♖a5+ 14 ♔c6 ♖a6+ 15 ♔b7 ♖f6 16 ♔c7 ♔h4 17 ♔d7 etc.

   11   **f7**   **♖xg7**
   12   **f8♕**

And White is winning. The best move must be:

   12   ...   **♔g6**

Now Black is threatening 13 ... ♔h7 with a known draw (cf diag QR18). But the

white king crosses the g-file with:

   13   **♔g4!**   **♔h7+**
   14   **♔h4**

with a theoretical win (cf diag QR19).

      Diagram 76a
   1   **♖d6**   **♖a4+**
   2   **♔e5**

Since the black king gets cut off on the back rank, White can simply play with the f- and h-pawns. Not 2 ♔g3 ♔g7 (2 ... ♖a3+? 3 ♔h4 ♔g7 4 f6+ wins) 3 f6+? ♔f7 4 ♖d7+ ♔xf6 5 ♖h7 ♖a6!! 6 ♖xh6+ ♔g5=.

   2   ...   **♖xg4**

Obviously Black cannot do better than this.

   3   **♖f6+**   **♔e7**

3 ... ♔g7 4 ♖g6+ ♖xg6 5 hxg6 but not 5 fxg6??= (cf diag 19a).

   4   **♖xh6**

And White wins fairly easily (cf diags 34, 35 and 38a). For example:

   4   ...   **♖g1**

If 4 ... ♔f7 5 ♖f6+ ♔e7 6 ♖a6 etc; or 4 ... ♖h4 5 ♖h7+ ♔f8 6 ♔f6 ♔g8 7 ♖g7+ ♔h8 8 ♖a7 ♖h1 9 ♔f7! ♔h7 (9 ... ♖xh5 10 ♔g6!) 10 f6 ♖xh5 11 ♔f8+ wins.

   5   **♖h7+**   **♔f8**
   6   **♔f6**   **♔g8**
   7   **♖d7**   **♖b1**

Or 7 ... ♖h1 8 ♖d8+ ♔h7 9 ♔e6 etc.

   8   **h6**

And we have a winning position similar to diag 35.

Rook v Rook

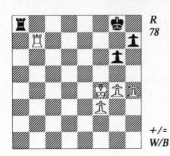

R 78

+/=
W/B

This ending is normally drawn unless there is a good reason why not.

Although Black's king is cut off on the back rank in diag 78, with the move he draws quite easily. White to play however, can force the win.

A.
White to play:

1	♔g5	♖a3
2	♔h6	♖xf3
3	♖g7+	♔f8
4	♔xh7	♖h3
5	♔xg6	♖xh4
6	g5	

and White wins (cf diag 11).

B.
Black to play:

1	...	♖a5

Cutting off the white king. 1 ... ♖f8+?! and 1 ... h6?! also seem okay, but this is the most thematic and sensible move.

Note that if the white rook were on e7 then 1 ... h6? would already be very dubious after 2 ♔e5 and if 2 ... ♖a5+ 3 ♔f6 there are no flank

checks - with the rook on b7 if 1 ... h6 2 ♔e5 ♖a5+ 3 ♔f6 ♖a6+ 4 ♔e7 should still hold.

2	♖d7	♖b5

Now 2 ... h6 is an alternative aiming always to answer h5 with ... g5.

3	♔e4	

White can also try 3 ♖e7 ♖a5 4 h5 gxh5 5 g5, but then 5 ... ♖a4+ 6 ♔g3 h6! draws easily enough.

Or 3 ♖d6 ♔g7 4 h5 gxh5 5 g5 ♖b4+ 6 ♔e3 ♖b3+ 7 ♔f2 ♖b5 8 f4 ♖b3! 9 ♖h6 ♖a3 10 ♖xh5 ♔g6 11 ♖h6+ ♔f5 12 ♖xh7 ♔xf4 13 g6 ♖a8=.

3	...	♖a5
4	♖d5	♖a7
5	♔e5	

Again 5 h5 is possible; but even 5 ... gxh5?! (5 ... ♔g7) 6 ♖xh5 is drawn - albeit Black would have to be a little more careful after this capture.

5	...	♔f7!
6	♖c5	♖e7+
7	♔d6!?	♖e3
8	♖c7+	♔g8

Not 8 ... ♔f6 9 g5+ ♔f5 10 ♖f7 mate.

9	f4	♖e4
10	f5	♖xg4=

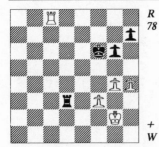

R 78

+
W

Szabo - Keres
Moscow 1956
As we saw, Black to move would be fine after simply 1 ... ♔f7 allowing his king to be cut. But White to move can cut the king the other way with

1	♖c7!	h6

Or 1 ... h5 2 g5+ ♔e6 3 ♖g7 ♔f5 4 ♖f7+ ♔e5 5 ♖f6 ♖d6!? 6 f4+ ♔d5 7 ♖xd6+ ♔xd6 8 ♔f3 ♔e7 9 ♔e4 ♔e6 10 f5+ gxf5+ 11 ♔f4 ♔f7 12 ♔xf5 ♔g7 13 ♔e5 etc. (see di-

ag P23).

2	♖h7	♖d6

Or 2 ... h5 3 g5+! etc. as in the note above.

3	h5!	

No doubt 3 ♖xh6 ♔g7 4 g5 would also win in the end, but this is much simpler.

3	...	♔g5
4	♖g7	♔h4

4 ... ♔f4 5 ♖xg6 ♖d2+ ♔h3 is even easier for White.

5	♖xg6	♖d2+
6	♔f1	♔g3

And White won easily: 7

♖f6 ♖a2 8 ♔e1 ♖h2 9 ♔d1
♖g2 10 ♔c1 ♖h2 11 ♔b1 ♖g2
12 ♖xh6 ♔xf3 13 ♖g6 ♔e4

14 h6 ♖h2 15 g5 ♔d3 16 ♖g7
♔c3 17 h7 ♔b3 18 ♖b7+ 1-0.

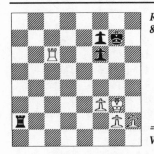

R
80

Suetin - Kholmov
USSR 1954
Although Black's pawns are
doubled they are perfectly
good for defensive purposes.

1	h4	♖b2
2	♖c5	♖a2
3	♔h3	♖b2
4	g4	♖b4
5	h5	♖a4
6	♔g3	♖b4
7	♔f2	♖a4
8	♔e3	♖b4
9	♖d5	♖a4
10	♖d4	♖a5
11	f4	

11 ♔f4 does not achieve

anything since with the king
on f4 White cannot oppose
rooks on the fifth rank.

| 11 | ... | ♖b5 |
| 12 | ♔e4 | f5+!? |

Black could also play 12 ...
♖a5 13 ♖d5 ♖a6 14 ♔f5 ♖b6
15 g5 fxg5 16 fxg5 ♖b8!.

13	gxf5	♔h6
14	♖d7	♔xh5
15	♖xf7	♔h6
16	♖d7	♖a5
17	♖d5	♖a6
18	♔e5	♔g7
19	♖d7+	

and Black drew easily (see
diag 44 for the continuation).

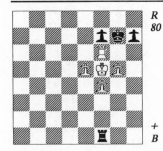

R
80

Gligoric - Euwe
Zürich Ct 1953
This position is a theoretical
win. Black has two possible
defensive ideas.

**A. Passive from behind the
pawns.**
This is the plan which Euwe
actually adopted:

1	...	♖f1
2	♖c6	♔f8
3	♖c8+	♔g7
4	♖d8!	

This is zugzwang! Black is
forced to reduce the distance
between his rook and the
white king and pawns.

| 4 | ... | ♖f2 |

If 4 ... h6 5 gxh6+ ♔xh6 6
♖g8 and White wins by 7
♖g4 and 8 ♔f6.

Or if 4 ... ♖a1 5 ♖d7 ♖a6 (5
... ♔f8 6 ♔f6 ♖a6+ 7 ♖d6; or
5 ... ♖e1 6 ♖e7!; or 5 ... ♖a5 6
♔g4 ♔f8 7 ♖d8+ ♔g7 8 f5!)
6 ♔g4 h6 7 f5! ♔g8 8 ♖d8+

♔h7 9 g6+ fxg6 10 f6! and
wins. These lines with 4 ...
♖a1 are an inferior version of
B (see below). Black hasn't got
time to both put his king on
f8 and get the rook to the best
possible square.

| 5 | ♖d1! | ♖f3 |

Or 5 ... ♖a2 6 ♖d7 etc. as
above.

6	♔e4	♖f2
7	♔e3	♖a2
8	f5!	♖g2

Or 8 ... ♖a7 9 ♔e4 ♖b7 10
♖d8 etc.

| 9 | ♖d7 | ♖xg5 |

Or 9 ... ♔f8 10 f6 ♔e8 11
♖e7+ ♔f8 12 ♖a7 ♔e8 13
♖a8+ ♔d7 14 ♖f8 ♔e6 15
♖e8+ ♔f5 16 e6! and wins.

10	♔f4	♖g1
11	e6	♖f1+
12	♔e5	♖e1+
13	♔d6	h5
14	♖xf7+	♔g8
15	♔e7	

And Euwe resigned in view

of 15 ...h4 16 ♔f6 h3 17 ♖g7+ ♔h8 18 ♖g3 etc.

B. Flank pressure

1	...	♖a1
2	♖c6	♖a4
3	♖c7	♔f8

Remember that having chosen variation A Black would not reach even this relatively favourable position.

4	♔g4	♖a1

Or 4 ... ♖a5 5 ♔f3 ♖a3+ 6 ♔e4 ♖a4+ 7 ♔e3 ♖a3+ 8 ♔d4 ♖a4+ 9 ♖c4 ♖a1 10 f5 ♖g1 11 ♔d5 ♖xg5 12 f6 ♔e8 13 ♔d6 ♔d8 14 ♖a4 and wins.

5	f5!	♖g1+

And White wins by first sheltering his king on c8:

6	♔f4	♖f1+
7	♔e4	♖e1+
8	♔d5	♖d1+
9	♔c6	♖c1+
10	♔d7	♖d1+
11	♔c8	♖d5
12	f6!	♖xe5

And then forcing the exchange of rooks to reach a dead won pawn ending:

13	♔d7	♖d5+
14	♔c6	♖d8
15	♖d7	♖a8
16	♔b7	♖e8
17	♔c7 and wins	

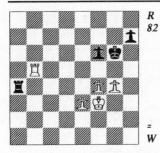

R 82

=
W

Here Black has got in ... f6 which is a great boon. The position is drawn, viz.

1	♖b7

If 1 g5 f5!; or 1 f5+ ♔g7 2 ♖b7+ ♔g8 3 ♖g3 ♖a1. 1 ♖b6 h6 2 e4 ♖a3+ 3 ♔f2 ♔g7! is also drawn, e.g. if 4 e5 fxe5 5 fxe5 ♖a5 6 ♖e6 ♔f7!.

1	...	h5!
2	f5+	

If 2 g5 fxg5 3 ♖b6+ ♔g7 4 f5!? (or 4 fxg5) 4 ... g4+ 5

♔g3 ♖e4=; or 2 gxh5+ ♔xh5 3 ♖g7 ♔h6 4 ♖g2 f5!=.

2	...	♔h6
3	gxh5	♔xh5
4	♖g7	♖b4
5	♖g6	♖b6
6	♔e4	♖a6
7	♔d5	♖a3
8	e4	♖a6
9	e5	♖a5+
10	♔e6	♖xe5+
11	♔xf6	♖a5=

cf diag 5 etc.

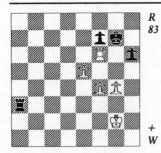

R 83

+
W

Capablanca - Yates
Hastings 1930
In this position, intermediate between diags 80 and 81, White to play can still win but extreme accuracy is required.

1	♖b6?!

1 ♖d6 was better so that if 1 ... ♖a2+ 2 ♔f3 ♖a3+ 3 ♔e4 ♖a4+ (or 3 ... ♖g3 4 ♔f5 ♖a3 5 ♖d7 ♖a6 6 ♔e4) 4 ♖d4 and the white king does not get boxed in as in variation A.

A.
The game continued:

1	...	♖e3
2	♖b4	♖c3
3	♔f2?	

This allows 3 ... h5! when if 4 gxh5 ♖h3 or 4 g5 h4 with counterplay; analysis has shown that this would be enough to draw (cf diag 83b) 3 ♖b8! was correct.

3	...	♖a3
4	♖b7	♔g8?!

If 4 ... ♔g6 5 f5+ ♔g5 6 ♖xf7 and wins, but Black should start flank checks with 4 ... ♖a2+ 5 ♔g3 ♖a3+ 6 ♔h4 ♖e3! (see diag 83b) - 6 ...

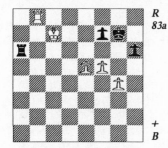

R
83a

R
83b

+
B

+
W

♖e3! is better than 6 ... ♔f8 7 ♖b6! ♖f3 (or 7 ... ♔g7 8 ♖b8!) 8 f5 ♖e3 9 e6! and wins.

    5   ♖b8+   ♔g7
    6   f5

Now White is clearly winning.

    6   ...   ♖a2+
    7   ♔e3

He could also hide the king on h4 via 7 ♔g3 ♖a3+ 8 ♔h4 since Black cannot keep it boxed in there due to the threat of f6+, i.e. if 8 ... ♖e3 9 ♖e8 ♖e1 (White to move would have had e6! in this position) 10 ♔g3 etc.

    7   ...   ♖a3+
    8   ♔e4   ♖a4+
    9   ♔d5   ♖a5+

Or 9 ... ♖xg4 10 f6+ ♔h7 11 ♖f8 ♔g6 12 ♖g8+ ♔f5 13 ♖xg4 ♔xg4 14 e6 etc.

    10   ♔d6   ♖a6+
    11   ♔c7 (83a)
    11   ...   ♔h7

If 11 ... ♖a1 (11 ... ♖a7+ 12 ♔b6 ♖a1 13 f6+) 12 f6+ ♔h7 13 ♖f8 ♖a7+ 14 ♔d6 as in the game.

    12   ♔d7   ♖a7+
    13   ♔d6   ♔g7

He cannot keep on checking since the white king could head to f6 or f8.

    14   ♖d8   ♖a5
    15   f6+   ♔h7
    16   ♖f8   ♖a7
    17   ♔c6

Another winning plan is to play the king to f5 and then sacrifice the rook with ♖xf7+!.

White now won very easily; the game continued: 17 ... ♔g6 18 ♖g8+ ♔h7 19 ♖g7+ ♔h8 20 ♔b6 ♖d7 21 ♔c5 ♖c7+ 22 ♔d6 ♖a7 23 e6 ♖a6+ 24 ♔e7 ♖xe6+ 25 ♔xf7 ♖e4 26 g5 hxg5 27

♔g6 1-0.

The important point about this variation is that once White gets in f5 and his rook gets to the eighth with the black king on g7, then he is winning.

Diagram 82b

As pointed out in the notes to variation A, Yates could have defended better. One critical line (note to 4 ... ♔g8) leads to this position.

White's plan is to try to get in f5. In order to do this he will have to either:

a) defend the e-pawn with the rook;

b) through zugzwang persuade the black rook to stop its observation of the e-pawn.

The problem with plan "a" is that at the critical moment Black can plan 1 ... h5. With the black rook on the eighth rank 2 gxh5 won't work. The alternative 2 g5 wins if either:

a1) White can avoid getting his king cut off on the second rank; or

a2) White gets in f5 before Black can play ... h4.

But as Kopaev has shown, plan "b" can be made to work.

B.

    1   ♖b8   ♖e1
    2   ♖a8

If 2 ♔g3 h5!? (2 ... ♖g1+ leads to the main line) and:

a) 3 gxh5 ♖g1+! 4 ♔f3 ♖f1+ 5 ♔g4 ♖g1+ 6 ♔f5 ♖h1! 7 ♔g4 ♖g1+ 8 ♔f3 ♖f1+! (but not 8 ... ♖h1? 9 f5 ♖xh5 10 ♔g4 ♖h1 11 f6+ wins, since if 11 ... ♔h7 12 e6! or 11 ... ♔g6 12 ♖g8+) 9 ♔e3 (or 9 ♔e4 ♖e1+ 10 ♔d5 ♖d1+

287

Rook v Rook

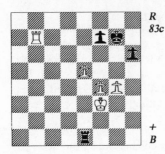

R
83c

+
B

11 ♔c6 ♖f1 12 ♖b4 ♖h1=) 9 ...
♖e1+ 10 ♔f2 ♖h1 11 f5
♖xh5=.

b) 3 g5! ♖e3+ 4 ♔f2 (if 4
♔h4 ♖e4! forces repeti-
tion) 4 ... ♖a3!. In this position
Black is a tempo away from
drawing. On the move he
would play 5 ... h4 and if then
6 ♖b7 ♔g8! or 6 f5 ♖g3!.
White ends up with his king
cut off on the third rank and
unable to advance his pawns.

But White to move could
force the win with 5 f5 threatening 6 f6+, 7 ♖g8+, 8 g6;
and if 5 ... ♖a2+ 6 ♔g3 ♖a3+
7 ♔h4 ♖f3 8 e6! (8 f6+ ♔g6
9 ♖g8+ ♔f5 10 g6 fxg6 11 f7
g5+!=) 8 ... fxe6 9 f6+ wins; or
if 5 ... ♖a7 simply 6 ♔g3 etc.

2   ...   ♖h1+
3   ♔g3   ♖g1+

Now if 3 ... h5 4 g5 ♖g1+ (4
... h4+ 5 ♔g4 h3 6 ♖a2 wins)
5 ♔f3 h4 6 ♖a6 and with his
king not cut off White wins
easily, e.g. 6 ... ♖g3+ 7 ♔e4
h3 8 ♖h6 ♖a3 9 ♔f5 ♖g3 10
♖h4 ♔g8 (10 ... ♖a3 11 ♔g4)
11 e6 fxe6+ 12 ♔xe6 ♔g7 13
♔f5 ♔f7 14 ♖h7+ ♔g8 15 g6
(not 15 ♔g6? ♖g4!) 15 ... ♔f8
16 ♔f6 ♔g8 17 f5 ♖a3 18
♔g5 ♖g3+ 19 ♔f4 ♖a3 20
♔g4 ♖a4+ 21 ♔xh3 ♖f4 22
♖f7 and wins.

4   ♔f3   ♖e1
5   ♖b8

Hoping for zugzwang.

5   ...   ♖f1+!
6   ♔e3

If 6 ♔e4 ♖e1+ 7 ♔d5 (7
♔f5 ♖g1 see diag 83c) 7 ...
♖d1+ 8 ♔c6 h5!=.

6   ...   ♖e1+
7   ♔f2

7 ♔d3 ♖d1+ 8 ♔e2 ♖g1!
and if 9 f5? ♖xg4 10 f6+
♔h7!= since the white king is

on the e-file.

7   ...   ♖e4
8   ♔f3   ♖e1
9   ♖b7!! (83c)

But this really is zugzwang.
Not however 9 ♖e8? ♖f1+ 10
♔e3 (or 10 ♔g3 ♖g1+) 10 ...
h5! 11 g5 h4 12 ♖a8 h3 13 ♖a2
♔g6=, e.g. 14 ♖a6+ ♔f5 15 g6
fxg6 16 ♖f6+ ♔g4 17 ♖xg6+
♔h4 18 ♔e4 h2 19 ♔f5 h1♕
20 ♖h6+ ♔g3 21 ♖xh1
♖xh1=.

9   ...   ♔f8

Alternatively:

a) 9 ... ♖a1 10 e6! (but not 10
f5? ♔f8!=) 10 ... ♔f6 11 exf7
(also 11 ♖xf7+) 11 ... ♔g7 12
♖b6 (threatening 13 ♖xh6 or
13 ♖f6) 12 ... ♖a8 13 ♔g3 ♖f8
14 ♔h4 ♖xf7 15 f5 wins easily.

b) 9 ... ♖h1 10 e6 ♔f6 11
exf7 ♔g7 12 ♖d7 ♖h2 (or 12
... ♖a1 13 ♖d6 as above) 13
♔e4 ♖a2 14 ♔e5 wins easily
cf variation c below.

c) 9 ... ♖f1+ 10 ♔e4 ♖a1 (if
10 ... ♖e1+ 11 ♔f5 threatening
12 ♖e7 ♖a2 13 e6 wins, e.g. 11
... ♖e2 12 ♖e7 ♖a2 13 c6 etc.)
11 f5. Black could hold this position if his king could get to
e7 but that is impossible:

c1) 11 ... ♖a4+ 12 ♔d5
♖a5+ 13 ♔d6 etc. as in A;

c2) 11 ... ♔f8 12 ♖b8+ ♔e7
13 f6+ ♔d7 14 ♖f8 ♖e1+ 15
♔d4 ♖d1+ 16 ♔e3! wins;

c3) 11 ... ♖e1+ 12 ♔d4 (or 12
♔d5-c6-d6-e7!) 12 ... ♖d1+ 13
♔e3 etc.

10   ♖b4!   ♔g7

Or 10 ... ♖a1 11 ♖b8+ ♔e7
(11 ... ♔g7 12 f5 etc. see the
column) 12 ♖b6! ♖h1 13 ♔e4
(threat 14 ♔f5, 15 ♖b7+) 13 ...
♔f8 14 ♖b8+ (or simply 14
♔f5 ♔g7 15 ♖b7+)14 ... ♔g7
15 f5 and wins.

288

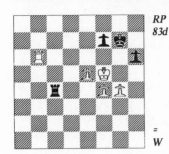

RP
83d

=
W

| 11 | ♔f2! | ♜a1 |
| 12 | ♖b8 | ♜a2+ |

If 12 ... h5 13 g5 h4 (or 13 ... ♜a3 14 f5 wins - see the notes to ♜a8 in variation B) 14 ♔f3 h3 15 ♖b2! wins.

13	♔g3	♜a3+
14	♔h4	♜e3
15	♖e8	

White is an invaluable tempo ahead of diag 83b.

| 15 | ... | ♜e1 |
| 16 | f5 and wins | |

C.

After Capablanca's 1 ♖b6 in diag 83, Yates should have started checking:

| 1 | ♖b6 | ♜a2+ |
| 2 | ♔f3 | |

If 2 ♔g3 ♜a3+ 3 ♔h4 ♜a4! (but not 3 ... ♜f3 4 f5 ♜e3 5 e6 fxe6 6 ♖xe6 and wins because of the *tempo*) 4 f5?! (4 ♔g3 ♜a3+, or 4 ♖f6 ♜b4 and White cannot unravel) 4 ... ♜a5! 5 e6 fxe6 6 ♖xe6 ♜a1!= (cf diag 57, the game Smyslov - Keres).

2	...	♜a3+
3	♔e4	♜a4+
4	♔f5	♜c4! *(83d)*

This position is very close. White can try:

i)

5	♖b7	♔g8
6	♖d7	♜a4
7	e6	fxe6+
8	♔e5	

Now Black would like to head for diag 58 variation B, e.g. by 8 ... ♜a5+ 9 ♔xe6 ♜a6+ 10 ♔f5? ♔f8=. But with the white rook already on d7 this appears to be impossible here.

| 8 | ... | h5! |

If 8 ... ♜a5+ 9 ♔xe6 (9 ♔f6 ♜a4) 9 ... ♜a4 (or 9 ... ♜a6+

10 ♖d6 ♜a4 11 ♔f5 transposes) 10 ♔f5 ♔f8 11 ♖d6 ♔g7 12 ♖g6+! ♔h7 13 ♖e6 ♔g7 14 ♖e7+ ♔f8 (14 ... ♔g8 15 ♔g6!) 15 ♔e4 ♜a6 16 ♖e6 ♜a7 17 ♔g6 ♜g7+ 18 ♔h5 and wins.

Or if 8 ... ♜b4 9 ♖e7 and Black simply can't improve on a transposition into the line above.

| 9 | g5 | h4 |
| 10 | ♖e7! | h3 |

If 10 ... ♜a6 11 ♔f6! threatens 12 ♖e8+ and 13 g6+ and 14 ♖h8 mate.

11	♖xe6	♜a7!
12	♖e8+	♔g7
13	♔f5	h2
14	♖e1	♜a2
15	♖h1	♜g2
16	♔e4	

And remarkably it seems that Black is just holding, viz: 16 ... ♔g6 17 ♔f3 ♜a2 18 ♔g3 ♔f5 19 ♖xh2 ♜a3+ 20 ♔h4 ♜a1!. Black will always check the white king when it is on the third rank - I can see no other way for White to improve his position here.

ii)

| 5 | ♖b7 | ♔g8 |
| 6 | ♖b3 | |

If 6 g5 hxg5 7 ♔xg5 ♜c5=.

6	...	♔g7
7	♖e3	♜c6!
8	♔e4	

For if 8 ♖e4 (intending 9 ♜a4, 10 ♔e4) then 8 ... f6!.

| 8 | ... | ♜c4+ |

But not 8 ... f6? 9 ♔d5!.

| 9 | ♔f3 | ♜c6 |
| 10 | f5 | |

White's problem is that he cannot improve his rook since if 10 ♜a3 f6! just holding, e.g. 11 ♜a7+ ♔f8 12 ♔e4 fxe5 13 ♔xe5 ♖b6 14 ♖d7 ♜g6!= (cf

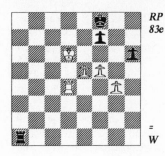

RP 83e

= W

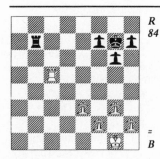

R 84

= B

diag 58).

However, White could try first 10 ♔g3 ♖a6 11 ♖b3 and if 11 ... f6? 12 ♖b7+ ♔g8 13 exf6 ♖xf6 14 ♖b4! (not 14 f5? h5) 14 ... ♔g7 15 ♔h4 ♖a6 16 ♔h5 ♖a5+ 17 f5 ♖a1 18 ♖b7+ ♔f6 19 ♖b6+ ♔g7 20 ♖g6+! and wins. In any case 10 f5 is interesting since it demonstrates what White must avoid.

| 10 | ... | ♔f8! |
| 11 | ♖a3 | ♖c1 |

This position is just drawn since White has weakened his position with f5 without preventing the black king from reaching e7.

If at once 12 ♖a8+ ♔e7 13 f6+ ♔e6 14 ♖e8+ ♔d5 15 e6 ♖c6! draws; and slower methods do not work since both of Black's pieces are active. For instance even if White reaches the relatively favourable looking diag 83e the position is still drawn.

Diagram 83e
Capablanca tried:

| 1 | e6 |

If 1 f6 ♔e8 2 ♖b4 ♖d1+ 3 ♔c5 ♖c1+ 4 ♔d4 ♖d1+ 5 ♔c4 (5 ♔c3 ♖e1! 6 ♖b8+ ♔d7 7 ♖b7+ ♔e6 8 ♖e7+ ♔d5 9 ♖xf7 ♖e3+ 10 ♔d2 ♖xe5 11 ♖e7 ♖e6!=) 5 ... ♖c1+ 6 ♔d3 ♔d7 7 ♖b7+ ♔e6=.

Or 1 ♔d7 ♖e1 2 ♖d5 ♖e4 3 ♖a5 ♖d4+ 4 ♔c6 ♖xg4 5 ♖a8+ ♔e7 6 f6+ ♔e6=.

| 1 | ... | ♖e1! |

In the game Black was lost after 1 ... ♖a6+? 2 ♔e5 fxe6 3 f6! ♔g8 4 ♖d6 ♖a1 5 ♔xe6 ♖e1+ 6 ♔f5 ♖g1 7 ♖d8+ ♔f7 8 ♖d7+ ♔f8 (or 8 ... ♔g8 9 g5! wins - also 9 ♖g7+ and 10 g5 - see diag 57c) 9 ♖h7 and wins.

1 ... ♖a7 would also be a sufficient defence.

2	♔d7	♖e2
3	♖d6	♖e4
4	♔d8	♖e1
5	exf7	♖e4
6	♔d7	♔xf7!=

This ending is of considerable theoretical and practical importance - it has arisen in master games dozens of times.

Usually "Black" should be able to draw but there is plenty of play. Diags 81 and 83 in particular are obviously positions which Black should avoid.

Petrosian - Keres
Moscow 1951

| 1 | ... | h5! |

If the defender can get this in then his task is eased considerably.

2	♖c2	♔g7
3	♔g2	♖b5
4	♔f3	♔f6
5	h4	

5 h3 and 6 g4 would only simplify the position.

5	...	♖f5+
6	♔g2	♖a5
7	♔h3	♖a4
8	♖d2	♔e5
9	♖b2	♔f6
10	♖b5	♖a2
11	♔g2	♖a4
12	♔f3	♖a3
13	♔f4	♖a2
14	f3	♖e2
15	e4	

White finally decides to push his pawns; but Black is not really in any trouble.

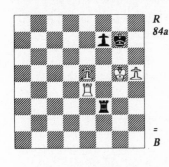

R
84a

=
B

15	...	♖e1
16	♖b6+	♔g7
17	♖a6	♖b1
18	♖c6	♖g1
19	♖c2	♔f6
20	♖a2	♔g7
21	♖e2	♔f6
22	♖e3	♔g7
23	e5	♔f8
24	g4	hxg4
25	fxg4	♔g7
26	♔g5	♖f1

27	♖e4	♖f3
28	h5	

And not 28 e6?? f6 mate.

28	...	gxh5
29	gxh5 (84a)	
29	...	f6+
30	♔g4	♖f1
31	h6+	♔g6!

But not 31 ... ♔xh6?? 32 e6!
f5+ 33 ♔h3 fxe4 34 e7 and
wins.

½-½

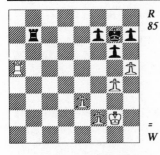

R
85

=
W

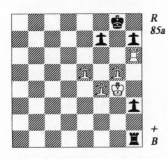

R
85a

+
B

Gligoric - Euwe
Zürich Ct 1953
Here White has got in h5 himself which makes the position
much more critical.

1   g5!?

Gligoric played this now
since they had still to make
the time control, i.e. this was
White's 38th move. But from
a technical point of view it
would be better to improve
the kingside first with e.g.
♔g3, f3, e4 and ♔f4.

1   ...   gxh5?!

1 ... h6! would draw relatively easily.

2   ♖a6!   ♖b3?

2 ... ♖e7! forced a draw at
once since if 3 ♔g3 ♖e6! and
4 ... h6, or 3 ♖h6 ♖e5 4 ♖xh5
♔g6 5 ♖h6+ ♔g7=.

3	♖h6	♖a3
4	♔g3	♖a1
5	e4	

Not 5 ♖xh5 ♔g6 6 ♖h6+
♔xg5 7 ♖xh7 ♔g6=.

5	...	♖g1+
6	♔f4	♖h1
7	e5	h4?

The decisive mistake. Now
White can round up the h-
pawn and this eventually
forces diag 80. Black should
have remained passive with 7
... ♔g8, keeping control of g4.

8	♔g4	♖g1+

9	♔f5	♖h1
10	♔g4	♖g1+
11	♔f5	♖h1
12	f4!	h3

If 12 ... ♖h2/♖h3 then 13
♔g4!; or if 12 ... ♔g8 either 13
♔g4 or 13 ♔f6 h3 14 f5 h2 15
♖h4.

13	♔g4	♖g1+
14	♔f3!	♖f1+
15	♔g3	♖g1+
16	♔f2	♖h1
17	♖f6!	♖a1
18	♔g3	♖h1
19	♔g4	♔g8

If 19 ... ♖h2 20 ♖h6 wins
the h-pawn at once.

20   ♖h6 (85a)

By excellent manoeuvring
Gligoric has forced the black
king back to g8. Euwe now
played

20   ...   h2

At the time of the game this
was thought to be a decisive
error. However if 20 ... ♖g1+
21 ♔xh3 ♖h1+ 22 ♔g4 ♖xh6
23 gxh6 f6 Maizelis pointed
out a win in this apparently
drawn ending, viz: 24 exf6
♔f7 25 ♔f5 ♔f8 (or 25 ...
♔e8 26 ♔e6 ♔f8 27 ♔d7
♔f7 28 ♔d8 ♔f8 29 f7!) 26
♔e6 ♔e8 27 f7+ ♔f8 28
♔d6 ♔xf7 29 ♔d7! and wins
(see diag P35).

21   ♔g3   ♖g1+

22	♔xh2	♖g4
23	♖f6	♔g7
24	♔h3	♖g1
25	♔h4	♖h1+

Black cannot keep the white king cut off on the g-file since White can play ♔h5 and ♖a6

- a7 threatening e6 and if then ... ♔g8, f5 will win.

26	♔g4	♖g1+
27	♔f5	

We have reached the won diag 81.

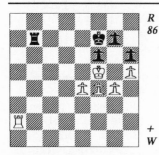

R 86

Botvinnik - Najdorf
Moscow 1956

As a result of the excellent position of his king and the deplorable state of Black's kingside, White is able to force a win.

1	♖a5	♖c7
2	♖d5	♖a7
3	e5	fxe5
4	fxe5	♔e7

White theatened 5 ♖d7+! and 6 e6+.

5	e6	♖a4

If 5 ... ♖a6 6 ♖d7+ ♔f8 7 ♔g6! ♖xe6+ 8 ♔h7 and Black loses both his pawns.

6	g5!	

Not 6 ♖d7+ ♔f8 7 e7+ ♔e8! 8 ♖b7 ♖a5+=; nor 6 ♖d7+ ♔f8 7 ♖f7+ ♔g8 8 g5 ♖a5+! (8 ... hxg5? 9 ♔g6) 9 ♔e4 ♖a6!=.

6	...	♖a7! *(86a)*

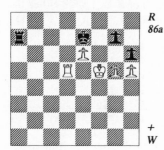

R 86a

In the game White won easily after 6 ... hxg5? 7 ♖d7+ ♔f8 8 ♖f7+ ♔g8 9 ♔g6 g4 10 h6 gxh6 11 e7 ♖a8 and Black resigned in view of the unstoppable ♖f6-d6-d8.

7	♖e5!	

The only way to win. If 7 ♖d7+? ♖xd7 8 exd7 ♔xd7 9 ♔g6 hxg5=.

7 gxh6 comes very close but Kopaev has shown in a long analysis that Black can just draw, viz: 7 ... gxh6 8 ♖b5 ♖c7 9 ♖b6 ♖c5+ 10 ♔g6 ♖e5! 11 ♔xh6 ♔f6 12 ♖a6 ♖f5 13 ♖a1 ♔xe6 14 ♔g6 ♖f6+ 15 ♔g7 ♖f7+ 16 ♔g8 ♖b7 17 ♖f1 ♖b5 18 h6 ♔g5+ 19 ♔f8 ♖h5 20 ♖a1 ♖f5+ 21 ♔e8 ♖b5 22 ♖a6+ ♔f5 23 h7 ♖b7 24 ♖h6 ♖b8+ 25 ♔d7 (25 ♔e7 ♖b7+) 25 ... ♖h8 26 ♔e7 ♔g5 27 ♖h1 ♔g6= (cf diag 24a).

7	...	hxg5

Or if 7 ... ♔d6 8 gxh6 gxh6 9 ♔f6, or 7 ... ♖a6 8 ♔g6! ♖xe6+ 9 ♖xe6+ ♔xe6 10 ♔xg7! and wins.

8	♔xg5	♖a1

If 8 ... ♖a6 9 ♔g6 ♔f8 10 ♔h7!, or 8 ... ♔f8 9 ♔g6 ♖e7 10 h6! gxh6 - or 10 ... ♔g8 11 ♖e1 etc. - 11 ♔f6 and wins; 11 ... ♖f7+ is impossible with the h-pawn on the board.

Finally if 8 ... ♔d6 9 ♔f5! (9 ♖e1 ♖a5+ 10 ♔g6 ♔e7!=) 9 ... ♔e7 (or 9 ... ♖a8 10 e7 ♖e8 11 h6!) 10 h6! gxh6 11 ♔f6 and wins.

9	♔g6	♖f1

9 ... ♖g1+ 10 ♖g5 is worse for Black.

10	♔xg7	♖g1+
11	♔h6!	♖g2
12	♖g5	♖f2
13	♔g7	♔xe6
14	h6	♖f7+
15	♔g8 and wins	

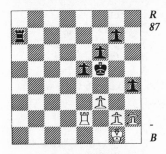

R 87

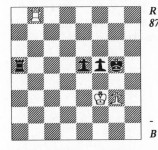

R 87a

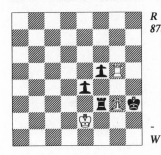

R 87b

Harandi - Vaganian
Rio de Janeiro 1979

In addition to the extra pawn, Black has several positional advantages. His king is already active, his h-pawn is very well placed and most importantly: *the position of the white f-pawn gives Black a very dangerous pawn lever with ... g4.*

It would appear that these additional advantages probably add up to a win.

   1   ...   ♖a4!
   2   ♔f2

If 2 ♖b2 g5 3 ♖b6 Black can still play 3 ... g4 and if 4 fxg4+ ♖xg4.

   2   ...   g5
   3   g4+!?

This was suggested by Kasparov as a possible improvement. If 3 h3 ♔f4 we've reached diag 86 with colours reversed. The game actually continued 3 ♖b2 g4 4 fxg4+ ♔xg4 5 ♖b6 ♖a2+ 6 ♔g1 f5 7 ♖g6+ ♔f4 8 ♖h6 ♔e3 9 h3 (Black threatened mate) 9 ... e4 10 ♖xh4 f4 11 ♖h8 ♖a1+ 12 ♔h2 ♔f2 13 ♖f8 f3 14 h4 ♖g1! 15 gxf3 ♖g2+ 16 ♔h1 e3 17 ♖e8 ♖g3 18 ♔h2 ♖xf3 0-1.

In principle such a passive defence ought to lose if Black can force a passed pawn. Kasparov's suggestion is much more challenging for Black:

   3   ...   hxg3+

Not 3 ... ♔f4? 4 h3=.

   4   hxg3

If 4 ♔xg3 g4! and Black gets two connected passed pawns.

   4   ...   g4
   5   ♖b2   ♔g5
   6   ♖e2   gxf3
   7   ♔xf3   ♖a5!
   8   ♖b2

If 8 ♖e4 f5 9 ♖h4 ♖a3+ 10 ♔f2 f4 11 ♖h3 ♖a2+ 12 ♔f3 e4+! 13 ♔xe4 ♔g4 and wins since if 14 ♖h8 fxg3; or 14 ♖h4+ ♔xg3 15 ♖xf4 ♖a4+.

   8   ...   f5
   9   ♖b8 *(87a)*

As Kasparov points out this position arose with colours reversed in Lyskov - Selezniev, USSR 1956.

   9   ...   e4+!

In that game Lyskov played "1 ♖a3+" which is weaker.

   10   ♔e3

If 10 ♔g2 ♖a2+ 11 ♔h3 e3 12 ♖e8 (12 ♖g8+ also loses) 12 ... e2 13 ♖e6 ♖b2 (zugzwang) 14 ♖e3 ♖a2 15 ♖e8 ♖b2 (zugzwang) 16 ♖e3 (16 ♔h4 e1♕! or 16 ... ♖b4+ - e4) 16 ... f4! 17 gxf4 ♖b3 18 ♖xb3 e1♕ with a theoretical win.

   10   ...   ♖a3+
   11   ♔f2   ♖a2+
   12   ♔e3   ♔g4
   13   ♖g8+   ♔h3
   14   ♖g5   ♖a3+
   15   ♔e2   ♖f3 *(87b)*
   16   ♔e1!

As we shall see Black wants to get the opposition - so this is better than 16 ♔d2? ♔h2.

   16   ...   ♔h2
   17   ♔d2

If 17 g4 f4 Black wins by at least a tempo in all variations.

   17   ...   ♔h1!
   18   ♔d1

Or if 18 ♔e1 ♔g1 19 ♔e2 ♔g2 20 ♔e1 ♖f2 as in the main line.

   18   ...   ♖f2!
   19   ♔e1   ♔g2
   20   ♔d1

If 20 ♖g8 ♔f3 etc; or 20 ♖h5 ♔xg3 21 ♖g5+ ♔h4!.

   20   ...   ♔f1

And the e-pawn queens.

R
88

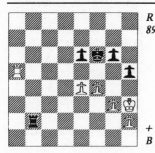

R
88a

+
W

+
W

Timman 1979

Here again, White's additional positional advantages are sufficient to force the win.

1	g4	hxg4
2	fxg4	♖c4

Or 2 ... ♖b7 3 e5+!.

3	g5+	♔f7
4	♖a7+	♔f8
5	♔e5 and wins	

Diagram 87a

Now if 1 g4? would be ineffective after 1 ... hxg4 2 fxg4 ♖f1+. Instead White has:

1	e5+	♔f7
2	♖a7+	♔f8
3	g4	hxg4
4	fxg4	♖e1
5	♔g5	♖e4!

If 5 ... ♖xe5+ 6 ♔f6 wins at once.

6	♔xg6	♖xg4+
7	♔f6	♖f4+
8	♔xe6	♖xh4
9	♖a8+	♔g7
10	♔e7	♖b4
11	e6 and wins	

See diag 6.

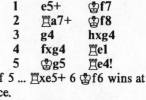

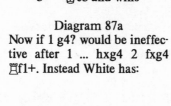

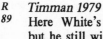

R
89

+
B

Timman 1979

Here White's task is harder but he still wins. Black has to defend against the threat of 1 e5+ ♔f7 2 ♖a7+ ♔f8 3 ♔h4 ♖xh2+ 4 ♔g5 ♖g2 5 ♔f6 ♔g8 6 ♖g7+ and wins. There are two possibilities:

A.

1	...	♖f2

Stopping 2 e5+? ♔f5 3 ♖a8 g5! and if 4 ♖f8+ ♔e4 the f-pawn is pinned.

2	♖b5!	

Zugzwang.

2	...	♖a2

If 2 ... ♔f7 3 ♖b7+ ♔f6 4 e5+ ♔f5 5 ♖f7+ ♔e4 6 ♖f6 and wins.

Or 2 ... ♖f1 3 e5+ ♔f5 4 ♖b8 g5 5 ♔g2! ♖a1 6 ♖f8+ and wins.

Or 2 ... h4 3 ♔xh4 ♖xh2+ 4 ♔g4 ♖g2 5 e5+ ♔f7 6 ♖b7+ ♔f8 and either 7 ♔g5 ♖xg3+ 8 ♔f6 or simply 7 ♖b3 and 8 ♔g5 wins.

3	e5+	♔f7
4	♖b7+	♔f8
5	♔h4!	etc.

B.

1	...	e5

This brilliant idea also just fails to draw.

2	♖xe5!	

Timman has shown that 2 ♖a6+ and 3 f5 is just insufficient to win.

2	...	♖e2
3	♖e8	♔f7
4	♖a8	♖xe4
5	♔h4	♔f6

If 5 ... ♖e2 6 ♔g5 (not 6 h3? ♖h2!=) 6 ... ♖xh2 7 ♖a7+ ♔e8 8 ♔xg6 ♖g2 9 ♖h7 ♖xg3+ 10 ♔f6 ♖g4 11 f5 h4 12 ♖h8+ ♔d7 13 ♔f7 and wins since the black h-pawn isn't dangerous - Black's king cannot possibly support it in time and the black king is on the *long* side of the f-pawn.

6	♖a6+	♔f5
7	h3!	g5+

If 7 ... ♖e1 8 g4+ hxg4 9 hxg4+ ♔xf4 10 ♖f6+ ♔e5 11 ♖xg6 and wins since the black king is cut off along a rank.

8	♔xh5	gxf4
9	g4+	♔e5
10	♔g5	f3

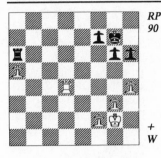

RP 90

RP 90a

An Extra Outside Passed Pawn

In this case the positioning of the rooks is of paramount importance. As we shall see:

a) If the "white" rook is behind the passed pawn, the position is usually won;

b) It is also quite favourable to defend the pawn from the side; but

c) If the rook is in front of its pawn the the win is much more problematic.

a) The attacking rook behind the passed pawn

Alekhine - Capablanca
34th Match Game 1927
Alekhine won this very famous ending to become World Champion.

1   ♖a4!

With the white rook on this beautiful square the black rook must remain totally passive until it is relieved by its king.

1	...	♔f6
2	♔f3	♔e5
3	♔e3	h5
4	♔d3	♔d5
5	♔c3	♔c5
6	♖a2!	

This is zugzwang - the black king is forced to give way. Putting the opponent into zugzwang is the normal technical procedure in positions such as this, where he cannot move his rook.

| 6 | ... | ♔b5 |

11	♖f6	♖e3
12	h4!	

And White's pawns are much too quick - but not the overelaborate 12 ♖f4 ♖a3 13 h4 ♖a8! 14 ♖xf3 (14 ♖f5+ and 15 h5) 14 ... ♖g8+=.

7	♔d4	♖d6+
8	♔e5	♖e6+
9	♔f4	♔a6

Black has succeeded in changing the guard and thus activating his rook. But the lone rook cannot really be expected to defend the whole kingside against the white king - the only piece that can ever really do that successfully is an "opposite bishop".

10	♔g5	♖e5+
11	♔h6	♖f5 (90a)

If 11 ... ♖e7 12 ♔g7 ♖d7 13 ♔f6 ♖c7 14 ♖e2! ♔xa5 15 ♖e7 ♖c2 16 ♖xf7 ♖xf2+ 17 ♔xg6 ♖g2 18 ♖f3 etc.

| 12 | f4?! | |

Although this looks natural, Capablanca is now able to pose further problems by withdrawing his rook to the second rank.

The best plan is to play for zugzwang. The obvious way to do this is 12 ♔g7 ♖f3 13 ♔g8. Now if 13 ... ♖f6 14 f4 ♖f5 15 ♔g7 and wins; or 13 ... ♖f5 14 f4 ♖f6 15 ♔f8! etc. But Black can create some minor technical problems with 13 ... f5 14 ♔g7 f4 when presumably 15 ♔xg6 would win but not utterly trivially.

White can circumvent even this minor inconvenience by playing 12 ♔h7! ♖f6 (after 12 ... ♖f3 13 ♔g7 etc, or 12 ... ♖d5 13 ♔g7 also wins easily) 13 ♔g8! ♖f5 14 f4 ♖f6 15 ♔g7 ♖f5 16 ♖a3 etc.

And another good line is 12 ♔g7 ♖f3 13 ♖d2! ♚xa5 14 ♖d5+ and if 14 ... ♚b6 15 ♖d6+ - f6 or 14 ... ♚b4 15 ♖d4+ - f4.

12	...	♖c5!
13	♖a3	♖c7
14	♔g7	♖d7
15	f5?!	

15 ♔f6 is simpler: 15 ... ♖c7 16 f5 ♖c6+ 17 ♔xf7 gxf5 18 ♖f3 etc.

| 15 | ... | gxf5 |
| 16 | ♔h6 | f4! |

There are now some technical problems but despite his inaccuracies Alekhine did succeed in winning:

17	gxf4	♖d5
18	♔g7	♖f5
19	♖a4	♚b5
20	♖e4!	♚a6
21	♔h6	♖xa5?

If 21 ... ♚b7! then 22 ♖e7+ still leaves the position messy after 22 ... ♚a6 23 ♖e5 ♖xf4 24 ♔xh5 f6; and 22 ♖e5 ♖xf4 23 ♖xh5 f5 24 ♔g5 ♖a4 25 ♖h7+ ♚a6 is similarly a bit confused.

But White could play simply 22 ♔g7 ♚a6 (23 ♖e7+ was threatened) 23 ♔g8 ♚b7 (23 ... ♖f6 24 ♔f8 ♖g6 or 24 ... ♖f5 25 ♔g7 - zugzwang - 25 ♔xf7 ♖g4 26 ♖e6+ ♚xa5 27 f5 wins easily) 24 ♖e7+ ♚c6 25 ♖xf7 ♖xa5 26 ♔g7 ♚d6 27 ♔g6 and with his king cut off, Black has no way of reaching a reasonable ending of ♖f+h v ♖.

22	♖e5	♖a1
23	♔xh5	♖g1
24	♖g5!	♖h1
25	♖f5	♚b6
26	♖xf7	♚c6
27	♖e7!	1-0

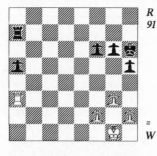

R 91 =W

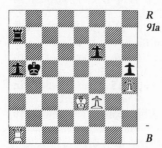

R 91a -B

Botvinnik - Borisenko
USSR Ch 1955

Although the position is very similar to the previous one the defender is doing better here since:

a) With the move Botvinnik is able to blockade the outside passed pawn on the fourth rank (rather than the fifth as in Alekhine - Capablanca);

b) Black's king is temporarily rather far from the action on the queenside which gives White some breathing space to try to organise a king side diversion.

c) Black's kingside pawns are very slightly weakened which improves White's prospects of organising counterplay against them.

1 ♖a4!

It is vital to keep the passed pawn back as far as possible.

With it only on the fourth rank White may be able to to activate his rook for one final burst of activity. (i.e. 1 ♖moves a4 2 ♖xpawn a3 3 ♖-1st rank a2 4 ♖a1).

With the passed pawn already on a4 this would be completely out of the question.

A.

1 ... ♔g5

This very obvious move was played in the game, however it is a mistake since it facilitates White's kingside counterplay.

2 f3! ♔f5?

Now White is clearly okay. 2 ... f5! was better, but after 3 ♔f2 ♔f6 4 ♔e3 ♔e5 5 h4 ♔d5 6 g4 fxg4 7 fxg4 ♔c5 (not 7 ... hxg4 8 ♖xg4 ♖a6 9 ♔d3 threatening 10 ♖g5+) 8 ♔d3 ♚b5 9 ♖e4 ♖c7 10 gxh5! (10 ♖e6?! ♖c6 11 ♖e5+ ♖c5 12

Re6 g5! 13 hxg5 hxg4 14 g6
Rg5!) 10 ... gxh5 11 Re8
White's active pieces give him
good drawing chances.

	3	g4+	hxg4?!

This is also somewhat dubious since now White gets a passed h-pawn - just what he needs. But if 3 ... Ke6 4 gxh5 gxh5 5 Kf2 White should have sufficient counterplay against Black's weakened kingside, e.g. 5 ... Kd6 6 Ke3 Re7+ (otherwise the white king will go on the rampage) 7 Kd3 Re5 8 Rf4 f5 9 Rh4! Kd5 10 Rxh5 f4 11 Rh4 Re3+ 12 Kd2 Rxf3 13 Rh5+= (Smyslov and Levenfish).

	4	fxg4+	Ke5

Black can reach an ending of R+2 vs R+1 with 4 ... Kg5 5 Kg2 Kh4 6 Kg1! Kh3 7 Kh1 Re7 (7 ... f5 8 gxf5 gxf5 9 Kg1) 8 Ra3+! Kxg4 9 Rxa5. Although this is theoretically drawn it is far from easy as we saw in diags 57 and 58.

	5	h4!	Kd5
	6	h5	gxh5
	7	gxh5	Ke6

Or 7 ... Kc5 8 h6 Kb5 9 Rh4 Rh7 10 Rh5+ Kb4 11 Rh4+ Kb3 12 Rh3+ Kb2 13 Rh4!=.

	8	h6	Kf7
	9	Rg4!	Kf8
	10	Rf4	Ra6
	11	Rg4	Ra7
	12	Rf4	Kg8
	13	Rxf6	a4
	14	Rf2	Kh7
	15	Ra2	Kxh6
	16	Kf2	Kg5
	17	Ke3	½-½

B.

	1	...	Kg7!

This is a better route for the black king since it does not come under fire from the enemy pawns. Nevertheless, Black must play very carefully to win.

	2	f3	

He must activate his pawns immediately. If 2 Kg2 Kf7 3 Kf3 Ke6 4 h4 (4 g4 h4! 5 g5 fxg5 6 Kg4 Kf6 7 h3 Ra8 zugzwang and White is quite lost) 4 ... f5 5 Kf4 (if 5 Ke3 Kd5 6 f3 intending 7 g4 White is an invaluable tempo down - he has played Kg1 - g2 f3 - e3) 5 ... Kd5 6 Kg5 Ra6 7 f3 Kc5 8 g4 fxg4 9 fxg4 hxg4 10 Kxg4 Kb5 and wins.

	2	...	Kf7
	3	h4!	

Not 3 g4? h4, but White could also have played 2 h4 and 3 f3.

	3	...	Ke6!

If 3 ... f5 4 Kf2 Ke6 5 Ke3 Kd5 6 g4 transposes to line A, the note to 2 ... Kf5?.

	4	g4	Kd5
	5	gxh5	gxh5
	6	Kf2	Kc5
	7	Ke3	Kb5
	8	Ra1	(91a)

But not 8 Rf4? a4 and wins.

	8	...	Re7+!

He must give priority to protecting his kingside. If e.g. 8 ... a4? 9 Kf4 Kc4 10 Kf5 Ra5+ (10 ... Ra6 11 Kg6 or 10 ... a3 11 Kxf6 transposes) 11 Kxf6 a3 (11 ... Kd4 12 Ra3!=) 12 f4 Kd4? (trying to win the f-pawn) 13 f5 Ke4 14 Kg6! and White is even better!

	9	Kf4	

Alternatively:

a) 9 Kd4 a4 10 Rb1+ Kc6! (10 ... Ka5 is very messy since the king is bad on the edge) 11 Ra1 (if e.g. 11 Rb8 Ra7 the white king cannot stop the a-pawn) 11 ... ♖a7 12 ♔e4 ♖a5! and wins;

b) 9 ♔d3 a4 10 ♖b1+ ♔c6! (10 ... ♔c5 should also win but this is much simpler) 11 ♖a1 (11 ♖b8 ♖a7 12 ♔c2 a3 13 ♔b1 ♖b7+) 11 ... ♖a7 12 ♔e4 ♖a5! etc.

9	...	♖e5
10	♖b1+	♔c5
11	♖c1+	♔b4
12	♖c6	

Better not to drive the king forward, e.g. if 12 ♖b1+ ♔c3 13 ♖c1+ ♔b2 14 ♖c6 ♖b5 15

♖a6 ♔b3 16 ♖xf6 a4 Black is even better placed than in the main line.

12	...	a4
13	♖xf6	♖a5
14	♖b6+	♖b5
15	♖a6	a3
16	♔e4	♔b3
17	f4	a2
18	♖xa2	

Black threatened 18 ... ♖b4+ - a4.

18	...	♔xa2
19	f5	♖b4+

And wins since he retains his h-pawn.

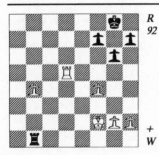

R 92

+ W

b) The rook defends the passed pawn from the side

Although the best place for a rook is usually behind the passed pawn, it can also be quite well placed defending it from the side.

*Andersson - Christiansen
Hastings 1978/79*

Here White has a "b-pawn" (rather than an "a-pawn") which is to his advantage. The winning plan must consist of bringing the king across to support the passed pawn. But with the pawn one file nearer the kingside the journey both to and from the queenside will be one move less. So, the b-pawn is virtually *two tempi* more favourable to White than an a-pawn.

Andersson won the position with great ease.

1	b5	h5
2	♔e3	♖b2
3	♔d4!	

As always in such a position White must sacrifice some of the kingside pawns in order to activate his king.

3	...	♖xg2

4	b6	♖b2

Not 4 ... ♖xh2 5 b7 ♖b2 6 ♖d8+ etc.

5	♔c5	♖c2+
6	♔b5	

Even better than 6 ♔d6 ♖xh2 7 b7 (7 ♖b5 ♖d2+) 7 ... ♖b2 8 ♔c6 ♖xb7 9 ♔xb7 - though no doubt that also wins. White's plan is to win the black rook with his king *as near the kingside as possible.*

6	...	♖xh2
7	♖d4!	♖e2

7 ... ♖b2+ 8 ♖b4 ♖e2 9 b7 ♖e8 10 ♖c4 transposes a move later.

8	b7	♖e8!
9	♖c4	♔g7
10	♖c8	♖e1
11	b8♕	♖b1+
12	♔c4	

Black has managed to prevent White from creating a permanent new queen but in fact he resigned here at once. After 12 ... ♖xb8 13 ♖xb8 the proximity of White's king to the kingside makes Black's position utterly hopeless.

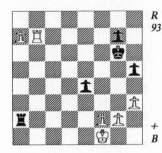

R
93

+
B

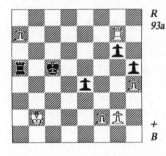

R
93a

+
B

Tartakower - Nimzowitsch
Berlin 1928

White's plan is simply to transfer his king to b8 and queen the a pawn. Black can oppose that with his king but only at the cost of abandoning his kingside. Although this position is won for White, Black can put up stiff resistance and in the event Tartakower faltered and only drew.

1	...	♔f6
2	♔e1	g6

If 2 ... g5 3 ♔d1 g4 4 hxg4 hxg4 5 g3! (he must not allow ... g3 creating a passed e-pawn) 5 ... ♔e5 6 ♔c1 e3 7 fxe3 ♔e4 8 ♖f7! ♔xe3 9 ♔b1 ♖a6 10 ♔c2 ♔d4 11 ♔b3 ♔c5 12 ♖f5+! ♔d4 (if 12 ... ♔b6 13 ♖f6+ ♔xa7 14 ♖xa6+ the pawn ending is won for White) 13 ♖f4+ and 14 ♖a4 wins.

3	♔d1	♔e5
4	♔c1	♔d5
5	♔b1	♖a6
6	♔b2	♔c6
7	♖g7	♔c5!
8	h4	

The black king is effectively defending the queenside so White now turns his attention to the other half of the board. Before undertaking decisive action, he improves his pawn structure. If at once 8 ♖xg6

♖xa7 9 ♖g5+ ♔d4 10 ♖xh5 ♖f7!=.

8	...	♖a5! *(93a)*

Here Tartakower was seduced by the brilliant trap which Nimzowitsch has just set. He played 9 g4? hxg4 10 h5 g3! 11 fxg3 e3! 12 ♖xg6 ♖xa7 13 ♔c2 ♖a2+ 14 ♔d1 ♔d4 15 h6 e2+ 16 ♔e1 ♔e3=. (Note that White had to be a strong player in order to fall into this!)

Instead White could force the win with:

9	g3	♖a6
10	♔c3	♖a3+

If 10 ... ♖a2 11 ♖xg6 now wins: 11 ... ♖a3+ (or 11 ... ♖xa7 12 ♖g5+) 12 ♔d2 ♖xa7 13 ♔e3 etc.

11	♔d2	♔d4
12	♖d7+	♔c5

Or 12 ... ♔e5 13 ♔c2 ♔e6 14 ♔b2 ♖a6 15 ♖g7 ♔d5 16 ♔c3 ♔c5 17 ♖xg6! and wins. By this rather roundabout manoeuvring White gained a vital tempo.

13	♔e2	♔c6
14	♖g7	♔d5
15	♖xg6	♖xa7
16	♖g5+	♔d4
17	♖xh5	♖a2+
18	♔f1	e3
19	fxe3+	♔e4
20	♖g5	♔f3
21	♔g1	and wins

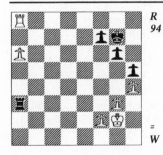

R
94

=
W

c) The rook in front of the passed pawn

This is clearly the worst position for the rook and very often presages a draw.

Ilivitsky - Krogius
Kislovodsk 1956

Despite White's extra pawn, the position is completely

drawn and indeed the players agreed to draw in this adjourned position without resumption. White has two conceivable winning plans:

a) To play a7. This would win if there were something for the white king to attack on the kingside (cf diag 67). Here, however, that is obviously not the case. After 1 a7 White could never support the a-pawn with his king since as soon as he played ♔b6 it would immediately be checked away. Hence 1 a7 would be totally useless.

b) White leaves the pawn on a6 and move his king towards the queenside. Now there is a shelter on a7 but the Black rook is not chained to the a-file. It can therefore maraud on the kingside.

As we shall see the a-pawn is simply *too far away* for this plan to promise White anything but trouble, e.g.

1	♔f1	♖a2!
2	♔e1	♔f6
3	f3	

If 3 ♔d1? ♖xf2 4 ♔c1 ♖a2 5 ♔b1 ♖a5 6 ♔b2 ♔f5 7 ♔b3 ♔g4 8 ♔b4 ♖a1 9 ♔b5 ♔xg3 and it is only White who is in danger - indeed lost presumably.

3	...	♖a3
4	♔e2	♔g7
5	♔d2!?	♖xf3
6	♔c2	♖xg3
7	♔b2	♖g2+
8	♔b3	♖g1

And here it would be most advisable to take a draw with 8 ... ♖g1 9 ♔b2 ♖g2+ 10 ♔b3 ♖g1 11 ♔b2=. If instead:

9	♔b4?	♖a1
10	♔b5	g5!
11	hxg5	h4
12	♖c8	h3
13	♖c2	♔g6
14	♖h2	♖a3!

And Black has magnificent winning chances.

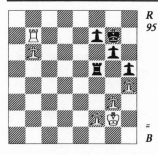

R
95

=
B

Bronstein - Romanishin Erevan 1975

Here White has an extremely significant extra advantage in that he has a "b-pawn" rather than an "a-pawn". As discussed in the introduction to diag 92 this gives him *two extra tempi*. Moreover, after Romanishin's very natural but weak first move the white king is several tempi more active than was its counterpart in the previous diagram.

1	...	♖b5?

1 ... ♖f6 was correct if then 2 ♔f1 ♖e6! White has no way of activating his king except by playing the useless ♖b8 and b7 when, as we know, ... ♖b6 leads to a dead draw.

2	♔f3	♖b2
3	♔e4!	♖xf2
4	♖c7	♖b2
5	b7	♔f6

Not only has Black been unable to capture a second pawn on the kingside but his king is also not very active. After:

6	♔d5	

He therefore had to sacrifice back a pawn.

6	...	♔f5!
7	♖xf7+	♔g4
8	♖g7!	♔xg3
9	♖xg6+	♔xh4

Black has levelled material, but his king is stuck in front of his passed pawn. Due to this, White wins by a tempo.

10	♔c6	♔h3
11	♖g5!	♖xb7

Forced since if 11 ... h4 12 ♖b5 wins at once.

12	♔xb7	h4
13	♔c6	♔h2
14	♔d5	h3
15	♔e4	1-0

Black resigned in view of 15 ... ♔h1 16 ♔f3 h2 17 ♖a5 ♔g1 18 ♖a1 mate.

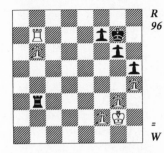

R 96 = W

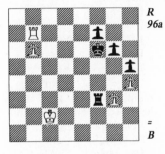

R 96a = B

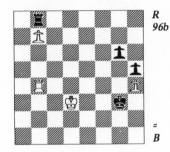

R 96b = B

Hollis - Florian
Corr. 1979
As we saw in the previous diagram a "b-pawn" confers very definite winning chances. Here, however, White's king is very bad, for Black has got his rook optimally placed as in diag 94.

Diag 96 is extremely close - the result certainly hangs on one tempo. Hollis won the game and published analysis claiming that the position is indeed won. However, later analysis suggests that with perfect play Black can just hold.

1   ♔f1   ♖b2!
2   ♔e1   ♔f6
3   f3   ♖b3
4   ♔d2!   ♖xf3
5   ♔c2 *(96a)*

This move highlights the advantage of a "b-pawn" over an "a-pawn". The black rook has already got to work to get back to the b-file.

Black can now try:

A.

5   ...   ♖xg3

This is possible since if 6 ♖xf7+ ♔xf7 7 b7 ♖f3 8 b8♕ ♔g7 9 ♕b7+ ♖f7 Black has a fortress. He will put the rook on f5 and can then safely pass with his king forever.

6   ♖c7!   ♖g2+
7   ♔b3   ♖g1
8   ♔b2

8 b7 would be too slow, e.g. 8 ... ♖b1+ 9 ♔c4 ♖c1+ (but not 9 ... g5? 10 hxg5+ ♔xg5 11 ♖c5+ and 12 ♖b5) 10 ♔d5 ♖b1 11 ♔c6 g5 12 hxg5+ ♔xg5 13 ♖c8 h4 14 b8♕ ♖xb8 15 ♖xb8 h3 16 ♔d5 ♔f4 17 ♖h8 ♔g3 18 ♔e4 h2 19 ♔e3 ♔g2 20 ♖g8+ ♔f1!=

cf diag RP12.
8   ...   ♖g4
9   ♖c3   ♖xh4
10   b7   ♖b4+
11   ♖b3   ♖xb7
12   ♖xb7

This position is extremely close. See diag RP29.

B.

5   ...   ♖f5

This was the game continuation.
6   ♖c7   ♖b5
7   b7   ♔e6

If 7 ... ♔f5 not 8 ♖xf7+? ♔g4= but 8 ♔c3! ♖b1 (8 ... ♔g4 9 ♔c4+ ♔xg3 10 ♖b4 wins; or 8 ... f6 9 ♔c4 intending 10 ♔c5+, 11 ♔b5) 9 ♖xf7+ ♔g4 10 ♖f4+! and 11 ♖b4.

8   ♔c3   f6
9   ♔c4   ♖b1
10   ♔c5   ♔f5

White threatened 11 ♖c6+ - b6.
11   ♖d7!   ♖c1+

Due to White's threat to interpose on the b-file, Black must start checking.
12   ♔d6   ♖b1
13   ♔c7   ♖c1+
14   ♔d8   ♖b1
15   ♔c8   ♔g4
16   ♖d6   g5
17   ♖xf6   gxh4
18   gxh4   ♔xh4
19   ♖g6!   ♔h3
20   ♔c7!   1-0

Black resigned since, in view of the threat of 21 ♖b6, he must take at once on b7 (if 20 ... h4 21 ♖b6 ♖xb6 22 ♔xb6 ♔g2 23 b8♕ h3 the h-pawn is only on the sixth rank). But after 20 ... ♖xb7+ 21 ♔xb7 White wins by a tempo exactly as in diag 95.

A very fine technical performance by Hollis!

C.

5	...	♖e3!

This is best. Although the black rook ends up very passive on b8 there will be no threats of interposition on the b-file. And therefore White would have to spend a lot of extra time winning the rook - in fact so slow would this be that White must try a different plan.

6	♖c7	♖e8
7	b7	♖b8
8	♔d3	♔f5
9	♖xf7+	

If 9 ♔e3 f6 10 ♔f3 g5 11 ♖e7 ♖d8 12 ♔e3 ♖b8 13 ♖b3 ♔e5 14 ♔e3 ♔d5 and Black holds without too much trouble.

9	...	♔g4
10	♖f4+	♔xg3
11	♖b4 *(96b)*	
11	...	g5!

Black must play actively.

Hollis gave only passive defence with 11 ... ♔h3. But this loses since White can use zugzwang to cross the fourth rank without allowing ... ♔xh4, viz: 12 ♔e2 (but not 12 ♔c2 ♔g3 13 ♔b3 ♔h3 14 ♔a4 ♔g3 15 ♔a5 ♖xb7!=) 12 ... ♔g3 (12 ... ♔g2 13 ♖b3!) 13 ♔e3 ♔h3 14 ♔f3 ♖f8+ 15 ♔e4 and wins.

12	hxg5	h4
13	g6	h3
14	g7	h2
15	♖b1	♔g2
16	♔e4	h1♛
17	♖xh1	♔xh1

This position would be won if the pawns were closer together but here its dead drawn.

18	♔d5	♔h2
19	♔c6	♖g8!=

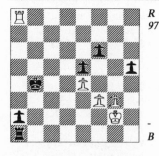

R 97

Nunn - Smejkal
Lucerne Ol 1982
This extremely difficult position arose in a game from the 1982 Olympiad. Black started nearly 40 moves ago(!) with the pawn on a3. But clearly that promises nothing and after extensive adjournment analysis Smejkal was finally ready to join battle.

1	...	♔b3
2	♖b8+	♔c3
3	♖c8+!	

Not 3 ♖a8? ♖d1! 4 ♖xa2 (4 ♖a3+ ♔b2) 4 ... ♖d2+ 5 ♖xd2 ♔xd2 and the pawn ending is won for Black, viz: 6 ♔h3 ♔e3 7 g4 hxg4+ 8 ♔xg4 ♔f2 9 f4 ♔e3 10 fxe5 fxe5 11 ♔f5 ♔d4 and wins.

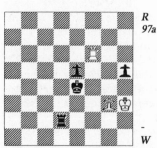

R 97a

3	...	♔d3
4	♖a8	♔c4
5	♖c8+	♔d3
6	♖a8	♖d1!

This is the only way to make progress. If 6 ... ♔e2 7 ♖a7 ♔e1 (threatening 8 ... ♖d1) 8 ♔g1! ♖d1? (8 ... ♔e2+! transposing back into the game) 9 ♖xa2 ♔d3 10 ♖a1+! (not 10 ♔g2?? ♖d2+) 10 ... ♔e2 11 ♔g2=.

7	♖a3+!	

Not 7 ♖xa2? ♖d2+! and wins.

7	...	♔e2
8	♖xa2+	♔e3!

Black has returned his extra pawn in order to force his pieces to extremely active squares. In view of the ever

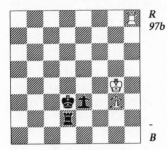

present threat of ... ♖d2+ White cannot now defend passively so:

9	♖a3+	♖d3
10	♖a6	♖d2+
11	♔h3	♔xf3
12	♖xf6+	

♔xe4 *(97a)*

| 13 | ♖h6 | |

If 13 ♔h4 ♖h2+ 14 ♔g5 ♖g2 15 ♔h4 ♔e3 16 ♖a6 e4 17 ♖a3+ ♔f2 and wins.

Or 13 g4 hxg4+ 14 ♔xg4 ♖g2+ 15 ♔h3 ♖g8 16 ♖f1 ♔d3 and wins.

Given that everything else really does lose there is even something to be said for the seemingly utterly absurd 13 g4 hxg4+ 14 ♔g3. As we saw in diags 42 - 43 the ending of ♖e+g v ♖ is sometimes far from easy. However, presumably Black wins quite easily if he plays sensibly, e.g. 14 ... ♖d1 and if 15 ♖a6 ♔f5 the position is theoretically winning or 15 ♔f2 ♖a1! taking the important a-file (cf diags 4 - 6 especially for the significance of this).

| 13 | ... | ♔d3! |

If 13 ... ♔f3? 14 ♖xh5 e4 15 ♖f5+ ♔e2 16 g4 e3 17 ♔g3 ♔d3 18 ♖f8 e2 19 ♔f2=.

| 14 | ♖xh5 | e4 |
| 15 | ♖h8 | |

But here if 15 ♖d5+ ♔e2 gains a tempo on the rook: 16 ♖e5 e3 17 ♔g4 ♖d4+ 18 ♔f5 ♔f3 19 ♖e8 (19 g4 ♖f4+!) 19 ... ♖d5+ 20 ♔f6 ♖d3 wins.

Or 15 g4 e3 16 ♔g3 (16 ♖d5+ ♔e4 wins) 16 ... e2! 17 ♔f2 ♖d1 18 ♖d5+ ♔e4 and wins. This is the *key variation*. Due to it White is unable to play the natural 15 g4 and must therefore lose an invaluable tempo.

15	...	e3
16	♔g4 *(97b)*	
16	...	♖d1!

As in most such endings, the attacker's priority must be, not to promote his own pawn, but to harass the enemy creating threats against his pawn. If instead 16 ... e2? 17 ♖d8+ ♔e3 18 ♖e8+ ♔f2 19 ♖f8+ ♔g2 20 ♖e8 ♖d4+ 21 ♔f5 ♔f3 22 ♖xe2! ♔xe2 23 g4 and draws by a tempo.

| 17 | ♖d8+ | ♔e2 |
| 18 | ♖f8 | |

18 ♖e8 ♖d4+ 19 ♔f5 ♔f3 20 ♖e5 ♖a4! (zugzwang) 21 ♖e8 (or 21 g4 ♖f4+) 21 ... ♖a5+ 22 ♔f6 ♖a3 and wins.

| 18 | ... | ♖g1! |
| 19 | ♔h4 | |

19 ♔h3 ♖f1! (19 ... ♔e1? 20 ♖d8 e2 21 ♔h2 ♖f1 22 ♔g2 ♖f2+ 23 ♔g1 ♖f7 24 ♔g2 ♖a7 25 ♖e8! ♖d7 26 g4 ♔d2 27 ♔f2 ♖f7+ 28 ♔g3 e1♕+ 29 ♖xe1 ♔xe1 30 g5=) 20 ♖a8 ♔f2 21 ♖f8+ ♔g1 22 ♖e8 ♖f3 23 ♔h4 ♔f2 24 g4 e2 25 ♖xe2+ ♔xe2 26 g5 ♔e3 27 ♔g4 ♖f4+ 28 ♔h5 ♔e4 and wins.

19	...	♔d2
20	♖d8+	♔e1
21	g4	e2

And Black is just winning - see diag RP33.

Due to this extensive analysis, much of it found by the English and Czech teams during the Lucerne Olympiad and thus sorted out by Nunn later, it would appear that diag 97 is actually lost for White!

Rook v Rook

Underlying Elements of Rook Endgames

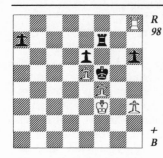

R
98

+
B

Tactics
The rook is a powerful piece and rook and king together can be a formidable attacking force. So it is not suprising that tactical ideas are often of extreme importance in rook endings.

Checkmate
Novak - Ryc
Czechoslovakia 1978
Although Black has a passed pawn, the dominant factor here is the unfortunate position of his king. The game

continued:

| 1 | ... | ♚g6 |

If 1 ... a5 2 ♖xh6 a4 3 h4! etc. as in the game. Or if 1 ... ♖b7 2 ♖f8+! ♚g6 3 ♖f6+ winning easily.

| 2 | ♖e8! | ♚f5 |
| 3 | h4 | a5 |

Or 3 ... h5 4 ♖g8 and mates on g5.

4	h5	a4
5	♖h8!	a3
6	♖xh6	a2
7	♖g6!	a1♛
8	♖g5 mate.	

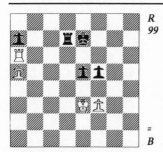

R
99

=
B

Piskalnietis - Berzins
USSR 1962
After:

| 1 | ... | f4+ |

White incautiously played:

| 2 | ♚e4?? | |

2 ♚e2 should hold since the white rook is very active on

a6.

| 2 | ... | ♖d6! |

But now 3 ♖xa7+ ♚e6 and the threat of 4 ... ♖d4 mate wins a rook. Or 3 ♖xd6 ♚xd6 leads to a completely lost pawn ending. So White had to resign.

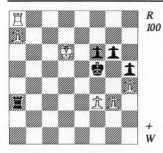

R
100

+
W

Unzicker - Lundin
Amsterdam 1954
White won easily by the technical procedure of playing a his king round to h6 and then giving up the a-pawn to annihilate Black's kingside,

i.e. 1 ♖b8 ♖xa7 2 ♖b5+ and 3 ♚xg6 etc. But he could have won on the spot with:

1	♖c8!	♖a6+
2	♖c6	♖xa7
3	♖c5 mate!	

R
101

Stalemate

This is a very important defensive idea. When it works it can save seemingly hopeless positions. See for example diag 60. Here are some further examples:

Bernstein - Smyslov
Groningen 1946

B

Black is winning easily. But he blundered with:

| 1 | ... | b2?? |
| 2 | ♖xb2! | |

And it turns out that after the intended skewer 2 ... ♖h2+ 3 ♔f3 ♖xb2 is stalemate.

After 2 ... ♔g4 3 ♔f1 the draw was soon agreed.

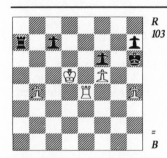

R
102

Meduna - Speelman
France 1979
(Analysis variation)

This somewhat unusual position arose during adjournment analysis - though not actually in the game! White is threatening to disrupt Black's defences with 1 ♖d6 and therefore a possible defensive move

=
B

is:

| 1 | ... | ♖f6 |

At the time I was concerned about:

| 2 | ♖d8 | |

But later Jonathan Mestel found the defence:

| 2 | ... | ♖e6+!! |
| 3 | ♔d7 | ♖e4 |

drawing easily.

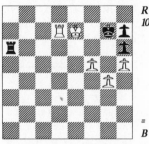

R
103

Korchnoi - Petrosian
Moscow 1971
(Analysis variation)

Black's position looks very difficult. But there is a hidden defence:

| 1 | ... | ♖a4! |

=
B

| 2 | ♔c6 | |

Or 2 ♔e6 c5!.

| 2 | ... | ♔h5 |
| 3 | ♔xc7 | h6! |

And the threat of 4 ... ♖xb4! 5 ♖xb4 stalemate forces a draw.

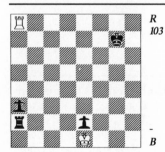

R
103

The Skewer

As the knight's primary tactical ability is to fork, so the *rook's main talent is the skewer*. We have already seen many examples of this, see especially diags 20 and 67. Here are a couple more.

| 1 | ... | ♖a1+! |
| 2 | ♔xe2 | a2 |

B

Now the white king has nowhere to hide. If he wishes he can give a few checks but the black king will simply go to the b-file. So instead he might try:

| 3 | ♔f2 | |

If 3 ♔ - third rank 3 ... ♖ checks and wins. And 3 ♔d2 is met as in the text by:

| 3 | ... | ♖h1! |
| 4 | ♖xa2 | ♖h2+ |

and wins.

Rook v Rook

♖ V ♜

R
105
+
W

Erinas - Ilmaz
Turkey 1976
Everything is set up for the skewer. But first White played:
    1   ♔b7!
    But not 1 d6? ♔xd6 2 ♖d8+? (2 ♔b7!=) 2 ... ♔c6 3 h8♕ ♖a4 mate! One must always look for *tactics for one's opponents* as well as for oneself!
    1   ...   b5
There is nothing better.
    2   ♖c8!   ♔d6
Or 2 ... ♖xh7 3 ♖xc7+, the skewer, and wins easily.

    3   ♖d8+
This is unnecessary but doesn't spoil anything.
    3   ...   ♔c5
    4   h8♕   ♖xh8
    5   ♖xh8   ♔xd5
    6   ♔xc7   ♔c4
    7   ♔b6
and Black loses by a tempo: (cf diags RP5 and RP6 - note that it takes White five more moves to get in ♔a2 but and ♖b8 but Black six to queen his pawn ie b5 - b4 - b3 - b2 - b1, ♔c4 - c3 - c2).

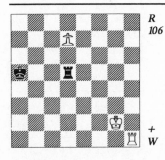

R
106
+
W

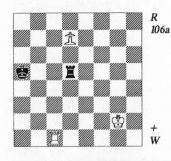

R
106a
+
W

The Pin
This is a very powerful weapon for a rook *against minor piece.* But a rook cannot ordinarily pin another rook and so pins don't usually arise in rook endings except in one very typical circumstace - cf diag 46 etc.
    1   ♖h5!   ♖xh5
    2   d8♕+ and wins.

The Fork
    Diagram 106a
If the white rook is on c1 then it can deflect the enemy rook from the other side with a *fork*.
    1   ♖c5+!   ♖xc5
    2   d8♕+
But although rooks very often fork pairs of pawns, this is the only reasonable scenario in which rook forks king and rook.

R
107
+
B

Interposition (discovered attack)
This is an extremely important strategical and tactical theme. The idea is that a rook, supported by its own king, or possibly a pawn, can cut the line of action of an enemy rook.
    Diag 107 is one of the two

main lines in the Lucena position diag 3. As we know after
    1   ...   ♖e1+
    2   ♖e4! wins at once
2 ♖e4 was an *interposition.* It is a tactical device which achieves a strategic aim: the black rook's checks are brought to an end.

Rook v Rook

R
108

Kozlov - Tukmakov
USSR 1977
Here Black has another tactical device, *discovered attack* to achieve his interposition. (I think that the question of whether an interposition is tactical or strategic would depend on an exact definition of those terms. For the moment I shall use them rather loosely.)

    1   ...   ♖b4!
   So that if 2 ♖xa2 ♔b3 *check.*

| 2 | ♔e5 | ♔b3 |
| 3 | ♖xa2 | |

Forced, since Black threatened the *interposition* 3 ... ♖a4 after which White cannot prevent the pawns from queening: 4 ♖b8+ ♔a3 etc.

3	...	♔xa2
4	♔f6	♔b3
5	♔g7	♖b7+
6	♔f6	♔c4
7	g4	♔d5
8	f5	♖a7
9	fxg6	♖a6+

0-1

R
109

Some Underlying Strategic Ideas

Properties of the Rook
a) The rook is a powerful attacking piece but a poor defender. It is therefore usually correct to play *actively* in rook endings. (see numerous examples: especially 125);

b) It is normally best to place your rook *behind* passed pawns. See diags 69, 71, 90-91 etc.);

c) Specific properties of the rook:
    A. Cutting;
    B. Rook on the seventh rank;
    C. Checking distance;
    D. Pressure from behind.

A. Cutting
Since it controls whole ranks and files, a rook can completely exclude the enemy king from the proceedings. This ability to *cut off* the king is extremely valuable.

In diag 109 Black is threatening to get his king in front

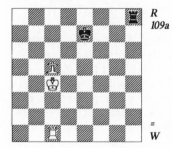

R
109a

of the pawn with 1 ... ♔d7. But White to move can exclude him from the struggle with:

    1   ♖d1!   ♔e7
  Or 1 ... ♖c8 2 ♔b5 ♖b8+ 3 ♔a6 ♖c8 4 ♔b6 ♖b8+ 5 ♔c7 and wins. The rook had *insufficient checking distance;* see C. below.

Diagram 109a
If, however, the black king starts on e7 then he can draw:

    1   ♖d1   ♖d8!
  Opposing the file. This is the thematic way to neutralise a rook which is cutting off your king.

    2   ♖xd8
If 2 ♖d5/♖d4 ♖xd5/d4=. Or if the rook moves away, Black simply plays 2 ... ♔d7.

| 2 | ... | ♔xd8 |
| 3 | ♔b5 | ♔c7= |

The strategic weapon of *opposing the file* is very closely allied to *interposition* (see diags 108 - 109). In each case the idea is to *neutralise the enemy rook by placing your*

Rook v Rook

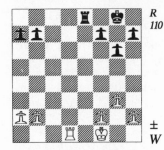

R 110

± W

B. Rook on the Seventh Rank

Until quite late in the game there are likely to be several pawns unmoved. A rook on the seventh rank will therefore be extremely inconvenient for the opponent.

White to move in diag 110 can seize considerable advantage with:

    1   ♖d7!

Black must now choose between:

a) Passive defence with 1 ... ♖b8;

b) A pawn sacrifice to activate his rook.

Normally, one would want to activate the rook. However, I can't see any very sensible way to do this. So, perhaps Black should try a), i.e. 1 ... ♖b8.

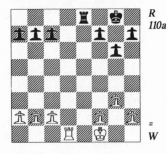

R 110a

= W

Although White then has rather a free hand, Black has no other disadvantages and I don't see a "clear winning plan". *At the right moment* Black will probably have to *go active*. See diag 118. But it will be hard for White to keep sufficient control to prevent this from being effective. Note that in this position, Black has no way of evicting the rook - he will have to "play around it".

Diagram 110a

Here, however, Black is more fortunate:

1	♖d7	♖c8
2	♔e2	♔f8
3	♔e3	♔e8

And the rook is evicted without doing any real damage.

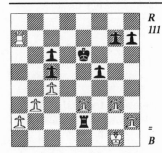

R 111

= B

Lilienthal - Smyslov
USSR 1941

Black is already a pawn down and his queenside pawns in particular are extremely weak. But he has a rook on the seventh rank.

In this case the white king is *cut off on the first rank* - a particularly serious case of cutting.

As a result Black drew extremely easily:

    1   ...   g5!

He must play actively. 1 ... ♔f6 would be quite wrong.

2	♖xh7	♖xa2
3	♖h6+	♔e5
4	♖xc6	♔e4
5	♖xc5	f4!

The key move, creating *shelter* for the black king

    6   exf4   ♔f3

As a result of the bad position of his king and the *active* black pieces, White is now threatened with mate.

    7   h3   ♖a1+
        ½-½

Since Black gains *perpetual check*.

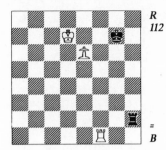

R 112

= B

R 113

= B

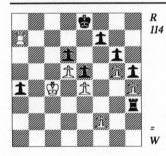

R 114

= W

C. Checking Distance

It quite often happens that a player has to defend by check-ing the enemy king repeatedly. In that case it is vital that the rook is placed *as far away as possible* from the enemy king, i.e. *rooks need room ("checking distance") in or-der to function effectively* - c.f. especially diags 4, 5, 6, and 13 (and diag 108).

Thus in diag 112, Black to move draws with:

   1   ...   ♖a2!

   2   e7

Or 2 ♖c1 ♖a7+ 3 ♖c7 ♖a8 4 e7 ♔f7= (cf diag 5).

   2   ...   ♖a7+!=

As in diag 4.

But only 1 ... ♖a2 will do. If e.g.

   1   ...   ♖b2??

Or 1 ... ♖d2+ 2 ♔e7 ♖a2 3 ♖g1+.

   2   e7 wins

Thus Black has *insufficient checking distance* and loses (cf diag 4a).

Similarly in diag 113 Black to move only draws with 1 ... ♖h8! (see diag 12 variation B). For if

   1   ...   ♖h7?

   2   ♔b4!

But not 2 c5? ♖d7!= oppos-ing the file.

   2   ...   ♖b7+

Or 2 ... ♖d7 3 ♖xd7 ♔xd7 4 ♔b5! and wins.

   3   ♔a5   ♖c7

   4   ♔b5   ♖b7+

   5   ♔c6   ♖b8

   6   c5 and wins

After 1 ... ♖b7, the black rook had *insufficient checking distance*.

D. Pressure from Behind

In diag 113, the black rook defended by exerting pressure from in front of the pawn. In certain positions, it is possible to restrain the pawn by exerting pressure from *behind the pawn* (see diag 2).

Since diag 2 makes the point so well, I shan't repeat it here. But I should point out that this method of defence will tend to work only in very simplified positions. For if a rook is pressurizing a pawn from behind, there will often be an extremely convenient square for the enemy king in front of the pawn. That is, the king will have *cover*. Which brings me to:

Cover for the King

In order to move the king to an active position one must have some way of hiding it from checks from the enemy rook. Essentially, there are two possibilities:

a) One can interpose one's rook to stop checks;

b) One can find cover - either from one's own or enemy pawns.

It will usually be best if the king can find its own cover, leaving the rook free to forage (cf diags 20 and 21: note the essential difference between these and diags 50 and 51, where a king found artificial shelter.

Savon - Jeliadinov
Riga 1964

Although he is a pawn up, Black is in great danger since

the white king and rook are enormously active.

1   **♔b5**

Here Black played the obvious 1 ... ♖xh4, but he soon succumbed to a combined attack by White's king and rook and soon-to-be-passed d-pawn: 2 ♔c6 ♖xe4 3 ♔xd6 ♔f8 (mate was threatened) 4 ♖a8+ ♔g7 5 ♔e7 ♖d4 6 d6 e4 (if 6 ... h4 7 d7 h3 8 d8♕ ♖xd8 9 ♖xd8 is also winning for White) 7 d7 e3 8 fxe3 ♖e4+ 9 ♔d6 ♖xe3 10 d8♕ ♖d3+ 11 ♔e5 1-0.

Instead, rather surprisingly, Black could have defended passively.

1   **...**   **♖c3!**

Cutting off the enemy king.

2	♖xa4	♔d7
3	♖a7+	♔e8
4	♔b6	♖c2
5	♖c7	

Interposition, as is normal against a rook which is cutting off your king.

5   **...**   **♖a2!**

And although it has very little room the rook is able to prevent the white king from achieving anything since there is *no shelter*:

6	♔c6	♖a6+!
7	♔b5	

Or 7 ♔b7 ♖a2.

7	...	♖a2
8	♖b7	♖c2!=

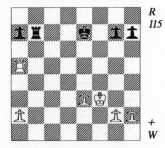

R 115

+ W

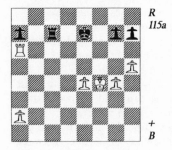

R 115a

+ B

Further Examples - Material Advantage

Rubinstein - Lasker
St Petersburg 1909

Not only is White a pawn up, but he also has a positional advantage - his rook is much more active than Black's.

Diag 115 is winning for White, but it would be perfectly possible to mess such a position up. This example is instructive mainly for the supremely *calm* way in which Rubinstein demonstrated the win.

1   **♖a6!**

Severely restricting the black king. Black cannot now free his rook from the burden of defending the a-pawn by playing his king to b8, since the white e-pawn would be too strong. So he must remain passive.

1	...	♔f8
2	e4	♖c7
3	h4	

Rubinstein plans to advance

his kingside in a unit. Once the h- and g-pawns are far enough up the board, Black will have to weaken his kingside to deal with them: then the white king will get additional possibilities.

Note also that by advancing his whole kingside together, White prevents Black from "going active", i.e. abandoning the pawns to free his rook. For example, 3 ♔f4? (instead of 3 h4) 3 ... ♖c2! 4 ♔f3 ♖c3+! and White is considerably embarrassed.

3	...	♔f7
4	g4	♔f8
5	♔f4	♔e7
6	h5 (115a)	
6	...	h6

Of course Black does not want to create a weakness on g6, but if he does nothing then White will advance his pawns further, e.g. 6 ... ♔f7 7 ♔f5 ♔e7 8 g5 ♔f7 9 e5 ♔e7 10 g6 h6 (if 10 ... hxg6+ 11 ♔xg6 the white king is much

too active) 11 a3 (zugzwang) 11
... ♖b7 12 ♖e6+ ♚d7 (or 12 ...
♚f8 13 ♖c6 ♚e7 14 ♖c8 and
wins) 13 ♖f6! ♚e8 (13 ... gxf6
14 g7 etc.) 14 ♖f7! ♖xf7+ 15
gxf7+ ♚xf7 16 e6+ ♚e7 17
♚e5 and wins easily.

7	♚f5	♚f7
8	e5	♖b7
9	♖d6	♚f8
10	♖c6	♚f7
11	a3!	

A calm and elegant move.
By preventing ... ♖b4 Rubinstein forestalls any possible
counterplay against the g4-

pawn. Here Lasker actually resigned. He is in zugzwang, i.e.

If 11 ... ♖e7 12 e6+ ♚g8 13
♚g6 ♖e8 14 e7!.

Or 11 ... ♚e7 12 ♚g6 ♚f8
13 ♖c8+ ♚e7 14 ♚xg7 etc.

Or 11 ... ♚f8 12 ♚g6 ♖b3
(note that 12 ... ♖b4 is impossible because of 11 a3) 13
♖c8+ ♚e7 14 ♚xg7 ♖xa3 15
♚xh6 winning easily.

Finally, if 11 ... a5 12 ♖a6
♖b5 13 ♖a7+ ♚g8 14 a4 ♖c5
15 ♚e6 is also quite hopeless -
the e-pawn soon queens.

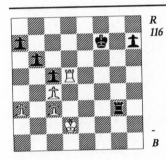

R
116

B

Kasparian - Botvinnik
Moscow 1931

Black is an outside passed
pawn up and the white queenside pawns are shattered.
Botvinnik won quickly and
easily by the simple expedient
of *advancing his h-pawn*. The
white rook simply does not
have time to inflict real damage on the queenside - especially given the woeful state of
White's pawns.

1	...	♚g6!
2	♖d7	h5
3	♖xa7	h4
4	♖b7	h3
5	♖xb6+	♚g5
6	♖b1	

Or if 6 ♖b8 ♖g4! wins, preparing to *interpose* on the h-
file.

6	...	♚g4

7	♚c2	

If White had reasonable
queenside pawns then he
would be able to set up a
passed pawn and get some
chances of drawing with ♚+P
vs ♚+♖. But here, although
he does have a passed pawn,
the case is hopeless. There is
no conceivable way of eliminating the black c-pawn.

7	...	h2
8	♖h1	♚h3
9	a4	

Or 9 ♚b3 ♖g1 10 ♖xh2+
♚xh2 11 ♚a4, hoping to
reach the c-pawn via b5, 11 ...
♖b1! and wins.

9	...	♖g1
10	♖xh2+	♚xh2
11	♚d3	♖e1!

0-1

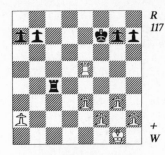

R
117

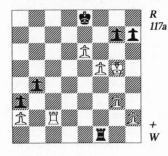

R
117a

+
W

Konstantinopolsky - Shaposh-
nikov
Sochi 1952
In this more unbalanced position, White should eventually
be able to set up two connected passed pawns on the
kingside. But on the other
hand, Black can get a passed
pawn on the queenside and
thus obtain counterplay.

1	♖b5	b6
2	♖b2!	

Correctly defending the
queenside before undertaking
kingside play.

2	...	♚e6
3	♚g2	♚d5

He could also have tried to
impede White's advance with
3 ... g5. But after 4 ♚h3 h5 5
f4 ♚f6 (if 5 ... ♖c5 6 a4 - to
threaten ♖b5 again - 6 ... ♖c4
7 a5 bxa5 8 ♖b5 g4+ 9 ♚h4
a4 10 ♖xh5 should win) 6 ♖b5
g4+ 7 ♚h4 ♖c2 8 ♖xh5
♖xh2+ 9 ♚xg4 ♖xa2 10 e4
and White must win the race
fairly easily.

4	♖d2+	♚c6

To support his pawn. If 4 ...
♚e4? 5 ♖d7 is much too
strong.

5	f4	a5
6	♚f3	b5
7	f5	a4
8	e4	♖c1

He must attend to White's
e-pawn. If 8 ... b4 9 e5 b3 10
axb3 axb3 11 e6 ♖c2 (or 11 ...
♖c1 12 ♖e2!) 12 e7 wins easily.

9	e5	♖e1

If 9 ... ♖f1+ 10 ♚e4 ♖e1+ 11
♚d4 merely improves White's
king position. Or 9 ... b4 10 e6
♖e1 11 ♖d4! (not now 11 ♖e2??
♖xe2 12 ♚xe2 b3 13 axb3 a3!)
11 ... ♚c5 12 ♖e4 winning.

10	♖e2	♖f1+
11	♚g4	♚d7
12	♚g5	a3
13	e6+	♚e8
14	♖c2	b4 *(117a)*
15	♖c8+	

Utilising the position of
Black's king to reposition his
rook with tempo.

15	...	♚e7
16	♖a8	

Black was threatening 16 ...
b3 17 axb3 a2.

16	...	♖e1

This may look rather tame
but really there was nothing
for Black to do. If 16 ... ♖f2 17
♖a7+ ♚d6 (or 17 ... ♚f8 18
♖f7+ ♚g8 19 ♖b7 wins eas-
ily) 18 ♖xg7 ♖xa2 19 ♖b7
wins by at least a tempo.
So Black keeps his rook on
the eighth rank still hoping to
get in his breakthrough ...

17	♖a4	

i.e. if 17 ♖a7+ ♚d6 18
♖xg7?? b3 would have fol-
lowed - this is possible only
with the rook on the eighth
rank.

17	...	♖e2

Acquiescing in a rather
hopeless exchange, but if 17 ...
♖b1 White could simply start
the plan he later played in the
game with 18 h4 intending h5,
♖+, h6 etc.

18	♖xb4	♖xa2
19	♖b7+	♚f8
20	♖f7+	♚g8
21	♖a7	♚f8
22	h4!	♖a1
23	h5	1-0

White threatens 24 h6 to
free for his king i.e. if 23 ... a2
24 h6! gxh6+ (or 24 ... ♖g1 25
hxg7+ ♚g8 26 ♖a8+ ♚xg7
27 f6 mate!) 25 ♚f6 etc.
And if 23 ... h6+ 24 ♚g6 a2
25 e7+ ♚e8 26 ♚xg7 wins
easily.

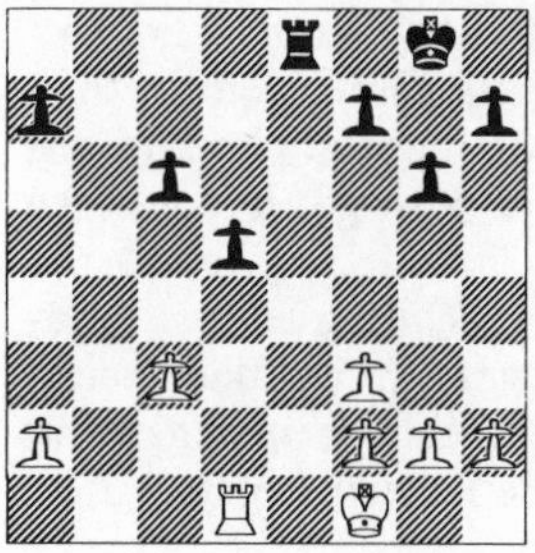

R 118

∓ B

Fuster - Bronstein
Moscow v Budapest 1949

As a result of the doubled f-pawns Black is effectively a pawn up. These pawns would be okay defensively but cannot be used to make a passed pawn.

A.

In the game Bronstein won extremely easily. He:

a) Seized the distant open file - the b-file;

b) Centralised his king; and

c) Then penetrated the white position using the a-pawn almost as a battering ram - or perhaps a tin opener?

1 ... ♖b8
2 ♖d2 ♔f8
3 ♔e2 ♔e7
4 ♔d3 c5
5 ♔c2 ♔d6
6 ♖e2 a5!

Already starting phase 3 of his plan.

7 ♔c1

If 7 a3 a4 and ... ♖b3xa3: or 7 a4 d4 seizing b4 for the rook.

7 ... a4
8 ♖d2 a3
9 c4!?

Trying to block the position. But White is already clearly lost.

9 ... d4
10 ♔c2 g5

White's idea is that if 10 ... ♖b2+ 11 ♔moves ♖xd2+ then the black a-pawn will be weak. But Bronstein simply ignores him, improving his position on the kingside.

11 ♔d3 f5
12 ♔c2 h5
13 ♔d3 h4
14 h3 ♖b1

Eyeing amongst others the g-pawn.

15 g4 ♖c1!
16 gxf5 ♔e5
17 ♖c2 ♖xc2
18 ♔xc2 ♔xf5
19 ♔d3 ♔f4
20 ♔e2 d3+
0-1

B.

But in the initial position after 1 ... ♖b8, I think that White should have created counterplay immediately with:

2 c4! dxc4
3 ♖c1

Now if 3 ... ♖b2 4 ♖xc4 ♖xa2 5 ♖xc6 is only a draw so Black play the obvious:

3 ... ♖b4
4 ♖c2

When Black must choose between:

a) 4 ... ♔f8 5 ♔e2 ♔e7 6 ♔d2 ♔d6 7 ♔c3; and

b) 4 ... ♖a4 5 ♔e2 ♖a3 (5 ... ♔f8 6 ♔e3!) 6 ♔e1 c3 7 ♔e2 ♔f8 8 ♔d3 ♔e7 9 ♔c4. In each case Black is much better - I think that I marginally prefer b) for him. But White has reasonable drawing chances.

It is quite wrong for White to sit back and let Black activate his centre without a fight. He should have taken what steps he could immediately before Black could get organised.

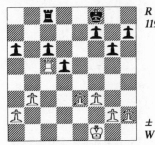

R 119

± W

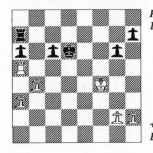

R 119a

+ B

Positional Features

We shall look at the following types of advantage:

 A. Better pawn structure;
 B. Better passed pawns;
 C. Active vs Passive pieces.

A. Better pawn structure

Diag 118 brought us nicely on to this matter. As usual, pawns can be weak because they either:

 a) are subject to attack and capture; or

 b) cripple a pawn majority of which they are part.

Diag 118 was a good instance of b) - as were, for instance, diags 76 and 111. In the next few pages we will examine some instances of a).

Flohr - Vidmar
Nottingham 1936

Although White has a clear advantage due to Black's shattered queenside pawns, Black has quite a solid position elsewhere.

If Black can choose the *right moment to "go active"* then he will have good drawing chances.

But this is always very difficult and in the game Vidmar allowed Flohr to get a complete stranglehold on the position after which he was demonstrably lost ...

 1 ♔e2 ♔e7
 2 ♔d3 ♔d6
 3 ♖a5!

Not 3 ♔d4? ♖b8 breaking the blockade at once, e.g. if 4 ♖a5 c5+ is possible.

 3 ... ♖a8
 4 ♔d4

White has cemented his advantage by preventing ...c5. At the moment he has no particular threats; but given time he could create play on the kingside with g4, h4 and then e4.

Since White intends to play e4 eventually, Vidmar decides to make this as expensive as possible in terms of pawn exchanges.

 4 ... f5!?
 5 b4 ♖b8?

This is the first good chance to *"go active"*: 5 ... ♔c7 6 ♔c5 ♔b7 7 ♔d6 ♖e8 8 ♖a3 d4! 9 exd4 ♖e2 10 ♖c3 ♖xg2 11 ♖xc6 ♖xh2 12 a4 g5!= (Smyslov and Levenfish).

 6 a3 ♖a8

6 ... ♖b6? would be very bad since the rook would have no pass move and so Black could easily fall into zugzwang. Moreover, on b6 it would be two more moves away from activity - as distinct from one on a8.

 7 e4! fxe4
 8 fxe4 dxe4
 9 ♔xe4 ♖a7?

This was Black's final chance to *"go active"*: 9 ... ♔c7 10 ♖e5 (10 ♔f4 ♖f8+! 11 ♔g3 ♔b6=) 10 ... ♔b6 11 ♖e7 a5! 12 ♖xh7 axb4 13 axb4 ♖a4 14 ♖g7 ♖xb4+ 15 ♔f3 ♖h4 16 h3 ♖h6! 17 ♔g4 c5 18 ♔g5 ♖h8 19 ♖xg6+ ♔b5 20 ♖g7 c4 21 h4 ♖c8! and the c-pawn gives drawing chances.

 10 ♔f4 *(119a)*

Black's pawn weaknesses have mutated from one backward pawn and one isolated to two isolated pawns.

Although this would have been very difficult to judge in a game, Black should have gone active either on move 5 or, if he missed that opportu-

R
119b

+
B

nity, on move 9. For now it would appear that Black is lost by force.

    10 ... h6

This is weakening. But understandably he didn't want to allow the white king into h6, e.g.

a) 10 ... ♖a8 11 ♔g5 ♖a7 12 ♔h6 ♔e6 13 g4 ♔d6 14 h3!? (if 14 h4 ♔e6 15 h5 gxh5 16 gxh5 ♔d6 17 ♖g5 ♖e7! intending 18 ♖g7 ♖e3! is also rather messy though White may just be winning) 14 ... ♔e6 15 h4 ♔d6 (15 ... ♔f6? 16 ♖c5 ♖c7 17 a4!) 16 h5 gxh5 17 ♖xh5 (17 ♔xh5 ♔c7) 17 ... ♖e7 18 ♖a5 ♖e4!? (if 18 ... ♖a7 19 g5 ♔e6 20 a4! wins) 19 ♔g5 ♖e5+?! (19 ... ♖e1!) 20 ♖xe5 ♔xe5 21 ♔h6 ♔f4 22 g5 ♔f5 23 a4 ♔g4 24 a5 ♔f4 25 ♔xh7 ♔xg5 26 ♔g7 ♔f5 27 ♔f7 and wins by a tempo!;

b) 10 ... ♔c7 11 ♔g5 ♔b6 12 ♔h6 ♖e7 13 g4 ♖e4 14 h3 ♖e7 15 h4 ♖e4 16 ♖g5! ♖e7 17 h5 gxh5 18 gxh5 ♖d7 19 a4! ♖d4 20 a5+ ♔c7 21 ♔xh7 wins easily.

    11 h4 ♔e6
    12 ♔g4 ♖a8

If 12 ... ♔f7 White still plays 13 h5!.

    13 h5! g5

Or 13 ... gxh5+ 14 ♔xh5 ♖g8 15 g4 ♔d6 16 ♖xa6 etc.

    14 g3 ♖a7
    15 ♔f3 ♖a8
    16 ♔e4 ♖a7
    17 ♖e5+! *(119b)*

Now Black must choose which way to go with his king - but unfortunately both choices lose:

    17 ... ♔d6

Or if 17 ... ♔f6 18 ♖c5 ♖c7 19 ♖a5 ♖a7 20 ♔d4 ♔e6 21 ♔c5 ♖d7 (21 ... ♔d7 22 ♔b6 is hopeless) 22 ♖xa6 ♖d3 23 ♖xc6+ ♔f7 24 a4 ♖xg3 25 ♖xh6 etc.

    18 ♖e8 c5
    19 ♖d8+! ♔c6

Or if 19 ... ♔c7 20 ♖h8 cxb4 21 ♖h7+ ♔b6 22 ♖xa7! ♔xa7 23 axb4 ♔b6 24 ♔f5! and White queens one move too soon.

    20 ♖c8+ ♔b6
    21 ♖xc5 ♖h7
    22 ♖e5 ♔c6
    23 ♖e6+ ♔b5
    24 ♔f5 ♖f7+
    25 ♖f6 1-0

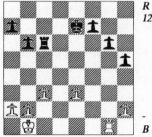

R
120

-
B

Schlechter - Rubinstein
San Sebastián 1912
In this much clearer position Rubinstein won exceedingly quickly:

    1 ... ♖e6

Forcing the white rook into a passive position.

    2 ♖e1 ♖f6!
    3 ♖e2 ♔e6

Now the black king advances.

    4 ♔c2 ♔e5
    5 c4

Or 5 ♔d3 ♖d6+, forcing the black king to e4 anyway.

    5 ... ♔e4
    6 b4 g5

With his king beautifully centralised Rubinstein now starts to mobilise his pawns. Although White also gets a passed pawn, it *cannot be supported by his king* and is therefore harmless.

    7 ♔c3 g4
    8 c5 h4
    9 ♖g2 ♖g6
    10 ♔c4 g3
    11 hxg3 hxg3
    12 ♔b5 ♔f3
    13 ♖g1 bxc5

Rook v Rook

14 bxc5 a6+!
Cutting the white king off from his passed c-pawn. The g-pawn, however, beautifully supported by king and rook, will quickly cost White his rook, so:
0-1

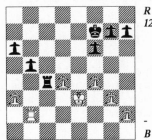

R 121

Marshall - Chigorin
Barmen 1905
In this position too, White's ragged pawn structure gives Black a huge advantage.

First Black must *blockade* the d-pawn.
1 ... ♔e6!
Centralising the king. But he must resist the temptation to take the a-pawn immediately. If 1 ... ♖c3+? 2 ♔e4 ♖xa3 (or 2 ... ♔e6 3 f5+ ♔d6 4 a4!) 3 ♔d5! and the d-pawn has been transformed from a sickly weakling into a redoubtable warrior *supported* as it is now by the king.
2 ♖b3
2 ♔e4 is an idea, trying to disrupt Black a little. But after 2 ... f5+ 3 ♔d3 ♔d5 4 ♖b4!? Black can play 4 ... ♖c1! (4 ... ♖xb4 5 axb4 isn't clear, e.g. 5... g6 6 h3 h6 7 g4! - cf

diags P43, P44) and if 5 a4 ♖c4 6 ♖xc4 bxc4+ 7 ♔c3 a5 8 h3 h5 9 h4 g6 and wins.
2 ... ♔d5
3 ♖d3 f5
4 h3 h5
5 ♔e2
White was in zugzwang. Obviously 5 h4 g6 does not help him. And if 5 ♖d1 ♖c3+ 6 ♖d3 ♖xd3+ 7 ♔xd3 a5, the pawn ending is an easy win for Black.
5 ... ♖xd4
Black is now a pawn up and has retained his positional advantage. He won easily: 6 ♖c3 ♖e4+ 7 ♔d2 h4! 8 ♖c7 hxg3 9 ♖xg7 ♖xf4 10 ♖xg3 ♔e5 11 ♔e2 ♖c4 12 ♖g6 ♖a4 13 ♖g3 f4 14 ♖b3 ♖c4 15 ♔d1 ♔e4 16 h4 f3 17 ♔e1 ♔f4 18 h5 ♖c1+ 19 ♔f2 ♖c2+ 20 ♔e1 ♔g3 0-1

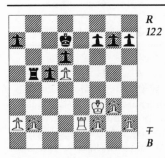

R 122

Chekhover - Budo
USSR 1937
The white pawn on d5 is weak since it is cut off from the rest of White's army. Moreover, Black's c5-pawn in particular is very strong; and his rook is much more active than White's.

Black therefore has a considerable positional advantage. But his position too is not without slight weaknesses and White should have reasonable chances if he can find the right moment to *go active*.
1 ... ♖b4
Threatening ... ♖d4xd5.
2 ♖d2 ♔e7

3 ♔e3 ♔f6
4 f4
This is slightly weakening but he must prevent the black king from settling on e5.
4 ... ♔f5
This is extremely natural, but also possible is 4 ... g5 at once fighting for the e5-square.
5 ♔f3 h5
6 b3
Alternatively:
a) If 6 h3 g5 and:
a1) 7 fxg5 ♔xg5 8 b3 ♔f6! 9 ♖e2 ♖d4 (9 ... h4!? if 9 ... a5 10 ♖e4) 10 ♖e8 ♖xd5 11 ♖a8 gives reasonable drawing chances.

R
122a

-
W

a2) 7 g4+ hxg4+ 8 hxg4+ ♔f6 9 f5! ♖f4+ 10 ♔g3 ♔e5 (not 10 ... ♖d4? 11 ♖xd4!) 11 ♖h2 ♖b4 12 ♖h7 ♖b7! is now good for Black and reasonably under control;

b) 6 ♖e2!? is interesting and:

b1) 6 ... g5?! 7 ♖e7 gxf4 (7 ... g4+!? 8 ♔e3 f6) 8 ♖xf7+ ♔e5 (8 ... ♔g6!?) 9 gxf4+ ♔xd5 10 b3! a5 11 ♖a7 prevents the creation of two connected passed pawns;

b2) 6 ... ♔f6! 7 b3 (7 ♖d2 g5!) 7 ... ♖d4 8 ♖e8 ♖xd5 9 ♖a8 ♖d2 10 ♖xa7 ♖xh2 is very pleasant for Black.

6 ... a5

He could also play 6 ... g5 at once.

7 ♖d3

This is deplorably passive. Perhaps he should have tried 7 ♖e2 a4 8 ♖e7 (8 bxa4 ♖xa4 9 ♖e7 ♖a3+ 10 ♔e2 ♖xa2+ 11 ♔e3 comes to more or less the same thing) 8 ... axb3! 9 axb3 ♖xb3+ 10 ♔e2 (10 ♔f2 ♖d3!). But after e.g. 10 ... ♖b2+ 11 ♔e3 (11 ♔f3 ♖d2!) 11 ... f6 White's position is very bad.

7 ... a4
8 bxa4

Maybe he should leave it. But Black's plan in any event will be to force his king to e5.

8 ... ♖xa4

9 a3 g5!
10 fxg5 ♔xg5
11 ♔e2 ♔f5
12 ♔d2

If 12 ♖e3 ♖e4!? 13 h4 ♖xe3+ 14 ♔xe3 ♔e5 15 g4 (15 a4 f5 wins) 15 ... hxg4 16 a4! c4 17 a5 c3 18 a6 c2 19 ♔d2 g3 20 a7 g2 21 a8♕ c1♕+ 22 ♔xc1 g1♕+ and Black must win.

Or 12 ♖f3+ ♔e4 13 ♖xf7 ♖xa3 is hopeless for White.

12 ... ♔e4 *(122a)*

This position is already quite hopeless for White. The connected passed c- and d-pawns will win easily. The game concluded:

13 ♔c2 c4
14 ♖c3 ♔xd5
15 ♖f3 ♔c6
16 ♔b2 ♖a7
17 ♖f5 d5
18 ♖xh5 ♖b7+
19 ♔c2 ♖b3
20 ♖h6+ ♔c5
21 ♖a6 ♖f3
22 h4 ♖xg3
23 h5 ♖h3
24 h6 f6
25 ♖xf6 ♖xa3
26 ♖f8 ♖h3
27 ♖h8 ♔d4
28 h7 ♖h2+
0-1

(cf Diag 62a).

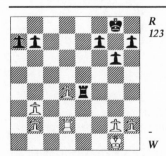

R
123

-
W

Torre - Miles
Amsterdam 1977

The white pawn is passed and supported from behind by the rook. Nevertheless it lacks any punch since the black king can blockade it - indeed it is really a weakness. Moreover the doubled b-pawns are very weak, subject to attack from the black rook.

Black therefore has a considerable advantage.

1 d5!?

The d-pawn isn't really dangerous for Black and this opens up the rank for the black rook. But maybe this is correct anyway. If White waits then Black would merely centralise his king and win the d-pawn and it seems very hard to find a good moment to *"go active"*, e.g. 1 ♔f2 ♔f8 2 ♔f3 f5 3 ♖c2?! (3 b4) 3 ... ♖xd4 4 ♖c7 ♖b4 5 ♖xh7 (hoping to profit from the bad position of the black king) 5 ... a5 6 h4 ♖xb3+ 7 ♔f4 ♖xb2 8 ♔g5 ♖b6 and Black wins easily.

> 1   ...   ♔f8!
> 2   d6   ♔e8
> 3   ♖c2

He must abandon the d-pawn, hoping to use the time Black must spend to take it to get some compensating advantage.

> 3   ...   ♖b4
> 4   ♖c7   ♖xb3
> 5   ♖e7+   ♔f8?

Presumably in time trouble, Miles repeats moves. 5 ... ♔d8 was right at once.

> 6   ♖c7?

Better was 6 ♖e2 ♖d3 7 ♖e7! with reasonable drawing chances since if 7 ... b6!? 8 ♖d7! (8 ♖xa7 ♖xd6) 8 ... a5 9 ♖d8+! ♔g7 10 ♔f2 ♔f6 11 ♔e2 ♖d5 12 d7! and White will force the exchange of his d-pawn for the black b-pawn.

> 6   ...   ♔e8
> 7   ♖e7+   ♔d8!

The d6-pawn is now entirely harmless and Black's queenside pawns can easily carry the day.

> 8   ♔f2

Or 8 ♖xf7 ♖xb2 9 ♖xh7 a5.

> 8   ...   a5!

There is no hurry to take the b-pawn and free the white king.

> 9   ♖xf7   a4
> 10   ♖xh7   ♖xb2+
> 11   ♔f3   a3
> 12   h4

Or 12 ♖h8+ ♔d7 13 ♖a8 a2 followed by b5 - b4 - b3 etc.

> 12   ...   ♖b6!
>   **0-1**

White resigned in view of 13 ♖h8+ ♔d7 14 ♖a8 ♖a6!.

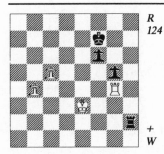

R 124

+ W

Better Passed Pawns
Keres - Alekhine
AVRO 1938

White is better simply because his pawns are further advanced; and moreover it is his move:

> 1   c6!   ♔e7

If 1 ... ♖c2 2 b5 ♖c5 3 ♖b4! and the threat of 4 b6 ♖xc6 5 b7 is decisive.

A.

The game now continued:

> 2   b5?

Keres had analysed up to move 7 and decided that Black was in zugzwang, but:

> 2   ...   ♖b2
> 3   ♖c4   ♔d8
> 4   ♖c5   g4
> 5   ♔f4   ♖b4+

> 6   ♔g3   ♔c7
> 7   ♔h4   ♔c8!

He'd simply missed that Black can move his king. With neither player able to support his passed pawns further the game soon ended in a draw.

> 8   ♖h5   ♔c7
> 9   ♖h7+   ♔c8
> 10   ♖b7   ♖c4
> 11   ♔g3   f5
> 12   ♔h4   ♖c5
>   ½-½

B.

> 2   ♖d4!

Cutting the black king off from the white passed pawn.

> 2   ...   ♖c2

If 2 ... ♖b2 3 ♔d3 ♖b1 4 ♔c2 ♖a1 5 c7 ♖a8 6 b5 and

wins.

3	b5	♖c5
4	♖b4!	

Much the strongest move - though analysis has shown 4 ♖d7+ would also lead to a win.

| 4 | ... | ♔d8 |

5	b6	♔c8
6	b7+	♔b8
7	♖b6	f5

Or 7 ... ♖a5 8 c7+!.

8	♖a6	♔c7
9	♖a8	♖b5
10	♖c8+! and wins	

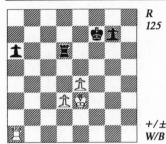

R 125

+/±
W/B

Alekhine - Alexander
Margate 1937

This is from another Alekhine game. White's *connected passed pawns* are immeasurably stronger *in a rook ending* than Black's disconnected ones. On the move, Black would have got some chances with 1 ... g5 intending 2 ... ♖g6. But it was White's move and he completely squashed Black after:

1	♖a5!	♖b6

Maybe he could have tried 1 ... ♖h6. But after 2 d4 ♖h3+ 3 ♔f4 ♖h4+ 4 ♔f3! (not 4 ♔f5?? ♖h5+) 4 ... ♖h6 (the a-pawn was hanging) and e.g. 5 ♔g4 or 5 d5, Black's position is pretty grim all the same.

2	d4	♖b3+
3	♔f4	♖b4
4	d5	

But not 5 ♔e5?? ♖b5+! and in the *pawn ending* Black wins! (6 ♖xb5 axb5 7 ♔d6 b4 8 ♔d7 b3 9 e5 b2 10 e6+ ♔f6 11 e7 b1♕ 12 e8♕ ♕b5+! 13 ♔d8 ♕xe8+ 14 ♔xe8 ♔e6!).

4	...	♖b6
5	♖c5	♖b4

Or 5 ... ♖b7 6 e5 ♖a7 7 ♖c8 a5 8 e6+ etc.

6	♖c7+	♔f8
7	♖a7	1-0

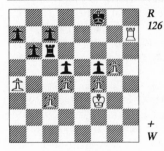

R 126

+
W

Active v passive pieces

The activity of pieces is always an important factor in all chess positions - and one which can sometimes balance or outweigh material considerations. This is especially so in rook endings.

King position

The king is an extremely powerful piece. A big disparity in the effectiveness of the two kings can sometimes outweigh a large material disadvantage.

Capablanca - Tartakower
New York 1924

This is a very famous example. White is a pawn down and his c-pawn is doomed, but the black king is badly cut off on the back rank. Capablanca demonstrated the overwhelming importance of king position with

1	♔g3!	♖xc3+
2	♔h4	♖f3

Also losing are:

a) If 2 ... ♖c1 3 ♔h5! will win (but not 3 g6? ♖h1+ 4 ♔g5 ♖xh7 5 gxh7 ♔g7 6 ♔xf5 c5!=) e.g. 3 ... c5 4 ♖d7 cxd4 5 ♖xd5 ♖d1 6 ♔g6 d3 7 ♔f6 ♔e8 8 g6 d2 9 g7 winning;

b) If 2 ... a5? 3 g6 b5 4 axb5 a4 5 ♔g5 a3 6 ♔f6 wins easily;

c) 2 ... a6 is a somewhat better attempt - a tempo slower than b), but Black keeps control of c6. However, even after

Rook v Rook

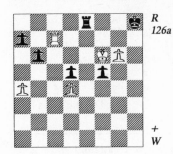

R
126a

+
W

e.g. 3 g6 (better is 3 ♖d7!) 3 ...
b5 4 axb5 axb5 5 ♖f7+ ♔g8 6
♔g5 b4 7 ♖xf5 b3 8 ♖xd5 b2
(8 ... ♖c6 9 f5 b2 10 ♖d8+
♔g7 11 f6+! wins) 9 ♖b5 ♔g7
(9 ... ♖c2 10 f5 wins) 10 ♖xb2
♖g3+ 11 ♔f5 ♖xg6 White
must win, for instance, 12
♖c2 c6 13 ♖b2 is one very
good plan.

3   g6   ♖xf4+
4   ♔g5   ♖e4

Not 4 ... ♖xd4 5 ♔f6 ♔g8 6
♖d7 and Black is actually
mated.

5   ♔f6!
But not 5 ♔xf5? ♖xd4=.

5   ...   ♔g8
6   ♖g7+!   ♔h8
7   ♖xc7   ♖e8 (126a)
8   ♔xf5

Note how White has avoided
taking this pawn (i.e. on move
5) until he had improved the
position of his rook. Now
Black was threatening to advance the f-pawn - hence its
capture

8   ...   ♖e4
9   ♔f6!   ♖f4+
10 ♔e5   ♖g4
11 g7+!   ♔g8

Obviously the pawn ending
after 11 ... ♖xg7 would be
hopeless.

12 ♖xa7   ♖g1
13 ♔xd5   ♖c1
14 ♔d6   ♖c2
15 d5   ♖c1
16 ♖c7   ♖a1
17 ♔c6   ♖xa4
18 d6   1-0

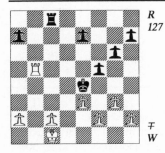

R
127

∓
W

Botvinnik - Kopylov
Moscow 1951
White is a pawn up but unfortunately the black king is extremely active and White's
kingside pawns are weak.

1   ♖b7   ♖e8!
2   ♖xa7?

Taking a second pawn. But
now Black's kingside pawns,
supported by the king, will be
overwhelming.

White should have played
instead 2 ♔d2 ♔f3 3 ♔e1 and
now Black can easily force a
"draw" (uncomfortable only
for White) with e.g. 3 ... ♖c8 4
♖xe7 ♖xc2 5 ♖xa7 ♖xf2 6
♖xh7 ♖xa2 7 h4 ♔xe3 8
♖e7+ ♔f3 9 ♖e6!=. But perhaps he can do no better, e.g.
if 3 ... e5 4 e4!? is very ra-
tional, intending to evict the
black king or maybe 4 ♖b3
and if 4 ... e4 5 c4.

2   ...   ♔f3
3   a4   ♔xf2
4   a5   g5

5   a6   ♔xe3
6   ♖b7   e5
7   a7   ♖a8

Since White's queenside
pawns are *isolated*, it takes
many moves to create any serious threat there. As a result,
Black's *connected pawns supported by the king* easily
carry the day.

8   ♖xh7

Or 8 ♖b5 (8 ♖b3+ ♔e2!
merely loses a tempo) 8 ... e4 9
♖xf5 ♖xa7 10 ♖xg5 ♔e2 and
the e-pawn will cost White his
rook.

8   ...   f4
9   gxf4   gxf4
10 ♔d1   f3
11 c4

If 11 ♔e1 ♖g8 12 ♔f1 ♖d8!
and wins.

11 ...   ♖d8+
12 ♔c2   f2
13 ♖f7   ♖a8!

And Botvinnik resigned in
view of the unanwserable
threat of 14 ... ♖xa7!.

R 128

= W

General activity and rook position

Lasker - Levenfish
Moscow 1925
White's position looks completely hopeless. The black rook is excellently posted *behind* the passed pawn, and it would appear that White has absolutely no counterplay to offset the pawn's triumphant advance.

However, White can obtain counterplay - by a *pawn breakthrough* to create a passed pawn on the kingside after which the king which was previously doing nothing on g7 suddenly becomes active.

1 f5!

In the game Lasker played 1 ♔f6? ♔b5 2 ♖a1! a4 and only then 3 f5. As a result he lost a vital tempo and with it the game, which ended 3 ... exf5 4 e6 fxe6 5 ♔xg6 f4 6 h5 f3 7 h6 e5 8 ♖e1! a3 9 ♖xe5+ ♔c4 10 ♖e1 a2 11 h7 ♖a8 12 ♔g7 f2 13 ♖a1 ♔b3 14 ♖f1 a1♕+ 15 ♖xa1 ♖xa1 16 h8♕ ♖g1+ 0-1.

Lasker later stated that he "instinctively wanted to avoid the discovered check with ♔f6". However this does sound a little odd.

1 ... exf5

If 1 ... gxf5? then the h-pawn is already passed.

2	**e6**	**fxe6+**
3	**♔xg6**	**♔b5**
4	**♖a1**	**f4**
5	**h5**	**e5**

If 5 ... f3 6 ♖f1! a4 7 ♖xf3 a3 8 ♖f1 a2 9 ♖a1 ♔c4 10 h6 ♔b3 11 h7 ♖a8 12 ♖e1! ♔b2 13 ♖e2+ ♔b3 14 ♖e1 and draws.

6 ♖e1! ♔c4

Or 6 ... a4 7 ♖xe5+ ♔c6 8 ♖e4 a3 9 ♖xf4 a2 10 ♖f1 a1♕ 11 ♖xa1 ♖xa1 12 h6=.

7	**♖xe5**	**♔d3**
8	**h6**	**f3**
9	**h7**	**♖xh7**

Not 9 ... ♖a8 10 ♖xa5.

10	**♔xh7**	**f2**
11	**♖f5**	**♔e3**
12	**♖f8!**	**a4**
13	**♖e8+**	**♔f3**
14	**♖f8+**	**♔g2**
15	**♖g8+**	**♔h2**
16	**♖f8=**	

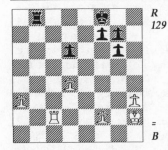

R 129

= B

Spielmann - Rubinstein
St Petersburg 1909
This famous position is very difficult. Black has much the better pawn structure with a nice compact position against White's four isolated pawns. On the other hand, the passed a-pawn could become very dangerous.

1 ... ♖a8!

It would be wrong to look for immediate material gain. After 1 ... ♖b3? 2 ♖a2 ♖d3 3 a4 ♖xd4 4 a5 White is certainly not worse. Now, however, White faces a difficult choice.

2 ♖c3?!

Here the rook is a little passive. It seems that 2 ♖a2 would have been better, viz. 2 ... ♖a4 3 ♔g3 ♔e7 4 ♔f3 ♔e6 5 ♔e4 g5 (5 ... d5+ 6 ♔d3 ♔d6 7 ♔c3 ♔c6 8 ♔d3 ♔b5 9 ♖b2+=) 6 ♖a1 f6 7 ♖a2 f5+ 8 ♔d3 ♔d5 9 ♔c3 ♖c4+ 10 ♔b3 ♖xd4 11 a4 *(129a)*. At last the a-pawn gets going, justifying the placement of the rook *behind the passed pawn*. White should draw after either:

a) 11 ... ♖d3+ 12 ♔b4 ♖xh3

Rook v Rook ♖ V ♜

R
129a

R
129b

R
129c

=
B

=
B

=
W

13 a5 ♖h8 14 a6 ♔e4 15 a7 ♖a8 16 ♔b5 ♔f3 17 ♔b6; or

b) 11 ... ♔c6 12 a5 ♔b7 13 a6+ ♔a7 14 ♖a5 ♖f4 15 ♖d5 ♖xf2 16 ♖xd6 ♖f3+ 17 ♔c4 ♖xh3 18 ♖g6 g4 19 ♔b5 ♖b3+ 20 ♔a5. However this was an immensely hard decision - of course Spielmann was well aware that rooks should go behind passed pawns - and one certainly should not criticise White too much for it.

2   ...   ♖a4
3   ♖d3   ♔e7
4   ♔g3

4 d5 is an attempt to confuse matters but after 4 ... g5! (not 4 ... ♔f6 5 ♖f3+; nor 4 ... f5 5 ♖e3+) 5 ♔g3 ♔f6 6 ♖f3+ ♔g6 7 ♖d3 f6 Black is very much in control. And in any case, White was clearly aiming for diag 129b.

4   ...   ♔e6
5   ♔f3   ♔d5
6   ♔e2? (129b)

A serious mistake, allowing Black to set up a very strong kingside pawn chain; and fix the h-pawn on a vulnerable square. Instead he ought to have blockaded Black's kingside pawns with 6 h4.

6   ...   g5!

Of course not 6 ... ♖xd4? 7 ♔e3 ♖xd3+ 8 ♔xd3 and the outside passed pawn guarantees at least a draw.

7   ♖b3   f6!

If 7 ... ♖xd4? 8 ♖d3 or conceivably 8 ♖b5+; or 7 ... ♔xd4 8 ♖b7 f6! (8 ... ♖xa3 9 ♖xf7 ♖xh3 10 ♖xg7 is easier for White) 9 ♖xg7 ♖xa3 10 h4! gxh4 11 ♖g4+ with excellent drawing chances.

8   ♔e3   ♔c4
9   ♖d3

If 9 ♖b7 ♖xa3+ 10 ♔e4 d5+ 11 ♔f5 ♖xh3 12 ♖xg7 ♖f3+ and wins.

9   ...   d5

Now, after systematically strengthening his position and, most important of all, improving the position of his king, Black is ready for this advance.

10   ♔d2   ♖a8
11   ♔c2   ♖a7
12   ♔d2   ♖e7! (129c)

White is now in zugzwang. If:

a) 13 ♖e3? ♖xe3 14 fxe3 f5!-+;

b) 13 ♔c2? ♖e2+ 14 ♖d2 ♖xd2+ 15 ♔xd2 ♔b3!;

c) 13 f3? ♖a7 14 ♔c2 ♖a8 15 ♔d2 ♖h8. He mus therefore choose between:

d) 13 a4 and the game continuation. At first sight, 13 a4 has little point. However, I now believe it may be best:

d1) If 13 ... ♖a7 14 ♖a3 and:

d11) If 14 ... ♔xd4 White is a tempo up on the game and can play the very useful 15 a5!;

d12) 14 ... ♖a5? blockades the pawn but allows 15 ♔e3 and if 15 ... ♔b4 16 ♖a1 ♖xa4 17 ♖b1+ is very annoying;

d13) 14 ... ♔b4 is natural but after 15 ♖c3! in return for the a-pawn White is able to cut the black king off on the b-file: 15 ... ♖xa4 16 ♖c5 ♖a5 17 ♖c7 ♖a2+ and both 18 ♔e1!? ♖a3 19 ♖c5 ♖xh3 20 ♖xd5 ♔c4 21 ♖d7; and 18 ♔e3!? ♖a3+ 19 ♔d2 ♖f3 20 ♔e2 ♖c3 21 ♖xg7 ♔c4 22 ♖g6 looks adequate to draw;

d2) 13 ... ♔b4 is also possible at once but White can play 14 ♖c3 (also 14 a5!? at

322

R 129d

W

once, 14 ... ♔xa5 15 ♖c3) and if 14 ... ♖e4 15 a5! ♖xd4+ 16 ♖d3 Black must try 16 ... ♖f4 17 ♔e2 since the pawn ending after 16 ... ♖xd3+ 17 ♔xd3 is drawn, viz. 17 ... ♔xa5 18 ♔d4 ♔b4 19 ♔xd5 ♔c3 20 ♔e6 ♔d3 21 ♔f7 ♔e2 22 ♔xg7 ♔xf2 23 ♔xf6 ♔g3 24 ♔xg5 ♔xh3.

13	♖c3+!?	♔xd4
14	a4	♖a7
15	♖a3	♖a5
16	♖a1	♔c4
17	♔e3?!	

Smyslov and Levenfish claim that this is the decisive mistake. Certainly, after it White is lost. But the alternative of offering the a-pawn to misplace the Black king may also be insufficient. 17 ♖c1+!? ♔b4 18 ♖b1+ (not 18 ♖c7 ♖xa4 19 ♖xg7 ♔c5 20 ♖f7 ♖f4 and Black is back in control) 18 ... ♔xa4 (if 18 ... ♔a3 19 ♖b7 ♖xa4 20 ♖xg7 ♖f4 21 ♔e2 ♔b3 22 ♖c7!) 19 ♔d3 ♖c5 and now if:

a) 20 ♖b7 ♖c4 21 ♖xg7 ♔b5 22 ♔e3 ♖e4+ (22 ... ♔c5 23 ♖c7+ ♔d6 24 ♖xc4 dxc4 25 ♔d4) 23 ♔d3 ♔c5 should be winning;

b) So Smyslov and Levenfish proposed 20 ♔d4 ♖c2 21 ♖b7 ♖xf2 22 ♖xg7 but Kasparov has continued this analysis: 22 ... ♖d2+ 23 ♔c5 ♔b3 24 ♖g6 ♔c3 25 ♖xf6 d4 with a winning position.

17	...	d4+!
18	♔d2	

If 18 ♔e4 ♖e5+ 19 ♔f3 d3

20 a5 d2 21 a6 ♖e1.

18	...	♖f5
19	♔e1	♔b4
20	♔e2	♔a5!
21	♖a3	♖f4
22	♖a2	♖h4!
23	♔d3	

Or 23 ♖a3 ♔b4. Note how Black's *extremely solid structure* on the kingside allows him to play there with just a rook and the king far distant. That is one of the advantages of a good pawn structure: if Black's kingside pawns had been at all weak, White could easily have liquidated to a draw. A further point is that this adamantine solidity is due in no small measure to his getting in ... g5 - see the note to 6 ♔e2?.

23	...	♖xh3+
24	♔xd4	♖h4+
25	♔d3	♖xa4 *(129d)*

Now it only remains for the black king to work its way back to the kingside. Rubin-stein won quite easily.

26	♖e2	

Or 26 ♖c2 ♔b6.

26	...	♖f4
27	♔e3	♔b6
28	♖c2	♔b7
29	♖c1	♖a4
30	♖h1	♔c6
31	♖h7	♖a7
32	♔e4	♔d6
33	♔f5	g6+!
34	♔xg6	♖xh7
35	♔xh7	♔e5
36	♔g6	g4
	0-1	

Two Rooks v Two Rooks 🨤🨣 v 🨫🨪

Although double rook endings have many similarities with single rook endings and of course usually transpose into them sooner or later there are certain distinct differences.

Extra Fire Power

A rook by itself can't usually checkmate the enemy king unless heavily supported. In single rook endings, therefore, one requires either rook and king or rook and several pawns or some freak accident in order to create serious mating threats. However, two rooks are an extremely powerful force. *Mating attacks* therefore play a very important part in double rook endings and bad positions can be saved by *perpetual check* more frequently than in single rook endings.

"Small Advantages"

With so much power on the board it is very difficult to identify and classify generic positions, e.g. $2🨣 + P v 2🨣$ in the same way as in simpler endings since so much depends on the exact placement of the pieces. However, one can make the general observation that:

A small advantage, e.g. an extra pawn on one side of the board, is much more likely to be exploitable with two pairs of rooks on than in a single rook ending.

The reason for this is that the extra pawn should provide *cover* for the king which is at a premium - but which is not so important in single rook endings. Moreover, weak pawns are relatively more vulnerable with the extra material.

RR 1
+
W

Underlying Tactical Ideas

Mating Attack
Rinck 1921
Although there are no pawns left, White to move has a mating attack. Henri Rinck produced dozens of studies with this material balance. Even if not very game-like, they do illustrate the vast power of two rooks working together.

1   🨣d6+   ♚f7

Or 1 ... ♚g5 2 🨣a5+ ♚h4 3 🨣h6 mate.

2   🨣a7+   ♚e8
3   🨣h6   🨫c3+

Or 3 ... 🨫b3+ 4 ♚e4 🨫e2+ 5 ♚d4 🨫d2+ 6 ♚c4 🨫f3 7 🨣h8+ 🨫f8 8 🨣a8+.

4   ♚e2   🨫b2+
5   ♚d1   🨫d3+
6   ♚c1   🨫f2
7   🨣h8+   🨫f8
8   🨣a8+ and wins

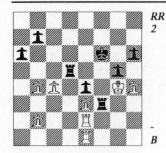

RR 2
-
B

Sahovic - Korchnoi
Biel 1979
Although Black is obviously much better White seems still to be fighting. But Korchnoi wins at once with a beautiful mating attack:

1   ...   h5+!
2   ♚xh5   🨫d8!
3   hxg5+

Or if 3 ♚g4 gxh4! is similarly quite disastrous, e.g. 4

🨫c2 🨣g8+ 5 ♚h5 🨣g5+ 6 ♚xh4 (or 6 ♚h6 🨫ff5!) 6 ... ♚f5 7 🨣h2 🨣g8!; or 4 🨣h2 🨣g8+ 5 ♚h5 🨫f5+ 6 ♚xh4 🨫h8+ 7 ♚g3 🨣g5+.

3   ...   ♚f5
4   ♚h6   🨣h3+
5   ♚g7   🨫d7+
6   ♚g8   ♚g6
7   🨣f2   🨣g7+
8   ♚f8   🨣h8 mate

Two Rooks v Two Rooks ♖♖ v ♜♜

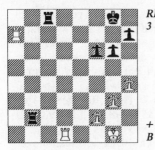

RR 3

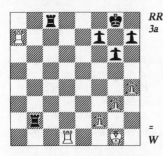

RR 3a

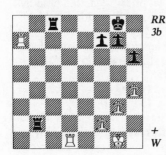

RR 3b

+ B

= W

+ W

Doubled Rooks on the Seventh Rank

These are one of a chessplayer's dreams. But to be operative they must clear the rank of protectable pawns.

J. Speelman 1984

Although it is Black to move in diag 3 he is in terrible trouble since he can't challenge White's absolute control of the seventh rank. Perhaps the best he can do is to evacuate his pawns, e.g.

1 ... h6!
2 ♖dd7 g5

Now White's best seems to be:

3 h5!

3 ♖g7+ ♔h8 4 ♖h7+ ♔g8 5 ♖xh6 gxh4 6 ♖xh4 is much less clear.

3 ... f5!?
4 ♖g7+ ♔h8
5 ♖h7+ ♔g8
6 ♖ag7+

Not 6 ♖xh6? ♖c1+! 7 ♔g2 ♖cc2=.

6 ... ♔f8
7 ♖f7+ ♔g8
8 ♖hg7+ ♔h8
9 ♖g6 f4
10 ♖xh6+!

If 10 gxf4 g4!? 11 ♖xg4 ♖c1+ 12 ♔g2 ♖cc2.

10 ... ♔g8
11 ♖f5 fxg3
12 ♖xg5+ ♔f7
13 ♖xg3

with excellent winning chances.

Diagram 3a

However if the *black f-pawn is on f7* then even with the move after 1 ♖d7 ♖f8 White has no advantage whatsoever. With the seventh rank closed

the doubled rooks are only beating the air.

A plausible alternative to 1 ♖d7 is:

1 ♖d4

Now, e.g. 1 ... h5 is quite equal, but not

1 ... ♖cc2?

If he must double rooks then better is 1 ... ♖c1+ 2 ♔g2 ♖cc2 but 3 ♖f4 f5 is still not nice for Black.

2 ♖f4!

Here the rook is perfectly placed; it both defends the white f-pawn and attacks the enemy one.

In general the only way to play against two rooks on the seventh rank is to *protect one of the pawns in their path*. And it is almost always best to do this actively with the rook in front of the pawn aiming down the board at the enemy position.

Now Black is forced into the abject:

2 ... f5

But he does seem just about to survive since if 3 ♖d4 ♖d2! 4 ♖c4 ♖(either)c2 etc. Or if 3 h5 ♖a2! (chasing the rook on the seventh rank) 4 ♖b7 ♖(either)b2.

Diagram 3b

If Black's kingside pawns are f7, g7, h6, then any sensible move will draw easily, e.g. 1 ... h5. But not

1 ... ♖cc2??
2 ♖d8+! ♔h7
3 ♖xf7

White has managed to protect the f-pawns from the front and has tremendous winning chances.

Two Rooks v Two Rooks ♜♜ V ♜♜

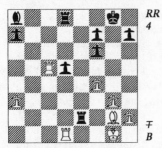

RR 4

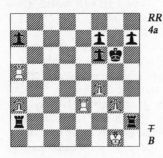

RR 4a

Miles - Timman
Linares 1983

1   ...   d4!

An excellent move returning the extra pawn to make his control of the seventh rank absolute.

2   ♗xa8   ♖xa8
3   ♖xd4   ♖b8
4   ♖d1   ♖bb2

Although Black has a great advantage his winning chances are reduced by the shattered state of his kingside pawns. In the play which follows White attempts and finally succeeds in *jettisoning a pawn or two in order to exchange off one pair of rooks*.

5   ♖h5

5 ♖c3 was an alternative intending to put that rook on f3 and thus activate the one on d1.

5   ...   ♖a2
6   ♖f1   ♔g7!

But not 6 ... ♖xa3? 7 ♖f2 and White has got off lightly.

7   ♖f3

White would like to maintain his rook on h5 with 7 f5, but then 7 ... ♖xa3! is much stronger since 8 ♖f2 ♖xf2 9 ♔xf2 ♖a4! leaves the h5-rook stranded.

7   ...   ♖g2+
8   ♔h1   ♔g6
9   ♖a5

Not 9 ♖h4? f5!.

9   ...   ♖xh2+
10   ♔g1   ♖hg2+
11   ♔f1   ♖gb2
12   ♖e3

If 12 ♔g1? f5! when if 13 ♖xa7? ♔h5 14 ♖xf7 ♔g4 and wins.

12   ...   ♖f2+
13   ♔g1   ♖fc2
14   ♔f1   ♖h2
15   ♔g1 *(4a)*

This critical position occurred just after adjournment (move 43). Here Timman decided to cash in on his positional advantage for material gain with 15 ... ♖hc2 16 ♔f1 ♖c1+ 17 ♖e1 ♖c3 18 ♖e2 ♖axa3 (If 18 ... ♖f3+ 19 ♔g2) 19 ♖xa3 ♖xa3 20 ♔g2. Although Black is much better this position is defensible. Miles fought his way to ♖ vs ♖+f+h and drew on move 105.

Instead Black should perhaps have played:

15   ...   ♖hg2+!?

Now White would like to play 16 ♔f1. However: 16 ... ♖af2+ 17 ♔e1 ♖h2!! and there is no defence to the threat of 18 ... ♖a2 followed by execution with either ... ♖a1+ or ... ♖h1+.

Therefore White would have had to answer 15 ... ♖hg2+ with:

16   ♔h1!   ♖gb2
17   ♖e1

However, even with White in this state of abject passivity there is nothing absolutely clear for Black, e.g.

a) 17 ... ♖h2+ 18 ♔g1 ♖hg2+ 19 ♔h1 ♖xg3 20 ♖g1!;

b) 17 ... ♖h2+ 18 ♔g1 ♖ag2+ 19 ♔f1 ♖f2+ (19 ... ♖xg3!?) 20 ♔g1 ♖hg2+ 21 ♔h1 ♖xg3 22 ♖g1! ♖xg1+ 23 ♔xg1 ♖xf4 24 ♖xa7;

c) 17 ... f5 18 ♖xa7 ♔h5 19 ♖xf7 ♖h2+ 20 ♔g1 ♖ag2+ 21 ♔f1 ♔g4 22 ♖b1! h5 23 ♖h7!;

d) 17 ... h5 18 ♖xa7 ♔f5 19 ♖ae7 (19 ♖xf7? ♔g4 20 ♖h7 ♖h2+ 21 ♔g1 ♖ag2+ 22 ♔f1 ♔f3) 19 ... ♔g4 20 ♖7e3 ♖h2+ 21 ♔g1 ♔h3 22 g4+!.

Two Rooks v Two Rooks ♖♖ v ♜♜

RR 5

₸ B

Endings with Limited Material

Ivanka - Gaprindashvili
Thessaloniki Ol 1984
If we removed any pair of (opposite coloured) rooks then this ending would be dead drawn. But here Black has the huge additional advantage that whereas her king is quite safe the white one is in mortal danger.

1 ... ♖e8!
2 h4

If 2 ♖g3 ♖f1+ 3 ♔g4 ♖e4+ 4 ♔h5 ♖f3! 5 ♖xf3 - there's nothing better - 5 ... g6 mate!

Or 2 ♖f3 g5+! 3 ♔f5 ♖f8+ 4 ♔e4 ♖e1+ 5 ♖e3 ♖e8+ wins a rook.

Or 2 ♖cc3 ♖f8+ 3 ♔e4 ♖g6 4 ♖f3 ♖e6+ 5 ♔d5 ♖fe8 and with the white king cut off so far from the kingside, Black is winning easily.

2 ... ♖f8+
3 ♔e5 ♖g4
4 ♖h3

Horrible but forced since if 4 h5 ♖g5+ 5 ♔d4 ♖f4+ 6 ♔e3 ♖xc5 7 ♔xf4 ♖xh5 etc.

4 ... ♖e8+
5 ♔d5?!

Obviously if 5 ♔f5 it gets mated. But 5 ♔d6 is better and if 5 ... ♖g6+ 6 ♔d5! (not 6 ♔d7 ♖a8 and ... ♖f6 with a mating threat) when 6 ... h5 is less good than with the rook on g4.

5 ... h5!

Fixing the weakness.

6 ♔d6 ♔h6
7 ♖c1

White must prepare to defend the h-pawn with the horrible ♖ch1.

7 ... ♖d8+
8 ♔e5 ♖dd4
9 ♖ch1 ♔g6?

In her opponent's time trouble Gaprindashvili misses a trick: 9 ... g6! won at once since the threat 9 ... ♔g7 and ... ♖ge4 mate wins the h-pawn for nothing.

10 ♖g3! ♖de4+
11 ♔d5 ♔f5
12 ♖gh3

If 12 ♖xg4?! hxg4 or 12 ♖f3+ ♖ef4 13 ♖xf4+ ♔xf4 the endings are lost - the latter has more chances. But perhaps she should have tried that anyway since the double rook ending is obviously hopeless.

12 ... ♖a4
13 ♖f3+ ♔g6
14 ♖fh3 ♔h6
15 ♔e5

Or 15 ♔c5 ♖a5+ 16 ♔b6 ♖f5 intending ... ♖g6+ and ... ♖f7+ etc, but still she should have tried that.

15 ... ♖ad4

Reforming the mating net she let slip on move 9.

16 ♔e6 ♔g6

Of course 16 ... g6 had the same effect.

0-1

In view of 17 ♔e7 ♖ge4+ 18 ♔f8 ♖d8 mate.

Two Rooks v Two Rooks ♖♖ v ♜♜

RR 6
+
W

Petrosian - Larsen
Biel IZ 1976
Much the same comments apply (with colours reversed) as to diag 5. An 'easy draw' suddenly becomes quite untenable because of the extra pair of rooks.

1 ♖d8+ ♚f7
2 ♖hh8

Here Petrosian in *Informator* indicates that White is actually winning. The immediate threat is 3 ♖de8 followed by either 4 ♖hf8+, 5 h5+ 6 ♖h8 mate or first 4 h5.

2 ... ♖b7

Defending against the threat since if now 3 ♖de8 ♖e7!.

3 ♖hf8+ ♚e7

Of course if 3 ... ♚g6? 4

h5+ and mate next move.

3 ... ♚e6 is a possible alternative but simply 4 f5+ ♚e7 5 ♔h5 is very strong, e.g. 5 ... ♖g2 (If 5 ... ♖2b3 6 g4 ♖3b4 7 g5! fxg5 8 ♔g6 wins; or 5 ... ♖7b4 6 ♖de8+ ♚moves 7 ♖e3!) 6 ♖de8+! (6 g4 ♖b4 is a bit problematical) 6 ... ♚d6 7 ♖e3 and Black's kingside disintegrates in a few moves.

4 ♚f5 ♖2b3
5 g4 ♖g3

White was threatening 6 ♚g6 and 7 ♖fe8. Note that if 5 ... ♖d7 6 ♖fe8+! ♚f7 7 ♖xd7+ ♚xe8 8 ♖xg7 wins.

6 ♖de8+ ♚d6
7 g5 fxg5
8 hxg5 ♖b5+
9 ♚g6 1-0

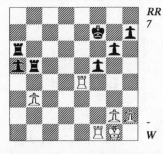

RR 7
-
W

Inkiov - Alburt
Thessaloniki Ol 1984
White decided to eliminate some pawns with:

1 g4?!

But in retrospect he felt that 1 ♖e3 was better.

1 ... ♖xb3
2 gxf5 g5!

The f-pawn can be surrounded later. This is much better than 2 ... gxf5? when White could draw quite easily.

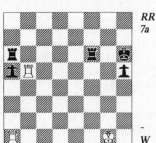

RR 7a
-
W

3 ♖c4 ♖b7
4 ♖a1 ♚f6
5 h4!

Having embarked on simplification he must continue before Black can consolidate on the kingside.

5 ... ♖b5

Taking control of the fifth rank - but 5 ... h6 seems more natural to help the g-pawn, e.g. 6 hxg5+ hxg5 7 ♖c5 a4 8 ♚f2 ♖b4! (not 8 ... a3 9 ♖h1 with counterplay) when if 9 ♖h1 ♖h4. Nevertheless Inkiov,

who should know, gives 5 ... ♖b5 an ! in *Informator*.

6 hxg5+ ♚xg5
7 ♖c7 h5
8 ♖g7+ ♚h6

If 8 ... ♚xf5 9 ♖f1+ White gets too active.

9 f6 ♖f5

If 9 ... ♖xf6 10 ♖a7!

10 ♖b7 ♖fxf6
11 ♖b5 *(7a)*

A very unusual "theoretical position". White has drawing chances because he can sometimes exchange a pair of rooks getting to ♖ v ♜ + two pawns cf diags R40-41.

11 ... ♖f4?!

He should have shifted the enemy rook at once with 11 ... ♖g6+! and 12 ... ♖g5.

12 ♚h2

Of course not 12 ♖(either)xa5 ♖g6+ 13 ♚h2 ♖h4 mate.

12 ... a4
13 ♖a3!

Black's problem now is that

if he brings the f4-rook to the fifth rank, e.g. 13 ... ♖g4 14 ♖c5 ♖g5 then simply attacking the a-pawn with 15 ♖c4 will force either repetition with 15 ... ♖g4 or the silly 15 ... ♖ga5. That's why he should have shifted the white rook in diag 7a - before White was organised. Now he has to transfer the a6-rook to White's fourth rank. But White has time to construct a watertight defence.

13	...	♖g6
14	♖a5	♖h4+
15	♖h3	♖gg4
16	♖a6+	♔g5
17	♖a5+	♔g6
18	♖a6+	♔f7
19	♖a5	♔e6
20	♖xh5	♖xh5
21	♖xh5	

This position which is outside the present domain (*double rook endgames*) is just drawable, cf diag R21. The game ended 21 ... ♔d6 22 ♔h3 ♖g1 23 ♖a5 ♖a1 24 ♔g2 ♔c6 25 ♖f5! ♖d1 (25 ... a3 26 ♖f3!) 26 ♖a5 ♖d4 27 ♔f3 ♔b6 28 ♖a8 ♔b5 29 ♔e2 ♖b4 30 ♖b8+ ♔c3 31 ♖c8+ ♔b2 (31 ... ♖c4 32 ♖xc4+!) 32 ♖b8+ ♔a2 33 ♖b7 ½-½

RR 8

+ B

Bolbochan - Markeluk
Israel 1981

White is a pawn up and has an excellent rook on d7 but the rest of his pawns are rather scattered. One feels that Black ought to have reasonable drawing chances though it will certainly be difficult for him. In the game he started a barrage of checks which only succeeded in driving the white king into a better position.

1	...	♖c2+

I suspect that 1 ... ♖b8 at once would be better since White's men are hard to coordinate even given time.

2	♔d5	♖d2+
3	♔e5	♖f5+

If 3 ... ♖xd7 4 ♔xf6 ♖d6+ 5 ♔g5 (5 ♔e5!?) the ending is just winning for White, viz. 5 ... ♖b6 6 ♖a7 ♖c6 7 a4 ♖d6 8 a5 9 a6 (not 9 ♖b7 ♖a6 10 ♖b6 ♖xa5+ 11 ♔xg1 ♖a1! 12 f5 ♖g1+ 13 ♔f6 ♔g8!=) 9 ... ♖b6 10 ♔h6 ♖c6 11 ♖a8+ ♔f7 12 a7 ♖a6 (12 ... ♖c5 13 ♖f8+!) 13 ♖h8 ♖a5! 14 f5! ♖xf5 15 ♖f8+ and wins.

4	♔e6	♖e2+

4 ... ♖xd7 5 ♔xd7 followed by 6 ♔e4 and 7 a4 is dreadful.

5	♔d6	♖f6+
6	♔c7	♖c2+
7	♔b7	♖b2+
8	♖b4!	♖f2

If 8 ... ♖xb4+ 9 axb4 ♖xf4 10 b5 White wins because of the appalling position of the black king.

9	♖c4	♖b2+
10	♔a7!	

As mooted in the introductory paragraphs Black has really succeeded in driving the enemy king where it wants to go.

10	...	♔e8
11	♖b7!	♖d2
12	♖h7	♔d8
13	♖b4	

This is the point of White's 11th move deflecting the Black rook from the b-file.

13	...	♖d7+

Obviously now totally forced.

14	♖xd7+	♔xd7
15	♔b7	

And White is winning. The

game ended:

15	...	♜f5
16	♖d4+	♚e6
17	♚c6!	♜f8

17 ... g5 18 ♖e4+! ♚f7 19 fxg5 ♖xg5 20 a4 is winning.

18	a4	♜c8+
19	♚b7	♜c5
20	♚b6	♜c8
21	a5	♜b8+
22	♚c6	♜b1
23	a6	♜c1+
24	♚b5	♜a1
25	♖a4	♜b1+
26	♚a5	1-0

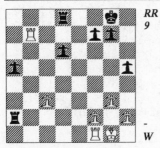

RR 9 - W

Further examples

Christiansen - Larsen
Lone Pine 1977
Although White is a pawn down he has reasonable drawing chances. One of his rooks (on b7) is extremely active and Black's pawns are fairly scattered.

1 ♖e1

White plans to tie down one black rook with 2 ♖ee7 and then go after the enemy pawns, but Larsen found an excellent riposte.

1 ... h4!

Now if 2 ♖ee7 h3 is very uncomfortable so:

2 ♚g2

If 2 gxh4 ♜a4 3 ♖ee7 ♜f4 is very pleasant for Black. As mentioned before, cf diag 3b, the ideal way to defend against doubled rooks on the seventh rank is with a pawn blocking the rank defended by a rook *in front of it*.

2 ... ♜c8!

So that now if 3 ♖ee7? h3+ 4 ♚f3? (Or 4 ♚xh3 ♜xf2) 4 ... ♜xc3+ 5 ♚g4 ♜xf2 and Black still manages to defend the f-pawn with an active rook.

3 gxh4!?

Acceding to his opponent's wishes - perhaps he could have tried instead 3 ♖e3 (threat 4 ♖f3) 3 ... h3+ 4 ♚f3 since the h-pawn might be surrounded later. But that would be very sharp and it is understandable that he preferred 'damage limitation' to an unknown degree of danger.

3 ... ♜a4
4 ♖ee7 ♜f4

Reaching the ideal position - Black now has a *permanent advantage* and good winning chances.

5 ♚g3 ♜f5
6 ♖e3

Not 6 ♖ec7?? ♜xc7 7 ♖xc7 ♜c5.

6 ... ♜fc5

It is somewhat of a pity to move the rook now that it has got to f5 but this way he wins a pawn or forces White into terrible passivity. Normally one would try to activate *the other rook* as well but that seems difficult here, e.g. 6 ... ♜a8 7 ♖ee7 a4? (7 ... ♜c8! forces repetition with 8 ♖e3 etc.) 8 ♖a7 ♜a5 9 ♖ab7 ♜f5 10 ♖a7! etc.

7	♖ee7!	♜xc3+
8	f3	♜f8
9	♖a7	♜c5
10	♖ed7	♜d5
11	♚f4	

So Black has remained a pawn up but at the cost of one passive rook.

11	...	g6
12	h5!?	

White offers another pawn to clarify matters. If 12 ... gxh5? Black would be badly

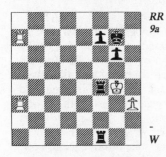

RR
9a

-
W

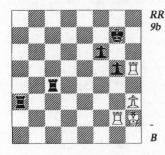

RR
9b

-
B

discoordinated and 13 ♔e4! ♖e5+ 14 ♔f4 wins a pawn back at once, so naturally he played:

12 ... ♖xh5!

The only question was whether White needed to sacrifice the h-pawn at all. If he had just waited, Black would probably have had to play ... ♖f5 to free his other rook - but maybe he could activate his king instead? This is another case of 'damage limitation' as at move 3. Christiansen shows he prefers to keep things clear (if unpleasant) rather than giving his opponent unknown scope.

13	♖xd6	♖f5+
14	♔g4	♖b8
15	♖d4	♖b1
16	f4	♖g1+
17	♔f3	♖a1
18	♔g3	♔g7
19	♖e4	♖a3+
20	♔g4	♖f6

It turns out that Black can do nothing whilst keeping the position, i.e. he can't defend both the a- and f-pawns and activate both rooks simultaneously. Therefore he plans to exchange the a-pawn for White's f-pawn reaching a position which would be drawn in a single rook ending but contains many chances in a double rook ending ... It takes another dozen moves to carry out this plan:

21	♖d4	♔h6
22	♖c4	♖f5
23	♖a8	♖a2
24	h3	♖a1
25	♖d4	♔g7
26	♖a7	♔h6
27	♖a8	

Not 27 ♖dd7?? ♖a4 28 ♖xf7 ♖axf4+!.

27	...	♖b5
28	♖d3	a4
29	♖a7	♔g7
30	♖dd7	♖f5
31	♖d4	a3
32	♖da4	♖f1
33	♖xa3	♖5xf4+

So we reach a 'theoretical position' (diag 9a) where Black has very reasonable winning chances.

34	♔g3	♔h6
35	♖7a4	♖f5
36	♖d3	

If 36 ♖a5 ♖g1+! 37 ♔h2 ♖ff1 Black manages to keep all the rooks on the board.

36	...	♖g1+
37	♔h2	♖b1
38	♖d2?!	

Surrendering the third rank after which his h-pawn becomes very weak, e.g. 38 ♖ad4 looks better.

38	...	♖b3
39	♖h4+	♔g7
40	♔g2	♖ff3
41	♔h2	♖a3
42	♖g2	♖fb3
43	♖e2	g5

After improving the positions of both of his rooks, Larsen now starts his attack. White's position is now extremely critical.

44	♖g2	f6
45	♖h5	♖b8
46	♖h4	♖b1
47	♖c4	♖bb3
48	♖h4	

Not 48 h4? ♖h3+ 49 ♔g1 ♖a1+ 50 ♔f2 ♖a2+ 51 ♔g1 ♖xg2+ 52 ♔xg2 ♖xh4.

48	...	♖c3
49	♖h5	♖c4 (9b)
50	h4!	

This is totally forced. Black was threatening 50 ... ♖a8 and 51 ... ♔g6 winning the rook. And if 50 ♖g4 ♖c2+ 51 ♖g2

Two Rooks v Two Rooks ♖♖ V ♜♜

♖xg2+ 52 ♔xg2 ♜a8 53 ♔g3 ♔g6 54 ♔g4 f5+.

| 50 | ... | g4 |
| 51 | ♜b2 | ♜cc3 |

Although he now has two connected pawns Black's position is far less comfortable than it was. Perhaps he is "theoretically winning" but the sequence h4 g4 has activated White's h5-rook and loosened the black position. Christiansen now succeeds in creating considerable confusion.

| 52 | ♖d5 | ♜h3+ |
| 53 | ♔g2 | ♔g6 |

But not 53 ... ♜xh4 54 ♖b4! ♔g6 55 ♖f4 intending 56 ♖df5 ♜a6 57 ♔g3=.

| 54 | ♖b4 | ♜a2+ |

Not 54 ... ♜ag3+ 55 ♔f2 ♜f3+ 56 ♔g2 ♜xh4? 57 ♖xg4+!=.

55	♔g1	♜g3+
56	♔h1	♜f2
57	h5+	♔h6
58	♖d8!	♜fg2

White's idea is that if 58 ... ♔xh5? he would then jettison both rooks to achieve stalemate, e.g. 59 ♖h8+ ♔g5 60 ♖b5+ ♔g6 61 ♖g8+ ♔f7 62 ♖b7+! ♔xg8 63 ♖g7+!=.

59	♖b1	♜a2
60	♖g8	♜h3+
61	♔g1	♜g3+
62	♔h1	♜a6
63	♖b5	♔h7
64	♖c8	

Not 64 ♖g6? ♜h3+ 65 ♔g2 ♜xh5! 66 ♖xf6 ♜a2+ wins.

64	...	♜a1+
65	♔h2	♜h3+
66	♔g2	♜a2+
67	♔g1	♜g3+
68	♔h1	♜e3
69	♖c1	♜f3
70	♔g1 (9c)	

| 70 | ... | ♔h6? |

Completely natural but he missed a trick. As Benko pointed out 70 ... ♜ff2! would keep control after which Black could improve his king and kingside pawns with a won game. The main point is that after 70 ... ♜ff2 71 ♖f1? allows mate in three. Now, however Christiansen found:

| 71 | ♖f1!! | ♜aa3 |
| 72 | ♖f5! | |

Now if 72 ... ♜xf1+ 73 ♔xf1 ♜f3+ 74 ♔xf3 gxf3 75 ♔f2 ♔xh5 76 ♔xf3 ♔g5 77 ♔g3=. Exchanging just one pair of rooks is obviously no good so Black had to try:

| 72 | ... | ♜g3+ |
| 73 | ♔h2 | ♔g7? |

With this (actually his 102nd move) he throws away everything. Black had to play 73 ... ♜h3+ 74 ♔g2 ♜ag3+ 75 ♔f2 ♜f3+ 76 ♔e1! (not 76 ♔g2 ♜hg3+ 77 ♔h2 ♜xf1 78 ♖xf1 ♜h3+ 79 ♔g2 ♔g5! and wins) 76 ... ♜e3+. But it seems that both 77 ♔d2 and 77 ♔f2 draw anyway, e.g. 77 ♔f2 ♔g7 78 ♖f4! ♜hf3+ 79 ♔g1! (but not 79 ♔g2? ♜e2+ 80 ♔h1 ♜h3+ 81 ♔g1 ♜g3+ 82 ♔h1 ♜gg2!) and Black can't make any progress. Hence the decisive error was probably 70 ... ♔h6.

| 74 | h6+ | |

Obviously Larsen had overlooked this, seeing only 74 ♖xf6?? ♜h3+ 75 ♔g2 ♜ag3+ 76 ♔f2 ♔xf6.

74	...	♔h7
75	♖xf6	♜h3+
76	♔g2	♜ag3+
77	♔f2	♜c3
78	♔g2	½-½

Rook v Knight   ♖ V ♞

Without Pawns

RN
1

RN
2

=
W

RN
2a

+
W

+
W

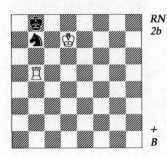

RN
2b

+
B

Horwitz and Kling 1851

1	♔f6	♘h7+
2	♔g6	♘f8+
3	♔h6	♔h8
4	♖f7	♔g8
5	♖g7+	♔h8
6	♖g1	♘d7!

Not 6 ... ♘h7? 7 ♔g6! ♔g8
8 ♖g2 ♘f8+ 9 ♔f6+ ♔h8 10
♔f7 or 6 ... ♘e6 7 ♔g6!

♘f8+ 8 ♔f7 ♘h7 9 ♖g8+.

7	♔g6	♔g8
8	♖d1	♘f8+
9	♔f6	♘h7+
10	♔g6	♘f8+

And Black holds the draw.
Note that this type of ending
can arise from Rook v
Pawn(s) (see diag RP13, 20
and 21).

**Arabic manuscript 1257!
analysis by Frink and Averbakh**

1	...	♘a5+
2	♔b5	♘b7

After 2 ... ♘b3 3 ♖d8 the
knight is trapped.

3	♖h5!	

Quickest.

3	...	♔b8

Alternatively:

a) 3 ... ♘d6+ 4 ♔c6 and
now:

a1) 4 ... ♘c4 (2a). A key position of Averbakh's which often features in analysing rook
v knight 5 ♖c5 ♘e3 6 ♖a5+
♔b8 7 ♖a4 ♘f5 8 ♖e4 ♘g3 9
♖b4+ ♔a7 10 ♖b7+ ♔a8 11
♔c7.

a2) 4 ... ♘e4 5 ♖h7+ ♔b8 6
♖b7+ ♔a8 7 ♖b4 ♘f6 8 ♖f4
♘h5 9 ♖f5 ♘g3 10 ♖f3 ♘h5

11 ♔c7.

b) 3 ... ♘d8 4 ♖d5 ♘e6 (4 ...
♘b7 5 ♖d7) 5 ♔c6 ♔b8 (5 ...
♘f4 6 ♖d7+ ♔b8 7 ♖d8+
♔a7 8 ♖e8) 6 ♖d6! ♘g5 (6 ...
♘f4 7 ♖d8+ ♔a7 8 ♖e8 ♘d3
9 ♖e4 ♘f2 10 ♖a4+ ♔b8 11
♖b4+! ♔a7 12 ♖b7+ ♔a8 13
♔c7) 7 ♖d8+ ♔a7 8 ♖d7+
♔a6 9 ♖d3 ♔a7 10 ♖e3 ♔b8
11 ♔d7 ♘f7 12 ♖e7 ♘h6 13
♔e6 ♘g4 14 ♖e2 ♔c7 15
♔f5 ♘h6+ 16 ♔g6 ♘g4 17
♔g5.

4	♔c6	♘d8+
5	♔d7	♘b7
6	♖b5 (2b)	

A key position, identical to
w♔b5, ♖d7; b♔a7, ♘b7.

6	...	♔a7
7	♔c7	♔a8
8	♖b3 and wins	

333

Rook v Knight

RN
3

+
W

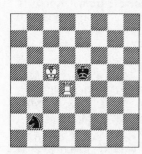

RN
3a

=/+
W/B

Averbakh
1	♔d5	♞f6
2	♔c6!	

Not 2 ♔c5? ♔e5!= when due to zugzwang, the knight escapes. This position is diagram *(3a)* with White to play; it represents a key defensive motif: 3 ♖d2 ♞a4+ 4 ♔b4

♞b6 5 ♔c5 ♞a4+.

| 2 | ... | ♔e5 |

This is the only move - White threatened ♔b5 and ♖d2.

3	♔c5 *(3a)*	
3	...	♔f5
4	♔b5	

And 5 ♖d2 winning.

RN
4

+
W

Welin - Benjamin
Reykjavik open 1986
76	♖b4	♔a6
77	♖c4	

This is the Averbakh position (see diag 2a) moved one rank back.

77	...	♞e2
78	♖a4+	♔b7
79	♖e4	

79 ♖a3 would be the analogous method, but here White has more difficulty switching to attack the king. By contrast, now the knight has less room to run. It would appear that 79 ♖a3 hunts down the knight as well: 79 ... ♞f4 80 ♖e3 ♞g2? (80 ... ♔c7!? 81 ♖e7+ ♔d8 82 ♔d6 ♔c8 83 ♖e4 ♞d3 84 ♖d4 ♞e1 85 ♖d2 ♔b7 86 ♔d5 ♞f3 87 ♖f2 ♞g5 88 ♖f5 ♞h3 89 ♔e4) 81 ♖e4 ♔c7 82 ♔c4 ♔c6 83 ♔c3! ♔d5 84 ♔d3 ♔c5 85 ♔d2 ♔d5 86 ♖g4.

| 79 | ... | ♞g3 |

Or 79 ... ♞c3 80 ♖e3 ♞a4+

(80 ... ♞d1 81 ♖f3 ♔a6 82 ♔b4) 81 ♔b5 ♞b6 (81 ... ♞b2 82 ♔b4 ♞d1 83 ♖f3) 82 ♖e7+.

| 80 | ♖g4 | |

White can play so directly since his king is well centralised and the black king rules out the knight escaping along the b-file.

| 80 | ... | ♞f5 |

Alternatively: 80 ... ♞e2 81 ♔c4; or 80 ... ♞f1 81 ♔d4 ♞d2 (81 ... ♔c6 82 ♖g2) 82 ♔e3 ♞b3 83 ♖b4+; or 80 ... ♞h5 81 ♔d6 ♞f6 82 ♖f4 ♞e8+ 83 ♔d7 ♞g7 (83 ... ♞c7 84 ♖b4+) 84 ♔e7 ♞h5 85 ♖g4.

| 81 | ♖g5 | ♞h4 |

81 ... ♞e3 fails to 82 ♔d4 ♞c2+ 83 ♔d3 and 81 ... ♞h6 to 82 ♔d5.

| 82 | ♔d5 | ♞f3 |
| 83 | ♖g2 | ♞h4 |

Or 83 ... ♞e1 84 ♖b2+ ♔c7 85 ♔e4.

| 84 | ♖g7+ | ♔c8 |

85	♔e4	♔d8	86	♖g4	1-0

RN 5

Geller - Am. Rodriguez
Amsterdam OHRA 1987
This is very nearly a lost Arabian position (cf diag 2). Note the defence.

87	♔f6	♞e8+!

87 ... ♞h5+ 88 ♔g5 ♞g7 89 ♖a7 (al-Adli).

88	♔e7	♞g7

=
W

89	♔f7	♞h5!

89 ... ♞f5 90 ♔f6.

90	♖c6	♞g7
91	♔f6	♞e8+
92	♔f5	♔g7
93	♔e6	♞f6
94	♖c1	♞h5
95	♔f5	♔f8
½-½		

RN 6

Berg - Kuijf
Græted 1990

85	♞g7+	♔f6
86	♞e8+	♔g6
87	♞d6	♖d7
88	♞e8	♖f7+
89	♔g8	♖f1
90	♞d6?	

W

This would lose immediately if the position were one file to the right. Here it leads to the Arabian position (diag 2).

Better is 90 ♞c7 ♖c1 (90 ... ♔f6 91 ♔f8) 91 ♞e8 ♖c8 92 ♔f8.

90	...	♔f6
91	♞e8+	♔e7
92	♞g7	

Compare with the Arabian position.

92	...	♖f7

92 ... ♖e1 is also possible:

a) 93 ♞f5+ ♔f6 94 ♞d6 (94 ♞h6 ♔g6) ♖e6 95 ♞c4 ♖c6 96 ♞e3 ♖c5 97 ♔h7 ♔g5 98 ♔g7 ♔f4;

b) 93 ♔h7 ♔f6 94 ♔h6 (94 ♞h5+ ♔g5 95 ♞g7 ♖e7 96 ♔g8 ♔g6 97 ♔h8 ♖a7) ♖h1+ 95 ♞h5+ ♔f5;

c) 93 ♞h5 ♖e5 94 ♞g7 (94 ♞f4 ♔f6 95 ♔h7 ♖f5 leads to diag 2) 94 ... ♖g5 95 ♔h7 ♔f7 96 ♔h8 ♖g1.

93	♔h8	

Not 93 ♞h5 ♖f5 94 ♞g7 ♖g5.

93	...	♖f8+
94	♔h7	♔f6
95	♞h5+	♔g5
96	♞g7	♖a8
97	♞e6+	♔f5
98	♞g7+	♔f6
99	♞h5+	♔g5
100	♞g7	♖a5

This is diag 2 (rotated and reversed) after 3 ♖h5!.

101	♔g8	♔f6
102	♞e8+	♔e7
103	♞g7	♖g5
104	♔h7	♔f7
105	♔h8	♖g1
	0-1	

Rook v Knight   ♖ V ♞

Rook and One Pawn v Knight

RN 7

=
W

Averbakh
> 1   ♖c5

A classic position which demonstrates the only saving grace with this material balance - White's extra pawn being isolated/too far advanced.
> 1   ...   ♞e7!

Not 1 ... ♞b6 2 ♔d4 and:
a) 2 ... ♞c8 3 ♖c6 ♞d7 (3 ... ♞a8 4 ♔c5) 4 ♔d5 ♞f8 5

♔d6;
b) 2 ... ♞c8 3 ♔c4 ♔d6 4 ♔b5 ♔d7 5 ♔a6 ♔d6 6 ♔b7.
> 2   ♔e4   ♞c8
> 3   ♔d5   ♞e7+
> 4   ♔c4   ♔c8!
> 5   ♔b5   ♔b7!
> 6   ♖e5   ♞c8

White cannot make progress - his king cannot reach the pawn.

RN 8

=
B

Averbakh
Here, Black can safely round up the pawn.
> 1   ...   ♞b5
> 2   ♔f3   ♔b3
> 3   ♔g4   ♔a4

> 4   ♔f5   ♞a3
> 5   ♔e5   ♔b5!
> 6   ♔d5   ♞c2

and draws
See also diag 9.

RN 9

=
W

Em. Lasker - Ed. Lasker
New York 1924
This is probably the most famous and memorable such ending, which focused attention on the defensive possibilities.
> 1   ♞a4   ♔d4
> 2   ♞b2   ♖f3
> 3   ♞a4   ♖e3
> 4   ♞b2   ♔e4

> 5   ♞a4   ♔f3
> 6   ♞a3   ♔e4

Or 6 ... ♔e2 7 ♔b2 with the idea of ♞c5.
> 7   ♔b4!   ♔d4
> 8   ♞b2   ♖h3
> 9   ♞a4   ♔d3

Black acknowledges that he cannot make progress.
> 10   ♔xb3   ♔d4+
> ½-½

RN 10

+
W

La Bourdonnais - Macdonnell
> 1   ♖a4!

This move was found by Berger (the starting position is La Bourdonnais - Macdonnell London 1834).
> 1   ...   ♞c6

Not 1 ... ♔c6? 2 ♖b4.
> 2   ♔d5   ♞a7
> 3   ♔d6   ♞b5+
> 4   ♔d7   ♞a7

Not 4 ... ♔a7 5 ♔c6 ♞c3 6

♖c4 ♞b1 7 ♖c1 ♞d2 8 ♔b5.
> 5   ♖a1   ♞b5
> 6   ♔c8   ♔a7

Or 6 ... ♞a7+ 7 ♔b8 ♞c6+ 8 ♔a8.
> 7   ♖a5   ♞d6+
> 8   ♔c7   ♞c4
> 9   ♖a2   ♞b6
> 10   ♔c6   ♞c4
> 11   ♔c5   ♞b6
> 12   ♔b5 and wins

Rook v Knight ♖ v ♘

Rook and Pawn v Knight and Pawn

RN 11

=
B

Stein - Bobotsov
Moscow 1967
The f-pawn is distraction
enough to hold the draw.

47	...	♘d3+
48	♔e2	f3+
49	♔d2	f2
50	♔e2	♔d4
51	♖b8	♔c4
52	♔f1	

Or 52 ♖c8+ ♔d4? (52 ...
♔b4!) 53 ♖d8+ (53 b3!) 53 ...
♔e4 54 ♖xd3 f1♕+.

52	...	♔d4
53	♖b7	♔c4
54	♔e2	♔d4
55	♖d7+	♔e4

Not 55 ... ♔c4?? 56 b3+.

| 56 | ♖b7 | ♔d4 |
| 57 | ♖b8 | |

Not 57 b3 ♔c3.

| 57 | ... | ♔c4 |
| 58 | ♖c8+ | ♔b4! |

Black plays to surround the
b-pawn, not falling for the tactic in the earlier note.

59	♖c2	♘c5
60	♔xf2	♘a4
61	♔e3	♔b3
62	♖c8	♘xb2=
63	♔d4	♘a4
64	♖c6	♔b4
65	♖c4+	♔b5
66	♖c1	♘b6
67	♖c5+	♔b4

½-½

RN 12

+
B

Dokhoian - Shirov
Klaipeda 1988

| 79 | ... | ♘g5 |

Black tries to provoke h4,
presumably to create counterplay by advancing the king towards the more exposed h-
pawn.

| 80 | ♔g4 | |

White's play in the game is
rather aimless. 80 ♖g3 is met
by 80 ... ♔h5 with the idea of
81 ... ♔h4. 80 h4 looks critical, aiming for positions similar to diag 13:

a) 80 ... ♘f7 81 ♖h3 ♔h5
(81 ... ♘d6 82 h5+ ♔h6 83
♖h2 ♔g7 84 ♖d2) 82 ♔f5
♘e5 83 ♔xf6 ♘g6 84 ♔f5
♘xh4+ 85 ♔f4;

b) 80 ... ♘e6+ 81 ♔g4 and
White wins as in (the notes to)
Bertona - Soppe:

b1) 81 ... ♘g7 82 ♖d6 ♘h5
83 ♖d5 ♘g7 84 h5+ ♔h6 85
♖a5 ♔h7 (85 ... f5+ 86 ♔h4
♘xh5 87 ♖a6+) 86 ♖a6;

b2) 81 ... f5+ 82 ♔g3 ♔h5

(82 ... ♘g7 83 ♖d6+) 83 ♖d6
with the idea of ♖f6.

80	...	♘e4
81	♖e3	♘g5
82	♖g3	♘e4
83	♖g1	♘g5
84	♖g2	♘e6
85	♖e2	♘g5
86	♖e8	♘f7
87	♔f4	♘g5
88	♔g4	♘f7
89	♖g8+	♔h7
90	♖b8	♔g6
91	♖a8	♘e5+
92	♔f4	♘d3+
93	♔e3	♘e5
94	♖g8+	♔h5
95	♔e4	♔h4
96	♖h8+	♔g5

97 ♔d5 ♘f3 98 ♔d6 ♘e5
99 ♔e6 ♘f3 100 ♔e7 ♘e5
101 ♖a8 ♘g6+ 102 ♔f7 ♘f4
103 ♖a3 f5 104 ♖c3 ♘xh3 105
♖xh3 ♔g4 106 ♖h6 f4 107
♖g6+ ♔h3 108 ♖f6 ♔g3 109
♔e6 f3 110 ♔e5 f2 111 ♔e4
♔g2 112 ♔e3 f1♕ 113 ♖xf1
♔xf1 ½-½

337

Rook v Knight   ♖ v ♞

RN 13

-

W

Bertona - Soppe
Argentine Ch 1990

  67   ♘e3

67 f3!? and transferring the knight to e4 would give Dokhoian - Shirov (diag 12).

67	...	♚g5
68	♘g2	♖g4+
69	♔h3	♖a4
70	♔g3	h5
71	♔h3	

71 f3 h4+ 72 ♔h3 ♖a1 73 ♔h2 ♖a3 wins.

71	...	♖a3+
72	♘e3	♖a1
73	♔g3	h4+
74	♔h3	♖a3
75	♔g2	♖a2
76	♔f3	♖d2
77	♔g2	♖d8!
78	♔h3	♖f8!
79	♔g2	♖h8!

80	♘f1	

80 ♔h3 ♖f4 81 ♘d5+ (81 ♘g2+ ♔f3 82 ♘xh4+ ♔f4) 81 ... ♔f3 82 ♘e7 ♖h7 83 ♘f5 ♖h5 84 ♘g7 ♖h6 85 ♘f5 ♖h7-+ (zugzwang).

80	...	♔f4
81	♘d2	h3+
82	♔h2	♖h5
83	♘f1	♔f3
84	♘g3	♖h8
85	♘g1	h2+
86	♔h1	♔xf2
87	♘e4+	♔f3
88	♘d2+	♔f4
89	♘f3	♔g3
90	♘d4	♖a8
91	♘e2+	♔g4
92	♘d4	♔h3
93	♘c2	♖g8

0-1

RN 14

+

W

Jansa - Gausel
Oslo 1988

73	♖a4!	♔e7
74	♔g6	♔f8
75	♖c4?	

75 ♖d4 transposing to the analysis of diag 38.

75	...	♔e7
76	♔g7	♘e3
77	♖e4	♘f5+
78	♔g6	♘h4+
79	♔g5	♘f5
80	♖a4	♘e3
81	♖e4	♘f5

82	♖e5	♘d4
83	♖e3	♘f5
84	♖e4	♘d6
85	♖a4	♘b5
86	♖c4	♔f7
87	♖c5	♘d6
88	♖c7+	♔f8
89	♖a7	♘b5
90	♖d7	♔e8
91	♖h7	♘c3
92	♔f6	♘e2
93	♔g5	♔f8
94	♖h2	1-0

RN 15

=

W

Averbakh

1	♖a5	♘c5
2	♖a3	

2 ♖xc5+ dxc5+ 3 ♔e5 ♔c7 4 ♔d5 ♔b6 5 ♔d6 ♔b7 6 ♔xc5 ♔c7=.

2	...	♘e6+
3	♔c3	♘c5
4	♔b4	♔b6

5	♖a8	♘d3+
6	♔c3	♘c5
7	♔d4	♔c6

'with a draw' - Averbakh. Black's knight is excellently placed and can prevent White's king from maintaining a threatening post.

Rook v Knight ♖ V ♞

RN 16
+ W

Ehlvest - Khalifman
USSR Ch 1987
    61   ♖a4   ♞c6
    61 ... ♞e6 62 ♖a5+ ♔f6 63 f5.
    62   ♔f3
An example of how easy it is to win when the defenders are not optimally placed.
    62   ...   g6

    63   ♖c4   ♞d8
    64   ♖c7   ♔f6
    64 ... ♞e6 65 ♖f7+.
    65   ♔e4   ♞e6
    66   ♖c6   ♔f7
    67   ♔e5   ♞g7
With the idea of ... ♞h5(+) (see also diag 17).
    68   ♖f6+   1-0

RN 17
+ W

Taimanov - Bronstein
Leningrad 1946
    1   ♖a7+
This position demonstrates that even if Black had managed to erect the optimal position in the previous example he would still have lost.
    1   ...   ♔f8
    2   ♖d7!
Found after the game by Bronstein and Averbakh. 2 f5? only led to a draw in the game.
    2   ...   ♔g8
    2 ... ♔e8 3 ♖h7 with the idea of f5+-.
    3   ♔e6!!
A rare case of rook winning against knight and pawn.
    3   ...   ♞xf4+
Or 3 ... ♔f8 4 ♖f7+ ♔g8 (4

... ♔e8 5 ♖f6! ♔d8 6 ♔f7) 5 ♔e7 ♔h8 6 ♔f8 ♞g3 7 ♖g7 ♞h5 8 ♖xg6.
    4   ♔f6   g5
Instead 4 ... ♞h5+ 5 ♔xg6 ♞f4+ 6 ♔g5 transposes, whilst 4 ... ♔h8 5 ♖d4! g5 6 ♖d7 g4 (6 ... ♔g8 transposes to other lines) 7 ♖d4 ♞g2 8 ♖xg4 ♞e3 9 ♖e4 ♞d5+ 10 ♔f7.
    5   ♔xg5   ♞e6+
    6   ♔f6   ♞f4
    7   ♖d4   ♞e2
    8   ♖g4+   ♔f8
    9   ♖c4   ♔g8
    10   ♔g6   ♔f8
    11   ♔g5   ♞g3
    12   ♔g4   ♞e2
    13   ♔f3   ♞g1+
    14   ♔g2   ♞e2
    15   ♔f2   1-0

RN 18
= W

Larsen - Tal
Bled 1965
White has a good defensive formation against the black king's approach to the front of the pawn. Black cannot make progress on the kingside so the king changes sides.
    54   ♔f3   ♔f7
    55   ♞g3   ♔e6
    56   ♔f4   ♖a4+
    57   ♔f3   ♔e5
    58   ♞h5! *(18a)*
This is the ideal position against the Black king's ap-

proach - it is given by Averbakh as a drawing formation.
    58   ...   ♖a8
    59   ♔e3   ♖b8
    60   ♔f3   ♖e8
    61   ♞f4   ♔d4
    62   ♞h5   ♖e1
    63   ♔f2   ♖e4
    64   ♔f3   ♔e5
    65   ♔g3   ♖e3+
    66   ♔f2   ♖b3
    67   ♔g2   ♖b7
    68   ♔f3   ♖b8
    69   ♔e3   ♖g8
    70   ♔f3   ♖h8

RN 18a

= B

With the idea of ... f5.

71	♘g3	♖h7
72	♔e3	♖h8
73	♔f3	♖h2
74	♔e3	♖b2
75	♘h5	♖b3+
76	♔f2	♖d3
77	♔g2	♔e4
78	♘xf6+	♔f4
79	♔f2	♖d2+
80	♔e1	♖d6

Black's last hope is to isolate the knight.

81	g5!	♔f3
82	♘h7	♔e3
83	♘f6	♔f3
84	♘h7	♖d5
85	g6	♖d7
86	♘g5+	♔e3
87	♘e6	♖d2
88	♘f4	♖h2
89	♘d5+	♔f3
90	♔d1	♖g2
91	g7	½-½

A very important ending, illustrating the entire range of winning attempts.

RN 19

- B

Tal - Ciocaltea
Riga 1967

66	...	♖c1?

Black underrates White's ability to achieve a fortress. Winning was 66 ... ♔d6 67 ♔g3 (67 ♔g4 ♖c3 68 ♔f5 ♖f3+ 69 ♔g5 ♔c5) 67 ... ♖c3+ 68 ♔f2 (68 ♔g4 ♔c5 69 ♔f5 ♔d4 70 ♘g4 ♖a3 71 ♘f6 ♖f3+ 72 ♔e6 ♖xf6+) 68 ... ♔c5.

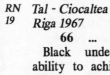

RN 19a

= W

67	♘g4	♔d6
68	♔g3	♖f1 *(19a)*
69	♔g2	♖f8

Or 69 ... ♖f4 70 ♘f2 ♔c6

(70 ... ♖f8 71 ♘d3=) 71 ♔g3 ♔b5 72 ♘d3! ♖xe4 73 ♔f3.

70	♔g3	♖e8
71	♔f3	♔c5
72	♔e3	♔c4
73	♘h2	♖a8
74	♘f3	

Finally, White reaches a theoretically drawn position.

74	...	♖a5
75	♔e2	♔c3
76	♔e3	♔c2
77	♔e2	½-½

Black can no longer coordinate his pieces against e4 due to the pressure against e5.

RN 20

= B

Barle - Neverov
Voskresensk 1990

Another version of the Tal-Ciocaltea (diag 19) ending. The shift of one file makes no difference to the result. Black's ideally placed pieces hold draw.

76	...	♔d6
77	♖h5	♔c6
78	♔b3	♔d6
79	♖h7	♔c6
80	♔c3	♘a4+
81	♔c2	♘b6
82	♔d3	♔d6
83	♖h1	♔c6
84	♖c1	♔d6
85	♔e4	♔c6
86	♔e5	♘d7+
87	♔e6	♘b6
88	♖c2	♔c7
½-½		

Rook v Knight ♖ V ♞

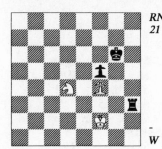

RN
21

-
W

Shirov - Fishbein
Kerteminde 1991
This is a good example of the defender needing to achieve a key position.

51 ♔e2

White has trouble getting the knight to e3: the knight cannot release the pressure against f5 without allowing the black king in.

51 ... ♖a3!
52 ♘c2

52 ♔d2 ♖a5 53 ♘c2 ♔h5 54 ♘e3 ♔h4 or 52 ♔f2 ♖d3 both lose.

52 ... ♖a2
53 ♔d3 ♖a4!

Not 53 ... ♔h5 54 ♘e3 ♖a5 (54 ... ♖a3+ 55 ♔e2 ♖xe3+ 56 ♔xe3 ♔g4 57 ♔e2 ♔xf4 58 ♔f2) 55 ♔e2 ♔h4 56 ♔f3=.

54 ♔e3

A major achievement for Black - the white king sits on the knight's ideal square.

54 ... ♖c4!

Driving the knight further from e3. (Not 54 ... ♔h5 55 ♔f3= when Black has no checks.)

55 ♘d4 ♖c3+
56 ♔e2 ♖c5

Preparing the invasion of the king.

57 ♘f3

57 ♔f3 ♔h5 wins easily.

57 ... ♔h5
58 ♘e5 ♖c3
59 ♔f2 ♔h4
60 ♔g2 ♖b3

The black king invades thanks to zugzwang.
0-1

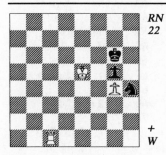

RN
22

+
W

Razuvaev - Lputian
Sochi 1987
Despite the lack of pressure against g4 Black can put up tremendous resistance since it is difficult for White to encircle the g-pawn.

74 ♖f1 ♘g2
75 ♖f6+ ♔g7
76 ♖f3

Or 76 ♔f5 ♘e3+ 77 ♔xg5 ♘xg4.

76 ... ♔g6
77 ♔e4 ♔g7
78 ♖f2 ♘h4
79 ♔e5 ♔g6
80 ♔e6 ♔g7
81 ♔d7 ♔g6

Not 81 ... ♘g6 82 ♖f5 ♘h4 (82 ... ♔h6 83 ♔e8 is analogous to the game) 83 ♖xg5+ ♔f6 84 ♖h5 ♘g2 85 ♖f5+ ♔g6 86 ♖e5! (86 ♔e6 ♘e3) ♔f6 87 ♔d6.

82 ♔e7 ♔g7
83 ♔e8 ♘g6
84 ♖f5 ♘h4
85 ♖f7+

85 ♖xg5+ ♔f6 86 ♖g8 (or 86 ♖a5 ♘g2) 86 ... ♘g6. In both cases White must beware of having the pawn surrounded before the ♔e8 returns to the game. Razuvaev is more methodical.

85 ... ♔g6
86 ♔f8 ♘g2
87 ♖e7! ♔f6
88 ♖e4 ♘f4
89 ♔g8 ♔g6
90 ♖e1

Zugzwang - the encirclement is finally complete.

90 ... ♔f6

Or 90 ... ♘d5 91 ♖e6+ ♘f6+ 92 ♔f8.

91 ♔h7 ♘d3
92 ♖f1+ 1-0

Rook v Knight

Rook and Pawn v Knight and Two Pawns

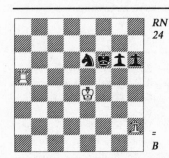

RN 23

Bronstein - Podgaets
USSR 1974

46	...	♖c6
47	♔e4	

47 ♔d5 ♔d7 - Bronstein and Lepeshkin.

47	...	♔d7
48	♔e5?	

48 ♔d5!= - Bronstein and Lepeshkin.

48	...	♖e6+
49	♔d5	♖e7
50	♔c4	♖e8
51	♔d5	f6
52	♘d6	♖e5+
53	♔d4	♔xc7
54	♘e4	♖f5
55	b5	♔b6
56	♔e3	♔c7
57	♔d4	♖f1
58	♔c5	

58 ♔e3! - Bronstein and Lepeshkin.

58	...	f5
59	b6+	♔b8
60	♘f6	f4
61	♔d4	♖e1
62	♘d7+	♔c8
63	b7+	♔xb7
64	♘c5+	♔c6
65	♘d3	f3
66	♘xe1	f2
67	♘d3	f1♕

0-1

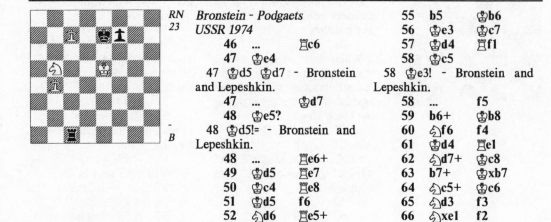

RN 24

Romanishin - Am. Rodriguez
Moscow 1985

54	...	♘g5+
55	♔f4	♘e6+
56	♔e3	h5

56 ... ♘g7 is suggested by Rodriguez.

57	♔e4	♘g5+
58	♔f4	♘e6+
59	♔e3	♘g5

59 ... ♘g7 is met by 60 ♔e4 ♘f5 61 ♔f4 with the idea of ♖a6, ♔g5 (Rodriguez).

60	h4	♘e6?

60 ... ♘f7! draws according to Rodriguez.

61	♔e4	g5
62	♖f5+	♔g6
63	♔e5	gxh4
64	♔xe6	h3
65	♔e5	h2
66	♖f1	♔g5
67	♖h1	♔g4
68	♖xh2	h4
69	♖g2+!	♔f3
70	♖a2	**1-0**

70 ... h3 71 ♔f5 ♔g3 72 ♖a3+ ♔g2 73 ♔g4 h2 74 ♖a2+ ♔g1 75 ♔g3+- (Rodriguez).

Rook and Two Pawns v Knight and Two Pawns

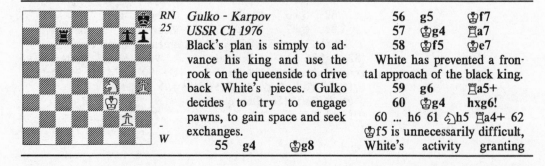

RN 25

Gulko - Karpov
USSR Ch 1976

Black's plan is simply to advance his king and use the rook on the queenside to drive back White's pieces. Gulko decides to try to engage pawns, to gain space and seek exchanges.

55	g4	♔g8
56	g5	♔f7
57	♔g4	♖a7
58	♔f5	♔e7

White has prevented a frontal approach of the black king.

59	g6	♖a5+
60	♔g4	hxg6!

60 ... h6 61 ♘h5 ♖a4+ 62 ♔f5 is unnecessarily difficult, White's activity granting

Rook v Knight

♖ V ♞

counterplay.

61	♘xg6+	♔f6

Despite the reduced material the activated king decides.

62	♘f8	♖a4+
63	♔h5	

Or 63 ♔g3 ♔f5 64 ♘h7

♖a3+ 65 ♔g2 ♔g4.

63	...	♖a8
64	♘h7+	♔f5
65	♘f8	♖a5
66	♘h7	♖a6
	0-1	

Rook and Two Pawns v Knight and Three Pawns

RN 26
+
W

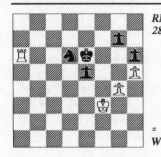

RN 27
=
B

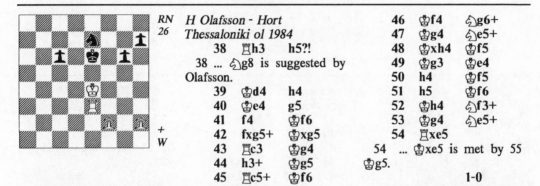

RN 28
=
W

H Olafsson - Hort
Thessaloniki ol 1984

38	♖h3	h5?!

38 ... ♘g8 is suggested by Olafsson.

39	♔d4	h4
40	♔e4	g5
41	f4	♔f6
42	fxg5+	♔xg5
43	♖c3	♔g4
44	h3+	♔g5
45	♖c5+	♔f6
46	♔f4	♘g6+
47	♔g4	♘e5+
48	♔xh4	♔f5
49	♔g3	♔e4
50	h4	♔f5
51	h5	♔f6
52	♔h4	♘f3+
53	♔g4	♘e5+
54	♖xe5	

54 ... ♔xe5 is met by 55 ♔g5.

1-0

Korchnoi - Mark Tseitlin
USSR Ch 1970

43	...	♔h4
44	♔e1	e5
45	♖e2	♔g3
46	♔f1	♔f4
47	♖f2+	♔g5
48	♖e2	♔f4

Black experiences no difficulties, thanks to his space control, which allows him to monitor White's pawns as well as defend his own. (Compare with diag 28).

½-½

Neckar - Makarichev
Balasiha 1977

An ending silently assessed as "=" in *Informator*. White's kingside space gives him play, and Black is restricted to passive defence.

59	♖c6	♔d7
60	♖b6	♔e6
61	♖a6	♔e7
62	g5!	

The only try - again the activity of the pieces is more important than material.

62	...	hxg5
63	♔g4	e4

Or 63 ... ♘f7 64 ♔f5.

64	♔xg5	e3
65	♖a1?	

65 ♔g6 looks most dangerous, when the draw is problematic, e.g.

a) 65 ... e2 66 ♖a1 ♘e4 (66 ... ♔f8 67 ♖e1 ♘c8 68 ♖xe2 ♘e7+ 69 ♔h7 ♘d5 70 ♖f2+ ♘f6+ 71 ♔g6 ♔g8 72 h6) 67 ♔xg7;

b) 65 ... ♔e6 66 ♔xg7 and

343

now:

b1) 66 ... e2 67 Ra1 Nf5+ 68 Kg6 Nh4+ 69 Kg7 Nf5+ 70 Kg6 Nh4+ 71 Kh7 Kf6! (71 ... Nf3 72 Kg7 e1Q 73 Rxe1+ Nxe1 74 h6+-) 72 h6 and:

b11) 72 ... Kg5 73 Rg1+! Kh5 74 Re1 Nf5 75 Rxe2 Nxh6 76 Rh2++-;

b12) 72 ... Nf5! 73 Re1 (73 Rg1 Kf7 74 Re1 Ng3= 75 Kh8 Kg6 76 h7 Kf7 77 Ra1 Kf8) 73 ... Kg5 74 Rxe2 Nxh6=;

b2) 66 ... Ke5 67 Kg6 Nf5 (67 ... e2 68 Ra1 Nf5 69 Re1) 68 Ra5+ Ke6 69 h6.

65	...	Kf7
66	Rf1+	Ke6
67	Kg6	Nf5!
68	Re1	Ke5
69	Rf1	e2!
70	Re1	

Or 70 Rxf5+ Ke6 71 Rf8 Ke7.

70	...	Ng3
71	Kg5	Kd4
72	Kg4	Nxh5
73	Rxe2	Nf6+

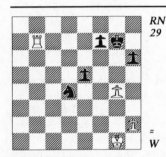

RN 29
Tal - Andersson
Tilburg 1980
=
W

43	Rb6	f6
44	Kf2	Kg6
45	h4	Nc2
46	Kf3	Nd4+
47	Ke3	Nc2+
48	Ke4	Nd4
49	Rb8	Nc6!

Andersson envisages a neat positional draw.

50	h5+	Kg5
51	Rg8+	Kh4
52	Rg7	Nd4
53	Rg6	Kh3!
54	Rxf6	Kxg4
55	Rxh6	

Or 55 Kxe5 Nf3+ (55 ... Kg5!?) 56 Kd5.

55	...	Nf3
56	Kd5	Ng5
57	Rh8	Nf7
58	Rh7	Ng5
59	Rh6	Kh4!

½-½

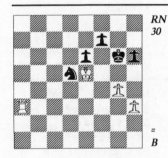

RN 30
Karpov - Ftacnik
Thessaloniki ol 1988
=
B

74	...	h5
75	gxh5+	Kxh5
76	Rg3!	Kh6

76 ... Kh4 77 Rf3.

77	Kd6	Nf4
78	Ke7	Kh5
79	Kf6!	

79 Kxf7 e5 80 Kf6 Kh4.

79	...	Nd5+
80	Ke5	

80 Kxf7 Kh4 81 Rf3 e5 82 Ke6 e4 is given by Karpov.

80	...	Kh4?!

After 80 ... Kh6! (Karpov) White should not be able to progress.

Now we reach a tough rook v knight position.

81	Rf3	Nb6
82	Rxf7	Kxh3
83	Kxe6	Nc4

Karpov gives this a "?" but this seems harsh. Instead he gives 83 ... Kg3! 84 Rc7! (84 Ke5 Nc4+= - Karpov) 84 ... Kf3=. Really? The following variation seems to demonstrate that Black is indeed lost: 85 Rc3+! (85 Ke5? Ke3 86 Rc3+ Kd2 87 Kd4 Na4 88 Rb3 Kc2 89 Ra3 Nb2 and the knight escapes) 85 ... Ke2 (85 ... Ke4 86 Rc6) 86 Rc6 Na4 87 Rc4! Nb6 88 Rb4 Nc8 89 Rb7.

84	Rf3+	Kg4

Karpov gives 84 ... Kg2 85 Rc3 Na5 86 Kd5 Nb7 87 Ra3

♘d8 88 ♖a7+-.

85 ♖d3! ♔g5

85 ... ♘a5 86 ♔d5; 85 ... ♘b6 86 ♖b3 ♘c8 87 ♖b7; and 85 ... ♘b2 86 ♖d2 all lose (Karpov).

86 ♔d5 ♘b6+

86 ... ♘b2 87 ♖d4 ♔f5 88 ♔c6 is a familiar motif; after 88 ... ♔e5 89 ♔c5 we reach a zugzwang.

87 ♔e5! ♘c4+

88 ♔e4 ♘b6

If instead 88 ... ♔f6 89 ♖d4 and now:

a) 89 ... ♘a5 90 ♔d5 and;

a1) 90 ... ♘b7 91 ♔c6 ♘a5+ 92 ♔b5 ♘b3 (92 ... ♘b7 93 ♖d7) 93 ♖d3 ♘c1 94 ♖e3 ♔f5 95 ♔c4 ♔f4 96 ♖e1;

a2) 90 ... ♘b3 91 ♖d1 ♔e7 92 ♖b1 ♘a5 93 ♖b5;

b) 89 ... ♘a3 90 ♖b4 ♘c2 91 ♖b2 ♘a3 92 ♔d3;

c) 89 ... ♘b2 90 ♔f3 ♔e5 91 ♔e3 ♔f5 92 ♔d2.

89 ♖d8 ♘c4

89 ... ♘a4 90 ♔d4 ♘b6 91 ♔c5 ♘a4+ 92 ♔b4 or 89 ... ♔g4 90 ♔d4 (Karpov).

90 ♖d4! ♘b6

90 ... ♘a3 is met by 91 ♔d3 with the idea of ♖b4, whilst 90 ... ♘b2 91 ♔e3 ♔f5 92 ♔d2 ♔e5 93 ♔c3 also wins for White.

91 ♔e5 ♘c8

92 ♔e6 ♘a7

Or 92 ... ♘b6 93 ♔d6.

93 ♔d7 1-0

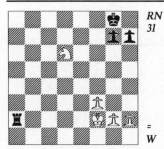

RN 31

= W

**Vidmar - Alekhine
San Remo 1930**

Fine gives this as probably won, but Averbakh demonstrates a draw.

38 ♔g3 ♔f8

39 h4 ♔e7

40 ♘e4 h6

41 ♘f2?

41 ♔h3 ♔e6 (or 41 ... ♖a3 42 ♔g4 ♔e6 43 ♔f4 g6 44 g4) 42 g4! (see diags 32, 343 42 ... ♔e5 43 ♔g3 g6 (not 43 ... ♔d4 44 h5 ♔e3 45 ♘d6) 44 ♘f2 ♖a3 45 ♘h3 ♖a4 46 ♔f2! (46 ♘f2 ♔d4 47 ♘h3 ♔e3) 46 ... h5 47 gxh5 ♖xh4 48 hxg6!=.

41 ... ♔e6

42 ♘d3 ♔f5

43 ♘f4 ♖a4

44 ♘d3 ♖c4

45 ♘f2 ♖c6

46 ♘h3 ♔e5

47 h5

'... without g4 this moves is a serious mistake, which simplifies Black's task' - Averbakh. Averbakh demonstrates

the following winning technique against passive defence: 47 ♘f4 ♖c2 48 ♘h3 ♖d2 49 ♘f4 ♖a2 50 ♘h3 ♔d4 51 ♘f4 ♔e3 52 ♘e6 ♖a7 53 ♘f4 ♖a6! 54 ♘h3 ♔e2 55 ♘f4+ ♔f1 56 h5 (56 ♘h3 ♖a2 57 ♘f4 g5 58 hxg5 hxg5 59 ♘e6 ♖xg2+ 60 ♔h3 ♔f2) 56 ... ♖a5 57 ♔h2 ♔f2 58 ♔h3 ♖b5 59 ♔h4 ♔e3.

47 ... ♖c2!

48 ♘f4 ♖d2

49 ♘h3 ♔d4

50 ♘f4 ♔e3

51 ♘e6

Not 51 ♘h3 ♖b2 52 ♘f4 ♖b5 53 ♘e6 ♖e5 or 51 ♔g4 ♖d4 52 g3 ♖a4.

51 ... ♖d5

52 f4

52 ♔h4 ♖e5! 53 ♘xg7 ♖g5 54 ♘e6 ♖xg2 was given by Alekhine.

52 ... ♖f5

53 ♔g4 ♖f6

54 f5 ♖f7

A better try was 54 ... ♔e4! 55 ♘xg7 (55 ♘c5+ ♔d5 56

♘d3 ♔d4 57 ♘f4 ♔e4) ♖f7 56 ♘e6 ♖xf5 57 ♔h4 (57 g3 ♖e5 58 ♘d8 ♖g5+ 59 ♔h4 ♔f3 60 ♘f7 ♖g4+ 61 ♔h3 ♖xg3+ 62 ♔h4 ♔f4 63 ♘xh6 ♖g7 64 ♔h3 ♖h7) 57 ... ♔e5 58 ♘c5 ♖f4+ 59 ♔h3 ♖d4 60 g3 ♔d6 (a familiar scene from rook v knight - the knight has strayed) 61 ♘b3 ♖d1 62 ♔h4 (62 ♔g4 ♔d5 63 ♔f5 ♖d3) 62 ... ♔d5 63 g4

♖d3 64 ♘c1 (64 g5 ♖xb3 65 gxh6 ♔e6 66 h7 ♖b8 67 ♔g5 ♔f7) 64 ... ♖e3 65 g5 ♖e4+ (Alekhine).

55 g3

55 ♘d8! ♖f6 56 ♘e6 ♔e4! leading to previous note.

55	...	♔e4
56	♘c5+	♔d4!
57	♘b3+	♔e5
	0-1	

RN 32

Leykin 1940

Leykin's analysis here and in diag 33 is a reaction to Vidmar's loss to Alekhine and shows the correct defensive array (See also diag 37a).

1	♘g2+	♔e2
2	♘f4+	♔f1
3	♘e6	♖a7
4	♘d4	♖d7
5	♘f5	♔e2
6	♔g2	

And Black cannot strengthen his position due to pressure against g7.

= W

RN 33

Leykin 1940

| 1 | ♘f4 | ♖a6 |

If 1 ... g5 2 hxg5 hxg5 3 ♘h3 ♖a5 4 f4.

2	♔f2	♖f6
3	♔g3	♖a6
4	♔f2	♖d6
5	♔g3	♔e3
6	♘g2+	♔d4
7	♘f4	

With a positional draw (½-½).

= W

RN 34

Fischer - Robatsch
Vinkovci 1968

39	♔g3	♘e4+
40	♔f4	♘f6
41	♔e5	

After 41 g4 g6 Black can defend as in the game.

41	...	h5
42	♔d6	g6
43	♔e5	♔g7

The simplest fortress with knight and three vs rook and two.

44	♖a4	♘d7+
45	♔d6	♘f6
46	♖f4	♘g8
47	♔e5	♘h6
48	♖f1	♔f8
49	♖a1	♔g7
50	♖a7	♘g8
51	♖a6	♘h6
52	♖c6	♘g8
53	g4	hxg4
54	hxg4	♘h6
55	g5	♘f5
56	♖c7	♘g3
57	♖a7	♘h5

After 58 ♖a3 f6+ and 58 ♔d6 ♘g3 White is stuck.

½-½

= W

Rook v Knight

Rook v Knight: Numerous Pawns

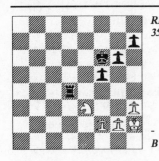

RN 35	*Geller - Mikhalchishin,*	
	USSR Ch 1985	

With three pawns each the knight has little hope, succumbing either to a pawn storm or the king and rook ganging up on one of the pawns, leading either to win of material or involuntary exposure.

B

39	...	🨢d2

40	🨴g3	g5
41	🨴f3	h5
42	g3	🨢a2
43	♘g2	🨴e5
44	h4	🨢a3+
45	🨴e2	f4
46	gxf4+	gxf4
47	f3	🨢a2+
48	🨴f1	🨢xg2!
49	🨴xg2	🨴d4

0-1

RN 36	*Plachetka - Kovacevic*
	Sombor 1976

40	🨴f2?	

Better is 40 g4! a3 (not 40 ... ♘b7 41 🨢e4 a3 42 🨢a4 🨴e5 43 🨢xa3 🨴xd5 44 🨢h3 or 40 ... h6 41 🨢e3!) 41 🨢a2 🨴e5 42 🨢xa3 🨴xd5 43 🨢h3 (Kovacevic).

40	...	h5
41	🨴f3	a3
42	🨢c2	

Here White should have played 42 d6! ♘d7 43 🨴f4 and now:

a) 43 ... ♘c5 44 🨢a2 g5+ 45 🨴e3 🨴e6 46 🨢xa3 🨴xd6 47 🨢a8 ♘d7 (47 ... 🨴e6 48 🨢h8 🨴f5 49 🨢xh5 - Kovacevic) 48 🨴e4 (Kovacevic);

b) 43 ... g5+ 44 🨴f3 🨴f5 45 🨢a2 ♘e5+ 46 🨴e2 🨴e6 47 🨢xa3 🨴xd6 48 🨢a6+ ♘c6 49 🨴e3 f5 (49 ... 🨴d5 50 🨢a8) 50 h4+- (Kovacevic).

42	...	♘a4=
43	🨴f4	

Not 43 🨴e4?? a2 44 🨢c1

RN 36a	

B

♘c5+ 45 🨴e3 ♘b3 (Kovacevic).

43	...	g5+
44	🨴e3	🨴e5
45	d6	🨴xd6
46	🨴d4	f6

46 ... f5 is suggested by Kovacevic.

47	🨢a2	

Or 47 🨢c4 ♘b6 48 🨢c3 a2 49 🨢a3 🨴e6 50 🨴e4 ♘c4 51 🨢xa2 ♘d6+ 52 🨴d4 ♘f5+= (Kovacevic).

47	...	♘c5
48	🨢xa3	*(41a)*
48	...	f5
49	🨢a8	♘e6+
50	🨴d3	🨴e5
51	🨢h8	f4
52	🨢xh5	🨴f5
53	🨢h6	♘c5+
54	🨴e2	fxg3
55	hxg3	♘e4
56	🨴f3	g4+
57	🨴g2	🨴g5
58	🨢h8	♘d6

½-½

RN 37

Tukmakov - Gulko
Erevan 1976

    42   ♘d3

White should be able to defend as in the three pawns against two endings. His structure is ideal, with no weaknesses and with h4 ready to exchange against a pawn advance.

42	...	♔e6
43	♘f4+	♔e5
44	♘h3	h6
45	♘f4	♔d4
46	e3+	♔c3
47	g4	♖d6
48	♔e2	♔c2
49	♘h3	♖d2+
50	♔f1	♖d1+
51	♔g2	♖a1
52	g5	

This is risky according to Tukmakov. White could safely wait.

52	...	♖a4
53	♔g3	

53 ♘f4? hxg5 54 hxg5 ♖a5 55 ♘h3 ♔d3 is very dangerous for White, e.g. 56 ♔g3

♔e4 57 ♔g4 and now:

a) 57 ... ♖a2?! 58 ♔g3 ♔f5 59 f3! (59 ♔f3? ♖a4 60 ♔g3 ♖b4 61 ♔f3 ♖g4 62 ♔e2 ♖h4 63 ♘g1 ♖h1 64 ♘f3 ♖a1 65 ♔d2 ♖a7 and ... ♔g4 will cost White the g-pawn) 59 ... ♖e2 60 e4+ ♔e5 61 ♘f4 and White is still fighting;

b) 57 ... ♖b5! 58 ♘f4 ♔f5 59 ♘h3 ♔f3 with zugzwang.

53	...	h5

Not 53 ... hxg5 54 ♘xg5! = (Tukmakov).

54	♘f4	♔d2
55	♔g2	♖e4
56	♔f3	♖c4
57	♔g2	♖c6
58	♔f1	♖c1+
59	♔g2	♖d1
60	♘d5	♔d3
61	f3	♖d2+
62	♔g3	♔e2
63	e4	

Black should now play 63 ... ♔d3=, but not 63 ... ♔f1 64 ♘f4 with the idea of e5-e6!+= (Tukmakov).

    ½-½

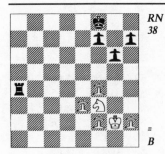

RN 38

Korchnoi - Kotov
USSR Ch 1958

Even with ruptured pawns, a four pawns against three advantage should be enough for the knight to draw.

46	...	♔e7
47	♔g3	♖a2
48	♔g2	♔d6
49	♔g3	♔d5
50	♔g2	f6
51	♔g3	♔e4
52	h4!	

Guaranteeing that any Black pawn advance will entail maximum exchanges.

52	...	♖a5

53	♘d2+	♔d3
54	♘f3	♖h5
55	♘d4	♖d5
56	♘f3	♔e2
57	♔g2	♖d1
58	♘d4+	♔d3
59	♘f3	♔e4
60	♔g3	♔f5
61	♘d4+	♔e4
62	♘f3	♖d5
63	♔g2	h6
64	♔g3	♖d1
65	♔g2	♔f5
66	♔g3	h5

    ½-½

Black has no way to make progress.

Rook v Knight

Rossetto - Gligoric
Havana 1967

31	...	♔e5
32	♖d7	♞d5
33	♔e1	

Or 33 ♖xf7 ♔d4 34 ♔e1 a4 35 ♖a7 (after 35 ♖xg7 ♔e3, whilst 35 ♔d2 ♞f6 transposes to the game) 35 ... ♔e3.

33	...	♔d4
34	♔d2	a4
35	♖xf7?	

Gligoric gives 35 ♖a7 ♞c3 36 ♖d7+= but 35 ... ♞b6! and 36 ... ♞c4+ still wins for Black.

35	...	♞f6!

Now the d-pawn becomes strong enough to paralyse White's entire army. The a-pawn becomes a decisive distraction while White's pawns are far too slow.

36	♖xg7	♞e4+
37	♔c1	♔e3
38	♖d7	

38 ♖e7 fails to 38 ... a3.

38	...	a3
39	g4	d2+
40	♔c2	a2
41	♔b2	♞f2
	0-1	

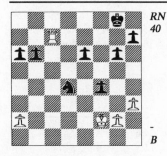

Velimirovic - Haag
Vrnjacka Banja 1966

Sometimes an excellently-placed rook is worth more than a knight and three pawns. This practical ending shows the value of rook activity.

26	...	h5
27	♖d7	e5

Trying to keep the white king out. If 27 ... ♞f5 28 ♖b7 (28 ♔f3! e5 29 ♔e4 ♞h4 30 ♔xe5 ♞xg2 31 ♔f6 and again all of Black's pawns fall) 28 ... b5 29 ♖a7 ♞d4 30 ♖xa6 ♔f7 and Black has coordinated his position.

28	♖e7	b5

Or 28 ... ♞c6 29 ♖e6 ♞b4 30 ♖xb6 (30 a3) 30 ... ♞xa2 31 ♖xa6? (31 ♖xg6+ ♔f7 32 ♖g5) 31 ... ♞c3 32 ♖xg6+ ♔f7 33 ♖h6 ♞e4+ 34 ♔f3

♞f6.

29	♖xe5	♔f7
30	♖d5	

The knight cannot cope with the rook.

30	...	♞e6
31	♖d6	a5

Not 31 ... ♞c5 32 ♔f3.

32	♔f3	b4
33	♖a6	g5
34	♖xa5	♔f6
35	♔e4	g4
36	hxg4	hxg4
37	♖f5+	♔e7
38	♖xf4!	♞xf4
39	♔xf4	♔f6
40	♔xg4	♔e5
41	♔h5	♔d4
42	g4	♔c3
43	g5	♔b2
44	g6	♔xa2
45	g7	b3
46	g8♕	♔a1
47	♕a8+	1-0

Rook v Knight

Rook v Knight and Two Pawns

RN
41

Von der Lasa 1843

    1   ♚e1

This position demonstrates that *White's best defensive array is king in front of pawns, rook working from behind* (compare with rook vs bishop). Even with connected central pawns on the sixth rank, Black cannot win by force.

1	...	d2+
2	♚e2	♞c4
3	♜c8+	♚b3
4	♜d8	♞c3+
5	♚xe3 and draws	

W

RN
42

Averbakh

    1   ♜d7

Again White's simplest path to a draw consists of moving the king in front and rook behind. (Not 1 ♚e1? c2 2 ♜c8 ♞c3.)

1	...	♚c4
2	♜d8	♞b4
3	♜c8+	♚b3
4	♚e2	♞d5
5	♚d3	

With the idea of ♜xc3+.

W

RN
43

Agdestein - Browne
Taxco IZ 1985

Since the most dangerous position (two central pawns on the sixth rank) is drawn, lesser versions of this ending are rare in practice. Here Black keeps the rook active both from back and side, and the pawns do not even make it to the sixth.

68	...	♚e7
69	♚g4	♚f7
70	♞g5+	♚e7
71	e6	♜e1
72	♚f4	♜a1
73	♞e4	♜a4

Or 73 ... ♜a4 74 ♚e5 ♜a5+ 75 ♚f4 ♜a4 76 ♚f3 ♜a5 77 ♚g4 (77 ♞g3 ♜xf5+) 77 ... ♜a4 78 ♚f4 ♜b4.

½-½

B

Rook v Bishop

Without Pawns

Generally this is a draw, though with the defending king caught on the edge of the board, disaster can result.

RB 1

=/=
W/B

Safe corner

When defending with a bishop against a rook the king should retreat towards the corner of the opposite colour to the bishop, as this gives rise to stalemate possibilities.

1   ♖d8+   ♔g8
2   ♖b8 stalemate

Of course 2 ♔g6 is also stalemate. In the safe corner the king is totally secure.

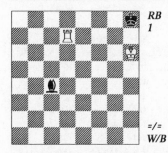

RB 2

+/+
W/B

Dangerous corner

Horwitz and Kling 1851
In the wrong corner, however, the position is a loss.

1   ...   ♗g1!

The threat was 1 ♖d7 ♗b6 2 ♖b7 ♗c5 3 ♖b8+ ♗f8 4 R(any)8 and 5 ♖xf8 mate.

2   ♖f1

After 2 ♖d7? ♔f8 3 ♔f6 ♗b6!! White cannot maintain threats without allowing a liberating check - a very useful defensive idea. (3 ... ♔e8? seems to escape but instead runs into an essential attacking manoeuvre: 4 ♔e6 ♔f8 5 ♖f7+ ♔g8 6 ♔f6 and 7 ♔g6 when White will return to the winning position.)

2   ...   ♗h2
3   ♖f2   ♗g3

The bishop stays in shadow, avoiding a rook fork threatening the bishop and check on the last rank.

4   ♖g2   ♗e5

Alternatively, 4 ... ♗h4 5 ♔h5+ or 4 ... ♗d6 5 ♖d2 ♗e7 6 ♖c2 (an important motif - the bishop prevents the king from fleeing successfully to e7 via f8).

5   ♖e2

Not 5 ♔f5+? ♗g7.

5   ...   ♗d6
6   ♖e8+   ♗f8
7   ♖a8 and wins

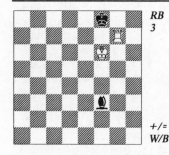

RB 3

+/=
W/B

Horwitz and Kling 1851

1   ♖g3

Black to move draws with 1 ... ♔e8, running away with his king.

1   ...   ♗e4

Alternatively, 1 ... ♗h5 2 ♖h3 ♗f7 3 ♖h8+ ♗g8 4 ♔g6

or 1 ... ♗c6 2 ♖c3 ♗d7 3 ♖b3 ♔g8 4 ♖b8+ ♔h7 5 ♖b7.

2   ♖e3   ♗g2
3   ♖e2!   ♗f3
4   ♖f2

And White wins by direct analogy with the previous diagram.

Rook v Bishop ♖ v ♝

Rook and Pawn v Bishop

Normally this is an easy win. Here we discuss two straightforward examples and some exceptional cases in which a draw can be made.

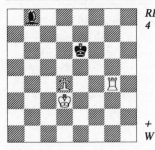

RB 4

+ W

Mills - Winkler
Novi Sad Women's ol 1990
A practical example of a basic position analysed as long ago as 1777 (Philidor). White experiences no practical difficulties by prefacing the advance of the pawn with a piece escort. Note, however, that advancing a pawn without support will lead to problems.

58 ♔e4 ♝h2

59	♖g6+	♔d7
60	♔d5!	♔e7
61	♖a6	

The immediate 61 ♔c6 and the advance of the d-pawn also wins.

61	...	♝b8
62	♔c6	♝e6
63	d5+	♔e7
64	♖a8	♝f4
65	♖a7+	1-0

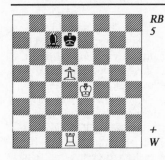

RB 5

+ W

Cheron, after Guretzky-Cornitz 1860
Here we see that the win is much harder if the pawn has advanced ahead of the other pieces.

1 ♖g1!

Much better than Fine's co-operative 1 ♔d4 ♝g3 2 ♖a1 ♝f4? when Black neglects to drive the white king from its flexible post on d4.

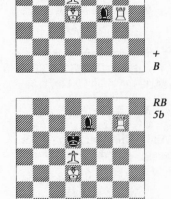

RB 5a

+ B

1 ... ♝a5

White's task is clear - he must invade with the king to c5 or e5 when it is simple to accomplish either d6 or rook to the seventh rank check, pushing Black off the board. But by constantly threatening to check back the white king Black can render this problematic, e.g. 1 ... ♝b8 2 ♖g7+ ♔d6 and now:

a) 3 ♔d4 ♝a7+! 4 ♔c4 and White must begin again. (Not 4 ♖xa7?? stalemate);

b) 3 ♖f7 ♝c7 4 ♖f6+ ♔d7 (4 ... ♔e7 5 ♖g6) 5 ♔d4 ♝h2 (5 ... ♝d8 6 ♖g6 ♝e7 7 ♖g7! transposes to diag 5b - see Black's fourth move options

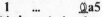

RB 5b

+ W

whilst 5 ... ♝b8 6 ♖f7+ ♔d6 7 ♔c4 transposes to the main line) 6 ♖g6! ♝f4 7 ♖g4! (Another key position) (5a)
7 ... ♝d2 (7 ... ♝h2 is met by 8 ♖g7+ - the coming pair of checks is a thematic device that conquers the d6-square, allowing the white king to invade - 8 ... ♔d6 9 ♖g6+ ♔d7 10 ♔c5 bringing d6 and g1 under control - mission accomplished) 8 ♖g2 and:

b1) 8 ... ♝b4 9 ♖b2 ♝a3 10 ♖b3 ♝f8 (10 ... ♝c1 11 ♔e5+-) 11 ♖b7+ ♔d6 12 ♔e4 with a mirror win to the main line: 12 ... ♝e7 13 ♖b6+ ♔c7 14 ♖a6;

b2) 8 ... ♝f4 9 ♖f2! again transposing to the main line.

Other first moves for Black are also insufficient:

a) 1 ... ♝h2 2 ♖g7+ ♔d6 3 ♖g6+ ♔d7 4 ♔d4 transposes to 1 ... ♝b8;

b) 1 ... ♝d8 2 ♖g7+ ♔d6 3 ♖g6+ ♔d7 4 ♔e5 ♝c7+ 5 d6 ♝b8 6 ♔d5+-;

c) 1 ... ♝b6? 2 ♖g7+ ♔d6 3 ♖g6+ ♔c7 4 ♖xb6 ♔xb6 5 ♔e5+-.

352

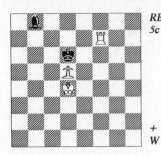

RB
5c

+
W

d) 1 ... ♔d6 2 ♖g6+ ♔d7 3 ♔d4 ♝f4 4 ♖g4 transposes to 1 ... ♝b8.

2   ♖g7+   ♔d6
3   ♖g6+   ♔d7
4   ♔d4

Threatening to accomplish the mission of safely posting the king on c5/e5. Note that d4 is the ideal post, eyeing both key squares, *and* that White only occupies d4 when Black cannot immediately repel the king with checks.

4   ...   ♝d2

After 4 ... ♝b4 5 ♖g1 ♝e7 6 ♖g7 ♔d6 leads to another key position. (5b)

Because of the limited room on this flank White must avoid a few tricks:

a) 7 ♖g6+?! ♔d7 8 ♔e5 ♝f8! 9 ♖e6 (9 d6? ♔c6!=) 9 ... ♝g7+ 10 ♔f5 ♝f8 and surprisingly Black has prevented White from achieving his ideal array;

b) 7 ♔e4! ♝f6 (7 ... ♝f8 8 ♖g6+ ♔d7 9 ♔e5 ♝e7 10 ♖g7) 8 ♖g6 ♔e7 9 d6+ ♔f7 10 ♖xf6+ ♔xf6 11 ♔d5+-.

Instead, 4 ... ♝e1 5 ♖g7+! ♔d6 6 ♖g2 ♝b4 7 ♖g6+

♔d7 8 ♖g1! simply transposes 4 ... ♝b4 and 4 ... ♝c7 loses to 5 ♔c5.

5   ♖g2   ♝f4
6   ♖f2!   ♝b8

After 6 ... ♝g3 the procedure is thematic: 7 ♖f7+ ♔d6 8 ♖f6+ ♔e7 (8 ... ♔d7 9 ♔c5+-) 9 ♖g6 ♝d6 (9 ... ♝f2+ 10 ♔e5+-) 10 ♖g7+ ♔f6 11 ♖d7 ♝a3 12 ♔c4 and the white king reaches c6.

7   ♖f7+

When the bishop is driven behind the ♔d6 (i.e. b8/c7/e7) the lack of coordination in the Black camp spells imminent defeat. Compare with 1 ... ♝b8.

7   ...   ♔d6 (5c)
8   ♔c4   ♝c7
9   ♖f6+   ♔e7

Or 9 ... ♔d7 10 ♔c5.

10   ♖g6   ♝d6
11   ♖g7+

Also 11 ♔b5 ♔d7 12 ♖g7+ ♝e7 13 ♔b6 ♔d6 14 ♖xe7 ♔xe7 15 ♔c7+- (JT).

11   ...   ♔f6
12   ♖a7   ♔e5
13   ♖a6   ♝f8
14   ♖e6+ and wins

RB
6

=/=
W/B

Special draws

In nearly all positions with rook and pawn against bishop White has excellent chances of winning as long as he is not immediately losing back his pawn. Exceptions to this may occur when the pawn is a

rook's pawn (diags 11-16), and the special cases discussed here.

Averbakh 1978
A very sad sight - White can do nothing to utilise his extra pawn.

Rook v Bishop

♖ V ♝

RB 7

Averbakh 1978

> 1   ♖h6   ♝c5

The same pathetic picture,

this time for a pawn defended along the rank.

=/=
W/B

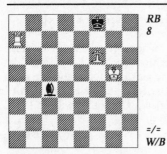

RB 8

del Rio 1750

> 1   ♖c7   ♝d5

After 1 ... ♝b5? 2 f7! ♚g7 3 ♚f5 ♝a4 4 ♖b7 ♝d1 5 ♚e6 ♝h5 Black is on much too short a diagonal, i.e. 6 ♖c7

♝g6 7 f8♕+! ♚xf8 8 ♚f6.

> 2   ♖d7   ♝b3

Black maintains a check to answer ♚g6, and answers f7 with ... ♚g7!, so White cannot make progress.

=/=
W/B

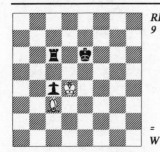

RB 9

Elekes (end of study) 1936

> 1   ♝b4   ♚d7
> 2   ♝a5   ♚c8
> 3   ♝e1   ♚c7
> 4   ♚c3

This is a positional draw - the black king cannot relieve the rook of guard duty. The

white king can always shoulder it out.

This shows that caution must be used when the king is separated from the pawn, even when defended from the rear. (Compare with exceptional ♘ vs ♖+P.)

=
W

RB 10

Averbakh, from praxis, 1978

> 1   ♖c6+?

Instead, White should play 1 ♖g4! ♝g7 2 ♚g3 ♚e7 3 ♚h4 ♚f8 4 ♚h5 ♚g8 5 ♖b4 ♝c3 6 ♖b7 ♝d4 7 g7! ♚h7 (7 ... ♝xg7 8 ♚g6 with a winning rook against bishop position) 8 ♖f7 ♝c3 (8 ... ♝xg7 9 ♚g5

♚g8 10 ♚g6 wins) 9 g8♕+ ♚xg8 10 ♚g6 winning.

> 1   ...   ♚g5!

And Black draws with ... ♝g7-f6. This positional drawing theme is worth noting. Moral: *a pawn with a rook behind it cannot be surrounded like this.*

+
W

354

Rook v Bishop ♖ V ♗

RB 11

+
W

Rook and Rook's Pawn vs Bishop

Dangerous Corner

Averbakh 1978, after Guret-zky-Cornitz 1863
The win is normally straight-forward if the queening square is of the same colour as the bishop.

1	♔f5	♗d2

2	h6!	♗e3
3	♖g7+!	♔xh6
4	♖g6+	♔h7

Or 4 ... ♔h5 5 ♖g3.

| 5 | ♔f6 | |

And 6 ♔f7, reaching diag 2 (rotated) which is a win.

See also diags 22a-c, in which the pawn is blockaded and in some danger, causing some technical problems.

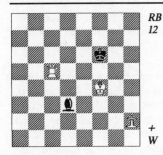

RB 12

+
W

Safe Corner
The ending of rook and wrong rook's pawn presents consider-able technical difficulties and is only winning by force if the pawn has not advanced past h4 or if the defending king can be cut off.

Averbakh 1978
Even with the 'right' bishop for the corner the position is still an easy win if the king can be cut off.

1	♖g5!	♗g6
2	h4	♗d3
3	h5	

There is no fear about advancing now that the black king is cut off.

3	...	♗h7
4	h6	♗g6
5	♖g3	♔f7

If Black moves the bishop then 6 ♖g7-a7 and h7 is deci-sive.

6	♖g1!	♔f6
7	♖a1	♗h7
8	♖a7!	

Otherwise ... ♔f7 crawls back to safety.

8	...	♗g6
9	♔e5	♗xh6
10	♔f6	

With one of the basic ♖ v ♗ winning positions (rotated).

RB 13

=
W

Cozio 1766

| 1 | ♖c7 | ♗e4 |

This highlights the impor-tance of the safe corner. White's extra pawn is mean-ingless - Black's king cannot be evicted from the corner so the position is a draw. As al-ways, the pawn rushing ahead of the king is a mistake.

355

Rook v Bishop ♖ V ♗

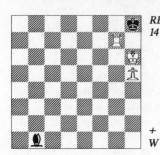

RB 14 +W

Lequesne 1858

1 ♖b7!

The only move, since the rook's pawn is again too far advanced to win by "normal" means. So, if 1 ♖c7 ♚g8 2 ♖g7+ ♚f8! and White cannot make progress: 3 ♖g4 ♗c2 4 ♖d4 ♗b1 5 ♖d8+ ♚f7 6 ♖d2 ♗e4 7 ♖f2+ ♚g8. (Compare with the rook's pawn on the fourth rank.)

1 ... ♗a2
2 ♖b8+ ♗g8
3 ♚g5 ♚g7
4 ♖b7+ ♚h8
5 ♚g6 ♗d5

6 ♖h7+!

Vital - White robs the bishop of the g8-square.

6 ... ♚g8
7 ♖e7

Threatens mate while preventing check.

7 ... ♚h8

Or 7 ... ♚f8 8 ♚f6 ♗c4 9 h6 ♚g8 10 h7+ ♚h8 11 ♚g6.

8 h6 ♗a2
9 h7 ♗b1+
10 ♚h6

The "Lequesne manoeuvre" is essential to solving rook and rook's pawn against bishop.

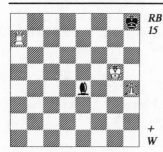

RB 15 +W

Guretzky-Cornitz 1863

1 ♚h6 ♚g8

1 ... ♗d5 leads to methodical death by Lequesne: 2 ♖d7 ♗e6 3 ♖d8+ ♗g8 4 ♚g5 ♚g7 5 ♖d7+ ♚h8 6 ♚g6 ♗b3 7 ♖h7+ ♚g8 8 ♖c7 ♚h8 (8 ... ♚f8 9 ♖g7 and cutting by one file with the black king out wins easily) 9 h5 ♗d5 10 ♖h7+ ♚g8 11 ♖e7 ♚h8 12 h6 ♗a2 13 h7.

2 ♖g7+ ♚f8

2 ... ♚h8 3 ♖e7 leads to Lequesne.

3 ♖g5

Now White needs to extract his king. He threatens 4 ♚h5 ♗f3+ 5 ♚g6 since 5 ... ♚g8 6 ♚h6+ and 7 ♖f5 wins. If 3 ♖g3 ♗c2! 4 ♚h5 ♚f7 we reach diag 16 with *White* to move. This is a problem, as we shall see.

3 ... ♚f7
4 ♖g3

With the idea of 5 ♚g5 since 5 ... ♚g7 fails to 6 ♚f4+.

4 ... ♗c2
5 ♚h5

Zugzwang! See comments

to diag 16 below. This appears to be a helpful clarification point that has not been noted before. Here, with Black to move, the win is achieved after:

5 ... ♚f6

Alternatively: 5 ... ♚f8 6 ♖g5 ♗d1+ 7 ♚g6 ♚g8 8 ♖c5! ♚f8 9 ♖c8+ ♚e7 10 h5; 5 ... ♗d1+ 6 ♚g5 ♚g7 7 ♖c3! (a key point is that Black cannot get onto the b1-h7 diagonal before the h-pawn crashes through) 7 ... ♗e2 8 h5 ♗b5 9 h6+ ♚h7 10 ♖c7+ ♚h8 11 h7; 5 ... ♗a4 6 ♚g5 ♚g7 7 ♖c3 and again there is no way back to the b1-h7 diagonal in time; or 5 ... ♗b1 6 ♖g5 and Black can no longer hinder ♚g4 with successful extraction.

6 ♖g5 ♗d1+

6 ... ♗f5 is the only other method of preventing 7 ♚g4, but after 7 ♚h6 ♗c2 8 ♖g2 and 9 ♖f2(+) Black will cede the f-file.

7 ♚h6 ♚f7

Otherwise the rook retreats with tempo on the bishop and

then checks on the f-file.

8 ♖g7+! ♚f6

The difference now is that Black must guard g6 with his king since the bishop has left the diagonal. After 8 ... ♚f8 9 ♚g6-f6 wins.

9 ♖g1 ♝e2
10 ♖g2 ♝d3
11 ♖f2+ and wins

RB 16

=/+
W/B

Mutual zugzwang

This is a key position in rook and rook's pawn against bishop.

1 ♖g5

It appears that the starting position is a type of mutual zugzwang. With Black to move, as in the previous example after 5 ♚h5, he was forced to either cede g6 or get

cut off one more file. Here, White cannot force such obligations.

1 ... ♝d1+
2 ♚h6 ♝c2
3 ♖g7+

Or 3 ♖g2 ♝d3 4 ♚g5 (4 ♖f2+ is met by 4 ... ♚g8) 4 ... ♚g7.

3 ... ♚f8!
with a draw

Rook and Pawn v Bishop and Pawn

RB 17

-
B

Enevoldsen 1949

1 ... ♖f2+
2 ♚e1

2 ♚g1? loses immediately after 2 ... ♖f7 3 ♝e6 ♖e7.

2 ... ♚g2
3 ♝d7 ♖f7

The beginning of an inevitable hunt and drive process against the white king.

4 ♝g4 ♖e7+
5 ♚d2 ♚f2
6 ♚d3 ♖e5
7 ♝c8 ♖e3+
8 ♚d4 ♚f3
9 ♝d7 ♚f4
10 ♝g4 ♖g3

11 ♝d7 ♖g7
12 ♝e6 ♖g6
13 ♝c8 ♖d6+
14 ♚c5 ♚e5

14 ... ♖d2 intending ... ♚g3 and ... ♖h2xh3 looks simpler than the original solution to me (JT).

15 ♝g4 ♖d4
16 ♝h5 ♖d3
17 ♝g4 ♖c3+
18 ♚b4 ♖c1
19 ♚b3 ♚f4
20 ♚b2 ♖h1
21 ♚c2 ♚g3
22 ♚d2 ♖xh3
and wins

RB 18

=
W

D Cramling - Winsnes
Stockholm open 1988

A practical example of an Averbakh position. The weakness of the g5-pawn disallows the freedom necessary to mount threats.

71 ♝b2+ ♚g6
72 ♝d4 ♖b8
73 ♚f3 ♖b3+
74 ♝e3 ♚f6

75 ♚e4 ♖b5
76 ♚f3 ♚e6
77 ♚e4 ♖e5+
78 ♚f3 ♚d5
79 ♝c1 ♚c4
80 ♝b2 ♖b5
½-½

Note that even if we place the white king on f3 and the black king on c2 in diag 18 White draws by 1 ♝xg5! ♖xg5

2 ⊕f4 ♖g8 3 g5 ⊕d3 4 ⊕f5
⊕d4 5 g6 ⊕d5 6 ⊕f6 ⊕d3 7
⊕f7.

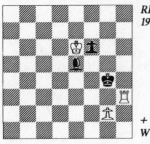

RB
19

+
W

Korchnoi - Speelman
Brussels 1985
    68   ♖h8

An interesting ending with
adjacent pawns. First White
prepares the advance of the g-
pawn.

    68   ...   ⊕g3
    69   ♖g8+   ⊕f4
    70   ♖g7   ♗b8
    71   ♖g6

Obviously not 71 ⊕xf6??
♗e5+.

    71   ...   ♗e5
    72   ♖g8   ♗c3
    73   g3+   ⊕e4
    74   ♖g4+   ⊕f3
    75   ♖c4   ♗d2
    76   g4   ♗g5
    77   ⊕f5

The first stage is complete.
Now White manoeuvres to
combine pressure against f6
and drive the black king from
attacking g4.

    77   ...   ⊕g3
    78   ♖c8   ♗d2
    79   ♖g8   ♗c3
    80   ♖d8!

The bishop proves surprisingly vulnerable on the long
diagonal.

    80   ...   ⊕h4
    81   ♖d3   ♗b2
    82   ♖d1

Preventing 82 ... ♗c1 and
getting checking room.

    82   ...   ♗c3
    83   ♖h1+   ⊕g3
    84   ♖c1   ♗b2

Also possible is 84 ... ♗d2

85 ♖g1+ ⊕f2 86 ♖d1 ♗g5
(86 ... ⊕e2? 87 ♖xd2+ ⊕xd2
88 ⊕xf6 or 86 ... ♗c3 87 ♖d3
♗a1 88 ♖a3 ♗d4 89 ♖a4 ♗c3
90 ♖a6 ⊕g3 91 ♖a3) 87 ♖d8
⊕g3 88 ♖g8 ♗h4 (88 ... ⊕h4
89 ♖g6) 89 ♖g7 ⊕f3 (89 ...
⊕h3 90 ♖h7 ⊕g3 91 ♖h5
⊕h3 92 ⊕f4) 90 ♖h7 and
now:

a) 90 ... ♗e1 91 ♖h6 ♗c3 92
♖h3+;

b) 90 ... ♗f2 91 ♖h6! (91
♖h3+ ♗g3 92 ♖h6 ♗e5 93 g5
fxg5 94 ⊕xe5 g4 95 ♖f6+
⊕e3) 91 ... ♗d4 92 ♖h3+ ⊕e2
(92 ... ⊕f2 93 ♖d3 and wins
as in earlier notes) 93 ♖a3 and
the bishop on d4 will not be
able to maintain the diagonal;

c) 90 ... ♗g3 91 ♖h3 ⊕g2 92
♖h6;

d) 90 ... ⊕g3 91 ♖h5 and
wins as in the note above.

    85   ♖c2   ♗d4
    86   ♖d2   ♗c5

Or 86 ... ♗a1 87 ♖a2 ♗d4 88
♖a3+ and:

a) 88 ... ⊕f2 89 ♖a4! ♗c3
(89 ... ♗e5 90 g5) 90 ♖a6 ⊕g3
91 ♖a3;

b) 88 ... ⊕h4 89 ♖a4 and 90
g5+.

    87   ♖d5   ♗e7
    88   ♖d3+!   ⊕h4
    89   ♖d4   ⊕g3
    90   ⊕e6

Now the f-pawn falls: 90 ...
♗a3 91 ♖d3+.

                        1-0

RB 20

Groszpeter - Inkiov
Palma de Mallorca 1989
Another adjacent pawns ending with Black attempting
counterplay against White's
pawn. White wins smoothly
here.

+
W

  50 ♖d6   ♗d3

Or 50 ... ♔e4 51 ♔b2 ♗e3
52 ♔a3 ♔e4 53 ♔b4 ♔e3 54
♖d4 ♗e2 55 ♖d5+-.

51	♖e6+	♗e4
52	♖e5	♔d3
53	♔b2	♗c6

This defensive diagonal is

no better than a6-f1.

54	♖c5	♗e8
55	♖e5	♗c6
56	♔b3	♔d2
57	♖c5	♗e8
58	♖d5+	♔c1
59	♖e5	♗c6
60	♖c5	♗e8
61	♖e5	♗c6
62	♔b4	♔c2
63	♖e2+!	♔d3

Or 63 ... ♔c1 64 ♖c5 ♗d7
65 ♖e7.

| 64 | ♖e6 | ♗g2 |
| 65 | ♖b6 | 1-0 |

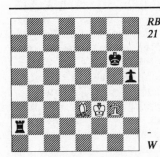

RB 21

Fischer 1969
This position could have
arisen in Reshevsky - Fischer,
Los Angeles 1961.

  1 ♗f4

Not 1 ♔f4 ♖a5! 2 ♗d2
♖f5+ 3 ♔e4 ♔f6 4 ♗f4 ♖a5
and Black's king reaches f5 after ... ♖a4+.

-
W

1	...	♔f5
2	♗d6	♖b2
3	♗f4	♖b3+
4	♔g2	♔g4
5	♗d6	♖b2+
6	♔g1	♔h3
7	♗e5	♖b4!
8	♗c7	

Or 8 ♗f4 h4.

8	...	♖g4
9	♔f2	♔h2
10	♗e5	♔h1
11	♔f3	♖g8

| 12 | ♗f4 | ♖f8? |

Better is 12 ... ♔g1! and
White cannot prevent ... ♔f1,
the rook taking the f-file and
winning as in Fischer's intended solution. (White will
be obliged to play g4 when ...
h4 really does win.)

  13 ♔f2?

Both 13 g4! h4 14 g5 h3 15
g6 and 15 ♔g4 are drawn.

13	...	h4
14	♔f3	h3
15	♔f2	h2
16	♔f1	♖a8
17	♔f2	♖a2+
18	♔f1	♖a3
19	♔f2	♖f3+!!
20	♔xf3	♔g1
21	♗e3+	♔f1

and wins

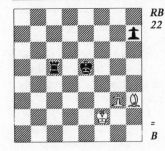

RB 22

Ftacnik - Murey
New York open 1987

| 60 | ... | ♖c2+ |
| 61 | ♔g1?? | |

61 ♔f3 draws.

61	...	♔e4
62	♗g2+	♔e3
63	♗d5	h6
64	♗b7	h5
65	♗d5	♖c5
66	♗b7	♖g5

=
B

| 67 | ♔h2 | |

Or 67 ♔g2 h4 68 g4 ♖xg4+
with a straightforward win
(see diag 11).

67	...	♔f2
68	♔h3	♖xg3+
69	♔h4	♖g7
70	♗c6	♖h7
71	♗d5	

Not 71 ♗e8 ♔f3 72 ♗xh5+
♔f4-+.

Rook v Bishop

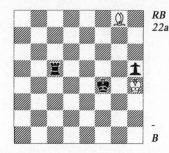

RB
22a

-
B

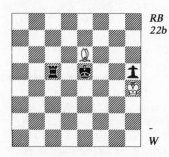

RB
22b

-
W

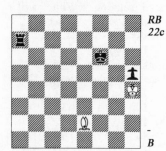

RB
22c

-
B

71	...	♔e3
72	♗g8	♖h8
73	♗f7	♔f4
74	♗b3	♖b8

Not 74 ... ♔f5 75 ♗c2+ ♔f6 76 ♗d1!.

75	♗c4	♖c8
76	♗e6	♖c6
77	♗d5?	

Instead, 77 ♗f7 ♖c5 78 ♗g8! transposes into a 1924 study by Vancura, with colours reversed. (22a)

Black wants this position with White to move.

a) 78 ... ♖e5(!!) is given by Ftacnik: 79 ♗b3 (79 ♗f7 ♔f5 80 ♗xh5 ♔f4 81 ♗g6 ♖g5 82 ♗d3 ♖d5 83 ♗g6 ♖d8-+) 79 ... ♖a5 80 ♗g8 ♖c5! (reaching the desired position) 81 ♗b3 (81 ♗e6 transposes to variation c below, whilst 81 ♗h7 ♖c7 82 ♗d3 ♖d7!-+ JT) 81 ... ♔f5-+ 82 ♗xh5 ♖c3;

b) 78 ... ♔f5? 79 ♔xh5 ♖c8 80 ♗h7+=;

c) 78 ... ♖a5 79 ♗b3 ♖e5 80 ♗g8 ♖c5! 81 ♗e6 ♔e5 (22b):

c1) 82 ♗f7 ♖f5 83 ♗e8 (83 ♗xh5 ♔f4 84 ♗g6 ♖c8!-+) 83 ... ♖f6 84 ♗e8 ♖e7 85 ♗xh5 (85 ♗a4 ♔g6-+) 85 ... ♖h7-+;

c2) 82 ♗d7 ♖c7 (82 ... ♔f6?! 83 ♗e8! ♖c8! 84 ♗xh5 ♖h8 85 ♔g4 and Black is in zugzwang!). 83 ♗h3 (83 ♗e8 ♔f5!) 83 ... ♖h7 84 ♗g2 (84 ♗f1 ♔f6!) 84 ... ♔f5! 85 ♗f1

♗f6! This critical position is mutual zugzwang:

c21) 86 ♗d3 ♖d7 87 ♗e2 ♔f5-+ will lead to main line;

c22) 86 ♗g2 is not considered by either Ftacnik or Vancura but is no simpler than other tries, it seems to me, after 86 ... ♖g7 and:

c221) 87 ♗c6 ♖g5 (intending ... ♔g6-h6) 88 ♗e8 ♔f5 89 ♗f7 (89 ♔h3 ♖g8-+ intending ... ♔g5) 89 ... ♖g4+ 90 ♔xh5 ♖g7;

c222) 87 ♗f3 ♔f5 88 ♗c6 (88 ♗e2 ♖d7 89 ♗f3 ♖d2 transposes and 88 ♗d1 is met by 88 ... ♖c7 89 ♗e2 ♖d7) 88 ... ♖g5 89 ♗e8 ♖g8 90 ♗c6 ♖d8!-+ JT;

c23) 86 ♗a6 ♖a7 87 ♗e2 (22c) (87 ♗d3 ♖a5 and ... ♔g6-♔h6, whilst 87 ♗b5 loses to 87 ... ♖a1! 88 ♗c6 ♔g6 89 ♗e8+ ♔h6-+).

This is one of the main positions Black is aiming for. 87 ... ♖e7! 88 ♗d1 (88 ♗xh5 ♖h7 89 ♔g4 ♖h8! - now White is in zugzwang! - 90 ♔h4 ♔f5) 88 ... ♖d7 89 ♗e2 ♔f5 90 ♗f3 ♖d2 91 ♗c6 ♖h2+ 92 ♔g3 ♖c2 and ... ♔g5 finally wins.

77	...	♖c2
78	♔h3	♔g5
	0-1	

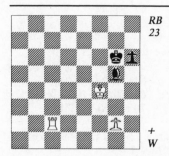

RB
23

+
W

Eingorn - Zaichik
Riga 1980

59 ♔e4

Again the critical factor in this ending will be White's ability to penetrate with the king.

59	...	♗e7
60	♖c7	♗b4
61	♖b7	♗d2

| 62 | ♖b5 | ♗c1 |

62 ... h5 must be tougher with a similar position to diag 30, although White's g-pawn is less vulnerable so probably White should win: 63 ♖b8 ♗c3 (or 63 ... ♗h6 64 ♖g8+ ♔h7 65 ♖g3 ♗d2 66 ♔f5 ♗e1 67 ♖e3 ♗f2 68 ♖e2 ♗g3 69 ♔g5 h4 70 ♖e7+ ♔g8 71

360

Rook v Bishop　　　♖ V ♝

♔g6 ♚f8 72 ♖e4) 64 ♖g8+ ♚f7 65 ♖c8 and now White invades as Black has no counter target with the pawn on g2 instead of g3.

63	♖d5	♝a3
64	♔f4	♝c1+
65	♔g4	♚f6
66	♔h5	♝g5
67	♖a5	♝d2

68 ♖a6+

Black is hopelessly lost: 68 ... ♚g7 (68 ... ♚f5 69 g4+ wins) 69 ♖g6+ ♚h7 70 ♖d6 ♝e3 71 ♖d7+ winning.

1-0

Rook and Two Pawns v Bishop and Two Pawns

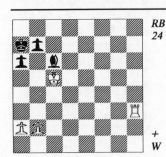

RB 24

Fine 1941

This is a typical winning position.

1　♔d6　♝b8

Black must keep the white king out of c7. (Not 1 ... ♚b6 2 ♖b3+.)

2	♖h8+	♚a7
3	♔c7	♝d5
4	a3	♝c6

Not 4 ... b5 5 ♔d6 ♝f3 6 ♔c5 ♝e4 7 ♖e8 ♝f3 8 ♖e7+ ♝b7 9 ♖g7 ♚b8 10 ♔b6.

| 5 | ♖h6 | ♝f3 |
| 6 | ♖b6 | |

White has achieved maxi-

+ W

mal grip. Now follows the decisive pawn storm.

6	...	♝e4
7	b4	♝f3
8	a4	♝e4
9	b5	axb5
10	axb5	♝d5
11	♖d6	♝c4

Or 11 ... ♝e4 (other moves on the diagonal fail to other forks) 12 ♖d4.

12	♖a6+!	bxa6
13	b6+	♚a8
14	b7+	♚a7
15	b8♕ mate	

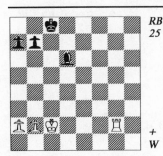

RB 25

Fine 1941

Another typical winning position, this time with a bishop which does not control the corner square.

| 1 | ♔c3 | ♚c7 |
| 2 | ♔c4 | a6 |

Or 2 ... ♚c6 3 ♖g6 b5+ 4 ♔d4 ♚c7 5 ♔d5 ♝f8 6 ♖f6 ♝e7 7 ♖f7 ♚d7 8 ♖xe7+ ♚xe7 9 ♔c5 ♚d7 10 ♔xb5 ♚c7 11 ♔a6 winning.

| 3 | ♔d5 | ♝f4 |
| 4 | ♖f2 | ♝e3 |

Or 4 ... ♝g3 5 ♖f7+ ♚b6 6

+ W

♔e6 ♚c6 7 ♖f3 ♝h2 8 ♖c3+ ♚b6 9 ♖h3 ♝f4 10 ♔d7 and wins as in main line.

5	♖f7+	♚b6
6	♔d6	♝d4
7	b3	♝c5+
8	♔d7	♚b5
9	♔c7	b6
10	♖f4	♝e3
11	♖e4	♝c5
12	♔b7	♝g1
13	a3	♚c5

Else 14 ♖e5+ and 15 b4.

14　♔xa6 and wins

361

RB 26

=/=
W/B

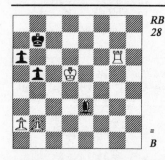

RB 27

+
W

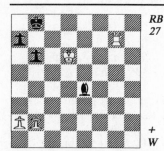

RB 28

=
B

RB 29

+
B

Fortress position No.1

Averbakh 1978

However, it is possible to establish fortress positions in this endgame, as the next few examples show.

1	♖g7+	♚b8
2	♚d6	♝f3
3	a4	

3 a3 looks more testing, planning:

a) 3 ... ♝e4?! 4 b4 axb4 5 ♖g4 ♝d3 6 ♖xb4 ♚a7 7 ♚c6 with winning chances;

b) 3 ... ♝h1 4 ♖g4 (4 b4 axb4 5 axb4 ♝f3 with a fortress) 4 ... ♝b7 5 b4 axb4 6 ♖xb4 ♝f3 7 ♖f4 ♝g2 8 ♖f7+ ♚a6=.

| 3 | ... | ♝h1 |

Or 3 ... ♝e4 4 b4 axb4 5 ♖g4 ♝f3 6 ♖xb4 ♚a7 7 ♚c7 ♚a6 8 ♖xb6+ ♚a5 and Black succeeds in drawing.

4	b4	axb4
5	♖g4	♚a7
6	♖xb4	♚a6
7	♚c7	♚a5

And the pawns are soon exchanged with a draw.

Averbakh 1978

| 1 | b4! | |

Preventing 1 ... a5 reaching the fortress draw of the previous diagram.

| 1 | ... | ♝f3 |

1 ... a5?! weakens the pawns too much, e.g. 2 bxa5 bxa5 3 ♚c5 a4 4 ♚b6 ♚c8 5 ♖c7+ ♚d8 6 ♖c4.

| 2 | a4 | ♝e4 |
| 3 | a5! | |

With the idea of 4 a6.

3	...	bxa5
4	bxa5	a6
5	♚c5	♝d3
6	♚b6	♚c8

and wins

See diag 17.

Fortress position No.2

Averbakh 1978

| 1 | ... | ♝f2 |

This creates a fortress. By analogy to the other fortress Black's pawns control white squares and his pieces are opti-mally placed. White cannot make progress, except by a Black error. (Note that 1 ... ♝b6? is an error with the white king on d5 - see diag 29)

Averbakh

| 1 | ... | ♝b6? |

Not 1 ... ♝a7?? 2 ♖g7+ ♚b8 3 ♖xa7! ♚xa7 4 ♚c6+-.

2	♖g7+	♚b8
3	b3	♝f2
4	♚c6	♝e3
5	b4	

Better is 5 ♖g4!.

5	...	♝d4
6	♖g3	♝f2
7	♖f3	♝d4
8	a4	bxa4
9	♖a3	♚a7
10	♖xa4	

And b5 +-.

RB 30

Nikolic - Kasparov
Niksic 1983

61	...	♔e2
62	h5	

Otherwise ... f6, ... ♖g7..

62	...	gxh5
63	♗f3+	♔e3
64	♗xh5	♖a2+
65	♔h3	

After 65 ♔g1 f6:

a) 66 ♗g4 ♔e4 67 ♗h5 f5 68 ♔h1 (68 ♗g6 ♔f3) 68 ... ♔e3 69 ♔g1 ♖b2 and Black's

king invades, i.e. 70 ♔h1 ♔f2 71 ♔h2 ♔f1+ 72 ♔h3 ♔g1;

b) 66 ♔f1 ♖h2 67 ♗g4 h5 and ... h4.

65	...	f6
66	♗e8	♔f2
67	♔h4	♖a8!
68	♗c6	♖g8
69	g4	♔e3
70	♔g3	f5
71	♗f3	h5
72	g5	h4+

0-1

RB 31

Kholmov - Tseshkovsky
USSR Ch S-F 1973

1	...	♖c2+
2	♔e3?	

Better is 2 ♔g1! trying to reach Kholmov's analysis in diag 34 (which may be difficult due to the incessant danger of ... ♖xg2+ and a winning pawn ending).

2	...	f5!
3	♗f1	♔d5
4	♗a6	♖b2!
5	♗f1	♖b3+
6	♔f2	♔d4
7	♗h3	♖b1!
8	♔f3	

Not 8 ♗f1 ♖xf1+!.

8	...	♖g1!
9	♔f2	♖h1
10	♗g2	♖h2!

And Black forces a won pawn ending.

0-1

Analysis by Kholmov.

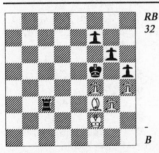

RB 32

Kholmov 1973

1	...	♖c2+

The insertion of ... h5 considerably complicates the winning process, since the simple plan of playing ... g5 to expose the weakness at g3 is no longer decisive.

2	♔f1	

2 ♔e3 is again hazardous due to pawn endings, e.g. 2 ...

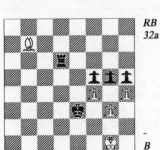

RB 32a

♖h2 and now:

a) 3 ♗e2 ♖xe2+ 4 ♔xe2 ♔g4 5 ♔f2 ♔h3 6 ♔f3 (6 f5 gxf5 7 ♔f3 f6 8 ♔f4 ♔g2) 6 ... f5 7 ♔f2 ♔h2 8 ♔f3 ♔g1;

b) 3 ♗d5 ♔g4 4 ♗xf7 ♖g2 5 ♗xg6 ♖xg3+ 6 ♔e4 ♔xh4 and:

b1) 7 ♔f5 ♖a3 8 ♗e8 ♖a8 9 ♗c6 (9 ♗d7 ♖f8+ 10 ♔e5

♔g3 11 f5 ♔g4 12 ♗e6 ♔g5 13 ♔e4 h4 14 ♔f3 ♖a8 15 ♗g2 ♖a3 16 ♔h2 ♔e3 17 ♗d7 h3 18 f6 ♔h4 19 f7 ♖e2+ 20 ♔g1 h2+) 9 ... ♖f8+ 10 ♔e5 ♔g3 11 f5 ♔g4;

b2) 7 ♗e8 ♖g8 8 ♗d7 ♔g3 9 f5 ♖f8 10 ♗e6 (10 ♔e5 ♔g4) 10 ... h4 11 ♔e5 h3 12 f6 h2 13 ♗d5 ♔g4;

c) 3 ♗d1 ♖g2 4 ♔f3 ♖d2 5 ♗a4 ♖d3+.

2	...	♔e6
3	♗e4	♖b2
4	♔g1	♔d6
5	♔f1	♔c5
6	♗f3	♔d4
7	♗c6	♔e3
8	♗d5	f5
9	♗c6	♖d2
10	♔g1	♖d6

11	♗b7	g5!! (32a)	16	g6 (16 ♔h5 ♗d3 17 ♔h6
12	hxg5			♖h3+ 18 ♔g6 ♖g3) 16 ... ♖d8.

Or 12 fxg5 f4 13 gxf4 ♔xf4 14 ♔f2 ♖d2+! 15 ♔e1 ♖h2 16 g6 ♖xh4 17 ♗c8 ♔f3! (17 ... ♖h2 18 ♗g4!!) 18 ♔d2 ♖d4+ 19 ♔c3 (19 ♔e1 ♖e4+ 20 ♔d2 ♖e5) 19 ... ♖d1.

			13	...	♗xf4
12	...	h4	14	♔g2	♗c8
13	gxh4				

Alternatively, 13 ♔g2 hxg3 14 ♔xg3 ♖d4 15 ♔h4 ♔xf4

14 ♔g2 ♖d2+ 15 ♔h3 ♖d3+ 16 ♔h2 ♗g4 17 ♗c8 ♖d2+ 18 ♔g1 ♗g3 19 ♔f1 f4 20 g6 f3 21 ♔e1 f2+.

14	...	♗g3
15	♔f1	f4

and wins

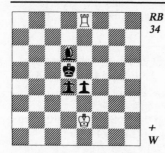

RB 33

Averbakh 1978
The active position of the black king enables him to win quickly.

1	...	♔d3
2	♔f1	

If 2 ♔f3 then 2 ... ♖f6+ 3 ♗f4 h6 5 ♔g2 ♖xf4 6 gxf4 ♔e4 7 ♔g3 f5 with a won pawn endgame.

2	...	♖a1+
3	♔g2	♔e2
4	♗d4	♖a3
5	♗c5	♖f3
6	♗d4	h6
7	♗c5	g5
8	hxg5	hxg5
9	♗d4	f5
10	♗c5	f4

With a straightforward win.

Rook v Bishop and Two Pawns

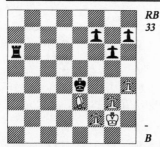

RB 34

Connected Pawns
Averbakh 1978,
after Cheron 1926

1	♖d8!	

When the pawns have reached the fifth rank, the rook must take accurate and decisive action from the rear. The text is the only defence against 1 ... d3+ 2 ♔e3 ♗c5+ 3 ♔d2 ♔d4 4 ♖d8+ ♔c4 5 ♖e8 e3+ and the (centre) pawns on the sixth must win.

1	...	♔c6
2	♔d2	♗b4+
3	♔e2	♗c5

Or 3 ... ♔c5 4 ♖e8 ♗d5 5 ♖d8+ ♔c4 6 ♖e8 d3+ 7 ♔e3 ♗c5+ 8 ♔xe4=.

4	♔d2	♗b5
5	♖e8!	♗b4+
6	♔e2	d3+
7	♔e3	d2
8	♖d8	♗c6
9	♖xd2!	with a draw

Not 9 ♔xe4?? ♗d6.

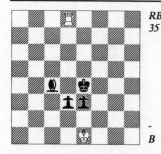

RB 35

Klausen 1963,
after Von der Lasa 1843

1	...	♗d5
2	♖e8+	♔d4
3	♖d8	♔c5
4	♔d1!	

Klausen. Not 4 ♖e8? d2+ 5 ♔e2 ♗f3+ or 4 ♖c8+? ♔b4 5 ♖b8+ ♔c3 6 ♖c8+ ♗c4 and

wins.

4	...	♗c4
5	♖d7	♔b4
6	♖d8	

White must pass on the d-file. Where he passes affects the winning procedure slightly, but not the result.

6	...	♔c3

7   ♖d6   ♗b3+!

Not 7 ... d2 8 ♖d3+!= or 7 ... e2+ 8 ♔e1=.

8   ♔e1

This is a key position which could be reached with the rook on d8 or d7. See next diags: 36 and 37.

8   ...   ♗f7!

The winning idea is to place the bishop so that it has two routes that influence the advance of the pawns. Now the threat of transfer to h5 - d1 is decisive. (Not 8 ... ♗c2 9 ♖d7 ♔b2 10 ♖d8 ♔c1 11 ♖xd3!=.)

9   ♖c6+

For 9 ♖d8 ♗e6 see diag 36 and for 9 ♖d7 ♗e6 see diag 43.

9   ...   ♗c4

and wins

RB 36

Klausen 1963

1	...	♗e6
2	♖d6	♗g4
3	♖c6+	♔d4
4	♖d6+	♔c4
5	♖d8	

- B

Alternatively, 5 ♖c6+ ♔d5 or 5 ♔f1 d2.

5   ...   ♔c3

Winning - there is no check on c8.

RB 37

Klausen 1963

| 1 | ... | ♗e6 |
| 2 | ♖c7+ | |

2 ♖d8 ♗g4 transposes to the previous example.

2   ...   ♗c4

White has prevented the transfer to h5 - d1 but loses

- B

due to his king position. If the king were on d1 then ♖d7 would defend as before. The point of ... ♗b3+! is that Black threatens both the transfer of the bishop and the array ♔c3/♗c4.

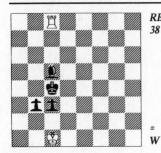

RB 38

Klausen 1963

1	♖c7	♔d5
2	♖c8	♗d4
3	♖c7	♔e4
4	♖c8	♔d3
5	♖c7	♗e3+

Not 5 ... c2 6 ♖c3+!.

| 6 | ♔b1 | ♔d2 |

Black does not have room to create threats of ... ♗a3, or to use the king on the queenside.

=
W

7	♖d7+	♔e2
8	♖c7	♔d3
9	♖c6	♗d4
10	♔c1! drawing	

Black's inability to combine threats prevents him from making progress. So defence from the rear holds against all but centre pawns on the sixth rank.

Rook v Bishop

♖ V ♝

RB 39

Von der Lasa 1843

  1   ♖a8   ♔b5

After 1 ... a2 2 ♔b2 ♔b5 3 ♖b8+ ♝b6 4 ♖a8! Black cannot progress.

2	♖b8+	♔c4
3	♖a8!	♔b5
4	♖b8+	♝b6
5	♖a8! drawing	

= W

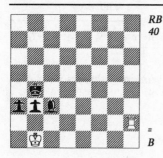

RB 40

Fine 1940

  1   ...   ♔c4

The weakness of the knight's pawn/rook's pawn duo means that Black cannot mount threats to advance from both sides of his pawn phalanx. Here White can draw even with his passive rook.

2	♖g2	♝d4
3	♖h2	♔d3
4	♖b2!	

A common motif in this type of ending.

4	...	♔c3
5	♖e2	♝c5
6	♖b2	♝e3
7	♖h2	♝d2
8	♖h3+	♔b4
9	♖h4+	♔b5
10	♖h3	

Black is not making progress.

= B

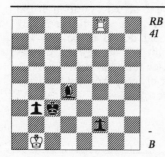

RB 41

Unconnected Pawns

Averbakh 1978

  1   ...   ♔d3!

1 ... b2 is drawn since Black's king's forthcoming attempt to help the f2-pawn is met by ♖xf2 ♝xf2, ♔xb2. With two isolated pawns, the key is whether or not the side with the pawns can move his king across to the pawn which is being stopped by the rook.

2	♖f7	♔e2
3	♖e7+	♔f1
4	♖e8	b2!
5	♔c2	♔g2
6	♖g8+	♔f3
7	♖f8+	♔e2
8	♖e8+	♝e3
9	♖f8	♝c1!
10	♖e8+	♔f3
11	♖f8+	♝f4

and wins

- B

Rook v Two Knights

♖ v ♞♞

Rook and One Pawn v Two Knights

+ W

RNN Rinck 1923

1 This time the rook dominates the two knights.

    1   ♖f1

Threatening ♖f3 winning the ♞h3.

    1   ...   ♞e7

Alternatively:

a) 1 ... ♚b6 2 ♖f3 and ♖g3 next, skewering;

b) 1 ... ♞h6 2 ♖h1.

    2   ♖f3   ♞g5

Or 2 ... ♞g1 3 ♖g3 ♞e2 4 ♖e3.

    3   ♖g3

Now White forces a skewer winning a piece: 3 ... ♞e6 4 ♖e3; 3 ... ♞e4 4 ♖e3; 3 ... ♞f7 4 ♖g7; 3 ... ♞h7 4 ♖g7.

Rook and Two Pawns v Two Knights

+ W

RNN Gavrikov - Peshina

2 *USSR 1981*

A rare example of this material balance in pure form.

52	g4	♚d7
53	♖a6	♞e6+
54	♚h4	♚e7
55	♚g3	♞f1+
56	♚g2	♞e3+
57	♚f3	♞c4
58	h4	♞e5+
59	♚g3	♚f6
60	♖a1	♞c4
61	♖e1	♞d6

Here 61 ... ♞e5 62 g5+ ♚f5 63 ♖f1+ ♚e4 64 ♖f6 clears a path for the pawns.

62	♖f1+	♚g6
63	♖d1	♞f7
64	♖d5	♚f6
65	♖f5+	♚g6
66	♖f1	♚g7
67	♚f3!	

Black has an ideal defensive position, so White manoeuvres to drive the black king away from in front of the pawns.

    67   ...   ♚f6

Or 67 ... ♞e5+ 68 ♚e4 ♞xg4 69 ♖g1.

68	♚e4+	♚g6
69	♖b1	♚f6

70	♖b6	♚e7
71	♖b7+	♚f6
72	♖b1!	♚e7

Alternatively, 72 ... ♚g6 73 ♖b6 ♚f6 74 g5+ ♚e7 75 ♚f5 ♞d6+ 76 ♚g4 and the pawns will advance successfully.

    73   ♖f1!

Now that Black has reacted to threatened pressure on the sixth rank, White switches to cut off the black king from frontal defence. (Not 73 ♖b6 ♞d6+ 74 ♚d5 ♞f4+ 75 ♚e5 ♞g6+.)

73	...	♞d6+
74	♚d5	♞c7+
75	♚e5	♞e6
76	♖e1	♞f7+
77	♚d5	♞fd8

This clumsy knight array spells the end of defensive cohesion.

78	g5	♚f7
79	♖f1+	♚g7
80	♚e5	♞f8
81	♚f5	♞f7
82	♖d1	♞g6
83	h5	♞f8
84	♖a1	♞h7
85	g6	♞h6+
86	♚e5	♞f8

Rook v Two Knights

87	♖a7+	♔g8	90	♖a8	♞f3+
88	♔f6	♞g4+	91	♔f6	1-0
89	♔g5	♞e5			

Rook and Two Pawns v Two Knights and Two Pawns

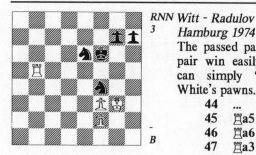

RNN Witt - Radulov
3 Hamburg 1974

The passed pawn and knight pair win easily. The knights can simply 'gang up' on White's pawns.

44	...	g5
45	♖a5	h5
46	♖a6	♞d3
47	♖a3	♞e5
48	♖a6	♔f5
49	♖a5	

Or 49 ♖d6 h4+ 50 ♔g2 ♞f4+ and the f3 pawn falls.

49	...	♞d4
50	♖a8	♞e2+
51	♔g2	♞f4+
52	♔h1	♞xf3
53	♖f8+	♔g4
54	♖a8	♞e5
55	♖a4	♞ed3
56	♔g1	♔f3
57	♖a5	♞xf2
58	♔h2	

Or 58 ♖xg5 ♞4h3+.

58	...	g4
59	♖a3+	♞4d3

0-1

RNN Averkin - Bronstein
4 USSR 1974

When both sides have passed pawns great tactical complications may arise.

51	...	c4
52	♔f3	

Or 52 ♖h7 c3 53 a7 ♞xa7 54 ♖xa7 c2 55 ♖a1 (55 ♖c7 ♞c4) 55 ... ♔d4 56 ♔f2 ♔c3 57 ♔e3 ♔b2 58 ♖h1 c1♛+ 59 ♖xc1 ♞xc1 60 ♔d4 ♞d2 61 ♔e5 ♞f7+ 62 ♔f6 ♔e3 63 ♔xf7 ♔f4-+.

52	...	c3
53	♔e2	♞e4
54	♔d1	♔c4
55	♖c6+	

55 ♖b6!? is a tricky defensive try and probably best: 55 ... ♞d4 56 a7 c2+ 57 ♔c1 ♞c5 (57 ... ♔c3 58 ♖c6+) 58 ♖c6 (58 ♔d2 ♞d3) 58 ... ♞xc6 59 a8♛ ♞d4 60 ♛c8 (60 ♛g8+ ♔c3) 60 ... ♔d3 61

♔b2 and now:

a) 61 ... ♞a4+ 62 ♔a3 ♞b6 63 ♛a6+ ♞c4+ 64 ♔a2 c1♛ (64 ... c1♖ 65 ♛g6+ and 66 ♛d3+!) 65 ♛g6+ ♔c3 66 ♛d3+ ♔b4 67 ♛b3+ ♔c5 68 ♛b6+ ♔d5 69 ♛d6+ ♔e4 70 ♛e5+ ♔d3 (70 ... ♔f3 71 ♛g3+ ♔e2 72 ♛e1+=) 71 ♛e4+ ♔c3 72 ♛d3+=;

b) 61 ... ♞cb3! 62 ♛c3+ ♔e2 63 ♛c4+ ♔f2 64 ♔a2!? and White has stalemate defences if the c-pawn queens, though ... c1♖!? should win.

55	...	♞c5
56	♔c1	♔b4
57	♖b6	♞b3+
58	♔d1	♔c4
59	♖c6+	♔d3
60	♖c8	♞3d4
61	♔c1	♞a7
62	♖d8	♞ac6
63	♖d7	c2

0-1

Rook v Two Knights

Rook v Two Knights: many pawns

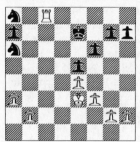

RNN 6

± B

Kasparov - Seirawan
Thessaloniki ol 1988

This complex ending illustrates how two knights can succeed in or fail to coordinate properly.

Note that, in general, knight work best side by side, and the array where the knight protect each other is the clumsiest.

23 ...   ♘b6?!

Better was 23 ... ♘6c7! Kasparov analyses 24 b4 (24 ♖b8!? may be most accurate, as it is harder for the ♘a8 to come into play, e.g. 24 ... ♘b6 25 ♖b7 ♔d7 26 b3!) 24 ... ♔d7 and now:

a) 25 ♖g8?! (In principle one of the rook's main weapons in this type of ending is a foray on the flank opposite his outside passed pawn, to force either gains on this side or to coerce the black king to abandon the fight against the passed pawn. But here the white rook gets tied up) 25 ... ♘e8 26 ♔d3 ♘ac7! 27 a4 ♘e6 28 g3 (28 ♔c4 ♘d6+ 29 ♔b3 a6! 30 ♖a8 ♘c7=) 28 ... ♘g5! 29 f4 ♘f7 intending 30 ... ♘fd6=;

b) 25 ♖b8 ♘b6 26 ♔d3 ♘c8 27 b5 ♘d6 28 a4 ♘e6 29 ♔c3 ♔c7 30 ♖g8 (30 ♖a8? ♘c8!).

24 ♖g8 ♔f7
25 ♖h8 ♘c5
26 ♖b8 ♔e7
27 b4 ♘c4+?

Better is 27 ... ♘cd7 28 ♖b7 ♘c4+ 29 ♔d3 ♘xa3 30 ♖xa7 (30 ♔c3 ♔d6!) 30 ... ♘b5 31 ♖a5.

28 ♔e2 ♘d7
29 ♖g8!+- g5
30 a4 a5
31 bxa5 ♘xa5
32 ♖a8?!

Here White goes astray. He should play 32 ♖g7+ ♔e6 33 ♖xh7 ♘c6 34 g3 ♘b6 35 h4 gxh4 36 gxh4 ♘xa4 37 h5 ♘d8 38 ♖c7! ♘f7 39 ♖c4! ♘b2 40 ♖b4+-.

32 ...   ♘c6
33 a5 ♔d6
34 g3 h5
35 h4 gxh4
36 gxh4 ♘c5
37 a6 ♔c7?

A better try was 37 ... ♘e6! 38 ♖h8 ♘c7 (38 ... ♘f4+ 39 ♔f2) 39 ♖xh5 ♘xa6 40 ♖h7! ♔e6 41 h5 ♘d8 42 ♖a7.

38 a7 ♘b7?

A blunder, but Black would also lose after 38 ... ♔b7 39 ♖c8!+- or 38 ... ♔b6 39 ♖h8 ♔xa7 40 ♖xh5+-.

39 ♖c8+   1-0

Analysis based on Kasparov's notes.

Rook v Bishop and Knight

Rook and Two Pawns v Bishop and Knight

RBN 1

= B

Mnatsakanian - Ermenkov
Varna 1986
An interesting and rare theoretical position. I would imagine that this must be the worst connected pair for the rook. First the rook is restricted to one side since the pawns are not central, and second, the rook and a5-pawn against bishop is drawn. White manages to get even less.

41	...	♗e5
42	♖c5	♔b6
43	♖d5	♗g7
44	♖g5	♗f6
45	♖h5	♗g7
46	a3	♗f8
47	♔c2	♔a6
48	♔d3	♔b6
49	♖g5	♗e7
50	♖f5	♗d6
51	♔c4	♘e7
52	♖f6	♔c6
53	b4	♘c8
54	♖h6	

White is so intent on doing nothing that the game is eventually drawn by repetition. There are (at least) three approaches:
a) advancing b5;
b) advancing first with a4;
c) cutting Black's king on the c-file and achieving ♔a4 or ♔a5. Even worse is 54 b5+? ♔b6 55 a4 ♔a5 56 ♔b3 ♔b6 57 ♖h6 ♔a5 58 ♖h7 ♔b6 59 ♖d7 ♗g3 and White cannot lift the blockade.

54	...	♘b6+
55	♔b3	♘d5
56	♖g6	♘f4
57	♖g4	♘d5
58	♖g5	♘e7
59	♖h5	

Here 59 a4 is slightly more dangerous since Black's pieces are rather loose, but the pawns will also become blockaded or overextended with correct defence: 59 ... ♘d5 (59 ... ♔b7 and ... ♘c6) 60 b5+ ♔c5 and now:
a) 61 b6 ♔c6 62 b7 ♗b8!= intending ... ♘c7 (not 62 ... ♘b6? 63 ♖g6 ♘d7 64 a5 ♘c5+ 65 ♔c4 ♘xb7 66 a6+-);
b) 61 a5 ♗f4 62 ♖f5 ♔xb5 63 ♖xd5+ ♔a6 is a theoretical draw - cf RB13.

59	...	♘d5
60	♔c4	♘e3+
61	♔b3	♘d5
62	♖h6	♘b6
63	♖h1!	

Ermenkov considers the threat of ♖c1, and the occupation of the c-file in general, to be winning. However, he does not analyse the ending at all. As noted earlier, if this is lost, then all rook and two connected pawns v bishop and knight should win. 63 ... ♘d5 Or 63 ... ♔b5. 64 ♖c1+ ♔b6 65 ♔c4 Ermenkov suggests 65 ♖c2!? intending 65 ♖c2 ♔c6 66 ♔a4 winning. (Even here 66 ... ♘b6+ simply drives the white king back.) But the basic idea of using ♔a4 to help advance the pawns is the most threatening, and makes it difficult for Black to maintain piece coordination: 65 ... ♗e7 66 ♔a4 ♗f8 67 ♖d2 and now:
a) 67 ... ♘c7 68 ♖f2 ♗e7! (68 ... ♗d6?! 69 ♖f6 ♔c6 70 ♔a5 and Black is in danger of having to misplace his king on the d-file) 69 ♖f7 ♗h4 70

♖h7 ♗g5 71 ♖g7 ♗e3 72 ♖g6+ ♚b7 73 ♚a5 when Black has again regrouped efficiently. This array takes much of the punch out of the white king advancing on the a-line;

b) 67 ... ♘c3+ (keeping the king from a4/a5 seems safest, though not essential) 68 ♚b3 ♘b5 69 a4 (69 ♖f2 ♗e7 70 ♖f7 ♗d6 71 ♖f6 ♚c7 72 a4 ♘d4+ 73 ♚c4 ♘c6 74 b5 ♘a5+ 75 ♚d5 ♗b4) 69 ... ♘c7 70 ♖d8 ♗e7 71 ♖d7 ♗h4

72 ♖d6+ ♚b7 73 ♚c4 ♗f2 and Black has reorganised his defence. White is sorely handicapped by the fact that the advance a5 allows the knight to sacrifice itself for the b-pawn. The advance of the b-pawn invites a blockade, and has little punch since the a5-advance is then difficult to achieve.

65	...	♘e3+
66	♚b3	♘d5
67	♖c2	♗e7
68	♖c1	♗d6

½-½

RBN Neverov - Pähtz
2 **Tbilisi 1985**

45	...	♘b4+
46	♚d2	♗e1+!
47	♚e2	♗c3

Another interesting theoretical position. Black has established a blockade. White finds no way to mobilise the pawns, or approach them with his king.

48	♖h5	♚d6
49	♚e3	♚c6
50	♚e4	♚d6

= B

51	♖h3	♗b2
52	♖h6+	♚c5
53	♖h5+	♚d6
54	♖h3	♚c5
55	♖h5+	♚d6
56	♖b5	♗c3
57	♚f5	♗e1
58	♚f6	♗c3+
59	♚f7	♚d7
60	♖h5	♗d2
61	♖h1	♗e3
62	♖d1+	♚c7
63	♚e6	♗f4

½-½

RBN Tisdall 1993
3

1		♗d5+	♚f5
2		♘g3+	

Or 2 ♘c1 e4.

2		...	♚g4
3		♘e4	f5
4		♘f2+	♚g5
5		♗b7	

This is safer than 5 ♘h3+?! and now:

a) 5 ... ♚f6 6 ♘f2 ♖a3+ 7 ♚e2 ♚g5 (7 ... ♚e7 8 ♗b7 and White can threaten f5 from c8 or h3 etc. which makes the idea of ... ♚d4 impractical) 8 ♗b7 (White tries to maintain the option of either sacrificing on e4 or blockading if ... f4. Not 8 ♗c6

= W

♚h4 9 ♘d3 e4 10 ♘c5 ♖c3 11 ♗xe4 ♖xc5.) 8 ... ♚h4 9 ♘d3 ♖a5 (9 ... e4 10 ♘c5 e3 11 ♚f3=) 10 ♚f3 ♚g5 11 ♘f2 and Black has not made progress;

b) 5 ... ♚h4 6 ♘f2 ♖a3+ 7 ♚e2 ♚g3 8 ♗e6 and:

b1) 8 ... ♖f3 9 ♘d3 e4 10 ♘e5 ♖f2+ (10 ... ♖a3 11 ♗xf5 ♚f4 12 ♗xe4) 11 ♚e3=;

b2) 8 ... ♚f4 9 ♘d3+ ♚e4 10 ♘f2+ ♚f4 11 ♘d3+ ♚g5 12 ♘xe5 ♚f6 13 ♘xf5;

b3) 8 ... f4! 9 ♘e4+ ♚g2 10 ♘g5! (This is clearly a most dangerous ... f4 position, but White can still organise a defence. Not 10 ♗d5 f3+ 11 ♚d2

371

Rook v Bishop and Knight ♜ V ♝♞

f2-+ or 10 ♘d2 ♖e3+ 11 ♔d1 ♔f2 12 ♗d5 ♖d3 13 ♗c4 ♖d4 14 ♔c2 e4-+) 10 ... ♖e3+ 11 ♔d2 ♔f2 (11 ... ♔g3 12 ♗d5 ♔g4 13 ♘e4) 12 ♗d5 and White has organised a blocka

ade. (But not 12 ♘h3+? ♖xh3 13 ♗xh3 e4-+.)

5	...	f4+
6	♔e2	♖a2+
7	♔f3	♖a3+
8	♔g2 with a draw	

RBN 4

Szymczak - Sznapik
Polish ch 1983
Here the pawns are split, and Black's king is distant, so White has chances to erect a piece barrier similar to the one in diag 6, or to cross with his king.

45 ... ♖d4

This cuts the king.

46 ♘c2 ♖d7

Instead 46 ... ♖d6 47 ♘e3 ♔f6 48 ♗c2 transposes into the game.

47 ♘e1 ♔g6?!

Much better was: 47 ... ♔f6! and now:

a) 48 ♗c2!? (trying to build a bridge to cross with the king looks the best idea) 48 ... h5 (48 ... ♔g5 49 ♘f3+ ♔f4 50 ♘h4=) 49 ♗d3 h4 (49 ... ♔g5 50 ♔d2 ♔g4 51 ♔e2 f4 52 ♔f2 and White will achieve ♗e2 and ♘f3, when he should hold) 50 ♔d2 h3 51 ♘f3 ♖h7 52 ♘h2 ♖g7 53 ♗f1 ♖g3 (53 ... ♔e5 54 ♗xh3 ♖h7 55 ♘f3+ ♔f4 56 ♗xf5=) 54 ♔e2 ♔e5 55 ♔e1 ♔e4 (55 ... ♔f4 56 ♔f2 mutual zugzwang!?) and:

a1) 56 ♗e2 ♖g1+ 57 ♔f1 (57 ♘f1 h2; 57 ♔d2 ♖g2-+) 57 ... ♖h1;

a2) 56 ♔f2? ♔f4 57 ♔e2 ♖g1 58 ♗xh3 (58 ♘f3 ♖xf1) 58 ... ♖h1-+;

a3) 56 ♔e2! f4 57 ♔f2 ♖b3 58 ♗e2 and White gains the f3 square for the knight on h2. White appears to hold if he tries to erect this fortress in time;

b) 48 ♘f3 h5 49 ♗c2 (this is reminiscent of the defensive tries in diag 6) 49 ... f4 (49 ... ♖d5 50 ♘h4 will force ... f4) 50 ♗d1 ♖d3 51 ♗e2 ♖d8 (51 ... ♖d6 52 ♘d2 ♖d5 53 ♔d1) 52 ♘h4 ♔g5 53 ♘f3+ ♔g4 54 ♘d2+ ♔h4 55 ♔d1 ♖e8 56 ♔e1 ♔g3 57 ♔f1 h4-+. White does not succeed in using the king in defence.

48 ♘f3 ♖d6?

48 ... ♔f6 still looks better, aiming for the previous note.

49	♗c2	♔f6
50	♘h4	f4
51	♘f5	♖d5
52	♘xh6	♔g5
53	♘f7+	♔h4
54	♘h6	♔h5
55	♘f5	♔g5
56	♘e7	♖c5
57	♔d2	f3
58	♗e4	

Here the players agreed a draw since 58 ... ♔f4 (58 ... f2 59 ♔e2 ♖e5 60 ♔xf2 ♖xe4 61 ♘d5=) 59 ♗xf3 ♔xf3 60 ♔d3 and in both cases the knight regains contact with the king.

½-½

Rook v Bishop and Knight

Rook and Two Pawns v Bishop, Knight and One Pawn

RBN
5

Tal - Geller
Moscow 1967

88 ... &d6(?)

88 ... ♘c5!? makes it harder for White to organise a defence. In fact, I do not see how the white king can get back in time to isolate the a-pawn from the black king: 89 ♖e3 (89 ♖h4 &e6) 89 ... &d6 90 &f7 (90 &f5 &d5 and White does not get his king back) &d5 91 &e8 &d4 and now:

a) 92 ♖h3 ♗c3 93 &d8 (93 ♖h4+ &d3 is impossible) 93 ... ♘xb3 94 &c7 &c4 95 &b6 &b4 and ... ♗d4 -+;

b) 92 ♖g3! ♗c3 93 ♖g4+ &d3 94 &d8 ♘xb3 95 &c7 ♘d4 (95 ... ♗d4) 96 &b6 &c4 97 ♖g5 ♘b3 and:

b1) 98 ♖g4+ ♗d4+ 99 &a6 &b4 100 ♖g5 ♘c5+!-+ (100 ... &xa4?? 101 ♖xa5+=);

b2) 98 ♖b5 and:

b21) 98 ... ♗d2 99 &b7 ♘c5+;

b22) 98 ... ♗b4 99 ♖h5;

b23) 98 ... ♗f6! 99 ♖xb3 (99 ♖h5 ♗d4+ and ... &b4 -+ or 99 &a6 ♗d8 100 ♖b8 ♘c5+ 101 &a7 ♗f6-+) 99 ... ♗d8+

and Black wins.

89 &f5 ♘c5
90 ♖e8!

The b3-pawn is doomed so White prevents a black king invasion. (Not 90 ♖e3 &d5 91 ♖h3 &d4 and ... ♘c3 will win the b3-pawn.)

90 ... ♘xb3

Not 90 ... &d5 91 ♖d8+.

91 &e4 ♘c5+
92 &d4 ♘xa4
93 &c4 ♘b6+
94 &b5

In this position, Black has no chance of creating a coordinated unit to advance the pawn - his king is unable to participate. The result now is a trivial draw.

94 ... &c7
95 ♖e6 ♘d5
96 ♖a6 ♘c3+
97 &c4 &b7
98 ♖e6 ♘b1
99 &b5 &c8
100 ♖a6 ♘c3+
101 &b6

Agreed drawn in view of 101 ... a4 102 ♖xa4 ♘xa4+ 103 &b5=.

Rook v Bishop and Knight: many pawns

RBN
6

Arshansky - B. Gruzman
corr 1969

White's (marginal) hopes are based on a lack of entry squares for the black king and a vague resemblance to diag 4.

51 ... d5
52 &f1 f4
53 &e1 d4

Selling the d-pawn to get access to e5.

54 ♘xd4 &e5
55 ♘f3+ &e4
56 ♘d2+

56 ♗e6!? offers better chances to coordinate a defence. White's resources are certainly greater than shown by the game, where Black is

373

Rook v Bishop and Knight    ♖ V ♗♘

RBN 6a

= B

allowed to improve his king position without a struggle.

56 ... ♖g2 and now:

a) 57 ♔f1 ♖b2 (White has lost the checking circuit with ♘d2) 58 ♘h4 (58 ♘g5+ ♔e3 59 ♗d5 ♖b5) 58 ... f3 59 ♗d7 (Not 59 ♗f7 ♖h2!-+ or 59 ♗c8 ♔e3 60 ♘f5+ ♔f4 61 ♘h4 ♖h2 62 ♘f5 ♖c2 63 ♘e7 ♖e2-+ when Black either achieves ... ♔g3, or drives the bishop from the defence of the knight on f5, as in the main variation) 59 ... ♔e3 60 ♘f5+ ♔f4 61 ♔g1 ♖d2 62 ♗c8 ♖d8 and:

a1) 63 ♗e6 ♖d1+! (63 ... ♔e5 64 ♘g7 ♔f6 65 ♘xh5+ ♔xe6 66 ♔f2 ♖f8 67 ♘g3 ♔e5 68 ♔e3 and White should reach a drawn version of rook and one pawn vs knight. This illustrates that Black should always beware of decentralising the king, even if this involves winning a piece. This kind of variation is White's main hope.) 64 ♔f2 ♖d2+ 65 ♔f1 ♔e5 66 ♗c8 (66 ♘g7 ♔f6 67 ♘xh5+ ♔xe6-+) 66 ... ♖d8 67 ♘e7 ♔f6-+;

a2) 63 ♘e7 ♖e8 64 ♘d5+ ♔g3;

b) 57 ♘d2+ ♔d3 and:

b1) 58 ♗c4+ and now:

b11) 58 ... ♔c3?! (this looks in the wrong direction) 59 ♗e2 h4 (59 ... ♔c2 60 ♘f3 and White threatens ♔f1-f2, maximising his defensive position - the king aids in the fight against the pawns and Black's king has been walled out. This is White's ideal posi-

tion.) 60 ♘f3 h3 (60 ... ♖g4) 61 ♗f1 ♖g3 62 ♔f2 *(6a)*. A mutually clumsy position. Black's pawns are too exposed to win so an ending with rook against minor piece and no pawns looks inevitable, e.g. 62 ... ♔b4 63 ♘e5 h2 64 ♗g2 ♖c3 65 ♘g4 ♖c2+ 66 ♔f1 ♖c1+ 67 ♔f2 h1♕ 68 ♗xh1 ♖xh1 69 ♔f3 ♖f1+ 70 ♔e4 and ♘f3 draws;

b12) 58 ... ♔e3 (in general, Black aims at maintaining a central king and rook on the seventh, which should ensure the advance of the pawns without allowing White to reach problematic endings with minor piece against rook) 59 ♘f1+ ♔d4 60 ♗e2 h4 61 ♘d2 h3 62 ♗f1 (62 ♗f3 ♔e3) 62 ... ♔e3 63 ♘c4+ ♔f3 64 ♘d2+ ♖xd2 65 ♔xd2 h2 66 ♗b5 ♔f2 67 ♗c6 f3-+;

b2) 58 ♗f5+ ♔e3 59 ♘f1+ ♔d4 60 ♘d2 h4 61 ♗d7 ♔e3 62 ♘f1+ ♔d3 63 ♗b5+ ♔c3 64 ♗c6 h3 65 ♗e4 ♔d4 66 ♗c6 ♖c2 67 ♗b7 h2 68 ♗f3 ♔e5 69 ♗b7 ♔f5 70 ♗f3 ♔g5 71 ♗e4 ♔g4 and Black will arrange ... f3.

56	...	♔e3
57	♘f1+	♔f3
58	♘d2+	♔g3
59	♗e6	♖a5

Now after 60 ♔f1 f3 61 ♘e4+ ♔f4 62 ♘d2 ♖b5 Black wins by combining the advance of the a-pawn with threats to the minor pieces, e.g. 63 ♗b3 (63 ♘c4 ♔g3 64 ♘d2 ♖e5 65 ♗c4 f2 66 ♗e2 h4-+) h4 64 ♔f2 h3 65 ♗d1 ♖b2-+.

Rook v Bishop and Knight

RBN 7
±B

Karpov - Kasparov
World ch (2), Moscow 1985
    50 ...   a3!

According to Kasparov, the pawn is as safe here as on a4 and is obviously one move closer to promotion. "Black's only chance is to break into White's rear with his rook, threatening to attack the knight on a2 and the kingside pawns" (Kasparov).

51 ♗c3

Or 51 ♘c3 ♖b8.

    51 ...   f6
    52 ♗b4   ♔f7?!

Better was 52 ... ♔h7!? when the defensive method used by White in the game may lose: 53 ♗c3 ♖b8 54 ♗b4? (54 ♘b4! ♖b5 55 g4 ♖b8 56 ♔d3! ♖a8 57 ♘a2 ♖a4 58 ♗b4 ♔h6 59 ♗d2+ "... and the fortress cannot be taken" - Kasparov) 54 ... ♖b5! 55 g4 ♖b8! (zugzwang) 56 ♔d3 (56 ♗c3 ♖b1) 56 ... ♖d8+ 57 ♔c2 hxg4 58 hxg4 ♖d4 59 ♗xa3 ♖a4! 60 ♔b3 ♖xg4 61 ♗c1 ♖g3+ 62 ♘c3 ♖f3 63 ♔c2 ♖xf5 64 ♔d3 when: "It

is not possible to give a definite assessment of this ending (I have been unable to find anything similar in the books), but Black would have had excellent practical chances" (Kasparov).

    53 ♘c3   ♖b8
    54 ♘a2   ♖b5
    55 g4   ♖b8
    56 ♔d3   ♖d8+
    57 ♔c4   ♖d1
    58 ♗xa5

Or 58 gxh5=.

    58 ...   ♖a1
    59 ♔b3   ♖h1

Not 59 ... h4?? 60 ♘c1! trapping the rook.

    60 gxh5   ♖xh3+
    61 ♘c3   ♖f3
    62 ♗c1!   ♖xf5
    63 h6   g6

63 ... g5 also leads to a draw: 64 ♘e4 ♔g6 65 h7 ♖f3+ (65 ... ♔xh7 66 ♘xf6+ ♖xf6 67 ♗xg5=) 66 ♔c4 ♖h3 67 ♘xf6! ♔xf6 68 h8♕+ ♖xh8 69 ♗b2+.

    64 ♘e4   ♖h5
    65 ♗b2   ½-½

Due to 65 ... f5 66 h7!=.

Rook v Bishop, Knight and One Pawn

RBN 8
=W

Fedorowicz - W. Watson
Hastings 1985

White is handicapped by a wrong rook's pawn. Once the black king reaches the corner the rook can hunt the knight forever.

    62 ♗b4   ♔d7
    63 ♔b5   ♔c7
    64 ♘c3   ♖c1
    65 ♘e4   ♖h1
    66 ♗a5+

White's handicap is best illustrated by the variation 66 a4 ♖h5+ 67 ♗c5 ♔b7 68 a5

♔a8 69 ♘c3 ♖h4 70 ♘d5 ♖h5 71 ♘b4 ♖h4 72 ♘a6 ♖h6 73 ♗b6 ♖h5+ 74 ♔c6 ♖h6+ 75 ♔b5 ♖h5+ 76 ♔c4 ♖h4+ 77 ♗d4 ♖h5 78 ♔c5 ♖h6 79 ♘b4 (79 ♘c7+ ♔b7 80 ♘e8 ♖e6=) 79 ... ♖h4+ 80 ♗d4 ♖h5 81 ♗b6 ♖h4+ 82 ♗d4 ♖h5 83 a6 ♖a5 84 ♔c3 (84 ♔b3 ♖b5) 84 ... ♖a4=.

    66 ...   ♔b8
    67 ♗b6   ♖b1+
    68 ♔c6   ♖a1

And a draw was agreed due to 69 ♘c3 ♖c1=.

Rook v Two Bishops

Rook and One Pawn v Two Bishops and One Pawn

RBB 1

±
B

RBB 1a

+
W

Tal - Fernandez Garcia
Malaga 1981

Tal had spent a long time manoeuvring before reaching this position. The fact that White's king has been allowed across the fifth rank gives him excellent chances.

    96 ...   **♖b7**
    97 ♗f5?

Missing a chance to reach the basic winning position, though the fifty move rule would have thwarted him anyway: 97 ♗d3! ♖b8 (97 ... ♖b6+ 98 ♔c5 ♖b7 99 ♗e2 ♖b6 100 ♗c7 ♖b7 101 ♔d6) 98 ♗c7 ♖b6+ 99 ♔c5 ♖b7 100 ♔d6.

    97 ...   **♖b8!**

This resource makes it clear that Black is not to be driven easily from the defence of the b-pawn.

    98 ♔c5

Alternatively:

a) 98 ♗xb8 stalemate;

b) 98 ♔c7 ♖b7+ 99 ♔d8 ♖g7 100 ♗c8+ (100 ♗c5) 100 ... ♔b6 101 ♗c5+ ♔c6 102 ♗f5 ♔b7.

    98 ...   **♖d8**
    99 ♗c7   **♖h8**
    100 ♔c6   **♖h6+**

Drawn by the fifty move rule. Tal's only comments about this ending were that Black should not have allowed White's king to cross the d-file (56 ... ♖d5!), and that the final position is winning for White. He does not give any clues as to why, but I sug-

gest 101 ♗d6 ♖h8 102 ♔c7 ♔a7 103 ♗c8 ♖h7+ 104 ♔c6 ♖h6 105 ♗g4! ♔a6 106 ♗e2+- and the b-pawn finally falls.

Black has other possibilities on move 100:

a) 100 ... ♖f8 101 ♗d3 ♖b8 102 ♗e2 ♖b6+ 103 ♔c5 ♖b7 104 ♔d6 and wins as in the above line;

b) 100 ... ♖b8 (This is the basic nut White has to crack in order to prove a win.) and now:

b1) 101 ♗d6 ♖g8 (101 ... ♖b6+ 102 ♔c5 ♔b7 103 ♗d7 ♔a6 104 ♗c7+-) 102 ♔c7 (again intending ♗c8+, ♗c5+ winning) 102 ... ♖g7+ 103 ♗d7 ♖h7 (103 ... ♔a7 104 ♔c6 ♖g6 105 ♗f5 ♖f6 106 ♗d3) 104 ♔c6 ♖h8 is less than convincing for White (but not 104 ... ♖h6 105 ♗c8+ ♔a7 106 ♗g4+-);

b2) 101 ♗d3 ♖b6+ 102 ♔c5 ♖b7 103 ♔d6! ♔a7 (103 ... ♖a7 104 ♗e4) 104 ♗e4+-.

c) 100 ... ♖g8 101 ♗d3 ♖g5 (101 ... ♖b8 102 ♗e2 and wins as in other lines) 102 ♗d6 ♖h5 103 ♗f4+-.

    Diagram 1a
Tisdall 1993
(by analogy to this game)
  1   ♗e6   ♖c6+
  2   ♔d5   ♖c7
  3   ♗f2   ♖c6
  4   ♗d7   ♖c7
  5   ♔d6 and wins

Rook v Two Bishops ♖ v ♝♝

Rook and Two Pawns v Two Bishops and Two Pawns

RBB
2
-
B

Basman - Gligoric
Hastings 1973

| 47 | ... | a4 |

White's pawns are more advanced but frustrated by the domination of both vital diagonals. The best White can reach is an ending with rook against bishop and pawns in which the passed pawns win handily.

| 48 | ♖b6+ | ♚d5 |
| 49 | g6 | a3 |

| 50 | ♖b8 | ♝xg6 |
| 51 | ♖xb5+ | |

Or 51 h8♕ ♝xh8 52 ♖xh8 a2 53 ♖a8 ♝b1 54 ♚f2 b4 55 ♚e1 b3 56 ♚d2 b2.

51	...	♚c4
52	♖a5	♚b3
53	♖b5+	♚a4
54	♖d5	♝c3
55	♖c5	♝e1+
56	♚g4	♝xh7

0-1

RBB
3
=
B

Balashov - Tukmakov
USSR ch 1977

61	...	♚e4
62	♝e6	g3
63	hxg3	hxg3
64	♝c4	½-½

Black's passed pawn ties up White just enough to allow the black king to approach the b-pawn. (Also drawn is 64 ♝d7 ♚d5 and ... ♚c4=.) The finish might have been 64 ♝c4 ♚d4 65 ♝f1 ♖b3 66 ♝d6 (66 ♝e7 ♖e3 67 ♝d6 ♖b3) 66 ... ♚d5 67 ♝xg3 ♚c5 68 ♝f2+ ♚b4 and ... ♚a5=.

Rook v Two Bishops: many pawns

RBB
4
±
W

Ljubojevic - V. Kovacevic
Bugojno 1984

An interesting theoretical position with three against three on the same side.

46	♚e3	♖d8
47	♝e2	♖d7
48	♝f3	♖d8
49	♝d4	♖d7
50	♚d3	♖c7
51	♝e5	♖a7
52	♚c4	♖a5
53	♚b4	♖a2
54	♚c5	♖d2
55	♝d5	

White has no difficulty improving his king position, but he must create a pawn weakness to generate winning chances.

55	...	♖d1
56	♚d6	♖d3
57	♚e6	♖d2
58	♝f3	♖a2
59	♚f7	♖a7+
60	♚f8	♖d7
61	♚e8	♖a7
62	♚f8	

Another try is 62 g4!? hxg4 (62 ... ♖a3 63 gxf5 ♖xf3 64 f6 ♖a3 65 f7 ♖a8+ 66 ♚e7 ♖a7+ 67 ♚f6 ♖a6+ 68 ♚g5 ♖a8 69 ♝d6+-) 63 hxg4 fxg4 (63 ... ♖a3 64 gxf5! and Black can choose between a lost ending after 64 ... ♖xf3 65 f6 and wins as in the previous note, or 64 ... gxf5 reaching di-

Rook v Two Bishops

ag 2) 64 ♗xg4 (Black now faces a difficult defence but has several advantages over the type of ending in diag 2. The f4-pawn is more vulnerable and the black king can become active via h6, and also press against f4.) 64 ... ♖a5 65 ♗f6 ♖a4 66 ♗g5 ♔g7 67 ♔e7 ♖b4 68 ♗d7 ♖e4+ 69 ♗e6 ♖a4 70 ♗f6+ ♔h6 71 ♗e5 (White needs to mount pressure on g6, probably with ♔f7,♗e7 and ♗d3, though Black can try to defend that position with a rook shuttling on the sixth rank.) 71 ... ♖a7+ 72 ♔f6 ♔h5. The g4-break is an interesting practical try, though I feel a draw is the most likely correct result.

62	...	♖d7
63	♗c6	♖d2
64	♔f7	♖a2
65	h4?	♖a6
66	♗f3	♖a7+
67	♔f8	♖d7
68	♗e2	♖a7
69	♗b5	♖a8+
70	♔e7	♔h6
71	♗d4	♔h7
72	♗e8	♔h6

73	♗c6	♖c8
74	♗d5	♖c7+
75	♔f6	♖d7
76	♔e6	♖d8
77	♗e5	♖c8
78	♗b7	

Alternatively, 78 ♔f7 ♔h7 79 ♔f6 ♔h6 80 ♗d6 ♖d8 81 ♔e7 ♖c8 82 ♔f7 ♖d8 83 ♗f8+ ♔h7 84 ♔e6 and now:

a) 84 ... ♖d2 85 ♗e7 ♖xg2 (85 ... ♖b2) 86 ♗f8+-;

b) 84 ... ♖a8 85 ♗e7 ♔h6 (Best is 85 ... ♖a7! 86 ♗f6 ♖a6. The text illustrates a dangerous variation.) 86 ♗g5+ ♔h7 87 g4 fxg4 88 f5 ♖a7+ 89 ♔f6 gxf5 90 ♗xf5+ ♔g8 91 ♔g6 g3 92 ♗h3 ♔f8 93 ♔xh5 ♖a2 94 ♔g4 g2 95 ♗e3 ♖a4+ 96 ♔f3 (96 ♔g5 ♖a3 97 ♗c5+ ♔f7= or 96 ♔h5 ♖a5+ 97 ♔h6 ♖a6+ 98 ♔h7 ♖a4 99 h5 ♖h4) 96 ... ♖a3=.

78	...	♖d8
79	♗c6	♖c8
80	♗b7	♖d8
81	♔e7	♖d2
82	♗c6	♖c2
83	♗d5	♖c8
½-½		

Rook v Two Bishops and One Pawn

RBB 5

Benjamin - A. Ivanov
Philadelphia 1988
Two bishops and a pawn win easily against the rook.

54	...	♗f5
55	♖a7	g5
56	♖a5	♗g6
57	♖a7	g4

White is playing without a king. If the rook stops the pawn, the black king assists the pawn and wins easily. A sample line is 58 ♖a1 g3 59 ♖f1 (to try to force the bishops to yield an approach for the white king) 59 ... ♗h5 60 ♔e4 (60 ♖xf4 g2) 60 ... ♗c7 61 ♖g1 (otherwise ... ♗b6) 61 ... ♔g7 62 ♔f5 ♗f3 63 ♔g5 g2 64 ♔h4 ♗h2 (64 ... ♗b6?? 65 ♔g3 ♗xg1 66 ♔xf3=) and wins.

Rook and Knight v Rook   ♖♘ v ♖

Introduction

Like rook and bishop v rook, this ending is generally drawn. However, in marked contrast to the suffering engendered in the former case, it is quite easy to draw against a rook and knight. Indeed, this ending is seldom played on really seriously. Naturally, there are some winning positions. But these tend to involve not only a misplaced king on the edge of the board but also some additional factor: either the defending rook also being misplaced or (and this comes to more or less the same thing) a particularly free hand for the attacker.

It is interesting to speculate why it should be so much easier to draw against a rook and knight. I can identify at least three reasons:

a) There is a considerable risk of stalemate as the attacker closes in: more so, perhaps, than with the other minor piece;

b) If the knight provides shelter for the attacking king, e.g. ♔d6 ♘d5 vs ♔d8, then:

b1) Only the three squares on c7, d7 and e7 are covered on the second rank so the defending king, depending on other circumstances, may be able to run in either direction (in contrast a bishop on d5 would cover both b7 and f7);

b2) Without additional support from the rook, the knight cannot block flank checks on the sixth rank (i.e. on b6 or d6), whereas a bishop, supported by the king, can interpose on either c6 or e6.

RNR *Centurini 1853*
1

  1   ♖d3!

Temporising so as to force the enemy rook to c4 before improving the white rook's position.

  1   ...   ♖c2
  2   ♖d1   ♖c4
  3   ♖h1

Now the rook can get some space since of course if 3 ... ♔c8 4 ♘d6+.

  3   ...   ♖c2
  4   ♘d4!   ♖b2+

Not 4 ... ♖c3 5 ♖h8+.

  5   ♔c6

Threatening 6 ♖h8+ ♔a7 7 ♘b5+.

  5   ...   ♔a8

+
W

The only move.

  6   ♖h3   ♖b1
  7   ♖h2

Again waiting to force the black rook to the fourth rank.

  7   ...   ♖b4
  8   ♘b5   ♖c4+
  9   ♔b6   ♔b8

Or 9 ... ♖c8 10 ♘c7+ ♔b8 11 ♘a6+ ♔a8 12 ♖a2! (not 12 ♖h7? ♖c6+!). Here we have almost the same position as after White's third move except that now his rook has more room.

  10   ♘d6   ♖b4+
  11   ♔c6   ♔a8
  12   ♖h8+   ♖b8
  13   ♘c8! and wins

RNR *Centurini 1850*
2

White's plan is to transfer the knight to c6 after which mate will quickly follow. Alternatively, if he can get the knight to b6 with the king on a6 then that will suffice. In order to move the knight he must control the sixth rank.

  1   ♔b6   ♖f8

Alternatively, 1 ... ♔b8 2

+
W

♘f7 ♖e8 3 ♘e5!; 1 ... ♖b8+ 2 ♔a6 ♖b1 3 ♘b5; or 1 ... ♖d8 2 ♘b5 ♖b8+ 3 ♔a6 ♖f8 4 ♖a7+ ♔b8 5 ♖b7+ ♔c8 6 ♘a7+ ♔d8 7 ♘c6+ ♔c8 8 ♖b8+.

  2   ♖h7!   ♖g8
  3   ♖f7   ♖h8
  4   ♖f6   ♖d8

If 4 ... ♔b8 5 ♘b5 and now:

a) 5 ... ♔a8 6 ♘a7 ♖b8+ 7

♔a6 ♖h8 (7 ... ♖b1 8 ♘b5) 8
♘c6;
   b) 5 ... ♔c8 6 ♖d6! ♔b8 7
♘a7 etc.

5	♔c7	♖h8
6	♖f5	♖h7+
7	♘f7 and wins	

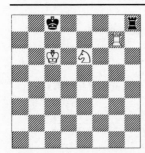

RNR *Centurini 1853*
3

Although the black king is
badly placed, his rook is more
active than in diag 1. White is
unable to transfer his rook
from the c-file without freeing
the black king and as a result
the position is drawn.

    1   **♔c6**   **♖b2!**

Not 1 ... ♔c8? 2 ♘d6+ ♔b8
(2 ... ♔d8 3.♖e1) 3 ♖h1 and
wins as in diag 1.

= W

| 2 | ♘d6 | ♖b3 |
| 3 | ♖c2 | ♖b1 |

Not 3 ... ♖b4?? 4 ♖h2 and
wins since the knight controls
c4; or 3 ... ♖h3? 4 ♖b2+ ♔a8
5 ♖g2 ♖h8 6 ♖g7 and wins as
in diag 2.

4	♘c4	♖h1
5	♖g2	♖h6+
6	♘d6	♔a7!

drawing

RNR *Centurini 1850*
4

    1   **♖f7**

The black pieces are both
badly placed. White wins by
waiting until the enemy rook
goes to an even worse square -
e8, after which it will have no
check on the sixth rank.

    1   ...   **♖g8**

Or 1 ... ♔b8 2 ♔b6 ♔a8 3

+ W

♖a7+ ♔b8 4 ♖b7+ ♔c8 5
♖c7+ (5 ♔a7? ♖h7!) 5 ...♔b8
6 ♘d4.

2	♖h7	♖e8
3	♘c5	♖g8
4	♖c7+	♔d8
5	♘e6+	♔e8
6	♔d6 and wins	

RNR *Centurini 1878*
5

In contrast to diag 4, here the
black rook is actively placed,
pinning the knight. As a result, Black is able to hold.

    1   **♖c7+**

Or 1 ♔a7 ♖h7!.

= W

1	...	♔b8
2	♖c6	♖h1!
3	♘d4	♖b1+
4	♘b5	♖b2
5	♖c1	♖b4=

cf diag 3.

RNR *Centurini 1878*
6

The stalemate defences make
this rather complicated,
though in the end White is
able to transform it into a less
cramped winning position
where Black's king has
enough air to avoid stalemate,
but insufficient space to sur-

+ W

vive.

1	...	♖g3+
2	♔f7	♖g7+
3	♔e6	♖b7

3 ... ♖g1 4 ♖d7 ♖e1+ 5
♔f7+- is analogous to the
main line.

    4   **♖g2**   **♖b6+**

4 ... ♖e7+ is worse since the

rook ends up misplaced on the e-file: 5 Kf5 Re5+ 6 Kg6 Re2 7 Rg5 Rg2 (7 ... Re5 8 Rg4+-) 8 Ng4 Ra2 9 Re5+-.

5	Kf5	Rb5+
6	Kg6	Rb2
7	Rg5	Rb5

Or 7 ... Rg2 8 Ng4.

8	Nd5	Rb7

Alternatively, 8 ... Kg8 9 Re5 Rb8 (9 ... Kf8 10 Rf5+) 10 Nf6+.

9	Kf6	Rg7

Both 9 ... Rd7 10 Ne7 Rd6+ 11 Kf7 Kh7 12 Rg7+ and 9 ...

Ra7 10 Rg1 Rb7 11 Ra1 Rd7 12 Ne7 Rd6+ 13 Kf7 Kh7 (cf diag 1) are winning for White.

10	Re5	Rd7
11	Ne7	Rd6+
12	Kf7	Kh7
13	Re1	Ra6
14	Rh1+	Kh6
15	Ra1	Rh2

For 15 ... Rb6 cf diag 1.

16	Ng8	Rf2+
17	Nf6+	Kh6
18	Rg1	Rg2
19	Ng4+ and wins	

RNR 7

+ W

Nunn 1992

1	Rh4!	

It is very interesting that in order to make progress the rook must abandon the seventh rank! (1 Nc6? fails to 1 ... Rg7! and 1 Kb6 to 1 ... Rb8+ 2 Kc7 Rc8+!).

1	...	Rb8

Alternatively:

a) 1 ... Rg6 2 Nc6 Rg7 3 Ra4+ Kb7 4 Ra7+ Kc8 5 Ne7+ Kd8 (5 ... Kb8 6 Kb6) 6 Kd6 Ke8 7 Ke6 Kd8 8 Rd7+ Ke8 9 Rc7;

b) 1 ... Rg1 2 Kb6 Rb1+ 3 Kc7 Rg1 4 Rh5 Rg2 5 Re5! (threatening 6 Nc6 to meet a rook check by 7 Ne7) 5 ...

Rb2 6 Re1 Ka7 7 Ra1 Ka6 8 Nc4+.

2	Nc6	Rb1
3	Rh7	Rc1+
4	Kd6	Rd1+
5	Kc7	Rh1
6	Rd7	

And White wins; cf diag 6. Using his database Nunn has shown that the longest line is: 6 ... Rd1 7 Nd4 Rb1 8 Rd5 Rb7+ 9 Kc6 Rb4 10 Nb5 Rc4+ 11 Kb6 Kb8 12 Rh5 Rc1 13 Rh8+ Rc8 14 Rh1 Rc2 15 Nd4 Rb2+ 16 Kc6 Ka8 17 Rg1 Rb4 18 Nb5 Rc4+ 19 Kb6 Kb8 20 Nd6 Rb4+ 21 Kc6 Ka8 22 Rg8+ Rb8 23 Nc8 etc.

RNR 9

+ W

The longest win

Nunn 1992

Using the database, Nunn kindly provided a longest win - it takes 33 moves!

1	Ra8+	Kd7
2	Ra7+	Kc8
3	Kd6	Rd8+
4	Kc6	Kb8
5	Rb7+	Ka8
6	Rh7!!	

Not 6 Rg7? Rc8+ 7 Kb6 Rb8+ 8 Kc5 (8 Ka6 Rb1 9 Nc4 Ra1+ 10 Kb6 Rb1+=) 8

... Rh8 9 Rg4 Kb8 10 Nc6+ Kc8 and because the rook is on h8 and not g8, 11 Ne7+ is harmless so Black can draw.

6	...	Rc8+

6 ... Rd1 7 Kc7! Rc1+ 8 Nc6 etc; or 6 ... Rg8 7 Nc4 Rg6+ 8 Nd6 Kb8 9 Rd7+-.

7	Kb6	Rb8+
8	Kc5!	Rg8
9	Rh4!	

And we have reached diag 8 in which White wins in 24 more moves.

Rook and Bishop v Rook

Introduction

In contrast to most other endings without pawns, rook and bishop against rook frequently arises in tournament play. Most positions are drawn; but they require accurate defence especially against a knowledgable opponent.

When Professor Thompson's database was set loose on this ending, it transpired that unfortunately some positions take more than 50 moves to win; and in fact the maximum is 59. In an act of bureaucratic lunacy, FIDE then decreed that "White" should have 100 moves. This was exceedingly unpleasant for the defender and led to a high percentage of wins. Indeed I remember at 3 or 4 am on the last night of the Dubai Olympiad in 1986, coming back into the playing hall to find two different victims trying to defend, albeit against different coloured bishops: by dawn both had lost.

Now we have passed back via 75 (which was in force for a year or so) to 50 moves. And a competent defender ought to be able to last this fairly easily. Indeed with the return of sanity to the rules, we may well see fewer of these endings in practice since potential torturers will eschew what ought definitely to be drawn, in favour of some less technical winning attempt.

RBR 1

+W

Theoretical Positions

Philidor 1747

This is the fundamental winning position. With the enemy king cut off on the back rank in opposition to his king, the attacker wins on every file except for some cases on the b- or g-files.

1 ♖f8+ ♖e8
2 ♖f7 ♖e2!
3 ♖h7

This waiting move forces the black rook to a worse square. The sixth rank is worst of all so first he tries the eighth.

3 ... ♖e1
4 ♖b7 ♖c1

4 ... ♔c8 leads to a typical winning sequence: 5 ♖a7 ♖b1 6 ♖h7 ♔b8 7 ♖h8+ ♔a7 8 ♖a8+ ♔b6 9 ♖b8+ (cf diag 2).

5 ♗b3!

By controlling d1 White forces the enemy rook to the sixth rank.

5 ... ♖c3

5 ... ♔c8 loses somewhat faster: 6 ♖b4 ♔d8 7 ♖g4 ♖e1 8 ♗a4! ♔c8 9 ♗c6 ♔b8 10 ♖a4 ♖d1+ 11 ♗d5. After 5 ... ♖c3 White returns his bishop to d5 with tempo after which the rook on the sixth rank is dominated - both b3 and f3 are unavailable.

6 ♗e6! ♖d3+
7 ♗d5 ♖c3

And with the black rook embarrassed it is possible to get the white rook to b4 with tempo.

8 ♖d7+ ♔c8

If 8 ... ♔e8 9 ♖g7 wins at once.

9 ♖h7 ♔b8
10 ♖b7+ ♔c8
11 ♖b4! ♔d8

Or 11 ... ♖d3 12 ♖a4.

12 ♗c4!

And mate follows.

Rook and Bishop v Rook ♖♗ V ♜

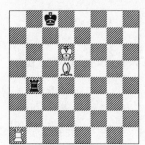

RBR
2
A typical combination
A very similar position arose in the note starting 4 ... ♔c8 in the Philidor position (diag 1). White wins since when the black king flees it is hampered by the edge of the board.
    1   ♖a8+

+ W

White cannot win instantly since the rook is well placed on b4. But it is easy to shift the rook - a waiting move e.g. 1 ♖a2 or 1 ♖a3 would be as good. But not 1 ♖h1? ♔b8 2

♖h8+?? (2 ♖a1+-) 2 ... ♔a7 after which the position is drawn in view of 3 ♔c5 ♖b5+!.
    1   ...   ♖b8
    2   ♖a4!   ♖b6+
Or 2 ... ♖b1 3 ♖h4 ♔b8 4 ♖h8+ etc.
    3   ♗c6   ♖b1
    4   ♖h4   ♔b8
If 4 ... ♖d1+ 5 ♗d5 ♔b8 6 ♖a4.
    5   ♖h8+   ♔a7
    6   ♖a8+   ♔b6
    7   ♖b8+ winning

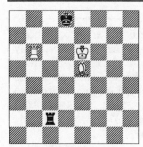

RBR
3
Szen
In contrast to the previous examples, this is a well-known drawing position since the black king has enough space to run to on the queenside.
    1   ♖b8+   ♔c8
    2   ♖b7
2 ♗f6+ ♔c7 3 ♗e5+ ♔d8 achieves nothing.
    2   ...   ♖c2

= W

2 ... ♖c6+ 3 ♗d6 ♖c1 is just as simple: 4 ♖b2 ♖e1+ 5 ♔e5 ♖c1=. And now if 3 ♖h7 ♔c8 (or 3 ... ♖c6+ 4.♗d6 ♔c8=) 4 ♖h8+ ♔b7 5 ♖b8+ either 5 ... ♔a6 or 5 ... ♔a7 is quite sufficient. So White should per-

haps try something more 'sneaky' but the draw is well within bounds, e.g.
    3   ♖b6   ♖c1
    4   ♖b2   ♖c4?!
4 ... ♖c6+ 5 ♔d6 ♖c1 is simpler.
    5   ♔d6   ♔e8
5 ... ♔c8 also draws and if 6 ♔e7 ♖b4!= is the only move but good enough.
    6   ♖f2   ♖a4!
By now 6 ... ♖b4 is the only other move to draw.
    7   ♔e6   ♖a7!
The only move.
    8   ♗d6   ♖e7+!=

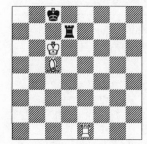

RBR
4
Lolli 1763
The play is similar to the Philidor position but the proximity of the a-file makes for differences.
    1   ♖e8+   ♖d8
    2   ♖e7
A.
    2   ...   ♖d2

+ W

2 ... ♖h8? loses quickly to 3 ♗d6 ♔d8 4 ♖a7 ♔e8 5 ♖a8+ but 2 ... ♖g8 is a reasonable defence - see B. below.
    3   ♖h7   ♖d1

    4   ♖a7   ♖b1
    5   ♗a3!
This is like 5 ♗b3! in the Philidor position of rook and bishop v rook above.
    5   ...   ♖b3
If 5 ... ♔b8 6 ♖e7 ♔a8 7 ♖e5! (not 7 ♗c5? ♖b7! when 8 ♖e8+! is the only move but it still takes 28 more to win!) 7 ... ♖b7 8 ♗f5! (zugzwang) and Black loses quickly, viz: 8 ... ♖h7 (if 8 ... ♖b1 9 ♖a5+ ♔b8 10 ♗d6+; or 8 ... ♔b8 9 ♖f8+

♔a7 10 ♗c5+) 9 ♖f8+ ♔a7
10 ♗c5+.

	6	♘d6	♜c3+
	7	♗c5	♜b3
	8	♖c7+	♔b8
	9	♖h7	♔a8
	10	♖h4	

and wins

B.

| | 2 | ... | ♜g8 |
| | 3 | ♗d6! | |

3 ♖a7 is slightly slower:
a) 3 ... ♔b8 4 ♖b7+ ♔a8 5
♗d6 ♜c8+ 6 ♗c7 ♜f8 7 ♖b1
♜f6+ 8 ♗d6 ♜f7 9 ♖e1 ♜g7

10 ♖e8+ ♔a7 11 ♗c5+.

| | 3 | ... | ♔d8 |
| | 4 | ♖e6! | |

The only move to win. If 4
♖e1 ♜g7=.

| | 4 | ... | ♜h8 |

4 ... ♔c8 5 ♖e1 ♔d8 6 ♗c7+
♔c8 7 ♖a1.

	5	♗e5	♜f8
	6	♗c3	♜g8
	7	♗f6+	♔c8
	8	♖e1	♜f8
	9	♗g7	♜g8
	10	♖a1	♔b8
	11	♗e5+ and wins	

RBR 5 *von Lasa 1843* **+ W**

It turns out that because of stalemate defences White cannot win straightforwardly. Instead he must force transposition to Lolli's position (diag 4) above.

  1   ♖e1!

If 1 ♖c8+? ♔b8 2 ♖c1 (2 ♖c7 loses time to 2 ... ♜b7! 3 ♖c8+ ♔b8 4 ♖c6!) 2 ... ♜e8 3 ♖c6 ♜f8 (not 3 ... ♔b8? 4 ♗b4 ♔a8 5 ♗d6 ♜d8 6 ♔b6 ♜g8 7 ♖c4) and White cannot arrange to get his bishop to d6 in view of a stalemate defence, viz. 4 ♗b4 ♜b8! and it still takes 26 moves to win since 5

♗d6?? draws after 5 ... ♜b6+!. Instead, he can belatedly transpose back into the main line with 4 ♖e6 ♜g8 5 ♗c3 ♜c8 6 ♗f6 (6 ♗e5?? ♜c6+!) 6 ... ♜b8 7 ♗d4 ♜c8 8 ♗c3 ♜b8 9 ♖e4 ♜b7 10 ♗a5 ♜b1 11 ♖e6 etc.

	1	...	♜b1
	2	♖e6	♜b2
	3	♖h6	♜b1
	4	♗b6	♜a1+
	5	♔b5	♔b7
	6	♖h7+	♔c8
	7	♔c6	♜c1+
	8	♗c5	♜d1

White has transposed into Lolli's position.

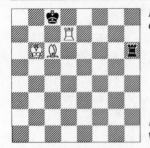

RBR 6 = W

Before turning to the extremely difficult case of the drawn "pseudo-Philidor" position on the b-file, we shall examine some less complex positions.

Kling and Kuiper 1846
White is unable to set up the Philidor position, e.g.

  1   ♖g7   ♔d8!?

He could equally play 1 ...
♜d6 avoiding line B below -

and White could have played 1 ♖e7 to force 1 ... ♜d6.

A.

	2	♖d7+	♔c8
	3	♖e7	♜d6
	4	♖e3	♜d1
	5	♖e2	♜b1+!?

This is still quite okay; but he could also pass with 5 ... ♜d3.

| | 6 | ♔c5 | ♜d1!= |

Or 6 ... ♔c7/♔b8/♜f1 or

Rook and Bishop v Rook ♖♗ V ♜

♖g1=). But not 6 ... ♜c1+? 7 ♔d6 and White reaches the Philidor position.

B.

    2 ♔c5   ♜h5+

Lots of other moves also draw here (2 ... ♔c8 and ♜h4/

h3/h2/f6/e6/even h8!).

    3 ♔b6

But now there is absolutely no latitude. The only drawing move is:

    3 ...   ♜h6!

For instance, if 3 ... ♜h2? we reach diag 7.

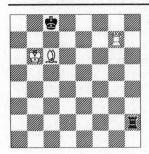

RBR 7

    1 ♖d7+   ♔c8
    2 ♖d6!

The only move. Now:

A.

    2 ...   ♜b2+
    3 ♗b5   ♜b1
    4 ♖d2

Zugzwang.

    4 ...   ♜b4

Or 3 ... ♜b3 4 ♖e2.

    5 ♖c2+   ♔b8
    6 ♖h2 and wins

B.

    2 ...   ♜h8

White can now win by manoeuvring to get his rook to the seventh rank against

Black's king on b8 and rook on the back rank. The only stipulation is that the black rook should not be on f8 or c8. If it is on d8, then the king cannot run. Whilst on g8 or h8 it falls victim to the skewer ♖a7-a8+. However if it is on f8 then 1 ... ♔c8 is sufficient to draw. And with the rook on c8, 1 ... ♜c7! holds.

    3 ♗e4   ♔b8
    4 ♗f5   ♜f8
    5 ♖e6   ♜d8
    6 ♖f6   ♜e8
    7 ♖f7   ♔a8
    8 ♗e4+   ♔b8
    9 ♗c6 etc.

RBR 8

Centurini 1867

If diag 6 is moved left one file (i.e. ♔c6 ♗d6 ♖e7 v ♔d8 ♜h6) then it is still a draw. But if we go two files over then the black rook runs out of space. In diag 8, Black, having only one square for his rook on the eighth rank, quickly falls into zugzwang.

    1 ♖f1   ♜g6
    2 ♖f2   ♜h6

    3 ♖a2!   ♔f8
    4 ♖g2!

Forcing the rook onto the back rank.

    4 ...   ♜h8
    5 ♔d7   ♜h7+
    6 ♔d8   ♜h8

If 6 ... ♜g7 7 ♖f2+; whilst the "50 percenter" 6 ... ♜d7+ fails to 7 ♗xd7!.

    7 ♖g1   ♜h2
    8 ♖g8 mate

Rook and Bishop v Rook

RBR
9

= W

RBR
9a

= W

Lolli 1763

"The pseudo-Philidor position"

This position was originally examined by Lolli. But from the analysis which follows its obvious that only with a database can one really hope to make sense of it. Black is able to hold the draw against all winning attempts; but in the play which starts here and continues in diag 10 below he has to find up to 15 'only' moves in a row!

1	♖d8+	♖c8
2	♖d7	♖c2
3	♖f7	

In play analogous to that in the Philidor position proper, White forces the enemy rook to an inconvenient square. But because of the lack of a file to the left of the a-file, he is unable to carry out the winning manoeuvre in diags 1 and 4 and must turn to other ideas.

3	...	♖c3
4	♗a4	♖c1
5	♗c6	♖b1+
6	♔c5	♖b2!!

The database shows that this is the only drawing move:

a) 6 ... ♖c1+?, 6 ... ♖a1 and 6 ... ♖e1 all lead to the Philidor position, e.g. 6 ... ♖c1+ 7 ♔d6 ♖g1 8 ♗e4 ♖d1+ 9 ♗d5 etc;

b) So does 6 ... ♔c8? though in fact this loses several moves faster since after 7 ♔d6 ♖d1+ 8 ♗d5 Black is immediately forced into 8 ... ♔b8 9 ♖b7+ ♔c8 10 ♖a7 etc. as in diag 2;

c) The remaining moves are much more complicated. They lose because Black is in the very long term unable to prevent White from setting up the Philidor position. But the database shows that they take: 6 ... ♖g1 47 moves, 6 ... ♖d1 45 moves and 6 ... ♖b3 45 moves respectively!

Rather than get involved in the incredibly complex lines which clearly belong later under the section on database positions, I will deal only with: 6 ... ♖b3? 7 ♗d5 and now after 7 ... ♖g3! 8 ♗e4 and White can win in 44 more moves; but the attempt to follow the drawing line below with 7 ... ♖h3? loses immediately to 8 ♔b6! ♔c8 9 ♗e6+.

| 7 | ♗d5 | |

Or 7 ♔d6 ♖h2! (the only move).

7	...	♖h2
8	♖b7+	♔c8
9	♖e7	♔b8 (9a)

and now:

A.

| 10 | ♔b6 | |

10 ♔d6 ♖h6+! makes life easy for Black.

| 10 | ... | ♖c2 |

This and all of the following black moves in this variation are unique.

| 11 | ♗b3 | |

Not 11 ♗e4 ♖c7!.

11	...	♖c1
12	♖d7	♔c8
13	♖d2	♖b1
14	♖d3	♖b2
15	♔c6	♖b1
16	♗e6+	♔b8
17	♖d8+	♔a7
18	♖d7+	♔b8

Not 18 ... ♔a8? 19 ♗d5 ♔b8 20 ♔d6 etc., as in the Philidor position.

19	♗d5	♖c1+
20	♔d6	♖c7!=

B.

| 10 | ♔c6 | |

This also poses extremely difficult defensive problems. Except where indicated otherwise, all of Black's moves in the main line of the following variation are forced:

  10 ...   ♖h6+
  11 ♗e6   ♖h1!

The best alternative is 11 ... ♖h2 but this loses in 43!

  12 ♖b7   ♔a8
  13 ♖b2

If 13 ♖g7 Black can choose between 13 ... ♖h6 utilising the fact that the rook has moved from e7: 14 ♖e7 ♖h1 or 14 ... ♖h2=; and 13 ... ♔b8 14 ♗f5 ♖h6+ 15 ♗g6 ♖h3=.

  13 ...   ♖c1+

Also 13 ... ♔a7 and 13 ... ♖a1 draw.

  14 ♔b6   ♔b8
  15 ♗f5   ♖c4
  16 ♖b5   ♖h4

Also 16 ... ♖a4.

  17 ♔c6+   ♔a7

Or 17 ... ♔a8=.

  18 ♗d3   ♖f4
  19 ♖b7+   ♔a8
  20 ♖g7   ♔b8
  21 ♖g8+   ♔a7
  22 ♖g6   ♖f7

Here ♖h4, d4, and f8 also draw.

  23 ♗e4   ♖c7+!=

But 23 ... ♖b7/♖f8 are also okay.

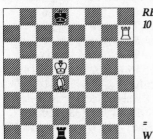

RBR 10

=
W

Important drawing methods

Cochrane

When the defender has time, this is one of the best set-ups to aim for. White cannot of course play 1 ♔d6 in view of 1 ... ♖xd4+. To untangle he must move his king to one side in which case Black runs in the opposite direction, e.g. 1 ♔c5 ♔e8 or 1 ♔e5 ♔c8. Of course if 1 ♖h4 ♔d7! is 'best'.

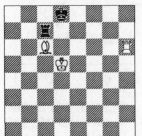

RBR 11

=
W

The second rank defence

This type of position looks very alarming but in fact Black defends without too much trouble. The main point is the stalemate defence:

  1 ♔d6   ♖d7+!

and now if:

  2 ♔e6!?   ♖e7+

... is not forced but is consistent with his defensive idea. So White must try to reset more favourably, e.g.

  3 ♔d6   ♖d7+
  4 ♔c5   ♖g7

Alternatively:

a) Not 4 ... ♖c7?? 5 ♖h8+ ♔e7 6 ♔b6+-;

b) 4 ... ♖e7!? is playable but after 5 ♔b6 ♖g7 6 ♖e6 ♖g8 (the only move) Black can still defend but has had to change defences.

  5 ♖e6   ♖e7
  6 ♖d6+   ♔c7
  7 ♖h6   ♖e5+
  8 ♗d5   ♖e7
  9 ♖a6   ♔d8
  10 ♖a8+   ♔c7=

In the final position if it were Black's move then either 1 ... ♔d7 or 1 ... ♖d7 would defend.

Rook and Bishop v Rook

RBR 12

+ W

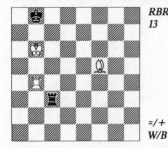

RBR 13

=/+
W/B

Database Positions

It has been shown that the longest win is 59 moves. Moreover, there are 17 fundamentally different positions of mutual zugzwang.

The very long wins appear to me to arise from the fact that the extremely unfavourable diags 9 and 10 are drawn albeit only with absolutely perfect defence. There are various positions, more suitable for machines than people, in which "White" cannot immediately force the Philidor position: but on the other hand, "Black" cannot reach a proper defensive set-up - not even one as unfavourable as diags 9-10. In this case a very lengthy duel ensues.

A longest win - 59 moves found by Thompson

This is one example of a longest win (numbers in brackets indicate how many moves it is to the win):

1   Bf5! (58)
1   ...   Rh4!

If 1 ... Rg7? (24), best play goes 2 Kc6 Rg3 3 Ra2+ Kb8 4 Be4 Rg7 5 Rf2 Rc7+ 6 Kd6 Rc8 7 Ra2 Rd8+ 8 Kc6

(17) and White forces the Philidor position.

2   Bd3!

Luring the black rook to the f-file. But not 2 Be4+? Kb8 3 Rb2 Ka7 4 Bd5 Rh3!=.

2   ...   Rf4
3   Be4+ (56)
3   ...   Ka7!

If 3 ... Kb8? (18) White succeeds in forcing the Philidor position immediately, viz. 4 Rb2 Ka7 5 Bd5 Rf6 6 Kc5 Rg6 7 Rb1 Rh6 8 Rb7+ Ka6 9 Rb8 (12) etc.

4   Bc6   Rg4

But not 4 ... Rf6+? (7!) 5 Kc7 Rf7+ 6 Bd7 Rf6 7 Be6! Ka6 8 Re5 (3) and wins.

5   Kc7   Rg7+
6   Bd7   Rg6
7   Be6   Rg7+
8   Kc6   Rg1
9   Ra2+   Kb8
10   Rb2+   Ka8! (49)

If 10 ... Ka7? (39) 11 Rb7+ (38) when Black must defend with 11 ... Ka8! (38) and not 11 ... Ka6? (16) 12 Bc4+ Ka5 13 Kc5 (14) etc.

11   Kb6   Rc1
12   Bf5   Rc3
13   Rb1   Kb8
14   Rb4! (45)

Zhitogorsky 1843

Mutual zugzwang! We have reached a position which was first investigated by L. Zhitogorsky in 1843. It is in fact mutual zugzwang. The reason for this is that Black has got to abandon the c-file after which White can get in Bd7. But this is only important with the rook on the fourth rank to support the cut Bc4 if necessary.

14   ...   Ra3

15   Bd7   Ra2! (44)

Instead:

a) if 15 ... Rc3? (7!) 16 Re4 Rb3+ 17 Bb5 Rc3 18 Bc4 Kc8 19 Rd4 (3) and wins; and

b) 15 ... Ra1? (16) is too far away from the king and therefore allows 16 Kc6+! (15) Ka7 17 Kc7 Ka6 18 Rb6+ Ka5 19 Rb5 Ka6 20 Rc5 (11) etc.

16   Rh4!

Now 16 Kc6+? Ka7 leads to a draw since after 19 Rb5+ as in b) above Black can play

Rook and Bishop v Rook

RBR
13a

=/+
W/B

19 ... ♔a4!.

16	...	♖b2+
17	♗b5	♖c2
18	♗c4	♖b2+
19	♔c6	♖c2
20	♖h8+	♔a7
21	♖h7+	♔b8
22	♖b7+	♔a8 (37)

Not 22 ... ♔c8? (17) 23 ♖b4 ♔d8 (23 ... ♖d2 24 ♗d5 ♔d8 25 ♔d6) 24 ♔d6 ♖d2+ 25 ♗d5 etc.

23	♖b4	♖g2!

23 ... ♖h2? (13) loses much quicker because after White's next move he cannot go to h7: 24 ♗d3! ♖f2 (24 ... ♖h3? 25 ♔c7!) 25 ♗e4 ♔a7 26 ♖b7+ ♔a6 (26 ... ♔a8 27 ♖b1 ♔a7 28 ♔c5 ♖a2 29 ♖b7+ ♔a6 30 ♖b8 ♖a5+ 31 ♔c6 ♔a7 32 ♖b7+ ♔a8 33 ♖e7 ♔b8 34 ♔b6) 27 ♗d3+ ♔a5 28 ♔c5 ♔a4 29 ♗c4 ♔a3 30 ♖b3+ ♔a4 31 ♖c3 ♖f5+ 32 ♗d5 ♖h5 33 ♖e3 ♖g5 34 ♖e7 ♔a3 35 ♖e2.

24	♗d3	♖g3
25	♖d4	♖f3
26	♗c4!	

26 ♗e4? ♖f6+ 27 ♔c7+ ♔a7=.

26	...	♖h3

Not 26 ... ♖f6+ 27 ♔c7.

27	♖d8+	♔a7
28	♗d5	♖h2
29	♖d7+!	♔b8
30	♖b7+	♔a8!

30 ... ♔c8? (16) 31 ♗e6+ ♔d8 32 ♔d6 ♖d2+ 33 ♗d5 etc.

31	♖b1!	

31 ♖b3? ♖c2+ 32 ♔b6+ ♔b8 33 ♗e6 ♖c1 34 ♗f5 ♖c4 35 ♖b2 ♖h4!= (the only move).

31	...	♖c2+
32	♔b6+	♔b8
33	♗e6!	*(13a)*

This is another zugzwang position!

White to move could only draw after (numbering from diag 15) 1 ♖b4 ♖c1 (only move) 2 ♖b3 ♖a1 or 2 ... ♖h1=. But Black to move must leave the c-file in unfavourable circumstances:

33	...	♖d2! (26)

Alternatively:

a) 33 ... ♖c7? 34 ♔a6+ ♔a8 35 ♗d5+;

b) 33 ... ♖c3? 34 ♖d1;

c) if 33 ... ♖h2? - 33 ... ♖g2 is even worse - 34 ♖c1! and 'relatively best' is 34 ... ♖h8 (6) since if 34 ... ♖b1+ 35 ♔a6! wins instantly; but

d) 33 ... ♖e2 (26) 34 ♔c6+ ♔a7 35 ♖a1+ ♔b8 36 ♗d5 ♖h2 37 ♖b1+ ♔a7 38 ♗e4 ♖h6+ 39 ♔c5 transposes back into the main line.

34	♔c6+	♔a7
35	♖a1+	♔b8
36	♗d5	♖h2
37	♖b1+	♔a7
38	♗e4	♖h6+ (21)

38 ... ♖h4? (9) 39 ♖a1+ ♔b8 40 ♖a4! ♖h3 41 ♔d6 (6) etc.

39	♔c5	♖b6!
40	♖h1	♖a6
41	♖h8	

The only move.

41	...	♖a5+
42	♔c6	♖g5
43	♖h7+ (16)	
43	...	♔a6

43 ... ♔b8? (7) 44 ♔b6 ♔c8 45 ♗c6 ♔d8 46 ♖d7+ ♔c8 47 ♖e7.

44	♗d5	

The only move.

44	...	♔a5
45	♔c5	♖g6 (14)

And the rest is simply the Philidor position: 46 ♖h2 ♖g4 47 ♖b2 ♖h4 48 ♖b7 ♖h6 49 ♗f7 ♖f6 50 ♗c4 ♖f5+ 51 ♗d5 ♖f6 52 ♖b5+ ♔a6 53 ♖b2

Rook and Bishop v Rook ♖ ♗ V ♜

♚a7 54 ♖b7+ ♚a6 55 ♖e7 ♚a5 56 ♗e6 ♚a6 57 ♗c4+   ♚a5 58 ♖a7+ ♖a6 59 ♖xa6 mate.

RBR 15

= W

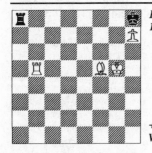

RBR 15a

=/+ W/B

H Olafsson - Petursson
Akureyri 1988

My final example is from the era of 100 moves and is an extremely grimmer affair. Petursson kept pressing Helgi Olafsson for 86 moves before giving up. In fact, in an exemplary defensive display Helgi kept a drawn position at all times except for one slip on move 98.

Partly to remind the reader of the full horror of the 100 move rule and partly to avoid renumbering so many moves, I am retaining the original move numbers: 75 ♖b2 ♖xe6+ 76 ♔f2 ♗c4 77 ♖d2 ♔e4 78 ♖b2 ♖f6+ 79 ♔e1 ♖f1+ 80 ♔d2 ♔d4 81 ♖c2 ♖g1 82 ♖b2 ♖h1 83 ♖c2 ♗b3 84 ♖b2 ♖h3 85 ♔c1 ♔c4 86 ♖f2 ♖d3 87 ♖d2 ♖c3+ 88

♔b2 ♔b4 89 ♖d4+ ♗c4 90 ♖d2 ♗d3 91 ♖f2 ♔e4 92 ♖e2 ♗d5 93 ♖c2 ♖a3 94 ♖d2 ♗c4 95 ♖c2 ♔d3 96 ♖f2 ♖a8 97 ♖d2 ♔c4 *(14a)*

In this version of the second rank defence, White must be extremely careful. Here the only move to draw was 98 ♖f2! so that if 98 ... ♖b8+ he can run with 99 ♔c1!. (In fact with Black to move diag 14a would be winning in 26 moves starting with 1 ... ♖b8+.)

98 ♔c1? ♔d4?

After 98 ... ♖a1+! 99 ♔b2 ♖h1 100 ♖g2 (or 100 ♔a3 ♔c3) 100 ... ♖b1+ 101 ♔a2 ♔c3 (Black forces Philidor's position).

After the text Margeir tried in vain to win for another 62 moves.

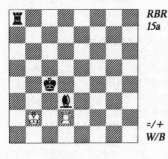

RBR 15

+ W

Endings with pawns

Normally, if the attacker has pawns as well then he should win quite easily. But there are some exceptional positions.

Of course, White cannot exchange rooks due to the wrong rook's pawn. It is well known that with the pawn any further back this ending is winning, e.g. if the pawn is on h6 White wins very easily by putting his rook on e7 and bishop on f7. With the pieces like this there is no stalemate defence and the threat of ♔g6 followed by ♗e6 as soon as the black rook vacates f8, can only be averted for a couple of moves.

1	♖b7	♖g8+
2	♗g6	♖a8

3	♗f7	♖d8

Or 3 ... ♖a5+ 4 ♔f6 ♖a8 5 ♖e7 etc.

4	♖e7	♖b8
5	♔g6	♖f8
6	♖d7	♖b8
7	♗e6	

In contrast some sources claim that if the rook's pawn is on the seventh it is a draw: but in fact White can force a win as long as there is no immediate forced draw.

1 ♖c5!

Before undertaking anything else, White must take the a-file as we shall see later.

1	...	♖b8

Or:

a) 1 ... ♔g7 2 h8♕+ ♔xh8 and White wins quickly after 3 ♗e6! ♖a3 4 ♔f6 ♖f3+ 5

♘f5 ♖g3 6 ♖c4 etc;

b) 1 ... ♖e8 2 ♗a5 ♔g7 (if Black is going to allow h8♕+ then this is the best square for the rook to be on but he still loses with best play in 26 moves – with the rook on f8 it would be 24 (cf diags 4-5) viz. 3 h8♕+ ♔xh8 4 ♔h6 ♖f8 5 ♖a6 ♔g8 6 ♖b6 ♖f8 7 ♖d6 ♖g8 8 ♗e4 ♖f8 9 ♗f3 ♖g8 10 ♖d4 ♖g7 11 ♗h5 and now as in diag 5: 11 ... ♖g3 12 ♖d6 ♖g2 13 ♗g6 ♖h2+ 14 ♔g5 ♔g7 15 ♖d7+ ♔f8 16 ♔f6 etc.

	2	♖a5!	♖e8
	3	♔f6	♖f8+
	4	♔g6	♖f6+

4 ... ♖e8 5 ♔g5 is one move quicker.

	5	♔g5	♖f8
	6	♗e6	♖e8

6 ... ♔xh7 leads to a win in 23: 7 ♖a7+ ♔h8 8 ♗f7 ♔g7 9 ♗g6+ ♔h8 10 ♖h7+ ♔g8 11 ♖e7 ♖d8 12 ♗f5 ♔f8 13 ♔f6 with the Philidor position etc.

	7	♔f6	♖f8+
	8	♔e7!	

8 ♗f7? is wrong because although White can force Black to take the h-pawn the resulting ending is only drawn – White needs the bishop on e6 after ... ♔xh7, viz. 8 ... ♖b8 9 ♖g5? ♖b2 10 ♖g8+ (10 ♗e6 ♖f2+ 11 ♗f5 ♖g2!) 10 ... ♔xh7=.

	8	...	♖f1

Or 8 ... ♖b8 9 ♖a1 (zugzwang) 9 ... ♖b7+ 10 ♔f6 ♖b8 11 ♖g1 ♖b2 12 ♖g8+ ♔xh7 13 ♖a8 and wins.

	9	♗f5	♖e1+
	10	♔d7!	

Not 10 ♔f7? ♖a1! 11 ♖b5 ♖b1 12 ♖e5 ♖e1 13 ♗e4 ♖f1+ and the battle continues.

	10	...	♖d1+
	11	♔c7	♖c1+
	12	♔b7 and wins.	

But if the rook were on the b-file then there would be nowhere to hide without blocking the rook.

RBR *Finegold - Illescas,*
16 *Amsterdam OHRA B 1989*
Although Black has only one pawn for the bishop, his exceptionally solid structure and the lack of pawn breaks due to the doubled g-pawns are sufficient to draw. White had already tried to do something with the rook and bishop for about 20 moves. And now he finally brought in the king.

	1	♗f4	♖a3+
	2	♔e4	♖a2
	3	g3	♖e2+
	4	♔d5	♖e8
	5	♖c4	♖e7
	6	♔d6	♖e1
	7	♖c7	♖e2
	8	♖e7	♖xe7!
	9	♔xe7	f5
	10	♔e6	fxg4
	11	♗e5	h5
	12	♗f4	

And a draw was agreed in view of 12 ... h4! 13 gxh4 ♔h5 14 ♗g3 g5!.

Queen v Pawn(s)

♛ V ♟(♟)

Queen v One Pawn

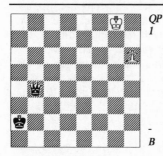

QP 1 – B

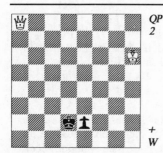

QP 2 + W

QP 2a + W

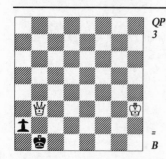

QP 3 = B

Queen against pawn is normally an easy win. Exceptions can arise when the pawn reaches the seventh rank just a square away from promotion, the other king being distant or the other king and queen obstructing each other.

Stalemate possibilities enable the side with either an a-pawn, a c-pawn, an f-pawn or an h-pawn sometimes to deny the side with a queen a win.

For the queen to win against a b-, d-, e- or g-pawn poised on the seventh there are three steps: first with the aid of checks, attacks and pins in the vicinity of the pawn, force the black king onto the promotion square and thus temporarily prevent the pawn's advance;

Second, use the breathing space gained to bring the other king one square nearer; repeat this until the king is close enough to help to win the pawn or to checkmate.

Step one:

1	♕d5+	♔c2
2	♕c4+	♔d2
3	♕d4+	♔c2
4	♕e3	♔d1
5	♕d3+	♔e1

Endings of king and queen versus king and either a- or h-pawn can be complicated by stalemate factors.

In diag 3 after:

Black wins from diag 1 with a series of encroaching moves:

1	...	♕g4+
2	♔h8	♕f5!?

Hoping for 3 h7 ♕f8 mate!

3	♔g7	♕g5+
4	♔h7	

... and now the useful waiting move ...

4	...	♔b3
5	♔h8	♕xh6+

After 6 ♔g8 Black can force mate in another six moves.

Step two:

6	♔g5	♔f2

Repeat step one:

7	♕d2	♔f1
8	♕f4+	♔g2
9	♕e3	♔f1
10	♕f3	♔e1

Repeat step two:

11	♔f4	♔d2	(2a)

Again as in step one:

12	♕f2	♔d1
13	♕d4+	♔c2
14	♕e3	♔d1
15	♕d3+	♔e1

Step two:

16	♔f3 and wins

The pawn is lost and mate is only two further moves away.

It is not easy to shorten this procedure without help from the opponent.

1	...	♔a1!

... the black king is in a stalemate; White needs to release this and has no time to bring the king nearer.

QP 4

= B

After:

| | 1 | ... | ♚a1! |
| | 2 | ♛xc2 | stalemate |

The black king cannot be forced in "front" of the pawn; the white queen has to be used to stop promotion, e.g. 2 ♛c3+; there is no time to bring the white king nearer.

Diagram 4a

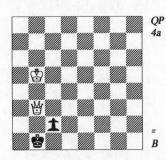

QP 4a

= B

In diag 4, the white king was way out of action. In contrast, here it is close at hand and while Black can still draw he

must play accurately:

1	...	♚a1
2	♛e3	♚b2
3	♛e2	

Of course if 3 ♚d2 ♚b1 is forced but now Black must avoid the natural-looking 3 ... ♚b1 4 ♚b4 c1♛ 5 ♚b3 and mates.

Instead Black must play:

| 3 | ... | ♚a1! |
| 4 | ♚b4 | |

Or 4 ♚d2 ♚b1!.

| 4 | ... | c1♛= |

QP 5

= B

Lolli 1763
This is an early published example of the complexities of the a-/h-pawn battle.

| | 1 | ... | ♚c2! |

1 ... ♚a1?? loses to the freak line 2 ♚b6! ♚b1 3 ♚c5+ (or 3 ♚a5+) bringing the king near enough to set up mating threats - see diag 5a.

2	♛a6	♚b2
3	♛b5+	♚c2
4	♛a4+	♚b2
5	♛b4+	♚c2
6	♛a3	♚b1
7	♛b3+	♚a1!

And the stalemate idea enables Black to hold the draw.

Diagram 5a

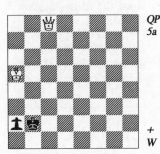

QP 5a

+ W

With his king close enough to come to b3, White wins by gradually bringing the queen so as to check along the rank from d2, forcing the black

king to b1 and then allowing the a-pawn to be promoted. Play could continue 1 ♛b7+ ♚c2 2 ♛g2+ ♚b1 3 ♛f1+ ♚b2 4 ♛e2+ ♚b1 5 ♛d1+ ♚b2 6 ♛d2+ ♚b1 7 ♚b4 a1♛ 8 ♚b3 and mates.

If we return to diag 5, but place the king on e4, we find it is then near enough to help give mate:

Diagram 5b

Here the white king is near enough to help mating after:

1	...	♚c2
2	♛c7+	♚b2
3	♛b6+	♚c2
4	♛c5+	♚b2
5	♛f2+	♚b1

5 ... ♚b3 6 ♛f6 and 7 ♛a1 is one way to win.

| 6 | ♚d3 | a1♛ |
| 7 | ♛c2 | mate |

Queen v Pawn(s)

♛ V ♟(♟)

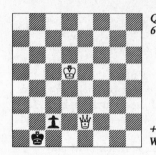

QP 6

+ W

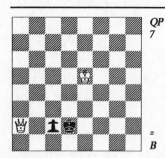

QP 7

= B

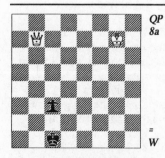

QP 8a

= W

QP 9

= W

Provided the white king can be brought to b3, directly opposite the black king on the move immediately after the pawn is queened at c1, this type of king and queen against king and pawn position can be won. This is a lesson learnt from diag 5.

This condition can be fulfilled if the white king is initially on a5, b5, c5, d5 or nearer to b3.

Watch that the pawn cannot be promoted to a knight that forks.

From the diagram play goes:

 1 ♔c4 c1♛+

If 1 ... ♔a1 of course not 2 ♔b3?? c1♘+ but White can win easily with 2 ♛d2 ♔b2 3 ♔b4 ♔b1 4 ♔b3 etc.

 2 ♔b3 and wins

The white king on e5 is one square too far away from the action. If it were on either e4 or d5 then White would be winning. However, here Black to move can draw.

 1 ... ♔c3!

And not 1 ... ♔d1? 2 ♔d4 c1♛ 3 ♔d3 and wins.

 2 ♛a3+ ♔d2
 3 ♛b2
 3 ... ♔d1

Now this is possible since after 4 ♔d4 c1♛ White would have no time for 5 ♔d3.

 4 ♛d4+ ♔c1

And, for example:

 5 ♔d5 ♔b1
 6 ♛d3 ♔b2
 7 ♛d2 ♔b1
 8 ♛b4+ ♔a2
 9 ♛c3 ♔b1
 10 ♛b3+ ♔a1!=

cf diag 4.

If the black king is badly placed there may be winning chances even with the white king on e5, cf diag KP16 - a superb study by Grigoriev.

Lemaire 1973

Normally with the pawn two squares away from queening White would win easily. For example if we started with the king on f7 *(8)* the process could go 1 ♛h1+ ♔b2 2 ♛h8! ♔b3 3 ♛h6 ♔b2 4 ♛f6 ♔b3 5 ♛f4 ♔b2 6 ♛b4+ etc.

However, with the king on g7, there is no way for White to activate the queen successfully since the a1-h8 diagonal is blocked, i.e.

 1 ♛h1+ ♔b2
 2 ♛b7+ ♔c1! etc.

If instead 1 ♔f6 c2 2 ♔e5 ♔d2= (cf diag 7).

Troitsky 1935

An example of the possible obstruction between the black king and queen.

 1 ♔e6! ♔f4+
1 ... ♔d4+ 2 ♔d7=.
 2 ♔f7=

394

Queen v Pawn(s)

♕ v ♟(♟)

Queen v More Pawns

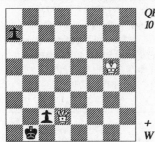

QP 10

+
W

Berger 1889, based on Walker 1841

1	♕b4+	♚a2
2	♕c3	♚b1
3	♕b3+	♚c1

If 3 ... ♚a1 4 ♕xc2 and mates in no more than five moves by 5 ♕c1.

4	♚f4	a5
5	♚e3	a4
6	♕a3+	♚d1

Or 6 ... ♚b1 7 ♚d2.

7	♕xa4	and wins

QP 11

=
W

Grigoriev 1932, based on Berger 1889

1	♕b4+	♚c1!!

Berger analysed 1 ... ♚a2 2 ♕c3 ♚b1 3 ♕b3+ ♚c1 4 ♚g5 a5 5 ♚f4 a4 6 ♕b4 a3 7 ♚e3 a2 8 ♕c3 ♚b1 9 ♚d2 as winning.

2	♚g5	a5
3	♕b6	♚d2
4	♕d4+	♚c1
5	♕a1+	

5 ♚f4 ♚b1 6 ♕d3 ♚b2 7 ♕b5+ ♚a2 8 ♕a4+ ♚b2= as the square b4 is unavailable.

5	...	♚d2
6	♕b2	

6 ♕xa5+ ♚d1 7 ♕a4 ♚d2 8 ♕d4+ ♚c1 9 ♚f4 ♚b1 10 ♕d3 ♚b2 11 ♕d2 ♚b1 (not 11 ... ♚a1 12 ♕c1+) 12 ♕d3 ♚a1 drawing.

6	...	♚d1=

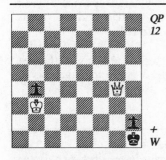

QP 12

+
W

Sometimes it is better for the defending side to have only one pawn rather than two! In diag 12 the b-pawn prevents Black from stalemating himself.

1	♕f3+	♚g1
2	♕g3+	♚h1
3	♚c4	b3
4	♕f2	b2
5	♕f1 mate	

QP 13

=
B

*J. Kossak - G. Kramer
New Jersey 1988*

60	...	♕f1+

The game went violently 60 ... ♕c5?! 61 b7 ♕c7 62 b8♕ ♕xb8 stalemate!

61	♚a7

If 61 ♚b7 ♕e4 62 a6 ♚d5 63 a7 ♕f7+ 64 ♚a6 ♕e8 65 ♚b7 ♕d7+ 66 ♚b8 ♚c6! 67 a8♕+ ♚xb6 and Black wins (Benko).

61	...	♕f2
62	♚a6	♕e2+
63	♚a7	♕e3
64	a6!	

If 64 ♚a6? ♕e5! 65 b7 ♕b8 wins.

64	...	♚e4
65	♚a8!	♕xb6
66	a7	

With a theoretical draw as

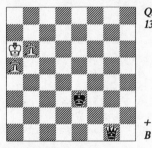

QP
13a

the black king is still too far away (Benko).

Diagram 13a
Pal Benko 1989
With the black king one square closer on e3 rather than f3 a win can be forced.

| 60 | ... | ♚d4 |
| 61 | b7 | ♛g6+ |

+
B

62	♔a7	♛f7
63	♔a8	♛d5
64	a6	♚c5
65	♔a7	♛d7
66	♔a8	♚c6!

66 ... ♚b6 67 b8♛+ ♚xa6 68 ♛d6+! ♛xd6 stalemate.

| 67 | ♔a7 | ♛b6+ |

and wins

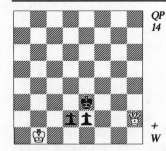

QP
14

Kling and Horwitz 1851
White wins by means of an elegant manoeuvre.

| 1 | ♛h6+ | ♚d3 |
| 2 | ♛d6+ | ♚e3 |

+
W

3	♛c5+	♚d3
4	♛c2+	♚e3
5	♛c3+	♚f2
6	♛xd2 winning

QP
15

This is a sample queen against three pawns that should help to form judgements.
Berger 1914

| 1 | ♚b2 |

Now:

1 ... f3 2 ♛b8.

1 ... g3 2 ♛f3 ♚g5 3 ♚c2/c3 g2 4 ♛f2 ♚g4 (4 ... f3 5 ♛g3+) 5 ♚d2 f3 6 ♚e3.

1 ... h2 2 ♛g2 g3 3 ♛f3 holds up the pawns and con

+
W

tinues ♚c2, ♚d2, ♚e2.

1 ... ♚g3 2 ♛h1.

1 ... ♚g5 2 ♛d8+ ♚g6 (2 ... ♚h5 3 ♛f6 f3 4 ♛f4 paralyses the pawns) 3 ♛h4 ♚f5 4 ♛h5+ and the pawns start to fall.

1 ... ♚h5 2 ♛h8+ ♚g5 (if 2 ... ♚g6 3 ♛h4 as in the last note) 3 ♛d8+ and again as in the last note.

QP
16

Dorogov and Kuznetsov 1970
A positional draw! White's king simply oscillates between c1 and c2, while if the queen

=
B

goes to the e-file, the king moves instead between d1 and d2. This is the end of a study.

Queen v Queen

Queen v Queen: No Pawns

Q 1

+ W

These occur mostly as a result of both sides queening a pawn. They should normally be a draw, but exceptions occur when there are mating possibilities, as in diags 1 and 2.

1   ♕b2+   ♔g3

2   ♕g7+   ♔h3
3   ♕h6+   ♔g2
4   ♕g5+   ♔f1
5   ♕f4+   ♔g2
6   ♕g4+   ♔h2

6 ... ♔f1 7 ♕e2+ ♔g1 8 ♕f2 mate.

7   ♔f2 and wins

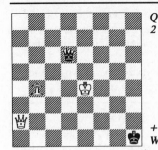

Q 2

+ W

Neumann - NN
Vienna 1887

1   ♕d5!   ♕xb4+

1 ... ♕g3 2 b5! ♕g6+ (2 ... ♔g1 3 ♕d1+ ♔f2 4 ♕d2+ ♔g1 5 ♕e3+ ♔h1 6 ♕f3+! and exchanges queens; 2 ... ♔h2 3 ♕e5; or 2 ... ♔g2 3 ♕d2+ and will exchange queens) 3 ♔f4+ ♔h2 (3 ... ♔g1 4 ♕g5+) 4 ♕e5! ♔h1! 5 ♕h5+ ♔g1 6 ♕d1+ ♔g2 7 ♕e2+ ♔g1 8 ♕e3+ ♔h1! 9 ♕f3+ etc.

1 ... ♕g6+ 2 ♔f4+! ♔h2 3 ♕e5! ♕d3 (if 3 ... ♕h6+ 4

♔f3+ wins; or 3 ... ♕c6 4 ♕e2+ ♔g1 5 ♕e1+ ♔g2 6 ♕g3+ and 7 ♕f3+ swaps queens; or 3 ... ♕f7+ 4 ♔g4+ ♔g1 5 ♕g3+) 4 b5! and Black has no good move, e.g. 4 ... ♕d2+ 5 ♔f3+ ♔h1 6 ♕e4 with a zugzwang.

2   ♔f3!   ♔h2

Or 2 ... ♕c3+ 3 ♔f2+ and mates; equally 2 ... ♕f8+ 3 ♔g3+.

3   ♕h5+   ♔g1
4   ♕g5+   ♔f1
5   ♕g2+   ♔e1
6   ♕e2 mate

Queen and Pawn v Queen

Endings with queen and a single pawn against queen arise fairly frequently in practice. Unless the defending king can get in front of the pawn, an immediate perpetual check can be forced, or we are dealing with a "rook's pawn", most positions will be winning. However, the nearer the pawn gets to the edge, the harder it will tend to be, since a more advanced pawn provides only limited shelter from checks.

In common with other endings with very limited material, this ending has been put onto a database. As a result, various positions have been discovered in which it takes more than 50 moves to advance the pawn a single square: but happily FIDE has not attempted to modify the fifty-move rule in accordance with this.

We shall deal with the material starting with centre pawns and then moving gradually out towards the "rook's file". Mostly, the pawn is already on the seventh rank: but there are a few examples in which it starts further back. And in fact, the most difficult positions to deal with are those with the pawn on the brink of queening; for then it is close to the top (or bottom) of the board and badly placed to shelter the attacking king.

General features

As in most queen endings, the attacking side has to work to avoid checks from the defender. This can be done either by hiding behind shelter - in this case his lone pawn; or by threatening to cross-check (cf diag 8). And in order to escape it is vital to centralise the queen as much as possible so as to dominate the defending queen. Improving one's pieces is often a higher priority than pushing the pawn (cf diagram 9a Alekhine - Stoltz when e7 is wrong).

The pawn on the seventh rank

When the pawn has reached the seventh rank, then unless the defending king can get to it or there is an immediate perpetual check, we will see a duel between the defending queen and the two attacking pieces.

In this duel, apart from checking the attacking king, the defender's main weapon is pinning. In general, it is better to pin along a diagonal than along a rank. This is because it is easier to escape successfully from a diagonal, than from a horizontal pin.

If, for example, the e-pawn is pinned along the rank and the attacking queen covers the f-file: then the defender must be able to deal with ♔f7-f8 forcing a diagonal pin as the only defence. Whereas if the pin is along the a3-f8 diagonal, then ♔f8-f7, as well as allowing a pin along the rank, may expose the king to checks along the b1-f7 diagonal.

Although it may not be easy to prove the win, however, these static positions in which the defender has abandoned checks in favour of pinning will almost always be won in the end.

Q 3

The pin on a pawn, one square away from promotion, against the attacking king, principally along the longer diagonal, but also along the rank, creates many technical problems. It is not possible to place the supporting queen to oversee all the pinning squares except by being on that diagonal itself.

Other factors like perpetual and harassing checks also have to be guarded against.

Despite sterling analytical work by the Russian grandmaster Yuri Averbakh and the Czech Jaroslav Pospisil, game analyses by Paul Keres and Mikhail Botvinnik and access to computer programs like BELLE these endings are often beyond human capability.

Queen and Centre Pawn v Queen

Q 4

= B

We concentrate on such endings when the pawn is already advanced to the seventh.

The great majority of such queen and d- or e-pawn versus queen endings should be won. Exceptions arise from the inability to escape perpetual checking or difficulties in pushing the pawn to the eighth because the defending sides king is near.

BELLE, after Speelman, after Averbakh

Black perpetually checks by 1 ... ♕c6+ 2 ♔f7 (2 ♔f8 ♕f6+ 3 ♕f7 ♕h8+) 2 ... ♕f3+! (Averbakh had analysed 2 ... ♕c4+ to a White win after 3 ♔f8 ♕f4+ 4 ♕f7+ ♕h6+ 5 ♔g8 ♕g5+ 6 ♕g7 ♕d5+ 7 ♔f8 ♕f5+ 8 ♕f7 ♕c5 9 ♕f4+ etc.) 3 ♔g7 ♕c3+! 4

Q 4a

+ W

♔g6 (4 ♔f8 ♕f6+ 5 ♔f7 ♕h8+ etc.) 4 ... ♕g3+ 5 ♔h7 ♕h3+ 6 ♔g7 ♕c3+ 7 ♔f7 ♕f3+ 8 ♔e8 ♕c6+. Black's access to the two tracks c6, f3, g3, h3 and c6, f6, h8 assures the draw.

Diagram 4a
Averbakh

Averbakh gives 1 ♔f8 ♕f4+ 2 ♕f7 ♕h6+ 3 ♔g8 ♕g5+ 4 ♕g7 ♕d5+ 5 ♔f8 ♕f5+ 6

♕f7 and the black queen is shunted onto an inferior network; after the diagonal pin 6 ... ♕c5 follows 7 ♕f4+ and if 7 ... ♔d7 8 ♕g4+ ♔c7 White changes which player is to move by 9 ♕g3+ ♔d7 10 ♕h3+ ♔c7 11 ♕g4; now Black has a choice - 11 ... ♕a3 12 ♕c4+ ♔b7 (12 ... ♔d7 13 ♕a4+) 13 ♕d5+ preparing 14 ♔f7; or 12 ... ♔b6 13 ♕d5.

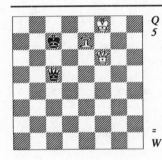

Q 5

= W

Averbakh 1962, BELLE 1985

Here the defending king is too near.

1	♕f4+	♔d7
2	♕g4+	♔c7
3	♕g3+	♔d7
4	♕h3+	♔c7
5	♕g4	♕f2+!
6	♔e8	♕c5

If 6 ... ♕f6 7 ♕c4+ ♔b6 8 ♔d7 ♕g7 9 ♕h4 (threatening ♔d8) 9 ... ♕f7 10 ♕d4+ ♔b7 11 ♔d8 wins (Averbakh).

7	♕f4+	♔c8
8	♔f7	♕h5+

Averbakh stopped in his analysis at 8 ♔f7; Bell Laboratories (Ken Thompson) BELLE program advanced 8 ... ♕h5+. White cannot expect to win - the Black king is *close* enough to help contain the pawn and the black queen is on its best square.

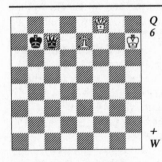

Q 6

+ W

White can force the win in only a few moves by interposing on the seventh rank. Both 1 ♕f7 and 1 ♕g7 win. However, one of them is much easier.

1 ♕g7!

This is correct because Black is unable to set up a diagonal pin. (If 1 ♕f7?! ♕h2+! 2 ♔g8 ♕g3+! 3 ♔f8 ♕d6 (3

... ♕a3 4 ♕d5+ ♔b8 5 ♔f7 ♕a7 6 ♕d8+ and wins) is diag 7.

1	...	♕c2+
2	♔h8	♕h2+
3	♔g8	♕a2+
4	♕f7	♕g2+
5	♔f8	and wins

Unfortunately, there is no square west of a2 so White wins immediately.

Q 7

+ W

The black queen is rather badly placed on d6 since it is easy to dominate it with the white queen in such a way that ♔f7 can only be met by a pin on the rank.

1 ♕f3+

Now:

A.

1 ... ♔a6

Instead 1 ... ♔c7 2 ♔f7 ♕d7 3 ♕f4+ ♔b7 4 ♔f8; or 1 ... ♔c8 2 ♔f7 ♔c7 3 ♕a8+ are easy. Or 1 ... ♔a7 2 ♔f7 ♕d7 (2 ... ♕c7 3 ♕a3+ ♔b7 4 ♕b4+ ♔a7 5 ♔f8) 3 ♕a3+ ♔b6 4 ♕b4+ ♔a6 5 ♕c5 (threatening 6 ♕f8) 5 ... ♕b7 6 ♕a3+ etc. And if 1 ... ♔b6 2 ♔f7 ♕c7 3 ♕b3+ ♔a5 4 ♕a3+ ♔b5 5 ♕d3+ etc. - see 4 ♕d3+ in the column.

	2	♔f7	♕c7

If 2 ... ♕d7 3 ♕f6+ ♔b7 4 ♔f8.

	3	♕a3+	♔b5

In order to avoid the standard procedure of ♕b4+ and ♔f8 after which the black queen is dominated: he is forced to advance his king (i.e. if 3 ... ♔b6 4 ♕b4+ ♔a6 5 ♔f8).

	4	♕d3+	♔a4

Black is forced onto the fifth rank since all other moves allow an immediate exchange of queens.

	5	♕d4+	♔b3
	6	♔f8 and wins	

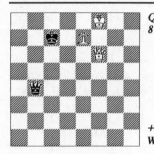

Q 8

+ W

BELLE 1985

In contrast to diag 7, here White is able to force the win since he can improve the position of the queen before running his king to cover.

	1	♕f5!	

BELLE found that strictly speaking this is best since it wins in the fastest manner. The following main line is BELLE's but we have fleshed it out with Carbon-based (and hence possibly fallible) side lines.

Instead 1 ♕e5+ was analysed by Averbakh in 1962. He continued: 1 ... ♔b7 (1 ... ♔d7 2 ♕b5+!) 2 ♔g7 ♕g4+ 3 ♔f6 ♕f3+ 4 ♔f5 ♕c6+ 5 ♔f7 ♕c7 6 ♕e4+ ♔a6 7 ♕a4+ ♔b7 8 ♕b4+ as in diag 10 above.

After 1 ♕f5 there are two main variations:

B.

	1	...	♔b8
	2	♔f7	♕c7
	3	♕b3+	♔c8

3 ... ♔a7 would allow White to force his queen to b4 with tempo: 4 ♕a4+ ♔b7 5 ♕b4+ ♔a7 6 ♔f8.

	4	♕b4	

Threatening 5 ♔f8.

	4	...	♕a7

Or 4 ... ♕d7 5 ♕c5+ ♔b7 6 ♔f8.

	5	♕c4+	

And the precarious nature of the pin allows White to force the queen to d8 with checks.

	5	...	♔b8
	6	♕b5+	♔c8
	7	♕c6+	♔b8
	8	♕d6+	♔c8
	9	♕d8+ and wins	

A.

	1	...	♔b7

If 1 ... ♕d6 2 ♔f7 *and* there is no pin and no check, whilst 1 ... ♔c6 is wrong since it runs into a cross-check: 2 ♔f7 ♕b3+ 3 ♕e6+ (the same objection applies to 1 ... ♔b6). Or 1 ... ♕a3 2 ♕e5+ (planning 3 ♔g7) 2 ... ♔c8 (2 ... ♔d7 3 ♕d5+ ♔c8 4 ♔f7 ♕a7 5 ♕d8+) 3 ♔g7 ♕a7 4 ♔h8! and wins.

	2	♔f7	♕c4+

If 2 ... ♕b3+ 3 ♔g7 ♕c3+ (or 3 ... ♕g3+ 4 ♔f8 ♕d6 5 ♔f7) 4 ♔h7 as in the note to 3 ... ♕d4+ below.

	3	♔g7	♕d4+

Instead 3 ... ♕c3+ 4 ♔h7 ♕c7 5 ♕d5+ transposes back to the main line a move quicker.

	4	♔g6	♕b6+
	5	♔h7	♕c7
	6	♕d5+	

6 ♕f7 also wins but slightly slower, viz: 6 ... ♕h2+ 7 ♔g8 ♕g3+ 8 ♔f8 ♕d6 (8 ... ♕a3 9 ♕d5+ ♔b8 10 ♔f7 ♕a7 11 ♕d8+) 9.♕f3+ wins as in diag 10).

  6   **♔a7**

If 6 ... ♔b8 7 ♕d8+; or 6 ... ♔c8 7 ♕a8+; or 6 ... ♔b6 (6 ... ♔a6 is the same) 7 ♕f7 ♕h2+ 8 ♔g7.

  7   **♕d4+**   **♔b7**
  8   **♕g7**

And wins as in diag 9.

B.

  1   **♔b8**

This turns out to be very slightly less resilient than 1 ... ♔b7 since it's easier to get the white queen to g7.

  2   **♔f7**   **♕b3+**

Instead 2 ... ♕c4+ 3 ♔g7 ♕d4+ (3 ... ♕c3+ transposes directly to line B) 4 ♔g6 ♕b6+ 5 ♔h7 ♕c7 6 ♕f8+ ♔b7 7 ♕g7 is diag 9 again.

  3   **♔g7** and now:

a) 3 ... ♕g3+ 4 ♔f8 ♕a3 (4 ... ♕d6 5 ♔f7 ♕c7 6 ♕b5+ ♔c8 7 ♕b4 etc. as in diag 10 line B) 5 ♕e5+ ♔c8 6 ♔g7;

b) 3 ... ♕c3+ 4 ♔h7 ♕c7 5 ♕f8+ ♔b7 6 ♕g7!.

Q 9

W

Alekhine - Stoltz
Salzberg 1942
This spawns many instructive positions. Play continued:

  65   **♕f7+**   **♔d6**
  66   **♕d7+**   **♔c5**
  67   **♔g6** *(9a)*

67 e7 immediately allows endless checks after 67 ... ♕f6+.

After 67 ♔g6 Stoltz faced a dilemma between trying for checks or aiming for a centralised queen.

Stoltz played:

  67   **♕g1+?**

Keres in *Practical Chess Endings* criticised this strongly "... ill-considered, purposeless checks ... disastrous ... no way improves the position of Black's queen ... White a useful tempo by forcing his king to go where it wants to go! ... active centralised queens are called for in this kind of ending, and as White has not been able to centralise his own queen, ... Black to take his chance of playing 67 ... ♕e5!".

"As Alekhine himself ad-

mitted after the game, 67 ... ♕e5 would have given Black a draw ..."

At least White should not win by 68 e7 because of the carefully positioned checking pattern 68 ... ♕g3+ 69 ♔f7 ♕f4+ 70 ♔e8 ♕b8+ 71 ♕d8 ♕b5+ 72 ♔f7/f8 ♕f1+ with a perpetual.

Nor by 68 ♕a7+ or 68 ♕c8+ losing the pawn after 68 ... ♔d6. And Black can frustrate efforts for the white king to escape to the queen's wing, viz. 68 ♔f7 ♕h5+ 69 ♔e7 ♕h4+!.

After 67 ... ♕g1+:

  68   **♔f7**   **♕h1**

Or 68 ... ♕f1+ 69 ♔e8 ♕f4! would attempt to reach a similar draw to that in the last note, but White could preserve winning chances by 70 ♕a7+ before pushing 71 e7.

"Black's most stubborn defence is 68 ... ♕f2+ 69 ♔e8 ♕h2 but after 70 ♕e7+ and 71 ♕f6 White can advance his pawn when Black would hardly be able to hold the position." - Keres.

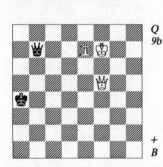

Q 9a

= B

Q 9b

+ B

Queen v Queen

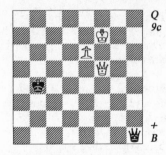

Q
9c

+
B

Q
9d

+
B

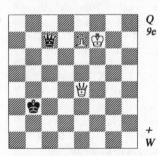

Q
9e

+
W

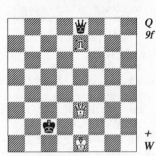

Q
9f

+
W

69 ♕c7+   ♚b5?!

69 ... ♚b4 would allow White to demonstrate a further method of flight from checks after 70 ♕f4+ ♚a3 71 e7 ♕h7+ (otherwise 71 ... ♕d5+ 72 ♚g7 ♕d7 73 ♚f8) 72 ♚e6 ♕h3+ 73 ♚d6 ♕d3+ 74 ♚c7 ♕c3+ 75 ♚b7 ♕b2+ 76 ♚a7 when after 76 ... ♕g7, 77 ♕d6+ and 78 ♚a6 wins.

70 ♕e5+   ♚a4

If 70 ... ♚a6/b6/c6 after 71 e7 ♕h7+ 72 ♚g7 White has a cross-check lined up.

71 ♕d4+

According to Keres this is needless; the white queen stands no better after this move.

71 ♕f5! wins more quickly, e.g. 71 ... ♕b7+ 72 e7 (9b) and now:

a) 72 ... ♕a7 73 ♚f8;

b) 72 ... ♕b3+ 73 ♚f8 ♕b4 (73 ... ♕a3 allows the swap of queens after 74 ♕d7+) 74 ♕e5 with zugzwang, e.g. 74 ... ♚b3 75 ♚g8 and queens.

c) 72 ... ♚a3 73 ♕f4!? (threat ♚f8) 73 ... ♕a7 (or 73 ... ♕d5+ 74 ♚g7 ♕g2+ 75 ♚f8) 74 ♚e6! ♕a8 75 ♕d6+ ♚b2 (75 ... ♚a4 76 ♕d7+; 75 ... ♚a2/b3 76 ♕d5+) 76 ♕e5+ with either ♕b5+ and e8♕ or ♕d5+ coming up;

d) 72 ... ♕c7 73 ♕e4+ ♚b3, or 73 ... ♚a3 74 ♕d4 (threat 75 ♚f8) 74 ... ♕b7 75 ♕c3+ (covering squares b4 and f3) 75 ... ♚moves 76 ♚f8 achieving White's strategic aim.

71 ...   ♚a3
72 ♕d3+   ♚b4
73 ♕f5! (9c)
73 ...   ♕c6

If 73 ... ♕b7+ 74 e7 when 74 ... ♕a7 allows 75 ♚f8, and 74 ... ♕c7 would follow like

the column after 74 ... ♕c7.

74 e7 (9d)
74 ...   ♕c7

Or 74 ... ♕c4+ 75 ♚f8.

75 ♕e4+   ♚a3

For the continuation after 75 ... ♚b3 see diag 12e below.

Else 75 ... ♚a5 76 ♚f6 ♕d6+ 77 ♚e6! when possible cross-checks bring Black's activity to a halt.

76 ♕d4!

Threatening 77 ♚f8.

76 ...   ♕h2
77 ♕c5+   ♚a2
78 e8♕   ♕f4+
79 ♚g7   ♕g3+
80 ♚f8!

This avoids the last trap of 80 ♕g6 ♕c3+! with a stalemate.

1-0

From diag 9e, after 75 ♕e4+ ♚b3!?:

76 ♕e3+

White creates a safe area for the white king in the f3/h3/f1/e1 box.

76 ...   ♚c2

Or 76 ... ♚a2 77 ♚f6 wins.

77 ♚g6   ♕c6+

If 77 ... ♕d6+ 78 ♚g5 ♕d5+ 79 ♚h4! ♕c4+ (79 ... ♕h1+ 80 ♚g3!) 80 ♚g3 ♕g8+ 81 ♚f2 ♕f7+ 82 ♚e1! and the white king has a safe haven on the open board.

78 ♚g5   ♕g2+
79 ♚f4   ♕h2+

On 79 ... ♕f1+ again 80 ♚g3.

80 ♚f3   ♕h5+

80 ... ♕h3+ 81 ♚f2 ♕h2+ 82 ♚f1 ♕h1+ 83 ♚g1! wins.

81 ♚g2   ♕g6+

Other checks are 81 ... ♕g4+ 82 ♚f1 ♕d1+ 83 ♚e1! and 81 ... ♕d5+ 82 ♚f1 ♕h1+ 83 ♕g1! ♕h5 84 ♕f2+ ♚d3

85 ♕g3+ enabling White to shepherd the pawn home in a few moves.

82	♔f1	♛e8
83	♔e1! *(9f)*	

Black would have no answer to ♕d2/d3+ and ♕d8.

Queen and Bishop's Pawn v Queen

Q 10

+
W

This is very similar to the ending with a centre pawn.

Pospisil 1955

1   ♔h7   ♛d7

Pospisil gave 1 ... ♛h1+ which is slightly less resilient: 2 ♔g7 ♛a1+ 3 ♔g8 ♛a2 4 ♕e4 ♔b6 5 ♔g7 ♛a1+ 6 ♔h7 ♛a3 7 ♕e6+ ♔b7 8 ♕d7+ ♔b8 9 ♕d8++- and 10 f8♕ winning.

2	♕g3+	♔b7
3	♕f3+	♔a7
4	♕e3+	♔a6
5	♕f4	♔a7
6	♔g7	♔b6
7	♕e3+	♔a6
8	♕e4	

Threatening 9 ♔g8.

8	...	♛c7
9	♕d3+	♔a7
10	♔g8 and wins	

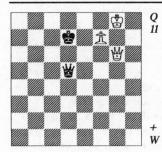

Q 11

+
W

The analagous position shifted over to the centre file was mutual zugzwang (see diag 5). Here White to move is able to win. But it's more difficult than Pospisil's position above since 1 ♔h7? would invite 1 ... ♔e7.

1	♕f6	♛g2+
2	♔h7	♛h3+
3	♕h6	♛f5+
4	♕g6	♛c5
5	♕f6	♛h5+
6	♔g8	♛g4+
7	♕g7	♛c4
8	♕g2	♔e7

9	♕b7+	♔d8

If 9 ... ♔f6 10 ♕b2+ ♔e7 (10 ... ♔g6 11 ♕g7+ ♔f5 12 ♔h8; or 10 ... ♔f5 11 ♕g7 threatening ♔h8 and wins) 11 ♕b4+!.

10	♕f3	♔c7
11	♔g7	♛d4+
12	♔h7	♛d7
13	♕f4+	♔b6
14	♔g7	♔a7
15	♕e3+	♔a6
16	♕e4	♛c7
17	♕d3+	♔a7
18	♔g8 and wins	

Queen v Queen

Q
12

+
W

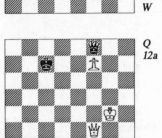

Q
12a

+
W

Stepushin and Malyshev
1962

1	♔g7	♛b2+

1 ... ♛a1+ 2 ♔g6.

2	♔g6	♛b6+
3	♔h5	♛c5+
4	♔g4	

Now Black's checks have dried up.

| 4 | ... | ♛f8 (12a) |
| 5 | ♕f5 | ♛b4+ |

If 5 ... ♛g7+ 6 ♔h5 ♛h8+ 7 ♔g6 ♛f8 8 ♕f6 and then af-

ter 8 ... ♛d7 White wins by 9 ♔h7 ♛c7 10 ♕g7.

Or 5 ... ♛d8 6 ♔h5 ♛e7 7 ♔g6 and Black must give way.

| 6 | ♔h5 | ♛f8 |
| 7 | ♕f4+ | |

Ensuring no ... ♛d6 with check.

| 7 | ... | ♔moves |
| 8 | ♔g6 | |

and White wins (like in the note 5 ... ♛g7+) by ♕f6, ♔h7 and, in time ♕g7.

Queen and Knight's Pawn v Queen

Q
13

+
W

After the considerable coverage we have given to centre and bishop's pawns we shall only give a fairly cursory treatment to the knight's pawn as the principles are basically the same.

It is still harder to win with a knight's pawn since the pinning diagonal is longer and there is less room to manoeuvre next to the pawn. Nevertheless, most positions are winning in the end.

van Vliet 1888
Louis van Vliet's study lifts Q+P vs Q endings out of their supposed methodical approach.

| 1 | ♕b4 |

This restricts the black king

without leaving a stalemate combination. The black queen must be kept on the h1-a8 diagonal.

White can cleverly win by a cascade of skewer checks.

After 1 ... ♛d5 (or 1 ... ♛b3) 2 ♕a4+ ♔b6 3 ♕b3+! sets up a skewer.

On 1 ... ♛g2 another arises after 2 ♕a3+ ♔b6 3 ♕b2+!.

1 ... ♛h1! puts the black queen further away from these skewers, but after 2 ♕a3+ ♔b6 3 ♕b2+ Black can choose between 3 ... ♔c6 allowing White a second queen, or 3 ... ♔a6 4 ♕a2+ ♔b6/b5 leading to a further skewer 5 ♕b1+, or have yet another skewer diagonally after 3 ... ♔c7 4 ♕h2+!.

404

Q 14

+ W

Averbakh 1959 (corrected by database)

White wins by improving his queen's position and then walking his king to a8 where it can escape the checks.

1	♕d2	♔a1

If 1 ... ♕e7 2 ♕d1+ ♔a2 (2 ... ♔b2 3 ♕d4+ ♔b1 4 ♔h8) 3 ♕d5+ ♔a1 4 ♔g6 ♕e8+ 5 ♔f6 wins; or 1 ... ♕f7 2 ♕d6 ♔a2 3 ♔h6 ♕g8.

2	♕d4+	♔b1
3	♔g6	♕c2+

3 ... ♕g3+ 4 ♔f5 (Averbakh) 4 ... ♕f3+ is one move quicker for White.

4	♔g5	♕g2+
5	♔f5	♕f3+
6	♔e5	♕g3+
7	♔d5	♕g5+
8	♔c4	♕g2!
9	♔c5	♕g5+
10	♔b6	♕g6+
11	♔a5	♕f5+
12	♔b4	♕g6
13	♕d7	♕g2
14	♕f7	♕e4+
15	♔a5	♕a8+
16	♔b6	♕b8+
17	♕b7	♕g3
18	♔a7+	♔a1
19	♔a8	

Finally reaching perfect shelter; but Black can still resist for a couple of moves with a stalemate defence.

19	...	♕b3!
20	♕h1+!	

If 20 ♕a7+ ♔b1 21 ♕b8 ♔a1 then White can win with 22 g8♖ but 22 g8♕ invites 22 ... ♕d5+!.

20	...	♔b2
21	♕g2+	♔a1
22	g8♕ and wins	

Q 15

+ W

Komissarchik and Futer 1973 (with amendments by BELLE)

This is an example of the longest win. It was originally analysed by a Soviet database but amendments were later made by BELLE.

1	...	♕b4+
2	♔e6	♕g4+
3	♔f6	

3 ♔f7? ♕f5 draws.

3	...	♕f4+
4	♔g6	♕e4+
5	♔g5	♕e3+
6	♔h5	♕f3+
7	♔h6	♕h1+
8	♔g5	♕d5+
9	♔f6 (15a)	

Q 15a

+ B

10	...	♕d4+
10	♔f7	♕d7+
11	♔g6	♕g4+
12	♔h7	♕h3+
13	♔g8	

Not 13 ♔h6 ♕d7!=.

13	...	♕f5

13 ... ♕b3+ 14 ♔f8 is easier.

14	♕a2+	♔c1
15	♕h2!	♕d5+
16	♔h8	♕d4
17	♕c7+	♔b1
18	♔h7	♕e4+
19	♔h6	♕e3+
20	♔g6	♕e6+
21	♔g5	♕d5+
22	♔f6	♕f3+
23	♔e7	♕e4+
24	♔d8	♕a8+
25	♔d7	♕d5+
26	♔c8	♕e6+
27	♔b8	♕e8+
28	♔a7	♕a4+
29	♔b6	♕b3+
30	♔a6	♕a2+
31	♕a5	♕g8
32	♕b4+	♔a2
33	♕d4 (15b)	
33	...	♕e6+

The BELLE program produced 33 ... ♕c8+ which takes one move less.

34	♔b5	♕e8+

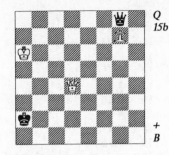

Q
15b

+
B

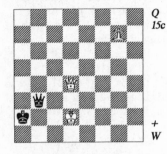

Q
15c

+
W

Q
16

+
W

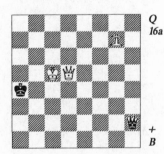

Q
16a

+
B

35	♔b4	♛b8+

BELLE produced 35 ... ♛e1+ 36 ♔c4 ♛e2+ 37 ♔d5 ♛b5+ 38 ♔e6 ♛e8+ 39 ♔f6 ♛c6+ 40 ♔e4 ♛e8+ and the position coincides with Komissarchik's and Futer's work (after Black's 45th move).

36	♔c3	♛g3+
37	♔d2	♛g2+
38	♔e1	♛h1+
39	♔f2	♛h2+
40	♔f3	♛h3+
41	♔f4	♛h2+
42	♔g5	♛g3+
43	♔f6	♛f3+
44	♔e6	♛c6+
45	♔e5	♛e8+
46	♔f4	♛f7+
47	♔g3	♛g6+
48	♔h3	♛h7+
49	♔g2	♛g6+
50	♔f1	♛b1+
51	♔e2	♛b5+
52	♔d2	♛b3 (15c)
53	♛a7+	

BELLE gives 53 ♛d3 ♛g8 54 ♛a6+ ♔d3 55 ♛b5+ ♔a3 56 ♛b7 ♛a2+ 57 ♔d3 ♛g8 58 ♔c3 ♛e6 59 ♛a8+ (or 59 ♛a7+, 59 ♛b4+ or 59 ♛b2+) 59 ... ♛a6 60 ♛xa6 mate.

53	...	♔b2
54	♛f2	♛g8
55	♛b6+	♔a3
56	♛b7	♔a4

56 ... ♛a2+ 57 ♔d3 ♛g8 58 ♔c3 wins.

57	♔c3	♔a5
58	♛b4+	♔a6
59	♛c4+	

Exchanging queens and winning.

Botvinnik - Minev
Amsterdam Olympiad 1954
A famous, deeply-analysed and instructive queen and knight's pawn v queen ending that contributed to, but did not resolve the debate as to where to place the defending king.

The game continued:

73	♔g5	♛d8+

Sealed.

74	♛f6!	

If 74 ♔h6 ♛h4+ 75 ♔g7 ♛h3.

74	...	♛d5+
75	♛f5	♛d8+
76	♔h5	♛e8

76 ... ♛h8+ 77 ♔g4 ♛g7 (77 ... ♛d4+ 78 ♛f4 pins) 78 ♛f7 ♛c3 (otherwise White forces an exchange of queens) 79 g7 ♛c8+ 80 ♛f5 ♛g8 (80 ... ♛a8 81 ♛c2+ ♔b4 82 ♛b2+ ♔c5 - 82 ... ♔c4 83 ♛a2+ with a skewer - 83 ♛c3+ ♔d6 84 ♛f6+ ♔c5 85 ♛f8+ wins) 81 ♛d7+

♔moves 82 ♔g5 followed by 83 ♔g6 and 84 ♛f7.

77	♛f4+	

BELLE gives 77 ♔g4! ♛e2+ as winning for White.

77	...	♔a5?

77 ... ♔a3= BELLE.

78	♛d2+	♔a4
79	♛d4+	♔a5
80	♔g5	♛e7+
81	♔f5!	♛f8+
82	♔e4	

Again checks are ended. The white king is excellently placed in the centre.

82	...	♛h6
83	♛e5+	♔a4
84	g7	♛h1+
85	♔d4	♛d1+
86	♔c5	♛c1+
87	♔d6	♛d2+

87 ... ♛h6+ 88 ♔d5!

88	♔e6	♛a2+
89	♛d5	♛e2+
90	♔d6	♛h2+
91	♔c5!! (16a)	

A memorable final position.

Queen v Queen

Queen and Rook's Pawn v Queen

Success in winning this ending is generally through the exploitation of the bad position of the opponent's king. Otherwise these endings are mostly drawn. Most endgame books tend to dwell on exceptions.

Analysis generated by Ken Thompson's BELLE Algorithm in the Bell Laboratories, New Jersey dominates and corrects many of the 37 positions chosen by *Encyclopaedia of Chess Endings* on this endgame.

The difficulties for possible successful outcomes are shown in two of *Roycroft's 5-Man Chess Endgame* series. These positions with a white pawn on a2 are shown as needing 16-17 moves to bring about the first effective advance of the a-pawn (a2-a3 or a2-a4). It could really take a long time for the pawn to advance all the way to the eighth rank!

Q 17

Averbakh 1962
In this position White can win because the black king is vulnerable to cross-checks.

| 1 | ♕g8+ | ♚b7 |
| 2 | ♕f7+ | ♚c8 |

If, for example, 2 ... ♚a6 3 ♔g7.

| 3 | ♕e8+ | ♚b7 |
| 4 | ♔g8 | ♕g3+ |

+ W

| 5 | ♔f8 | |

There are no good checks now.

| 5 | ... | ♕c3 |

If 5 ... ♕h3 6 ♕f7+ ♚a8 7 ♕g8 or 6 ... ♚a6 7 ♔g7 wins.

6	♕f7+	♚a6
7	♕g6+	♚a5
8	♕h5+	♚b4
9	h8♕ and wins	

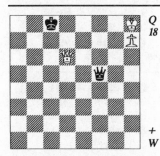

Q 18

Staleraytis 1980 and Averbakh 1982
Again the black king is poorly placed.

1	♕e7!	♕f4
2	♕e8+	♚b7
3	♔g7!	♕d4+

Or 3 ... ♕g5+ 4 ♕g6 ♕e5+ 5 ♕f6 ♕g3+ 6 ♔f8 ♕b8+ 7

+ W

♔f7 when 7 ... ♕c7+ allows the pin 8 ♕e7 and 3 ... ♕g3+ and 3 ... ♕g4+ are met by 4 ♔f8 and if 4 ... or 4 ... ♕d4, 4 ... ♕c3 5 ♕f7+.

4	♔g8	♕g4+
5	♔f8	♕d4
6	♕f7+ and wins	

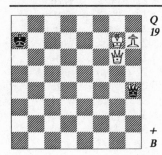

Q 19

Staleraytis 1980
With the black king on the seventh or eighth ranks the white king should go to f8 and g8 to construct cross-checks and pins, e.g. after:

1	...	♕d4+
2	♕f6	♕g4+
3	♔f7	♕c4+

Or 3 ... ♕h5+ 4 ♔g8 ♕e8+ 5 ♕f8 stops the checks.

| 4 | ♕e6 | ♕f4+ |
| 5 | ♔g7 | ♕d4+ |

+ B

On 5 ... ♕g5+ 6 ♔f8 ♕d8+ 7 ♔f7! ♕h8 8 ♕e7+ and check next move exchanges queens.

5 ... ♕g3+ is controlled by 6 ♔f8 ♕c3 (6 ... ♕b8+ 7 ♕e8!) 7 ♕f7+ ♚a6 (or 7 ... ♚a8 8 ♕g8!) 8 ♕g6+ ♚a5 9 ♕h5+ escorts the pawn home.

| 6 | ♔g8 | ♕g1+ |

Or 6 ... ♕d8+ 7 ♔f7 wins.

| 7 | ♔f8 | ♕d4 |
| 8 | ♕f7+ wins | |

8 ... ♚a8 (or 8 ... ♚b8) 9 ♕g8; or 8 ... ♚a6 9 ♕g6+ ♚a5 (or 9 ... ♚b5) 10 ♕h5+ or 9 ... ♚a7 (or 9 ... ♚b7) 10 ♕g7+.

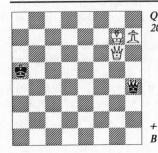

Q 20
+ B

Staleraytis 1980
With the defending king on a5 White's king should usefully be played to g6 and h6.

1 ... ♕e7+

If 1 ... ♕d4+ 2 ♔f6 ♕d7+ 3 ♔h6 ♕h3+ 4 ♔g6 ends Black's checks.

2 ♔h6 ♕f8+
3 ♔g5! and now:

A.

3 ... ♕e7+
4 ♔h5 ♕f8

If 4 ... ♕e2+ 5 ♔h6.

5 ♕e6! ♕f3+

Or 5 ... ♕h8 6 ♕g8.

6 ♔g5 ♕g3+
7 ♕g4 ♕e3+

If 7 ... ♕b8 8 ♕f5+.

8 ♕f4 ♕e7+

Or 8 ... ♕g1+ 9 ♔h5 ♕d1+ 10 ♔g6 with cross-checks.

9 ♔g6 ♕e8+
10 ♕f7 ♕c6+

11 ♕f6 ♕e8+
12 ♔h6 and wins

B.

3 ... ♕h8
4 ♕f7 ♔a4
5 ♔g6

Planning 6 ♕g8.

5 ... ♕e5

Or:
a) 5 ... ♕d4/c3/b2/a1 6 ♕e8+ and 7 ♕h8♕;
b) 5 ... ♕a8? 6 ♕a2+;
c) 5 ... ♕b8/c8/d8 6 ♕a2+, 7 ♕b2+ and 8 ♕h8♕.

6 ♕a7+ ♔b3
7 ♕b7+ ♔a2
8 ♕a8+ ♔b1
9 h8♕

Can the perpetual be avoided?

9 ... ♕g3+
10 ♔f7 ♕c7+
11 ♔e8 and wins

Yes!

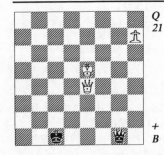

Q 21
+ B

BELLE 1985

1	...	♕c5+
2	♔f6	♕f8+
3	♔g6	♕d6+
4	♔h5	♕d1+
5	♔h4	♕d8+
6	♔g3	♕g5+
7	♔f3	♕g7
8	♕f4+	♔d1
9	♕f5	♕c3+
10	♔g4	♕g7+
11	♔h5	♕c3
12	♕e6	♔c2
13	♔g5	♕g3+
14	♕g4	♕e3+
15	♔f6	♕b6+
16	♕e6	♕d4+
17	♔g6	♔d1
18	♔f7	♕a7+
19	♕e7	♕d4
20	♕c7	♕d5+
21	♔e8	♕e4+
22	♕e7	♕g6+
23	♔d8	♕b6+
24	♕c7	♕f6+
25	♔c8	♕a6+
26	♕b7	♕c4+
27	♔d8	♕h4+
28	♕e7	♕h5
29	♔c8	♔c1
30	♕g7	♕h3+
31	♔b8	♕b3+
32	♕b7 and wins	

Queen v Queen

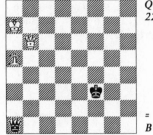

Q
22
=
B

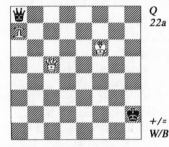

Q
22a
+/=
W/B

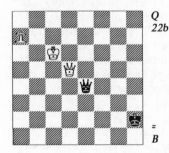

Q
22b
=
B

van der Wiel - Fedorowicz
Student Teams, Graz 1981

97 ... ♔e2

A key question for the defence is where best to place the king, i.e. where it does not impede the queen's ability to check and where it is least susceptible to cross-checks. The answer varies according to the progress of the passed pawn. When it is at a7 opinions vary between e1, f1, g1, h2, h3 and h4.

98 ♕e6+ ♔f1
99 ♕f5+ ♔e1?!

Van der Wiel proposed 99 ... ♔g1 to go to h2 as better.

100 ♔b6 ♕b2+
101 ♔c6 ♕c3+
102 ♔d6 ♕b4+
103 ♕c5 ♕b8+
104 ♔e7 ♕b7+
105 ♔f6 ♕f3+
106 ♕f5 ♕a8
107 ♕e6+ ♔f1
108 a6 ♔g1
109 ♕b6+

Possibly critical. In his notes to the game van der Wiel considered 109 ♔g7!?. We have not seen BELLE's reaction.

109 ... ♔h2
110 ♕c7+ ♔g1
111 ♕c5+ ♔h2
112 a7 (22a)

When the pawn has reached the seventh rank its king has the least shelter and is most likely to be exposed to constant checks.

Both van der Wiel and the BELLE algorithm regarded the diagrammed position after 112 a7 as tenable (=).

112 ... ♕h8+
113 ♔g5 ♕g7+
114 ♔f5 ♕h7+
115 ♔f4 ♕f7+

Also 115 ... ♕h4+=

(BELLE).

116 ♔e3 ♕b3+
117 ♔e4 ♕b7+!

The only move according to BELLE.

118 ♔d3 ♕a6+
119 ♔e3 ♕e6+

Also 119 ... ♕h6+= (BELLE).

120 ♔d4 ♕g4+!

Another only move (BELLE).

121 ♔c3 ♕f3+!

Again the only move (BELLE).

122 ♔d2 ♕g2+

Also possible is 122 ... ♕f4+ despite its dangerous appearance.

123 ♔e1 ♕e4+!
124 ♔d1 ♕f3+
125 ♔c1 ♕h1+

Also 125 ... ♔h1.

126 ♔b2 ♕b7+!
127 ♔a3 ♕f3+!
128 ♔b4 ♕e4+!
129 ♔b5 ♕e2+

Also 129 ... ♕e8+ and 129 ... ♕b1+.

130 ♔c6 ♕e8+
131 ♔b6 ♕e6+!
132 ♔b7 ♕e4+
133 ♔c7 ♕h7+
134 ♔c6 ♕e4+!
135 ♕d5 (22b)
135 ... ♕a4+
136 ♔b7 ♕b4+!
137 ♔c7 ♕e7+

Also 137 ... ♕c3+.

138 ♕d7 ♕c5+
139 ♔b8 ♕f8+

Also 139 ... ♕b6+ and 139 ... ♕b4+.

140 ♕c8 ♕b4+
141 ♔a8 ♔g1

Also 141 ... ♕a3/♕a5/♕d2= (BELLE).

142 ♕c1+ ♔f2
143 ♕b2+!? ♕xb2

stalemate

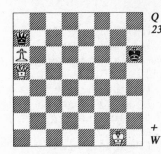

Q
23
+
W

BELLE 1985

In diag 23 White needs 71 more moves in the longest line of play to force a winning advance of the pawn from a6 to a7! That's the message from the BELLE program.

Queen v Queen: Many Pawns

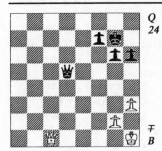

Q
24
干
B

Pawns all on one Flank

Endings in which all the pawns are on one flank arise fairly frequently. With one extra pawn, winning chances depend on the possibility of activating the attacking king; and the pawn structure particularly of the defender.

If it is possible to move the king into the defender's guts or he has weak pawns which can be attacked; then there are good chances. Otherwise, up to three pawns v two, the defender ought presumably to be able to draw.

In the case of endings of four v three, however, an extra pawn even without other additional advantages must afford good winning chances.

Delaney - Speelman
Bath Zonal 1987

With his pawn structure intact, White ought to be able to draw. But in the end I forced my way through:

39	♕c3+	♔h7
40	♕c7	g5
41	♕b8	♕d4

Taking control of the long diagonal. White could have resisted this for a while with, e.g. ♕c3, but obviously not in-

definitely.

42	♕c8	♔g7
43	♔h2	h5
44	♔h1	♕e3

Black would like to play ... g4 with the queen on f4. However, if 44 ... ♕f4 at once then 45 ♕c3+ is annoying. The text move also sets a trap 45 ♕f5?? ♕c1+ 46 ♔h2 ♕f4+. Black shouldn't play 44 ... g4 immediately since after 45 hxg4 hxg4 46 ♕f5! the white queen is extremely inconvenient.

45 ♔h2?!

Rather falling in with the opponent's plan. 45 ♕c4 was possible, preventing ... g4 for the moment. 45 ♕a6!? is another option, intending 45 ... g4 46 hxg4 hxg4 47 g3!.

45	...	♕f4+
46	♔h1	

Natural, but 46 ♔g1 would have been a good idea as after 46 ... g4 47 hxg4 hxg4 48 ♕c3+ ♔g6 White can play 49 g3!.

46	...	g4!?
47	hxg4!?	

Opening up the h-file, but White is still probably drawing.

47	...	hxg4
48	♕c3+	♔g6?!

49 ♕d3+ ♚h6?!/?

Now 50 g3 loses easily to 50 ... ♕f3+ ⁻ hence the advantage of 46 ♚g1. However, here White can still probably draw with 50 ♕a6+! to be followed against all replies by 51 g3! when 51 ... ♕xg3 will allow White to draw by stalemate. It was vital to get the white queen on a square covering f1, otherwise g3 would have been met by ... ♕f1+, ... ♕h3+ and ... ♕xg3+ etc. Presumably this means that Black should play either 48 ... ♚h6 or 49 ... ♚g5. *After* getting in g3 safely White should draw since it will be almost impossible for Black to activate his king while the squares h4, g4 and f4 are all forbidden territory.

50 ♕d8? g3

White's position is now demonstrably lost. Black has to avoid stalemate with his queen on the a7-g1 diagonal but this turns out to be fairly simple.

51 ♕b6+

If 51 ♕h8+ ♚g6 52 ♕g8+ ♚f6 53 ♕d8+ ♚g7 54 ♕d4+ ♕f6 55 ♕g4+ ♕g6 56 ♕d4+ ♚h7! and wins. 56 ... f6?

would be a serious mistake in view of 57 ♕d7+ ♚h6 58 ♕d2+ ♕g5 59 ♕e3! reaching the position arising in the game after 52 ... ♕g5, but with Black to move. As a result Black is in a most annoying zugzwang and in analysis after the game we could see no way for him to lose a move; so the position may well be drawn.

51 ... f6
52 ♕e3! ♕g5!

Now it is White who is in zugzwang and he loses immediately.

53 ♕c5 ♕h5+

Of course 53 ... ♕h4+ 54 ♚g1 ♕h2+ 55 ♚f1 ♕h1+ also won, but why not go straight for the king and pawn ending?

54 ♕xh5+ ♚xh5
55 ♚g1 ♚g4
56 ♚f1 ♚f4
57 ♚e2 ♚e4
58 ♚d2 f5
59 ♚e2 f4
60 ♚e1 ♚e3
61 ♚f1 ♚d2
0-1

After 62 ♚g1 ♚e2 63 ♚h1 f3 64 gxf3 ♚f2 wins.

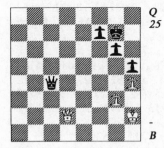

Q 25

B

Ciocaltea - Unzicker
Moscow 1956

The black king is brought into the white half with ideas of mating nets, cross-checks, the further weakening of the white pawns, and of being well-placed to exploit the exchange of queens.

59 ... ♚f6
60 ♕d8+ ♚e6
61 ♕e8+ ♚f5
62 ♕d7+ ♚e4
63 ♕e7+ ♚d3
64 ♕d7+ ♚c2

65 ♕e7 ♚d2
66 ♕d7+ ♚e2
67 ♕e7+ ♕e6
68 ♕b7 ♚f2
69 ♕g2+ ♚e1
70 ♕g1+ ♚e2
71 ♕g2+ ♚d3
72 ♕f3+ ♚d2
73 ♕f4+ ♚e2 (25a)
74 ♕c7 f5
75 ♕c2+ ♚f3
76 ♕g2+ ♚e3
77 ♕b2 ♕c4
78 ♕a3+ ♕d3
79 ♕c5+ ♚f3

Q 25a

W

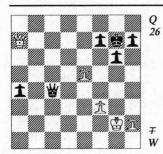

	80	♕c6+

Or 80 ♕g1 f4! 81 ♕g2+ ♔e3 82 ♕g1+ ♔d2 83 gxf4 ♕e2+; 81 gxf4 ♕c2+ 82 ♔h1 ♕e4! 83 ♕g5 ♕b1+ 84 ♔h2 ♕c2+ 85 ♔h1 ♕c1+ 86 ♔h2 ♕xf4+.

80	...	♕e4
81	♕c3+	♔f2
82	♕c5+	

Or 82 ♕d2+ ♔f1 83 ♕d1+ ♕e1 84 ♕d5 ♕e2+ 85 ♔h3

♔g1.

82	...	♕e3
83	♕c2+	♕e2
84	♕c6	♔f1+
85	♔h3	♔g1
86	♕c5+	♕f2
87	♕e3	f4!

Avoiding stalemate and reaching after 88 ♕c1+ ♕f1+ an easily won pawn ending.

0-1

Q 26

F W

Zapata - Speelman
Mexico City 1980
After White's first move, Black is forced to exchange down to three pawns vs two.

48	e6!	♕xe6
49	♕xa4	♕e2+
50	♔g3	♕e5+
51	♔g2	♕e3
52	♕b4	♕e5
53	♕d2	♔f6
54	♕d8+	♔f5

54 ... ♔g7!

55	♕g8!	♕e2+
56	♔g3	♕e1+
57	♔g2	♕d2+
58	♔g3	♕g5+
59	♔f2	♕h4+
60	♔g2	♔e6

60 ... ♕e7? 61 ♕xh7 ♔f4 62 ♕h6+ g5 63 ♕b6! ♕e2+ 64 ♔f2.

61	♕e8+

Or 61 ♕c8+ ♔e7 62 ♕c5+ ♔f6 63 ♕f8 ♕g5+ 64 ♔f2 ♕d2+ 65 ♔g3 ♕e1+ 66 ♔g2 h5 67 h4.

61	...	♕e7
62	♕c6+	♔f5
63	♕d5+	♔f6
64	♕d4+	♕e5
65	♕d8+	♔g7!
66	♕d2	♔f6

66 ... h5 67 h4!.

67	♕b4	♔h6
68	♕c4	

68 ♔f2 ♕g5 69 ♕f8+, 68 ...

g5!?.

68	...	♕g5+
69	♔f2	f6
70	♕d3	

70 ♕f7!?; 70 ♕c7!?.

70	...	♕f4
71	♔g2	♔h5
72	♕d7	h6
73	♕d3	♔g5
74	♕c2	♕e3

74 ... h5? 75 ♕c5+!.

75	♕c4	

75 h4+ ♔h5 (75 ... ♔xh4? 76 ♕c4+ ♔h5 77 ♕g4+).

75	...	f5
76	♕b4	

76 h4+??.

76	...	♔h5
77	♕c4	f4

77 ... g5? 78 ♕f7+ ♔h4 79 ♕xf5.

77 ... ♕d2+? 78 ♔h3 ♕f2 79 ♕g4+!! fxg4+ 80 fxg4+ ♔g5.

78	♕d5+	g5

78 ... ♔h4 79 ♕d8+ g5 80 ♕d1 h5!? 81 ♕c2 g4 82 ♕d1! ♕e5 (82 ... gxf3+ 83 ♕xf3 ♕xf3+ 84 ♔xf3=; 81 h3?? ♕e6) 83 ♕d2.

79	♔h3!?

79 ♕d1 ♔h4 80 ♕c2 g4 (80 ... ♕e1 81 ♕d3 h5 82 ♕c2 g4 83 ♕d3) 81 ♕d1!.

79	...	♕e7
80	♕f5	♕e8!
81	♕f6??	

81 ♕d5 ♛c8+ 82 ♔g2 ♔h4
83 ♕d2.

81	...	♛c8+
82	♔g2	♛c2+

83	♔h3	♛c4
84	♕b2	♛f1+
85	♕g2	♛xg2+
86	♔xg2	0-1

Q
27
+
W

Averbakh - Suetin
USSR Ch Kiev 1954
Here Black has an additional weakness in the e-pawn. Moreover, there is a juicy square on g5 for the white king to target. Averbakh won quite quickly by advancing his king to that square and creating mating threats.

42 g4! ♕d2

Black cannot play 42 ... e4 43 ♔g3 e3 to expose the white king because of 44 ♕h5+ ♔g8 45 ♕e8+ and 46 ♕xe3.

43	♔g3	♛c3+
44	♔h4	♕d4

45	♕f5+	g6

If 45 ... ♔g8/h8 then 46 f3 followed by ♔h5 preparing the mating net g5 - g6.

46	♕f7+	♔h6
47	♕f6	♔h7
48	♔g5	♕d2+
49	f4	exf4

The pawn ending after 49 ... ♕xf4+ is calculably won for White.

50	♕f7+	♔h8
51	♔h6!	

If 51 ... f3+ 52 g5 closes the tent door and shuts out the wild elements.

1-0

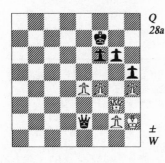

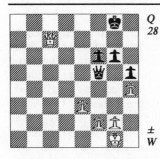

Q
28
±
W

Q
28a
±
W

Sämisch - Maroczy
Carlsbad 1929
With four pawns against three, White has excellent winning chances. In the end, though, Maroczy, who was extremely good at queen endings, held the draw.

47	f3	♕d3
48	e4	♕d2
49	♔h2	♕b2
50	♕g3	♔f7
51	f4	♕e2 *(28a)*
52	♕b3+	

Alternatively:

a) Velickovic analysed instead 52 e5 when:

a1) if 52 ... fxe5 he gives a win with 53 fxe5 ♕a6 54 ♕f4+ ♔e7 55 ♕e4 ♔f7 56 ♔g3 ♕e6 57 ♔f4 ♕g4+ 58 ♔e3 ♕e6 59 g3 ♔e7 60 ♕b7+ ♔d8 61 ♕b8+ ♔d7 62 ♔d4 ♕c6 63 ♕b3 ♔e7 64 ♕c4 ♕d7+ 65 ♔e3 ♕f5 66 ♕c7+ ♔e8 67 ♕d6 ♔f7 68 ♔d4 ♕f2+ 69 ♔c4 ♕a2+ 70 ♔b4 ♕b2+ 71 ♔a5 ♕a2+ 72 ♔b6 and wins;

a2) He claims that 52 ... ♕e4 holds after 53 ♕f3 ♕e1 54 ♕b7+ ♔g8 55 ♕d5+ ♔g7=;

b) If 52 f5 gxf5 53 exf5 ♕e5! 54 ♕xe5 fxe5 55 g4 hxg4 56 ♔g3 e4 57 ♔xg4 e3 58 ♔f3 ♔f6= (Cabrilo).

52	...	♔g7
53	♕b7+	♔f8
54	♕c8+	♔e7
55	♕c7+	♔e6
56	♕c6+	♔e7
57	♕c5+	♔f7
58	♕d5+	♔e7
59	♕b7+	♔e8
60	♕c6+	♔e7
61	♕c5+	♔f7
62	♕c7+	♔e6
63	f5+	gxf5
64	♕c8+	♔e7
65	♕xf5	♔f7
66	♔h3	♕d3+
67	♕f3	♕d7+
68	♔h2	♕b5

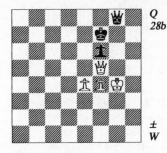

Q
28b

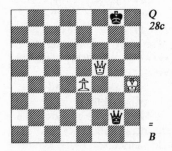

Q
28c

±
W

	69	♕f4	♕e2		85	♔g4	♕e6+
	70	♕f3	♕b5		86	♔h5	♕e5+
	71	g4	hxg4		87	♔g4	♕e6+
	72	♕xg4	♕b2+		88	♕f5	♕g8+
	73	♔g3	♕c3+		89	♔f4	♕f7
	74	♔f3	♕c7+		90	♕d5	♕g6
	75	♔g4	♕d7+		91	h5	♕h6+
	76	♔h5	♕e8!		92	♔g4	♔e7!
	77	♕f5	♕h8+				
	78	♔g4	♕g8+ *(28b)*				
	79	♔f4					

79 ♔f3 would have stopped 79 ... ♕g2 in the note to the next move.

79 ...   ♕b8+

Fine gives 79 ... ♕g2 80 ♕d7+ ♔f8 81 ♔f5 ♕f3+=.

80	♔g4	♕g8+
81	♔f3	♕g1
82	♕d7+	♔f8
83	♕h7	♕d1+
84	♔f4	♕d6+

=
B

If 92 ... ♕g7+ 93 ♔f5 ♕g5+ 94 ♔e6+-. Now after 93 ♕c5+ ♔d7 94 ♕f5+ ♔e7 95 ♕f4 ♕g7+ 96 ♔h4 ♕g2 97 h6 ♔f7 98 ♕c7+ ♔g8 99 ♕d8+ ♔h7 100 ♕e7+ ♔xh6 101 ♕xf6+ ♔h7 102 ♕f7+ ♔h8 103 ♕h5+ ♔g8 104 ♕f5 *(28c)* the players finally agreed a draw. The exchange of queens last move by 104 ♕g4+ ♕xg4+ 105 ♔xg4 led only to a draw after 105 ... ♔f8! 106 ♔f4 ♔e8=.

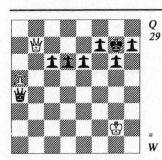

Q
29

=
W

Outside passed pawns

Outside passed pawns are especially valuable in queen endings and can often outweigh a material disadvantage. There are two specific reasons for this:

a) A queen cannot blockade a passed pawn against a queen and pawn since one can always arrange to hit her with the other queen supported by the pawn (e.g. in diag 30 Black cannot maintain the queen on c8 in view of ♕d8);

b) The option of sacricing a piece for the monster and then carrying on playing is not normally available since the only piece that one can sacrifice is the queen herself.

Here despite five(!) extra pawns, Black has no winning chances after

1   a6

i.e. the speed of queening outweighs the number of pawns.

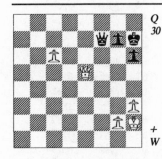

Q
30

+
W

Averbakh 1982

White wins easily.

1	c7	♕d7
2	♕e4+	g6

2 ... ♔h8 3 ♕a8+ ♔h7 4 c8♕ ♕d6+ 5 g3 ♕d2+ 6 ♔g2.

3	♕c2	♕c8
4	♕c5	h5

4 ... ♔g7 5 ♕e7+ ♔g8 6 ♕d8+;

4 ... ♔g8 5 ♕a7 ♕e6 6 ♕b8+ ♔g7 7 c8♕;

4 ... g5 5 ♕c2+ ♔g7 6 ♕b2+ ♔h7 7 ♕b8.

5	♕e7+	♔h6
6	h4	♕h8

6 ... ♕a6 7 ♕f8+ ♔h7 8 c8♕.

7	♕e3+	♔h7
8	♕e6	♕d4
9	♕e7+	♔h6
10	♕g5+	♔g7
11	c8♕	and wins

Q 31
+
W

Marjanovic - Schüssler
Trstenik 1979
White is able to transfer the queen with checks to a better defensive location, after which Black's desperate attempts to create counterplay in the form of checks are much too slow.

1	♕b8+	♔h7
2	♕b1+	f5
3	♕a2	h5

3 ... f4 4 exf4 gxf4 5 ♕c2+ followed by ♕c7+ and ♕xf4 wins.

4	a6	h4
5	a7	hxg3+
6	fxg3	♕a8
7	♕xe6	♕xa7
8	♕xf5+	♔h6
9	♕f6+	♔h7
10	♕xg5	1-0

Q 32
=
W

Alekhine - Reshevsky
AVRO 1938
If the pawn had been on f2 then White would have been able to create perfect shelter for his king with 44 ♕e4! after which White should win analogously to diags 35 and 36. But with the second rank open, he has to take constant care of his king and Reshevsky managed to save the draw.

44	♕a2	♔g8
45	a4	♕c6
46	a5	♕a6

And it appears that in this position White can make no progress.

47	g4	

The immediate atttempt to evict the blockader led to 47

♕d5 ♔g7 48 ♕d4+ ♔g8 49 ♕b6 ♕e2+. Therefore White decided to improve his pawn structure first.

47	...	g5
48	♔f2	♕d6
49	♔f1	♕a6+
50	♔g2	♔g7
51	♕b2+	♔g8
52	♕b8+	♔g7
53	♕e5+	♔g8
54	♔f2	♕a7+
55	♔e2	♕a6+
56	♔d2	♕c4!

Black must block the white king's path.

57	♕f5	♕d4+
58	♔e2	♕b2+
59	♔d3	♕b3+
60	♔e2	♕b2+
	½-½	

Q 33
-
B

Korchnoi - Anand
Tilburg 1991
This is more difficult than the previous example. But after a certain amount of manoeuvring Anand broke through.

82	♕b8+	♔c5
83	♕f8+	♔d5
84	♕f3+	♔d6
85	♔a3	

85 ♕f8+ ♔c7 86 ♕e7+ ♔b6.

85	...	♕a1+

86	♔b3	♕f6
87	♕d3+	♔e7
88	♕g3	♕d6
89	♕h4+	♔f6
90	♕g3	♔e6
91	♔c4	♕f1+
92	♔c3	

92 ♔c5 ♕b5+.

92	...	♕c1+
93	♔b3	♕b1+
94	♔a3	♕a1+
95	♔b3	♕e5
96	♕h4	♔d5
97	♕f2	♕f6

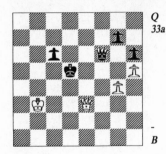

Q
33a

-
B

	98	♕e3 *(33a)*
	98	...	♛e6
	99	♕f4	♚c5+
	100	♚a3	♛d6
	101	♕e3+	♚c4+

The black king penetrates with the aid of discovered checks.

	102	♚a2	♛d5
	103	♕b6	c5
	104	♚a3	♛d3+
	105	♚a2	♛d2+
	106	♚a1	♛b4

	107	♕e6+	♚c3
	108	♕e3+	♚c2
	109	♕f2+	♛d2
	110	♕f5+	

110 ♕xc5+ ♚c3+ and Black, with this counter-check, forces the exchange of queens and wins the pawn ending.

	110	...	♚b3
	111	♕f7+	c4

0-1

Either mate follows or the queens are exchanged.

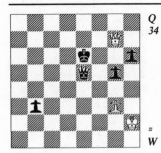

Q
34

=
W

Chiburdanidze - Gaprindashvili Tbilisi 1984

Black has excellent winning chances. But Chiburdanidze defends very resourcefully and eventually manages to hold an ending of two pawns against one on the same side.

	64	♕g8+!	♚f5
	65	♕f7+	

If 65 ♕xb3? ♛e2+ 66 ♚g1 ♚g4 would win.

| | 65 | ... | ♚g4 |

Or 65 ... ♛f6 66 ♕d5+ ♚g4 67 ♕d1+ ♚f3 68 ♕d7+ with perpetual.

On 65 ... ♚e4 White should be able to draw after 66 ♕xb3.

	66	♕c4+	♚f3
	67	♕f1+!	

Not 67 ♕xb3+ ♛e3 and the black king can be wormed further into the vicinity of the white king with threats to ex

change queens if not mating.

	67	...	♚e4
	68	♕b1+	

Black retains good winning chances after 68 ♕c4+ ♛d4 69 ♕xb3 ♛f2+ (or 69 ... ♛e3).

| | 68 | ... | ♚f3 |

If 68 ... ♚d4 69 ♕a1+.

| | 69 | ♕f1+ | ♚e3 |

70 ♕e1+ ♚d4 71 ♕b4+ ♚d3 72 ♕xb3+ ♚c3 73 ♕e6 ♛d2+ 74 ♚h3 ♛e3 75 ♕a6+! (not falling into 75 ♕xh6 g4+!) 75 ... ♚d2 76 ♕a2+ ♚e1 77 ♕a1+ ♚f2 78 ♕f6+ (78 ♕b2+ allows 78 ... ♛e2) with the ability to reach eventually ... ♚g1 followed by interpositions ... ♛f2 and ... ♛f1) 78 ... ♛f3 (If 78 ... ♚e2 79 ♕a6+! ♛d3 80 ♕xh6=) 79 ♕b6+ ♛e3 80 ♕f6+ ♛f3 81 ♕b6+ ♚e1 82 ♕b4+ ♚f2 83 ♕b6+ ½-½

Q
35

-
W

Flohr - Levenfish Moscow 1936

Material is level, but the outside a-pawn gives Black serious winning chances.

	62	♛d3	♛a5
	63	♕a3	♛d2+
	64	♚h3	♛d1
	65	♕c5	

If 65 ♚g2 ♛b3 66 ♕c5 ♛d3 will enable Black to advance the outside passed pawn.

	65	...	♛d3
	66	♕a5!	

For if 66 ... a3 67 e4! fxe4 68 ♕f5+ ♚g8 69 ♕e6+ ♚f8 70 f5 leads to major complications.

66 ...   ♛e4!

Zugzwang!? On 67 ♔h4 Black has 67 ... g5+ 68 ♔h3 ♔g6 threatening both 69 ... ♔h5 and 69 ... g4+ leading to mate and meeting 69 ♕c7 with 69 ... ♛f3 and another mate!

67 ♕a7   ♛b4!
68 ♕f7   ♛a5

White can no longer blockade the pawn and must seek the advance of kingside pawns for counterplay.

69 e4   fxe4

Not 69 ... a3 70 exf5 ♛a6 71 g4 a2 72 f6 with a last ditch draw.

70 ♕e8   ♛f5+
71 ♔g2   ♛d5??

71 ... a3 72 ♕a8 e3! 73 ♕xa3 ♛e4+ 74 ♔f1 (74 ♔h3 e2) 74 ... ♛f3+ led to checkmate.

Now the game ended in a draw after 72 ♕xa4 e3+ 73 ♔g1 ♛d3 74 ♕e8 ♛b1+ 75 ♔g2 ♛c2+ 76 ♔h3 ♛f5+ (76 ... e2 77 ♕e6) 77 ♔g2 ♛d5+ 78 ♔h3 ♛f3 79 ♕e6 ♛f1+ 80 ♔h4 ½-½.

Q 36
+ B

R. Maric - Quinteros
Vinkovci 1970

Amid the tactical battles White's advanced passed a-pawn plays the decisive role.

1 ...   ♛c7

The game itself continued instead 1 ... h5 2 ♕e4! h4 3 ♕f3 ♔f5 4 ♕g4+ ♔e4 5 ♕e6+ ♔d3 6 ♕b3+ ♔d2 (if 6 ... ♔e4 7 ♕b7+ ♔d3 8 a7 wins) 7 ♕a2+ ♔e3 8 a7 f3 9 gxf3! ♕c7+ 10 ♔h1 ♛g3 (or 10 ... ♛c1+ 11 ♔g2) 11 ♕g2 1-0 *(36a)*.

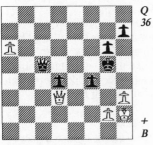

Q 36a
+ B

2 ♕e4!

Not 2 g3 ♛c2+ 3 ♔g2 d3.

2 ...   ♔h6

Or instead:

a) 2 ... f3+ 3 g3 f2 4 ♕g4+ followed eventually by ♕xd4+;

b) 2 ... h5 3 h4+ ♔g4 (if 3 ... ♔xh4 4 a7 wins; if 3 ... ♔h6 4 ♕xd4 f3+ 5 ♔g1 ♛c1+ 6 ♔f2 wins) 4 ♕b7 ♛e5 5 ♕f3+ ♔f5 6 ♕d3+ ♔f6 7 a7 and White escapes the perpetuals;

c) 2 ... ♛b6 3 ♕e7+ ♔h6 4 a7 wins easily;

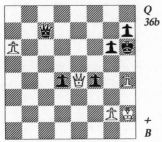

Q 36b
+ B

d) 2 ... ♛c5 3 h4+! ♔xh4 4 ♕xf4+ ♔h5 5 ♔h3 ♛c3+ 6 g3 g5 7 ♕f7+ ♔h6 8 ♔g4!

♛c8+ 9 ♕f5 ♛xf5+ 10 ♔xf5 d3 11 a7 d2 12 a8♕ d1♕ 13 ♕f8+ and mates in three.

3 h4! *(36b)*
3 ...   g5

If 3 ... ♔h5 4 ♕b7 ♛e5 5 ♕f3+ and 6 a7 wins. Or 3 ... f3+ 4 g3 ♛b6 5 ♕f4+ ♔g7 6 ♕e5+ ♔h6 (on 6 ... ♔g8 7 ♕d5+ forces the exchange of queens) 7 ♕g5+ ♔g7 8 ♕e7+ and now:

a) 8 ... ♔h6 9 ♕f8+ ♔h5 10 ♕xf3+ ♔h6 11 ♕f8+ ♔h5 12 ♕f4! ♛b5 13 ♔h3 and mates;

b) 8 ... ♔g8 9 ♕b7 ♛a5 10 a7! ♛a2+ 11 ♔h3 ♛g2+ 12 ♔g4 h5+ 13 ♔f4 with ♔xf3, ♔g2, ♔g1 and ♔h2 as a convenient route to escape checks.

4 ♕b7   ♛e5
5 ♕f3   ♛c7

If 5 ... ♛a5 6 ♕c6+ ♔h5 7 ♕b7 gains a critical tempo.

6 ♔h3   d3

6 ... ♛c8+ is met by 7 ♕g4 preparing ♕xg5 mate.

7 hxg5+   ♔xg5
8 ♕d5+   ♔h6

Or 8 ... ♔f6 9 ♕xd3 ♛b6 10 ♔g4! and with further care wins.

9 ♕xd3   ♔g7

9 ... ♔g5 allows the clever

10 g4!   11   a7 and wins

     10   ♕d4+   ♔g6   Analysis by Rudolf Maric.

Q 37

+ W

Tactics

The queen is a powerful piece and queen endings are naturally full of tactics.

Skewers, Pins, Forks and Cross-Checks

The only normal way for a queen to win another queen is by a skewer. A particularly good example of multiple skewers is diag 13.

Pinning is one of the main ways of defending against a passed pawn supported by its king. There are countless examples of this in the sections on queen and pawn against queen. A queen cannot, strictly speaking, fork a king and queen though it will frequently fork two or more pawns. However, there is a very important motif: the cross-check, whereby a player in check arranges to interpose his queen with check. Obviously by doing so he is effec

tively forking the enemy king and queen. Crosschecking is one of the main ways of averting perpetual check. For example:

Diagram 36

This position could arise at the very end of a queen and g-pawn ending. After 1 ♔h7! White wins at once since 1 ... ♕h1+ and 1 ... ♕b1+ are met by the cross-checks 2 ♕h6+ and 2 ♕g6+ respectively; whilst 1 ... ♕a7 fails to the skewer 1 ... ♕e3+/1 ... ♕g1+.

Cross-checking is in itself an extension of interposition: stopping the checks by putting one's queen in the way.

Checkmate

Since a queen is such a powerful attacking force, the threat of checkmate is a very common theme in queen endings. A good example of this was diag 2.

Q 38

= B

Borisenko - Simagin
Moscow 1955

     1   ...   ♕f1+

White has an extra outside passed pawn but his king is very exposed and this factor enables Black to hold the draw. For example, after 1 ... ♕f1+ 2 ♔h2 (2 ♔h4 ♕e2! threatens mate and forces a repetition) 2 ... ♕e2+ 3 ♔g1 ♕e1+ 4 ♔g2 ♕e2+ 5 ♔f2 ♕e4+ 6 ♔h2 ♕c4! there is no way White

can improve his position. White chooses another plan to try to get his king over to the queenside to support the passed pawn but there is a major defect.

     2   ♔g4?   f5+!

     3   gxf6

Or 3 ♔h4 ♕h1 mate.

     3   ...   ♕f5+

     4   ♔h4   ♕h5

        mate

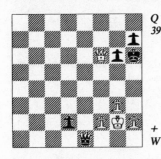

Q
39

+
W

Kartanaite - Kutavitshyene
Vilnius 1983

    1   ♕f8+   ♚h5

1 ... ♚g5 allows mate in two.

    2   ♕f4

Threatening mate!

    2   ...   g5

If 2 ... ♕e7 3 g4+ ♚h4 4 h3! intending ♕h6 mate.

    3   ♕f7+   ♚h6

    4   ♕f6+   ♚h5

    5   g4+   ♚h4

Or 5 ... ♚xg4 6 ♕f3+ and mates.

    6   ♕f3   ♕e4

To prolong the resistance.

    7   ♕xe4   d1♕

    8   h3   ♕d7

8 ... h6 9 ♕e5 to play 10 ♕g3+.

    9   ♕f3   1-0

Mate in two.

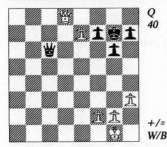

Q
40

+/=
W/B

Perpetual Check

With a queen to check with, the defender can often threaten perpetual check if the stronger side's king is at all exposed.

The threat of perpetual, however, can usually be averted by centralising the queen so as to hinder the defender's own queen. In some cases, the king will then have to walk in order to escape the checks. It can either find total shelter or aim for a square on which it escapes by threatening to interpose the queen either with a pin or a cross-check.

A.

Black to move forces immediate perpetual with:

    1   ...   ♕c1+

    2   ♚h2   ♕f4+

    3   ♚g1   ♕c1+

    4   ♚h2   ♕f4+

    5   g3   ♕xf2+=

B.

White to move must not play 1 e8♕? since the perpetual still works. But he can win in several ways, one of them being 1 ♕b8.

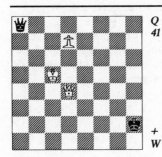

Q
41

+
W

Wheel Checks

"Star" checks going round the twinkling points of a star or "wheel" checks revolving like the spokes of a wheel are shown in diag 41. They are a form of perpetually checking the king and queen. Play could go:

    1   ...   ♕a7+

    2   ♚c4   ♕a4+

    3   ♚c3   ♕a1+

    4   ♚d3   ♕d1+

    5   ♚e3   ♕g1+

    6   ♚e4   ♕g4+

    7   ♚e5   ♕g7+ etc.

Queen v Queen

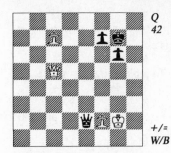

Q 42

+/=
W/B

A.

Black to move draws with:

1	...	♛g4+
2	♔f1	♛d1+
3	♔g2	♛g4+

| 4 | ♔h2 | ♛h4+= |

B.

With *White to move* 1 c8♘ covers g4.

Q 43

=
B

Lolli 1763

1	...	♛h4+
2	♛h7	

Or 2 ♔g8 ♛d8+, ... ♛d7+, ... ♛d4+, ... ♛g4+, ... ♛h4+ etc.

2	...	♛d8+
3	g8♛	

3 g8♖ is the same; if 3 g8♘ ♛d4+ 4 ♛g7 ♛xg7.

| 3 | ... | ♛f6+= |

Q 44

-
B

Stalemate

Stalemate, or the threat of stalemate, is an extremely common theme in queen endings: after all, a queen can stalemate a king in the corner all by itself.

Sometimes it is necessary to under-promote; see for example QRQ2.

Pilnick - Reshevsky
USA Championship 1942
Reshevsky blundered with:

92	...	g4??

This allowed:

93	♛f2!	½-½

Now stalemate cannot be avoided.

Instead of the impatient 92 ... g4 Reshevsky could have continued 92 ... ♛c1+ 93 ♔g2 and then 93 ... ♔b8 is an idea to explore, e.g. 94 ♛e5+ ♔c7 95 ♛h8+ (95 ♛xg5 ♛g3+ reaches a winning pawn ending) 95 ... ♔a7 96 ♛d4+ ♔a8 97 ♛h8+ ♔b8 98 ♛e4 g4!.

Queen v Queen v

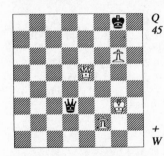

Q
45
+
W

Lehmann - Pfeiffer
Germany 1958
   1   ♚h4!
   This enables White to parry the stalemate idea that decided actual play - 1 ♚g4? ♛xg6+ 2 ♛g5 ♚h8! (3 ♛xg6 stalemate) to lead into a "drawable" end-ing.

1	...	♛xg6
2	♛g5	♚h8
3	♛h5+!	

Now the exchange of queens - forced - gives White a won pawn ending.

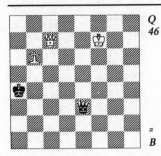

Q
46
=
B

Podgaets - Klovan
USSR 1969
   1   ...   ♚a5
   The surprising point! Instead of giving a series of futile checks which would only drive the king over to support the pawn, Black encourages White to promote.

2	b7+	♚a6
3	b8♘+	

White had to advance his pawn since otherwise he would just lose it. If 3 b8♛ ♛e6+ 4 ♚g7 ♛h6+ 5 ♚g8 ♛h8+ 6 ♚f7 ♛f6+ is perpetual check or stalemate; hence the knight promotion, but White still has no winning chances.

3	...	♚b5

½-½

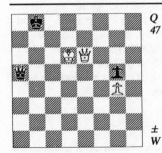

Q
47
±
W

J. Polgar - Tolnai
Budapest 1991
White's obvious plan is to swap queens and win the pawn ending.
   However, after:
   1   ♛e5!?
Black can frustrate the first step by:

1	...	♛c7+
2	♚e6	♚a8

and if
   3   ♛xc7 stalemate!
Instead White would, of course play 3 ♛xg5 and might win a long drawn-out ending.
   The game actually continued with 1 ♛e5!? ♛b6+? 2 ♚d5+ ♚b7 3 ♛e7+ ♚a8 4 ♛e8+ ♚b7 5 ♛d7+ 1-0 since after 5 ... ♚b8 6 ♛d6+ ♚a8 7 ♛c6+!

Q
48
+
B

Liquidation
Queen and pawn endings are complicated by the presence of such powerful units on the board; so it is always a good idea to transpose to a pawn ending, provided you are sure about the result.
K. Solja 1989
   White forces the exchange of queens with a series of checks.

1	...	♚f4
2	♛f8+	♚e4
3	♛e7+	♚f3
4	♛f6+	♚e4
5	♛c6+	♚f4
6	♛d6+	♚f3
7	♛d5+	♚e2
8	♛e4+ and wins	

Queen v Queen ♕ V ♛

Q
49
+
W

Kolchurin - Dryabkin
Kazan Ch 1929
Kolchurin forced the exchange of queens and achieved a winning pawn ending by the precise manoeuvre:

1 ♕d4+ ♔c2
Or 1 ... ♔c1 2 ♕c3+ ♔d1 3 ♕e1+.
2 ♕c5+! ♔d2
On 2 ... ♔d1 3 ♕d5+.
3 ♕a5+! and wins.

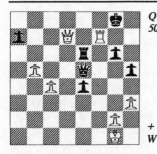

Q
50
+
W

Kasparov - Salov
Dortmund 1992
In contrast to the previous positions, this is an example of liquidation into rather than out of a queen ending. Kasparov forced the exchange of rooks with:

48 ♖g7+ ♕xg7
49 ♕xe6+ ♔h7
50 ♕xe4 ♕c3
51 ♕e7+ ♔h6
52 ♕xa7 ♕c1+
53 ♔h2 ♕xc4
54 ♕b8 1-0

Q
51
=
B

Levitt - Watson
London WFW 1990
While we're on the subject of liquidation, I must stress that it is vital to check the resultant pawn endings. In diag 51, as you can see, there were rooks on the board; but if we changed both pieces to queens then the principle would equally apply. After 38 ... ♖c4?? 39 ♖xc4+ ♔xc4 40 f5 gxf5 41 e6 Black had to resign since the pawn breakthrough forces a queen!

Queen v Queen: Further Examples

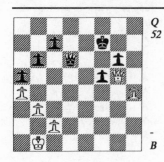

Q
52
-
B

Kostic - Capablanca
match 1919
Queen endings don't have to be long and tortuous. With an extra pawn and a totally sound position Capablanca won easily.

1 ... ♔e8
Intending ... ♔d7 - c8 - b7 sheltering.
2 ♔a2 ♕e6

3 h5 gxh5
4 ♕xh5+ ♔d7
5 ♔b1 ♔c6
6 ♔c1 ♕e3+
7 ♔d1 f4
8 ♕g5 ♕d4+
9 ♔e2 ♕e4+
10 ♔d2 ♕d5+
Exchanging queens and winning.

0-1

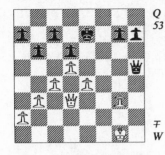

Q
53
W

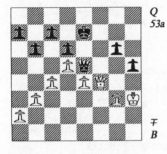

Q
53a
B

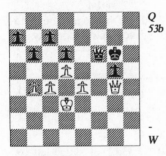

Q
53b
-
W

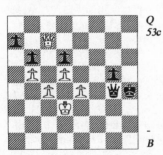

Q
53c
-
B

Keres - Alekhine
Dresden 1936
Black has a big advantage in view of his centralised position and much better pawn structure. Despite protracted resistance Keres was unable to save the game.

30 ♔g2

More resistant perhaps is 30 ♕f1!? meeting 30 ... ♕e5 with 31 ♕f4 as the queen swap leads to a tenable pawn ending.

30 ... ♕e5!

Two factors stand out in this position: the dominating position of the black queen and Black's pawn majority on the king's wing.

31 ♕f3 h5
32 ♔h3

If 32 ♕f4 not 32 ... g5 33 ♕xe5+ reaching a pawn ending with no king entries, but first 32 ... ♕f6.

32 ... g6

Preparing ... ♕f6.

33 ♕f4 *(53a)*

The pawn ending after 33 g4 hxg4+ 34 ♕xg4 ♕h5+! is lost for White.

33 ... ♕f6
34 ♕h6 ♔f7!
35 ♔g2

Ink has been spilt over possibilities after 35 a3 ♕f1+ 36 ♔h2 ♕e2+.

35 ... ♕b2+
36 ♔h3

36 ♔f3!? ♕c3+ 37 ♔f2 ♕c2+ 38 ♔f3 ♕d3+ 39 ♔f2 ♕xe4 40 ♕h7+ ♔f6 41 ♕xc7 leaves Black the initiative but not a clear method of winning.

36 ... ♕a1!
37 ♕f4+ ♔g7
38 ♕f3 ♕f6

38 ... ♕xa2 39 ♕c3+ fol-

lowed by e5 obtains good counterplay.

39 ♕e2 ♔h6
40 ♔g2 g5
41 b4 ♕e5

41 ... h4 is premature, e.g. 42 gxh4 gxh4 43 ♕g4 ♕g5 44 ♔h3 ♕xg4+ 45 ♔xg4 with a tricky pawn ending; a sample line is 45 ... ♔g6 46 ♔xh4 ♔f6 47 ♔g4 ♔e5 48 ♔f3 ♔d4 49 ♔f4 ♔xc4 50 ♔f5 and Black should be content with a draw (Grigoriev).

42 ♕f3 ♔g6
43 g4?

Though after the less committal 43 a3 ♕b2+ 44 ♔g1 ♕f6 45 ♕e3 ♕a1+ 46 ♔g2 ♕a2+ and 47 ... ♕xc4 Black should also have long term winning chances.

43 ... hxg4
44 ♕xg4 ♕b2+
45 ♔f3 ♕a3+!
46 ♔e2 ♕xa2+
47 ♔d3 ♕b3+
48 ♔d4 ♕b2+
49 ♔d3 ♕f6 *(53b)*

Besides the passed g-pawn, Black has the possibility of ... a7-a5.

50 b5

If 50 50 ♕c8 ♕f4 51 ♕xc7 Black runs with the g-pawn.

50 ... ♕f4
51 ♕e6+ ♔h5
52 ♕h3+ ♕h4
53 ♕f3+ ♕g4
54 ♕f7+ ♔h4
55 ♕xc7 *(53c)*
55 ... ♕f3+
56 ♔d4 ♕f6+

Protecting d6 as a necessary preliminary to pushing the g-pawn.

57 ♔d3 g4
58 ♕h7+ ♔g5
59 ♕g8+ ♔f4
60 ♕e6 ♔g5!

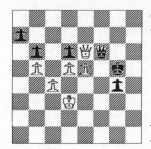

Q
53d

B

If 60 ... ♕e5 61 ♕f7+ ♔g3 62 ♕xa7 the win is doubtful.

61 e5 (53d)

On 61 ♕g8+ ♕g6 62 ♕d8+ ♔f4 Black wins easily.

61	...	♕xe5
62	♕xe5+	dxe5
63	♔e4	♔f6
64	♔e3	♔f5
65	♔f2	e4
66	♔e2	g3
67	♔e3	♔g4

Without critical calculation is the methodical 67 ... ♔e5 68 ♔e2 ♔d6 69 ♔e3 (69 ♔f1

e3) 69 ... ♔c7 70 ♔e2 ♔b7 71 ♔e3 a5 72 bxa6+ ♔xa6 73 ♔e2 ♔b7 74 ♔e3 ♔c7 75 ♔e2 ♔d6 76 ♔e3 b5 eliminating White's assets.

68	d6	g2
69	♔f2	♔h3
70	d7	e3+
71	♔f3	g1♕
72	d8♕	♕f2+
73	♔e4	e2
74	♕d7+	♔g2
75	♕g4+	♔f1

0-1

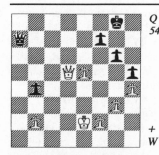

Q
54

+
W

Smyslov - Lilienthal
Moscow 1947
This is an example of transformation of an advantage.

1 e6! fxe6

If 1 ... ♕e7 2 ♕d7 ♕xe6+ 3 ♕xe6 fxe6 4 ♔d3 and wins.

2 ♕e4! ♔f7

In the game Black played 2 ... ♕a6+!? 3 ♕d3 ♕b6 4 ♕g6+ ♔f8 5 ♕xh5 and thus lost two pawns. White won in another 16 moves.

3 ♕xb4

And the b-pawn should be enough to win comfortably.

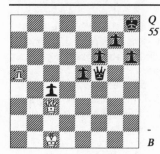

Q
55

B

Lasker - Capablanca
Moscow 1936
A classic endgame. Despite Black's four extra pawns, White has some swindling chances in view of the huge passed a-pawn. But Capablanca wrapped up the game with only two more accurate moves.

53 ... ♕f2

53 ... ♕c8 54 ♕a3 ♕a6 55 ♕c5 c3! 56 ♕xc3 (56 ♕b6 ♕e2) 56 ... e4 57 ♔d2 (57 ♕a3 e3!) 57 ... f5 overturns previous thinking and also wins (Minev).

53 ... e4 54 a6 ♕c5 55 ♕b2 c3 56 ♕b8+ (if 56 ♕b7 ♕f2! wins) 56 ... ♔h7 57 a7 ♕e3+ 58 ♔b1 ♕d3+ 59 ♔a2 c2 60 a8♕ (60 ♔b2 ♕d2 61 ♕h8+

♔g6! 62 ♕e8+ ♔g5 63 ♕b5+ f5 wins) 60 ... ♕c4+ 61 ♕b3 c1♘+! wins.

54 ♕a3?!

If 54 ♕d2, as suggested by Lasker, 54 ... ♕c5! (zugzwang!) 55 ♕c3 e4 takes control.

Or 54 ♕xc4 ♕e1+ 55 ♔c2 ♕xa5 when Black can give up two pawns and avoid the checks after 56 ♕c8+ ♔h7 57 ♕f5+ ♔g8 58 ♕e6+ ♔f8 59 ♕d6+ ♔e8 60 ♕e6+ ♔d8 61 ♕g8+ ♔e7 62 ♕xg7+ ♔e6 63 ♕g8+ ♔d6 64 ♕f8+ ♔d5 65 ♕xf6 by 65 ... ♕a4+! (planning 66 ... ♕f4), thus winning (Capablanca).

54 ... ♔h7!
0-1

If 55 a6 c3! 56 ♕xc3 ♕f1+.

Queen v Queen

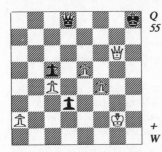

Q
55

+
W

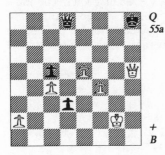

Q
55a

+
B

Sax - Franzoni
Thessaloniki ol 1984
This ending is an illustration of the skilful use of queen and pawns as an attacking force and incorporates mating and stalemate ideas and careful transitions to pawn endings.

    48   ♕h5+   ♔g8

For 48 ... ♔g7 see diag 71a below.

    49   e6!   d2

If 49 ... ♕f6 50 ♕f7+.

    50   ♕f7+   ♔h8
    51   e7   ♕xe7

Instead if 51 ... ♕a8+ 52 ♕d5 ♕xd5+ 53 cxd5 d1♕ 54 e8♕+ ♔g7 55 ♕e7+ ♔h6 (after 55 ... ♔g8 perhaps 56 ♕xc5 is simplest) 56 ♕f6+ and now:

a) 56 ... ♔h5 57 ♕g6+, 58 ♕g3+ and 59 ♕f3+ wins;

b) 56 ... ♔h7 57 ♕f7+ ♔h8 58 ♔g3 with the white king escaping into the black side of the board.

    52   ♕xe7   d1♕
    53   ♕e5+   ♔h7

Or 53 ... ♔g8 54 ♕d5+ reaching a won pawn ending.

    54   ♕e4+   ♔h8
    55   f5   ♕d2+
    56   ♔f3   ♕xa2

56 ... ♕c3+ 57 ♔f4 is another escape.

    57   f6   1-0

Diagram 55a

    48   ...   ♔g7

Instead of 48 ... ♔g8 as played.

    49   f5!

Instead 49 e6 d2 50 ♕f7+ ♔h6 51 e7 ♕a8+ enables Black to uncover two stalemate ideas, viz. 52 ♔h2 ♕h1+!! or 52 ♔g3 ♕f3+!!; the other continuation 52 ♕d5 ♕xd5+ 53 cxd5 d1♕ 54 e8♕ ♕xd5+ followed by ... ♕xa2 arrives at a level ending.

    49   ...   ♕a8+

If 49 ... d2 50 f6+ ♔g8 51 ♕g6+, 52 ♕g7+, 53 f7+ etc.

    50   ♔g3   ♕e4
    51   f6+   ♔f8

After 51 ... ♔g8 52 ♕g5+ ♔f7 53 ♕g7+ ♔e6 54 ♕e7+ ♔f5 55 ♕h7+ ♔xe5 White forces an easily won pawn ending by 56 ♕xe4+ ♔xe4 57 ♔f2!.

    52   ♕h8+

And wins similarly to previous note.

Analysis based on notes by Sax and Hazai.

Queen v Rook (and Pawns) ♕ V ♖(♙)

Queen v Rook: No Pawns

The ending of queen v rook without pawns is always winning unless the player with the rook to play can force a draw, or indeed, a win, immediately.

Until the advent of computer databases, this ending was thought to be fairly simple: although "Euclid", a certain Alfred Crosskill Beverley, devoted a whole book of 120 positions to it in 1895.

If the rook defends very accurately, however, the win can be quite difficult. In 1978, the American grandmaster Walter Browne took on a database. He failed to win the first time round and only won the replay on the fiftieth move.

If the defending king can be driven into the corner, the win is easy - see diag QR1. The main problem arises, however, if the defender manages to set up the third rank defence. In order to break this it is sometimes necessary to retreat the queen from an apparently superb position on the seventh rank, in order to switch flanks suddenly and so outwit the rook. The absolutely critical position is diag QR3.

QR 1
+B

Philidor 1777
From diag 1 flow a cascade of queen checks forking king and rook dependent on the square the rook is placed to seek safety.

White, in five moves, wins the rook or mates: If 1 ... ♔h6 2 ♕f8 pins and wins.
1... ♖g8 2 ♕h5 mate.
1... ♖b7 2 ♕e4+.
1... ♖g2 2 ♕e4+.

1 ... ♖g4 2 ♕h5+.
1 ... ♖g1 2 ♕e4+ ♔h8/g8 3 ♕a8+ ♔h7 4 ♕a7+.
1 ... ♖g3 2 ♕e4+ ♔g8 3 ♕c4+ ♔h7 4 ♕h4+.
1 ... ♖a7 2 ♕h5+ ♔g8 3 ♕d5+ ♔h8 4 ♕h1+ ♔g8 (4 ... ♖h7 5 ♕a8 mate) 5 ♕g1+.
1 ... ♖c7 2 ♕h5+ ♔g8 3 ♕d5+ ♔h7 4 ♕d3+ ♔g8/h8 5 ♕d8+.

QR 2
=B

Berger 1889
Exceptions to the winning process occur when there are possibilities for pinning the queen against its king or for stalemating. Play from diag 2

could go 1 ... ♖h7+ 2 ♔g2 ♖g7+ 3 ♔h3 ♖h7+ 4 ♔g4 ♖g7+ 5 ♔h5 ♖h7+ 6 ♔g5 ♖g7+ 7 ♔h6 ♖h7+ 8 ♔g6 ♖h6+ 9 ♔xh6 stalemate.

QR 3
+W

In diag 3 White is intent on driving the rook off its third rank and bringing up the king to confront the black king. After 1 ♔g5 the black rook has only one "safe" square at h8. If 1 ... ♖h2 2 ♕d6+; 1 ... ♖h1 2

♕c8+; 1 ... ♖b6 2 ♕d8+; 1 ... ♖a6 2 ♕c8+ - all forks. But after 1 ... ♖h8 2 ♔g6 (threatening 3 ♕d8) 2 ... ♖g8+ 3 ♔f6 Black can delay, but not stop, mate.

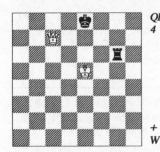

QR 4

+ W

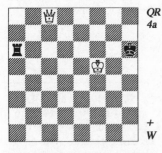

QR 4a

+ W

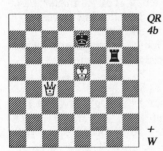

QR 4b

+ W

If we shift all the pieces in diag 3 one square towards the a-file we reach diag 4. The winning process is much more difficult here.

There is still the same need to eject the rook from the third frame (c6 - f6 - f3 - c3) and establish the attacking king thereon. One must find squares from which the queen will dominate and must be prepared to use the whole board.

The first phase is finding such a dominant queen position. Surprisingly the most effective is:

1 ♕c4

Already the rook has no further squares on its rank, viz. 1 ... ♖h6 2 ♕g8+ and 3 ♕g7+; 1 ... ♖b6 2 ♕c8+ and 3 ♕c7+.

And control is exercised over other rook moves: 1 ... ♖g2 2 ♕c6+; 1 ... ♖g1 2 ♕a4+ and eventually forking with ♕a7+; 1 ... ♖g3 2 ♕a4+ ♔e7/d8 (2 ... ♔f7/f8 3 ♕f4+) 3 ♕h4+; 1 ... ♖g5+/g7 allows 2 ♔f6 threatening mate; 1 ... ♔d7/d8 2 ♕d3+ forks.

After 1 ♕c4 Black is therefore limited to 1 ... ♔f8 and to 1 ... ♔e7.

A.

1 ... ♔f8

White can continue herding with:

2 ♔f5 ♔g7

Else:

2 ... ♖d6 allows the pin 3 ♕c5 and after 3 ... ♔e7 4 ♔e5 loses the rook.

2 ... ♖g1 (or 2 ... ♖b6) 3 ♕c5+.

2 ... ♖g2 3 ♕c8+ and 4 ♕b7+.

2 ... ♖g3 3 ♕c8+ and 4 ♕c7+.

2 ... ♖g7 (or 2 ... ♖g8) allows 3 ♔f6 gaining White's main objective.

After 2 ... ♖h6 White has a further powerful centralisation by 3 ♕d4!, e.g. 3 ... ♖h3 4 ♔g6 ♖g3+ 5 ♔f6 ♖f3+ 6 ♔e6 ♖h3 7 ♕f4+ ♔g7 8 ♕g4+ wins the rook, or if 3 ... ♔f7 White continues encroaching with 4 ♕d7+ ♔f8 5 ♔g5 ♖h8 6 ♔g6 ♖g8+ 7 ♔f6, or on 3 ... ♔g8 similarly 4 ♔g5 ♖h7 5 ♔g6.

3 ♕h4! ♖a6

Or 3 ... ♖h6 4 ♕e7+ ♔g8 5 ♕e8+ ♔g7 6 ♔g5 ♖h7 7 ♕e4 ♖h8 8 ♕e7+ ♔g8 9 ♔g6 and mate in two.

4	♕d4+	♔h7
5	♕d7+	♔h6
6	♕d8!	♔g7
7	♕c7+	♔h6
8	♕c8!	*(4a)*

White succeeds with a clever blend of threats to the rook and to mate.

8 ... ♖a5+!
9 ♔f6

And Black must throw the rook to the lions.

B.

Returning to diag 4 Black can play (after 1 ♕c4):

1 ... ♔e7 *(4b)*

Now one winning method is:

2	♕h4+	♔f7
3	♕h7+	♖g7
4	♕f5+	♔g8

After 4 ... ♔e8 5 ♔d6 establishes the white king on the "third frame" (c6-f6-f3-c3).

5	♔e6	♖b7
6	♕d5!	♖f7

Or 6 ... ♖b6+ 7 ♔e7+ ♔h7 8 ♕d3+ setting up the win of the rook.

| 7 | ♕d4! | ♖b7 |

8	♔f6	♖g7
9	♕d8+	♔h7
10	♕e8	

And White has reached the Philidor position (see diag 1).

There could follow 10 ... ♖c7 11 ♕h5+ ♔g8 12 ♕d5+ ♔h7 13 ♕d3+ ♔g8 14 ♕g3+ or 14 ♕d8+.

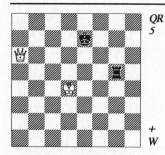

QR 5

+ W

A sample line illustrating the gradual 'herding' by the queen and king: 1 ♕c6 ♖h5 2 ♕c7+ ♔e6 3 ♕d8 ♔f7 4 ♕d6 ♖f5 5 ♔e4 ♖f1 6 ♕d3 ♖f6 7 ♕d7+ ♔g6 8 ♔e5 ♖f7 9 ♕g4+ ♔h6 10 ♔e6 ♖g7 11 ♕d4 ♖g5 12 ♔f6 ♖g6+ 13 ♔f7 ♔h5 14 ♕h8+ ♖h6 15 ♕c8 ♖h7+ 16 ♔f6 ♔h4 (16 ... ♖h6+ 17 ♔f5 ♔h4 18 ♕b7) 17 ♔g6 gains the rook, e.g. 17 ... ♖a7 18 ♕h8+ and forks next move.

QR 6

+ W

A Practical Example

Kamsky - Ljubojevic
Linares 1991

To win White needs to be able to cross the f-file with his king. Black's fortress is broken by:

80	h4	♖f3
81	h5!	gxh5

... so that the black rook has no secure post on the f-file. Play continued:

82	♕c8+	♖f8
83	♕c5	♖f1
84	♕xh5	♖e1+
85	♔f6	♖f1+
86	♔g6	♖g1+
87	♔h6	♖e1 *(7a)*

Now Kamsky won by 88 ♕g4+ ♔f7 89 ♕c4+ ♖e6+ 90 ♔g5 ♔e7 91 ♔f5 ♖h6 92 ♕c7+ ♔e8 ("Black has managed to reach his best defensive position with the rook on the sixth rank to hold back the white king." - Benko) 93 ♕f4 ♖c6 94 ♕a4 ♔d7 95 ♔e5 ♔c7 96 ♕a7+ ♔c8 97 ♔d5 ♖h6 98 ♕g7 ♖a6 99 ♕e7 ♖a2 (if 99 ... ♖b6 100 ♔c5 ♖a6 101 ♔b5 wins) 100

QR 6a

+ W

♕e8+ ♔c7 101 ♕c6+ ♔d8 102 ♕c4 ♖h2 103 ♕d4 ♖h6 104 ♔c5+ ♔c8 105 ♕g4+ 1-0.

The same position put on a queen v rook computer base gave the following moves:

88	♕d5+	

White now needs eight more moves to win.

88	...	♔f8
89	♕c5+	♔e8

Or 89 ... ♔g8 90 ♔g5! (90 ♔g6 takes four moves longer after 90 ... ♖e6+) 90 ... ♖e8 (90 ... ♔h7 91 ♕c2+ ♔g8 92 ♕c4+ wins the rook) 91 ♔f6 ♖f8+ 92 ♔g6 and wins in four more moves.

90	♔g7	♔d7

If 90 ... ♖e6 91 ♕c8+, 92 ♕c7+ and 93 ♕f7+.

91	♕b5+	♔c8

Or:
91 ... ♔e6 92 ♕e8+;
91 ... ♔e7 92 ♕b4+;
91 ... ♔d8 92 ♕a5+.

92	♕c4+	♔d7
93	♕a4+	♔c8
94	♕g4+	

With forks on h4, g3 and b4. So White would win much quicker than in the game.

Queen v Rook (and Pawns)

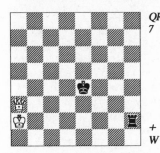

QR 7

+ W

QR 7a

+ W

The longest win

Diag 7 illustrates a queen v rook position setting the optimum difficulty to construct a win. White needs 31 moves to force mate or gain the rook. A sample line runs: 1 ♔a1 ♖f2 2 ♕b4+ ♔d3 3 ♔b1 ♖d2 4 ♕f4 ♔c3 5 ♕e3+ ♖d3 6 ♕c5+ ♔d2 7 ♕c1+ ♔e2 8 ♔c2 ♖d4 9 ♔c3 ♖d5 10 ♕g1 ♖a5 11 ♕b1 ♖a3+ 12 ♔d4 ♖a4+ 13 ♔e5 ♖g4 14 ♕c2+ ♔e3 15 ♕c1+ ♔e2 16 ♕c3 ♖g7 17 ♕c4+ ♔e3 18 ♔f5 ♖g2 *(7a)* (the white pieces are now optimally positioned ready to ease the opposing king back to the rim of the board and keep the rook tamed) 19 ♕f4+ ♔e2 20 ♔e4 ♖f2 21 ♕c1 ♖g2 22 ♕c2+ ♔f1 23 ♕d1+ ♔f2 24 ♔f4 ♖h2 25 ♕d4+ ♔g2 26 ♔g4 ♔h1 27 ♕e4+ ♔g1 28 ♔g3 ♖f2 29 ♕e3 ♔h1 30 ♕e1+ ♖f1 31 ♕xf1 mate.

Queen v Rook and Pawn(s)

Except in very exceptional positions, the queen is, of course, trying to win. "Black" can try to defend in two distinct ways:

a) By setting up a fortress;

b) By supporting the pawn far enough up the board to prevent the white king and queen from mounting a successful attack.

In practical play, fortresses predominate so we shall concentrate on them.

Fortresses

For the fortress to withstand siege it is necessary to keep the enemy forces behind the moat. And in practice this means that the queen must be prevented from getting behind the pawn.

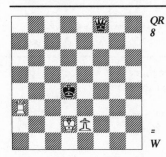

QR 8

= W

Conde, Duke of Olivares collection

The text of a 15th century Spanish manuscript, now in the Library of El Escorial, indicates that White draws by moving the rook between d3 and f3. Since the white rook has two excellent outposts on these two squares there is no way for the queen to get behind the pawn without a treasonous defence. The position is therefore absolutely drawn.

Queen v Rook (and Pawns)

QR
9

+
W

Halberstadt 1931

In contrast, here the pawn is on the third rank and so the white queen is able to infiltrate.

1	♕a1	♖b5
2	♕g7+	♔d8
3	♕f6+	♔d7
4	♕f7+	♔d8
5	♕e6	♔c7
6	♕e7+	♔c8
7	♕d6	♔b7
8	♕d7+	♔b6
9	♕c8	♖d5
10	♕b8+	♔c5
11	♕c7	♔b5
12	♕a7	♖h5

The next objective is to make Black relax the rook's barrier along the fifth rank so that the white king can cross to behind the pawn.

The remaining analysis stems from Cheron, 1950.

13	♔d3!	♖h3+

If 13 ... ♖d5+ 14 ♔c3 ♖c5+ (14 ... ♖h5 15 ♕b7+ ♔c5 16 ♕b4+ ♔d5 17 ♕d4+ ♔e6 18 ♕e4+ and at least the pawn drops) 15 ♔b3 ♖f5 16 ♕b7+ ♔c5 17 ♕b4+ ♔d5 18 ♕d2+ ♔e6 19 ♕d8 ♖d5 20 ♕c7 and Black's position is beginning to give.

14	♔d4	♖h4+
15	♔e5	♖h5+
16	♔f6	♖h6+
17	♔g5	♖h1
18	♕e3	♔a6
19	♔f5	♖h5+
20	♔e6	♖d5
21	♕g3	♔b7
22	♕a3	♖b5
23	♕e7+	♔b6
24	♔d7	♖d5+
25	♔c8	♖c5
26	♕e3	♔b5
27	♕b3+	♔a5
28	♔c7 and wins	

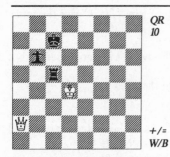

QR
10

+/=
W/B

Cheron 1950

If Black has a knight's pawn, there is no room on the flank and with the move it is possible for Black to draw. (White to move can force the win starting with 1 ♕a7+ ♔c6 2 ♕b8 though it is not by any means trivial.)

1	...	♔b7!

And White can make no progress, e.g.

2	♕f7+	♔b8
3	♕e6	♔b7
4	♕d7+	♔b8
5	♔e4	♔a8
6	♕a4+	♔b7
7	♔d4	♖c7!
8	♔d5	♖c5+
9	♔d6	♖c7
10	♕b5	♖c5
11	♕d7+	♔b8
12	♕g4	♖c7
13	♕e2	

Threatening 14 ♕a6.

13	...	♔b7! etc.

QR
11

=
B

L. I. Kubbel "Archives"

Theory tends to concentrate on positions in which the fortress is already built. But of course in practical play there is often a headlong rush to get the rook back into place; or the king or pawn to the right square. In Kubbel's study, Black is very close to the precipice but with exact play he can survive.

1	...	♖f1!

Of course not 1 ... ♖h1 2 ♕d8+ ♔f7 3 ♕d5+.

2	♕c5+	♔g8
3	♕d5+	

Of course White must prevent ... ♖f6 with an easy draw.

3	...	♖f7
4	♔g4	

Or 4 ♕e6 g6!.

4	...	g6!
5	♔g5	♔g7
6	♕d4+	♔h7
7	♕h4+	♔g7
8	♕h6+	♔g8
9	♔g4	

Instead 9 ♔xg6 fails to the

simple stalemate defence 9 ... ♖f6+!=. Black's position is now critical but the bad position of the white king allows him to evict the intruder.

9	...	♖h7!
10	♕d2	♖f7
11	♔g5	♔g7=

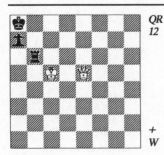

QR 12

+ W

J. Berger 1921

Although in general the defender will prefer to have his pawn as near to the edge of the board as possible, you can have too much of a good thing. Rook's pawns do *not* make a good foundation for a fortress since there is *only one anchor square*.

In diag 12 White can easily put Black into zugzwang.

1	♕d5+	♔b8
2	♕d7	♖h6

Or 2 ... ♔a8 3 ♕c8+ ♖b8 4

♕c6+ ♖b7 5 ♔d6 and the pawn falls.

3	♕e8+	♔b7
4	♕e7+	♔a6
5	♕g7!	

Now on:

a) 5 ... ♖h5+ 6 ♔c6 wins.

b) 5 ... ♖b6 6 ♕d7 ♖b2 7 ♕a4+ ♔b7 8 ♕e4+ ♔a6 9 ♕d3+ ♔b7 10 ♕f3+ ♔c7 11 ♕f7+ ♔b8 12 ♕f8+ ♔b7 13 ♕g7+ and the rook is gone.

c) 5 ... ♖h3 6 ♕f6+ ♔b7 7 ♕e7+ will fork the rook.

White wins.

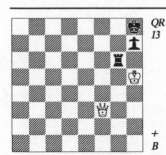

QR 13

+ B

Koblenc 1959

White is also winning with his king on h5.

1	...	♔g8
2	♕a8+	♔g7
3	♕b7+	♔h8

3 ... ♔g8 4 ♕e7!

4	♕f7!	♖h6+
5	♔g5	♖g6+
6	♔f5	♖g1
7	♕f8+	♖g8
8	♕f6+	♖g7
9	♕d8+	♖g8
10	♕d4+	♖g7
11	♕f6!	♔g8
12	♕d8+	♔f7
13	♕h8	

Winning the pawn.

QR 14

+ W

von Guretzky and Cornitz 1864

Leaving aside rook's pawns on the third for the moment, we pass on to diag 14, in which White wins easily by the familiar plan of infiltration from behind.

1	♕d5	♔a6
2	♕c6+	♔a7

Or 2 ... ♖b6 3 ♕a8+ ♔b5 4 ♔b3 ♖a6 5 ♕d5+ ♔b6 6 ♔a4 ♖a7 7 ♕d6+ ♔b7 8 ♔b5 a4 9 ♕b6+ ♔a8 10 ♕c6+, intending ♔b6, wins.

3	♔d3!	♖b6
4	♕c7+	♔a6
5	♕c8+	♔a7
6	♔c4	♖b7
7	♕d8	♔a6
8	♔c5	♖b5+
9	♔c6	

squeezes Black.

QR 15

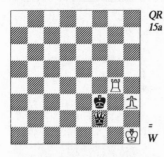

QR 15a

QR 15b

Pawn on the Third Rank

With the pawn further up the board, White is usually still winning. But we've never seen an example of this in actual play: whereas the case of the pawn on the third rank (or on the second and able to advance one square) has occurred several times. The defender can hold as long as he prevents the enemy king from settling on f1 or f2. The natural way to investigate this structure seemed to be to look at potential zugzwang positions:

Diagram 15

White can draw with 1 ♖g1, 1 ♖g4, 1 ♖g8 but not: 1 ♖g6? ♕e5+ 2 ♔h1 ♕h5; 1 ♖g5? ♕d2+; or 1 ♖g7? ♕e5+.

Diagram 15a

Here too, White has a choice: either 1 ♖g1, 1 ♖g6 or 1 ♖g8 draws but not: 1 ♖g5? ♕h4; or 1 ♖g7? ♕h4 2 ♔h2 ♕f4+

3 ♔h1 ♕h6.

Diagram 15b

von Guretsky and Cornitz (with colours reversed) 1864

This is what the defender must avoid. The enemy king can settle on f2 and as a result White falls into zugzwang:

| 1 | ... | ♔f2 |
| 2 | ♔h2 | |

Or 2 ♖g2+ ♔f1 3 ♖g4 ♕f2.

2	...	♕e3
3	♖g1	♕f4+
4	♔h1	♕f3+
5	♔h2	♕e3
6	♖g2+	♔f1
7	♖g4	♕e2+
8	♔h1	♕f2

A zugzwang position.

9	♖g8	♕f3+
10	♔h2	♕f4+
11	♔h1	♕e4+
12	♔h2	♕e5+
13	♔h1	♕d5+
14	♔h2	♕xg8

and Black wins.

QR 16

Ghitescu - Badea
Bucharest 1991
White had a choice as to which way to go with his king.

A.
Ghitescu chose:
55 ♔f3?
This looks natural, but as we now know Black was able to defend successfully. 55 ... ♖g5! 56 ♕e4 ♖g6 57 ♕e7+ ♔g8 58 ♔f4 ♖g5 59 ♕f6 ♔h7 60 ♕f7+ ♖g7 61 ♕f5+ ♔g8 62 ♕e6+ ♔h7 63 ♕e4+

♔h8 64 ♔f5 ♔h7 65 ♔f6+ ♔h8 66 ♕e8+ ♖g8 67 ♕e6 ♔h7 68 ♕e5 ♖g7 69 ♕d5 ♔h8 70 ♕e4 ♔g8 ½-½.

B.
55 ♔h3
This would have been correct since the necessity of keeping the white king out of h5 causes Black to fall into zugzwang.

55	...	♖g5
56	♕d4+	♔h7
57	♔h4	♔g8
58	♕d7	♔h8

Queen v Rook (and Pawns) ♕ V ♖(♟)

59 ♕f7

With a zugzwang. If 59 ... ♖a5 White zigzags checks to ♕d8/c7/b6 to win the rook.

| 59 | ... | ♖g7 |

60 ♕e8+ ♚h7 61 ♕e4+ ♚g8 62 ♚h5 and wins the pawn.

QR 17

= W

Sande - Bernstein (variation)
Malta ol 1980
Our final example of fortresses arises from analysis of a game from the 1980 Olympiad. Initially Liberzon thought he had found a nice win in this variation; but Ftacnik realised that White can head for diag 18.

49 ♚g2

Liberzon gave 49 ♚e2 ♕e4+ 50 ♚d2 ♕f4+ 51 ♚c3 ♚d5 52 h4 ♚c6 53 h5 ♚b6 54 h6 ♚a7 and wins.

49	...	♕b2+
50	♚h1	♚f6
51	♖g3	♕xb7+
52	♚g1	♕b1+

If 52 ... ♚f5 53 h3! sets it up at once.

53	♚g2	♕e4+
54	♚g1	♕e1+
55	♚g2	♚f5
56	h3!	♚f4
57	♖g4+	♚e3
58	♚h2=	

Analysis by Liberzon and Ftacnik.

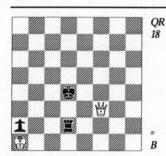

QR 18

= B

The Rook Defends Along the Rank
Henkin 1962
For Black to draw this and similar positions the king must be within the area b3, c3, c4-g4, g3 and h3 to help the rook maintain some square along the rank c2-h2.

Even the position with black king at c4, rook at c2 and white queen at e3 is lost after 1 ... ♚b4 2 ♕d3 giving zugzwang.

From diag 18:

| 1 | ... | ♖c2 |
| 2 | ♕f4+ | ♚d3 |

3	♕f5+	♚c3
4	♕e4	♚d2
5	♕f3	♚e1!
6	♕e3+	♚f1
7	♕d3+	♖e2
8	♕f3+	♚e1
9	♕f4	♖c2!

9 ... ♖d2 loses to 10 ♕e3+ ♚d1 11 ♕e4! ♖c2 (if 11 ... ♖h2 12 ♕g4+) 12 ♕d3+ ♚c1 13 ♕d4 ♖g2 14 ♕f4+ ♖d2 15 ♕f1+ ♚d1 16 ♕c4+ ♚d2+ 17 ♚xa2.

10	♕d4	♚e2!
11	♕e4+	♚d2
12	♕f3	♚e1

Repeating.

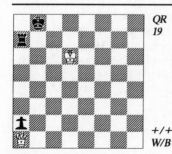

QR 19

+/+
W/B

Khenkin 1962
Difficulties winning are to be expected when the pawn, supported from behind by a rook, is far advanced and needs to be blockaded by the queen.

With *White to play:*

| 1 | ♕h8+ | ♚b7 |

| 2 | ♕g7+ | ♚b8 |

If 2 ... ♚b6 3 ♕b2+ or 2 ... ♚a6 3 ♕b2 win.

3	♕g8+	♚b7
4	♕f7+	♚b8
5	♕e8+	♚b7
6	♕c6+	♚b8
7	♕b6+	♚a8

7 ... ♖b7 is met by 8 ♕d8+.

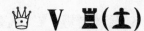
8	♔c6	♖h7

9   ♕a6+ and wins

Contrary to published theory, which says that *Black to play* is able to draw, White wins from the diagram after:

1	...	♖a6+
2	♔d7	♖a7+
3	♔d8	♔b7
4	♕g7+	♔b6
5	♕d4+	♔b7

Thus far Henkin's analysis; he continued 6 ♕b4+ ♔c6 7 ♕c4+ ♔b6 and could not progress further. *ChessBase* produced:

6	♕d7+	♔b6
7	♕d6+	♔b7

7 ... ♔b5 8 ♕b8+ while 7 ... ♔a5 8 ♕c5+ tranposes to the main line

8	♕c7+	♔a6
9	♕c8+	♔b6

Or 9 ... ♖b7 10 ♕c3 ♖b3!? 11 ♕c6+ winning the pawn.

10	♕b8+	♔a6

If 10 ... ♖b7 11 ♕d6+ and White will win the pawn with a forking check.

11	♕b2

This picks up the pawn and wins.

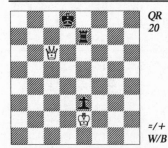

QR 20

=/+
W/B

Kling and Horwitz 1851
Black to move has to give ground in diag 20 after 1 ... ♖e8 2 ♕d6+ ♔c8 when White loses a move by 3 ♔f1 e2+ 4 ♔e1 and Black, in zugzwang, loses the pawn.
With *White to move* the black king and rook cannot be forced apart, e.g. 1 ♔f1 e2+ 2 ♔e1 ♖e8 3 ♕d6+ ♔c8 - so far and no further.

QR 21

=/+
W/B

Cheron 1926
Corrected by a database
Cheron believed that it was only with a bishop's pawn on the fifth supported from behind by a rook that a draw could be held giving diag 20 as an example.

Cheron had presumably missed the idea of temporarily blockading the pawn with the queen. The win is exceedingly complex and we give the main line with only minimal notes: 1 ... ♖c8 2 ♕e5 ♔b7 3 ♔b4! ♖c7 (3 ... c3 4 ♕b5+ ♔a7 5 ♕a5+ ♔b7 6 ♔b5 c2 7 ♕b6+ ♔a8 8 ♔a6) 4 ♕c3!

♔b6 5 ♔a3 ♖a7+ 6 ♔b2 ♖c7 7 ♔c2 ♔a6 8 ♔d2 ♖d7+ 9 ♔e1 ♔b5 10 ♕b2+ ♔a4 11 ♔e2 ♖d5 12 ♕b6 ♖d3 13 ♕b7 ♖b3 14 ♕c6+ ♔b4 15 ♕b6+ ♔c3 16 ♕a5+ ♔d4 17 ♔d1 ♖b1+ 18 ♔c2 ♖b3 19 ♔c1 ♖c3+ 20 ♔b2 ♖d3 21 ♔a2 ♖b3 22 ♕f5 ♖d3 23 ♕b5 ♖b3 24 ♕c6 ♔c3 25 ♕c5 ♖b2+ 26 ♔a3 ♖b3+ 27 ♔a4 ♖b2 28 ♕e3+ ♔c2 29 ♕d4 c3 30 ♕e4+ ♔c1 31 ♔a3 ♔d2 32 ♕d4+ ♔c2 33 ♕c4 ♔d2 34 ♕e4 ♖c2 35 ♕d4+ ♔e2 36 ♔b3 ♖c1 37 ♕f4 ♔d1 38 ♕f2 c2 39 ♔c3 ♖a1 40 ♕d2 mate.

Queen v Rook (and Pawns)

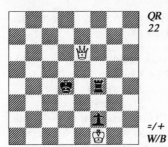

QR 22

=/+
W/B

Mutual Zugzwang
Prokop - Chess Amateur 1925
Prokop showed that with Black to move it is an easy win for White.

 1 ... ♖f3
Or 1 ... ♔d3 2 ♕e5.
 2 ♕g4+ ♔e3
 3 ♕c4 ♖f4
 4 ♕d5!

We shall look at this position with White to move in diag 25.

 4 ... ♖f3
 5 ♕e5+ ♔d3
 6 ♕e2+ and wins

This is all quite simple; but the further claim that the position is mutual zugzwang is infinitely harder to substantiate. I turned for help to John Nunn and his CD-ROM and together we worked through some of the variations which arise.

Since Black is short of room and White can play only with his queen it is not too surprising that there are at least two positions of mutual zugzwang: diags 22 and 23. And some of the tempo play which arises is quite splendid:

A.
 1 ♕e2

If 1 ♕e8 ♔d5= or 1 ... ♖f5=; but not 1 ... ♖f3? 2 ♕e7! with zugzwang (see diag 26).
 1 ... ♔d5
Alternatively:
a) 1 ... ♖f5 is also okay; but not
b) 1 ... ♖f7? 2 ♕b2+ ♔e4 3 ♕b4+ ♔e5 4 ♕b8+! and wins; or
c) 1 ... ♖f8? 2 ♕g4+ ♔e3 3 ♕e6+ ♔f3 4 ♕g6 ♖f4 5 ♕g2+ ♔e3 6 ♕d5! (see diag 25).
 2 ♕e7

If 2 ♕e3 ♖f5 or 2 ... ♖f6 or 2 ... ♖f8 still keep the draw. But now Black has only one move:
 2 ... ♖f5!
See diag 24.

B.
 1 ♕d6+ ♔e4
 2 ♕c5 ♔f3

2 ... ♖f3 and 2 ... ♖f5 are also sufficient.
 3 ♕g5

Of course if 3 ♕xf2+ ♔e4 or 3 ... ♔g4=; while if 3 ♕e5 ♔g4!.
 3 ... ♔e4!

The only move; but not 3 ... ♔e3 4 ♕d5! and wins (see diag 25).

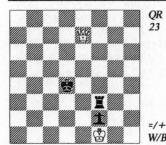

QR 23

=/+
W/B

This is also mutual zugzwang. White to play cannot do better than 1 ♕e6 ♖f4!= (as in diag 23) or 1 ♕e8 ♖f5!.

Black to move loses immediately after 1 ... ♖f5 2 ♕d6+ ♔e4 3 ♕e6+; whilst 1 ... ♖f4 2 ♕e6 is diag 23 with Black to move.

Queen v Rook (and Pawns)

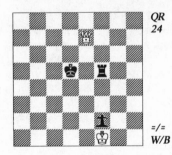

QR 24

=/=
W/B

However, diag 24 is drawn with either player to move. The critical difference between this and diag 25 is that the black pieces are further away from the e2-square. As we know already, even if he gets driven up one more file into diag 22 Black can draw if it is White to move. But of course, there is no such latitude in diag 22 since ♔d3 and ♖f3 both get forked by ♕e2+.

Thus with *Black to move* he must play:

  1   ...   ♖f4!

But not 1 ... ♖d4? 2 ♕d6+ ♔e4 3 ♕e6+.

  2   ♕g5+   ♔e4
  3   ♕c5

This transposes directly into diag 25 with White to move in line B. Black can draw with 3 ... ♔f3, 3 ... ♖f3 or 3 ... ♖f5.

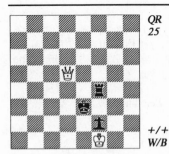

QR 25

+/+
W/B

CD-ROM, Nunn and Speelman
As we have seen already, this position is simple with Black to move, viz. 1 ... ♖f3 2 ♕e5+ and 3 ♕e2+.

With *White to move*, however, there is only one way to win. White has to triangulate with his queen so as to reach diag 22 with Black to move.

  1   ♕c6!!

If 1 ♕b7 ♔d4 or 1 ... ♖f3 both draw. However, after 1 ♕a8 only 1 ... ♔d4 is sufficient. The point is that after 1 ♕a8 ♖f3? 2 ♕a4! ♖f4 3 ♕c6 reaches the main line two moves late. With the queen on b7 this was not possible.

  1   ...   ♔d3
  2   ♕e8!   ♔d4
  3   ♕e6 and wins

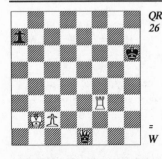

QR 26

=
W

Timman - Nunn
Wijk aan Zee 1982
An example of a good fortress is Timman - Nunn up to and including move 68.

56	♖a3	♕b4+
57	♔a2	♕c5
58	♔b2	♔g5
59	♖b3	♔f4
60	♖d3	♔e4
61	♖a3	a5
62	♖d3	a4

Reaching a position given in a 1917 study by Grigoriev. To draw White needs to keep the queen out of c1 and a1 and to maintain the rook on the rank using a3 and d3.

63	♖a3	♕b4+
64	♔a2	♔d5
65	♖d3+	♔c5
66	♖a3	♕c4+

QR 26a

+
W

67	♔b2	♔b4 *(26a)*

The fortress can be kept intact, e.g. 67 ♖d3 ♕e4 68 ♖a3 ♕e5+ 69 ♔a2 ♕f5 70 ♔b2 ♕g6 71 ♖d3 ♕h6 72 ♖a3!.

But tactical advances based on an advance ... a4-a3 have to be carefully monitored.

68	♖d3	♕e4

Against the try 68 ... ♕a6 Grigoriev gave 69 ♖a3! holding and avoiding 69 ♖f3? a3+ 70 ♔a2 ♕c4+ 71 ♖b3+ ♔a4 72 ♔a1! ♕f1+! 73 ♖b1 ♕f6+ 74 ♔a2 ♕c3 winning.

69	♔a2??	

69 ♖a3 holds.

69	...	a3!

0-1

If 70 ♖b3+ ♔c4 71 ♖d3 ♕e2 or 70 ♔b1 ♕e1+ 71 ♔a2 ♕c1 72 ♖b3+ ♔a4 winning.

Queen v Minor Pieces

These endings occur exceedingly rarely. There are now databases on all three endings which have demonstrated that: queen vs two bishops and queen vs bishop and knight are usually won; whereas two knights have somewhat better chances to defend themselves. I should like to thank John Nunn for giving me access to his databases - and even more important the knowledge which he has gleaned by working with them. One caveat, however, before we dive into the material. 'God Chess', which a database reproduces, is extremely alien and reminds me of nothing so much as solving a Rubik Cube. The pieces gradually become disorganised and suddenly, as if by magic, all is clear. Given the extreme rareness and complexity of these endings, It would take a quite disproportionate amount of time and energy to gain even a slight understanding of the absolute truth which a total analysis encompasses. I do have some vague ideas about what is going on; but really I feel more like an anthropologist investigating some rare species than a chessplayer!

Queen v Two Bishops

QBB
1

=/=
W/B

A fortress
I gave this known drawing position to John's database and we made some obvious winning attempts. It seems that Black should keep his bishop on c6 and play ... ♗a7-b6-a7 or if necessary ... ♚b7-b6.

1	♕e7+	♚c8
2	♚b4	♚b8
3	♕d6+	♚b7
4	♚c4	♗a7
5	♚b4	♗b6
6	♚c4	♗a7
7	♚b3	♗b6
8	♚b4	♗a7
9	♕e7+	♚b6
10	♕f7	♗b8
11	♕f2+	♚b7
12	♕c5	♗a7=

QBB
2

=/+
W/B

Mutual Zugzwang!
White to play must allow Black to set up the fortress, viz.

1	♕(any)	♗c7+
2	♚e7	♗b6

But Black to move loses a bishop immediately, e.g.

1	...	♗h2

If 1 ... ♗h1 2 ♕b5+ ♚a7 (or 2 ... ♚a8 3 ♕a6+) 3 ♕d7+.

2	♕b4+	♚a7
3	♕a3+	♚b8
4	♕b2+	

Winning.

QBB
3

+/=
W/B

Preventing the fortress
White wins only with ...

1	♕b1+!	

This prevents the fortress - after which we are informed that it takes another 60 moves to win.

Black to play can draw with either 1 ... ♗c7 or 1 ... ♗b8.

437

Queen v Minor Pieces

QBB 4

+ W

This is a straightforward winning position.

1 &d6!

This is much the quickest though 1 &d7 is also sufficient.

1 ... &a7

If 1 ... &c7+ 2 &c5 and, e.g.

2 ... &d8 3 ₩c6+ &a7 4 ₩d7+; or 1 ... &b5 2 ₩d5+ &a6 3 ₩a8+ &a7 4 &c7 etc.		
2	₩a2	&b7
3	₩f7+	&b8
4	&c6	&a5
5	₩e7	&a8
6	₩a3 and wins	

QBB 5

+ B

Finally, the longest win - 71 moves: 1 ... &d5+ 2 &b8 &d6+ 3 &a7 &c5+ 4 &a6 &c4+ 5 &a5 &e6 6 ₩h2 &d5 7 ₩f4 &d3 8 ₩d2 &e4 9 ₩c3 &d4 10 ₩e1+ &d5 11 &b4 &e4 12 ₩g3 &f5 13 ₩c7 &d3 14 ₩f4 &e4 15 ₩g5+ &e5 16 ₩g8+ &d4 17 ₩c4+ &e3 18 ₩e6 &d4 19 ₩b6+ &d5 20 ₩b7+ &d4 21 ₩a7+ &d5 22 ₩d7+ &d6+ 23 &c3 &g6 24 ₩b5+ &e6 25 &d4 &f7 26 ₩g5 &d7 27 ₩g7 &e7 28 &d3 &e6 29 &e4 &e8 30 ₩h6+ &e7 31 &f5 &d7+ 32 &g5 &e5 33 ₩b6 &e6 34 ₩c5+ &d6 35 ₩a7+

&d7 36 &g6 &e5 37 ₩a6 &e6 38 ₩c6 &d6 39 ₩b7+ &d7 40 ₩b2 &e8+ 41 &g5 &c6 42 ₩f6+ &d7 43 ₩f7+ &c8 44 ₩a7 &c7 45 &f5 &d7 46 ₩f6 &d6 47 ₩a3+ &d5 48 ₩e7 &b5 49 ₩b3+ &c5 50 ₩c3+ &c4 51 &d7 &f4 52 ₩f6 &b5+ 53 &e6 &c4+ 54 &e7 &c7 55 &d7 &a5 56 ₩f5+ &b6 57 ₩e5 &b5+ 58 &d6 &b4+ 59 &d5 &a6 60 ₩f6+ &b5 61 ₩c6+ &a5 62 &d4 &f1 63 ₩c7+ &a6 64 &d5 &d3 65 ₩e5 &a5 66 &c6+ &a4 67 ₩d5 &h7 68 ₩d1+ &a3 69 &b5 &c3 70 &c4 &b2 71 ₩b3+.

Queen v Bishop and Knight

QBN 1

= W

A static fortress

Although there are few exceptional positions, this is the only easy draw. Black's fortress is completely impregnable since he can always play either a king move, ... &g7-h8 or ... &h8-g7.

1	&e6	&g8
2	₩h5	&h8!
3	&e7	&g7
4	₩h3	&h8
5	₩c8+	&h7
6	&f8	&g7+
7	&e7=	

438

Queen v Minor Pieces

=/+
W/B

QBN
2

Mutual Zugzwang!
This position is mutual zugzwang. *White to move* is unable to free his king. If 1 ♕a3 ♗c8 the position has merely been reflected about the h1-a8 diagonal; and there is no way for White to "lose a move".

Black to move, however, is forced to release the white king after which a fairly typical winning process ensues. White gradually improves his pieces weaseling his king into position mainly along the black squares (the ones not controlled by the bishop). And

eventually Black runs out of squares for his pieces: 1 ... ♔e4 2 ♕f2 ♘d5 3 ♕a2+ ♗c4 4 ♕d2+ ♔c5 5 ♔b7 ♘d4 6 ♕g5+ ♗d5+ 7 ♔a6 ♘c6 8 ♕e3+ ♘d4 9 ♕a3+ ♔c4 10 ♔b6 ♗e6 11 ♔c5+ ♘d3 12 ♔c7 ♗g8 13 ♕h5 ♗b3 14 ♔d6 ♗c3 15 ♕h1 ♔b4 16 ♔e5 ♘b5 17 ♕e1+ ♔c4 18 ♕d2 ♔c5 19 ♕f4 ♗c4 20 ♕f8+ ♔c6 21 ♕f2 ♘c7 22 ♕h4 ♗a6 23 ♕f6+ ♔d7 24 ♕d6+ ♔c8 25 ♕e7 ♘b5 26 ♔d6 ♘e8+ 27 ♔c5 ♗a4 28 ♔b6 ♘d7 29 ♕e4 ♔d8 30 ♕h4+ ♔c8 31 ♕e7 ♗a4 32 ♕a3 ♘d1 33 ♕c1+ and wins.

+
B

QBN
3

This is an example of a longest win - 42 moves in all. It is interesting that from moves 19-35 Black is able to operate with a pseudo-fortress of ♘f3, bishop on the b1-h7 diagonal and king next to the knight.

1 ... ♗d5+ 2 ♔b8 ♘c6+ 3 ♔b7 ♘b4+ 4 ♔a7 ♘c6+ 5 ♔a6 ♗c4+ 6 ♔b7 ♘d8+ 7 ♔b8 ♘c6+ 8 ♔a8 ♗d3 9

+
B

QBN
3a

♕b7+ ♔d6 10 ♕c8 ♗e4 11 ♕f8+ ♔d5 12 ♕b7 ♘d4 13 ♔b6 ♘e6 14 ♕a8+ ♔e5 15 ♕a1+ ♔f5 16 ♕a5+ ♔f4 17 ♕h5 ♗f5 18 ♔c6 ♘d4+ 19 ♔d5 ♘f3 20 ♕f7 ♔g5 21 ♕c7 ♔g4 22 ♕d6 ♗d3 23 ♕b8 ♗f5 24 ♕c7 ♗b1 25 ♔e6 ♗d3 26 ♕c1 ♗e4 27 ♕e3 ♔g3 28 ♔f6 ♗b1 29 ♕e6

For the moment, Black is successfully defending his pseudo-fortress and over the next few moves White must manoeuvre to expel the bishop from the b1-h7 diago

nal.

29 ... ♗h7 30 ♕e7 ♗b1 31 ♕d6+ ♔g2 32 ♕d1 ♗h7 33 ♕d7 ♗c2 34 ♕b5 ♔g3 35 ♕c4 *(3a)*

Forcing the bishop off the diagonal, after which the rest is quite straightforward:

35 ... ♗d1

For if 35 ... ♗b1 36 ♕c6! (zugzwang) and:

a) 36 ... ♔g4 37 ♕c8+ ♔g3 (37 ... ♔h4 38 ♕c1) 38 ♕b8+;

b) 36 ... ♔g2 37 ♕b5 ♗h7 38 ♔g7;

c) 36 ... ♔f4 37 ♕c1+ or 36 ... ♔f2 37 ♕b6+ are simple;

d) 36 ... ♘d2/e1/g1 37 ♕c1! wins quickly;

e) 36 ... ♘h4 37 ♕c1 ♗e4 38 ♕e1+!;

f) 36 ... ♘h2 37 ♕c7+ ♔h3 38 ♕c3+ ♔h4 39 ♕e1+!.

36 ♕d3 ♗a4 37 ♔e7 ♔f2 38 ♔d8 ♔g2 39 ♕b1 ♔g3 40 ♔e7 ♘e5 41 ♕b8 ♔f4 42 ♔f6 and wins.

Queen v Minor Pieces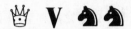

Queen v Two Knights

QNN
1

+
W

We are told that this is also won for the queen in almost 90% of starting positions. But whereas in the cases above the defender can draw *only* if he can reach a fortress, I understand from John Nunn that with two knights one will be able to draw some more fluid positions as long as the defender can get properly coordinated.

The important thing seems to be to have the knights, which must obviously be fairly near to the king, on different circuits. If they get stuck defending each other then the 'white' king can wedge himself between them with disastrous results, see diag 1.

A good example of poor coordination.

1 ♕h6 ♘b6 2 ♔c5 ♘8d7+ 3 ♔b5 ♘c8 4 ♕c1+ ♔d8 5 ♔c6 ♘e7+ 6 ♔d6 ♘c8+ 7 ♔e6 ♘f8+ 8 ♔f7 ♘d7 9 ♕f4 ♘cb6 10 ♔e6 ♘c8 11 ♕d4 ♘cb6 12 ♔d6

Now the two knights, chained together in self defence, become utterly immobilised. If the preliminary play was slightly obscure, the rest is readily comprehensible. White is able to confine the black king to the a-file after which he quickly falls into zugzwang:

12 ... ♔c8 13 ♔e7 ♔b7 14 ♔d8 ♔a6 15 ♔c7 ♔b5 16 ♕d4 ♔a5 17 ♕b2 ♔a6 18 ♕b3 ♔a5 19 ♕b1 ♔a4 20 ♔c6 ♔a3 21 ♔b5 and wins.

QNN
2

=
B

Here Black is well enough coordinated to draw. We tried some obvious winning attempts but White is never able to break Black's dynamic defence since he can neither chain the horses together nor approach with his king: 1 ... ♔h6 2 ♕f7 ♔g5 3 ♕e6 ♘h5+ 4 ♔f2 ♘f6 5 ♔g1

♘g4 6 ♕d5+ ♔f4 7 ♕e6 ♔g5 8 ♕e4 ♘f6 9 ♕e3+ ♔f5 10 ♔g2 ♘f4+ 11 ♔f1 ♘g6 12 ♔e1 ♘f4 13 ♔d2 ♘e6 14 ♔d3 ♘f4+ 15 ♔c4 ♘e6 16 ♔b5 ♘f4 17 ♔c6 ♘e4 18 ♔d7 ♘f6+ 19 ♔d8 ♘e6+ 20 ♔c8 ♘f4 21 ♕f3 ♘e4 22 ♔d7=.

QNN
3

=/=
W/B

There are some fortress positions and this is one of them. The white king cannot escape on its own; and since the

queen is unable to put Black into zugzwang it is an immediate draw.

Queen v Minor Pieces

♕ V ♝♞♞

QNN 4

Here, for interest's sake, is an example of a longest win (63 moves). Whilst I find it almost totally incomprehensible, it is clear that at no stage is Black quite able to set up a stable defensive position as in diag 2 above: 1 ... ♔d6 2 ♕d1+ ♔e6 3 ♕b3+ ♔f6 4 ♕b6+ ♔f5 5 ♕b1+ ♔e6 6 ♕a2+ ♔f6 7 ♕a6+ ♔f5 8 ♕f1+ ♔e6 9 ♕h3+ ♔d6 10 ♔e8 ♘hg6 11 ♕b3 ♔c6 12 ♕d1 ♔c5 13 ♕d2 ♔c4 14 ♕d6 ♔c3 15 ♕d5 ♘c4 16 ♕f3+ ♔b4 17 ♕b7+ ♔c3 18 ♕g7+ ♘ce5 19 ♔d8 ♔c4 20 ♔c7 ♔d5 21 ♕g8+ ♔d4 22 ♔d6 ♘c4+ 23 ♔e6 ♘f4+ 24 ♔f5 ♘d5 25 ♕g7+ ♔d3 26 ♕g3+ ♔d4 27 ♕h4+ ♔d3 28 ♕d8 ♔d4 29 ♔e6 ♘ce3 30 ♕h4+ ♔c5 31 ♕f2 ♔d4 32 ♔d6 ♔e4 33 ♕e1 ♔d3 34 ♕g3 ♘c3 35 ♔e5 ♔e2 36 ♕g6 ♔d2 37 ♕d6+ ♔c2 38 ♕c5 ♘ed1 39 ♔d4 ♔d2 40 ♕g5+ ♔c2 41 ♕g6+ ♔d2 42 ♕g2+ ♔e2+ 43 ♔e4 ♘dc3+ 44 ♔f3 ♔d3 45 ♕g6+ ♔c4 46 ♕a6+ ♔b4 47 ♔e3 ♘c1 48 ♕f1 ♘b3 49 ♕f4+ ♔b5 50 ♔d3 ♘a4 51 ♕c4+ ♔a5 52 ♕g8 ♔b4 53 ♕b8+ ♔a5 54 ♕c4 ♘d2+ 55 ♔d4 ♘b6 56 ♕e5+ ♔a6 57 ♕e2+ ♘dc4 58 ♔c5 ♔a7 59 ♕b5 ♘a3+ 60 ♔c6 ♘bc4 61 ♕e7+ ♔a6 62 ♕b7+ ♔a5 63 ♔c5 ♔a4 64 ♕b4 mate.

QNN 5

A Practical Example
van Scheltinga - Prins
Hastings 1938

1	♔e5	♔f3
2	♕g1	

2 ♕g5 ½-½! occurred in the game.

2	...	♔e2
3	♕g3	♔d2
4	♔d4 and wins	

e.g. 4 ... ♔e2 5 ♕g2+ ♔e1 6 ♕c2 ♔f1 7 ♕d2 ♔g1 8 ♔e2 ♔h1 9 ♕f2 stalemates the black king and zugzwangs the knights.

Queen v Three Minor Pieces

QBNN 1

Lautier - M. Gurevich
Munich 1993

Black's plan is to win the White h-pawn and then to shepherd his two pawns to promotion.

The first step is to bear on h4 by a knight from f5 and the bishop from f6, while keeping the king sheltered.

80	...	♗e5+
81	♔h3	♔g7
82	♔g2	♘h7
83	♔h3	♘f6
84	♕e6	♘g8
	0-1	

The knight would continue via h6 to f5.

White, not being able to save his pawn, resigned. The task of marshalling the black pieces to support the advance of his pawns is not difficult.

Queen v Two Rooks

At the ending stage in a non-critical position two rooks is equal to a queen plus a pawn. This is based on the simple calculation that two rooks lined up against a pawn protected by both its king and queen might well lead to an exchange to a levelish pawn ending.

However, other factors play an important role, and it is these factors on which we concentrate in diags 1-4.

Diag 1 illustrates a transition to a winning king and pawn versus rook ending; diag 2 shows both how the two rooks became tied up and a way for the rooks to be effectively regrouped; diag 3 is an example of two rooks lined up to prevent the advances of connected passed pawns; and diag 4 show the careful preparation and advance of passed pawns.

+
W

QRR
1

Yrjölä - Andersson (variation)
Finland - Sweden 1991

White wins by 1 ♔f4! ♖gf7
2 ♕xf7+ ♖xf7+ 3 ♔e5

eventually forcing Black to sacrifice rook for c-pawn and then White can win the a-pawn.

=
B

QRR
2

Jansa - A. Sokolov
Gausdal 1990

1 ... ♖c2!

The game continuation was 1 ... ♔xa6 2 ♕a8+ ♔b6 3 ♕b7+ ♔a5 4 ♕a7+ ♔b4 5 ♕e7 (paralysing Black) 1-0.

Also losing were 1 ... ♖c1? 2 ♕e7+ ♔xa6 3 ♕a3+ with a fork; and 1 ... ♖xc6 2 ♕d7+

♔b6 3 ♕b7+ wins the rook.

2 ♕e7+

Alternatively:
2 c7 ♖bc5= or 2 ♕c8 ♖bb2!=.

2	...	♔xa6
3	c7	♖bc5
4	♕xc5	♖xc5
5	♔xc5	♔b7
6	♔d6	♔c8=

=
W

QRR
3

Portisch - Smyslov
Havana 1964

32	♖e7	♕xe7
33	dxe7	♖xd1+
34	♔h2	♖e1
35	♕f5+	

Concentrating on setting up queenside passed pawns.

35	...	♔g8
36	♕d7	♖ce6
37	♕xb7	♖xe7
38	♕xb6	♖7e6
39	♕d4	♖1e4
40	♕d8+	♖e8
41	♕d5	♖8e5
42	♕d8+	♖e8
43	♕d3	♖e2

44	a4	♖xf2
45	a5	♖b2!

Not 45 ... ♖ee2 46 ♕d5 ♖a2 47 b5 and the pawns become unstoppable.

46	♕b5	♖e4
47	♕b8+	♔h7
48	b5	♖eb4
49	b6	♖b5
50	♕a7	f5
51	♕a8	♖b1
52	♔g3	♖1b3+
53	♔f2	♖b2+
54	♔g1	♖b1+
55	♔h2	♖1b2
56	♕a6	♖b1
57	♕a8	½-½

Queen v Two Rooks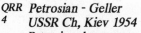

QRR
4

QRR
4a

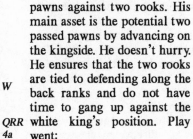

QRR
4b

+
W

Petrosian - Geller
USSR Ch, Kiev 1954

Petrosian has queen and two pawns against two rooks. His main asset is the potential two passed pawns by advancing on the kingside. He doesn't hurry. He ensures that the two rooks are tied to defending along the back ranks and do not have time to gang up against the white king's position. Play went:

```
43   h5!      g5
44   ♕c3+     ♚h7
45   ♕c2+     ♚g7
46   ♕f5      ♖de7
47   f4!      gxf4
48   exf4     ♖d6
49   ♚f3      ♖e1
50   ♕g4+     ♚f7
51   ♕c8      ♖e7
52   ♕f5+
```

52 ♕h8 is an interesting possibility.

```
52   ...      ♚g7
```

The next phase - up to move 70 - seems to be a "marking of time". The moves to then were 53 a4 ♖e1 54 ♕g4+ ♚f7 55 ♕c8 ♖e7 56 b4 ♖d3+ 57 ♚g4 ♚g7 (If 57 ... ♖ee3 58 ♕xb7+ ♚g8 59 ♕b8+ ♚g7 60 f5) 58 ♕f5 ♖d6 59 ♕c5 ♖dd7 60 ♚h4 ♖e6 61 ♕c3+ ♚h7 62 ♕c2+ ♚g7 63 ♕b2+ ♚h7 64 ♕b1+ ♚g7 65 ♕f5 ♖dd6 66 ♚h3 ♖e7 67 ♚g4 ♖ee6 68 ♚f3 ♖e7 69 ♕c2 ♖ee6 70 ♕f5 ♖e8 *(5b)*

```
71   b5       cxb5
72   ♕xb5     ♖e7
```

Now starts the decisive over-running of Black's position.

```
73   g4!      ♖f6
74   a5       ♖fe6
```

If 74 ... ♖ef7 75 ♕e5.

```
75   ♕b2+     ♚g8
76   ♕b3      ♚h7
77   ♕d3+     ♚g8
78   g5       hxg5
79   fxg5     ♖e5
80   ♚f4      ♖5e6
81   g6       b6
82   a6       1-0
```

Queen and Knight v Queen

QNQ 1 Working together in endgame positions, queen and knight can be a devastating team. Typical studies which illustrate this theme are diags 1 and 2.

Dehler 1908
This study features forks, skewers, discovered checks, a stalemate in the middle of the board coupled with the

+
W

1	♘c6+	♚f4
2	♕f2+	♚e4
3	♕e3+	

Not 3 ♕xf7 stalemating.

3	...	♚d5
4	♕b3+	♚e4
5	♕d3+	♚f4
6	♕e3+	♚f5
7	♕f3+	

White wins with either a knight fork or a skewer.

QNQ 2 *Joseph 1978*
David Joseph's study illustrates the need to find the right series of squares on which the attacking queen should work and is attractive for its aesthetic effect.

1	♕g2+	♕b7
2	♕g8+	♚a7

+
W

3	♕g1+	♚a8
4	♕a1+	♕a7
5	♕h1+	♕b7
6	♕h8+	♚a7
7	♕a1+	♕a6
8	♕g1+	♚a8
9	♕g8+	

White forks or mates.

QNQ 3 *Lengyel - Levy*
Cienfuegos 1972
This example was analysed extensively before the advent of databases. Now John Nunn has been able to clear it all up with the aid of a Silicon friend.

-
B

66	...	♕f4+!
67	♚e6	

QNQ 3a **A.**
In the game, Levy continued with:

67	...	♕h6+?

And in the end he won: though as John Nunn discovered there were several inaccuracies.

68	♚d7?	

-
B

If 68 ♚f5? ♕f4+! Black can transpose back to B below; but with 68 ♚e7! to prevent the

knight joining in with check he could have held the draw:
68 ... ♕g7+ 69 ♚e6 ♘c5+ (if 69 ... ♕g6+ 70 ♚e7 and Black has made no progress) 70 ♚f5! etc.

68	...	♕g7+?

68 ... ♘c5+! 69 ♚c7 ♕g7+ is the same as B 67 ... ♘c5+ below (68 ... ♘e5+ also wins but is slower than 68 ... ♘c5+).

69	♚c8?	

69 ♚e6! would still have been drawing.

69	...	♕f8+
70	♚b7	♘c5+
71	♚a7	♕e7+

71 ... ♕f7+! would have saved seven moves.

72	♚b6	♘d7+
73	♚c7	♘e5+
74	♚b8	♕d8+

This loses one move.

75	♔b7	♛d7+
76	♔b6	

Better was 76 ♔a6!.

76	...	♘c4+
77	♔a6	♛d6+
78	♔b7	♛d7+
79	♔b8	♛d8+
80	♔b7	♘d6+
81	♔a7	♛a5+
82	♔b8	♛b6+
	0-1	

B.

Instead, Black should have included his knight in the attack at the first opportunity; and the database shows that this leads to a forced win with checks: albeit a rather obscure sequence of them.

67	...	♘c5+
68	♔e7	♛h4+
69	♔f7	

If 69 ♔d6 ♛g3+ 70 ♔e7 ♛g7+ 71 ♔d6 ♛d7 mate.

69	...	♛h7+
70	♔f6	♘e4+
71	♔e6	♛g6+
72	♔e7	♛f6+
73	♔d7	♛f7+
74	♔c8	*(4a)*
74	...	♛g8+!
75	♔b7	♘c5+
76	♔a7	♛a2+

This was the reason for going to g8 on move 74.

| 77 | ♔b8 | ♛h2+! |

and wins

QNQ Nunn
4

+
W

Dr Nunn, with the aid of his queen and knight v queen database program concocted the position (diag 4), developed out of analysis of the 'mutual zugzwang' position arising from 1 ♘d6+ ♔b6 2 ♛f5. Here, whoever is to move must give ground.

The solution runs:

1 ♘d6+

If 1 ♘c5+? ♔b6 escaping from the gravitational power of the white king.

1 ... ♔a6

The mutual zugzwang position referred to above is reached after 1 ... ♔b6 2 ♛f5 with Black to move: now if 2 ... ♔a6 (2 ... ♔a7 3 ♔c7! ♛e7+ 4 ♔c6 wins) 3 ♔d8 (3 ♔c6!?) 3 ... ♔b6 (or 3 ... ♛b2 4 ♛d3+ forces 4 ... ♔a7 allowing 5 ♘c8+ and on 5 ... ♔b8 6 ♛d6+ at least skewering the black queen) 4 ♛d5! ♔a6 5 ♛b7+ ♔a5 6 ♛b3! (such quiet control moves are difficult to reach in calculations) 6 ... ♔a6 (if 6 ... ♛h5 7 ♘c4+ and mates) 7 ♔c7 ♛e7+ 8 ♔c6 ends Black's good checks; or 2 ... ♛a6 3 ♛f2+ ♔a5 4 ♛d2+ ♔b6 5 ♛b4+ ♔a7 6 ♔c7 completes the net.

2 ♛h3!

2 ♛f5 ♔b6 arrives at the mutual zugzwang with White to move. Progress is not possible, e.g. 3 ♛d5 ♛g4+.

Now if 2 ... ♔b6 3 ♛f5 is a critical zugzwang.

2 ... ♔a5 3 ♛a3+ ♔b6 would transpose to the main line after 5 ... ♔b6.

2 ... ♛b2 3 ♛d3+ ♔a7 4 ♘c8+ ♔b7 5 ♛d5+ ♔b8 6 ♛d6+ or 2 ... ♛e1 3 ♛d3+ ♔a7 4 ♘c8+ or 2 ... ♛a2 3 ♛d3+ ♔a7 4 ♛b5 would follow

2	...	♔a7
3	♘c8+	♔a6
4	♛a3+	♔b5
5	♘d6+	♔b6
6	♛b4+	♔a6
7	♛c3!	

Threat 8 ♔c7.

7 ... ♚b6

If 7 ... ♛g4+ 8 ♔c7 or 7 ... ♛h5 8 ♛a3+ ♚a5 (8 ... ♚b6 9 ♘c4+) 9 ♛d3+ ♚a7 10 ♛d4+ ♚a6 11 ♔c6 bags the black king.

8 ♔d8!

Avoids ... ♛g4 with check, while 8 ... ♛g4 without check permits 9 ♛c7+.

8 ... ♛h5

If 8 ... ♚a6 (or 8 ... ♚a7) 9 ♔c7; or 8 ... ♛g2 9 ♛b4+ ♚a6 10 ♛b5+ ♚a7 11 ♘c8+, or 8 ... ♛f1 9 ♘c4+ ♚b5 (9 ... ♚b7 10 ♛b4+ ♚a7 - or 10 ... ♚a8 - 11 ♛a5+ leads to mate) 10 ♛a5+ ♚c6 11 ♛b6+ and 12 ♘e3+ all win for White.

9	♘c4+	♚c6
10	♘e5++	♚b5
11	♛b3+	♚c5
12	♛c4+	♚b6
13	♛b4+	♚a6
14	♛a4+	♚b6
15	♘d7+	

Also 15 ♘c4+.

15	...	♚b7
16	♛b4+	♚c6
17	♛b6+	

and skewers the black queen.

QNQ 5

Ljubojevic - Hjartarson
Reykjavik 1991

White had just captured a pawn at g5 on move 70. Black now needs to be able to survive until after White's 120th to claim a draw under the 50 move rule: 70 ... ♚f7 71 ♔c5 ♛d3+ 72 ♔h4 ♛d8+ 73 ♔h5 ♛d1 74 ♔g5 ♛d8+ 75 ♔f4 ♛d2+ 76 ♔e4 ♛e1+ 77 ♔f5 ♛f1+ 78 ♔g5 ♛g2 79 ♛d6 ♚e8 80 ♛d3 ♛g1 81 ♛c4 ♚d8 82 ♔f4 ♛h1 83 ♛c5 ♛h4 84 ♛c6 ♚e7 85 ♛d5 ♛e1 86 ♛c5+ ♚d8 87 ♔f5 ♛e7 88 ♛c4 ♛d7+ 89 ♔g6 ♛d6+ 90 ♔h5 ♛d1 91 ♛c5 ♛e2 92 ♛d5+ ♚c7 93 ♔g5 ♛e7+ 94 ♘f6 ♛e3+ 95 ♔g6 ♛g1+ 96 ♔f7 ♛f2 97 ♛b7 ♛f3 98 ♛c5+ ♚b7 99 ♛e7 ♛c6 100 ♛b4+ ♚b6 101 ♛e4+ ♛c6 102 ♘d5 ♚b8 103

QNQ 5a

♛f4+ ♚b7 104 ♛d4 ♛b5 105 ♛e4 ♚c6 106 ♛b4+ ♚a7 107 ♛a3+ ♚b8 108 ♘f6 ♚b7 109 ♛b3+ ♛b6 110 ♛f3+ ♚c6 111 ♛f5 ♛h1 112 ♘e4 ♚a6 113 ♛e6+ ♚a7 114 ♛a2+ ♚b8 115 ♛b3+ ♚a7 116 ♛a4+ ♚b8 117 ♘f6 ♛b7+??! (5a)

So far until 117 ... ♛b7, Black according to Dr. John Nunn's *ChessBase* program for queen and knight v queen endings, has not been in danger of losing. Indeed he claims that the vast majority of these endings should be drawn.

118 ♘d7+ ♚c8 119 ♔e8 ♚c7 120 ♛a5+ ♚d6 ½-½

Black is able to claim a draw under the fifty-move rule despite mates by 121 ♛c5+ ♚e6 122 ♛e5 and by 121 ♛e5+ ♚c6 122 ♛c5.

Queen and Piece v Queen

Queen and Bishop v Queen

+
W

QBQ 1 This is normally a draw, since the queen and bishop do not cooperate well enough to create threats of both mate and winning the queen.

For the attacking side to win, the defending pieces need to be unfortunately placed.

Composer Unknown, corrected by Nunn

1 ♔h3!
1 ♔h5? ♕f7+!.
1 ... ♕g7
1 ... ♕f7 2 ♕d4+ ♔g7 3 ♕h4+ is a move shorter.

2	♕d8+	♔g8
3	♕f6+	♔g7
4	♕h4+	♔g8
5	♗c4+	♔f8
6	♕d8+	1-0

+
W

QBQ 2 *Centurini 1858*

1 ♕d4+ (1 ♕f2 and 1 ♕c3+ also win, by the same idea) 1 ... ♕b2 2 ♕d1+ ♔b1 3 ♕a4+ ♔b2 4 ♕b3+ ♔c1 5 ♕e3+ ♔b2 6 ♔b4 ♗a1+ (6 ... ♔c2 7 ♕a3+ ♔b1 8 ♗d3 wins) 7 ♗b3 ♔b2 8 ♕g1+ ♔b1 9 ♕a7+ ♔b2 10 ♕a3 mate.

+
B

QBQ 3 **The Longest Win**

Nunn CD-ROM 1993

1 ... ♔d8 2 ♗b6+ ♔e8 3 ♕e2+ ♔f7 4 ♕e7+ ♔g6 5 ♕e8+ ♔h7 6 ♕e4+ ♔g7 7 ♗d4+ ♔f7 8 ♕e7+ ♔g6 9 ♕e8+ ♔g5 10 ♗e3+ ♔h4 11 ♕e7+ ♔g3 12 ♕e5+ ♔g2 13 ♕b2+ ♔h1 14 ♕b1+ ♔g2 15 ♕g1+ ♔f3 16 ♕f2+ ♔e4 17 ♕f4+ ♔d3 18 ♕d4+ ♔e2 19 ♕b2+ ♔f3 20 ♕f6+ ♔e4 21 ♕d4+ ♔f3 22 ♕f4+ ♔e2 23 ♕f2+ ♔d3 24 ♕d2+ ♔c4 25 ♕c2+ ♔b4 26 ♗c5+ ♔a5 27 ♕a2+ ♔b5 28 ♕b2+ ♔c4 29 ♕b4+ ♔d3 30 ♕a3+ and wins the queen

+
W

QBQ 4 *Ivanchuk - Kamsky*

Dortmund 1992

76	♕a3+	♔d7
77	♕a4+	♔c7
78	♕c6+	♔d8
79	♕b6+	♔d7
80	♗c6+	♔d6
81	♗a4+	♔e7
82	♕c7+	♔f6

83	♕d6+	♔xf5
84	♗d7+	♔g5
85	♕f4+	♔g6
86	♗f5+	♔h5

86 ... ♔f6 87 ♕d4+ ♔xf5 88 ♕xg7 b1♕ 89 ♕h7+ skewering.

87	♗g4+	♔h4
88	♗e6+	1-0

Queen and Piece v Queen

Queen and Rook v Queen

QRQ
1

+ W

Roycroft

This position was discovered by the English study composer John Roycroft (actually White's king was on a different square).

1 g8♕ would be a mistake, for after 1 ... ♕c6+ 2 ♔b5 ♕c2+ 3 ♔a5 (3 ♕gb3 ♕c4+ 4 ♔a5 ♕c7+ 5 ♔b6 ♕a7+) 3 ... ♕c7+ 4 ♔b6 ♕c3+ and if 5 ♔a6 ♕c4+ or if 5 ♔b5 ♕b3+. In each case Black either forces stalemate or obtains perpetual check or wins a queen.

The correct move is:

1   g8♖!

When the stalemate possibilities disappear, Black is then able to obtain a barrage of checks, but these will run out if White's king can reach h1. That it can do so can be seen if we invoke some coordinate squares.

What happens if the king reaches h2? To prevent ♔h1 Black must check on the h-file, but on which square? If 1 ... ♕h5+ 2 ♔g3!; or 1 ... ♕h7+ 2 ♔g1; or 1 ... ♕h6+ 2 ♔g2 ♕c6+ 3 ♔g3! ♕c3+ 4 ♔h2 and wins. So the only good square is h4, i.e. ♔h2 co-ordinates with ... ♕h4+. Similarly ♔g1 must be met by ... ♕e1+ and then ♔g2 requires ... ♕e4+.

What about h3? If 1 ... ♕h6+ or 1 ... ♕h5+ then 2 ♔g2 will win; and if 1 ...

♕h7+ then 2 ♔g3 ♕d3+ 3 ♔h2 etc. Only 1 ... ♕h1+ remains, but then White has 2 ♕h2 ♕f3+ (or 2 ... ♕f1+ 3 ♔g2 ♕f5+ 4 ♔h2 ♕h5+ 5 ♔g1 ♕c5+ 6 ♕f2) 3 ♖g3 ♕h5+ 4 ♔g2 ♕d5+ 5 ♖f3 ♕d2+ 6 ♔h1.

So Black cannot fight successfully against ♔h3, and it is similarly sufficient for White's king to reach f1. But then ♔g2 will clearly win eventually.

It remains to be seen whether Black can keep White's king away from the kingside. It is fairly clear that this will be impossible. For example:

1	...	♕c2+
2	♔b4	♕e4+
3	♔c5	♕f5+
4	♔d4	♕f2+
5	♔e4	♕e2+
6	♔f4	♕f1+
7	♔g3	♕e1+
8	♔h3	♕h1+
9	♕h2	♕f3+
10	♖g3!	

It is not surprising that for any initial positions of White's king and Black's queen in diag 1 (apart from the unfortunate ♔h8 vs ♕h6!) Black will be unable to box in White's king completely. But in order to show that White is winning we needed to find a place where his king could hide and a precise way of getting there.